DISCOVERING OUR REDEMPTION

McDougal & Associates
Servants of Christ and Stewards of the
Mysteries of God

DISCOVERING OUR REDEMPTION

Being Transformed by the 52 Days that Changed the Universe

by

Donald C. Mann

DISCOVERING OUR REDEMPTION

Copyright © 2011, 2012, 2013 by Donald C. Mann

ALL RIGHTS RESERVED, AMERICAN, PAN-AMERICAN AND INTERNATIONAL.

This book is protected under the copyright laws of the United States of America and may not be copied or reprinted for commercial gain or profit. The use of short quotations or occasional page copying for personal or group study is permitted and encouraged. Permission will be granted upon request. No part of this publication may be stored in a retrieval system, transmitted, or reproduced in any way, including but not limited to photocopy, photograph, magnetic or other record, without prior agreement and written permission from the author.

Unless otherwise noted, all Scripture references are from *The Holy Bible, Authorized King James Version*. References marked "AMP" are from *The Amplified Bible*, copyright © 1954, 1958, 1962, 1964, 1965, 1987, the Lockman Foundation, La Habra, California. References marked "NKJV" are from *The Holy Bible, New King James Version*, copyright © 1982, Thomas Nelson, Inc., Nashville, Tennessee. References marked "KSW" are from *The New Testament: An Expanded translation by Kenneth S. Wuest*, copyright © 1961, Wm. B. Eerdmans Publishing Co., Grand Rapids, MI. Portions marked "RSV" are from **The Revised Standard Version of the Bible**, copyright © 1946, 1952, 1971, 1973 by the Division of Christian Education of the National Council of the Churches of Christ in the U.S.A. References marked "DBY" are from a literal translation of the Old Testament (1890) and the New Testament (1884) by John Nelson Darby (1800-82), in the public domain. References marked "WYM" are from the New Testament in Modern Speech by Richard Francis Weymouth © 2002, Christian Classics Ethereal Library, Grand Rapids, MI. References marked "Rotherham" are from the *Emphasized Bible* by Joseph Bryant Rotherham, public domain. References marked "MOF" are from *A New Translation of the Bible* by James Moffatt, copyright © 1954, 1964 by James Moffatt. References to Young's are from *Young's Analytical Concordance to the Bible*, copyright © 1984 by Hendrickson Publishers, Peabody, Massachusetts.

Non-Medical Advice: The information presented in this book is in no way intended as advice or instruction concerning the use of medicine, medical treatment, or the avoidance thereof. Each person is responsible to investigate all methods of remedy they are contemplating. No one has a right or responsibility to make your decision except you. Any reference to medicine or medical treatment is solely for historical or informational purposes.

The author is in no way responsible or liable for the successful application of the material or for the manner of the reader's application or future re-presentation of the material in this manual or their results. Nor is the author in any way a trained medical or psychological professional. By using this material for any purpose, the reader holds harmless the author of any liability.

Book Cover Photo: © 2010 by Donald C. Mann, all rights reserved

Excerpts taken from other books by the author include:
Battle Prayer for Divine Healing, Field Manual 2, The Mind Renewing Battle Prayer, The Prayer Cards and OK, God, Now What?

Published by:

McDougal & Associates
18896 Greenwell Springs RD
Greenwell Springs, Louisiana 70739
www.thepublishedword.com

McDougal & Associates is an organization dedicated to the spreading of the Gospel of the Lord Jesus Christ to as many people as possible in the shortest time possible.

ISBN 978-1-934769-50-8
Printed on demand in the US, the UK and Australia
For worldwide distribution

Dedication

This is for all the people who have never understood the depth and power of the great work of God in Jesus Christ. I found myself asking, "What exactly did Jesus accomplish in His great appearing and death 2000 years ago, and what does that mean to me now?"

My next great question was, "What is the awesome Jesus doing now that was not being done before He came, because, frankly, the world does not look in such great shape or a whole lot different?"

And another question: "Is there anything I can do to fulfill my part as a Christian to make Jesus more effective?"

If you are wondering how to build your faith so that you can enter deeper into the fullness God has for you, I trust that *Discovering Our Redemption* will become a valuable resource in your Christian growth.

Acknowledgments

I thank the ever-faithful Lord Jesus Christ of Nazareth, who purchased me with His blood and now intercedes for me by the will of Father God, and Holy Spirit who dwells within me.

I also thank my wife, Cindy, and our children Christina and Jonathan who have been used of the Lord to show me His goodness and love.

I also thank Margie and Carroll Harlow for being such good friends and for Margie's invaluable help in the final proofing of this work.

I also thank Harold McDougal who helped organize and edit my books for general publication.

Contents

About the Unique Editorial Style 9
Bible Book Abbreviations 10
Author's Foreword 11
Introduction 15

PART I: UNDERSTANDING OUR REDEMPTION MORE FULLY 23
1. Redemption: God's Answer to the Fall of Adam 25
2. Redemption Facts Are the Work of *Agape* Love 34
3. The Story of Redemption 37
4. Our Redemption Is a Finished Work 47

**PART II: UNDERSTANDING THE LEGAL ASPECTS OF
CHRIST'S SACRIFICE 55**
5. The Law of Covenant Identification 57
6. The Facts of Covenant Identification 76
7. Legal Action for Producing Vital Daily Living 83
8. Past Tense Language into a Present Reality 91

**PART III: UNDERSTANDING WHAT JESUS DID FOR US BY
CALVARY 95**
9. Jesus Was Made Sin for Us 97
10. Jesus Was Made Sick and Scourged for Us 105
11. Jesus Suffered for Us 127
12. Jesus Was Made Righteous for Us 134
13. Jesus Conquered Satan for Us 139
14. Jesus Became Our High Priest 153
15. Jesus Worked So the Veil Was Torn 160
16. Jesus Sat Down 181
17. Jesus and the 52 Days that Changed the Universe 194

PART IV UNDERSTANDING WHO WE ARE IN CHRIST 199
18. We Were Crucified with Jesus 201

19. We Died with Jesus 206
20. We Were Buried with Jesus 227
21. We Have Been Made Alive with Jesus 232
22. We Were Raised with Jesus 235
23. We Have Been Given a New Identity in Jesus 244
24. We Now Hold the Key 249
25. Because of Jesus, We Have Received a Great Inheritance 257

PART V: UNDERSTANDING WHAT IT ALL MEANS TO YOU 267
26. You Have the Name of Jesus 269
27. You Have Holy Spirit in You 284
28. You Have Been Made the Righteousness of God 306
29. You Have God's Wisdom 315
30. Why Satan Hates You So Much 322

PART VI: UNDERSTANDING WHAT WE NEED TO DO NOW 329
31. Knowing the Will of God 331
32. Having Faith in God 345
33. Destroying Sin-Consciousness 358
34. Working with the Wrath Of God 372
35. Facing Off Against the Devil 379
36. Dealing with the Burn-It-Now Process 387
37. Having God's Word Abiding in You 390
38. Working with Propitiation in Communion 402
39. Liberating the Ability of God within You 415
40. Following the *Agape* Path to Faith 421
41. Growing in Agape Love 443
42. Becoming Burden-Bearers 464
43. Becoming Gateways for God's Love 468
44. Examining How You Know You Got the Message 480

PART VII: THE CONCLUSION 485
45. Some Concluding Thoughts 487

APPENDICES 517
Bibliography and Recommended Reading 518
Glossary 520
Identified (A Redemption Song) by E.W. Kenyon 571

Ministry Page 572

About the Unique Editorial Style

Wherever a Scripture reference is underlined, any adjustments in tense, person, count or additions are italicized. This identifies what has been modified or added to the original translation's text. The original language Old or New Testament (i.e., Hebrew or Greek) words are added occasionally for emphasis in the format of *aiteo* or *aiteo*/ask.

Capitalization: Multiple scriptures after the same reference have the capitalization adjusted where there is no capitalization across verses, after commas, colons and semicolons except when the new word is either someone speaking or a quote from another part of the Bible.

Quotation Marks Around Scripture: Not used at the option of the author when in a prayer, affirmation, confession or a list of scriptures (see prayer example below). When no quotation marks are used, any added words between or after the scriptures are in italics to the end of the paragraph, as in the example below.

Additional meanings and expansions within Scripture are in parentheses and in italics. Also inserted implications are in brackets and in italics. Occasionally the punctuation is changed to fit the content.

For Example: Heb 3:12-13 as a prayer becomes: **Father, in the name of Jesus**, work in us so that I and those I pray for Heb 3:12 take heed, *among the* brethren, lest there be in any of *us* an evil heart of unbelief (*unpersuadableness, offense or lack of confidence*), in departing from *You,* Father, the *zao*/living God. 13 But *by Your grace in us we* exhort one another daily, while it is called To day; lest any of *us* be hardened through the deceitfulness of sin [*in corrupt thoughts, words and actions in believing that God is not your friend, helper, near or that His word cannot fail, and thus living in the mind of the carnal flesh and not in the spirit by the Word of God*]. *Thank You Father. In the name of Jesus, thank You!*

HOLY SPIRIT: You will notice that there is no "the" in addressing or describing Holy Spirit where written by the author. Holy Spirit is the third person of the Godhead; Holy Spirit is His revealed name. He is not an "it" but a person. The article *the* is not in the original Greek and, unless within the particular translation used, it is not used by the author to address Him. The King James Version often translates the Greek word *pneuma* as *ghost* or *spirit*. Holy Spirit is used by the author rather than Holy Ghost, recognizing that both are the same word.

Bible Book Abbreviations Used

For Old Testament Books

Gen	Genesis	Eccl	Ecclesiastes
Ex	Exodus	Song	Song of Solomon
Lev	Leviticus	Isa	Isaiah
Num	Numbers	Jer	Jeremiah
Deut	Deuteronomy	Lam	Lamentations
Josh	Joshua	Ezek	Ezekiel
Judg	Judges	Dan	Daniel
Ruth	Ruth	Hos	Hosea
1 Sam	1 Samuel	Joel	Joel
2 Sam	2 Samuel	Am	Amos
1 Kings	1 Kings	Ob	Obadiah
2 Kings	2 Kings	Jon	Jonah
1 Chron	1 Chronicles	Mic	Micah
2 Chron	2 Chronicles	Nah	Nahum
Ezra	Ezra	Hab	Habakkuk
Neh	Nehemiah	Zeph	Zephaniah
Esther	Esther	Hag	Haggai
Job	Job	Zech	Zechariah
Ps	Psalms	Mal	Malachi
Prov	Proverbs		

For New Testament Books

Matt	Matthew	1 Tim	1 Timothy
Mark	Mark	2 Tim	2 Timothy
Luke	Luke	Titus	Titus
John	John	Philem	Philemon
Acts	Acts	Heb	Hebrews
Rom	Romans	James	James
1 Cor	1 Corinthians	1 Pet	1 Peter
2 Cor	2 Corinthians	2 Pet	2 Peter
Gal	Galatians	1 John	1 John
Eph	Ephesians	2 John	2 John
Phil	Philippians	3 John	3 John
Col	Colossians	Jude	Jude
1 Thes	1 Thessalonians	Rev	Revelation
2 Thes	2 Thessalonians		

EXAMPLE: 2 Cor 5:17 refers to the book, 2 Corinthians and the scripture found in chapter 5, verse 17. 2 Cor 5:17-6:2 refers to the book 2 Corinthians with the passage starting at chapter 5, verse 17 and going through to chapter 6, verse 2 of that book.

AUTHOR'S FOREWORD

This book actually started some 35 years ago, when I first discovered the writings of E.W. Kenyon. I consumed the few books of his I had access to. At the same time I was discovering that much of the other materials I was exposed to had conflicts with each other and the Scriptures. As a newly excited believer, I decided to first go with the Word of God.

Back then, a lot of conversations started with, "xxxx teacher says ..." Very few of us said, "But/for the Word of God says ..." I decided that if the Scriptures were to be my authority and all these people said different things about the Scriptures, at least I could learn first what the Scriptures said and then discover the implications.

So I developed my own way to read Christian books. I would read a book and highlight all the scripture references and all the scriptural phases I could recognize. Then I would look them up. If it was missing, I would write the scripture reference in the book. I would read the book rather fast the first time through, marking the Scriptures, and then I would go back and read the book and the Bible at the same time. In the Bible, I would read the entire chapter a reference came from. Soon I found it was better to read two chapters before the referenced chapter, the referenced chapter itself and then two chapters following.

With this process, if I could verify that what the author was saying was consistent with the Scriptures, I kept what was said. If not, I marked it, much like a shoal warning, and moved on. I did the same for any conclusions the author drew. If I could not validate them with Scriptures, I marked them as warnings. Some books I just stopped reading as not worth the effort to mark all the shoals. Kenyon was one of the few authors for whom, at the time, I had no warning marks. This method slowed my reading considerably, but soon I became known as a walking Bible.

In this manner, I looked forward to reading the little book, *Identification* by E.W. Kenyon. I don't remember the exact details, but I came home after work on a Friday evening, put on a pot of coffee and started following the process I just described. I was probably also fasting, but I am not sure of that. So, with coffee, highlighter, Bible, pad, pen and *Strong's Concordance* on the table, I started. I finished some 18 hours later around 1 PM on Saturday afternoon.

I was "cramming" on the Word of God, just as I had done for years as a college student. I may even have written the scripture reference on the pad, or even the whole passage it came from. When finished I started to clean up the dirty dishes in the kitchen and put on another pot of coffee (remember I hadn't slept at all that Friday night). I was working away on the dirty dishes when I noticed the percolator was really bubbling. You may remember the kind. It had a ceramic bottom and sidewalls, a metal top, a plastic lid with a raised glass center so you could see when the coffee was percolating. For those who do not know, you had to watch when the coffee was percolating and then turn the heat down, or else you could get a small explosion, as the top burst and hot coffee and grounds went everywhere.

I reached over to grab the coffee pot, and as I picked it up, it erupted all over my hand. Coffee grounds and boiling coffee covered my hand. The hot coffee ran off quickly, but the coffee grounds stayed there, and I could feel my flesh burning. I had visions of third-degree burns with a swollen hand and flesh dropping off of it.

Then suddenly what I had been reading for 18 hours (my Identification with Christ in His death and resurrection and how, when He was raised from the dead, I was raised too, and death had no place in me) popped into my mind. I knew I was identified with His total healing, and this accident and burned flesh did not belong to me.

I recognized the voice in my head of the pain, swollen hand and loss of use of that hand was not God's. By the stripes of Jesus, I had been healed, and healed I was. Now you may not have responded the same way, but here is what I did. And I did it without thought.

I commanded my hand to be healed, the pain to go and the devil to shut up, all in the name of Jesus. I looked at my red hand, starting to swell, and said something like, "I am healed in Jesus. Hand, be whole. And that is that." Then I proceeded to put my hand in the scalding hot dishwater and finished washing the dishes, then cleaned up the stove and counter of all the spilled coffee and grounds.

Remember, I had been filling my head with the Word of God on our Identification in Christ for 18 hours non-stop, with book reading and Bible study. I knew what God's Word said. I knew His will about healing. I knew it so much that it took me until the next day, Sunday, in the late afternoon, to realize that I had been healed on Saturday. I looked at my hand, and there was nothing unusual there. It was as good as always.

After I had finished cleaning the kitchen and doing whatever else I did, then I went to sleep Saturday night. And I never even looked at my hand the rest of the day after those first few moments. I do remember that, as I went back to washing the dishes right after the accident, I heard a voice in my head saying, "That water is hot; it will make it even worse. That flesh will fall off in the water and on the dishes, and your hand will be ruined." I said something like, "Go, devil, I am healed in Jesus. Go!" I put my hand straight into the hot water coming out of the faucet, and then did not look at my hand again. It was not a struggle of faith; rather, I acted in certainty.

Ever since then I have been teaching this awesome truth of our Identification in Christ, and have often used E.W. Kenyon's books to lead Bible studies and also in my preaching. I am sure I often speak in his unique style of writing.

Discovering Our Redemption also follows the style of E. W. Kenyon where the scriptural facts are presented first and then the implications and ways to apply those facts follow. This book is a combination of what I learned in that little book, *Identification*, and additional teachings that have borne fruit over the years concerning our redemption by and in the blood of Jesus Christ.

As I wrote this book, I was strengthened in the power of these awesome truths once again. I trust Holy Spirit to do the same and even greater for you, as together we explore the work of Jesus in those Universe-changing 52 days stretching from the Last Supper to the Day of Pentecost.

I aim for 50% or more scripture in my writing, and my goal is to accurately describe what God is saying before I deal with the implications. As you read, you will see many of the same verses repeated. This is intentional. My goal is that, if you should also spend 18 or more hours reading this straight through but are not as diligent as I was that night, you will still have scripture for every comment in this book, to persuade you of these awesome truths.

I would like to say that from that Saturday on I was a power source of faith. My confidence in God did last about 5 days. By the 5th day or so I was back to my normal "hoping" style because I did not keep cramming on God's Word, and I was not in an environment that kept stressing our redemption in the blood of Jesus.

It was 30 years before I learned that cramming, while effective in the short term, is only good for 3 to 5 days after you stop saturating your mind, if you do not keep at it for at least 90 days. What I did in those 2 days was cognitive mind learning and did not keep at it long enough to write it on my heart. But I got the results I needed, and have repeated this many times.

I did learn a valuable tool, that when I did need answers, cramming on specific aspects of God's Word can work to build that path through which He can bless. What I lacked was good books that taught God's Word and had plenty of scriptures to keep my mind persuaded. That is when I started writing my own books, to provide those kinds of tools for myself and others.

Thus, *Discovering Our Redemption* is written so that as you saturate yourself in these redemption truths of the Scriptures, your confidence in God can grow to provide Him that path of faith He can use to bless you as needed per His covenant promises in the Bible.

Here is a powerful summary of the goal of this book: <u>1 John 5:13</u> "These things have I written unto you that believe on the name of the Son of God; that ye may know that ye have eternal *zoe*/life, and that ye may believe on the name of the Son of God. 14 And this is the confidence that we have in him, that, if we *aiteo*/ask any thing according to his will, he heareth us: 15 and if we know that he hear us, whatsoever we *aiteo*/ask (*require, demand and expect as due by Bible promise*), we know that we have the *aiteo*/petitions that we *aiteo*/desired of him."

Introduction

Welcome! Together we will take a journey. This journey will start in the pages of the Bible and take you to the vast realm of spiritual reality. We will look at recorded historical facts in the normal, sense-ruled physical world of flesh and blood, and enter into the usually invisible world of angels, demons and God Himself. Our goal is to pull back the spiritual curtain, so that the spiritual realities lead to new and greater levels of God's love in your life.

We are going on a journey to discover what Jesus came to do and how God accomplished our redemption unto the justification of *zoe*/life in Christ Jesus. That may be quite a mouthful, but it is a reality. In the process, we will discover amazing facts that will challenge your mind.

The key scripture for this book is Philem 6 "That the communication of thy faith may become effectual by the acknowledging of every good thing which is in you in Christ Jesus." We will discover what Jesus accomplished in the 52 days leading from the Passover Last Supper to the Day of Pentecost in Acts Chapter 2. The results of what Jesus and Father God accomplished are what we have in Christ, even before we are born-again. Then we receive from God His wondrous new creation, by faith in that work. This is our equipment to then live out our Christian lives.

Philem 6 tells us the key to an effective walk, by God's standard, is to first know, in intimate detail, every good thing we have in Christ and then use that information of what we have in Christ so that we become a master craftsman in producing the life of God in our own lives and in the lives of others around us. That is part of the meaning of the original Greek word translated here as, "acknowledging." With this foundation of practical expertise, we then can walk to the standard God has made us for, i.e., to be effective for Him in our Christian lives, i.e., "communication."

The practical aspect of this is that if you don't know what you already have in Christ and you need it, when you don't think you have it, you will spend an inordinate amount of time in prayer and other works trying to get what you already have. The result often seems to be like the tantrums or despondency of a teenager who wants to use the family car but thinks it is gone on a trip. There is an authorization note on the kitchen table with the car keys attached, and the car is in the garage ready to go. In all that drama, he just doesn't know yet that the car and permission slip were waiting for him all the time. Our goal is for you to know what we already have in Christ so you can go about the business of becoming a master craftsman in the things of God to His glory. So let's go on a quick drive through our new-creation redemption neighborhood.

We ask you to read with an open mind and let the reality of these great facts concerning our redemption in Jesus soak in. As you do so, you may realize that perhaps in your experience, you and those you know, may have much opportunity to expand your knowledge and use of these facts.

Some of you may get angry about why these truths have been hidden for so long. It may feel like you have been living in poverty and misery on the outside of a wonderful castle, but did not know the door was open to you all the time. Not only was it open, but you are a special invited guest. And not even just a guest, but a full citizen of this wondrous domain. And not just a citizen, but a part of the royal family! If you feel anything like this, please know that you have just received a prayer assignment from God. After prayer for God's truth to be set free in you and others, share this with others, and let God's Word set them free as well. Start a study group around this book.

We will show what God accomplished in His Mighty Arm, Jesus of Nazareth, in these 52 days leading from the New Covenant Passover Meal to the sending of the long-promised Holy Spirit on the Day of Pentecost. We will then discuss ways to apply this knowledge of Jesus' earth-shattering and Universe-changing work.

These 52 Days of Jesus can be grouped into three major areas:
- From the Last Supper to the Resurrection (Days 1 through 3, on the *"third day"*)
- The Teaching from the Scriptures to the Ascension (Days 3 through 43, *"40 days"*)
- The Coronation and sending forth of Holy Spirit on the Day of Pentecost (Days 43 through 52)

The actual days, from the Last Supper or Passover meal, is of some debate. For a more detailed discussion we refer you to the Bibliography (see Mann, Robertson and Thomas). Following the traditional celebration days of the Last Supper on Holy Thursday, Crucifixion on Good Friday, and Resurrection on Easter Sunday, we have 52 days from the Last Supper to the Day of Pentecost.

The term *Pentecost* is from the Jewish observance of the 50 Days of Omer, which are from the Feast of First Fruits (here on Resurrection Sunday) to the fiftieth day as celebration, when the Law was given by Moses, and on which Jesus poured out the gift of Holy Spirit in a new and different way than had ever been done before.

After the Resurrection, Jesus appeared to the disciples over a period of 40 days until the Ascension. Acts 1:1 "The former treatise have I [Luke] made, O Theophilus, of all that Jesus began both to do and teach, 2 until the day in which he was taken up, after that he through the Holy Ghost had given commandments unto the apostles whom he had chosen: 3 to whom also he shewed himself alive after his passion by many infallible proofs, being seen of them [*over a period of*] forty days, and speaking of the things pertaining to the kingdom of God."

The disciples apparently were in prayer in the Upper Room from the Ascension until Pentecost morning. Acts 1:10 "And while they [*the disciples*] looked stedfastly toward heaven as he [*Jesus*] went up, behold, two men stood by them in white apparel; 11 which also said, Ye men of Galilee, why stand ye gazing up into heaven? this same Jesus, which is taken up from you into heaven, shall so come in like manner as ye have seen him go into heaven. 12 Then returned they unto Jerusalem from the mount called Olivet, which is from Jerusalem a sabbath day's journey. 13 And when they were come in, they went up into an upper room, where abode both Peter, and James, and John, and Andrew, Philip, and Thomas, Bartholomew, and Matthew, James the son of Alphaeus, and Simon Zelotes, and Judas the brother of James. 14 These all continued with one accord in prayer and supplication, with the women, and Mary the mother of Jesus, and with his brethren."

So the disciples were in prayer in the Upper Room for nine full days after the Ascension, and on the morning of the tenth day, the Day of Pentecost, the fiftieth day from the Feast of First Fruits with the wave offering, while still in prayer, Holy Spirit was received in a new and different way than ever before. Acts 1:4 "And, being assembled together with them, [*Jesus*] commanded them that they should not depart from Jerusalem, but wait for the promise of the Father, which, saith he, ye have heard of me. 5 For John truly baptized with water; but ye shall be baptized with the Holy Ghost not many days hence."

The big issue we have to understand is the difference and the significance of physical events and spiritual events, that is, to understand the what and the how of the impact of the physical on the spiritual and the impact of the spiritual on the physical. The Bible records events occurring over some 4,000 years and is full of such spirit-physical interactions and some explanations. That is one of the things that sets the Bible apart from other books.

We have the most detail on the physical aspects of these 52 days of Jesus in the Gospels and Acts. What Jesus accomplished in the physical did not appear to change much. Even in our world today, we do not acknowledge much direct impact of it. Today, less than one third of the world's population professes the God of the Bible as the one true God who sent His Son, Jesus of Nazareth to redeem us from our sins. Still, the sun continues to rise like clockwork every day and still shines, even when hindered by clouds, the birds still fly through the air, and water still flows downhill.

But the Universe is spiritual first, and the physical is a manifestation of the spiritual. After all, according to Genesis chapter one, the Universe we see was made by spirit words mixed with Holy Spirit. Jesus, as seen in the Gospels, demonstrated that God's Spirit is greater than the physical and can change the physical. The rest of the New Testament shows that this is still a reality.

The understanding of what Jesus accomplished in the spirit that changed the Universe forever comes primarily from the revelation of Paul in his epistles. Eph 3:1 "For this cause I Paul, the prisoner of Jesus Christ for you Gentiles, 2 if ye have heard of the dispensation of the grace of God which is given me to you-ward: 3 how that by revelation he made known unto me the mystery; (as I wrote afore in few words, 4 whereby, when ye read, ye may understand my knowledge in the mystery of Christ) 5 which in other ages was not made known unto the sons of men, as it is now revealed unto his holy apostles and prophets by the Spirit; 6 that the Gentiles should be fellowheirs, and of the same body, and partakers of his promise in Christ by the gospel: 7 whereof I was made a minister, according to the gift of the grace of God given unto me by the effectual working of his power. 8 Unto me, who am less than the least of all saints, is this grace given, that I should preach among the Gentiles the unsearchable riches of Christ; 9 and to make all men see what is the fellowship of the mystery, which from the beginning of the world hath been hid in God, who created all things by Jesus Christ: 10 to the intent that now unto the principalities and powers in heavenly places might be known by the church the manifold wisdom of God, 11 according to the eternal purpose which he purposed in Christ Jesus our Lord."

Note in verse 10 that things can now happen that could not happen before. That means there was a change, or shift, that impacts all of creation (our Universe) some 2000 years ago.

While we have detail on that entire Passover day 2000 years ago, from the preparations for the Last Supper to the Crucifixion, we have almost no detail in the Gospels or Acts on what Jesus did in the belly of the Earth for 3 days until His resurrection. We are told the effect of His resurrection, but not specifically the details of how He did what He accomplished. We do learn some of this from the Psalms, as referenced in the Gospel record. The unseen spiritual events, while the apostles wept in unbelief and fear, and their significance is described in the Epistles.

Other than from the Epistles by inference, we do not know in detail what Jesus taught those 40 days after the resurrection or what He was doing in Heaven those 10 days after His Ascension until the Pentecost of Acts 2. For example, the Scriptures do not tell us when Jesus carried His blood to Heaven's Mercy Seat for the propitiation of the sin of mankind. We do know it happened, but not exactly how or when.

Pentecost means the 50th day after Passover and celebrates the giving of the Law by Moses. Jesus brought a new order to the Universe. John 1:16 "And of his (*Jesus'*) fulness have all we received, and grace for grace. 17 For the law was given by Moses, but grace and truth came by Jesus Christ."

From Acts we do have more physical detail and the spiritual explanations on the Day of Pentecost and the days immediately afterward in the lives of the disciples. Additional indications of the impact of the events of Pentecost are also found in the Epistles.

We will discuss the events and facts of redemption, along with the results, as described in the Scriptures. But we are warned not to stop there. Bible knowledge that does not lead to action can lead to deception. The Bible is a "learn-and-go-do" book. Not doing is to miss the prime message. The key is to use these facts for the calling we have received in our redemption. James 1:22 "But be ye doers of the word, and not hearers only, deceiving your own selves." 1 Cor 8:1 "Now as touching things offered unto idols, we know that we all have knowledge [*of religious and spiritual things*]. Knowledge puffeth up, but *agape*/charity edifieth. 2 And if any man think that he knoweth anything, he knoweth nothing yet as he ought to know. 3 But if any man *agape*/love God, the same is known of him."

You *agape*/love God by *agape*/loving your fellowman, especially those of the household of faith. And you cannot *agape*/love God and not *agape*/love your fellowman. 1 John 4:20 "If a man say, I *agape*/love God, and hateth his brother, he is a liar: for he that *agape*/loveth not his brother whom he hath seen, how can he *agape*/love God whom he hath not seen? 21 And this commandment have we from him, That he who *agape*/loveth God *agape*/love his brother also."

Jesus demonstrated how to *agape*/love our fellowman. Here is one summary: Acts 10:36 "The word which God sent unto the children of Israel, preaching peace by Jesus Christ: (he is Lord of all:) 37 that word, I say, ye know, which was published throughout all Judaea, and began from Galilee, after the baptism which John preached; 38 how God anointed Jesus of Nazareth with the Holy Ghost and with power: who went about doing good, and healing all that were oppressed of the devil; for God was with him."

And another summary: 1 John 2:3 "And hereby we do know that we know him, if we keep his commandments. 4 He that saith, I know him, and keepeth not his commandments, is a liar, and the truth is not in him. 5 But whoso keepeth his word, in him verily is the *agape*/love of God perfected: hereby know we that we are in him. 6 He that saith he abideth in him ought himself also so to walk, even as he (*Jesus*) walked."

So yes, as you implement these redemption facts, you will walk more effectively in the natural and the supernatural of God, to improve your own life and the lives of others for God. Besides the human level—good works of alms and other acts of kindness and mercy—we are told: James 1:26 "If any man among you seem to be religious, and bridleth not his tongue, but deceiveth his own heart, this man's religion is vain. 27 Pure religion and undefiled before God and the Father is this, To visit the fatherless and widows in their affliction, and to keep himself unspotted from the world."

While we discuss some methods and implications, size limits what we can do in one volume. For more application knowledge on how to use these redemption facts to manifest the glory of God more effectively in every part of your life, please refer to our other works (please visit www.CovenantPeaceMinistries.com for more information and resources).

Another goal of this book is to explain the Scriptures in a way that can help you effectively grow in the knowledge of Father God, Jesus and Holy Spirit. We are not after academic knowledge, but, rather, that which releases more of Jesus into your world in power, love and the mind of Christ. Therefore I have included many scriptures. This also means you do not need to have your Bible handy as you read, but I do recommend it highly. Rom 10:16 "But they have not all obeyed the gospel. For Esaias saith, Lord, who hath believed our report? 17 So then faith cometh by hearing, and hearing by the word (*you do*) of God [*the gospel of Christ in you, the present-tense hope of God manifesting His glory in the Earth through you, i.e., that our God reigns through men*]."

If you want to receive and make a greater impact, I suggest you first read *Discovering Our Redemption* through once, then go back and look up every scripture reference in your own Bible. Then, where possible, read the reference and then the Bible chapter of the reference and two chapters before the chapter the reference came from, the referenced chapter, and then two chapters following it, then the referenced chapter again to understand what God said in the Bible (and if I have described it accurately). For example, if I reference Isaiah 53:11, go read Isaiah 53:11; then read chapters 51, 52, 53, 54 and 55. Then go back and read Isaiah chapter 53 again and focus on the verse or verses referenced. If the reference is in the last chapter of a book, say, Ephesians 6, then read at least Ephesians 4, 5 and 6, or even a full five chapters, starting at chapter 2 and reading though to the end of chapter 6.

This may make the process go much slower, but for most, it is also a life-transforming process, as you persuade yourself in the awesome truths of our redemption in Christ. The facts of the cross do little if you do not know how to walk in the triumph of Christ we now have. Our redemption is complete and in past tense. Jesus is no longer on the cross, but He is on the Throne of God! The requirements of God become the path that God can inhabit when we do them. The first step is to know what God said in the Scriptures.

Acts 17:10 "And the brethren immediately sent away Paul and Silas by night unto Berea: who coming thither went into the synagogue of the Jews. 11 These were more noble than those in Thessalonica, in that they received the word with all readiness of mind, and searched the scriptures daily, whether those things were so. 12 Therefore many of them believed; also of honourable women which were Greeks, and of men, not a few."

This is one of the secrets to building your believing (your faith). When you hear or read something, go back to the Scriptures and see if what is said is really so. Then, if it is, make that truth a part of your life by writing it on your heart to do it.

Please note, if you find any areas for improvement, please send them to us at: Info@CovenantPeaceMinistries.com.

The final section of this book is a short glossary, as many of the key words and concepts used here may be unfamiliar to the reader. Those that are familiar may not be understood to practical application. In the Glossary, these words or phrases are explained in detail, and you may actually want to read that material first, to help you better understand what the Scriptures are saying.

For over 35 years I have watched this seemingly-incomprehensible truth release people into more love and the power of God. So this book is the fruit of watching the Word of God transform lives, when they are understood enough to be applied. I have designed this book from years of answering questions about these awesome redemption facts and how to walk in them. Typically the answer is either in the next few paragraphs of the book or in the Glossary. If that does not satisfy you, research your own Bible and please feel free to contact us at our website.

Now, hold onto your hats, open your heart, and let's explore God's Word of Redemption together.

Here is a prayer to get us started (with scripture text modified into the first person).

Father, I believe that You raised Jesus from the dead, and I come to You now in the name of Jesus, my Lord and *aiteo*/ask Eph 1:17 that *You,* the God of our Lord Jesus Christ, the Father of glory, may give unto *me Your* spirit of wisdom and revelation in the knowledge of *You:* 18 the eyes of *my* understanding being enlightened; that *I* may know what is the hope of *Your* calling [*for me*], and what the riches of the glory of *Your* inheritance in the saints [*including me*], 19 and what is the exceeding greatness of *Your* power *toward me* who *am a believer*, according to the working of *Your* mighty power, 20 which *You* wrought in Christ, when *You* raised him from the dead, and set him at *Your* own right hand in the heavenly places, 21 far above all principality, and power, and might, and dominion, and every name that is named, not only in this world, but also in that which is to come: 22 and hath put all things under *Jesus'* feet, and gave *Jesus* to be the head over all things to the church, 23 which is his body [*and of which I am a part*], the fulness of him that filleth all in all. 2:1 And *to know and understand to walking in Your glory, zealous for good works, by faith, working in* agape/love, *that You have* quickened *me,* who *was* dead in trespasses and sins; 2 wherein in time past *I* walked according to the course of this world, according to the prince of the power of the air, the spirit that now worketh in the children of disobedience: 3 among whom also we all had our conversation in times past in the lusts of our flesh, fulfilling the desires of the flesh and of the mind;

and were by nature the children of wrath, even as others. 4 But *You, Father* God, who *are* rich in mercy, for *Your* great *agape*/love wherewith *You* agape/loved us, 5 even when we were dead in sins, hath quickened us together with Christ *[2000 years ago]*, (by grace *we* are *sozo*/saved;) 6 and hath raised us up together *[including me]*, and made us sit together in heavenly places in Christ Jesus *[including me]*: 7 that in the ages to come *You* might shew the exceeding riches of *Your* grace in *Your* kindness toward us *[including me]* through Christ Jesus. 8 For by grace are *we sozo*/saved through faith; and that not of *ourselves*: it is the gift of *You, Father* God: 9 not of works, lest any man should boast. 10 For we are *Your* workmanship, created in Christ Jesus unto good works, which *You, Father* God, *hast* before ordained that we should walk in them." *I praise and thank You, Father God, for Your great work in Jesus. Help me to know how loved I am by You. Thank You. In the name of Jesus, thank You, Father God, thank You!*

Donald C. Mann
Landenberg, Pennsylvania

Part I

Understanding Our Redemption More Fully

Chapter 1

Redemption: God's Answer to the Fall of Adam

In the Bible, the need for our Redemption is the direct effect of Adam's sin. Sin is spiritual and legal, with the spiritual effects manifested in the physical Earth. These effects are called the curse of sin. God's great Redemption in Jesus initially addresses the legal and spiritual aspects, with the physical manifestation to come later. This is much like a contract, where the contract is first signed and paid for, and then the new owner takes possession and control.

The effect of Redemption is the removal of sin as an issue between God and man and reuniting man to God. Rom 3:23 "For all have sinned, and come short of the glory of God; 24 being justified (*just as if you had never sinned or will ever sin, so you are holy, blameless and unreproveable in the sight of God, just as Jesus is*) freely by his grace through the redemption that is in Christ Jesus: 25 whom God hath set forth to be a propitiation through faith in his blood, to declare his righteousness for the remission (*obliteration, washing, removal, purging and putting away*) of sins that are past, through the forbearance of God." It is the grace of God that gives us a level of Redemption that required Jesus as the ransom price. Even though it required the suffering of Christ, Jesus and the Father did it gladly. That immeasurable price is the level of value God sets on mankind.

DISCOVERING OUR REDEMPTION

Father God, Eph 1:5 "having predestinated us unto the adoption of children by Jesus Christ to himself, according to the good pleasure of his will, 6 to the praise of the glory of his grace, wherein he hath made us accepted in the *agape*/beloved. 7 In whom we have redemption through his blood, the forgiveness (*remission, removal, purging and putting away*) of sins, according to the riches of his grace; 8 wherein he hath abounded toward us in all wisdom and prudence; 9 having made known unto us the mystery of his will, according to his good pleasure which he hath purposed in himself." The Greek word *agape is* translated in the KJV as both love and charity. Please see the Glossary for more details on the meaning of *agape*.

Notice, in Ephesians 1:5, God intended to adopt man back into His family by the Redemption through the blood of Jesus. In order for an adoption to take place, there must have been a time when man was not in God's family. That time was when Adam sinned and lost his position as a son of God and, instead, became a son of darkness and death, for himself and the whole human race. Col 1:12 "Giving thanks (*continually*) unto the Father, which hath made us meet to be partakers of the inheritance of the saints in light: 13 who hath delivered us from the power (*authority, jurisdiction, lordship or kingdom*) of darkness, and hath translated us into the kingdom (*family and household*) of his *agape*/dear Son: 14 in whom we have redemption through his blood, even the forgiveness (*remission, washing, removal, purging and putting away*) of sins."

Eph 2:18 "For through him (*Jesus*) we both have access by one Spirit unto the Father. 19 Now therefore ye are no more strangers and foreigners, but fellowcitizens with the saints, and of the household of God." The use of household means you are back in the family of God.

Gal 4:4 "But when the fulness of the time was come, God sent forth his Son, made of a woman, made under the law, 5 to redeem them that were under the law, that we might receive the adoption of sons. 6 And because ye are sons, God hath sent forth the Spirit of his Son into your hearts, crying, Abba (*Daddy*), Father." When you receive that adoption, you become a permanent member of the family, based on the Father's love for you, your Redemption in Jesus, and not your performance.

A great wonder is that God would provide a legal adoption by faith, but also recreate the person into a new kind of being, where Holy Spirit, the Administrator of the power of God in this Universe, by a process called the new birth or the new creation, takes up permanent residence in them. God not only knows and adopts you legally, but recreates your spirit as His love child. So the Christian is a legal love child of God and a partaker of the very *zoe* life and nature of God. Now a human is the vessel by which the God of the Universe releases the Spirit and power of God to rule the Universe for God. Col 1:27 "To whom God would make known what is the riches of the glory of this mystery among the Gentiles; which is Christ in you, the hope of glory."

REDEMPTION: GOD'S ANSWER TO THE FALL OF ADAM

God first stated the law of sin and subsequent death, where death, in fast and slow forms, is the curse, or evil consequence, of breaking His laws. Gen 2:16 "And the Lord God commanded the man, saying, Of every tree of the garden thou mayest freely eat: 17 but of the tree of the knowledge of good and evil, thou shalt not eat of it: for in the day that thou eatest thereof thou shalt surely die."

God's Redemption is deliverance from the ownership of sin (death, darkness, and Satan). God's Salvation is the manifestation of this deliverance, into the Earth, from the consequence of sin and death, which includes any disease, danger or evil manifested in the Earth. Salvation is the manifestation of this deliverance from the curse of sin found in the law of sin and death, and entry into the state of divine well-being. Salvation is the manifestation of the goodness and glory of God in the Earth.

God is both our Savior, the one who implements Salvation, and our Redeemer, the one who buys us back from slavery and death. Isa 49:24 "Shall the prey be taken from the mighty, or the lawful captive delivered? 25 But thus saith the Lord, Even the captives of the mighty shall be taken away, and the prey of the terrible shall be delivered: for I will contend with him that contendeth with thee, and I will save thy children. 26 And I will feed them that oppress thee with their own flesh; and they shall be drunken with their own blood, as with sweet wine: and all flesh shall know that I the Lord am thy Saviour and thy Redeemer, the mighty One of Jacob."

Redemption includes not only a change of ownership due to sin, but a change of spiritual condition, where the curse, or penalty, for sin no longer applies. This release from sin and the curse of sin is so great that Holy Spirit can now come and dwell in the Christian. Gal 3:13 "Christ hath redeemed us from the curse of the law, being made a curse for us: for it is written, Cursed is every one that hangeth on a tree: 14 that the blessing of Abraham might come on the Gentiles through Jesus Christ; that we might receive the promise of the Spirit through faith."

That is the legal state, and it is brought to Earth by the exercise of faith in God. The curse is an evil condition with fear, torment, limitation, disease and death. Protection, healing or deliverance from that curse is called Salvation.

Salvation (Greek: *soteria*) is the state of being healed, made whole, delivered and without limitation; and *saved* (Greek: *sozo*) is the process by which the Kingdom of God comes to Earth and operates in specific events or things. *Soteria* is the noun form, and *sozo* the verb of the same Greek word. The fullness of this Salvation is described in Revelation chapters 21 and 22. Biblical Salvation is based on the results of our Redemption in Christ and covers our entire being, spirit, soul and body. 1 Thes 5:23 "And the very God of peace sanctify you wholly; and I pray God your whole spirit and *psuche*/soul (*life*) and body be preserved blameless unto the coming of our Lord Jesus Christ." Note: the Greek word for soul, *psuche*, is translat-

DISCOVERING OUR REDEMPTION

ed as both soul and life in English translations, depending on how the translators evaluated either English word in the context of the meaning.

A simple way to think of this is to know the blood of Jesus was for our Redemption from the bondage of sin, the curse of sin, and Satan as a source in your life; and what happened to Jesus' body was for our Salvation from the curse of sin to glorification with Jesus. Obviously the two elements, the body and the blood, are intertwined, as His blood could not be offered unless it came out of His body by the scourging and piercings on the day of His binding and crucifixion.

1 Pet 2:24 "Who his own self bare our sins in his own body on the tree, that we, being dead to sins, should *zao*/live unto righteousness: by whose stripes ye were healed." Manifestation in this Earth of this spiritual truth is Salvation or healing that you experience. The Greek word *zoe* is the noun form and is translated as life in the KJV. This is not the same as *psuche*, which is also often translated as life in the KJV. The verb form, *zao*, is translated as live and living. It means the life source powering your thoughts, words and actions. For the Christian, this *zoe* life is in your spirit and is released by faith, as you act according to God's Word.

Another way to understand this is that Redemption is the legal act, and Salvation is when you receive a part or the entire benefit of Redemption as the Salvation of God. When that benefit is manifested in the Earth it is called Salvation. So whether it is getting a small cut healed by God, or Heaven coming to Earth, as seen in Revelation 21 and 22, both are called acts of Salvation. And all the benefits, or manifestations, of Salvation are based on the Redemption in Jesus.

Another way to look at Salvation is that it is the total removal of any effect and control of Satan and the total presence and control of God on Earth. Rev 12:9 "And the great dragon was cast out, that old serpent, called the Devil, and Satan, which deceiveth the whole world: he was cast out into the earth, and his angels were cast out with him. 10 And I heard a loud voice saying in heaven, Now is come *soteria*/salvation, and strength, and the kingdom of our God, and the power of his Christ: for the accuser of our brethren is cast down, which accused them before our God day and night."

God removed man from the legal status of enemy (because sin against God is an enemy act against God), and made peace unto the status of full Reconciliation through the blood and body of Jesus. Col 1:20 "And, having made peace through the blood of his cross, by him to reconcile all things unto himself; by him, I say, whether they be things in earth, or things in heaven. 21 And you, that were sometime alienated and enemies in your mind by wicked works, yet now hath he reconciled 22 in the body of his flesh through death, to present you holy and unblameable and unreproveable in his sight."

The fruit of this Reconciliation in the body of Jesus is that man is made holy, unblameable and unreproveable to God. This is a good definition of being justified, made righteous or made the righteousness of God in Christ Jesus. So the fruit of Redemption is peace unto Reconciliation, unto the righteousness of God in Christ Jesus, unto eternal *zoe*/life, unto partaking of the divine nature of God, unto indwelling Holy Spirit, and unto the full Salvation of God.

2 Cor 5:18 "And all things are of God, who hath reconciled us to himself by Jesus Christ, and hath given to us the ministry of reconciliation; 19 to wit, that God was in Christ, reconciling the world unto himself, not imputing their trespasses unto them; and hath committed unto us the word of reconciliation. 20 Now then we are ambassadors for Christ, as though God did beseech you by us: we pray you in Christ's stead, be ye reconciled to God. 21 For he hath made him to be sin for us, who knew no sin; that we might be made the righteousness of God in him. 6 We then, as workers together with him, beseech you also that ye receive not the grace of God in vain. 2 (For he saith, I have heard thee in a time accepted, and in the day of *soteria*/salvation have I succoured thee: behold, now is the accepted time; behold, now is the day of *soteria*/salvation.)"

Rom 5:18 "Therefore as by the offence of one (*Adam*) judgment came upon all men to condemnation; even so by the righteousness of one (*Jesus*) the free gift came upon all men unto justification (*being made righteous just as if you had never sinned or will ever sin again, to the level of the righteousness of God in Christ Jesus and making you holy, unblameable and unreproveable in the sight of God*) of *zoe*/life."

This passage describes how that Redemption is the basis of our Salvation: Eph 1:12 "That we should be to the praise of his glory, who first trusted in Christ. 13 In whom ye also trusted, after that ye heard the word of truth, the gospel of your *soteria*/salvation: in whom also after that ye believed, ye were sealed with that holy Spirit of promise, 14 which is the earnest of our inheritance until the redemption of the purchased possession, unto the praise of his glory."

Concerning Salvation or being saved: Eph 2:4 "But God, who is rich in mercy, for his great *agape*/love wherewith he *agape*/loved us, 5 even when we were dead in sins, hath quickened us together with Christ, (by grace ye are *sozo*/saved;) 6 and hath raised us up together, and made us sit together in heavenly places in Christ Jesus: 7 that in the ages to come he might shew the exceeding riches of his grace in his kindness toward us through Christ Jesus."

In the realm of the Spirit, where the throne of God is, right now you are sitting beside Father God in Jesus, and when He looks at you, He only sees Jesus. This is the legal condition of all mankind because of the work of Jesus by the cross. We enter into this legal fact by faith in the work of Jesus.

Notice this *sozo*/saved, Salvation, is based on when Jesus was made alive, raised from the dead, and, later, bodily raised to be seated beside the Father in heavenly places. All of this is part of Salvation, made possible by our Redemption through the blood of Jesus. Salvation includes the manifestation of the will of God

DISCOVERING OUR REDEMPTION

into the Earth, based on spiritual truth. We enter the legal status of Redemption and the manifested benefits of Salvation by faith in the work of God in Jesus because God *agape*/loves all mankind, including you.

For example, sickness is the physical manifestation of a spiritual condition. Salvation is the state of being healed and the full goodness of the Kingdom of God in operation against or over that sickness. Biblically, the process of being healed is also called "being *sozo*/saved." In the process of "being saved," the exercise of the kingdom of darkness is stopped (death in any form, fast or slow), and God's life is now flowing to rescue and restore, and to allow continued blessing or life.

Here are two uses and forms of the Greek verb *sozo* (the process or action of being saved or healed), to show how it applied to events in the physical body. As Jesus hung on the cross, those who put Him there spoke: Matt 27:40 "And saying, Thou that destroyest the temple, and buildest it in three days, ***sozo*/save** thyself. If thou be the Son of God, come down from the cross. 41 Likewise also the chief priests mocking him, with the scribes and elders, said, 42 he ***sozo*/saved** others; himself he cannot ***sozo*/save**. If he be the King of Israel, let him now come down from the cross, and we will believe him. 43 He trusted in God; let him deliver him now, if he will have him: for he said, I am the Son of God."

Here *sozo*/saving is related to Jesus no longer bound on the cross but able to live a continued good life. Also note, the mocking leaders said "He *sozo*/saved others," meaning the healing of the sick, raising the dead, casting out devils, cleansing the lepers and restoring the maimed all as acts of "*sozo*/saving." These men understood that the bondage of sickness was at least as great as the physical and governmental bondage and assured death of Jesus on the cross, and called release from that bondage *sozo*/saving. They also understood that when someone got healed, that governmental and physical bondage and assured death was broken, and wholeness could come forth.

Matt 14:35 "And when the men of that place had knowledge of him (*Jesus*), they sent out into all that country round about, and brought unto him all that were diseased; 36 and besought him that they might only touch the hem of his garment: and as many as touched were made perfectly ***diasozo*/whole** (dia *meaning totally or throughout, and* sozo meaning *healed, made whole, as God designed them*)." Note this *diasozo* included any disease or disorder of any kind.

Here *saved* means healing of any and all kinds of unhappy or evil conditions throughout the crowd.

There are other Greek words translated as healed. The point here is that *sozo* is also a manifestation of healing, and Salvation includes physical healing, as described in the Bible.

Redemption and Salvation have two major parts. This follows the Jewish pattern of marriage where, first, there is a betrothal and then a consummation of the marriage a year later. A betrothal was a formal event and required a divorce to break. The event many seem to focus on, the consummation, is the eternal part with God, which is assured after the Day of Judgment. You enter into this legal state of betrothal with the subsequent consummation by faith in the blood of Jesus, or the resurrection of Jesus from the dead.

The other aspect of marriage, as the Bride of Christ, is this: in this life the betrothal, and the quality or character of your betrothal is not assured, except as faith in God by His Word is exercised by the Bride. As in a Jewish marriage, the bride is expected to make herself ready for the consummation of the marriage on the wedding event. Rev 19:7 "Let us be glad and rejoice, and give honour to him: for the marriage of the Lamb is come, and his wife hath made herself ready."

Jesus commanded us to always be preparing for that consummation day: Luke 21:27 "And then shall they see the Son of man coming in a cloud with power and great glory. 28 And when these things begin to come to pass, then look up, and lift up your heads; for your redemption draweth nigh." Here Jesus gets the Bride He paid so dearly to ransom from the Prince of Darkness.

A reminder to God, and the hope of Jesus and the Christian, is that we are sealed with Holy Spirit as our engagement ring! Eph 4:30 "And grieve not the holy Spirit of God, whereby ye are sealed unto the day of redemption."

Holy Spirit is sealed to the Christian until that Day, and His ride in you is not guaranteed to be happy for Him, but He cannot go anywhere until that Day comes. So whatever your theology about sin and the Christian, you must deal with the fact that even when the Christian sins, Holy Spirit is sealed to the Christian, the betrothed, the engaged Bride-to-be of Christ throughout our life on this Earth, unto the fulfillment of that Day. But it is God's goal that this betrothed one will make herself ready and fully pleasing to her Lord for that Day.

Part of the process of "making ready" is the good acts, in God, of the saints, in faith, working through *agape*/love in this life, to bring the Kingdom of God to Earth. Gal 5:6 "For in Jesus Christ neither circumcision availeth anything, nor uncircumcision; but faith which worketh by *agape*/love."

For example, in this betrothed condition, a redeemed, saved Christian can still be sick, unless faith (like Jesus told us to use) will either prevent them from getting sick and/or get them healed directly by Holy Spirit. So there is a legal position that is eternal, and there is a present-life condition that is temporary ... until the eternal is manifested.

In this present life condition, the amount of God's goodness you experience is based on knowledge of the legal facts of our Redemption and Salvation in Jesus and our betrothal, as applied by the believer, in faith, as needed to produce the blessings in this life, as promised by God.

DISCOVERING OUR REDEMPTION

3 John 2 "*Agape*/beloved, I wish (*pray*) above all things that thou mayest prosper and be in health, even as thy *psuche*/soul (*life*) prospereth."

Sin is not the issue with God, if Jesus did His job: Gal 1:1 "Paul, an apostle, (not of men, neither by man, but by Jesus Christ, and God the Father, who raised him from the dead;) ... 3 Grace be to you and peace from God the Father, and from our Lord Jesus Christ, 4 who gave himself for our sins, that he might deliver us from this present evil world, according to the will of God and our Father: 5 to whom be glory for ever and ever. Amen." Notice that Paul states he is an apostle of God because God raised Jesus from the dead, and all of Paul's sins were taken care of in that resurrection.

1 Cor 15:17 "And if Christ be not raised, your faith is vain; ye are yet in your sins."

Rom 4:24 "But for us also, to whom it (*righteousness*) shall be imputed, if we believe on him that raised up Jesus our Lord from the dead; 25 who was delivered for our offences, and was raised again for our justification (*making mankind separated from our sins and made holy, unblameable and unreproveable to and in God*). 5 Therefore being justified (*separated from our sins and made holy, unblameable and unreproveable to and in God*) by faith, we have peace with God through our Lord Jesus Christ: 2 by whom also we have access by faith into this grace wherein we stand, and rejoice in hope of the glory of God."

Here we are told we are now redeemed through the remission of sin by the blood of Jesus, but the fullness (consummation) of that Redemption will not occur until later. Eph 1:6 "To the praise of the glory of his (*Father God's*) grace, wherein he hath made us accepted in the *agape*/beloved. 7 In whom we have redemption through his (*Jesus'*) blood, the forgiveness (*remission, removal, obliteration and putting away*) of sins, according to the riches of his grace; 8 wherein he hath abounded toward us in all wisdom and prudence. ... 13 In whom ye also trusted (*in God who raised Jesus Christ from the dead*), after that ye heard the word of truth, the gospel of your *soteria*/salvation: in whom also after that ye believed, ye were sealed with that holy Spirit of promise, 14 which is the earnest of our inheritance until the redemption of the purchased possession, unto the praise of his glory."

The believer's seal by and of Holy Spirit is the assurance God gets what He paid for in our Redemption, by the body and blood of Jesus Christ, on the Day of Redemption. It is also the believer's assurance for faith to exercise in this life to produce the benefits of Redemption and Salvation.

Since Redemption is about legal position and ownership, based on a price paid, the issue is, "who sets the price?" Obviously the one who sets the price is God.

One definition of *father* is the one who gives you value and significance. By that definition, it is no wonder that Father God is the greatest Father there is, be-

REDEMPTION: GOD'S ANSWER TO THE FALL OF ADAM

cause He spent Jesus, Maker of all things, in awful physical, soulish and spiritual suffering, as the price to buy back man in His great work of Redemption. There is no way to value Jesus, and thus your value assigned by God is immense and, equally, immeasurable.

1 Tim 2:5 "For there is one God, and one mediator between God and men, the man Christ Jesus; 6 who gave himself a ransom for all, to be testified in due time."

There is no doubt in Heaven or Hell that the price Father paid, Jesus, was more than sufficient to redeem man from the kingdom of darkness and translate us into His Kingdom of *agape*/love.

That all men, much less one man, is worth the price of Jesus is beyond imagination in value, yet Father God says we, as a race, are worthy of that awful price, and that each one of us, as an individual, is worth that awful price.

To Father God, you are worth the price of Jesus to get you back legally from the failure of Adam and the legal rule of death by Satan.

This is ultimate value and significance for each one of us. This is *agape* love in action.

John 3:16 "For God so *agape*/loved the world, that he gave his only begotten Son, that whosoever believeth in him should not perish, but have everlasting *zoe*/life. 17 For God sent not his Son into the world to condemn the world; but that the world through him might be *sozo*/saved."

As we understand what God reveals of this great work, keep your mind and heart focused on the fact that the source of all this is His love for you and yours. As that drives your sense of acceptance, care, significance, commitment and value, it will transform you from one in need, to confidence in Father God and His *agape*/love for you, and then to one who gives the *agape* love of God, as His agent, to others.

For those who already walk in the fullness of the knowledge of the Son, this will be a refreshing to always keep the work of Jesus in those 52 days ever in your remembrance. 2 Pet 1:14 "Knowing that shortly I must put off this my tabernacle, even as our Lord Jesus Christ hath shewed me. 15 Moreover I will endeavour that ye may be able after my decease to have these things always in remembrance. 16 For we have not followed cunningly devised fables, when we made known unto you the power and coming of our Lord Jesus Christ, but were eyewitnesses of his majesty."

CHAPTER 2

REDEMPTION FACTS ARE THE WORK OF AGAPE LOVE

The great work of Jesus is our Redemption. No wonder Paul prayed for us to understand these Redemption facts: Eph 1:16 "(*I, Paul,*) Cease not to give thanks for you, making mention of you in my prayers; 17 that the God of our Lord Jesus Christ, the Father of glory, may give unto you *[functioning new creation Christians]* the spirit of wisdom and revelation in the *epignosis*/knowledge of him: 18 the eyes of your understanding being enlightened; that ye may know what is the hope of his calling, and what the riches of the glory of his inheritance in the saints, 19 and what is the exceeding greatness of his power to us-ward who believe, according to the working of his mighty power, 20 which he wrought in Christ, when he raised him from the dead, and set him at his own right hand in the heavenly places, 21 far above all principality, and power, and might, and dominion, and every name that is named, not only in this world, but also in that which is to come: 22 and hath put all things under his feet, and gave him to be the head over all things to the church, 23 which is his body, the fulness of him that filleth all in all."

So that our *agape* love would grow in effectiveness, Paul teaches us also to pray: Eph 3:14 "For this cause I bow my knees unto the Father of our Lord Jesus Christ, 15 of whom the whole family in Heaven and Earth is named, 16 that he would grant you, according to the riches of his glory, to be strengthened with

Redemption Facts Are the Work of Agape Love

might by his Spirit in the inner man; 17 that Christ may dwell in your hearts by faith; that ye, being rooted and grounded in *agape*/love, 18 may be able to comprehend with all saints what is the breadth, and length, and depth, and height; 19 and to know the *agape*/love of Christ, which passeth knowledge, that ye might be filled with all the fulness of God."

God calls this great work of Jesus by the cross the Redemption, the buying back, the Reconciliation, the peace, the restoration to man's original value and position before Adam fell, and translating man back into the Kingdom of God, i.e., the Kingdom of Jesus. This is part of the great work of the Mighty Arm of God, Jesus of Nazareth, the Christ of God.

Notice this great work of Redemption through Jesus, as described by Holy Spirit:

<u>Luke 1:67</u> "And his (*John the Baptist's*) father Zacharias was filled with the Holy Ghost, and prophesied, saying, 68 Blessed be the Lord God of Israel; for he hath visited and redeemed his people, 69 and hath raised up an horn of *soteria*/salvation for us in the house of his servant David; 70 as he spake by the mouth of his holy prophets, which have been since the world began: 71 that we should be *sozo*/saved from our enemies, and from the hand of all that hate us; 72 to perform the mercy [*chesed*] promised to our fathers, and to remember his holy covenant; 73 the oath which he sware to our father Abraham, 74 that he would grant unto us, that we being delivered (*rescued, redeemed*) out of the hand of our enemies might serve him without fear, 75 in holiness and righteousness before him, all the days of our life."

Zacharias spoke with the voice of the prophetic future. Jesus had not redeemed man yet, but Zacharias was describing what Jesus would do. This is an example of God calling things that are not as if they were, and then they become. <u>Rom 4:17</u> "(As it is written, I have made thee (*Abraham*) a father of many nations,) before him whom he believed, even God, who quickeneth the dead, and calleth those things which be not as though they were."

This Redemption, this horn of Salvation, this deliverance out of the hand of our enemies is God's "big deal," planned from before the foundation of the Earth was laid. If you are going to deal with God, you have to deal with His "Great Work."

<u>1 Pet 1:18</u> "Forasmuch as ye know that ye were not redeemed with corruptible things, as silver and gold, from your vain conversation received by tradition from your fathers; 19 but with the precious blood of Christ, as of a lamb without blemish and without spot: 20 who verily was foreordained before the foundation of the world, but was manifest in these last times for you."

<u>1 John 3:5</u> "And ye know that he (*Jesus*) was manifested to take away our sins; and in him is no sin."

DISCOVERING OUR REDEMPTION

1 John 3:8 "He that committeth sin is of the devil; for the devil sinneth from the beginning. For this purpose the Son of God was manifested, that he might destroy the works of the devil."

Titus 2:13 "Looking for that blessed hope, and the glorious appearing of the great God and our Saviour Jesus Christ; 14 who gave himself for us, that he might redeem us from all iniquity, and purify unto himself a peculiar people, zealous of good works."

Rom 5:8 "But God commendeth his *agape*/love toward us, in that, while we were yet sinners, Christ died for us. 9 Much more then, being now justified by his blood, we shall be *sozo*/saved from wrath through him. 10 For if, when we were enemies, we were reconciled to God by the death of his Son, much more, being reconciled, we shall be *sozo*/saved by his *zoe*/life. 11 And not only so, but we also joy in God through our Lord Jesus Christ, by whom we have now received the atonement (*reconciliation*)."

By the end of this book, if you don't yet know you are loved, study it again until you walk in a confidence of love that can prevail in triumph over the very gates of Hades.

Chapter 3
The Story of Redemption

The story of Redemption is where God has revealed in the Scriptures how Jesus, the Lamb of God, accomplished His mission and took away, or remitted/ *aphesis*, the sins of the world and, thus, bought man's freedom from Satan, death and sin.

The story of our Redemption starts in Genesis and never ends, for it is eternal. It starts when Adam sinned and continues when Heaven comes to Earth and God dwells here with us. Rather than a full Bible survey, our focus will be on what happened during the 52 days from the Last Supper to the Garden of Gethsemane to the Day of Pentecost.

Eph 1:13 "In whom ye also trusted, after that ye heard the word of truth, the gospel of your *soteria*/salvation: in whom also after that ye believed, ye were sealed with that holy Spirit of promise, 14 which is the earnest of our inheritance until the redemption of the purchased possession, unto the praise of his glory."

Redemption, as a legal term, is to buy or pay a value, to change ownership and rights of possession.

In Redemption, we are dealing with the almost unknown fact of our Identification with Christ, not as a theological concept, for Identification has been talked about for centuries, but few have walked in its awesome meaning.

DISCOVERING OUR REDEMPTION

Identification is the chief mechanism through which God accomplished the taking away of the sins of the world by the Lamb of God, Jesus of Nazareth, whom God has declared as both Lord and Christ.

At once you ask, "What does Identification mean?"

It means either who others identify or unite you with, or who you unite or identify yourself with. Your personal self-identity is the basis of your self-esteem, the ability to overcome anything to get what you want. Your perceived identity is how others relate to you.

To God, Identification means our complete union with Jesus in His substitutionary sacrifice and glorification, i.e., His great redemptive work of reconciling man back to God. Thus, in this Identification, what Jesus went through, you went through, and what Jesus got, you got. Even more amazing, what Jesus is now, you are!

As God defines it, Identification = when He sees Jesus, He sees you + when God sees you, He sees Jesus + when you see Jesus, you see God + when you see God, you see Jesus.

For you to match God's Identification of you = when you see yourself, you see Jesus + when you see Jesus, you see yourself + when you see God, you see yourself in Jesus + when you see Jesus, you see yourself in God.

And for others = when you see others you see Jesus + when you see Jesus, you see others.

Or, as Jesus prayed: John 17:20 "Neither pray I for these alone, but for them also which shall believe on me through their word; 21 that they all may be one; as thou, Father, art in me, and I in thee, that they also may be one in us: that the world may believe that thou hast sent me. 22 And the glory which thou gavest me I have given them; that they may be one, even as we are one: 23 I in them, and thou in me, that they may be made perfect in one; and that the world may know that thou hast sent me, and hast *agape*/loved them, as thou hast *agape*/loved me."

Remember, the essence of covenant is Identification, where two now become one in a blood process.

For instance, this term is used: "I have been crucified with Christ" (Gal 2:20). This is our Identification with Christ in His crucifixion.

Paul reveals to us that each one of us can say:"I died with Christ."

"I was buried with Christ."

"I suffered with Christ."

"I was made alive with Christ."

"Now I am seated with Him."

Jesus is our *zoe*/life, our wisdom, our righteousness, our sanctification and our Redemption. Then it is not about us and our abilities, but about Him and His abilities in us, to the Father's will for us.

THE STORY OF REDEMPTION

1 Cor 1:30 "But it is from Him (*Father God*) that you have your *zoe*/life in Christ Jesus, whom God made our Wisdom from God, [revealed to us a knowledge of the divine plan of salvation previously hidden, manifesting itself as] our Righteousness [thus making us upright and putting us in right standing with God *now and forever as full sons of God with never again a writ to break our adoption by Him*], and our Consecration [making us pure and holy], and our Redemption [providing our *eternal* ransom from eternal penalty for sin *and the authority of Satan*]." AMP

Rom 8:28 "We are assured and know that [God being a partner in their labor] all things work together and are [fitting into a plan] for good to and for those who *agape*/love God and are called according to [His] design and purpose. 29 For those whom He foreknew [of whom He was aware and *agape*/loved beforehand], He also destined from the beginning [foreordaining them] to be molded into the image of His Son [and share inwardly *and outwardly* His likeness], that He might become the firstborn among many brethren. 30 And those whom He thus foreordained, He also called; and those whom He called, He also justified (acquitted, made righteous, putting them into right standing with Himself *as a permanent condition*). And those whom He justified, He also glorified [raising them to a heavenly dignity and condition or state of being *full of the Spirit of glory, Holy Spirit*]." AMP

If you are in Christ, you are: foreordained, called, justified, seated and glorified with Holy Spirit, in Him.

Eph 1:2 "Grace be to you, and peace, from God our Father, and from the Lord Jesus Christ. 3 Blessed be the God and Father of our Lord Jesus Christ, who hath blessed us with all spiritual blessings in heavenly places in Christ: 4 according as he hath chosen us in him before the foundation of the world, that we should be holy and without blame before him in *agape*/love: 5 having predestinated us unto the adoption of children by Jesus Christ to himself, according to the good pleasure of his will, 6 to the praise of the glory of his grace, wherein he hath made us accepted in the *agape*/beloved. 7 In whom we have redemption through his blood, the forgiveness (*remission, obliteration and putting away*) of sins, according to the riches of his grace; 8 wherein he hath abounded toward us in all wisdom and prudence; 9 having made known unto us the mystery of his will, according to his good pleasure which he hath purposed in himself: 10 that in the dispensation of the fulness of times he might gather together in one all things in Christ, both which are in heaven, and which are on earth; even in him."

If you are in Christ, you are: foreordained to God, called, justified, glorified with Holy Spirit, empowered for peace, blessed with all spiritual blessings in Heaven to bring to Earth, chosen, holy, without blame, *agape*/loved, adopted to Father God, in His good pleasure and will, accepted, redeemed, and your sins are remitted and put away, forgiven, gathered unto Him, in abounding, rich grace in Him, and you are forever joined to Him in Jesus.

DISCOVERING OUR REDEMPTION

This grace, this *agape* love in action, to give men all this, was not dependent upon men's ability to hear it and to live it right. God already did that with Adam and through the Law of Moses, and both failed. They were sources of life ... until Jesus could come. The source of life for Adam was lost when he sinned; and then this path of life returned partially in the Law of Moses and was made complete in Jesus.

Gal 3:12 "And the law is not of faith: but, The man that doeth them shall *zao*/live in them."

Rom 5:14 "(Nevertheless death reigned from Adam to Moses, even over them that had not sinned after the similitude of Adam's transgression, who is the figure of him that was to come. 15 But not as the offence, so also is the free gift. For if through the offence of one many be dead, much more the grace of God, and the gift by grace, which is by one man, Jesus Christ, hath abounded unto many. 16 And not as it was by one that sinned, so is the gift: for the judgment was by one to condemnation, but the free gift is of many offences unto justification. 17 For if by one man's offence death reigned by one; much more they which *(continually) lambano*/receive abundance of grace and of the gift of righteousness shall reign in *zoe*/life by one, Jesus Christ)."

Notice you walking and operating as a king for Jesus in the New Covenant depends on how well you *lambano*/receive this grace (which includes forgiveness and remission of sins and total Salvation) and the gift of righteousness. This is our work; God has already done His.

Under Moses, the life of God was dependent upon how well men lived under the Law. In the New Covenant this *zoe*/life is dependent upon God in the flesh, Jesus of Nazareth, once a carpenter, but now Lord of all lords and King of all kings in creation and in heavenly places.

1 John 5:10 "He that believeth on the Son of God hath the witness in himself: he that believeth not God hath made him a liar; because he believeth not the record that God gave of his Son. 11 And this is the record, that God hath given to us eternal *zoe*/life, and this *zoe*/life is in his Son. 12 He that hath the Son hath *zoe*/life; and he that hath not the Son of God hath not *zoe*/life. 13 These things have I written unto you that believe on the name of the Son of God; that ye may know that ye have eternal *zoe*/life, and that ye may believe on the name of the Son of God."

The whole intent is that man get *zoe*/life. We get this *zoe*/life as a gift from God, by faith, not the labors under the Law of Moses.

Rom 5:8 "But God commendeth his *agape*/love toward us, in that, while we were yet sinners, Christ died for us. 9 Much more then, being now justified by his blood, we shall be *sozo*/saved from wrath through him. 10 For if, when we were enemies, we were reconciled to God by the death of his Son, much more, being reconciled, we shall be *sozo*/saved by his *zoe*/life. 11 And not only so, but we also joy in God through our Lord Jesus Christ, by whom we have now received the atonement *(reconciliation)*."

The Story of Redemption

Notice, from Rom 5:10, it is this *zoe*/life that produces our Salvation, or Heaven coming to Earth, for and in us. And, from 1 John 5:13, believing on the name of Jesus releases this *zoe*/life into the Earth. Rom 10:11 "For the scripture saith, Whosoever believeth on him shall not be ashamed. 12 For there is no difference between the Jew and the Greek: for the same Lord over all is rich unto all that call upon him. 13 For whosoever shall call upon the name of the Lord shall be *sozo*/saved."

This great Reconciliation of Salvation is dependent upon Jesus and His holiness and not on man's ability to hear and obey God, but on our ability to believe that God did it for us in Jesus. Rom 10:4 "For Christ is the end of the law for righteousness to every one that believeth."

If Jesus is our wisdom, then our wisdom depends on Jesus, and not on us.

If Jesus is our righteousness, then our righteousness depends on Jesus, and not on us or on you.

If Jesus is our sanctification, our consecration, then our sanctification, our consecration, depends on Jesus, and not on us or on you.

If Jesus is our Redemption, then our Redemption depends on Him, and not on us or on you.

If Jesus is our Salvation, then our Salvation depends on Jesus, and not on us or on you.

If Jesus is our Reconciliation, then our Reconciliation depends on Jesus, and not on us or on you.

If Jesus is our adoption, then our adoption depends on Jesus, and not on us or on you.

If Jesus is our propitiation, then our propitiation depends on Jesus, and not on us or on you.

If Jesus is our peace, then our peace depends on Jesus, and not on us or on you.

If Jesus is our *zoe*/life, then our *zoe*/life depends on Jesus, and not on us or on you.

If Holy Spirit is our seal unto the Day of Redemption then our being sealed depends on Holy Spirit, and not on us or on you.

This state or royal position with God is dependent on Jesus for: Heb 13:8 "Jesus Christ the same yesterday, and to day, and for ever." Mal 3:6 "For I am the LORD, I change not; therefore ye sons of Jacob are not consumed."

God did this through the process that is called our covenant Identification with Christ in His awesome work by the cross.

We enter into this Identification of God, this Redemption of God, this Reconciliation of God, and this Salvation of God by faith in God, per His promise, His Word of the Gospel of Jesus Christ:

1 Cor 15:1 "Moreover, brethren, I declare unto you the gospel which I preached unto you, which also ye have received, and wherein ye stand; 2 by which also

DISCOVERING OUR REDEMPTION

ye are (*continuously being*) *sozo*/saved [*in your soul*], if ye keep in memory what I preached unto you, unless ye have believed in vain. 3 For I delivered unto you first of all that which I also received, how that Christ died for our sins according to the scriptures; 4 and that he was buried, and that he rose again the third day according to the scriptures."

Hear ye, hear ye, hear ye! God has solved the problem of every wrong action of man, every sin, in the death and resurrection of Jesus Christ! You may not understand it fully in this life, because it is a work worthy of God, and not of fallen man. But even if you believe in the smallest portion of it, the God who put the entire wrath due us on Jesus will use that to put you into His entire, so-great Salvation. He did it because He loves you. You are loved.

Isa 53:4 "Surely he hath *cabal*/borne our griefs, and *nasa*/carried our sorrows: yet we did esteem him stricken, smitten of God, and afflicted. 5 But he was wounded for our transgressions, he was bruised for our iniquities: the chastisement of our peace was upon him; and with his stripes we are healed."

This is about God's love for His fallen men, and He did such a work that it takes only the absolute minimum to enter into it, because of His *agape* love, but then it takes a lifetime of focus for us to walk in it.

Phil 2:12 "Wherefore, my *agape*/beloved, as ye have always obeyed, not as in my presence only, but now much more in my absence, work out your own *soteria*/salvation [*in this life, so the day of Christ is not a fear to you*] with fear and trembling [*knowing the sure judgment of that day*]. 13 For it is God which worketh in you both to will and to do of his good pleasure. 14 Do all things without murmurings and disputings: 15 that ye may be blameless and harmless, the sons of God, without rebuke, in the midst of a crooked and perverse nation, among whom ye shine as lights in the world; 16 holding forth the word of *zoe*/life; that I may rejoice in the day of Christ, that I have not run in vain, neither laboured in vain."

We do have a job to do. We are to labor to enter into this finished work of Christ, so we may bring Heaven to Earth, to the glory of God the Father, through Jesus Christ, our Lord.

Heb 4:1 "Let us therefore fear, lest, a promise being left us of entering into his rest, any of you should seem to come short of it. [*Being called a son of God and walking in less of it, to the glory of God that Jesus made available to us by the cross.*] 2 For unto us was the gospel preached, as well as unto them [*in the desert with the Law of Moses*]: but the word preached did not profit them, not being mixed with faith (*full persuasion and confidence*) in them that heard it. 3 For we which have believed do enter into rest, as he said, As I have sworn in my wrath, if they shall enter into my rest: although the works were finished from the foundation of the world. 4 For he spake in a certain place of the seventh day on this wise, And God did rest the seventh day from all his works. 5 And in this place again, If they shall enter into my rest.

6 Seeing therefore it remaineth that some must enter therein, and they to whom it was first preached entered not in because of unbelief: 7 again, he limiteth a certain day, saying in David, To day, after so long a time; as it is said, To day if ye will hear his voice, harden not your hearts. 8 For if Jesus (*Joshua*) had given them rest, then would he not afterward have spoken of another day. 9 There remaineth therefore a rest to the people of God. 10 For he that is entered into his rest, he also hath ceased from his own works, as God did from his. 11 Let us labour therefore to enter into that rest, lest any man fall after the same example of unbelief."

The message of the chosen people of God in the desert, those who would not trust and work with God to enter into their inheritance, although they had been chosen by God for attacking giants, vast armies and massive walled cities with the mere skills of slave mud-brick makers (keep mixing and stomping and building until you build a nation), died in the desert of unbelief. They saw the God who melts mountains and the great acts of power in Egypt, but soon forgot that this all-powerful God was with them to accomplish what He wanted done.

1 Cor 10:6 "Now these things were our examples, to the intent we should not lust after evil things, as they also lusted. 7 Neither be ye idolaters, as were some of them; as it is written, The people sat down to eat and drink, and rose up to play. 8 Neither let us commit fornication, as some of them committed, and fell in one day three and twenty thousand. 9 Neither let us tempt Christ, as some of them also tempted, and were destroyed of serpents. 10 Neither murmur ye, as some of them also murmured, and were destroyed of the destroyer. 11 Now all these things happened unto them for ensamples: and they are written for our admonition, upon whom the ends of the world are come."

Jude 5 "Now I want to remind you, though you were fully informed once for all, that though the Lord [at one time] delivered a people out of the land of Egypt, He subsequently destroyed those [of them] who did not believe [who refused *to be persuaded* to adhere to, trust in, and rely upon Him]. AMP

That destruction included sudden judgments by the devil and living only to the age of seventy or eighty years old. As Moses lamented: Ps 90:9 "For all our days are passed away in thy wrath: we spend our years as a tale that is told. 10 The days of our years are threescore years and ten; and if by reason of strength they be fourscore years, yet is their strength labour and sorrow; for it is soon cut off, and we fly away." They were close enough, right on the border, but did not enter into the Promised Land.

The message is simple: Just like a workman who mixes water, dirt and straw every day to make bricks for a city, if you are not mixing the Word of God with belief, you are mixing it with unbelief, and this is a day-by-day, minute-by-minute process. The children of Israel had God in a cloud by day, a fire by night and food every day, yet they could not get over their bitterness, disappointments, resentments, unforgiveness and offense, to see the goodness of the Lord. God did not bring them to the desert to die. They did that to themselves by hardened hearts that were exercised every day in war against God.

This is a fearful warning: Heb 4:7 "Again, he limiteth a certain day, saying in David, To day, after so long a time; as it is said, To day if ye will hear his voice, harden not your hearts."

The issue is not the message; the issue is how you receive it.

This message is repeated four times in over the course of Hebrews 3 and 4. It is not about God talking to us; it is about us hearing what God is saying. It is not about what God is trying to say, but what He is saying. The penalty is the same as for the children in the desert; they died, away from the Promised Land, for failure to take heed in their day.

If you are not in the work of believing, you are in the work of unbelieving.

You must labor with the Word of God to enter and stay in this Word of Identification, Reconciliation, Redemption, Adoption, Betrothal, and Salvation. Holy Spirit will help you. It is not the legal facts; they were set 2000 years ago. They set your eternal destiny with God on your small act of faith in getting born again into a new creation. John 1:12 "But as many as received him (*Jesus*), to them gave he *exousia*/power (*authority, power, ability, commission and the resources of Heaven*) to become the sons of God, even to them that believe on his name: 13 which were born, not of blood, nor of the will of the flesh, nor of the will of man, but of God."

The issue is *agape*/loving God enough to accomplish His purpose for you here and now, so you can earn rewards of silver, gold and jewels that have eternal value. He wants you to receive them, but you have to cooperate. It is the facts of Salvation that must become life in our hearts and minds, now, today, This process of making the Word of God life in us is called renewing the mind, mixing the Word of God with faith, and repentance.

So where do we start to walk in the *zoe*/life of God that Jesus came to give? John 10:10 "The thief (*Satan and his works*) cometh not, but for to steal, and to kill, and to destroy: I am come that they might have *zoe*/life, and that they might have it more abundantly. 11 I am the good shepherd: the good shepherd giveth his *psuche*/life (*soul*) for the sheep."

This *zoe*/life starts as we enter in this so-great Identification:

Rom 10:8 "But what saith it? The word is nigh thee, even in thy mouth, and in thy heart: that is, the word of faith, which we preach; 9 that if thou shalt confess with thy mouth the Lord Jesus, and shalt believe in thine heart that God hath raised him from the dead, thou shalt be *sozo*/saved. 10 For with the heart man believeth unto righteousness; and with the mouth confession is made unto *soteria*/salvation. 11 For the scripture saith, Whosoever believeth on him shall not be ashamed. 12 For there is no difference between the Jew and the Greek: for the same Lord over all is rich unto all that call upon him. 13 For whosoever shall call upon the name of the Lord shall be *sozo*/saved."

With the heart, you believe that God raised Jesus from the dead, unto the righteousness of God in Christ Jesus, which is *zoe*/life; and with confession, agreeing out loud, with your mouth, that it is true that Jesus is indeed Lord, you bring Heaven to Earth, that is, God's Salvation. Confession simply means to agree that it is true. Here the scripture specifically says to agree out loud, with your mouth, that Jesus is Lord, Owner and Rightful Ruler of all Creation.

In the process, we are sealed with Holy Spirit unto the Day of Redemption (as illustrated in Revelation 21 and 22).

Eph 1:11 "In whom (*Christ*) also we have obtained an inheritance, being predestinated according to the purpose of him who worketh all things after the counsel of his own will: 12 that we should be to the praise of his glory, who first trusted in Christ. 13 In whom ye also trusted, after that ye heard the word of truth, the gospel of your *soteria*/salvation: in whom also after that ye believed, ye were sealed with that holy Spirit of promise, 14 which is the earnest of our inheritance until the redemption of the purchased possession, unto the praise of his glory."

The good news is that your Salvation is already complete in Jesus, and when you believed that, then you were sealed, stamped and made qualified to go to the Day of Redemption by Holy Spirit.

For our understanding and righteous development in Christian growth, the process starts with our knowing: Rom 6:6 "Knowing this, that our old man [*was and, thus, forever*] is crucified **with him**, that the body of sin might be destroyed, that henceforth we should not serve sin. 7 For he that is dead is freed from sin. 8 Now if we be dead **with Christ**, we believe that we shall also *zao*/live **with him**."

This is one of those scriptures you must mix with faith every day to build your heart into what God has for you in His so-great Salvation, our Redemption in Jesus.

This little preposition "with" is the key that unlocks a long-hidden truth that is of vital importance to us.

The first two or three chapters of this book will lead you into the first steps of God's greatest revelation connected with the work of the Mighty Arm of God, Jesus, and the New Creation.

Jesus became as we were, so that we might become as He is. This is Identification.

2 Cor 5:21 "For he hath made him to be sin for us, who knew no sin; that **we might be made the righteousness of God in him**."

Rom 8:31 "What shall we then say to these things? If God be for us, who can be against us? 32 He that spared not his own Son, but delivered him up for us all, how shall he not with him also freely give us all things? 33 Who shall lay any thing to

DISCOVERING OUR REDEMPTION

the charge of God's elect? It is **God that justifieth**." Note: justification is the process of making one righteous.

Now that Jesus has accomplished His great work, we are still identified by God with and in Him:

1 John 3:2 "*Agape*/beloved, now are we the sons of God, and it doth not yet appear what we shall be: but we know that, when he shall appear, **we shall be like him**; for we shall see him as he is."

1 John 3:7 "Little children, let no man deceive you: he that doeth righteousness is righteous, **even as he is righteous**."

1 John 4:17 "Herein is our *agape*/love made perfect, that we may have boldness in the day of judgment: because **as he is, so are we** in this world."

That can only be because Jesus redeemed us by His blood 2000 years ago. Jesus got the job done, but it does us little good in this life until we hold on to it, no matter what.

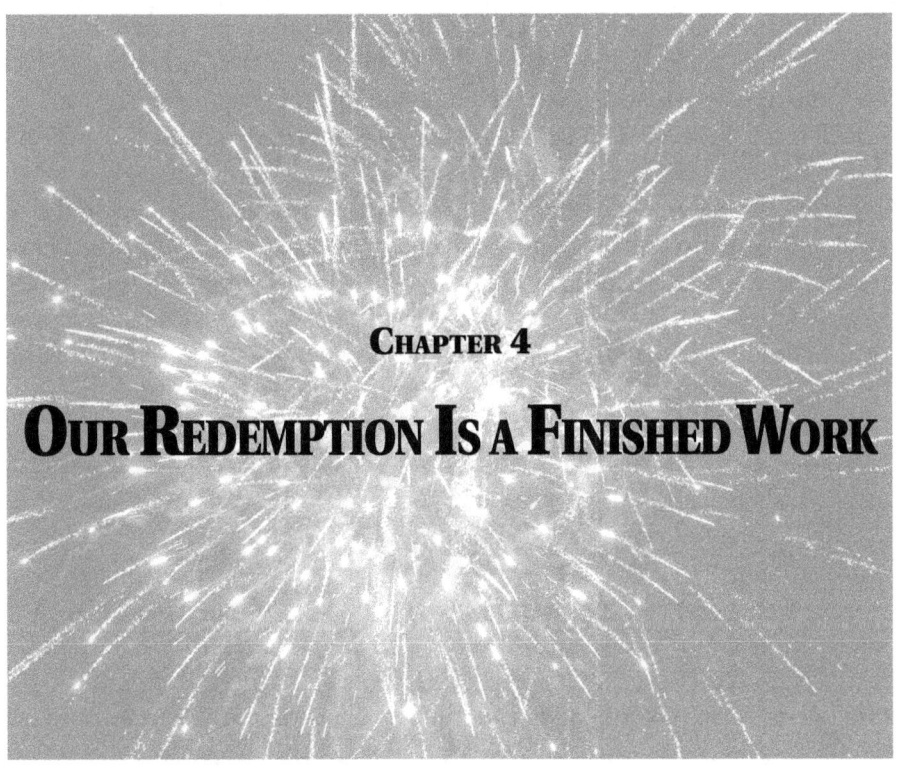

Chapter 4

Our Redemption Is a Finished Work

Jesus is the Lamb of God. Instead of being used by a priest to bear sin, Jesus was both the Lamb and the High Priest, when He bore the sin of mankind.

John 1:29 "The next day John seeth Jesus coming unto him, and saith, Behold the Lamb of God, which taketh away the sin of the world."

The core issue for us is this: Did He do that? Did He take away the sin of the world?

Was sin removed and healed 2000 years ago?

If not, what or who will bear and heal our sins now?

If Jesus did it, what does that mean to us now?

If this is the mighty act of God, how do we enter into it, and use it, as He desires, to His glory?

Why does the New Testament, in Acts and all the letters that follow it, never tell a person to ask God to forgive them when they have sinned? Instead, the Scriptures say this:

Acts 5:30 "The God of our fathers raised up Jesus, whom ye slew and hanged on a tree. 31 Him hath God exalted with his right hand to be a Prince and a Saviour, for to give (*render, to make happen, produce*) repentance to Israel, and forgiveness (*remission, removal, obliteration and putting away*) of sins."

DISCOVERING OUR REDEMPTION

Acts 13:37 "But he, whom God raised again, saw no corruption. 38 Be it known unto you therefore, men and brethren, that through this man is preached unto you the forgiveness (*remission, removal, obliteration and putting away*) of sins: 39 and by him all that believe are justified from all things, from which ye could not be justified by the law of Moses."

What an awesome statement! By Jesus, God exceeded the justification (being made right with God) that was available under the Law of Moses. The righteousness of the Law allowed men to be giants on the battlefield, crumble walled cities, singlehandedly put a thousand to flight, be giants in business and economy, be rich beyond measure, heal the sick, raise the dead and restore men and women from leprosy. The righteousness of the New Covenant is even greater and more complete!

This strains the imagination: Acts 13:39 "And by him all that believe are justified from all things, from which ye could not be justified by the law of Moses."

Justified means the removal of all things that could hinder any free flow of acceptance and love, now or forever. It is not just the removal of sin, but a state in which, when viewed, there is no remembrance of past sin, and no expectation of future sin. Col 1:21 "And you, that were sometime alienated and enemies in your mind by wicked works, yet now hath he reconciled 22 in the body of his flesh through death, to present you holy and unblameable and unreproveable in his sight."

When sin is put away under this work, there can be no more sin applied, as it was under Moses.

Under Moses, you got clean, and if you sinned again, had to get clean again. Jesus is greater than Moses, and His righteousness is greater than the righteousness of doing and being right. It is mind-boggling to the un-renewed mind and one of the primary focuses of how to renew our minds.

Jesus described the mission of Paul to the world. Acts 26:18 "To open their eyes, and to turn them from darkness to light, and from the power of Satan unto God, that they may *lambano*/receive (*hold on to, cling to and never let go of*) forgiveness (*remission, removal, obliteration and putting away*) of sins, and inheritance among them which are sanctified by faith that is in me (*Jesus*)." Notice that spreading this truth frees people from the control of Satan.

Eph 6:19 "And for me (*Paul*), that utterance may be given unto me, that I may open my mouth boldly, to make known the mystery of the gospel, 20 for which I am an ambassador in bonds: that therein I may speak boldly, as I ought to speak."

Col 1:25 "Whereof I (*Paul*) am made a minister, according to the dispensation of God which is given to me for you, to fulfil the word of God; 26 even the mystery which hath been hid from ages and from generations, but now is made manifest to his saints: 27 to whom God would make known what is the riches of the glory of this mystery among the Gentiles; which is Christ in you, the hope of glory: 28 whom we preach, warning every man, and teaching every man in all wisdom; that we may present every man perfect in Christ Jesus: 29 whereunto I also labour, striving according to his working, which worketh in me mightily."

So the central issue is not: did the Lamb of God do the job of taking away (remitting) the sins of the world? But, rather, convincing men, so they will *lambano/* receive it and not let go of this awesome fact, in spite of their many failures.

This scripture also makes it clear that forgiveness (*remission, removal, obliteration and putting away*) of sins by Jesus is of a whole different caliber, or capacity, than the forgiveness under Moses.

These scriptures next declare we are in a legal state where we already have the forgiveness/remission/taking away of sins paid for 2000 years ago, so the proper response is not asking for forgiveness when we sin, but knowing what God has already done and thanking Father God that we have remission, the taking away of sins, as the mighty work of Jesus, the Mighty Arm of God.

Eph 1:7 "In whom **we have redemption** through his blood, the forgiveness (*remission, removal, obliteration and putting away*) of sins, according to the riches of his grace; 8 wherein he hath abounded toward us in all wisdom and prudence."

Col 1:12 "Giving thanks (*continually*) unto the Father, which hath made us meet to be partakers of the inheritance of the saints in light: 13 who hath delivered us from the power of darkness, and hath translated us into the kingdom of his *agape*/dear Son: 14 in whom **we have redemption** through his blood, even the forgiveness (*remission, removal, obliteration and putting away*) of sins."

The word in these above scriptures translated as forgiveness in the KJV is the Greek word *aphesis*, which is much stronger and more complete than forgiveness. In other places in the KJV it is translated as remission. Occasionally, in the KJV, it is translated forgiveness, but where the KJV has remission, it is always *aphesis*.

To make this statement even more secure in your mind consider:

Heb 1:3 "Who being the brightness of his glory, and the express image of his person, and upholding all things by the word of his power, when **he had by himself purged our sins** (*remission, removal, obliteration and putting away*), sat down on the right hand of the Majesty on high."

Rev 1:5 "And from Jesus Christ, who is the faithful witness, and the first begotten of the dead, and the prince of the kings of the earth. Unto him that *agape*/loved us, and **washed us (*remission, removal, obliteration and putting away*) from our sins in his own blood**, 6 and hath made us kings and priests unto God and his Father; to him be glory and dominion for ever and ever. Amen."

Col 2:13 "And you, being dead in your sins and the uncircumcision of your flesh, hath he quickened together with him, having forgiven (*pardoned so the curse no longer applies and if you are in the curse, it stops now for*) you all trespasses."

DISCOVERING OUR REDEMPTION

If Jesus did not handle the sins of the world, of the entire human race, the sin from Adam to the last man or woman alive, then He could not be seated at the right hand of the Father, because He did not get the job done.

But praise God, the Scriptures declare boldly Jesus got the job done, once and for all time!

Heb 9:11 "But Christ being come an high priest of good things to come, by a greater and more perfect tabernacle, not made with hands, that is to say, not of this building; 12 neither by the blood of goats and calves, but by his own blood he entered in once into the holy place, **having obtained eternal redemption for us**. 13 For if the blood of bulls and of goats, and the ashes of an heifer sprinkling the unclean, sanctifieth to the purifying of the flesh: 14 how much more shall the blood of Christ, who through the eternal Spirit offered himself without spot to God, purge your conscience from dead works to serve the *zao*/living God? 15 And for this cause he is the mediator of the new testament, that by means of death, for the redemption of the transgressions that were under the first testament, they which are called might receive the promise of eternal inheritance."

Heb 9:24 "For Christ is not entered into the holy places made with hands, which are the figures of the true; but into heaven itself, now to appear in the presence of God for us: 25 nor yet that he should offer himself often, as the high priest entereth into the holy place every year with blood of others; 26 for then must he often have suffered since the foundation of the world: but now once in the end of the world hath he appeared to put away (*remove, remit, obliterate and purge*) sin by the sacrifice of himself."

Heb 10:10 "By the which will we are sanctified (*set apart for God*) through the offering of the body of Jesus Christ once for all. 11 And every priest standeth daily ministering and offering oftentimes the same sacrifices, which can never take away (*remit*) sins: 12 but this man, after he had offered one sacrifice for sins for ever, sat down on the right hand of God; 13 from henceforth expecting till his enemies be made his footstool. 14 For by one offering he hath perfected for ever them that are sanctified. 15 Whereof the Holy Ghost also is a witness to us: for after that he had said before, 16 This is the covenant that I will make with them after those days, saith the Lord, I will put my laws into their hearts, and in their minds will I write them; 17 and their sins and iniquities will I remember no more. 18 Now where remission (*removal, obliteration and putting away*) of these (*sins and iniquities*) is, **there is no more offering for sin."**

This purging, this remission of sin is the heart of the New Covenant of God with man by Jesus. This is the New Testament. We either have it or we don't. There is no middle ground, because if Jesus did not get the job done, then there must be more of God's blood that has to be shed to purge our sin (that which Jesus did not get done for all time, if, indeed, Jesus did not get the job done). The Scriptures declare: Heb 10:12 "But this man (*Jesus*), after he had offered one sacrifice for sins for ever, sat down on the right hand of God."

Jesus got the job done, our sins are purged, and we are sanctified, set apart from our sins and unto God. All the past, present and future sins of the whole human race were put on Jesus, and so they were removed from us. 1 Cor 1:30 "But of him (*Father God*) are ye in Christ Jesus, who of God is made unto us wisdom, and righteousness, and sanctification, and redemption: 31 that, according as it is written, He that glorieth, let him glory in the Lord."

God has solved the sin problem for the entire human race—past, present and future—through Jesus, and sin is no longer an issue with God.

1 John 2:2 "And he (*Jesus Christ*) is the propitiation for our sins: and not for ours only, but also for the sins of the whole world."

Col 1:21 "And you, that were sometime alienated and enemies in your mind by wicked works, yet now hath he reconciled 22 in the body of his flesh through death, to present you holy and unblameable and unreproveable in his sight."

This scripture declares that Jesus is our propitiation, the removal of sin unto aggressive release of blessing. That great blessing of God is God Himself dwelling in man by Holy Spirit. Notice that God's answer is not a thing, but a person, in this case, Holy Spirit, the Administrator of God and the Helper of man. Gal 3:13 "Christ hath redeemed us from the curse of the law, being made a curse for us: for it is written, Cursed is every one that hangeth on a tree: 14 that the blessing of Abraham might come on the Gentiles through Jesus Christ; that we might receive the promise of the Spirit through faith."

With Holy Spirit, the Administrator of God in man, then man becomes the channel or vessel of Holy Spirit to the universe. The Gospel is that God has made a way for God to reign through man, this is"Christ in you the hope of glory." As God's "on site" agents, He reigns through us.

Rom 5:17 "For if by one man's offence death reigned (*as a cruel king enforcing the law of sin and death*) by one; much more they which (*continually*) *lambano*/receive abundance of grace and of the gift of righteousness shall reign (*as kings for God*) in *zoe*/life by one, Jesus Christ.) 18 Therefore as by the offence of one judgment came upon all men to condemnation; even so by the righteousness of one the free gift came upon all men unto justification of *zoe*/life. 19 For as by one man's disobedience many were made sinners, so by the obedience of one shall many be made righteous. 20 Moreover the law entered, that the offence might abound. But where sin abounded, grace did much more abound: 21 that as sin hath reigned (*as king*) unto death, even so might grace reign (*as a greater king*) through righteousness unto eternal *zao*/life by Jesus Christ our Lord."

DISCOVERING OUR REDEMPTION

If Jesus is our propitiation, then our righteousness does not depend on us, but on Jesus. And our blessing does not depend on us, but on Jesus. This is included in the meaning of the word *propitiation*.

Heb 13:8 "Jesus Christ the same yesterday, and to day, and for ever."

Since Jesus is our propitiation, our propitiation in Jesus lasts from the past through to today and then forever into the future.

1 Cor 1:30 "But of him (*Father God*) are ye in Christ Jesus, who of God is made unto us wisdom, and righteousness, and sanctification, and redemption."

If Jesus is wisdom for us, then we have access to that wisdom.

If Jesus is righteousness for us, then we have access to that righteousness.

If Jesus is sanctification for us, then we have access to that sanctification.

If Jesus is Redemption for us, then we have access to that Redemption.

These are the facts of Redemption. The issue is our believing and holding on to this beyond-wonderful Good News of God's goodness by Jesus.

1 John 2:1 "My little children, these things write I unto you, that ye sin not. And if any man sin, we have an advocate (*continually in the face of, for our benefit*) with the Father, Jesus Christ the righteous: 2 and he is the propitiation (*removal, obliteration, putting away and purging, unto full release of blessing*) for our sins: and not for ours only, but also for the sins of the whole world."

Our issue is not so much the sins of 1 John 2:1, but the knowing we have our propitiation in verse 2. The propitiation wipes out the effect of the sins. That is what *propitiation* means.

Rom 3:24 "Being justified freely by his grace through **the redemption that is in Christ Jesus**: 25 whom God hath set forth to be a propitiation through faith in his blood, to declare his righteousness for the remission of sins that are past, through the forbearance of God; 26 to declare, I say, at this time his righteousness: that he might be just, and the justifier of him which believeth in Jesus."

This is not a man thing, but, rather, a God thing. Our Redemption is a work of God, not a work by mere men. God did it for Himself to recover man, and God did it for man because we were unable to do it for ourselves, and each human enters in by faith in the work of God in Jesus.

This is a thing God has done that is a once-for-all thing. He will not have to "re-do" what Jesus accomplished. The job was done right to the satisfaction and level of God the first time. What Jesus accomplished will never need to be accomplished again. The covenant with Moses was temporary; the covenant in Jesus is forever.

We enter in by faith, but it is a work of God, to the level and purposes of God. This is God's program for us, for His purposes, to His satisfaction.

1 Cor 6:19 "What? know ye not that your body is the temple of the Holy Ghost which is in you, which ye have of God, and ye are not your own? 20 For ye are

bought with a price: therefore glorify God in your body, and in your spirit, which are God's."

1 Cor 7:23 "Ye are bought with a price … ."

The Redemption of man is God's plan and purpose for the benefit of Himself first. He knows what He paid for it. He knows who enters in, and He is able to keep one who has received eternal justification by a onetime act of faith. This is not hard, for it is Father God, getting His family back. He knows we are children. The issue is not how hard can God make it, but how quickly and easily can God get people born again from the nature of Satan and back into His family, to satisfy His longing heart.

His plan is to get you born again right from your worst state as a sinner, and then, with you being made His righteousness in spirit, work with you to develop your soul, to walk in this redemption fully.

Rom 14:4 "Who art thou that judgest another man's servant? to his own master he standeth or falleth. Yea, he shall be holden up: for God is able to make him stand."

It gets even better as you learn to know Him in spirit and truth: 2 Tim 1:12 "For the which cause I also suffer these things: nevertheless I am not ashamed: for I know whom I have believed, and am persuaded that he is able to keep that which I have committed unto him against that day."

Phil 1:6 "Being confident of this very thing, that he which hath begun a good work in you will perform it until the day of Jesus Christ."

Notice again that mankind is redeemed (past tense) in the one act of Jesus we call the cross, but this act was a series of events that lasted from the Last Supper, to when they bound Him in the Garden, until the Day of Pentecost, when He sent Holy Spirit, so men could be born again. This all happened over the course of 52 days, and we call this our Reconciliation or Redemption.

The work of Jesus, from His binding in the Garden to His resurrection, is often called "the work of the cross," or "Christ's passion," but this work was not ended until Jesus took His blood to Heaven, was seated at the right hand of the Father, and sent Holy Spirit back, so men could enter into this Redemption, get born again, and get Holy Spirit dwelling in them.

This was God's way of keeping the promise He made to Abraham: Gal 3:16 "Now to Abraham and his seed were the promises made. He saith not, And to seeds, as of many; but as of one, And to thy seed, which is Christ." Notice the covenant of Abraham was really God's covenant with Christ, with Abraham as a substitute for Christ.

So the death and resurrection of Jesus were part of a greater process that did not consummate until the Day of Pentecost, when the Body of Christ was first created, with the 120 men and women in the Upper Room, and then shortly afterward with the first 3,000 converts.

DISCOVERING OUR REDEMPTION

The covenant of Abraham is without law, because it was made with Jesus, through Abraham, and Jesus could never fail. The goal was to get Holy Spirit in men, so men had to be born again of God, for this to happen.

Gal 3:8 "And the scripture, foreseeing that God would justify the heathen through faith, preached before the gospel unto Abraham, saying, In thee shall all nations be blessed. ... 13 Christ hath redeemed us from the curse of the law, being made a curse for us: for it is written, Cursed is every one that hangeth on a tree: 14 that the blessing of Abraham might come on the Gentiles through Jesus Christ; that we might receive the promise of the Spirit through faith."

This Redemption is timeless, not bound by time or when sin occurs, else Jesus would have to die many times to cover each person's sin. Heb 9:12 "Neither by the blood of goats and calves, but by his own blood he entered in once into the holy place, having obtained eternal (*timeless and not bound by time*) redemption for us."

Gal 1:3 "Grace be to you and peace from God the Father, and from our Lord Jesus Christ, 4 who gave himself for our sins, that he might deliver us from this present evil world (*system and order*), according to the will of God and our Father: 5 to whom be glory for ever and ever. Amen."

Let no one ever doubt: Jesus got the job done and delivered a greater Redemption than ever could be done under the Law of Moses. Acts 13:38 "Be it known unto you therefore, men and brethren, that through this man is preached unto you the *aphesis*/forgiveness (*remittance, purging, obliteration and removal*) of sins: 39 and by him all that believe are justified from all things, from which ye could not be justified by the law of Moses."

Jesus satisfied the cry of the ages: "How can sinful man be redeemed." The answer is by the blood of the Lamb of God! God so hated sin that He spent the greatest, Jesus, to redeem man from sin.

John 1:29 "The next day John seeth Jesus coming unto him, and saith, Behold (*ponder, consider until it fills your whole being and translates to a different perspective and way of life*) the Lamb of God, which taketh away the sin of the world." Yes, Jesus got the job done, once, for all time! Our Redemption is a finished work. Hallelujah!

Isa 11:9 ... For the earth shall be full of the knowledge of the Lord, as the waters cover the sea.

PART II

UNDERSTANDING THE LEGAL ASPECTS OF CHRIST'S SACRIFICE

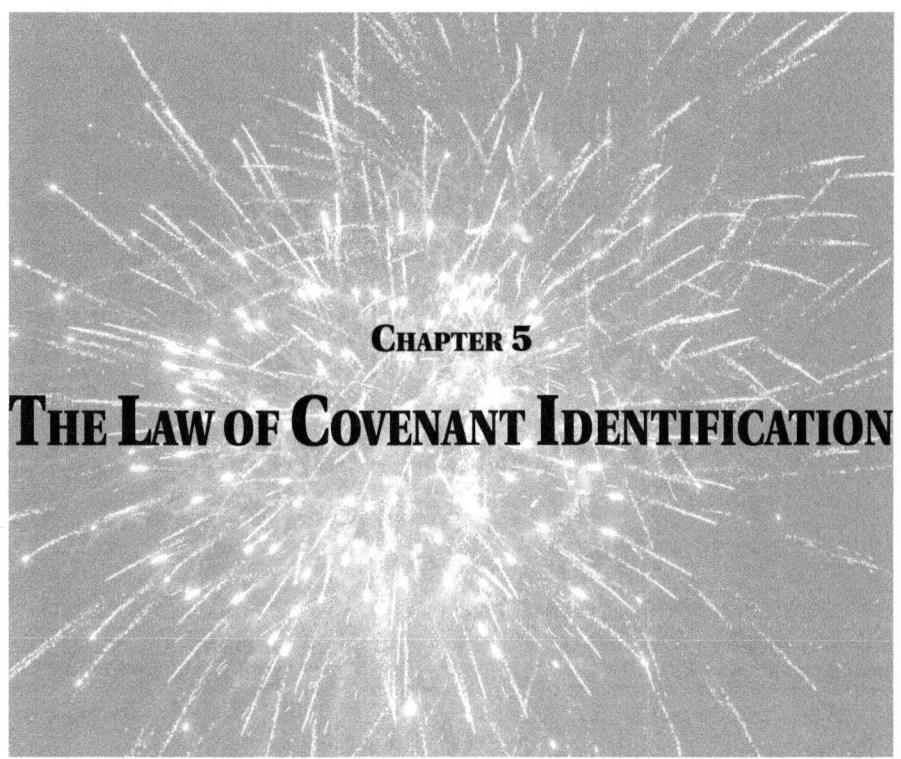

Chapter 5

The Law of Covenant Identification

The teaching of Identification is the legal side of our Redemption in Jesus. Our redemption and all its benefits are based on the law of covenant.

A covenant is a permanent agreement that cannot be broken. When a covenant is made, the members of the covenant lose their individual identities and become one. For legal and spiritual purposes, they are now one. Thus two individuals or two tribes or two nations become one in covenant relationship. In the condition of tribes, regions or nations, every individual is joined into the covenant by the substitute for each whole group. Each substitute goes through the covenant process for the whole people. Thus, once the covenant is cut by the substitutes, the two tribes or nations become one identity or individual. Their separate identities merge and become one. Thus, they are no longer two tribes in agreement; they are one tribe in covenant.

This is similar to what happens in marriage. The two become one. They lose their individual identities and now have, or are, one and the same identity. But unlike marriage today, covenant cannot be broken or repealed. Thus, the law of covenant is the law of Identification, in particular, our Identification in Christ.

During the covenant process, the two covenanting parties surrender and forgive all past wrongs against each other. These are also symbolized by slain animals and their blood being released. The blood signifies that the individual lives are now gone, and the parties are now one in the new relationship of covenant unity or common identity. It is a new life, different than the one they had before.

Also there is a third party to the covenant, whatever gods are invoked to recognize the two as one, and now that god or gods add their life to the relationship. Of course, this is why God told the Israelites not to make any covenant with other people. He was not about to enter into covenant with other gods, or idols, no matter what the Israelites did.

This is the meaning of this scripture: Hab 1:13 "Thou (*God*) art of purer eyes than to behold (*approve*) evil, and canst not look (*with pleasure*) on iniquity: wherefore lookest thou upon them that deal treacherously, and holdest thy tongue when the wicked devoureth the man that is more righteous than he?" God can see evil, as if in the distance, but He could not become one, or identified, with it.

That is … until Jesus came. God made Jesus sin so He could make Jesus the righteousness of God when He raised Jesus from the dead. In the process God made Jesus one with the entire human race, one with our sin and totally remitted sin from Jesus and healed Jesus and us at the same time. God did this all by covenant Identification. Jesus was made the substitute for the entire human race and the substitute for God at the same time. 2 Cor 5:21 "For he (*Father God*) hath made him (*Jesus*) to be sin for us, who knew no sin; that we might be made the righteousness of God in him (*Jesus*)."

This ancient Identification of covenant was so strong that if two men entered into covenant and then one wanted to marry the daughter of the other, he could not, as that would have been considered incest, after the covenant was made or cut.

A covenant was kept in force by those involved in the covenant and by the gods invoked. If one violated the covenant, then the other parties to the covenant would kill the one who had broken the covenant. God has kept His covenant with man, and Jesus suffered and was killed for man's violation of God's covenant in Adam and by Adam.

Jesus, identified totally with mankind as our covenant substitute, went to Hades (Hell) for us. Holy Spirit reveals part of Jesus' struggle in Hades for us: Ps 88:3 "For my soul is full of troubles: and my life draweth nigh unto the grave. 4 I am counted with them that go down into the pit: I am as a man that hath no strength: 5 free among the dead, like the slain that lie in the grave, whom thou rememberest no more: and they are cut off from thy hand. 6 Thou hast laid me in the lowest pit, in darkness, in the deeps. 7 Thy wrath lieth hard upon me, and thou hast afflicted me with all thy waves. Selah."

God has given Jesus as the covenant with man. Isa 42:5 "Thus saith God the Lord, he that created the heavens, and stretched them out; he that spread forth the earth, and that which cometh out of it; he that giveth breath unto the people upon

The Law of Covenant Identification

it, and spirit to them that walk therein: 6 I the Lord have called thee in righteousness, and will hold thine hand, and will keep thee, and give thee for **a covenant of the people**, for a light of the Gentiles; 7 to open the blind eyes, to bring out the prisoners from the prison, and them that sit in darkness out of the prison house."

Part of the process of making and re-affirming a covenant now includes a meal in which the bread represents the animals slain, and the wine represents the blood that seals and is the life of the covenant.

Lev 17:11 "For the life of the flesh is in the blood: and I have given it to you upon the altar to make an atonement for your souls: for it is the blood that maketh an atonement for the soul."

Animals were slain, showing that divided or independent physical life was gone, all past violations destroyed, and that in the eating of the bread, they now all shared the same life of the covenant. They were totally identified as one and in unity with this new life.

The blood removed all past barriers and penalties to new life in the covenant. So, in the drinking of the wine, everything that could have separated them was washed away and no longer could or ever would be present.

When men remembered, called to mind and reaffirmed the covenant, they repeated the covenant meal with bread and wine. This was a process of re-affirmation of their joint Identification, a statement that they "were" because of a past covenant, so now they could "be" or live in that covenant.

We see this with Abraham, after he had defeated the 5 kings, rescued Lot and brought back much treasure. Gen 14:16 "And he (*Abraham*) brought back all the goods, and also brought again his brother Lot, and his goods, and the women also, and the people. 17 And the king of Sodom went out to meet him after his return from the slaughter of Chedorlaomer, and of the kings that were with him, at the valley of Shaveh, which is the king's dale. 18 And Melchizedek king of Salem brought forth bread and wine: and he was the priest of the most high God. 19 And he blessed him, and said, Blessed be Abram of the most high God, possessor of heaven and earth: 20 and blessed be the most high God, which hath delivered thine enemies into thy hand. And he gave him tithes of all."

Abraham and Melchizedek reaffirmed their covenant with God in the bread and the wine. For Abraham, this reaffirmed the promise of God to him that God would make him prosperous. So Abraham first gave a tithe of the bounty to Melchizedek, the representative of God. This was recognizing the part God had provided in Abraham's victory.

Then Abraham spurned the king's offer to share the wealth, saying that he would get rich by the hand of God and not the generosity of the king. Gen 14:21 "And the king of Sodom said unto Abram, Give me the persons, and take the goods to thyself. 22 And Abram said to the king of Sodom, I have lift up mine hand

DISCOVERING OUR REDEMPTION

unto the Lord, the most high God, the possessor of heaven and earth, 23 that I will not take from a thread even to a shoelatchet, and that I will not take any thing that is thine, lest thou shouldest say, I have made Abram rich: 24 save only that which the young men have eaten, and the portion of the men which went with me, Aner, Eshcol, and Mamre; let them take their portion."

Jesus made a similar covenant meal in the Last Supper, prior to His becoming the covenant sacrifice and substitute. The same Greek word is translated as either covenant or testament, depending on the translation. When He took the bread and the wine at the Passover meal, He was declaring Himself to be the covenant substitute for all mankind. Like marriage, this was to be a total unification and identity transfer between man and God. So this was the betrothal statement of Jesus for all men.

Matt 26:26 "And as they were eating, Jesus took bread, and blessed it, and brake it, and gave it to the disciples, and said, Take, eat; this is my body. 27 And he took the cup, and gave thanks, and gave it to them, saying, Drink ye all of it; 28 for this is my blood of the **new testament (*covenant*)**, which is shed for many for the remission of sins."

The story of Redemption is the story and the power of the blood of Jesus. Eph 1:5 "Having predestinated us unto the adoption of children by Jesus Christ to himself, according to the good pleasure of his will, 6 to the praise of the glory of his grace, wherein he hath made us accepted in the *agape*/beloved. 7 In whom we have redemption through his blood, the forgiveness (*remission, removal, obliteration and putting away*) of sins, according to the riches of his grace."

In a covenant between two parties, animals are substitutes for the lives of the two parties. The animals are sacrificed, and the parties, the leaders of each party, or a substitute for each party, walks through the blood to show they have died individually and now live as one new identity. Jesus, thus, as man and God, was both the symbol and the substitute (for all that each party is) to rise again from the dead as one, man in God and God in man.

Like the rest of His brothers in the new creation, Jesus was the first one born again, made alive from the dead. Col 1:18 "And he (*Jesus*) is the head of the body, the church: who is the beginning, the firstborn from the dead; that in all things he might have the preeminence."

Thus, the law of covenant is the law of Identification. Just as Jesus is the way, the truth and the *zoe*/life, He is the covenant of God with man and the covenant of man with God. His very self (body, soul and spirit) is the covenant that God makes and reaffirms with man. This is total unity and Identification of God with man, and man with God.

Isa 49:5 "And now, saith the Lord that formed me from the womb to be his servant, to bring Jacob again to him, though Israel be not gathered, yet shall I be glorious in the eyes of the Lord, and my God shall be my strength. 6 And he said, It

The Law of Covenant Identification

is a light thing that thou shouldest be my servant to raise up the tribes of Jacob, and to restore the preserved of Israel: I will also give thee for a light to the Gentiles, that **thou mayest be my salvation** unto the end of the earth. 7 Thus saith the Lord, the Redeemer of Israel, and his Holy One, to him whom man despiseth, to him whom the nation abhorreth, to a servant of rulers, Kings shall see and arise, princes also shall worship, because of the Lord that is faithful, and the Holy One of Israel, and he shall choose thee. 8 Thus saith the Lord, In an acceptable time have I heard thee, and in a day of salvation have I helped thee: and I will preserve thee, and **give thee for a covenant of the people**, to establish the earth, to cause to inherit the desolate heritages; 9 that thou mayest say to the prisoners, Go forth; to them that are in darkness, Shew yourselves. They shall feed in the ways, and their pastures shall be in all high places. 10 They shall not hunger nor thirst; neither shall the heat nor sun smite them: for he that hath *racham*/mercy on them shall lead them, even by the springs of water shall he guide them. 11 And I will make all my mountains a way, and my highways shall be exalted."

Notice, in verse 6, Jesus not only obtained salvation for us, but He is our salvation. Whatever happened to Jesus happened to us also. His salvation from God is our salvation from God. This is Identification. This is part of Jesus being our covenant with God.

Notice the parallel idea of deliverance in Jesus' declaration of His mission to man, in Luke 4, that is also seen in Isaiah chapters 42 and 49: Luke 4:17 "And there was delivered unto him the book of the prophet Esaias. And when he had opened the book, he found the place where it was written, 18 the Spirit of the Lord is upon me, because he hath anointed me to preach the gospel to the poor; he hath sent me to heal the brokenhearted, to preach deliverance to the captives, and recovering of sight to the blind, to set at liberty them that are bruised, 19 to preach the acceptable year of the Lord."

This is a direct reference to Isaiah 42 and 49 and the redemption of man. That is to deliver man from him who hates him, Satan, and put man into the kingdom of His *agape*/love. As Zacharias said: Luke 1:68 "Blessed be the Lord God of Israel; for he hath visited and redeemed his people, 69 and hath raised up an horn of *soteria*/salvation for us in the house of his servant David; 70 as he spake by the mouth of his holy prophets, which have been since the world began: 71 that we should be *sozo*/saved from our enemies, and from the hand of all that hate us; 72 to perform the mercy promised to our fathers, and to remember his holy covenant; 73 the oath which he sware to our father Abraham, 74 that he would grant unto us, that we being delivered out of the hand of our enemies might serve him without fear, 75 in holiness and righteousness before him, all the days of our life."

Holy Spirit proclaims that today is the Day of Salvation that God had long promised. Notice the warning that we must seize this fact and use it to produce

DISCOVERING OUR REDEMPTION

God's salvation on the Earth: <u>2 Cor 6:1</u> "We then, as workers together with him, beseech you also that ye receive not the grace of God in vain. 2 (For he saith, I have heard thee in a time accepted, and in the day of *soteria*/salvation have I succoured thee: behold, now is the accepted time; behold, now is the day of *soteria*/salvation.)"

<u>Heb 2:1</u> "Therefore we ought to give the more earnest heed to the things which we have heard, lest at any time we should let them slip."

This is not just talking about going to Heaven; this is talking about our life on this Earth, in this Universe right now. Thus, it is entirely possible for anyone or all of us to let this redemption, salvation and covenant reality slip past us and not move into what God has ordained for us in this life. No wonder Jesus said: <u>Luke 18:8</u> "... Nevertheless when the Son of man cometh, shall he find faith on the earth?"

Redemption is part of the covenant of God with man, and the Redeemer comes to establish that covenant. <u>Isa 59:20</u> "And the Redeemer shall come to Zion, and unto them that turn from transgression in Jacob, saith the Lord. 21 As for me, this is my covenant with them, saith the Lord; My spirit that is upon thee, and my words which I have put in thy mouth, shall not depart out of thy mouth, nor out of the mouth of thy seed, nor out of the mouth of thy seed's seed, saith the Lord, from henceforth and for ever."

This is the essence of the New Covenant, as referenced in Hebrews chapters 8 and 10 and as seen in the writings of the prophet Jeremiah.

<u>Jer 31:31</u> "Behold, the days come, saith the Lord, that I will make a new covenant with the house of Israel, and with the house of Judah: 32 not according to the covenant that I made with their fathers in the day that I took them by the hand to bring them out of the land of Egypt; which my covenant they brake, although I was an husband unto them, saith the Lord: 33 but this shall be the covenant that I will make with the house of Israel; After those days, saith the LORD, I will put my law in their inward parts, and write it in their hearts; and will be their God, and they shall be my people. 34 And they shall teach no more every man his neighbour, and every man his brother, saying, Know the Lord: for they shall all know me, from the least of them unto the greatest of them, saith the Lord; for I will forgive their iniquity, and I will remember their sin no more."

<u>Heb 10:18</u> "Now where remission of these is (*iniquity and sin*), there is no more offering for sin."

<u>Heb 10:12</u> "But this man (*Jesus*), after he had offered one sacrifice for sins for ever, sat down on the right hand of God; 13 from henceforth expecting till his enemies be made his footstool. 14 For by one offering he hath perfected for ever them that are sanctified."

Genesis shows that it was the shedding of blood in a covenant-type sacrifice that addressed the problem of sin, and recovering of prosperity in a death-ruled

The Law of Covenant Identification

world. Starting with the shedding of blood after Adam sinned, the sacrifice of Abel that got him killed, and then Noah's offered sacrifice after the flood, the next recorded covenant of man and God is in Abraham. That all men sin and fall short of the glory of God is the basic condition of any and all men. Rom 3:10 "As it is written, There is none righteous, no, not one: 11 there is none that understandeth, there is none that seeketh after God. 12 They are all gone out of the way, they are together become unprofitable; there is none that doeth good, no, not one."

Rom 3:23 "For all have sinned, and come short of the glory of God."

The Israelites, through Abraham, had a specific covenant with God. When Jesus became the covenant for all men, He was made one with all the evil of man, to remove any violation of God's ways by man, for the entire human race, "a light to the Gentiles," and not just Israel. This included from the sin of Adam to the very last sin committed by man.

As Zacharias stated, in Luke 1:73, Jesus came in answer to that long-ago promise to Abraham, as well as the covenant with Abraham. A promise was made before the covenant was cut with Abraham. Heb 6:13 "For when God made promise to Abraham, because he could swear by no greater, he sware by himself, 14 saying, Surely blessing I will bless thee, and multiplying I will multiply thee. 15 And so, after he (*Abraham*) had patiently endured, he obtained the promise. 16 For men verily swear by the greater: and an oath for confirmation is to them an end of all strife. 17 Wherein God, willing more abundantly to shew unto the heirs of promise the immutability of his counsel, confirmed it by an oath: 18 that by two immutable things, in which it was impossible for God to lie, we might have a strong consolation, who have fled for refuge to lay hold upon the hope set before us: 19 which hope we have as an anchor of the soul, both sure and stedfast, and which entereth into that within the veil; 20 whither the forerunner is for us entered, even Jesus, made an high priest for ever after the order of Melchisedec."

In the process of being the covenant and making the new covenant, Jesus also became all that man is, in his failure toward God, sin, so that just as He was raised, man was redeemed back to God by Jesus, fully paying for the broken covenant laws, the sin of Israel under the Law, as well as all the evil of all men everywhere.

That is not all; when we sin, there are consequences. The curse of the law describes these. Jesus also became the curse due for the sins and, when Father God raised Jesus, He also healed us of all consequences, to make us totally right, or righteous, with God. Rom 4:25 "Who was delivered for our offences, and was raised again for our justification (*or when we were justified to a full status of justification of all the failures of all of mankind into the full blessing of God*)." If you are a human, you are included. It has been legally accomplished and now waits to be received by faith in Jesus.

DISCOVERING OUR REDEMPTION

The law of sin and death was first revealed when God commanded Adam: Gen 2:16 "And the LORD God commanded the man, saying, Of every tree of the garden thou mayest freely eat: 17 but of the tree of the knowledge of good and evil, thou shalt not eat of it: for in the day that thou eatest thereof thou shalt surely die."

Adam broke this law, and the result was that Satan was made the god of this world. Rom 5:19 "For as by one man's disobedience many were made sinners, so by the obedience of one shall many be made righteous. 20 Moreover the law entered, that the offence might abound. But where sin abounded, grace did much more abound: 21 that as sin hath reigned [*though the lordship of Satan, as the prince or god of this world*] unto death (*by every curse of the law, in slow and fast forms of death*), even so might grace reign (*as king*) through righteousness unto eternal *zoe*/life (*making Heaven on Earth in the abundance of the zoe/life of God, that even makes deserts bloom and raises the dead*) by Jesus Christ our Lord."

Matt 4:8 "Again, the devil taketh him (*Jesus*) up into an exceeding high mountain, and sheweth him all the kingdoms of the world, and the glory of them; 9 and saith unto him, All these things will I give thee, if thou wilt fall down and worship me."

2 Cor 4:3 "But if our gospel be hid, it is hid to them that are lost: 4 in whom the god of this world hath blinded the minds of them which believe not, lest the light of the glorious gospel of Christ, who is the image of God, should shine unto them."

Even though Adam sinned, God had a plan to solve the sin problem and buy back man from the bondage of sin and the lordship of the devil.

Rom 5:6 "For when we were yet without strength, in due time Christ died for the ungodly. 7 For scarcely for a righteous man will one die: yet peradventure for a good man some would even dare to die. 8 But God commendeth his *agape*/love toward us, in that, while we were yet sinners, Christ died for us."

In this act, Jesus broke the power of the devil and redeemed man from the power of the kingdom of darkness and redeemed him back to God. As we realize and know this truth, we will continually be: Col 1:12 "Giving thanks (*continually*) unto the Father, which hath made us meet to be partakers of the inheritance of the saints in light: 13 who hath delivered us from the power of darkness, and hath translated us into the kingdom of his *agape*/dear Son: 14 in whom we have redemption through his blood, even the forgiveness (*remission, removal, obliteration and putting away*) of sins."

Heb 9:11 "But Christ being come an high priest of good things to come, by a greater and more perfect tabernacle, not made with hands, that is to say, not of this building; 12 neither by the blood of goats and calves, but by his own blood he entered in once into the holy place, having obtained eternal redemption for us."

This eternal redemption lasts forever and needed to be paid for only once by Jesus. In order to receive a remission or forgiveness of sins different from that ob-

The Law of Covenant Identification

tained by Jesus 2000 years ago, there must be another shedding of blood, and Jesus would never die again. No other blood is sufficient, for the blood of Jesus is so identified with God that Holy Spirit declared that Jesus' blood is the blood of God.

Acts 20:28 "Take heed therefore unto yourselves, and to all the flock, over the which the Holy Ghost hath made you overseers, to feed the church of God, which he hath purchased with his own blood."

So, if the matter was not handled by God in Jesus 2000 years ago, it will never be handled by God again. Man has only one option for forgiveness, remission or full healing. It is what Jesus did 2000 years ago or nothing!

Heb 10:26 "For if we sin wilfully [*by denying that the only sacrifice for sin was in Jesus*] after that we have received the knowledge of the truth, there remaineth no more sacrifice for sins [*Jesus did it, or it will never be propitiated before God otherwise*], 27 but a certain fearful looking for of judgment and fiery indignation, which shall devour the adversaries [*who deny the effectiveness of the Mighty Arm of God in Jesus*]. 28 He that despised Moses' law died without mercy under two or three witnesses: 29 of how much sorer punishment, suppose ye, shall he be thought worthy, who hath trodden under foot the Son of God [*in denying the power of His death and resurrection as the only valid salvation of mankind as a free gift*], and hath counted the blood of the covenant, wherewith he was sanctified, an unholy thing, and hath done despite unto the Spirit of grace?" To deny the power of the blood of Jesus is to deny the grace of God in Jesus. To deny the covenant of Jesus, where Abraham was the substitute for Jesus, is to call God a liar and a covenant breaker.

Gal 5:1 "Stand fast therefore in the liberty wherewith Christ hath made us free, and be not entangled again with the yoke of bondage."

The letters to the Hebrews and the Galatians proclaim this great truth because the Hebrew Christians were going back to the temple to seek forgiveness of sin under the blood of bulls and goats and, thus, denying the propitiation of the blood of Jesus and His resurrection. The blood of Jesus did away with the blood of the temple. Your religion may look for other answers, but God only accepts that blood shed long ago.

Jesus shed His covenant-making and sin-cleansing blood in two major ways. First His blood was shed in bruises under the skin, where the blood vessels are broken but the blood generally stays in the body. This causes the typical black and blue marks. The second was where His blood was beaten out of Him with fists, thorns and scourging whips. Then there were scrapes and more piercings by that cruel crown of thorns, as He fell on the way to Golgotha. Next came the spikes driven into this hands and feet. Then there were scrapes again, as He pushed His back against the cross to breathe. And, finally, His blood was released by a spear piercing His side after He was dead.

DISCOVERING OUR REDEMPTION

The only "humane" bleeding was from this spear wound in His side. It was like the sacrificial lamb of that first Passover or the annual atonement of the single goat. All the rest were where He gave His body for us like the second-atonement goat that was led into the wilderness to be torn by wild animals.

Who could have believed that this oft-repeated cruelty of scourging and crucifixion was the awesome change God had long predicted? Isa 53:1 "Who hath believed our report? and to whom is the arm of the Lord revealed? ... 3 He is despised and rejected of men; a man of sorrows, and acquainted with grief: and we hid as it were our faces from him; he was despised, and we esteemed him not. 4 Surely he hath borne our griefs, and carried our sorrows: yet we did esteem him stricken, smitten of God, and afflicted. 5 But he was wounded for our transgressions, he was bruised for our iniquities: the chastisement of our peace was upon him; and with his stripes we are healed."

This cruel mistreatment of Jesus' body was what He took for us.

Matt 26:26 "And as they were eating, Jesus took bread, and blessed it, and brake it, and gave it to the disciples, and said, Take, eat; this is my body."

Mark 14:22 "And as they did eat, Jesus took bread, and blessed, and brake it, and gave to them, and said, Take, eat: this is my body."

Luke 22:19 "And he took bread, and gave thanks, and brake it, and gave unto them, saying, This is my body which is given for you: this do in remembrance of me."

This was to fulfill: Isa 53:5 "But he was wounded for our transgressions, he was bruised for our iniquities: the chastisement of our peace was upon him; and with his stripes we are healed." So we were healed before Jesus died on the cross. This is what He took for us in His body, His flesh.

With His blood, He remitted our sins, for our redemption.

Math 26:27 "And he took the cup, and gave thanks, and gave it to them, saying, Drink ye all of it; 28 For this is my blood of the new testament, which is shed for many for the remission (*purging, removal, putting away and obliteration*) of sins."

Mark 14:23 "And he took the cup, and when he had given thanks, he gave it to them: and they all drank of it. 24 And he said unto them, This is my blood of the *kainos*/new (*renewed, revitalized, renovated*) testament, which is shed for many."

Luke 22:20 "Likewise also the cup after supper, saying, This cup is the *kainos*/new (*renewed, revitalized, renovated*) testament in my blood, which is shed for you."

This is the New Covenant in the blood of Jesus: Heb 10:12 "But this man, after he had offered one sacrifice for sins for ever, sat down on the right hand of God; 13 from henceforth expecting till his enemies be made his footstool. 14 For by one offering he hath perfected for ever them that are sanctified. 15 Whereof the Holy Ghost also is a witness to us: for after that he had said before, 16 this is the covenant that I will make with them after those days, saith the Lord, I will put my laws into

The Law of Covenant Identification

their hearts, and in their minds will I write them; 17 and their sins and iniquities will I remember no more. 18 Now where remission (*purging, removal, putting away and obliteration*) of these (*sins and iniquities*) is, there is no more offering for sin."

This blood is the sealing blood of the renewed or newly invigorated testament of Abraham. God kept His promise to Abraham in Jesus. Luke 1:71 "That we should be *sozo*/saved from our enemies, and from the hand of all that hate us; 72 to perform the [*chesed*] mercy promised to our fathers, and to remember his holy covenant; 73 the oath which he sware to our father Abraham."

Heb 6:13 "For when God made promise to Abraham, because he could swear by no greater, he sware by himself, 14 saying, Surely blessing I will bless thee, and multiplying I will multiply thee."

Gal 3:8 "And the scripture, foreseeing that God would justify the heathen through faith, preached before the gospel unto Abraham, saying, In thee shall all nations be blessed."

Gal 3:13 "Christ hath redeemed us from the curse of the law, being made a curse for us: for it is written, Cursed is every one that hangeth on a tree: 14 that the blessing of Abraham might come on the Gentiles through Jesus Christ; that we might receive the promise of the Spirit through faith."

So, we see, God re-vitalized the promise and covenant He had actually made to Jesus when He made promise and covenant with Abraham. Gal 3:14 "That the blessing of Abraham might come on the Gentiles through Jesus Christ; that we might receive the promise of the Spirit through faith. 15 Brethren, I speak after the manner of men; though it be but a man's covenant, yet if it be confirmed, no man disannulleth, or addeth thereto. 16 Now to Abraham and his seed were the promises made. He saith not, And to seeds, as of many; but as of one, And to thy seed, which is Christ. 17 And this I say, That the covenant, that was confirmed before of God in Christ, the law, which was four hundred and thirty years after, cannot disannul, that it should make the promise of none effect." Verse 16 makes it clear that it was not to Abraham, but to Jesus Christ, the "seed of Abraham," the promise was made.

Little did the 11, sitting at that pivotal Passover meal, understand that the dream of the ages, the dream of Abraham for all mankind, was about to go into high motion for fulfillment. The great plan of God was Jesus coming to redeem man, in fulfillment of that promise made to Abraham so long ago. God had no other plan.

Jesus proclaimed that plan at that Last Supper and then proceeded to walk out (in His body, blood, soul and spirit) the awesome plan of God that would forever change the structure of the Universe, the "whole creation." Heb 10:12 "But this man, after he had offered one sacrifice for sins for ever, sat down on the right hand of God; 13 from henceforth expecting till his enemies be made his footstool."

DISCOVERING OUR REDEMPTION

The message is clear: Sin is so real and so terrible it cost Jesus His life. God was willing to have Jesus become one with man and sin, to heal mankind of sin. God only identifies our remission of sin and healing in Jesus 2000 years ago. You can do anything you want, but God only recognizes His great work, the work of the Mighty Arm of God, in Jesus, 2000 years ago.

Father God planned to solve the sin/lack of blessing problem in Jesus before He ever laid the foundation of the Earth. Titus 1:1 "Paul, a servant of God, and an apostle of Jesus Christ, according to the faith of God's elect, and the acknowledging of the truth which is after godliness; 2 in hope of eternal *zoe*/life, which God, that cannot lie, promised before the world began; 3 but hath in due times manifested his word through preaching, which is committed unto me according to the commandment of God our Saviour."

If you choose to forgo His great work, you are only left with the penalty of sin and no experiential remission or healing. If sin is not atoned for or propitiated, you are only left with the doom of the impending curse of that sin. If you are a Christian, you may be eternally *sozo*/saved, born again, but your Earth life will reflect a life without the power of the remission of sin, physical healing and earthly prosperity in Jesus. 3 John 2 "*Agape*/beloved, I wish (*pray*) above all things that thou mayest prosper and be in health, even as thy *psuche*/soul (*life*) prospereth."

If the apostle had to exercise faith, praying for prosperity and health from God and a prosperous-in-God soul, then earthly prosperity and health and a soul that operates like Jesus in the mind of Christ are not automatic in this life. Somebody has to labor in faith and truth to bring it to pass in this lifetime. It is available, as part of all the spiritual blessings in heavenly places (see Eph 1:3), but it takes active faith to bring it to the Earth. Which is exactly how Jesus said to pray:

Matt 6:8 "Be not ye therefore like unto them: for your Father knoweth what things ye have need of, before ye *aiteo*/ask (*require, demand and expect as due by covenant promise of*) him. 9 After this manner therefore pray ye: Our Father which art in heaven, Hallowed be thy name. 10 Thy kingdom come. Thy will be done in earth, as it is in heaven. 11 Give us this day our daily bread. 12 And forgive us our debts, as we forgive our debtors. 13 And lead us not into temptation, but deliver us from evil: For thine is the kingdom, and the power, and the glory, for ever. Amen. 14 For if ye forgive men their trespasses, your heavenly Father will also forgive you: 15 but if ye forgive not men their trespasses, neither will your Father forgive your trespasses."

Your mind and your heart are active 24 hours a day, 7 days a week. If you are not managing what goes into your mind, through your senses, someone else is. If you are not prospering your soul in the truth of God's great redemption, you are prospering it in the devil's great lies. Just like life, this is an all-day, everyday issue.

The Law of Covenant Identification

2 Cor 4:3 "But if our gospel be hid, it is hid to them that are lost (*death is reigning in either fast or slow death*): 4 in whom the god of this world hath blinded the minds of them which believe not, lest the light of the glorious gospel of Christ, who is the image of God, should shine unto them. 5 For we preach not ourselves, but Christ Jesus the Lord; and ourselves your servants for Jesus' sake. 6 For God, who commanded the light to shine out of darkness, hath shined in our hearts, to give the light of the knowledge of the glory of God in the face of Jesus Christ. 7 But we have this treasure in earthen vessels, that the excellency of the *dunamis*/power may be of God, and not of us."

If you are not walking just like Jesus, you are deceived and sinning in some way, and if you are not handling your sin and failure in Jesus, you are left only with the law of sin and death, as enforced by the devil. 1 Cor 15:56 "The sting of death is sin; and the strength of sin is the law. 57 But thanks be to God, which giveth us the victory through our Lord Jesus Christ."

If you walk, knowing the great work of God in His redemption through Jesus, your confession becomes: Rom 8:2 "For the law of the Spirit of *zoe*/life in Christ Jesus hath made me free from the law of sin and death."

In the Last Supper, Jesus made that Passover meal greater or fulfilled what it is before He became our Passover sacrifice. 1 Cor 5:7 "For even Christ our passover is sacrificed for us ... ."

That word Passover does not mean that the blood protected the people from an angry God while God destroyed the first-born of the Egyptians. It means the exact opposite.

First, it was not God that killed those first-born, just as with all the other plagues; it was evil angels of calamity and woe, i.e., from the devil. God Himself did not do these awesome and terrible things; the devil did them as the Egyptians put themselves under the curse. God, each time, limited the devil as to what he could do and, the entire time, protected the Israeli people. Yes, it was God that allowed it or could not stop it because of His laws. Ps 78:49 "He cast upon them the fierceness of his anger, wrath, and indignation, and trouble, by sending evil angels among them. 50 He made a way to his anger; he spared not their soul from death, but gave their life over to the pestilence; 51 and smote all the firstborn in Egypt; the chief of their strength in the tabernacles of Ham."

For the last woe, God specified that the Israelites put fresh blood from a newly slain lamb on the doorposts and lintels (which included the threshold at the bottom). This was a covenant act. They understood this blood was inviting God in to bless and protect them. He was to "pass over" or "leap over" the threshold and be "adopted" into the family and, thus, become their protector and blessing. (See H. Clay Trumbull, *The Threshold Covenant*, Christian Impact Books, Inc. USA,

DISCOVERING OUR REDEMPTION

2000). In our modern terms, perhaps "entered in" rather than "pass over" might explain it better.

The lamb that was sacrificed was to cover any sins, or issues, with God and make the people clean. They were to eat the lamb fully, to give them new life and a new identity. The blood path on their doorway and threshold allowed Holy Spirit to enter and bless the inhabitants. This was so effective that all of Israel was healed and made prosperous in the process. Ps 105:37 "He brought them forth also with silver and gold: and there was not one feeble person among their tribes."

The threshold has even more significance. If that threshold, usually a stone, extended to the corner of the house, because it had such significance then it was also called the *cornerstone*. Upon this type of *cornerstone* the whole physical and spiritual aspects of the house and, therefore, the family rested or was established. Jesus is our Cornerstone. Eph 2:19 "Now therefore ye are no more strangers and foreigners, but fellowcitizens with the saints, and of the household of God; 20 and are built upon the foundation of the apostles and prophets, Jesus Christ himself being the chief corner stone; 21 in whom all the building fitly framed together groweth unto an holy temple in the Lord: 22 in whom ye also are builded together for an habitation of God through the Spirit."

Because Jesus is our Cornerstone, God is building us up, individually and corporately, by our continual ingestion of the Word of God, so we can fulfill our calling as a royal priesthood, kings that are also to be priests. 1 Pet 2:2 "As newborn babes, desire the sincere milk of the word, that ye may grow thereby: 3 if so be ye have tasted that the Lord is gracious. 4 To whom coming, as unto a *zao*/living stone, disallowed indeed of men, but chosen of God, and precious, 5 ye also, as *zao*/ lively stones, are built up a spiritual house, an holy priesthood, to offer up spiritual sacrifices, acceptable to God by Jesus Christ. 6 Wherefore also it is contained in the scripture, Behold, I lay in Sion a chief corner stone, elect, precious: and he that believeth on him shall not be confounded. 7 Unto you therefore which believe he is precious: but unto them which be disobedient, the stone which the builders disallowed, the same is made the head of the corner, 8 and a stone of stumbling, and a rock of offence, even to them which stumble at the word, being disobedient: whereunto also they were appointed. 9 But ye are a chosen generation, a royal priesthood, an holy nation, a peculiar people; that ye should shew forth the praises of him who hath called you out of darkness into his marvellous light: 10 which in time past were not a people, but are now the people of God: which had not obtained mercy, but now have obtained mercy."

Jesus is that Way for God to enter and become one with man, so each of us can fulfill our purpose and our destiny. John 10:6 "This parable spake Jesus unto them: but they understood not what things they were which he spake unto them. 7 Then said Jesus unto them again, Verily, verily, I say unto you, I am the door of the sheep.

The Law of Covenant Identification

8 All that ever came before me are thieves and robbers: but the sheep did not hear them. 9 I am the door: by me if any man enter in, he shall be *sozo*/saved, and shall go in and out, and find pasture. 10 The thief cometh not, but for to steal, and to kill, and to destroy: I am come that they might have *zoe*/life, and that they might have it more abundantly. 11 I am the good shepherd: the good shepherd giveth his *psuche*/life (*soul*) for the sheep."

John 14:6 "Jesus saith unto him, I am the way, the truth, and the *zoe*/life: no man cometh unto the Father, but by me. 7 If ye had *ginosko*/known me, ye should have *ginosko*/known my Father also: and from henceforth ye *ginosko*/know him, and have seen him."

We are to grow, individually and corporately, into effective portals or gateways through which God can fill the Earth as the waters cover the sea. Isa 11:9 "They shall not hurt nor destroy in all my holy mountain: for the earth shall be full of the knowledge of the Lord, as the waters cover the sea. 10 And in that day there shall be a root of Jesse, which shall stand for an ensign of the people; to it shall the Gentiles seek: and his rest shall be glorious." Hab 2:14 "For the earth shall be filled with the knowledge of the glory of the Lord, as the waters cover the sea." Num 14:21 "But as truly as I (*the* Lord) live, all the earth shall be filled with the glory of the Lord."

This knowing of the Lord on His terms and to His satisfaction is a key part of the renewed covenant in Jesus. Heb 8:10 "For this is the covenant that I will make with the house of Israel after those days, saith the Lord; I will put my laws into their mind, and write them in their hearts: and I will be to them a God, and they shall be to me a people: 11 and they shall not teach every man his neighbour, and every man his brother, saying, Know the Lord: for all shall know me, from the least to the greatest. 12 For I will be merciful to their unrighteousness, and their sins and their iniquities will I remember no more."

We are required to participate in this process now in this life. 2 Pet 1:2 "Grace and peace be multiplied unto you through the *epignosis*/knowledge of God, and of Jesus our Lord, 3 according as his divine power hath given unto us all things that pertain unto *zoe*/life and godliness, through the *epignosis*/knowledge of him that hath called us to glory and virtue: 4 whereby are given unto us exceeding great and precious promises: that by these ye might be partakers of the divine nature, having escaped the corruption that is in the world through lust. 5 And beside this, giving all diligence, add to your faith virtue; and to virtue knowledge; 6 and to knowledge temperance; and to temperance patience; and to patience godliness; 7 and to godliness brotherly kindness; and to brotherly kindness *agape*/charity. 8 For if these things be in you, and abound, they make you that ye shall neither be barren nor unfruitful in the knowledge of our Lord Jesus Christ."

Barren means a land that is owned but is empty of things desired by the owner. Fruit is something that can be given away to others. We are to grow to become a

DISCOVERING OUR REDEMPTION

fruitful garden of the Lord. Isa 58:9 "Then shalt thou call, and the LORD shall answer; thou shalt cry, and he shall say, Here I am. If thou take away from the midst of thee the yoke, the putting forth of the finger (*accusing and finding fault with others without getting them healed*), and speaking vanity (*things that will not stand on the Day of Judgment*); 10 and if thou draw out thy soul to the hungry, and satisfy the afflicted soul; then shall thy light rise in obscurity, and thy darkness be as the noonday: 11 and the LORD shall guide thee continually, and satisfy thy soul in drought, and make fat thy bones: and thou shalt be like a watered garden, and like a spring of water, whose waters fail not (*in the midst of earthly famine and lack of effective knowledge of the Lord*). 12 And they that shall be of thee shall build the old waste places: thou shalt raise up the foundations of many generations; and thou shalt be called, The repairer of the breach, The restorer of paths to dwell in." Jer 31:11 "For the LORD hath redeemed Jacob, and ransomed him from the hand of him that was stronger than he. 12 Therefore they shall come and sing in the height of Zion, and shall flow together to the goodness of the LORD, for wheat, and for wine, and for oil, and for the young of the flock and of the herd: and their soul shall be as a watered garden; and they shall not sorrow any more at all." Ps 1:1 "Blessed is the man that walketh not in the counsel of the ungodly, nor standeth in the way of sinners, nor sitteth in the seat of the scornful. 2 But his delight is in the law of the Lord; and in his law doth he meditate day and night. 3 And he shall be like a tree planted by the rivers of water, that bringeth forth his fruit in his season; his leaf also shall not wither; and whatsoever he doeth shall prosper."

We can measure our progress in this growth process. 1 John 2:3 "And hereby we do know that we know him, if we keep his commandments. 4 He that saith, I know him, and keepeth not his commandments, is a liar, and the truth is not in him. 5 But whoso keepeth his word, in him verily is the *agape*/love of God perfected: hereby know we that we are in him. 6 He that saith he abideth in him ought himself also so to walk, even as he walked."

Anyplace we fall short in matters of heart or action, including answered *aiteo*, we are to know that Jesus is the Lamb of God, our Passover, where God was slain 2000 years ago and has entered into us when we got born again by Holy Spirit. And, by the New Covenant, Jesus not only enters in, but also makes Himself one with us by Holy Spirit. When Jesus died, He died for every aspect of our life that is not just like Jesus. By His stripes, we were healed in our physical or earthly aspects, and when He was raised again, all of our "inner man" issues (spirit, heart and soul) were then healed so Holy Spirit could now dwell in men in the new creation.

So, in any situation of apparent unanswered *aiteo*, whatever needs to be healed in us, to get that answer, was also healed 2000 years ago, for us to get, by faith, in the manner as described this way: 2 Cor 3:17 "Now the Lord is that Spirit: and where the Spirit of the Lord is, there is liberty. 18 But we all, with open face behold-

The Law of Covenant Identification

ing as in a glass (*mirror*) the glory of the Lord (*being manifested in us*), are changed into the same image from glory to glory, even as by the Spirit of the Lord."

Every failure was placed on Jesus, borne fully to completion by Jesus and healed in Jesus 2000 years ago, as promised by God: Isa 53:4 "Surely he hath *cabal/* borne our griefs, and *nasa/*carried our sorrows: yet we did esteem him stricken, smitten of God, and afflicted. 5 But he was wounded for our transgressions, he was bruised for our iniquities: the chastisement of our peace was upon him; and with his stripes we are healed. 6 All we like sheep have gone astray; we have turned everyone to his own way; and the Lord hath laid on him the iniquity of us all."

This is what Jesus accomplished 2000 years ago. 1 Pet 2:24 "[*Jesus*] who his own self bare our sins in his own body on the tree, that we, being dead to sins, should *zao*/live unto righteousness: by whose stripes ye were healed." Jesus did this for us, by becoming one with us in the covenant process, and thus became our Passover Lamb.

This "pass over" or "entering in" for the Jews was to be remembered every year in the bread and wine of the Passover meal celebrated by each family or household. As seen with Abraham, they could call to remembrance this covenant relationship and promise anytime they wanted to celebrate God's goodness or were in need. This was to be to a faith act in which they "remembered" in a covenant meal that God was identified with them and He would bless them. Jesus is the Lamb and the doorway for God to enter us. We Christians are to believe Him for the same benefits and even greater of healing, protection and blessing through Communion, for God has not just "entered in," but also has become one with those born again.

This was included when Jesus said: John 6:53 "Then Jesus said unto them, Verily, verily, I say unto you, Except ye eat the flesh of the Son of man, and drink his blood, ye have no *zoe*/life in you. 54 Whoso eateth my flesh, and drinketh my blood, hath eternal *zoe*/life; and I will raise him up at the last day. 55 For my flesh is meat indeed, and my blood is drink indeed. 56 He that eateth my flesh, and drinketh my blood, dwelleth in me, and I in him. 57 As the *zao*/living Father hath sent me, and I *zao*/live by the Father: so he that eateth me, even he shall *zao*/live by me. 58 This is that bread which came down from heaven: not as your fathers did eat manna, and are dead: he that eateth of this bread shall *zao*/live for ever."

We were commanded by Jesus to remember that we are in eternal and unbreakable covenant with Him (and through Him, with Father God) in the covenant meal we call Communion or The Lord's Supper. Failure to renew your covenant relationship in your heart in the ordnance of Communion means you will not keep this alive in your mind to control your life and, instead, while "saved," live as mere man without God, where the death, resurrection and glorification of Jesus are of little power for you in this life. 1 Cor 11:28 "But let a man examine himself, and so

DISCOVERING OUR REDEMPTION

let him eat of that bread, and drink of that cup. 29 For he that eateth and drinketh unworthily, eateth and drinketh damnation to himself, not discerning the Lord's body. 30 For this cause many are weak and sickly among you, and many sleep. 31 For if we would judge ourselves, we should not be judged. 32 But when we are judged, we are chastened of the Lord, that we should not be condemned with the world."

The judgment of God is like this: "You ignore or diminish My work by Jesus, have no faith in My Word, so you will live as if Jesus never did His work–without true knowledge of God and without a covenant of promise. Reaffirm my Word in your heart, the great work of Jesus, and enforce that over the devil, and you will live in my Kingdom, to set yourself and others free and bring my Kingdom to Earth."

The choice is ours, as the Scriptures say: 1 Cor 11:29 "For he that eateth and drinketh unworthily, eateth and drinketh damnation to himself, not discerning the Lord's body. 30 For this cause many are weak and sickly among you, and many sleep. 31 For if we would judge ourselves, we should not be judged. 32 But when we are judged, we are chastened of the Lord, that we should not be condemned with the world."

We are told that what happened to Jesus' body was for our earthly healing and prosperity. Isa 53:5 "But he was wounded for our transgressions, he was bruised for our iniquities: the chastisement of our peace was upon him; and with his stripes we are healed. 6 All we like sheep have gone astray; we have turned every one to his own way; and the Lord hath laid on him the iniquity of us all." This included sin and all the consequences of sin. Jesus bore it all on His body so we do not need to.

In Communion, the failure to judge properly the curse of sin currently in our lives, as taken by Jesus for and instead of us, means our physical life will be: 1 Cor 11:30 "For this cause many are weak and sickly among you, and many sleep." You will experience sickness, lack and an early death. That word *weak* can also include lack of wisdom and prosperity. The cure is to identify yourself in Jesus, as you take Communion.

Gal 3:13 "Christ hath redeemed us from the curse of the law, being made a curse for us: for it is written, Cursed is every one that hangeth on a tree: 14 that the blessing of Abraham might come on the Gentiles through Jesus Christ; that we might receive the promise of the Spirit through faith."

Rom 6:11 "Likewise reckon ye also yourselves to be dead indeed unto sin, but *zao*/alive unto God through Jesus Christ our Lord."

Knowing: 1 Cor 6:17 "But he that is joined unto the Lord is one spirit." This is ultimate Identification. We may not appreciate its full significance, but God does because it is His idea, and part of His Great Work of His Mighty Arm, Jesus of Nazareth, who is the Christ.

THE LAW OF COVENANT IDENTIFICATION

Man is in covenant unity with God by Jesus, our covenant substitute. He became one with all of mankind by the Passover Last Supper meal. God is not our problem; our ignorance and rebellion is.

Our growth in God depends on keeping these covenantal redemption facts constantly in our minds and our hearts. 2 Pet 1:9 "But he that lacketh these things (*of walking like Jesus in this life*) is blind, and cannot see afar off, and hath forgotten that he was purged (*remitted*) from his old sins."

Heb 3:14 "For we are made partakers of Christ, if (*as*) we hold the beginning of our confidence (*faith, believing*) stedfast unto the end."

No wonder the Scriptures say: Hos 4:6 "My people are destroyed for lack of knowledge ... ."

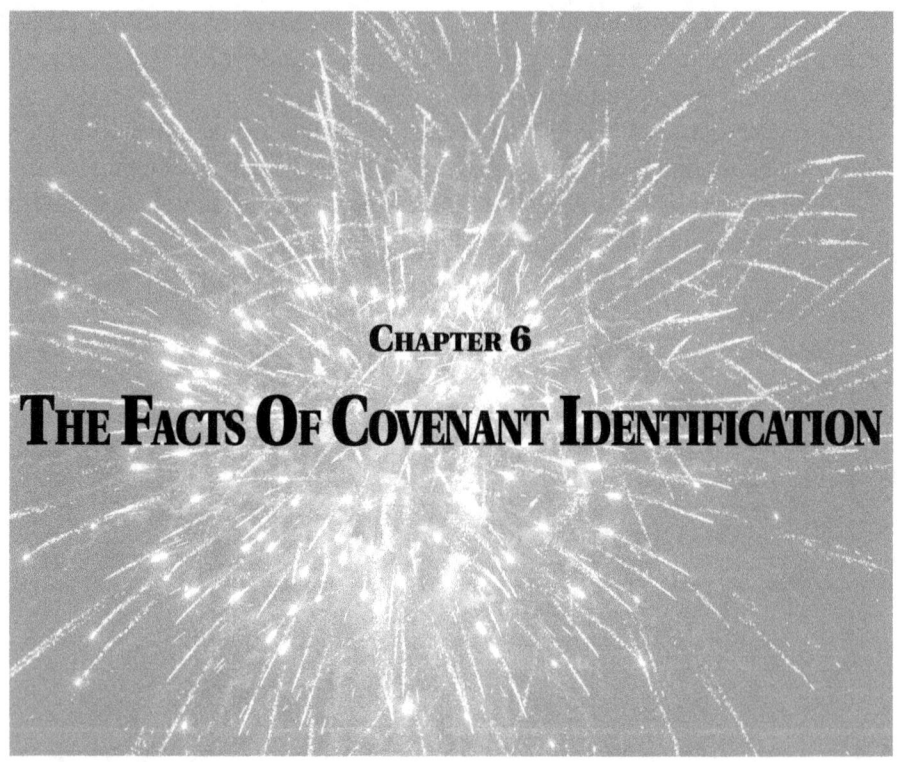

CHAPTER 6
THE FACTS OF COVENANT IDENTIFICATION

In the facts of covenant Identification, we have one of the richest phases of Redemption. Jesus did not redeem us as if He was helping those who He was not a part of.

It was not like a police rescue, where that is their job, and after your rescue, they are gone. No, Jesus rescued us as one with Himself, and then stays with us forever, to His delight.

Father God made us one in Jesus. So, when Jesus redeemed us, Father God made us totally one with Jesus in the process, bringing us back to our original position as sons of God, as Adam was before the fall, and then He gives us Holy Spirit in a manner apparently Adam did not have. Remember, Holy Spirit is sealed unto us unto the Day of Redemption. Eph 4:30 "And grieve not the holy Spirit of God, whereby ye are sealed unto the day of redemption." Holy Spirit may be grieved, but He cannot leave.

In the spirit, we are back in the house with Father God, in Jesus, seated at God's right hand in Jesus.

Eph 2:4 "But God, who is rich in mercy, for his great *agape*/love wherewith he *agape*/loved us, 5 even when we were dead in sins, hath quickened us together **with Christ**, (by grace ye are *sozo*/saved;) 6 and hath raised us up together, and made us sit together in heavenly places **in Christ Jesus**."

The Facts of Covenant Identification

We could have been with Him, and yet not been one with Him. But "in Christ" means we are one with Him, and He with us. This is fact, a past event, settled in Heaven and Hades forever 2000 years ago. The devil has to work overtime to keep these facts from us; else we will know we are masters over him in God.

God has never defined man by the fall of Adam, but He has always defined man by the covenant redemption through Jesus. Now He has manifested Jesus and His Redemption for man.

1 Pet 1:18 "Forasmuch as ye know that ye were not redeemed with corruptible things, as silver and gold, from your vain conversation received by tradition from your fathers; 19 but with the precious blood of Christ, as of a lamb without blemish and without spot: 20 who verily was foreordained before the foundation of the world, but was manifest in these last times for you, 21 who by him do believe in God, that raised him up from the dead, and gave him glory; that your faith and hope might be in God."

Titus 1:1 "Paul, a servant of God, and an apostle of Jesus Christ, according to the faith of God's elect, and the acknowledging of the truth which is after godliness; 2 in hope of eternal *zoe*/life, which God, that cannot lie, promised before the world began; 3 but hath in due times manifested his word through preaching, which is committed unto me according to the commandment of God our Saviour."

1 John 3:5 "And ye know that he (*Jesus*) was manifested to take away our sins; and in him is no sin."

Heb 2:9 "But we see Jesus, who was made a little lower than the angels for the suffering of death, crowned with glory and honour; that he by the grace of God should taste death for every man. 10 For it became him, for whom are all things, and by whom are all things, in bringing many sons unto glory, to make the captain of their *soteria*/salvation perfect through sufferings. 11 For both he that sanctifieth and they who are sanctified are all of one: for which cause he is not ashamed to call them brethren."

Because of His great work, Jesus is not ashamed to call the weakest Christian Brother or Sister.

Heb 2:10 "For it became him, for whom are all things, and by whom are all things, in bringing many sons unto glory, to make the captain of their *soteria*/salvation perfect through sufferings. 11 For both he that sanctifieth and they who are sanctified are all of one: for which cause he is not ashamed to call them brethren."

1 John 3:2 "*Agape*/beloved, now are we the sons of God, and it doth not yet appear what we shall be: but we know that, when he shall appear, we shall be like him; for we shall see him as he is. 3 And every man that hath this hope in him purifieth himself, even as he is pure."

DISCOVERING OUR REDEMPTION

This book is designed to help you know and understand the hope that sets and keeps you on the path of God's call for your life in Jesus, so you can *"purify yourself, even as he is pure."*

Jesus (and, through Jesus, God) gave Himself for us.

1 Tim 2:5 "For there is one God, and one mediator between God and men, the man Christ Jesus; 6 who gave himself a ransom for all, to be testified in due time."

Titus 2:13 "Looking for that blessed hope, and the glorious appearing of the great God and our Saviour Jesus Christ; 14 who gave himself for us, that he might redeem us from all iniquity, and purify unto himself a peculiar people, zealous of good works. 15 These things speak, and exhort, and rebuke with all authority. Let no man despise thee."

Paul made the great proclamation that when Jesus gave Himself for us, we were fully identified and one with Him. Gal 2:20 "I am (*have been*) crucified with Christ: nevertheless I *zao*/live; yet not I, but Christ *zao*/liveth in me: and the life which I now *zao*/live in the flesh I *zao*/live by the faith of the Son of God, who *agape*/loved me, and gave himself for me."

If Paul was there, we were all there too, when Jesus gave Himself for us all.

When He gave Himself, Jesus took all the sin of mankind, that men might have *zoe*/life, the life of God.

Matt 20:28 "Even as the Son of man came not to be ministered unto, but to minister, and to give his *psuche*/life (*soul*) a ransom for many."

John 6:51 "I am the *zao*/living bread which came down from heaven: if any man eat of this bread, he shall *zao*/live for ever: and the bread that I will give is my flesh, which I will give for the *zoe*/life of the world."

1 Pet 2:24 "Who his own self bare (*entirely*) our sins in his own body on the tree, that we, being dead to sins, should *zao*/live unto righteousness: by whose stripes ye were healed."

1 Pet 3:18 "For Christ also hath once suffered for sins, the just for the unjust, that he might bring us to God, being put to death in the flesh, but quickened (*made alive from death*) by the Spirit."

With Christ: Several times Paul uses the preposition "with" in connection with His Substitutionary teaching. This is covenant Identification where Jesus and mankind are one. He, as our substitute, makes the covenant by, for and with us, and us in Him.

Gal. 2:20 "I have been crucified WITH Christ ... ." AMP

Then he tells us that "he died WITH Christ," that "he was buried WITH Christ," and we "live WITH him." 1 Thes 5:9 "For God hath not appointed us to wrath, but to obtain *soteria*/salvation by our Lord Jesus Christ, 10 who died for us, that, whether we wake or sleep, we should *zao*/live together WITH him."

2 Tim 2:11 "It is a faithful saying: For if we be dead WITH him, we shall also *zao*/live WITH him."

The Facts of Covenant Identification

These are all part of our covenant identity in Christ, our covenant substitute. By covenant, we are counted as one with Him in every action of those mighty 52 days.

Notice, the three key "knowing"s of Romans 6 (verses 3, 6, and 9) allow us to do the proper "reckoning" of verse 11.

Rom 6:3 "**Know** ye not, that so many of us as were baptized into Jesus Christ were baptized into his death? 4 Therefore we are buried with him by baptism into death: that like as Christ was raised up from the dead by the glory of the Father, even so we also should walk in newness of *zoe*/life. 5 For if we have been planted together in the likeness of his death, we shall be also in the likeness of his resurrection."

Rom 6:6 "**Knowing** this, that our old man is crucified with him, that the body of sin might be destroyed, that henceforth we should not serve sin. 7 For he that is dead is freed from sin. 8 Now if we be dead with Christ, we believe that we shall also *zao*/live with him."

Rom 6:9 "**Knowing** that Christ being raised from the dead dieth no more; death hath no more dominion over him. 10 For in that he died, he died unto sin once: but in that he *zao*/liveth, he *zao*/liveth unto God."

Rom 6:11 "Likewise (*or therefore*) **reckon** (*count, as in a ledger book, or consider, as a new, unchangeable position*) ye also yourselves to be dead indeed unto sin, but [*reckon yourself to be*] *zao*/alive unto God through Jesus Christ our Lord."

Reckoning is something you do when it does not seem real but contrary to the current facts. When you still sin, are not walking just like Jesus, but you "reckon," or count, or call, as truth in spite of what you see, God's Word and God's view of you in the new creation. The "reckoning" is our part.

Notice there are two reckonings:
1. Reckon yourself, along with Jesus, as dead to sin.
2. Reckon yourself, along with Jesus, as now *zao*/alive to God, as Jesus is.

What do you do when you find yourself still sinning? To reckon either one without Jesus is to miss the point of Romans 6:1-10. To spend excessive time on reckoning yourself as dead to or trapped in sin is to miss the Gospel that you now are *zao*/alive to God, so that He sees you as *zao*/alive in Christ and not dead in the devil. You should spend at least twice if not 100 times considering yourself *zao*/alive to God as the amount of time you spend considering yourself dead to or trapped in sin. But you cannot do either until you have the "knowing" of Rom 6:3, 6 and 9.

Or, in the words of this verse: Philem 6 "That the communication (*outworked reality of life in Holy Spirit*) of thy faith may become effectual (*in producing the Kingdom of God right now in miracles, power, love and a mind operating just like Jesus*) by the acknowledging (*working as a master craftsman able to train others to the same level of master craftsmanship*) of every good thing which is in you in Christ Jesus."

DISCOVERING OUR REDEMPTION

Freedom from sin comes from, not just confession of sin, but also majoring significantly on what Jesus had already done in and for you to produce more of the blessings of God in your life. So you spend less time on your sins and a lot more time on who you are in Jesus right now, in spite of your sins. Thus, you spend little time focusing on the devil working in your life to produce sin, and a lot more time and effort on the reality of your new birth, made in righteousness and true holiness, like Father God.

2 Cor 6:1 "We then, as workers together with him, beseech you also that ye receive not the grace of God in vain. 2 (For he saith, I have heard thee in a time accepted, and in the day of *soteria*/salvation have I succoured thee: behold, now is the accepted time; behold, now is the day of *soteria*/salvation.)"

2 Cor 1:19 "For the Son of God, Jesus Christ, who was preached among you by us, even by me and Silvanus and Timotheus, was not yea and nay, but in him was yea. 20 For all the promises of God in him are yea, and in him Amen, unto the glory of God by us. 21 Now he which stablisheth us with you in Christ, and hath anointed us, is God; 22 (*and knowing it is God*) who hath also sealed us, and given the earnest of the Spirit in our hearts."

This knowing gives us the key that unlocks the great teachings of Identification.

Christ became one with us in sin by covenant Identification, that we might become one with Him in Righteousness by covenant Identification. For the unborn again, God, at best, is limited in you. For the born-again new creation, God is unlimited in you for His purposes, depending on your soul being renewed into the grace and truth of the Gospel.

He became as we were, to the end that we might be as He is now. 1 John 4:17 "Herein is our *agape*/love made perfect, that we may have boldness in the day of judgment: because as he is, so are we in this world." 1 Cor 6:17 "But he that is joined unto the Lord is one spirit." This is total Identification and unity at the deepest level of man.

Jesus died to give us *zoe*/life, the nature of God.

John 10:10 "The thief cometh not, but for to steal, and to kill, and to destroy: I am come that they might have *zoe*/life, and that they might have it more abundantly."

2 Pet 1:4 "Whereby are given unto us exceeding great and precious promises: that by these ye might be partakers of the divine nature, having escaped the corruption that is in the world through lust."

Jesus became one with us in death, that we might be one with Him in *zoe*/life. Rom 6:4 "Therefore we are buried with him by baptism into death: that like as Christ was raised up from the dead by the glory of the Father, even so we also should walk in newness of *zoe*/life."

1 John 5:11 "And this is the record, that God hath given to us eternal *zoe*/life, and this *zoe*/life is in his Son. 12 He that hath the Son hath *zoe*/life; and he that hath

not the Son of God hath not *zoe*/life. 13 These things have I written unto you that believe on the name of the Son of God; that ye may know that ye have eternal *zoe*/life, and that ye may believe on the name of the Son of God."

We have a two-fold oneness with Christ: first His oneness with our sin on the cross; second, our oneness with Him in His glory on the throne.

Eph. 2:6 "And raised us up with him, and made us to sit with him in the heavenly places, in Christ Jesus."

Jesus was made sin to make us righteous.

2 Cor 5:14 "For the *agape*/love of Christ constraineth us; because we thus judge, that if one died for all, then were all dead: 15 and that he died for all, that they which *zao*/live should not henceforth *zao*/live unto themselves, but unto him which died for them, and rose again. ... 21 For he (*Father God*) hath made him (*Jesus*) to be sin for us, who knew no sin; that we might be made the righteousness of God in him (*Jesus*)."

Rom 5:8 "But God commendeth his *agape*/love toward us, in that, while we were yet sinners, Christ died for us. 9 Much more then, being now justified by his blood, we shall be *sozo*/saved from wrath through him. 10 For if, when we were enemies, we were reconciled to God by the death of his Son, much more, being reconciled, we shall be *sozo*/saved by his *zoe*/life. 11 And not only so, but we also joy in God through our Lord Jesus Christ, by whom we have now received the atonement (*reconciliation*)."

Jesus became weak to make us strong.

Heb 12:2 "Looking unto Jesus the author and finisher of our faith; who for the joy that was set before him endured the cross, despising the shame, and is set down at the right hand of the throne of God."

2 Cor 13:4 "For though he was crucified through weakness, yet he *zao*/liveth by the power of God. For we also are weak in him, but we shall *zao*/live with him by the power of God toward you."

Jesus became poor, of no strength or value to men, that we might be rich.

2 Cor 8:9 "For ye know the grace of our Lord Jesus Christ, that, though he was rich, yet for your sakes he became poor, that ye through his poverty might be rich (*wealthy in every way*)."

Jesus suffered shame to give us glory.

Rom 8:29 "For whom he did foreknow, he also did predestinate to be conformed to the image of his Son, that he might be the firstborn among many brethren. 30 Moreover whom he did predestinate, them he also called: and whom he called, them he also justified: and whom he justified, them he also glorified. 31 What shall we then say to these things? If God be for us, who can be against us? 32 He that spared not his own Son, but delivered him up for us all, how shall he not with him also freely give us all things?"

DISCOVERING OUR REDEMPTION

Jesus went to Hell in order to take us to God. If we die before the throne of God comes to Earth, we go to Heaven, but ultimately we all come back to Earth after the events of Revelation 21 and 22 come to pass.

Heaven is a blessed warehouse for those returning to Earth. Our mission is to bring Heaven to Earth.

Jesus was condemned to the full curse of the Law in order to justify us. (See Deuteronomy 28 for a listing of the curses of the Law.)

Jesus was made sick in order that healing might be ours.

Isa 53:10 "Yet it was the will of the Lord to bruise (*crush, destroy, humble, and oppress*) Him; He has put Him to grief and made Him sick … ." AMP

Jesus was cast out from the presence of God in order to make us welcome there.

Heb 10:18 "Now where remission of these is (*sins and iniquities*), there is no more offering for sin. 19 Having therefore, brethren, boldness to enter into the holiest by the blood of Jesus, 20 by a new and *zao*/living way, which he hath consecrated for us, through the veil, that is to say, his flesh."

Heb 4:14 "Seeing then that we have a great high priest, that is passed into the heavens, Jesus the Son of God, let us hold fast our profession. 15 For we have not an high priest which cannot be touched with the feeling of our infirmities; but was in all points tempted like as we are, yet without sin. 16 Let us therefore come boldly unto the throne of grace, that we may *lambano*/obtain (*hold on to*) mercy, and find (*perceive*) grace to help in time of need."

Chapter 7
Legal Action for Producing Vital Daily Living

We are told all men fall short of God's standard, which is not just a "good" human, whatever that is, but the standard of God Himself, as seen in the life of Jesus. So until you walk just like Jesus, you fall short of the standard of God. Rom 3:10 "As it is written, There is none righteous, no, not one: 11 There is none that understandeth, there is none that seeketh after God. 12 They are all gone out of the way, they are together become unprofitable; there is none that doeth good, no, not one."

Rom 3:23 "For all have sinned, and come short of the glory of God."

So all men come to God, prior to their new birth, with a spirit united to Satan in death and a life that is less than just like God. This means the only acceptable standard is no sin whosoever in your life.

Since how you live is a function of the thoughts and attitudes of your soul, all men come to God in the new birth with a corrupt soul. His grace, through covenant, gives us a legal status when we are born again. Then we are to live out the life of Christ in us the hope of glory, in cleaning out our souls and keeping them clean before God. And as we do, we will walk and make alive the benefits of His so-great salvation in our lives.

James 1:21 "Wherefore lay apart all filthiness and superfluity of naughtiness, and *lambano*/receive with meekness the engrafted word, which is able to *sozo*/save

DISCOVERING OUR REDEMPTION

your souls. 22 But be ye doers of the word [*of your new creation in Christ, with Christ in you, the hope of the glorious free reign of Holy Spirit*], and not hearers only, deceiving your own selves. 23 For if any be a hearer of the word (*of your total salvation in Jesus*), and not a doer, he is like unto a man beholding his natural face in a glass: 24 for he beholdeth himself, and goeth his way, and straightway forgetteth what manner of man he was [*in the new birth, as a fully adopted son of God, and made after the image of God in the new creation*]. 25 But whoso looketh into the perfect law of liberty [*of your freedom from the devil, so God can dwell in you fully*], and continueth therein, he being not a forgetful hearer, but a doer of the work [*of walking in the fullness of Christ in you the hope of the free and glorious reign of Holy Spirit in and by you*], this man shall be blessed in his deed. 26 If any man among you seem to be religious, and bridleth not his tongue, but deceiveth his own heart, this man's religion is vain [*his vain works will not survive the Day of Judgment, and he will receive no reward from God for those vain works*]. 27 Pure religion [*your application of the saving grace of Jesus in your life*] and undefiled before God and the Father is this, To visit the fatherless and widows in their affliction, and to keep himself unspotted from the world." These are the works and attitudes that will survive the Day of Judgment, with eternal rewards of silver, gold and jewels, per 1 Corinthians, chapter 3.

The revelation of Paul in Redemption unveils to us what God did in Christ for us, from the time He instituted the Communion covenant meal and went to the Cross, until He sat down on the right hand of the Father. The revelation of these awesome 52 days details the legal action, done once for all time, in the Heavenly Halls of Justice, at the Bench of the Supreme Court of Creation, in the covenantal Redemption, the buying back of mankind from the slavery of the devil by the sin of Adam. Luke 19:10 "For the Son of man is come to seek and to *sozo*/save that which was lost."

This legal position is much like what happens in a court of law. The judge rules, and the case is settled. However, unless the winner of the court case does something to enforce the ruling, the loser may decide not to obey the court ruling. Unless the winner takes the judge's ruling (the Scriptures) and goes to the police (Holy Spirit) to enforce the ruling, it is as if there never was a court case. In the Halls of Heaven, it is settled, but unless we bring the ruling to Earth, by faith in the name of Jesus and His great work, we live as if Jesus had never accomplished His victory, until God comes and does it Himself on the Last Day.

Therefore God says: Hos 4:6 "My people are destroyed for lack of knowledge ...."

The vital side of Redemption, that which you walk in, possess in this life, is what Holy Spirit, through the Word of God, is doing in us right now to implement, or execute, this legal fact. Go to Heaven, and you will find your sins and the curse of sin buried and remitted in the eternal Blood of the Lamb of God, and all the consequences of sin fully healed unto prosperity. Go to the Earth, and men and devils will condemn you day and night. Isa 53:1 "Who hath believed our report? and to whom is the arm of the Lord revealed?"

Rom 10:16 "But they have not all obeyed the gospel. For Esaias saith, Lord, who hath believed our report? 17 So then faith cometh by hearing, and hearing by the word of God (*in Christ*)."

What word? Rom 1:16 "For I am not ashamed of the gospel of Christ: for it is the power of God unto *soteria*/salvation to every one that believeth; to the Jew first, and also to the Greek. 17 For therein is the righteousness of God revealed from faith to faith: as it is written, The just shall *zao*/live by faith."

Eph 1:13 "In (*Christ*) whom ye also trusted, after that ye heard the word of truth, the gospel of your *soteria*/salvation: in whom also after that ye believed, ye were sealed with that holy Spirit of promise, 14 which is the earnest of our inheritance until the redemption of the purchased possession, unto the praise of his glory."

How much we integrate our covenant Identification with Christ in His great Redemption of mankind 2000 years ago into our self-identity determines how much of His *zoe*/life actually manifests in us and out to others. This is the vital or "lived out" side of our Redemption. The great work of God in Jesus is eternal; how we reap the benefits of it in this life is up to us and how well we work with Holy Spirit in the process of "saving" our souls.

James 1:21 "Wherefore lay apart all filthiness and superfluity of naughtiness, and *lambano*/receive with meekness the engrafted word, which is able to *sozo*/save your *psuche*/souls (*lives*). 22 But be ye doers of the word, and not hearers only, deceiving your own selves."

1 Pet 1:9 "Receiving the end of your faith, even the *soteria*/salvation of your *psuche*/souls (*lives*)."

John 8:31 "Then said Jesus to those Jews which believed on him, If ye continue in my word, then are ye my disciples indeed; 32 and ye shall know the truth, and the truth shall make you free [*for God to move as freely in you as He does in Jesus*]."

John 15:7 "If ye abide in me, and my words abide in you, ye shall *aiteo*/ask (*require, demand and expect as due by covenant promise*) what ye will, and it shall be done unto you. 8 Herein is my Father glorified, that ye bear much fruit; so shall ye be my disciples."

John 16:22 "And ye now therefore have sorrow: but I will see you again, and your heart shall rejoice, and your joy no man taketh from you. 23 And in that day ye shall *aiteo*/ask (*require, demand and expect as due by covenant promise of*) me nothing. Verily, verily, I say unto you, Whatsoever ye shall *aiteo*/ask (*require, demand and expect as due by covenant promise*) the Father in my name, he will give it you. 24 Hitherto have ye *aiteo*/asked (*require, demand and expect as due by covenant promise*)

DISCOVERING OUR REDEMPTION

nothing in my name: *aiteo*/ask (*require, demand and expect as due by covenant promise*), and ye shall receive, that your joy may be full."

Notice the fruit of all this learning and heart writing is so that you can get answered *aiteo*, just like Jesus did and even greater than He did. Diplomas don't count; only a life of *agape*/love and answered *aiteo* that brings the Kingdom of God to Earth does. Just one of them is not enough; both are needed.

Your spirit is born again in the new creation. This is the basis of our eternal Salvation with God, who is spirit. You will get a new immortal body at your resurrection. The issue now is how much you work with Holy Spirit to make your soul (heart, mind, will and emotions) to be just like Jesus'.

Becoming like Jesus in your soul is "saving your soul." It is not just getting born again. Jesus is the living Word of God; we are to become living words of God, as members of His Body on the Earth. Our Earth success in Jesus depends on how much we work to "save" our souls, to be just like His.

1 John 3:1 "Behold (*pay attention and consider in a way that changes your worldview and present actions*), what manner of *agape*/love the Father hath bestowed upon us, that we should be called the sons of God: therefore the world knoweth us not, because it knew him not. 2 *Agape*/beloved, now are we the sons of God, and it doth not yet appear what we shall be: but we know that, when he shall appear, we shall be like him; for we shall see him as he is. 3 And every man that hath this hope in him purifieth himself, even as he is pure."

This will be reflected in what thoughts we allow, what words we speak and what our actions are. How we actually live is a function of our souls (hearts and minds). Whatever we speak and do in this world is controlled by our souls. In this life, we work with God to write His laws into our hearts and minds.

Heb 10:38 "Now the just shall *zao*/live by faith: but if any man draw back, my *psuche*/soul (*life*) shall have no pleasure in him. 39 But we are not of them who draw back unto perdition; but of them that believe to the *sozo*/saving of the *psuche*/soul (*life*)." Perdition means the effects of the law of sin and death are enforced in your life, in fast and slow forms of destruction. Again, we are not only eternally saved, but we now are on Earth with the job of saving our own souls till we think and act like Jesus.

God tells us life and death are up to us and in our tongues. If it were just up to God, He is the God of life, and there would be no death. That Day will come, but for now He says: Prov 18:21 "Death and life are in the power of the tongue: and they that love it shall eat the fruit thereof." The power is in our tongues to exercise for God unto life or for the devil unto death. God, as an act of sovereignty, has given this power to man and holds each one accountable as to how he uses it.

The apostle Paul warned Timothy, who was troubled by his circumstances: 2 Tim 1:6 "Wherefore I put thee in remembrance that thou stir up the gift of God, which is in thee by the putting on of my hands. 7 For God hath not given us the spirit of fear; but of *dunamis*/power (*God's impossible, unlimited and overcoming ability*), and of *agape*/love, and of a sound mind (*to think just like Jesus*)."

Notice Timothy had Holy Spirit, who is *dunamis* power, *agape*/love and the mind of Christ, yet Timothy had to stir himself up in God to release that *dunamis*/power and *agape*/love and operate in the mind of Christ. They were there, but inaccessible or limited, until he got his attitude right in his soul. You stir yourself up in spirit and soul much like a coach in a locker room with affirmations, confessions, proclamations, thanksgiving, praise and joy, with the Word of God in Christ. The Psalms and long, hard and fast tongues are great tools to use for this.

Our job is to *zao*/live by faith; that is, press in, by believing God in His Word over the circumstances of the devil. Failure to do that puts us in the category of those who died in the desert, living in the presence of God, but never taking possession of the things promised them. We must mix the Word with faith (persuadableness and confidence) to produce the results of believing God in His Word. We have to go to the Word and do this in the presence of God.

James 1:21 "Wherefore lay apart all filthiness and superfluity of naughtiness, and *lambano*/receive with meekness the engrafted word, which is able to *sozo*/save your *psuche*/souls (*lives*)."

Notice the things that stop your soul from receiving and holding on to that Word, that saving Word, are desires in your soul for filthy things of this earth or present world order, and vanity, things that will be destroyed on the Day of Judgment.

2 Cor 13:4 "For though he (*Jesus Christ*) was crucified through weakness, yet he *zao*/liveth by the power of God. For we also are weak in him, but we shall *zao*/live with him by the power of God toward you. 5 Examine yourselves, whether ye be in the faith; prove your own selves. Know ye not your own selves, how that Jesus Christ is in you, except ye be reprobates?" *Reprobate* means to be useless, like garbage, ineffectual in bringing the Kingdom of God to Earth. A reprobate Christian is one who is born again, with Holy Spirit dwelling in them, but is still in bondage to sin by not renewing their mind and not using the reality of Jesus living in them to release Jesus into the Earth in every aspect of life continually.

This command of Paul in 2 Cor 13:5 tells us it is possible to be born again, live in this world, and not know the effective reality of Jesus living inside you. That effectiveness is measured by how much *agape*/love we walk in and how much of the Kingdom of God we bring to Earth, with Holy Spirit, in answered *aiteo* prayers and requests.

There are some Christian groups that contend only the elect are saved, and they *are* the elect. If they are the elect, then they should be walking in the fullness of the Gospel, which means that they should never die, except as martyrs, and there

DISCOVERING OUR REDEMPTION

should be only temporary sick, defective or maimed among them, as they all will be healed and restored rather quickly, as Jesus showed in His Earth walk, and none should die of sickness. They should be prosperous in physical, spiritual and soulish wealth, and all the other benefits of what Jesus taught the first disciples to do. They can die by persecution or die still having a strong hand and eye (in the manner of Moses) and depart the body. All these were part of the covenant in Moses, and we have a better one in Jesus. If you are the elect, then you should manifest that fact.

You absolutely are the elect, but until you work with the Word of God and Holy Spirit to renew your mind, by writing God's laws on your hearts and minds, so that you know the Lord in walking in *agape*/love and answered *aiteo*, you are not walking in your election. 2 Pet 1:8 "For if these things (*of walking like Jesus*) be in you, and abound, they make you that ye shall neither be barren nor unfruitful in the *epignosis*/knowledge of our Lord Jesus Christ. 9 But he that lacketh these things is blind, and cannot see afar off, and hath forgotten that he was purged (*remitted*) from his old sins. 10 Wherefore the rather, brethren, give diligence to make your calling and election sure [*so you show up on the Day of Judgment, with no wood, hay or stubble, but only mountains of silver, gold and jewels*]: for if ye do these things, ye shall never fall: 11 for so an entrance shall be ministered unto you abundantly into the everlasting kingdom of our Lord and Saviour Jesus Christ. 12 Wherefore I will not be negligent to put you always in remembrance of these things, though ye know (*behold, perceive*) them, and be established in the present truth (*of the Gospel of Jesus Christ, where God reigns through men, just like He did in Jesus*)."

The Gospel of God in Jesus Christ is better than the one God provided for Job; and he was the richest man in the East. The Gospel is better than the one given Moses; and it made David and Solomon rich beyond measure and produced supermen, invincible in battle. The world absolutely deserves to have the Gospel preached, as Jesus preached it and as it was preached during the first 300 years of Christianity.

1 Cor 2:4 "And my speech and my preaching was not with enticing words of man's wisdom, but in demonstration of the Spirit and of *dunamis*/power: 5 that your faith should not stand in the wisdom of men, but in the *dunamis*/power of God."

A key to understand is the word translated *know* or *knowledge*. This Greek word, *epignosis*, does not mean just academic facts. It means to be expert at it, so you perform it as a master craftsman. A knowing that Jesus lives in us that produces an actual walking in Holy Spirit is key to our effectual life in Him.

LEGAL ACTION FOR PRODUCING VITAL DAILY LIVING

Eph 4:13 "Till we all come in the unity of the faith, and of the *epignosis*/knowledge of the Son of God, unto a perfect man, unto the measure of the stature of the fulness of Christ."

Gal 5:16 "This I say then, Walk in the Spirit, and ye shall not fulfil the lust of the flesh. 17 For the flesh lusteth against the Spirit, and the Spirit against the flesh: and these are contrary the one to the other: so that ye cannot do the things that ye would."

2 Pet 3:18 "But grow in grace, and in the *epignosis*/knowledge of our Lord and Saviour Jesus Christ. To him be glory both now and for ever. Amen."

James 1:21 "Wherefore lay apart all filthiness and superfluity of naughtiness [*In thinking and operating in the ways of the devil in this present world system*], and *lambano*/receive with meekness the engrafted word, which is able to *sozo*/save your *psuche*/souls (*lives*). 22 But be ye doers of the word [*of the Gospel of your salvation that Christ is now in you, the hope of the free and glorious reign of Holy Spirit, in and by you, to reign in this life, as Jesus would*], and not hearers only [*with no obedience and life-changing faith*], deceiving your own selves. 23 For if any be a hearer of the word [*unto obedience and life-changing faith of your Redemption by the blood of Jesus unto the righteousness of* zoe/*life, of Christ in you the hope of the free and glorious reign of Holy Spirit, in and by you, to reign in this life, as Jesus would*], and not a doer, he is like unto a man beholding his natural face in a glass (*mirror*): 24 for he beholdeth himself, and goeth his way, and straightway forgetteth what manner of man he was [*a fully adopted son of God by the Redemption in the blood of Jesus*]. 25 But whoso looketh into the perfect law of liberty [*in your Redemption in Christ, with the remission of sins, freedom from the curse of the law, being made the righteousness of God in Christ Jesus, and indwelling Holy Spirit, to bring the Kingdom of God to Earth in every realm of life*], and continueth therein [*in every part of life*], he being not a forgetful hearer [*of our salvation in Jesus for the purposes and benefit of God*], but a doer of the work [*of believing on and bringing Heaven to Earth by the name of Jesus and* agape/*loving one another*], this man shall be blessed in his deed [*of walking and reigning in every aspect of his life, like Jesus would*]."

In the same way, this truth of covenant Identity and Redemption is to lead us into walking in reality more like Jesus. 1 Tim 1:5 "Now the end of the commandment (*instruction, doctrine, and teaching*) is *agape*/charity out of a pure heart, and of a good conscience, and of faith unfeigned [*so it produces the results of Heaven on Earth*]."

Rom 6:22 "But now being made free from sin, and become servants to God, ye have your fruit unto holiness, and the end everlasting *zoe*/life. 23 For

DISCOVERING OUR REDEMPTION

the wages of sin is death; but the gift of God is eternal *zoe*/life through Jesus Christ our Lord."

Rom 6:5 "For if we have been planted together in the likeness of his death, we shall be also in the likeness of his resurrection: 6 *ginosko*/knowing this, that our old man is crucified with him, that the body of sin might be destroyed, that henceforth we should not serve sin. 7 For he that is dead is freed from sin. 8 Now if we be dead with Christ, we believe that we shall also *zao*/live with him."

CHAPTER 8
PAST TENSE LANGUAGE TRANSLATES INTO A PRESENT REALITY

This Redemption is past tense in Jesus, 2000 years ago, and we each enter into it by faith to live it out, in this life—now.

1 Pet 1:17 "And if you call upon Him as [your] Father Who judges each one impartially according to what he does, [then] you should conduct yourselves with true reverence throughout the time of your temporary residence [on the earth, whether long or short]. 18 You must know (recognize) that **you were redeemed** (ransomed) from the useless (fruitless, *doomed to destruction on the Day of Judgment*) way of *zao*/living inherited by tradition from [your] forefathers, not with corruptible things [such as] silver and gold, 19 but [**you were purchased**] with the precious blood of Christ (the Messiah), like that of a [sacrificial] lamb without blemish or spot." AMP

Gal 3:13 "Christ **hath redeemed us** from the curse of the law, being made a curse for us: for it is written, Cursed is every one that hangeth on a tree."

The story of Redemption in the Blood of Jesus is the "hidden-in-plain-sight" story of how Jesus accomplished this mighty work of God by the means of the cross.

In fact, the Scriptures warn us that our growth into Christ depends on our growing in the knowledge of our redemption. Thus we are to ever keep reminding ourselves of this awesome truth.

DISCOVERING OUR REDEMPTION

2 Pet 1:8 "For if these things be in you, and abound, they make you that ye shall neither be barren nor unfruitful in the *epignosis*/knowledge of our Lord Jesus Christ. 9 But he that lacketh these things is blind, and cannot see afar off, and hath **forgotten that he was purged from his old sins (*has remission*)**. 10 Wherefore the rather, brethren, give diligence to make your calling and election sure: for if ye do these things, ye shall never fall: 11 for so an entrance shall be ministered unto you abundantly into the everlasting kingdom of our Lord and Saviour Jesus Christ. 12 Wherefore I will not be negligent to put you **always in remembrance of these things**, though ye know them, and be established in the present truth."

Holy Spirit makes a point of telling us: if we will hear and learn the facts of Redemption and do not let them go, we will grow in Christ. Without them, you may grow in religion, but not for what you were created.

Heb 2:1 "Therefore we ought to give the more earnest heed to the things which we have heard, lest at any time we should let them slip."

2 Pet 1:2 "Grace and peace be multiplied unto you through the *epignosis*/ knowledge of God, and of Jesus our Lord, 3 according as his divine power hath given unto us all things that pertain unto *zoe*/life and godliness, through the *epignosis*/knowledge of him that hath called us to glory and virtue: 4 whereby are given unto us exceeding great and precious promises: that by these ye might be partakers of the divine nature, having escaped the corruption that is in the world through lust."

Partaking of the divine nature is to walk just like Jesus. 1 John 4:17 "Herein is our *agape*/love made perfect, that we may have boldness in the day of judgment: because as he is, so are we in this world."

Amazingly, God does not live in time. We do (for now), but He does not. The work of Jesus was done once for the entire world, from Adam to the last person, else Jesus would have had to die many times to handle each generation. The work Jesus accomplished was not bound by time, but is eternal, forever, and without time limits.

This applies to us personally today because Jesus died and then rose again 2000 years ago. Every act of sin we commit in our past, our right now, or in our future, were all future to that event 2000 years ago. So your sins tomorrow or next year or in the next hundred years are all future tense to the great work accomplished 2000 years ago. If Jesus died for sins once, then all our current sins were handled then, or else Jesus must die again at least once more, at the end of the world, to cover all the sins of the past, and that is not going to happen.

Heb 10:11 "And every priest standeth daily ministering and offering oftentimes the same sacrifices, which can never take away (*remit*) sins: 12 but this man, after he had offered one sacrifice for sins for ever, sat down on the right hand of God."

PAST TENSE LANGUAGE TRANSLATES INTO A PRESENT REALITY

This truth includes knowledge of our Redemption by the blood of Jesus as a past accomplishment, never-to-be-repeated fact before God in the Records of the Supreme Court of All Creation. Our job is to put it into our hearts and keep it ever-fresh there.

Philem 6 "That the communication of thy faith may become effectual by the acknowledging of every good thing which is in you in Christ Jesus." Or, in expanded form: "That the way you talk and act in the faith of God in our Salvation in Jesus may become effectual to bring Heaven to Earth, no matter what your circumstances, by you *epignosis*/acknowledging, until you are a master craftsman in walking in every good thing of this salvation that you have in Christ Jesus."

To make your faith effectual, to demonstrate the Kingdom of God, to partake of the divine nature, you must major in this great work of the Mighty Arm of God.

Don't major in the minor facts, until you get the major facts settled.

Luke 24:46 "And said to them, Thus it is written that the Christ (the Messiah) should suffer and on the third day rise from (among) the dead, [Hos 6:2.] 47 and that repentance [with a view to and as the condition of] forgiveness (*remission, removal, obliteration and putting away*) of sins should be preached in His name to all nations, beginning from Jerusalem." AMP

The Redemption of mankind was accomplished 2000 years ago; we enter in by faith in the working of God in Jesus, and walk it out in our lives now.

Instead of the bloody circumcision of the male, we now have the circumcision of the heart in men and women, by Holy Spirit in the new birth. The first was performed by men; the second is performed by God.

This circumcision is not made by the hands of men, but by God Himself. Circumcision under Abraham or Moses was never a sign of perfection, but of ownership or covenant relationship. So this New Covenant circumcision is a sign or permanent condition in the heart of God's ownership and eternal covenant relationship with the one who enters in by faith, however poor or fruitless that faith may be in this present life. God sets the measure of adequacy, not man. To God, the adequacy is found in Jesus, not in men. God is eager to get men back into His family, so He does the new-creation circumcision so it is done right, to His standard.

Col 2:11 "In Him (*Jesus*) also you were circumcised with a circumcision not made with hands, but in a [spiritual] circumcision [performed by] Christ by stripping off the body of the flesh (the whole corrupt, carnal nature with its passions and lusts). 12 [Thus you were circumcised when] you were buried with Him in [your] baptism, in which you were also raised with Him [to a new life] through **[your] faith in the working of God** [as displayed] when He raised Him up from the dead." AMP

Again, as the Scriptures say, we enter into this redemption unto righteousness, the effect of this Redemption, when we believe God raised Jesus from the dead.

DISCOVERING OUR REDEMPTION

Rom 10:9 "That if thou shalt confess with thy mouth the Lord Jesus, and **shalt believe in thine heart that God hath raised him from the dead,** thou shalt be *sozo*/saved. 10 **For with the heart man believeth unto righteousness**; and with the mouth confession is made unto *soteria*/salvation."

God is our Salvation, so it depends on God, and not us.

Ps 62:1 "Truly my soul waiteth upon God: from him cometh my salvation. 2 He only is my rock and my salvation; he is my defence; I shall not be greatly moved. 3 How long will ye imagine mischief against a man? ye shall be slain all of you: as a bowing wall shall ye be, and as a tottering fence. 4 They only consult to cast him down from his excellency: they delight in lies: they bless with their mouth, but they curse inwardly. Selah. 5 My soul, wait thou only upon God; for my expectation is from him. 6 He only is my rock and my salvation: he is my defence; I shall not be moved. 7 In God is my salvation and my glory: the rock of my strength, and my refuge, is in God."

Jesus is our Salvation: Acts 4:12 "Neither is there *soteria*/salvation in any other: for there is none other name *(Jesus)* under heaven given among men, whereby we must be *sozo*/saved."

As we grow in knowledge of what we have in Jesus, our faith is made more effectual and, indeed, we can grow to new depths and new heights of glory. John 1:29 "The next day John seeth Jesus coming unto him, and saith, Behold the Lamb of God, which taketh away the sin of the world."

Jesus got the job done!

Jesus is the Great King of God.

Ps 24:7 "Lift up your heads, O ye gates *(the authority of the Great Palace of God)*; and be ye lift up, ye everlasting doors *(the doors of the Great Palace of God, and of the human heart)*; and the King of glory shall come in. 8 Who is this King of glory? The Lord strong and mighty, the Lord mighty in battle. 9 Lift up your heads, O ye gates; even lift them up, ye everlasting doors; and the King of glory shall come in. 10 Who is this King of glory? The Lord of hosts, he is the King of glory. Selah."

Isa 11:9 ... For the earth shall be full of the knowledge of the Lord, as the waters cover the sea.

Part III

Understanding What Jesus Did for Us by Calvary

CHAPTER 9

JESUS WAS MADE SIN FOR US

In the great drama of our Redemption, as soon as Christ was nailed to the cross, with His crown of thorns, and with the howling mob that surrounded Him, justice continued to do its awful work behind the scenes.

Sense-knowledge men and women could see Jesus arrested in the Garden, dragged before the rulers, mocked, beaten, scourged and tormented. They could see His agony and blood.

But these sense-knowledge men and women, who surrounded the cross, could only see the physical man, Jesus, hanging there.

God could see His spirit.

Angels could see His spirit.

Demons could see the real man, hidden in that body.

Men only saw the supposedly invincible cruel Roman justice on flesh and blood.

Then came the dreadful hour in this process when 2 Cor 5:21 was fulfilled.

"Him (*Jesus*) who knew no sin he (*Father God*) made to be sin on our behalf; that we might become the righteousness of *Father* God in him (*Jesus*)." RSV

Isaiah 53:5 "He was wounded for our transgressions, he was bruised for our iniquities; the chastisement of our peace was upon him; and with his stripes we are

DISCOVERING OUR REDEMPTION

healed. 6 All we like sheep have gone astray; we have turned everyone to his own way; and Jehovah hath laid on him the iniquity of us all." RSV

Right after His great thrice-made prayer in the Garden, they came to take Jesus.

Luke 22:41 "And he was withdrawn from them about a stone's cast, and kneeled down, and prayed, 42 saying, Father, if thou be willing, remove this cup from me: nevertheless not my will, but thine, be done. 43 And there appeared an angel unto him from heaven, strengthening him. 44 And being in an agony he prayed more earnestly: and his sweat was as it were great drops of blood falling down to the ground. 45 And when he rose up from prayer, and was come to his disciples, he found them sleeping for sorrow, 46 and said unto them, Why sleep ye? rise and pray, lest ye enter into temptation. 47 And while he yet spake, behold a multitude, and he that was called Judas, one of the twelve, went before them, and drew near unto Jesus to kiss him."

Jesus went into prayer, struggling in His humanity, to suffer and risk the fullness of the will of God, the plan of the ages. Jesus arose from prayer a conqueror ready to go to battle, from arrest to death, to resurrection, to glorification, with His trust firmly established in His Father and in the Scriptures.

When they came to take Him and asked if He were the one, Jesus answered "I am," and the outflowing of glory showed He was not yet made sin. John 18:4 "Jesus therefore, knowing all things that should come upon him, went forth, and said unto them, Whom seek ye? 5 They answered him, Jesus of Nazareth. Jesus saith unto them, I am he. And Judas also, which betrayed him, stood with them. 6 As soon then as he had said unto them, I am he, they went backward, and fell to the ground."

While many debate the exact moment that Jesus became sin, there are many opportunities to split the details. What matters most is that the whole process accomplished what God desired, the Redemption of man. But the key is that before He died, by giving up His spirit, Jesus was made sin. And when He was made sin, He died in spirit. Then He could die physically.

The first opportunity for Jesus to become sin was on the way to the first priestly judgment. They bound Him in the garden. This binding would not have been a pleasant process. His bleeding probably started then or soon thereafter.

First they took Him to Annas. John 18:12 "Then the band and the captain and officers of the Jews took Jesus, and bound him, 13 and led him away to Annas first; for he was father in law to Caiaphas, which was the high priest that same year. 14 Now Caiaphas was he, which gave counsel to the Jews, that it was expedient that one man should die for the people."

Next they took Him to the High Priest, Caiaphas. Matt 26:62 "And the high priest arose, and said unto him, Answerest thou nothing? what is it which these

Jesus Was Made Sin for Us

witness against thee? 63 But Jesus held his peace. And the high priest answered and said unto him, I adjure thee by the *zao*/living God, that thou tell us whether thou be the Christ, the Son of God. 64 Jesus saith unto him, Thou hast said: nevertheless I say unto you, Hereafter shall ye see the Son of man sitting on the right hand of power, and coming in the clouds of heaven. 65 Then the high priest rent his clothes, saying, He hath spoken blasphemy; what further need have we of witnesses? behold, now ye have heard his blasphemy. 66 What think ye? They answered and said, He is guilty of death. 67 Then did they spit in his face, and buffeted him; and others smote him with the palms of their hands."

By this time, Jesus was receiving the wounding and bruising for us, the Just for the unjust. His body was definitely bruised and bleeding by now.

On the whipping post, at the scourging, He received the curse of all men, so that by His stripes all men could be healed.

Isa 53:5 "He was wounded for our transgressions, he was bruised for our iniquities; the chastisement of our peace was upon him; and with his stripes we are healed. 6 All we like sheep have gone astray; we have turned everyone to his own way; and Jehovah hath laid on him the iniquity of us all." RSV

1 Pet 2:24 "Who his own self bare our sins in his own body on the tree, that we, being dead to sins, should *zao*/live unto righteousness: by whose stripes ye were healed."

On that awful cross, He was not only sin, but He became a curse, for in Gal 3:13 Holy Spirit tells us, "Christ hath redeemed us from the curse of the law, being made a curse for us: for it is written, Cursed is every one that hangeth on a tree."

Jesus came as a Jew, under the Mosaic Covenant, to redeem all those who were under that Covenant from the curse of the Law. In the process, Father God extended Jesus to all men.

Isa 49:5 "And now, saith the Lord that formed me from the womb to be his servant, to bring Jacob again to him, though Israel be not gathered, yet shall I be glorious in the eyes of the Lord, and my God shall be my strength. 6 And he said, It is a light thing that thou shouldest be my servant to raise up the tribes of Jacob, and to restore the preserved of Israel: I will also give thee for a light to the Gentiles, that thou mayest be my salvation unto the end of the earth. 7 Thus saith the Lord, the Redeemer of Israel, and his Holy One, to him whom man despiseth, to him whom the nation abhorreth, to a servant of rulers, Kings shall see and arise, princes also shall worship, because of the Lord that is faithful, and the Holy One of Israel, and he shall choose thee. 8 Thus saith the Lord, In an acceptable time have I heard thee, and in a day of salvation have I helped thee: and I will preserve thee, and **give thee for a covenant of the people**, to establish the earth, to cause to inherit the desolate heritages."

When Jesus was hanging on the cross, He was not only sin, but He was also the curse of sin.

DISCOVERING OUR REDEMPTION

Every evil action on Earth is the result of Adam's sin. So whether men sin or not, sin reigns, unless we implement, by faith, God's solution for sin.

Jesus is our Salvation, the solution for the sin of man. In the process, He became sin, unrighteousness, ruled by Satan and one with Satan.

Is it any wonder that Jesus felt God had turned His back upon Him?

Is it any wonder He cried in His agony, "My God, my God, why hast thou forsaken me?"

Yet this was the plan of the ages, the work of the Mighty Arm of God!

1 Pet 1:18 "Forasmuch as ye know that ye were not redeemed with corruptible things, as silver and gold, from your vain conversation received by tradition from your fathers; 19 but with the precious blood of Christ, as of a lamb without blemish and without spot: 20 who verily was foreordained before the foundation of the world, but was manifest in these last times for you, 21 who by him do believe in God, that raised him up from the dead, and gave him glory; that your faith and hope might be in God."

Father God was keenly aware and made sure Jesus got all that man deserved. And because Jesus would take it all, Father could then reward Jesus. It was horrible, but God made sure it was all done to fullness, to remove any doubt that Jesus had not fully paid for and redeemed Father's beloved mankind.

Isa 53:10 "Yet it pleased the Lord to bruise him; he hath put him to grief: when thou shalt make his soul an offering for sin, he shall see his seed, he shall prolong his days, and the pleasure of the Lord shall prosper in his hand. 11 He shall see of the travail of his soul, and shall be satisfied: by his knowledge shall my righteous servant justify many; for he shall *cabal*/bear their iniquities. 12 Therefore will I divide him a portion with the great, and he shall divide the spoil with the strong; because he hath poured out his soul unto death: and he was numbered with the transgressors; and he *nasa*/bare the sin of many, and made intercession for the transgressors."

Jesus had taken the sinner's place in Judgment.

Jesus took my place and your place in Judgment.

His cry reflected the loss of man in his difficulty to perceive God, when the press of the circumstances declared Satan was lord, and there seemed to be no help in God.

We are promised troubles in this life ... until Heaven comes to Earth. Jesus bore, for every man, our difficulty to perceive God, when the press of evil circumstances declares Satan is lord, and there seems to be no help in God. If Jesus bore it, we were healed of it, so we can exercise faith to receive it in time of need. That total loneliness, that sense of loss and abandonment, that sense of the orphan, that sense that God cannot be trusted, that offense in God, Jesus bore so we might be free of it in time of trouble. Great is our God!

Jesus Was Made Sin for Us

All the forces of darkness had overwhelmed Jesus.

He was our sin Substitute.

Sin was not just reckoned to Him. Sin was not just set to His account. Jesus became sin.

2 Cor 5:21 "For he hath made him to be sin for us, who knew no sin; that we might be made the righteousness of God in him."

[Note: some add that Jesus was not sin, but, rather, simply a sin offering. All past sin offerings were a type of which Jesus was the real. In the Old Testament, sins were not removed, remitted, or put away; they were covered, atoned for. Under the Law of Moses this atonement was renewed each year. In Jesus, sin is removed, remitted, put away forever, and not just covered for a year. The Greek word for sin in this verse, *harmartia*, is used 173 times in the New Testament as sin or the sin nature. So in 2 Cor 5:21 *harmartia* does not mean sin offering, as if somehow Jesus was not made sin; for if used that way, it must also be used in the 171 other instances, and that does not make good sense.]

Our senses reel under the staggering thought that Jesus actually became sin and not just a symbol for it.

We cannot grasp it. And not just the obvious sins, like murder and slavery, but also the "invisible" sins, like pride, fault-finding, blame, indifference, self-centeredness, unbelief, offense, lust, evil thoughts, and lack of the knowledge of God.

With an un-renewed mind, only our spirits can fathom the depths of Jesus' condition and His agony.

We can hear Paul's cry, Phil 3:10 "That I may know him, and the power of his resurrection, and the fellowship of his sufferings, becoming conformed unto his death."

Paul's prayer amazes one.

He wanted to share in the death agonies of Christ.

He wanted to fellowship with His sufferings, that he might know that only in Jesus is there the righteousness of God. Phil 3:8 "Yea doubtless, and I count all things but loss for the excellency of the knowledge of Christ Jesus my Lord: for whom I have suffered the loss of all things, and do count them but dung, that I may win Christ, 9 and be found in him, not having mine own righteousness, which is of the law, but that which is through the faith of Christ, the righteousness which is of God by faith: 10 that I may know him, and the power of his resurrection, and the fellowship of his sufferings, being made conformable unto his death; 11 if by any means I might attain unto the resurrection of the dead. 12 Not as though I had already attained, either were already perfect: but I follow after, if that I may apprehend that for which also I am apprehended of Christ Jesus."

But only Christ could pay the suffering penalty for man; Paul could not do it.

It was God's own work that must be wrought. Ps 49:6 "They that trust in their wealth, and boast themselves in the multitude of their riches; 7 none of them can

DISCOVERING OUR REDEMPTION

by any means redeem his brother, nor give to God a ransom for him: 8 (for the redemption of their soul is precious, and it ceaseth for ever:) 9 that he should still live for ever, and not see corruption."

Jer 31:11 "For the Lord hath redeemed Jacob, and ransomed him from the hand of him that was stronger than he."

Hos 13:14 "I will ransom them from the power of the grave; I will redeem them from death: O death, I will be thy plagues; O grave, I will be thy destruction: repentance shall be hid from mine eyes."

Notice, in these verses, that ransom and redemption are similar and related to deliverance-freedom from that which is not like the presence of God, or Heaven on Earth. The word translated as *ransom* means to sever, to release, to deliver so there is no longer any connection to that which held one in bondage, by the giving of something of value. Here redeem or the redeemer is, according to the law of kinship, where one, as a *gaal* (the kinsman redeemer or avenger), could buy another out of bondage of any kind and deliver them back into the life of the family. Again, something of value had to be exchanged to set right a wrong or unhappy condition.

When Father God surrendered His Son to death, God unveiled a love that beggars description. Who could imagine the value God sets on man by paying such an exorbitant price as the Son of God for man's Redemption? Under almost any condition, you would not spend one trillion trillion dollars for a speck of dust, yet God spent the most wonderful creature of all, Jesus, God in the flesh, to redeem mankind. The incomparable Jesus was given in exchange for men who denied God and even deny that He exists.

Rom 5:5 "And hope maketh not ashamed; because the *agape*/love of God is shed abroad in our hearts by the Holy Ghost which is given unto us. 6 For when we were yet without strength, in due time Christ died for the ungodly. 7 For scarcely for a righteous man will one die: yet peradventure for a good man some would even dare to die. 8 But God commendeth his *agape*/love toward us, in that, while we were yet sinners, Christ died for us."

Our labor is to not believe in our ability or righteousness, but that Jesus did the perfect job for God and us, and that God is able and will perform His Word.

Rom 4:5 "But to him that worketh not, but believeth on him that justifieth the ungodly, his faith is counted for righteousness."

It awes the mind to think of such a thing, that God would set such a value on man, that He would pay one far greater than Satan to redeem from Satan that which had so easily been fooled by Satan.

Father God not only paid the price, but set us up with Him, to exercise His Lordship together with Him.

Rom 5:15 "But not as the offence, so also is the free gift. For if through the offence of one many be dead, much more the grace of God, and the gift by grace, which is by one man, Jesus Christ, hath abounded unto many. 16 And not as it was by one that sinned, so is the gift: for the judgment was by one to condemnation, but the free gift is of many offences unto justification. 17 For if by one man's offence death reigned (*as king*) by one; much more they which (*continually*) *lambano*/receive abundance of grace [*unto God's full salvation*] and of the gift of righteousness shall reign (*as kings*) in *zoe*/life by one, Jesus Christ.) 18 Therefore as by the offence of one judgment came upon all men to condemnation; even so by the righteousness of one the free gift came upon all men unto justification of *zoe*/life. 19 For as by one man's disobedience many were made sinners, so by the obedience of one shall many be made righteous. 20 Moreover the law entered, that the offence might abound. But where sin abounded, grace did much more abound: 21 that as sin hath reigned (*as king*) unto death, even so might grace reign (*as king*) through righteousness unto eternal *zoe*/life by Jesus Christ our Lord."

The unfathomable price of Jesus was paid, to reconcile man back to his original condition with God prior to Adam's fall, and make it possible for Holy Spirit to dwell in men and women by the new creation/new birth.

This price paid was so over the top, so fully abundant, that there can never be any suggestion that anything was not fully paid and healed in Jesus.

Rom 5:20 "But then Law came in, [only] to expand and increase the trespass [making it more apparent and exciting opposition]. But where sin increased and abounded, grace (God's unmerited favor) has surpassed it and increased the more and super abounded, 21 so that, [just] as sin has reigned (*as king*) in death, [so] grace (His unearned and undeserved favor) might reign (*as a greater and stronger king*) also through righteousness (right standing with God) which issues in eternal *zoe*/life through Jesus Christ (the Messiah, the Anointed One) our Lord." AMP

Few, since the time of Adam, have escaped the clutches of death. We know of two: Enoch and Elijah. Neither of them died, but went to be with God without death. The reign of grace offered us is so over the top, so super abundant, that what death has been able to do is nothing compared to what grace can do through us.

Rom 5:20 "Moreover the law entered, that the offence might abound. But where sin abounded, grace did much more abound: 21 that as sin hath reigned (*as king*) unto death, even so might grace reign (*as king*) through righteousness unto eternal *zoe*/life by Jesus Christ our Lord."

Eph 3:20 "Now to Him Who, by (in consequence of) the [action of His] power that is at work within us, is able to [carry out His purpose and] do superabundantly, far over and above all that we [dare] *aiteo*/ask or think [infinitely beyond our highest prayers, desires, thoughts, hopes, or dreams]." AMP

1 Tim 1:14 "And the grace (unmerited favor and blessing) of our Lord [actually] flowed out superabundantly and beyond measure for me, accompanied by faith and *agape*/love that are [to be realized] in Christ Jesus." AMP

DISCOVERING OUR REDEMPTION

Eph 1:6 "[So that we might be] to the praise and the commendation of His glorious grace (favor and mercy), which He so freely bestowed on us in the *Agape/beloved*. 7 In Him we have redemption (deliverance and salvation) through His blood, the remission (forgiveness, *removal, putting away, purging and obliteration*) of our offenses (shortcomings and trespasses), in accordance with the riches and the generosity of His gracious favor, 8 which He lavished upon us in every kind of wisdom and understanding (practical insight and prudence)." AMP

The vastness of Father God's riches, the abundance of His grace and the greatness of the price He paid beggars language to show that the blood of Jesus is more than sufficient to redeem us back to God from the hand of the enemy.

That price included the fact that Jesus must become sin that we might be made, not just covered with, but made, the substance of the very righteousness of God in Jesus.

2 Cor 5:21 "For he hath made him to be sin for us, who knew no sin; that we might be made the righteousness of God in him."

Chapter 10

Jesus Was Made Sick and Scourged for Us

The next element in this awful drama is found in Isaiah 53:3-5 "He was despised, and rejected of men; a man of pains, and acquainted with sickness (*sorrows, grief*): and as one from whom men hide their face he was despised; and we esteemed him not. Surely he hath *cabal*/borne our sicknesses, and *nasa*/carried our diseases; yet we did esteem him stricken, smitten of God, and afflicted." (From an RSV marginal note, giving alternate words or phrases.)

That word *acquainted* in verse 3 could also be translated as "in union with" or "fully understanding from all aspects, totally identified with, not only the sicknesses/griefs, but also the consequences." Jesus became and experienced the griefs, sorrows, and the sicknesses of man throughout the ages, all in one brief period of time. While the physical abuse He suffered was brutal, this "acquainted" with "grief" and "sickness" appears to have been a much larger spiritual component than mere physical torture.

It was not what the rulers of Israel, the Roman soldiers or the angry mob did in the flesh of Jesus that was so mighty. What man did was more about what Jesus (and Father God) allowed and required to fulfill the Scriptures. Jesus' body must bear the curse and receive the stripes, that we could be healed. The spiritual significance was all but invisible to all the people there that day.

DISCOVERING OUR REDEMPTION

It is recorded in the three synoptic gospels that Jesus warned and prophesied that He was to be scourged and killed and that He would rise from the dead in three days. Matt 20:17 "And Jesus going up to Jerusalem took the twelve disciples apart in the way, and said unto them, 18 Behold, we go up to Jerusalem; and the Son of man shall be betrayed unto the chief priests and unto the scribes, and they shall condemn him to death, 19 and shall deliver him to the Gentiles to mock, and to scourge, and to crucify him: and the third day he shall rise again."

Mark 10:32 "And they were in the way going up to Jerusalem; and Jesus went before them: and they were amazed; and as they followed, they were afraid. And he took again the twelve, and began to tell them what things should happen unto him, 33 saying, Behold, we go up to Jerusalem; and the Son of man shall be delivered unto the chief priests, and unto the scribes; and they shall condemn him to death, and shall deliver him to the Gentiles: 34 and they shall mock him, and shall scourge him, and shall spit upon him, and shall kill him: and the third day he shall rise again."

Luke 18:31 "Then he took unto him the twelve, and said unto them, Behold, we go up to Jerusalem, and all things that are written by the prophets concerning the Son of man shall be accomplished. 32 For he shall be delivered unto the Gentiles, and shall be mocked, and spitefully entreated, and spitted on: 33 and they shall scourge him, and put him to death: and the third day he shall rise again."

But even though they were warned by Jesus, the disciples could not "hear" what Jesus was saying. Luke 18:34 "And they understood none of these things: and this saying was hid from them, neither knew they the things which were spoken."

After the high priest and the Council, or Sanhedrin, had condemned Jesus, they took Him to Pilate, the Roman Governor.

Matt 27:1 "When the morning was come, all the chief priests and elders of the people took counsel against Jesus to put him to death: 2 and when they had bound him, they led him away, and delivered him to Pontius Pilate the governor."

Mark 15:15 "And straightway in the morning the chief priests held a consultation with the elders and scribes and the whole council, and bound Jesus, and carried him away, and delivered him to Pilate."

Luke 23:1 "And the whole multitude of them (*Sanhedrin, rulers and chief priests*) arose, and led him unto Pilate. 2 And they began to accuse him, saying, We found this fellow perverting the nation, and forbidding to give tribute to Caesar, saying that he himself is Christ a King."

John 18:30 "They (*Sanhedrin, rulers and chief priests*) answered and said unto him (*Pilate*), If he were not a malefactor, we would not have delivered him up unto thee. 31 Then said Pilate unto them, Take ye him, and judge him according to your law. The Jews therefore said unto him, It is not lawful for us to put any man to death: 32 that the saying of Jesus might be fulfilled, which he spake, signifying what death he should die."

Jesus Was Made Sick and Scourged for Us

Pilate tried to avoid the issue by sending Jesus to Herod, but Herod sent Jesus back to Pilate. Trying to avoid criticism for the death of Jesus, Pilate offered them the choice of Jesus or Barabbas. The crowd chose Barabbas. Matt 27:26 "Then released he (*Pilate*) Barabbas unto them: and when he had scourged Jesus, he delivered him to be crucified. 27 Then the soldiers of the governor took Jesus into the common hall, and gathered unto him the whole band of soldiers. 28 And they stripped him, and put on him a scarlet robe. 29 And when they had platted a crown of thorns, they put it upon his head, and a reed in his right hand: and they bowed the knee before him, and mocked him, saying, Hail, King of the Jews! 30 And they spit upon him, and took the reed, and smote him on the head. 31 And after that they had mocked him, they took the robe off from him, and put his own raiment on him, and led him away to crucify him."

Mark 15:15 "And so Pilate, willing to content the people, released Barabbas unto them, and delivered Jesus, when he had scourged him, to be crucified. 16 And the soldiers led him away into the hall, called Praetorium; and they call together the whole band. 17 And they clothed him with purple, and platted a crown of thorns, and put it about his head, 18 and began to salute him, Hail, King of the Jews! 19 And they smote him on the head with a reed, and did spit upon him, and bowing their knees worshipped him. 20 And when they had mocked him, they took off the purple from him, and put his own clothes on him, and led him out to crucify him."

John 18:39 "But ye have a custom, that I (*Pilate*) should release unto you one at the passover: will ye therefore that I release unto you the King of the Jews? 40 Then cried they all again, saying, Not this man, but Barabbas. Now Barabbas was a robber. 19:1 Then Pilate therefore took Jesus, and scourged him. 2 And the soldiers platted a crown of thorns, and put it on his head, and they put on him a purple robe, 3 and said, Hail, King of the Jews! and they smote him with their hands."

The sequence appears to be this: first they scourged Jesus, then abused Him with further beatings with a reed and their hands, put on Him a scarlet, or purple, robe and a crown of thorns. After beating and mocking Him, they took off the scarlet/purple robe and put Jesus' clothes back on Him, leaving the crown of thorns on His head, and led Him away to be crucified.

John added more detail. After they had scourged Jesus, He was brought back to Pilate and the chief priests one more time. Pilate tried to avoid responsibility for the death of Jesus again, but the Jewish leaders again demanded His death. John 19:1 "Then Pilate therefore took Jesus, and scourged him. 2 And the soldiers platted a crown of thorns, and put it on his head, and they put on him a purple robe, 3 and said, Hail, King of the Jews! and they smote him with their hands. 4 Pilate therefore went forth again, and saith unto them, Behold, I bring him forth to you, that ye may know that I find no fault in him. 5 Then came Jesus forth, wear-

DISCOVERING OUR REDEMPTION

ing the crown of thorns, and the purple robe. And Pilate saith unto them, Behold the man! 6 When the chief priests therefore and officers saw him, they cried out, saying, Crucify him, crucify him. Pilate saith unto them, Take ye him, and crucify him: for I find no fault in him. ... 15 But they cried out, Away with him, away with him, crucify him. Pilate saith unto them, Shall I crucify your King? The chief priest answered, We have no king but Caesar. 16 Then delivered he him therefore unto them to be crucified. And they took Jesus, and led him away. 17 And he bearing his cross went forth into a place called the place of a skull, which is called in the Hebrew Golgotha."

The Romans knew how to scourge a man to death or to leave him in a weakened condition. They scourged men often, and they were good at it. No doubt the scourging Jesus received was a dreadful and agonizing process. Without a doubt this was the major portion of the "stripes" He bore for us.

Part of the purpose of using crucifixion was that the suffering was long, so all the people could get the lesson of what it meant to challenge Imperial Rome. These experienced men were surprised that Jesus died so quickly on the cross.

Mark 15:44 "And Pilate marvelled if he were already dead: and calling unto him the centurion, he asked him whether he had been any while dead. 45 And when he knew it of the centurion, he gave the body to Joseph."

Just to make sure He was dead, apparently, in part, because Jesus died so quickly, He was pierced with a spear. John 19:33 "But when they came to Jesus, and saw that he was dead already, they brake not his legs: 34 but one of the soldiers with a spear pierced his side, and forthwith came there out blood and water."

This act of assurance was in fulfillment of the Scriptures: John 19:37 "And again another scripture saith, They shall look on him whom they pierced." (Zech 12:10)

Thus Jesus' body was mutilated after He had left His body. They speared a dead body. The suffering of His body was complete; the work of His spirit and soul had to continue into Hades. The next time Jesus would see His body was at the resurrection three days later. "By His stripes we were healed."

But He would not be gone from it long enough for His Body to rot. Acts 2:27 "Because thou wilt not leave my *psuche*/soul (*life*) in hell, neither wilt thou suffer thine Holy One to see corruption. 28 Thou hast made known to me the ways of *zoe*/life (*from the grip of death*); thou shalt make me full of joy with thy countenance." (Ps 16:10)

What is beyond imagination is what God did in the spirit. It was God, in the spirit realm, that completed the work of the Mighty Arm of God, Jesus of Nazareth.

The revelation of Paul shows some of the details of what God did in the spirit realm.

Paul tells us that, while the physical events and appearances of Jesus' death may capture our eyes and our mind, of far greater value is the spiritual realities,

JESUS WAS MADE SICK AND SCOURGED FOR US

even if they conflict with the physical events. 2 Cor 5:14 "For the *agape*/love of Christ constraineth us; because we thus judge, that if one died for all, then were all dead: 15 and that he died for all, that they which *zao*/live should not henceforth *zao*/live unto themselves, but unto him which died for them, and rose again. 16 Wherefore henceforth know we no man after the flesh: yea, though we have known Christ after the flesh, yet now henceforth know we him no more."

Paul, in part, is saying that even though the official Roman government convicted and executed Jesus, this did not stop Him from being the Son of God, the Savior of the world and the Mighty Arm of God. Just as we are to look at all men only by the standard of whether they are born again or not, and not by their outward behavior, we must not limit our view of Jesus to just His physical death on the cross.

As one man, Jesus could do little, *but* as the Son of God and the Substitute for all men, He was the Mighty Arm of God, in redeeming man from the kingdom of darkness. The spiritual reality outweighs the physical like a speck of dust is nothing compared to the Universe.

It shocks us when we realize that Jesus was stricken, smitten by God with our diseases and our sin. Sin and sickness are spiritual conditions manifested in the flesh. The spiritual suffering of Jesus, therefore, was beyond imagination in depth and power.

Not only was this spiritual suffering beyond imagination, but it was total and complete, to the satisfaction of Justice for all ages. It was a suffering and work that required and tested the caliber of the Son of God. Heb 5:7 "Who in the days of his flesh, when he had offered up prayers and supplications with strong crying and tears unto him that was able to save him from death, and was heard in that he feared; 8 though he were a Son, yet learned he obedience by the things which he suffered; 9 and being made perfect, he became the author of eternal *soteria*/salvation unto all them that obey (*believe*) him."

This is the One of whom Holy Spirit said: John 1:1 "In the beginning was the Word, and the Word was with God, and the Word was God. 2 The same was in the beginning with God. 3 All things were made by him; and without him was not any thing made that was made." This same One was made sin and sickness for us.

Phil 2:6 "Who, being in the form of God, thought it not robbery to be equal with God: 7 but made himself of no reputation, and took upon him the form of a servant, and was made in the likeness of men: 8 and being found in fashion as a man, he humbled himself, and became obedient unto death, even the death of the cross."

Heb 2:9 "But we see Jesus, who was made a little lower than the angels for the suffering of death, crowned with glory and honour; that he by the grace of God should taste death for every man. 10 For it became him, for whom are all things,

DISCOVERING OUR REDEMPTION

and by whom are all things, in bringing many sons unto glory, to make the captain of their *soteria*/salvation perfect through sufferings. 11 For both he that sanctifieth and they who are sanctified are all of one: for which cause he is not ashamed to call them brethren."

Heb 2:14 "Forasmuch then as the children are partakers of flesh and blood, he also himself likewise **took part of the same**; that through death he might destroy him that had the power of death, that is, the devil; 15 and deliver them who through fear of death were all their lifetime **subject to bondage**. 16 For verily he took not on him the nature of angels; but he took on him the seed of Abraham. 17 Wherefore in **all things it behoved him to be made like unto his brethren**, that he might be a merciful and faithful high priest in things pertaining to God, to make reconciliation for the sins of the people."

Jesus became one with all of man, so we could become one with Him. He became one with our sin and the bondage of our sin, with every form of death, fast and slow. And He did this perfectly, to the level of God.

Thus, there was laid upon Him the diseases and sicknesses of the human race.

Isa 53:10 "Yet it was the will of the Lord to bruise Him; He has put Him to grief and made Him sick ... ." AMP

God was not saddened to do this, but, rather, pleased, so that He could redeem man back to Himself, fully healed and fully justified. Father knew and was glad to pay the price to get His whole family back in the legal work of Redemption. Father God knew that the blood of bulls and goats had never done the job; they only covered the sin, like a thick paint. Although they allowed healing to flow, the sins were not put off and destroyed, and man's spirit was not made righteous unto *zoe*/life.

Gal 2:21 "I do not frustrate the grace of God: for if righteousness come by the law, then Christ is dead in vain."

Heb 10:3 "But in those sacrifices there is a remembrance again made of sins every year. 4 For it is not possible that the blood of bulls and of goats should take away (*obliterate, remit*) sins. 5 Wherefore when he cometh into the world, he saith, Sacrifice and offering thou wouldest not, but a body hast thou prepared me: 6 in burnt offerings and sacrifices for sin thou hast had no pleasure. 7 Then said I, Lo, I come (in the volume of the book it is written of me,) to do thy will, O God. 8 Above when he said, Sacrifice and offering and burnt offerings and offering for sin thou wouldest not, neither hadst pleasure therein; which are offered by the law; 9 then said he, Lo, I come to do thy will, O God. He taketh away the first (*in the Law of Moses*), that he may establish the second (*in Jesus*). 10 By the which will we are sanctified through the offering of the body of Jesus Christ once for all."

God fully knew the terrible price to be paid: 1 Pet 1:18 "Forasmuch as ye know that ye were not redeemed with corruptible things, as silver and gold, from your

Jesus Was Made Sick and Scourged for Us

vain conversation received by tradition from your fathers; 19 but with the precious blood of Christ, as of a lamb without blemish and without spot: 20 who verily was foreordained before the foundation of the world, but was manifest in these last times for you, 21 who by him do believe in God, that raised him up from the dead, and gave him glory; that your faith and hope might be in God."

Isa 53:4 "Surely he hath *cabal*/borne our griefs (*infirmities*), and *nasa*/carried our sorrows (*sicknesses*): yet we did esteem him stricken, smitten of God, and afflicted."

In Isaiah 53:4 the word translated as borne, *cabal*, means to labor or carry, so the full burden is carried to completion and so there is no longer anything to be done or paid. The word translated as carried, *nasa*, means to contain or carry so nothing is left out and nothing else remains to be done. So both words mean the entire fullness of something is satisfied in a way that there is nothing else to be done. It is fully complete and fully paid.

The word translated as griefs, *choliy*, means infirmities, disease, sickness, malady, anxiety and calamity. The word translated as sorrows, *makab*, means grief, pain, sickness, sorrow, anguish or that which is produced by affliction, improper operation to pain, suffering, limitation or pressure.

So Jesus took upon Himself for mankind the fullness of man's curse, so that everything that could cause grief, disease or sorrow was fully paid by God, and therefore man no longer has any need to be involved in it in any way.

Isa 53:3 "He was despised and rejected and forsaken by men, a Man of sorrows and pains, and acquainted with grief and sickness; and like One from Whom men hide their faces He was despised, and we did not appreciate His worth or have any esteem for Him. 4 Surely He has *cabal*/borne our griefs (sicknesses, weaknesses, and distresses) and *nasa*/carried our sorrows and pains [of punishment], yet we [ignorantly] considered Him stricken, smitten, and afflicted by God [as if with leprosy]. 5 But He was wounded for our transgressions, He was bruised for our guilt and iniquities; the chastisement [needful to obtain] peace and well-being for us was upon Him, and with the stripes [that wounded] Him we are healed and made whole." AMP

Thus, there is no legal sickness, lack or sorrow in the world ever since Jesus received those stripes and was raised, and healing has been paid for—past, present and future. For the future, from the time of Jesus to the last sin or sickness of mankind, it was all paid for in advance, like a vast sum in the bank, to be drawn out in the time of need. Fill out a check with what is needed, and present your check already signed in the blood of Jesus, and you can receive the blessing already paid for.

This is part of the rest we are to labor to enter into. Heb 4:11 "Let us labour therefore to enter into that rest, lest any man fall after the same example of unbelief (*unpersuadableness, calling God a liar and not faithful in love*)."

DISCOVERING OUR REDEMPTION

Our problem is not God; He paid the awesome and awful price for our Redemption. He has placed us in Christ, beside Himself on the throne. Remind Father God of this until your heart is stirred, and enforce this truth on the devil, in the name of Jesus, to get the manifestation of the promised blessing on the Earth. Anything between you and a promise of God is ignorance, deception or a devil. God is your Helper, not your enemy.

Rev 12:11 "And they overcame him (*Satan*) by the blood of the Lamb, and by the word of their testimony; and they *agape*/loved not their *psuche*/lives (*souls*) unto the death."

Having sufficient knowledge of the Lordship of Jesus and the great work of Redemption is our problem and our challenge. Start to *epignosis* (know it to walking like a master craftsman in the boldness, power, *agape* love and the sound mind of Christ), and the devil will flee.

You may be assaulted with feelings and thoughts that this cannot be true, but such feelings and thoughts cannot be from God. He declares that He cannot lie! Consider the source and put the promises of God in your mouth, until they are written forever on your heart and in your mind.

Holy Spirit applies the meaning of Isaiah 53 in the New Testament. Matt 8:16 "When the even was come, they brought unto him many that were possessed with devils: and he cast out the spirits with his word, and healed all that were sick: 17 that it might be fulfilled which was spoken by Esaias the prophet, saying, Himself took our infirmities, and bare our sicknesses." Matt 8:17 is a more accurate translation of Isaiah 53:4 than that found in the actual passage in the KJV.

In Matt 8:17, the Greek word translated as "took," *lambano*, means to hold on to, so it can never get away, to hold on to in full ownership and possession and to hold on to like a man in a storm holds on to a life preserver. This holding on to takes diligent and intense focus to maintain. Thus *lambano* is equally as strong or even stronger than the *cabal* of Isa 53 verses 4 and 12.

It was Father God's love to heal and redeem His mankind that made sure all that curse was held on to Jesus. It was the Great Shepherd's love that made sure He held on to that curse to heal and redeem mankind. Song 8:6 "Set me as a seal upon thine heart, as a seal upon thine arm: for love is strong as death ... ."

Part of Jesus' attitude was: "I will take this sickness upon Myself, per Isaiah 53, when I go to the cross. So, Father, perform Your Word now in them, and charge it to My account. And, since I now take it, it can never come back on them again. And, Father, You place it on Me so it can never get away, but be fully healed by You, when You raise Me from the dead. Thank You."

All of God's miracles and healings, since the foundation of the Earth were laid, and until Jesus was glorified and sent Holy Spirit back to Earth, were on credit, in anticipation of His work of Redemption. So, until Jesus took them and paid for them, they were all on credit. Once Jesus paid for it all with His stripes, healing and prosperity of any kind are more like drawing on a fully-funded bank account as funds are needed. Healing is a heavenly fact, to be manifested by faith into the Earth. You don't need faith for facts; you just need enforcement.

Jesus commanded the sickness and diseases to go, in a way that they can never return. This is what God meant in Isaiah 53:4. Jesus bore, or removed, or contained, them so they could not afflict man, and then exercised that promise in Matt 8:16, as He delivered "many that were possessed with devils: and he cast out the spirits with his word, and healed all that were sick."

The Greek word found in Matt 8:17 translated as bare, *bastazo*, means to bear away or remove so that it is no longer there and is much like the Hebrew word *nasa*. Again the message is that Jesus fully contained all the penalties for sin, the curse of the Law, in Himself, in a way that man is totally ransomed from the power of him who enforced the law of sin and death, the devil. The claims of justice for the penalty were fully paid by Jesus through His physical and spiritual act on the cross and by faith in the cross, as He ministered prior to it.

Matt 8:17 "That it might be fulfilled which was spoken by Esaias the prophet, saying, Himself *lambano*/took (*hold on to in complete and full ownership, never to let go*) our infirmities (*our griefs and that which causes us grief*), and *bastazo*/bare (*away or removed so that it is no longer there*) our sicknesses (*our sorrows and that which causes our sorrows*)."

So, for every person Jesus healed while He was here on Earth, it was like He was saying, "I will receive your curse, your sickness upon Me; I will *lambano* that problem, that work of the devil, until it is fully off of you, fully on Me and fully destroyed. And the sin that caused it (yours, another's or Adam's) is fully remitted, and, even as I will be healed of it, you be healed of it now. My stripes will be more than sufficient for your healing. Sin and its consequence are removed from you, taken by Me so it cannot get away, taken fully off of you and transferred fully onto or in me (*lambano*), and what I don't *lambano*, Father God will put on Me fully from you, and now you be free with the healing I will receive in My resurrection. Father, credit this to My account."

Or: "I will pay for that, for I know Father will heal Me of this, so I receive that healing for you now, so you can be free. Father, make it so, per My heart and Your Word, for You will do a complete work in and by Me, per Isaiah 53. This is an act of Your Kingdom. So, Thy Kingdom come, Thy will be done on Earth as it is in Heaven—now."

Jesus never said anything like this out loud, but this is included in: Matt 8:16 "When the even was come, they brought unto him many that were possessed with devils: and he cast out the spirits with his word, and healed all that were sick: 17 that it might be fulfilled which was spoken by Esaias the prophet, saying, Himself *lambano*/took our infirmities, and bare our sicknesses."

DISCOVERING OUR REDEMPTION

Remember, Jesus came to do only the Father's will.

John 5:30 "I can of mine own self do nothing: as I hear, I judge: and my judgment is just; because I seek not mine own will, but the will of the Father which hath sent me."

John 6:38 "For I came down from heaven, not to do mine own will, but the will of him that sent me."

And Jesus is the exact representation of how Father God really is.

Ps 103:6 "The LORD executeth righteousness and judgment for all that are oppressed."

Heb 1:1 "God, who at sundry times and in divers manners spake in time past unto the fathers by the prophets, 2 hath in these last days spoken unto us by his Son, whom he hath appointed heir of all things, by whom also he made the worlds; 3 who being the brightness of his glory, and the express image of his person, and upholding all things by the word of his power, when he had by himself purged our sins, sat down on the right hand of the Majesty on high."

This puts Jesus' prayer prior to raising Lazarus from the dead in perspective: John 11:41 "Then they took away the stone from the place where the dead was laid. And Jesus lifted up his eyes, and said, Father, I thank thee that thou hast heard me. 42 And I knew that thou hearest me always: but because of the people which stand by I said it, that they may believe that thou hast sent me. 43 And when he thus had spoken, he cried with a loud voice, Lazarus, come forth."

Jesus made it clear that sin and sickness are related, like opposite sides of the same coin, and He handled both with mercy. Mark 2:8 "And immediately when Jesus perceived in his spirit that they so reasoned within themselves, he said unto them, Why reason ye these things in your hearts? 9 Whether is it easier to say to the sick of the palsy, Thy sins be forgiven thee; or to say, Arise, and take up thy bed, and walk? 10 But that ye may know that the Son of man hath power on earth to forgive sins, (he saith to the sick of the palsy,) 11 I say unto thee, Arise, and take up thy bed, and go thy way into thine house. 12 And immediately he arose, took up the bed, and went forth before them all; insomuch that they were all amazed, and glorified God, saying, We never saw it on this fashion."

Jesus bore the fullness of our sin and the curse of sin, to set all men free; and He knew what He was doing and where He was headed even as He ministered. For Jesus said: John 3:13 "And no man hath ascended up to heaven, but he that came down from heaven, even the Son of man which is in heaven. 14 And as Moses lifted up the serpent in the wilderness, even so must the Son of man be lifted up [*as one cursed of God for the healing of men*]: 15 that whosoever believeth in him should not perish, but have eternal *zoe*/life. 16 For God so *agape*/loved the world, that he gave his only begotten Son, that whosoever believeth in him should not perish, but have everlasting *zoe*/life. 17 For God sent not his Son into the world to condemn the world; but that the world through him might be *sozo*/saved."

Jesus Was Made Sick and Scourged for Us

The serpent on the pole, in Numbers 21:4-9, was the consequence of sin, the curse, and God had that curse killed and had it hung on a stake by Moses, to show that if you looked to God for goodness, in spite of your sins, you could be healed. As the people stared at the snake, dead and impaled on the stake, they knew God did not want them dead, and that God would kill the thing that was killing them, and they would be healed.

They were sinning and thought it was fine. While they were sinning, they were in agreement with it and thought it natural and right. They knew they had sinned by the snake bite, the curse of sin. They knew they could be forgiven and healed by looking at the impaled and cursed snake on the stake. They could know God was not the source of the snake, because God treated the snake like an enemy, and God was the source of their healing. That word *beheld* means to recognize, acknowledge, behold and consider the facts and the implications of what they are looking at, and regard it with pleasure. As they "looked" or "beheld," fully expecting to be healed, they were healed.

Num 21:9 "And Moses made a serpent of brass, and put it upon a pole, and it came to pass, that if a serpent had bitten any man, when he beheld the serpent of brass, he lived."

Jesus became that curse that we might be healed. Even the serpent on the pole became a curse, by being put on the pole, or stake, just like Jesus was. Gal 3:13 "Christ hath redeemed us from the curse of the law, being made a curse for us: for it is written, Cursed is every one that hangeth on a tree: 14 that the blessing of Abraham might come on the Gentiles through Jesus Christ; that we might receive the promise of the Spirit through faith."

The only way the blessing of Holy Spirit dwelling in men could happen was if Jesus made us totally pure and healed in spirit by His mighty work of Redemption. Our true self is spirit, and Holy Spirit is spirit. They are made for each other. The work of Jesus by the Redemption of man made this possible by removing the consequence of Adam's sin and our own.

And, thus, Jesus had to pay the full price for sin and the consequences of sin, so it could never be paid again, so that this purity is now available for all men, for all time. We receive this purity in our spirit when we are born again in the new creation. 1 Cor 6:17 "But he that is joined unto the Lord is one spirit." Rom 5:18 "Therefore as by the offence of one judgment came upon all men to condemnation; even so by the righteousness of one the free gift came upon all men unto justification of *zoe*/life."

Jesus was not only made sin and separated from His Father, until His broken heart cried: "My God, my God, why hast thou forsaken me?" (Matt 27:46, Mk 15:34), but the diseases of the human race, the entire and full curse of sin, fell upon Him in such a way that man can never legally again carry it for any reason.

DISCOVERING OUR REDEMPTION

A notation on Isa 52:14 in the margin of the Cross-Reference Bible says, "Just as many were amazed over Him, and princes on His account shuddered, were astonished and appalled, amazed, frightened. His visage was so marred, unlike to a man, and His form unlike to the sons of man, so deformed was His appearance not to be a man, and His figure no longer resembled a man."

In the physical realm, Jesus was still a normal man on a cross. But this was more than just physical suffering; it was spiritual suffering. He started as one man, and then, in the spirit, became all men in the fullness of the penalty due for the sin of mankind. Who could recognize one man in the spirit when, in the spirit, He had become all the sin and sickness of the human race?

This was when the real man in Jesus, His spirit, became not only sin, but sickness, and every curse of the law for all mankind. To become our Salvation, He became our curse. The thing that was killing us was killed by God, as He managed the base instincts of sinful men, to crucify His beloved Son. 1 Cor 2:7 "But we speak the wisdom of God in a mystery, even the hidden wisdom, which God ordained before the world unto our glory: 8 which none of the princes of this world knew: for had they known it, they would not have crucified the Lord of glory."

Father God knew what ungodly men would do and used that to destroy the devil. The devil walked right into the ambush, or trap, set by God.

This was the spiritual side of the agony of the cross. Men could scourge and abuse Jesus' physical body, sacred as it was, and put Him on a cross, but only God could lay the entire burden of men, the curse and our sin, on Jesus. God is spirit, and this was a spiritual act.

Iniquity not only means our thoughts that are not like God's, but it includes the actions that these wicked thoughts produce and the consequences of those actions, the curse of sin. Jesus fully bore all this for us. And it pleased the Father, who wanted His creation, man, His beloved family back in the mighty work of the Mighty Arm of God. Jesus became man, not a man. By covenant Identification, He became all men, the entire human race, in order to suffer and die for the Redemption of mankind.

John 3:16 "For God so *agape*/loved the world, that he gave his only begotten Son, that whosoever believeth in him should not perish, but have everlasting *zoe*/life. 17 For God sent not his Son into the world to condemn the world; but that the world through him might be *sozo*/saved."

Isa 53:5 "But he was wounded for our transgressions, he was bruised for our iniquities: the chastisement of our peace was upon him; and with his stripes we are healed. 6 All we like sheep have gone astray; we have turned every one to his own way; and the Lord hath laid on him the iniquity of us all."

That word *laid* could also be stated as "the Lord hath violently and totally united and joined to Him the iniquity of us all."

Jesus Was Made Sick and Scourged for Us

This was the moment when our sin and diseases were laid upon and joined into Jesus' spirit.

His spirit was made sin.

His spirit was made sick.

His spirit died. Just as when Adam sinned, Jesus died in spirit, bearing the sin of all mankind.

Isa 53:3 "He is despised and rejected of men; a man of sorrows, and acquainted (*made one*) with grief (*sickness*): and we hid as it were our faces from him; he was despised, and we esteemed him not."

If our hearts could only take it in, that He was made sin, and that we were identified with Him, unified totally in and with Him on the cross, then we could grasp the reality of His covenant substitutionary work. As we grasp it, "behold it," then we will manifest that finished work in our lives and in the lives of those around us.

Heb 2:17 "So it is evident that it was essential that He be made like His brethren in every respect, in order that He might become a merciful (sympathetic) and faithful High Priest in the things related to God, to make atonement and propitiation for the people's sins." AMP

The word *atonement* means to cover sin so that the consequence is removed, even though the sin is still there. The atonement under the Law of Moses in all the sacrifices was temporary, awaiting the Messiah to bear away the sins, not just cover them. That word *propitiation* means not only to remove all hindrances to blessing, but to impel or push blessing (Holy Spirit and all His wondrous capabilities) onto men. Through the propitiation of Jesus, sin and its consequences are put away eternally and the force of grace applied. It is activated by faith.

Jesus could not be made "in every respect" until He became us, sin and the curse of sin, including going to Hades of the damned, as one who was damned. Because He was all men, He was the most damned One.

He became, in every respect, man, in every respect, sin, in every respect, unrighteousness and, in every respect, sickness and the curse of sin.

To most of us, this truth has been a mere academic doctrine rather than a daily reality.

Make it the dominate thought of your heart, and you will: Rom 6:12 "Let not sin therefore reign (*as king or lord*) in your (*current*) mortal body, that ye should obey it in the lusts thereof." This does not just include evil desires, but also sickness, disease, maimed bodies, early death, poverty, lack, fear, hate, etc. All of these are evil and cruel masters which Jesus came to destroy and did destroy, by His propitiation by the cross.

Lust and fear may assault your mind, but sickness rules the body with an iron grip, until either you die or you are healed.

DISCOVERING OUR REDEMPTION

Father God not only laid our sin on Jesus, but He laid us on (and in) Jesus.

2 Cor 5:15 "And that he died for all, that they which *zao*/live should not henceforth *zao*/live unto themselves, but unto him which died for them, and rose again."

Darby's translation makes it clear that we are now alive to God in Jesus. 2 Cor 5:15 "And he died for all, that they who *zao*/live should no longer *zao*/live to themselves, but to him who died for them and has been raised."

We now join with Paul's great confession for all mankind: Gal 2:20 "I *have been* crucified with Christ: nevertheless I *zao*/live; yet not I, but Christ *zao*/liveth in me: and the life which I now *zao*/live in the flesh I *zao*/live by the faith of the Son of God, who *agape*/loved me, and gave himself for me. 21 I do not frustrate the grace of God: for if righteousness come by the law, then Christ is dead in vain."

It took the death of Jesus by the crucifixion to make men the righteousness of God in Jesus, unto the *zoe* life of God. This had never happened before in the history of the human race.

The whole man was involved in this sacrifice of Jesus—His spirit, His soul, and His body. By covenant Identification, our whole spirit, soul and body were there also. What happened to Jesus happened to us, just as surely.

We were nailed to the cross with Him and in Him.

Our diseases were put on Him and made part of Him.

When this is written on the mind and the heart, it will be the end of the dominion of disease.

When this is written on the mind and the heart, it will be the end of the dominion of fear.

When this is written on the mind and the heart, it will be the end of the dominion of the spirit of the orphan, poverty and lack.

For if He was made sick with our sickness, Satan has no legal right to put diseases upon us or anyone and, in the name of Jesus, we can exert the power to free ourselves and others from Satan's power and bring the Kingdom of God to Earth.

True, for now we have mortal bodies, but this mortal body can be filled with the life of God.

2 Cor 5:4 "… That what is mortal may be swallowed up of *zoe*/life." RSV

Rom 6:14 "Sin shall not have dominion over you," or, literally, "Sin shall not lord it over you."

Or, even more direct: "Sin shall not reign as king in your mortal body, as a cruel master, in sickness, defeat and lack."

As we learn to reckon ourselves in the new creation in Jesus, neither disease nor pain shall lord it over us. Disease and pain are cruel taskmasters. Just look at a children's hospital ward, to see his cruelty in action.

We see now that if Satan has lost his dominion, he cannot legally place and keep disease upon us.

Jesus Was Made Sick and Scourged for Us

We understand that sickness is spiritual. It is manifested in our physical bodies as a disease. The world sees sickness in our bodies as a biological fact and process; this physical fact is merely a manifestation of the spiritual condition.

Matt 3:10 "And now also the axe is laid unto the root of the trees: therefore every tree which bringeth not forth good fruit is hewn down, and cast into the fire."

That root is sin and the curse of sin. The axe is the spirit, soul, body and blood of Jesus.

God deals with sickness as a spiritual condition that manifests itself in and through our physical life and body. The devil behind the sickness is the real root. So God's primary target is the devil causing the sickness symptoms or biology. Get rid of the devil, and the life of God will heal, restore or recreate as necessary, to put the body back into proper condition and health.

Working this Word: God calls the Word of God a seed, and we have been given the ministry of the Word of Reconciliation. As we speak of the grace of God, we put that grace to the root of sin, curse and self–righteousness, and God confirms this Word of reconciliation in Jesus, with signs and wonders following. 2 Cor 5:19 "To wit, that God was in Christ, reconciling the world unto himself, not imputing their trespasses unto them; and hath committed unto us the word of reconciliation. 20 Now then we are ambassadors for Christ, as though God did beseech you by us: we pray you in Christ's stead, be ye reconciled to God. 21 For he hath made him to be sin for us, who knew no sin; that we might be made the righteousness of God in him. 6:1 We then, as workers together with him, beseech you also that ye receive not the grace of God in vain. 2 (For he saith, I have heard thee in a time accepted, and in the day of *soteria*/salvation have I succoured thee: behold, now is the accepted time; behold, now is the day of *soteria*/salvation.)"

We minister the Gospel of Reconciliation, and God heals the sick, raises the dead, multiplies the food and provides money, as needed. This is the Gospel to the poor. We are the agents of God to speak this Word, and then God does mighty things in the spirit world, things which then translate to God's prosperity in the physical world, Heaven on Earth.

This spiritual power over physical manifestations of the devil is described in this Holy Spirit summary of Jesus' ministry: Acts 10:38 "How God anointed and consecrated Jesus of Nazareth with the [Holy] Spirit and with strength and ability and power; how He went about doing good and, in particular, curing all who were harassed and oppressed (*under the active dominion, reign and lordship*) by [the power of] the devil, for God was with Him." AMP

Jesus gave to the disciples this same spiritual power to destroy and crush physical sickness by power over the spirits behind them (and therefore to all subsequent believers). Luke 10:19 "Behold (*consider, ponder and let or make it change your life and world-view*)! I have given you authority and power to trample upon

DISCOVERING OUR REDEMPTION

serpents and scorpions, and [physical and mental strength and ability] over all the power that the enemy [possesses]; and nothing shall in any way harm you. 20 Nevertheless, do not rejoice at this, that the spirits (*causing these evil manifestations*) are subject to you, but rejoice that your names are enrolled in heaven. [Ex 32:32; Ps 69:28; Dan 12:1.]" AMP

God heals us through the Word which is spirit and *zoe*/life.

The anointing for healing is in the Word.

No Word of God is void of power. Isa 55:11 "So shall my word be that goeth forth out of my mouth: it shall not return unto me void, but it shall accomplish that which I please, and it shall prosper in the thing whereto I sent it."

God's life is in His Word.

John 6:63 "It is the spirit that quickeneth; the flesh profiteth nothing: the words that I speak unto you, they are spirit, and they are *zoe*/life."

Jesus spoke only the Father's words. What Jesus said is what Father God says.

When you speak like Jesus did, you are speaking the Father's Word for Him also.

God and His Word are one; Jesus and His Word are one.

The Word is God, in that He cannot lie, and He is His Word, and is true to His Word.

1 John 1:1 "That which was from the beginning, which we have heard, which we have seen with our eyes, which we have looked upon, and our hands have handled, of the Word of *zoe*/life; 2 (for the *zoe*/life was manifested, and we have seen it, and bear witness, and shew unto you that eternal *zoe*/life, which was with the Father, and was manifested unto us;) 3 that which we have seen and heard declare we unto you, that ye also may have fellowship with us: and truly our fellowship is with the Father, and with his Son Jesus Christ. 4 And these things write we unto you, that your joy may be full."

God's Word is greater than His name.

Ps 138:2 "I will worship toward thy holy temple, and praise thy name for thy *chesed*/lovingkindness and for thy truth: for thou hast magnified thy word above all thy name."

God's Word is settled forever in Heaven, so it can never be changed.

Ps 119:89 "For ever, O Lord, thy word is settled in heaven. 90 Thy faithfulness is unto all generations: thou hast established the earth, and it abideth."

The name *Jesus* means "the salvation of God is now," or "the Kingdom of God is released now."

His Word and God are the same.

The Word is Spirit, and it is Truth.

God is in His Word.

Heb 4:12 "For the word of God is quick, and powerful, and sharper than any twoedged sword, piercing even to the dividing asunder of *psuche*/soul (*life*) and

Jesus Was Made Sick and Scourged for Us

spirit, and of the joints and marrow, and is a discerner of the thoughts and intents of the heart. 13 Neither is there any creature that is not manifest in his sight: but all things are naked and opened unto the eyes of him with whom we have to do."

Jesus is the living/*zao* Word of God.

John 1:14 "And the Word was made flesh, and dwelt among us, (and we beheld his glory, the glory as of the only begotten of the Father,) full of grace and truth."

John 17:17 "Sanctify them through thy truth: thy word is truth."

The Word is spirit, and it is *zoe*/life, that all powerful *zoe*/life of God.

It is the Word that heals our spirits enabling us to be born of God.

It is the Word that recreates us.

When we preach the Word of grace in Jesus, God confirms His Word.

Mark 16:19 "So then after the Lord had spoken unto them, he was received up into heaven, and sat on the right hand of God. 20 And they went forth, and preached everywhere, the Lord working with them, and confirming the word with signs following. Amen."

Acts 14:3 "Long time therefore abode they speaking boldly in the Lord, which gave testimony unto the word of his grace, and granted signs and wonders to be done by their hands."

What Word of grace? We proclaim and decree the Word of Salvation by grace; the Word of Reconciliation, the Word of Redemption unto Remission of sin and the curse of sin by grace, through faith in the blood of Jesus, the Word that sin is cursed, condemned in the flesh, unto healing.

Rom 8:3 "For what the law could not do, in that it was weak through the flesh, God sending his own Son in the likeness of sinful flesh, and for sin, condemned sin in the flesh: 4 that the righteousness of the law might be fulfilled in us, who walk not after the flesh, but after the Spirit."

This is the Word of Reconciliation. The ministry of reconciliation is when we deliver that *agape*/love in wisdom, healing, prosperity, restoration and raising the dead.

Gal 2:16 "Knowing that a man is not justified by the works of the law, but by the faith of Jesus Christ, even we have believed in Jesus Christ, that we might be justified by the faith of Christ, and not by the works of the law: for by the works of the law shall no flesh be justified."

Rom 3:23 "For all have sinned, and come short of the glory of God; 24 being justified freely by his grace through the redemption that is in Christ Jesus: 25 whom God hath set forth to be a propitiation through faith in his blood, to declare his righteousness for the remission of sins that are past, through the forbearance of God; 26 to declare, I say, at this time his righteousness: that he might be just, and the justifier of him which believeth in Jesus."

DISCOVERING OUR REDEMPTION

If you have Jesus, you have *zoe*/life in the salvation of God, and have been made the righteousness of God in Christ Jesus. You are righteousness. Your new-creation self only wants to do, in purpose, thought and action, what Jesus would do, which is just what the Father wants done, the way He wants it done. This is to be born again by the Word of our Salvation in Jesus.

Eph 1:12 "That we should be to the praise of his glory, who first trusted in Christ. 13 In whom ye also trusted, after that ye heard the word of truth, the gospel of your *soteria*/salvation: in whom also after that ye believed, ye were sealed with that holy Spirit of promise, 14 which is the earnest of our inheritance until the redemption of the purchased possession, unto the praise of his glory."

You may not understand and appreciate it or even walk in it, but when that Word is done with you on the Day of Redemption, all creation will shout at what a great job God did in you!

The anointing is in the Word, and it is activated as we believe and, thus, obey it. We rejoice in our confession that "The word of *zoe*/life, of Reconciliation, of Redemption, of Peace, of Grace, of Righteousness, of Propitiation, of Adoption, of Betrothal, and of Salvation in Jesus alone, is growing in me more and more!"

1 Pet 1:23 "Being born again, not of corruptible seed, but of incorruptible, by the word of God, which *zao*/liveth and abideth for ever. 24 For all flesh is as grass, and all the glory of man as the flower of grass. The grass withereth, and the flower thereof falleth away: 25 but the word of the Lord endureth for ever. And this is the word which by the gospel is preached unto you."

That Word is all-powerful, pure, incorruptible, everlasting and is *agape*/love.

It is the Word that produces faith, believing.

That is why it is not about our holiness, but His. We speak the Word of grace in Jesus, in preaching. And, as you become more persuaded of that Word, you command, *aiteo*, and He confirms it with acts of peace, just like He did in the Gospels.

John 14:11 "Believe me that I am in the Father, and the Father in me: or else believe me for the very works' sake. 12 Verily, verily, I say unto you, He that believeth on me, the works that I do shall he do also; and greater works than these shall he do; because I go unto my Father. 13 And whatsoever ye shall *aiteo*/ask (*require, demand and expect as due by covenant promise*) in my name, that will I do, that the Father may be glorified in the Son. 14 If ye shall *aiteo*/ask (*require, demand and expect as due by covenant promise*) any thing in my name, I will do it."

John 15:7 "If ye abide in me, and my words abide in you, ye shall *aiteo*/ask (*require, demand and expect as due by covenant promise*) what ye will, and it shall be done unto you. 8 Herein is my Father glorified, that ye bear much fruit; so shall ye be my disciples."

Note that *faith* is the noun form of the Greek verb *pisteuo*, to believe. They are the same word, *faith* the noun from *pistis* and *believe*, the verb. To believe means to have faith, and to have faith means to believe. Believing is evidenced by what you say and do. What you actually say and do is what you really believe, what you are fully persuaded of and have confidence in. You proclaim, affirm, confess, give thanks, praise and profess to get to the point of believing.

This is not confidence in your words, but confidence that God moves by your words, as your words become His words. Your faith is in God, not yourself.

Beyond believing is knowing. You know if you are believing, but, in believing, you may not be knowing. Knowing is the end goal, not just believing. Believing is on the way to knowing. In knowing, you are an expert in believing, obeying or in having faith in God by His Word, just as apprenticeship and journeymanship are on the way to master craftsmanship.

Rom 10:16 "But they have not all obeyed the gospel. For Esaias saith, Lord, who hath believed our report? 17 So then faith cometh by hearing, and hearing by the word of God (*in Christ*)."

It is the Scriptures, especially in the Word of Christ, that wash our souls free, so we can relate in truth to God in Spirit.

It is the Word that goes past our mental-assent mind and gets into our believing heart.

Eph 5:25 "Husbands, *agape*/love your wives, even as Christ also *agape*/loved the church, and gave himself for it; 26 that he might sanctify and cleanse it with the washing of water by the word, 27 that he might present it to himself a glorious church, not having spot, or wrinkle, or any such thing; but that it should be holy and without blemish."

James 1:21 "Wherefore lay apart all filthiness and superfluity of naughtiness, and *lambano*/receive with meekness the engrafted word, which is able to *sozo*/save your *psuche*/souls (*lives*)."

It is the Word that purifies your heart in your soul that makes the difference for the long term.

It is the Word that unveils to us what we really are in Christ, new creations, His workmanship, His master craftsmanship.

2 Cor 5:14 "For the *agape*/love of Christ constraineth us; because we thus judge, that if one died for all, then were all dead: 15 and that he died for all, that they which *zao*/live should not henceforth *zao*/live unto themselves, but unto him which died for them, and rose again. 16 Wherefore henceforth know we no man after the flesh: yea, though we have known Christ after the flesh, yet now henceforth know we him no more. 17 Therefore if any man be in Christ, he is a new creature: old things are passed away; behold, all things are become new. 18 And all things are of God, who hath reconciled us to himself by Jesus Christ, and hath given to us the ministry of reconciliation."

DISCOVERING OUR REDEMPTION

All we need is enough believing in the resurrection of Jesus for God to get us born again. Just like any birth, it is a onetime event. Just like life in general, what you do with that new birth is up to you, but it does not change the fact that you are now here in your new birth. Do it right, and you can mature into the fullness of Christ.

Eph 4:13 "Till we all come in the unity of the faith, and of the *epignosis*/knowledge of the Son of God, unto a perfect man, unto the measure of the stature of the fulness of Christ: 14 that we henceforth be no more children, tossed to and fro, and carried about with every wind of doctrine, by the sleight of men, and cunning craftiness, whereby they lie in wait to deceive; 15 but speaking the truth in *agape*/love, may grow up into him in all things, which is the head, even Christ."

Everything you need is in the new creation, to mature you into Jesus by the Word of God.

Col 2:8 "Beware lest any man spoil you through philosophy and vain deceit, after the tradition of men, after the rudiments of the world, and not after Christ. 9 For in him dwelleth all the fulness of the Godhead bodily. 10 And ye are complete in him, which is the head of all principality and power."

Col 1:26 "Even the mystery which hath been hid from ages and from generations, but now is made manifest to his saints: 27 to whom God would make known what is the riches of the glory of this mystery among the Gentiles; which is Christ in you, the hope of glory: 28 whom we preach, warning every man, and teaching every man in all wisdom; that we may present every man perfect (*mature*) in Christ Jesus: 29 whereunto I also labour, striving according to his working, which worketh in me mightily."

The "all things" that we experience now in the new creation, does not refer to the physical body, unless you got healed when you were made a new creation. If you got healed, then it is just a taste.

And the "all things" of the new creation for now, does not refer to the soul. That is not changed in the new creation, as your memories remain intact.

What got transformed immediately in the new creation is your spirit, the real man.

Spirit relates to spirit, and God is spirit. God deals with our soul in the mind and heart, to get us to believe the Word of God, and then He makes us righteousness unto *zoe*/life in our spirit, as we believe that Word.

It is the Word, then, which is spirit and life, that brings healing, the physical reconciliation, to these sick bodies of ours.

Ps 107:19 "Then they cry unto the Lord in their trouble, and he saveth them out of their distresses. 20 He sent his word, and healed them, and delivered them from their destructions. 21 Oh that men would praise the Lord for his *chesed*/goodness, and for his wonderful works to the children of men!"

Jesus Was Made Sick and Scourged for Us

Sin is spiritual lies manifested in the flesh.

Sickness is a spiritual condition manifested in the physical body.

It takes the believed, fully-persuaded, confident Word of God to make the difference.

Heb 4:1 "Let us therefore fear, lest, a promise being left us of entering into his rest, any of you should seem to come short of it. 2 For unto us was the gospel preached, as well as unto them: but the word preached did not profit them, not being mixed with faith (*persuasion, confidence, reconciliation*) in them that heard it."

If Jesus was made sin, and if He put our sin away, we need not be ruled by it.

If He was made sick with our sickness, and if He put our diseases away, we need not be ruled by sickness and disease.

Isa 53:3 "He is despised and rejected of men; a man of sorrows, and acquainted (*made one*) with grief (*sickness*): and we hid as it were our faces from him; he was despised, and we esteemed him not."

Freedom from sickness is health and strength, and it takes the force of sin to keep sickness on us.

Sickness does not manifest itself in *agape*/love. The sick, in their misery are filled with self. They know they are sick, in pain, in fear, in dread and limited. The goal of sickness is to cause you to focus on self, accuse God with thoughts of "why me?" and experience limitation, so you cannot fulfill the work of God. Unhindered, sickness will kill you.

We, with our diseases and sicknesses, were nailed to the cross in Christ.

Gal 2:16 "Knowing that a man is not justified by the works of the law, but by the faith of Jesus Christ, even we have believed in Jesus Christ, that we might be justified by the faith of Christ, and not by the works of the law: for by the works of the law shall no flesh be justified."

Gal 2:20 "(*Knowing*) I am (*have been*) crucified with Christ: nevertheless I *zao*/live; yet not I, but Christ *zao*/liveth in me: and the life which I now *zao*/live in the flesh I *zao*/live by the faith of the Son of God, who *agape*/loved me, and gave himself for me. 21 I do not frustrate the grace of God: for if righteousness come by the law, then Christ is dead in vain."

If righteousness were possible, unto the righteousness of God in Christ Jesus, unto *zoe*/life in the new creation, without the death and resurrection of Jesus, then Jesus died in vain. This is what we get and become in the new birth, and it is only possible by the death and resurrection of Jesus.

Righteousness includes every promise of God being fulfilled in you up to and including Heaven in you and on Earth, which includes walking in Holy Spirit health, purpose, faith, hope, patience, righteousness, peace, joy, power, *agape*/love, sound mind, mercy, grace, truth and prosperity, all to the glory of God.

Because the end of sickness is death, Jesus took our death for us in Him. Partial death, living but still sick, was included.

DISCOVERING OUR REDEMPTION

When we recognize this, we will no longer struggle for faith, for confidence, for righteousness and holiness because we will know that we were nailed to the cross and died with Him, were buried with Him, suffered with Him, were made alive with Him, were justified with Him, conquered Satan with Him, were raised with Him and, finally, were seated with Him and glorified by Holy Spirit with Him.

The whole program of that Substitutionary Sacrifice or Redemption unto Salvation is made real in us by Holy Spirit through the Word. Then we deal on fact, spiritual fact, that is greater than worldly fact; by faith in God we can change the worldly condition to match the spiritual facts.

All these things are ours now. Eph 1:3 "Blessed be the God and Father of our Lord Jesus Christ, who hath blessed us with all spiritual blessings in heavenly places in Christ."

No wonder Jesus taught us to pray: Matt 6:9 "After this manner therefore pray ye: Our Father which art in heaven, Hallowed be thy name. 10 Thy kingdom come. Thy will be done in earth, as it is in heaven."

And as you pray this way, expect Father to draw you to His work of Redemption in the Scriptures, expect to hunger and thirst after the Word of our righteousness in the Jesus of the New Testament revelation, and for you to start to minister healing and other good works, just as Jesus did.

Just like Jesus, you become a bearer, a messenger, of the Word of God in Jesus = Salvation Now.

Acts 10:36 "The word which God sent unto the children of Israel, preaching peace by Jesus Christ: (he is Lord of all:) 37 that word, I say, ye know, which was published throughout all Judaea, and began from Galilee, after the baptism which John preached; 38 how God anointed Jesus of Nazareth with the Holy Ghost and with power: who went about doing good, and healing all that were oppressed (*under the active dominion, reign and lordship*) of the devil; for God was with him."

Peace means freedom from any oppression, dominion, reign, or lordship of the devil and you released into walking in the truth of God, to release God's *zoe*/life into the world at will.

Mark 16:19 "So then after the Lord had spoken unto them, he was received up into heaven, and sat on the right hand of God. 20 And they went forth, and preached everywhere, the Lord working with them, and confirming the word (*of our redemption in Jesus*) with signs following. Amen."

Here is what it looks like when we are walking in this truth: Acts 5:15 "Insomuch that they brought forth the sick into the streets, and laid them on beds and couches, that at the least the shadow of Peter passing by might overshadow some of them. 16 There came also a multitude out of the cities round about unto Jerusalem, bringing sick folks, and them which were vexed with unclean spirits: and they were healed every one."

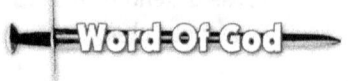

CHAPTER 11

JESUS SUFFERED FOR US

Jesus endured all that humanity could suffer, Deity suffering for humanity. First He suffered in soul and spirit in the Garden, then, in the torment and cruelly of that day, and, finally, as the most damned One in Hell for us.

Jesus suffered physically in the cruel beatings, mockery and scourging. He suffered with each lash of the cruel and vicious Roman whip. Blow after blow He took for our healing, His blood splattering all around Him each time that whip was pulled away, ripping flesh and spraying blood. His pain was ceaseless and multiplied with each stroke. He suffered in the piercing crown of thorns.

Then there was the awful slog from the whipping place to the cross, and then He suffered the agony of the cross. Jesus suffered for every breath He took, pushing His back against the rough tree and rising by forcing Himself upward with His feet, pushing against the nails that held Him there, just to get a breath. All of this was physical suffering. While it was Deity suffering for man, the entire curse of the Law did not fall on Jesus, in this process, on just His physical body. His suffering was physical, in His soul, and also spiritual; it was total man suffering.

Here is some of the suffering and how Jesus got through it on that terrible day: Isa 50:4 "The Lord God hath given me the tongue of the learned, that I should know how to speak a word in season to him that is weary: he wakeneth morning

DISCOVERING OUR REDEMPTION

by morning, he wakeneth mine ear to hear as the learned. 5 The Lord God hath opened mine ear, and I was not rebellious, neither turned away back. 6 I gave my back to the smiters, and my cheeks to them that plucked off the hair: I hid not my face from shame and spitting. 7 For the Lord God will help me; therefore shall I not be confounded: therefore have I set my face like a flint, and I know that I shall not be ashamed. 8 He is near that justifieth me; who will contend with me? let us stand together: who is mine adversary? let him come near to me. 9 Behold, the Lord God will help me; who is he that shall condemn me? lo, they all shall wax old as a garment; the moth shall eat them up. 10 Who is among you that feareth the Lord, that obeyeth the voice of his servant, that walketh in darkness, and hath no light? let him trust in the name of the Lord, and stay upon his God. 11 Behold, all ye that kindle a fire, that compass yourselves about with sparks: walk in the light of your fire, and in the sparks that ye have kindled. This shall ye have of mine hand; ye shall lie down in sorrow."

While it is not mentioned in the Gospels, verse 6 above states that Jesus gave His back to the smiters, which fits the Roman scourging, and His cheeks to them that plucked His hair and beard. These last two were common practices in a scourging. So whether this abuse happened as part of the scourging or during the mockery that followed, His beard and/or hair were pulled out by the roots in torment. John 19:1 "Then Pilate therefore took Jesus, and scourged him. 2 And the soldiers platted a crown of thorns, and put it on his head, and they put on him a purple robe, 3 and said, Hail, King of the Jews! and they smote him with their hands." That smiting could have included plucking out His hair, per Isaiah 50:6.

Just one case of leprosy can rot the entire body and one case of cancer can consume it or fill it with tumors. There is no way to imagine that the entire penalty for the sin of the human race could ever be satisfied by the wounding, the bruising, the chastisement, and the lacerations of Jesus' passion in the physical realm. His physical suffering was sufficient for our healing and prosperity, but just the physical part was not the plan of God. The fullness, restoring man again to the side of God, took place in the spirit realm, the realm of demons, a match between the devil and our Great God. Sin is spiritual but it results in physical effects; Jesus' sufferings were physical, leading to spiritual results. But then He was healed, justified in spirit, and then He rose physically from the tomb of Joseph of Arimathea.

The soul suffering can be seen in His cry of anguish: Matt 27:46 "And about the ninth hour Jesus cried with a loud voice, saying, Eli, Eli, lama sabachthani? that is to say, My God, my God, why hast thou forsaken me? 47 Some of them that stood there, when they heard that, said, This man calleth for Elias. 48 And straightway one of them ran, and took a spunge, and filled it with vinegar, and put it on a reed, and gave him

JESUS SUFFERED FOR US

to drink. 49 The rest said, Let be, let us see whether Elias will come to *sozo*/save him. 50 Jesus, when he had cried again with a loud voice, yielded up the ghost (*spirit*)."

Man can easily get lost in the physical sufferings, but the work of God was needed in the spiritual realm as well. This is the realm of the Mighty Arm of God.

A key element of our Christian faith is that Jesus suffered for us and then rose from the dead.

Heb 2:17 "Wherefore in all things it behoved him to be made like unto his brethren, that he might be a merciful and faithful high priest in things pertaining to God, to make reconciliation for the sins of the people. 18 For in that he himself hath suffered being tempted, he is able to succour them that are tempted."

Heb 5:7 "Who in the days of his flesh, when he had offered up prayers and supplications with strong crying and tears unto him that was able to *sozo*/save him from death, and was heard in that he feared; 8 though he were a Son, yet learned he obedience by the things which he suffered; 9 and being made perfect, he became the author of eternal *soteria*/salvation unto all them that obey him."

Heb 9:24 "For Christ is not entered into the holy places made with hands, which are the figures of the true; but into heaven itself, now to appear in the presence of God for us: 25 nor yet that he should offer himself often, as the high priest entereth into the holy place every year with blood of others; 26 for then must he often have suffered since the foundation of the world: but now once in the end of the world hath he appeared to put away sin by the sacrifice of himself. 27 And as it is appointed unto men once to die, but after this the judgment: 28 so Christ was once offered to bear the sins of many; and unto them that look for him shall he appear the second time without sin unto *soteria*/salvation."

Heb 13:12 "Wherefore Jesus also, that he might sanctify the people with his own blood, suffered without the gate."

1 Pet 2:21 "For even hereunto were ye called: because Christ also suffered for us, leaving us an example, that ye should follow his steps: 22 who did no sin, neither was guile found in his mouth: 23 who, when he was reviled, reviled not again; when he suffered, he threatened not; but committed himself to him that judgeth righteously: 24 who his own self bare our sins in his own body on the tree, that we, being dead to sins, should *zao*/live unto righteousness: by whose stripes ye were healed."

1 Pet 4:1 "Forasmuch then as Christ hath suffered for us in the flesh, arm yourselves likewise with the same mind: for he that hath suffered in the flesh hath ceased from sin; 2 that he no longer should *zao*/live the rest of his time in the flesh to the lusts of men, but to the will of God."

Rev 1:5 "… Jesus Christ, who is the faithful witness, and the first begotten of the dead, and the prince of the kings of the earth. Unto him that *agape*/loved us, and washed us from our sins in his own blood, 6 and hath made us kings and priests unto God and his Father; to him be glory and dominion for ever and ever. Amen."

DISCOVERING OUR REDEMPTION

Rev 1:17 "And when I saw him, I fell at his feet as dead. And he laid his right hand upon me, saying unto me, Fear not; I am the first and the last: 18 I am he that *zao*/liveth, and was dead; and, behold, I am *zao*/alive for evermore, Amen; and have the keys of hell and of death."

Many focus on His physical sufferings, which were, without a doubt, grievous. But it did not stop there; otherwise Jesus would only have dealt with sin and the curse on the physical level, which is not the root. The root is the spiritual realities in the realm of God, who is spirit.

As John said of the coming Messiah: Matt 3:10 "And now also the axe is laid unto the root of the trees: therefore every tree which bringeth not forth good fruit is hewn down, and cast into the fire."

Here is a description of Jesus' spiritual sufferings (Kenyon, *Identification*, Kenyon Gospel Publishing Society, USA, p24-26):

Ps 88:6 "He laid Him in the lowest pit, the pit of the underworld, in the dark places, in dense darkness. 6 Thy wrath lieth hard upon me. 7 Thy wrath presseth, thou hast laid thy fury upon me. All thy breakers thou has brought upon me. Thou hast let all thy waves strike me. Thou hast let come all thy breakers upon me." (Cross-Reference Bible, with margin notes) (See also Act 2:27-31, Jonah 2)

Ps 88:1 "I have called upon thee my God, day and night; and thou hearest me not." (Cross-Reference Bible)

Ps 88:3 "Full of trouble, weighted with evils. Thou hast brought me to Sheol, the kingdom of death. I am become a man without God." (Cross-Reference Bible)

To think that this is Jesus, Lord of All, Lamb of God, is beyond imagination.

The heart cannot take it in.

The mind stands dumb in the presence of truth like this.

Ps 88:15 "I was afflicted and close to death from my youth up; while I suffer Your terrors I am distracted [I faint].

"16 Your fierce wrath has swept over me; Your terrors have destroyed me.

"17 They surround me like a flood all day long; together they have closed in upon me.

"18 Lover and friend have You put far from me; my familiar friends are darkness and the grave." AMP

Jesus' body went to the grave, but His spirit and soul went to Hades, as one of the damned. Just as man had to suffer in Hades, so did Jesus. 1 Pet 3:18 "For Christ also hath once suffered for sins, the just for the unjust, that he might bring us to God, being put to death in the flesh, but quickened by the Spirit."

To the best of our knowledge, after Jesus gave up the ghost on the cross, He did not enter into His body again until that resurrection morning.

In the meantime, Jesus went to Hades for us and continued to suffer as the condemned for all men for 3 days in the "heart of the Earth." (Matt 12:40)

Four Divine Attributes Seen in Hell: Then we come to the most remarkable part of the suffering of Christ.

Jesus Suffered for Us

(Ps 88:10) He cried, "Wilt thou show wonders to the dead? Shall they that are deceased arise and praise thee?"

Down there in that awful place, God showed His wonders to the dead.

- His Power was displayed

He let them see the awfulness of sin and the absolute justice of God.

He let them see His resurrection power, when He made Jesus alive from being the sin and curse of sin for the human race.

Eph 1:19 "And what is the exceeding greatness of his power to us-ward who believe, according to the working of his mighty power, 20 which he wrought in Christ, when he raised him from the dead, and set him at his own right hand in the heavenly places, 21 far above all principality, and power, and might, and dominion, and every name that is named, not only in this world, but also in that which is to come: 22 and hath put all things under his feet, and gave him to be the head over all things to the church, 23 which is his body, the fulness of him that filleth all in all."

- His Love was displayed

More than that, He showed the lovingkindness of God.

(Ps 88:11) He said, "Shall thy *chesed*/loving kindness be shown in the grave?"

Jesus trusted God and saw His answer.

Acts 2:22 "Ye men of Israel, hear these words; Jesus of Nazareth, a man approved of God among you by miracles and wonders and signs, which God did by him in the midst of you, as ye yourselves also know: 23 him, being delivered by the determinate counsel and foreknowledge of God, ye have taken, and by wicked hands have crucified and slain: 24 whom God hath raised up, having loosed the pains of death: because it was not possible that he should be holden of it."

Matt 17:22 "And while they abode in Galilee, Jesus said unto them, The Son of man shall be betrayed into the hands of men: 23 and they shall kill him, and the third day he shall be raised again … ."

- His Eternal Faithfulness was displayed

(Ps 88:12a) "Or thy faithfulness in Destruction? Shall thy wonders be known in the dark?"

Jesus trusted in the absolute reliability of Him who cannot lie as He went to and through the cross to resurrection.

- His Righteousness was displayed

(Ps 88:12b) "And thy righteousness in the land of forgetfulness?"

Ps 9:1 "I will praise thee, O Lord, with my whole heart; I will shew forth all thy marvellous works. 2 I will be glad and rejoice in thee: I will sing praise to thy name, O thou most High. 3 When mine enemies are turned back, they shall fall and perish at thy presence. 4 For thou hast maintained my right and my cause; thou satest in the throne judging right."

Those demons saw Jesus, who had been made sin with our sin, and the curse with our curse, made as Righteous as He was before He was made sin.

DISCOVERING OUR REDEMPTION

But more than just Jesus, for Jesus had borne and been healed of the iniquity and curse on mankind. The devil knows what he lost in that battle, the world and all men.

Luke 24:44 "And he (*Jesus*) said unto them, These are the words which I spake unto you, while I was yet with you, that all things must be fulfilled, which were written in the law of Moses, and in the prophets, and in the psalms, concerning me. 45 Then opened he their understanding, that they might understand the scriptures, 46 and said unto them, Thus it is written, and thus it behoved Christ to suffer, and to rise from the dead the third day: 47 and that repentance and remission (*purging, obliteration, removal and putting away*) of sins should be preached in his name among all nations, beginning at Jerusalem."

In seeing Jesus made righteous, Satan must have witnessed the fact that righteousness was made possible for each human in the new creation.

Christ was made alive right there in the realm of death.

He was called "the firstborn out of death."

Col 1:18 "And he (*Jesus*) is the head of the body, the church: who is the beginning, the firstborn from the dead; that in all things he might have the preeminence. 19 For it pleased the Father that in him should all fulness dwell."

God said to Him, Acts 13:33 "Thou art my Son; this day have I begotten thee." (Also: Ps 2:7, Heb 1:5, Heb 5:5)

The hosts of Hell saw Jesus born out of death, first in His spirit, then in His body. They witnessed the triumph of God and the glory of our matchless Christ.

Ps 24:7 "Lift up your heads, O ye gates; and be ye lift up, ye everlasting doors; and the King of glory shall come in. 8 Who is this King of glory? The LORD strong and mighty, the LORD mighty in battle. 9 Lift up your heads, O ye gates; even lift them up, ye everlasting doors; and the King of glory shall come in. 10 Who is this King of glory? The LORD of hosts, he is the King of glory. Selah."

Wasn't it good of Him to give us this graphic picture, not only of His death and suffering, but also of His triumph and glory?

Throughout eternity, in the archives of the Supreme Court of the Universe, there will be records of the Son's visit to Hell, Jesus' suffering for and in the name of all mankind in Hell, of Satan's defeat and dethroning, Jesus' glorious triumph, and of man's legal Redemption and Glorification in Jesus.

As Jesus bore all mankind's sin, then the devil and all demons were enforcing all the curse of damnation on Jesus in Hell. This is the total Hell-suffering due all mankind forever. They saw Jesus put off from Himself the principalities and the powers of death. Col 2:15 "And having spoiled (*put off totally from Himself all their works on Himself and destroyed all their rulership*) principalities and powers, he made a shew of them (*Satan and all his empire*) openly, triumphing over them (*paraded captive in chains*) in it." Jesus submitted to death, to suffer for us, to triumph for us. We owed it; He paid for it. Case closed. Hallelujah!

They saw Jesus paralyze the death-dealing ability of Satan.

They saw Jesus conquer the hosts of the Black Leader.

Jesus Suffered for Us

As Mary said: <u>Luke 1:51</u> "He hath shewed strength with his arm; he hath scattered the proud in the imagination of their hearts. 52 He hath put down the mighty from their seats, and exalted them of low degree. 53 He hath filled the hungry with good things; and the rich he hath sent empty away."

As Zacharias said: <u>Luke 1:71</u> "That we should be *sozo*/saved from our enemies, and from the hand of all that hate us; 72 to perform the mercy promised to our fathers, and to remember his holy covenant; 73 the oath which he sware to our father Abraham, 74 that he would grant unto us, that we being delivered out of the hand of our enemies might serve him without fear."

They saw Jesus strip Satan of the authority and dominion he had robbed from Adam in the Garden.

<u>Luke 4:6</u> "And the devil said unto him (*Jesus*), All this power will I give thee, and the glory of them: for that is delivered unto me; and to whomsoever I will I give it." Now the tables were turned.

They saw Jesus strip Satan of the bonds of the curse of sin that held all men bound unto death.

They saw Jesus arise from the dead, a victor.

They knew it was the victory of the New Creation.

They saw us made alive with Jesus, justified with Him, raised with Him, and made victors with Him.

<u>Rev 1:17-18</u> was His song of victory:

"I am the first and the last, and the *zao*/Living one and I was dead, and behold, I am *zao*/alive for evermore; and I have the keys of death and of Hades." RSV

<u>Acts 17:2</u> "And Paul, as his manner was, went in unto them, and three sabbath days reasoned with them out of the scriptures, 3 opening and alleging, that Christ must needs have suffered, and risen again from the dead; and that this Jesus, whom I preach unto you, is Christ (*Messiah*)."

<u>Acts 26:23</u> "That Christ should suffer, and that he should be the first that should rise from the dead, and should shew light unto the people, and to the Gentiles."

<u>Heb 2:9</u> "But we see Jesus, who was made a little lower than the angels for the suffering of death, crowned with glory and honour; that he by the grace of God should taste death for every man. 10 For it became him, for whom are all things, and by whom are all things, in bringing many sons unto glory, to make the captain of their *soteria*/salvation perfect through sufferings."

Chapter 12

Jesus Was Made Righteous for Us

You surely noticed in the last chapter that Jesus was made alive and that we were made alive with Him in the mind of Justice.

That life was the nature of the Father, and when Jesus received that nature, He became righteous and righteousness once again.

He had been made sin.

Then the moment He was made alive, God justified Him.

Rom 6:23 "For the wages of sin is death; but the gift of God is eternal *zoe*/life through Jesus Christ our Lord."

Rom 5:16 "And not as it was by one that sinned, so is the gift: for the judgment was by one to condemnation, but the free gift is of many offences unto justification."

1 Pet 2:24 "Who his own self bare our sins in his own body on the tree, that we, being dead to sins, should *zao*/live unto righteousness: by whose stripes ye were healed."

Jesus was declared righteous because He had satisfied the claims of Justice. He had met every demand of the Supreme Court of the Universe that was against the human race.

Jesus Was Made Righteous for Us

Rom 4:24 "But for us also, to whom it (*righteousness*) shall be imputed, if we believe on him that raised up Jesus our Lord from the dead; 25 who was delivered for our offences, and was raised again for our justification (*and when we were justified*)."

Isa 53:10 "Yet it pleased the LORD to bruise him; he hath put him to grief: when thou shalt make his soul an offering for sin, he shall see his seed, he shall prolong his days, and the pleasure of the LORD shall prosper in his hand. 11 He shall see of the travail of his soul, and shall be satisfied: by his knowledge shall my righteous servant justify many; for he shall *cabal*/bear their iniquities. 12 Therefore will I divide him a portion with the great, and he shall divide the spoil with the strong; because he hath poured out his soul unto death: and he was numbered with the transgressors; and he *nasa*/bare the sin of many, and made intercession for the transgressors." Numbered with the transgressors includes the cross and in hell.

Jesus was made righteous with the *zoe* life of God, as we are made righteous in the new creation.

He was made so righteous that there was not a trace of the sin, the curse of sin, and the diseases that had become a part of Him in His awful judgment.

He was made so righteous, that He could enter into the presence of the Father with no sense of sin, guilt or inferiority, but totally holy, blameless and unreproveable.

The fact that He was righteous means there was no separation between Jesus and the Father, and Jesus was once again full of Holy Spirit and once again unified and experienced the free flow of Father God to the Earth by Holy Spirit.

When Jesus was overwhelmed with the presence of sin, His physical suffering, His spiritual anguish and His legal separation from the Father, He cried, Matt 27:46 "My God, my God, why hast thou forsaken me?"

Much like Noah, when there were only eight human beings living on the Earth, and yet they were not aware of God watching over and being with them, so Jesus, whom the Father was pleased to make sure every speck of sin and curse was laid upon, in the pressure of horrible circumstances, felt alone, yet, for sure, God was involved in every way He could be to work His good pleasure in Jesus to redeem mankind.

Isa 53:10 "Yet it pleased the LORD to bruise him; he hath put him to grief: when thou shalt make his soul an offering for sin, he shall see his seed, he shall prolong his days, and the pleasure of the LORD shall prosper in his hand."

Father was pleased then to proclaim Him alive, because Satan had illegally crucified and damned Him, who knew no sin, so justice could prevail for all sinful man. Father did not turn His face away; He looked to make sure every speck, every trace of sin and its consequences were fully paid for, and then fully removed.

But He could no longer be one with His Son, as Jesus was sin and united with death and Satan.

DISCOVERING OUR REDEMPTION

Then came that happy moment when God could make Jesus alive, as the full course had been borne and paid in full forever for all men, past, present and future.

2 Cor 5:21 "For he (*Father God*) hath made him (*Jesus*) to be sin for us, who knew no sin; that we might be made the righteousness of God in him (*Jesus*)."

When Jesus was made alive, God said of Him, Acts 13:33 "Thou art my Son; this day have I begotten thee."

Jesus stood before the angelic hosts as righteous and as pure as though He had never been made sin. The moment that He was made righteous, He was the absolute monarch of the Universe.

He was also the Master of the underworld and Master of Satan.

As long as He was spiritually dead, filled with sin and one with sin, Satan ruled over Him.

But when Jesus was made righteous, Jesus became the dominant master and ruler of Hell.

Col 2:15 "And having spoiled principalities and powers, he made a shew of them openly, triumphing over them in it."

Col 1:12 "Giving thanks (*continually*) unto the Father, which hath made us meet to be partakers of the inheritance of the saints in light: 13 who hath delivered us from the power of darkness, and hath translated us into the kingdom of his *agape*/dear Son: 14 in whom we have redemption through his blood, even the forgiveness (*remission, obliteration, removal and putting off*) of sins."

If He was made righteous, then all of us who believe God raised Jesus from the dead unto the righteousness of *zoe*/life are born again. We were automatically made righteous that moment, and can therefore dominate the forces of Hell in His name.

This is not just imputed righteousness, even though we have that also, just like Abraham, by believing God. This is being made the righteousness of God in Christ Jesus to the level of God's *zoe*/life. There is, in the spirit of the new creation, a desire and a will to perform the righteousness of God in any situation. It is now our new nature made in "righteousness and true holiness" the "workmanship of God" for and by God that "no man may boast." (Eph 2:1-10)

This is then made a reality in the Earth the moment:
- We believe in our heart God raised Jesus from the dead.
- Or we believe the good news of our salvation.
- Or we confess that Jesus is the Son of God.

Father God makes it easy to be made a new creation in righteousness and true holiness unto *zoe*/life. We then confess, agree, with our mouths that Jesus is Lord, (Ruler, Owner and Master of All), to bring His *soteria*/salvation to Earth.

Now our job is to continually grip tightly, against all resistance, labor, receive/ *lambano* eternal *zoe*/life. 1 Tim 6:12 "Fight the good fight of faith, *lambano*/lay hold on eternal *zoe*/life, whereunto thou art also called, and hast professed a good profession before many witnesses."

Rom 10:8 "But what saith it? The word is nigh thee, even in thy mouth, and in thy heart: that is, the word of faith, which we preach; 9 that if thou shalt confess with thy mouth the Lord Jesus, and shalt believe in thine heart that God hath raised him from the dead, thou shalt be *sozo*/saved. 10 For with the heart man believeth unto righteousness; and with the mouth confession is made unto *soteria*/salvation. 11 For the scripture saith, Whosoever believeth on him shall not be ashamed. 12 For there is no difference between the Jew and the Greek: for the same Lord over all is rich unto all that call upon him. 13 For whosoever shall call upon the name of the Lord shall be *sozo*/saved."

Rom 4:22 "And therefore it was imputed to him (*Abraham*) for righteousness. 23 Now it was not written for his sake alone, that it (*righteousness*) was imputed to him; 24 but for us also, to whom it shall be imputed, if we believe on him that raised up Jesus our Lord from the dead; 25 who was delivered for our offences, and was raised again for our justification (*or when we were justified in fullness to the level of Jesus*)."

1 Pet 1:18 "Forasmuch as ye know that ye were not redeemed with corruptible things, as silver and gold, from your vain conversation received by tradition from your fathers; 19 but with the precious blood of Christ, as of a lamb without blemish and without spot: 20 who verily was foreordained before the foundation of the world, but was manifest in these last times for you, 21 who by him do believe in God, that raised him up from the dead, and gave him glory; that your faith and hope might be in God."

1 Cor 15:15 "Yea, and we are found false witnesses of God; because we have testified of God that he raised up Christ: whom he raised not up, if so be that the dead rise not. 16 For if the dead rise not, then is not Christ raised: 17 and if Christ be not raised, your faith is vain; ye are yet in your sins. 18 Then they also which are fallen asleep in Christ are perished. 19 If in this life only we have hope in Christ, we are of all men most miserable. 20 But now is Christ risen from the dead, and become the firstfruits of them that slept (*and we are no longer in or one with our sins, for we are* zao *alive in God*)."

2 Cor 1:9 "But we had the sentence of death in ourselves, that we should not trust in ourselves, but in God which raiseth the dead: 10 who delivered us from so great a death, and doth deliver: in whom we trust that he will yet deliver us."

It is all of grace, not of works. We are God's workmanship, created in Christ Jesus. It is a work by and to the level of God.

You can do nothing to earn it, and no sin is so great as to prevent it. Grace trumps and crushes sin.

Eph 2:1 "And you hath he quickened, who were dead in trespasses and sins; 2 wherein in time past ye walked according to the course of this world, according

DISCOVERING OUR REDEMPTION

to the prince of the power of the air, the spirit that now worketh in the children of disobedience: 3 among whom also we all had our conversation in times past in the lusts of our flesh, fulfilling the desires of the flesh and of the mind; and were by nature the children of wrath, even as others. 4 But God, who is rich in mercy, for his great *agape/*love wherewith he *agape/*loved us, 5 even when we were dead in sins, hath quickened us together with Christ, (by grace ye are *sozo/*saved;) 6 and hath raised us up together, and made us sit together in heavenly places in Christ Jesus: 7 that in the ages to come he might shew the exceeding riches of his grace in his kindness toward us through Christ Jesus. 8 For by grace are ye *sozo/*saved through faith; and that not of yourselves: it is the gift of God: 9 not of works, lest any man should boast. 10 For we are his workmanship, created in Christ Jesus unto good works, which God hath before ordained that we should walk in them."

We are re-created in righteousness and holiness of truth.

Col 1:21 "And you, that were sometime alienated and enemies in your mind by wicked works, yet now hath he reconciled 22 in the body of his flesh through death, to present you holy and unblameable and unreproveable in his sight."

We still exist; we are not annihilated; we are transformed in spirit into the nature of God.

2 Pet 1:2 "Grace and peace be multiplied unto you through the *epignosis/*knowledge of God, and of Jesus our Lord, 3 according as his divine power hath given unto us all things that pertain unto *zoe/*life and godliness, through the *epignosis/*knowledge of him that hath called us to glory and virtue: 4 whereby are given unto us exceeding great and precious promises: that by these ye might be partakers of the divine nature, having escaped the corruption that is in the world through lust."

And what is this godliness? 1 Tim 3:16 "And without controversy great is the mystery of godliness: God was manifest in the flesh, justified in the Spirit, seen of angels, preached unto the Gentiles, believed on in the world, received up into glory."

This godliness is "Christ in you, the hope of glory." And what is this glory? It is the free reign of Holy Spirit within you, just like He reigns in Jesus.

Eph 4:17 "This I say therefore, and testify in the Lord, that ye henceforth walk not as other Gentiles walk, in the vanity of their mind, 18 having the understanding darkened, being alienated from the *zoe/*life of God through the ignorance that is in them, because of the blindness of their heart: 19 who being past feeling have given themselves over unto lasciviousness, to work all uncleanness with greediness. 20 But ye have not so learned Christ; 21 if so be that ye have heard him, and have been taught by him, as the truth is in Jesus: 22 that ye put off concerning the former conversation the old man, which is corrupt according to the deceitful lusts; 23 and be renewed in the spirit of your mind; 24 and that ye put on the new man (*in your new creation self identity and start acting like it*), which after God is created in righteousness and true holiness."

Chapter 13

Jesus Conquered Satan for Us

Heb 2:14 "Forasmuch then as the children are partakers of flesh and blood, he also himself likewise took part of the same; that through death he might destroy (*abolish, bring to no effect, make impotent, powerless, to do away, take away all well being*) him that had the power of death, that is, the devil; 15 and deliver them who through fear of death were all their lifetime subject to bondage. 16 For verily he took not on him the nature of angels; but he took on him the seed of Abraham. 17 Wherefore in all things it behoved him to be made like unto his brethren, that he might be a merciful and faithful high priest in things pertaining to God, to make reconciliation for the sins of the people."

Col 2:14 "Blotting out the handwriting of ordinances that was against us, which was contrary to us, and took it out of the way, nailing it to his cross; 15 and having spoiled (*to wholly put off from oneself, divest*) principalities and powers, he made a shew of them openly, triumphing over them in it."

This was one of the greatest events of the eternities.

The Mighty Arm of God had done His Mighty Work for Mankind. Satan had been brought to nought, his lordship abolished, when Jesus put off the devil and his armies from Himself and triumphed in that victory. That is, He led Satan captive as a slave trailing behind.

DISCOVERING OUR REDEMPTION

The Psalms describe it this way: Ps 9:1 "I will praise thee, O LORD, with my whole heart; I will shew forth all thy marvellous works. 2 I will be glad and rejoice in thee: I will sing praise to thy name, O thou most High. 3 When mine enemies are turned back, they shall fall and perish at thy presence. 4 For thou hast maintained my right and my cause; thou satest in the throne judging right. 5 Thou hast rebuked the heathen, thou hast destroyed the wicked, thou hast put out their name for ever and ever. 6 O thou enemy, destructions are come to a perpetual end: and thou hast destroyed cities; their memorial is perished with them. 7 But the LORD shall endure for ever: he hath prepared his throne for judgment. 8 And he shall judge the world in righteousness, he shall minister judgment to the people in uprightness. 9 The LORD also will be a refuge for the oppressed, a refuge in times of trouble. 10 And they that know thy name will put their trust in thee: for thou, LORD, hast not forsaken them that seek thee. 11 Sing praises to the LORD, which dwelleth in Zion: declare among the people his doings. 12 When he maketh inquisition for blood, he remembereth them: he forgetteth not the cry of the humble."

The eternal Son was made sin and death, then justified, made alive in spirit, and He put off from Himself the principalities and the powers, making a show of them openly, triumphing over them in it

Ps 68:1 "Let God arise, let his enemies be scattered: let them also that hate him flee before him. 2 As smoke is driven away, so drive them away: as wax melteth before the fire, so let the wicked perish at the presence of God. 3 But let the righteous be glad; let them rejoice before God: yea, let them exceedingly rejoice."

Jesus triumphed over Satan.

He conquered the hosts of Hell.

He dethroned Satan from his stolen empire.

He stripped Satan of the authority and dominion that he had taken from Adam at the Fall.

Jesus has also commanded that the devil must bow to His name in the mouths of believers.

Phil 2:9 "Wherefore God also hath highly exalted him, and given him a name which is above every name: 10 that at the name of Jesus every knee should bow, of things in heaven, and things in earth, and things under the earth; 11 and that every tongue should confess that Jesus Christ is Lord, to the glory of God the Father."

Acts 4:10 "Be it known unto you all, and to all the people of Israel, that by the name of Jesus Christ of Nazareth, whom ye crucified, whom God raised from the dead, even by him doth this man stand here before you whole. 11 This is the stone which was set at nought of you builders, which is become the head of the corner. 12 Neither is there *soteria*/salvation in any other: for there is none other name under heaven given among men, whereby we must be *sozo*/saved (*set free of every* hindrance, danger and limitation enforced or imposed by the devil, into the demonstration of the dominion of the Kingdom of God)."

Elders are to set others free in the name of Jesus of all oppressions, control, reign and rulership of the devil, so the Lord can heal them. James 5:14 "Is any sick among you? let him call for the elders of the church; and let them pray over him, anointing him with oil in the name of the Lord: 15 and the prayer of faith shall *sozo*/save the sick, and the Lord shall raise him up; and if he have committed sins, they shall be forgiven him."

Notice that the elder prays the prayer of faith, which includes commanding the devil to go, because we have been given the authority, commission and resources to tread on all the works and ability of the devil (see Luke 10:19). As the devil goes, healing comes from the Lord, "and then the Lord will raise the sick one up."

The great wonder is that, without confession of sin, any sins that the sick one may have committed are reconciled, in fellowship with the Lord. All this comes by asking for prayer for sickness.

These are the fruits of the victory Jesus won for us.

1 Cor 15:55 "O death, where is thy sting? O grave, where is thy victory? 56 The sting of death is sin; and the strength of sin is the law. 57 But thanks be to God, which giveth us the victory through our Lord Jesus Christ. 58 Therefore, my *agape*/beloved brethren, be ye stedfast, unmoveable, always abounding in the work of the Lord, forasmuch as ye know that your labour is not in vain in the Lord."

You were with Him and in Him when that battle took place.

1 Cor 2:6 "Howbeit we speak wisdom among them that are perfect: yet not the wisdom of this world, nor of the princes of this world, that come to nought (*being dethroned, destroyed, abolished from authority*): 7 but we speak the wisdom of God in a mystery, even the hidden wisdom, which God ordained before the world unto our glory: 8 which none of the princes of this world knew: for had they known it, they would not have crucified the Lord of glory."

You were identified with Christ by God in covenant relationship. Therefore what Jesus received, you received. What we were, He became, and what He is, now we are also.

You were loved by Him, who took all this for you and fought for you to gain your freedom from Satan and the law of sin and death, unto the freedom of the children of the light.

You were there in Christ, and He was there for you.

That deliverance is so great that, for the Christian: John 14:19 "... because I (Jesus) *zao*/live, ye shall *zao*/live also. 20 At that day ye shall know that I am in my Father, and ye in me, and I in you."

DISCOVERING OUR REDEMPTION

Just as you were identified with Jesus when He was crucified, when He died, when He was buried, when He was made alive, and when He was justified, you were also with Him in that victory over the adversary.

Therefore it was your victory, not just His.

He did not need to fight that battle; He did it for you, for all men.

He did it out of *agape*/love for all mankind.

Jesus did it out of *agape*/love, for the Father, to only please Him, and it was the Father's good pleasure to crush Jesus, that we might be free from the dominion of the devil and be transferred into the Kingdom of *Agape*/love.

John 8:29 "And he that sent me is with me: the Father hath not left me alone; for I do always those things that please him."

But you must make it yours.

John 12:31 "Now is the judgment of this world: now shall the prince of this world be cast out. 32 And I, if I be lifted up from the earth, will draw all men unto me. 33 This he said, signifying what death he should die."

The judgment written was executed in the spirit. Gen 3:15 "And I (*Father God*) will put enmity between thee and the woman, and between thy seed and her seed; it (*Jesus of Nazareth*) shall bruise (*crush, politically remove from power*) thy head, and thou shalt bruise his heel."

When Jesus conquered the adversary and stripped him of his authority, in the mind of the Father, it was as though you had done it. Father looks at you as more than a conqueror for Him because of Jesus' victory. You are totally identified in and with Jesus in His victory over the devil.

In Jesus, you are seated beside the Father, the place of kings. In Jesus, you are lord over the devil and have authority over his works, to bring Heaven to Earth.

Col 2:12 "Buried with him in baptism, wherein also ye are risen with him through the faith of the operation of God, who hath raised him from the dead."

We are commanded to continually dwell on this spiritual reality to bring it to Earth for God. Not to just think on, but put our heart of affections, desires and wants in that seat of God's governing power in Jesus. Thus this is a key element of renewing our mind.

Col 3:1 "If ye then be risen with Christ, seek those things which are above, where Christ sitteth on the right hand of God. 2 Set your affection on things above, not on things on the earth. 3 For ye are dead, and your *zoe*/life is hid with Christ in God. 4 When Christ, who is our *zoe*/life, shall appear, then shall ye also appear with him in glory."

God now commands us to think like Jesus, from our position of His authority in Him.

You are Satan's master today, just as Jesus was when He rose from the dead.

Col 2:15 "And having spoiled principalities and powers, he made a shew of them openly, triumphing over them in it."

Jesus Conquered Satan for Us

Just as Jesus conquered the adversary, during His Earth walk, you can conquer him today.

Eph 3:9 "And to make all men see what is the fellowship of the mystery, which from the beginning of the world hath been hid in God, who created all things by Jesus Christ: 10 to the intent that now unto the principalities and powers in heavenly places might be known by the church the manifold wisdom of God, 11 according to the eternal purpose which he purposed in Christ Jesus our Lord: 12 in whom we have boldness and access with confidence by the faith of him."

This means your mastery over all the works of Satan.

Matt 28:18 "And Jesus came and spake unto them, saying, All power is given unto me in heaven and in earth. 19 Go ye therefore, and teach all nations, baptizing them in the name of the Father, and of the Son, and of the Holy Ghost: 20 teaching them to observe all things whatsoever I have commanded you: and, lo, I am with you alway, even unto the end of the world. Amen."

Luke 10:19 "Behold, I (*Jesus*) give unto you power (*authority, commission and the resources of Heaven*) to tread on serpents and scorpions, and over all the power (*ability, lordship*) of the enemy: and nothing shall by any means hurt you. 20 Notwithstanding in this rejoice not, that the spirits are subject unto you; but rather rejoice, because your names are written in heaven."

It means that you are expected to do the works that Jesus began.

This is the path to end fear, defeat and failure, for those who believe.

This was the beginning of a new era. It is time that we appreciated what Father God has done for us in Christ.

It is time that we appreciated what it means to be a member of the Body of Christ, that we appreciate the position in which He has placed us, the authority He has given us in the Name of Jesus and the calling we have been given.

When Jesus defeated Satan, it was our victory.

1 Cor 15:57 "But thanks be to God, which giveth us the victory through our Lord Jesus Christ. 58 Therefore, my *agape*/beloved brethren, be ye stedfast, unmoveable, always abounding in the work of the Lord, forasmuch as ye know that your labour is not in vain in the Lord."

We are now the righteous victors.

We are Satan's masters in Jesus, for God.

We are made the righteousness of God, so God can have free access to bring His Kingdom to Earth through us as fellowlaborers, or co-laborers, just as Jesus was. We are sanctified from our sin in Jesus, so sin no long presents a limitation on how much of God can move in us. The only valve is our soul. The more renewed our mind into these Redemption truths, the more God can be released through us into the Earth. We make the path of God's Salvation to the Earth. No longer is man waiting on God; instead, it is the opposite. God is waiting on man to write these

DISCOVERING OUR REDEMPTION

Redemption truths into our hearts and minds, so we can be about our Father God's business on Earth, as Jesus did.

James 4:7 "Submit yourselves therefore to God. Resist the devil, and he will flee from you. 8 Draw nigh to God, and he will draw nigh to you. Cleanse your hands, ye sinners; and purify your hearts, ye double minded."

We can now reign as kings in the realm of *zoe*/life through Jesus Christ, our risen Lord. (see Rom 5:21)

Satan cannot lord it over us any longer, if we stand against him.

1 Pet 5:8 "Be sober, be vigilant; because your adversary the devil, as a roaring lion, walketh about, seeking whom he may devour: 9 whom resist stedfast in the faith, knowing that the same afflictions are accomplished in your brethren that are in the world."

James 4:7 "Submit yourselves therefore to God. [*Fight the devil and not the people involved in any situation.*] Resist the devil, and he will flee from you."

Eph 6:11 "Put on the whole armour of God, that ye may be able to stand against the wiles of the devil. 12 For we wrestle not against flesh and blood, but against principalities, against powers, against the rulers of the darkness of this world, against spiritual wickedness in high places."

Eph 6:16 "Above all, taking the shield of faith, wherewith ye shall be able to quench all the fiery darts of the wicked. 17 And take the helmet of *soteria*/salvation, and the sword of the Spirit, which is the word of God: 18 praying always with all prayer and supplication in the Spirit, and watching thereunto with all perseverance and supplication for all saints."

With that shield of faith, we can conquer "all the fiery darts," the attacks of the devil, whether they be in thoughts, evil words, sickness, disease or any other form of death, fast or slow.

Satan cannot stand against us, as we hold on to, do not let go of, *lambano* our righteousness and the super-abundance of grace in Jesus: Rom 5:17 "For if by one man's offence death reigned (*as king, in inflicting death, in fast and slow forms, from murder to war, to disease to poverty*) by one; much more they which (*continually*) lambano/receive abundance of grace and of the gift of righteousness shall reign (*to bring Heaven to Earth*) in *zoe*/life by one, Jesus Christ.)"

2 Tim 2:1 "Thou therefore, my son, be strong in the grace that is in Christ Jesus."

Salvation, deliverance from the devil in this life, is by grace and not by works. Eph 2:5 "Even when we were dead in sins, hath quickened us together with Christ, (by grace ye are *sozo*/saved;) 6 and hath raised us up together, and made us sit together in heavenly places in Christ Jesus: 7 that in the ages to come he might shew the exceeding riches of his grace in his kindness toward us through Christ Jesus."

This, right now, starts the age of Salvation, Redemption and the Deliverance of God in Jesus. 2 Cor 6:1 "We then, as workers together with him, beseech you also

Jesus Conquered Satan for Us

that ye receive not the grace of God in vain. 2 (For he saith, I have heard thee in a time accepted, and in the day of *soteria*/salvation have I succoured thee: behold, now is the accepted time; behold, now is the day of *soteria*/salvation.)"

It only gets better as we *lambano* the abundance of grace and the gift of righteousness by faith in Jesus. John 6:28 "Then said they unto him, What shall we do, that we might work the works of God? 29 Jesus answered and said unto them, This is the work of God, that ye believe on him whom he hath sent."

The devil and his works are under our feet, as we believe that Jesus is who He said He was, and what God said He accomplished, and that He will help you understand and obey the Scriptures, to His glory.

Acts 4:10 "Be it known unto you all, and to all the people of Israel, that by the name of Jesus Christ of Nazareth, whom ye crucified, whom God raised from the dead, even by him doth this man (*healed of infantile paralysis at the Gate Beautiful*) stand here before you whole. 11 This is the stone which was set at nought of you builders, which is become the head of the corner. 12 Neither is there *soteria*/salvation in any other: for there is none other name under heaven given among men, whereby we must be *sozo*/saved."

Disease is under our feet, in the name of Jesus.

Sickness is under out feet, in the name of Jesus.

Early and untimely death is under our feet, in the name of Jesus.

Poverty, lack and anything else that is not the peace of God is under our feet, in the name of Jesus.

Isa 52:14 "As many were astonied at thee; his visage was so marred more than any man, and his form more than the sons of men: 15 so shall he sprinkle many nations; the kings shall shut their mouths at him [*this includes the devil and all his works*]: for that which had not been told them shall they see; and that which they had not heard shall they consider."

Isa 53:4 "Surely he hath *cabal*/borne our griefs, and *nasa*/carried our sorrows: yet we did esteem him stricken, smitten of God, and afflicted. 5 But he was wounded for our transgressions, he was bruised for our iniquities: the chastisement of our peace was upon him; and with his stripes we are healed."

The spirits behind the diseases and troubles of man are under our feet, in Jesus.

1 Pet 3:21 "... by the resurrection of Jesus Christ: 22 who is gone into heaven, and is on the right hand of God; angels and authorities and powers being made subject unto him."

Jesus is Lord over the devil and all his forces; our job is to enforce this victory, as His Body, just as if Jesus were here. He is not, but you, a member of His body, are.

Matt 28:18 "And Jesus came and spake unto them, saying, All power is given unto me in heaven and in earth. 19 Go ye therefore, and teach all nations, baptizing them in the name of the Father, and of the Son, and of the Holy Ghost: 20 teaching

DISCOVERING OUR REDEMPTION

them to observe all things whatsoever I have commanded you: and, lo, I am with you alway, even unto the end of the world. Amen."

We are to exercise this authority, just as Jesus taught the disciples, and as He demonstrated in His own walk. We are the peacemakers of God, speaking and delivering His peace, His Kingdom.

Acts 10:36 "The word which God sent unto the children of Israel, preaching peace by Jesus Christ: (he is Lord of all:) 37 that word, I say, ye know, which was published throughout all Judaea, and began from Galilee, after the baptism which John preached; 38 how God anointed Jesus of Nazareth with the Holy Ghost and with power: who went about doing good, and healing all that were oppressed (*under the active dominion, reign or lordship*) of the devil; for God was with him."

Just as God is with Jesus, so is He with us now, to enforce this triumph over the devil.

Rev 1:5 "... Jesus Christ, who is the faithful witness, and the first begotten of the dead, and the prince of the kings of the earth. Unto him that *agape*/loved us, and washed us from our sins in his own blood, ... 17 and he (*Jesus*) laid his right hand upon me, saying unto me, Fear not; I am the first and the last: 18 I am he that *zao*/liveth, and was dead; and, behold, I am *zao*/alive for evermore, Amen; and have the keys of hell and of death."

Jesus took these keys, the symbols of authority and power, and now wields them to bring Heaven to Earth though His Body (the church, the new-creation people) to the glory of God, our Father.

Father God did not have Jesus born of a virgin in the flesh, suffer and be crucified, become one with us and our sin and the curse, become death and submit to the devil, suffer beyond imagination in spirit and soul, and then be made alive in mortal combat in Hades, to defeat the devil, just so we could answer theological questions in a Bible study. He did it so: Rom 16:20 "And the God of peace shall bruise Satan under your feet shortly (*as shattered glass*). The grace of our Lord Jesus Christ be with you (*to think, know, be and do this*). Amen."

Eph 3:9 "And to make all men see what is the fellowship of the mystery, which from the beginning of the world hath been hid in God, who created all things by Jesus Christ: 10 to the intent that now unto the principalities and powers in heavenly places might be known by the church the manifold wisdom of God, 11 according to the eternal purpose which he purposed in Christ Jesus our Lord: 12 in whom we have boldness and access with confidence by the faith of him."

We are new-creation sons.

We are, like our Father, warriors. Ex 15:1 "Then sang Moses and the children of Israel this song unto the Lord, and spake, saying, I will sing unto the LORD, for he hath triumphed gloriously: the horse and his rider hath he thrown into the sea. 2 The LORD is my strength and song, and he is become my salvation: he is my God, and I will prepare him an habitation; my father's God, and I will exalt him. 3 The LORD is a man of war: the LORD is his name."

The Lord has destroyed our true enemy, just as He destroyed Pharaoh. Ex 15:1 "Then sang Moses and the children of Israel this song unto the LORD, and spake, saying, I will sing unto the LORD, for he hath triumphed gloriously: the horse and his rider hath he thrown into the sea."

This becomes our praise song to our Father: Ex 15:11 "Who is like unto thee, O LORD, among the gods? who is like thee, glorious in holiness, fearful in praises, doing wonders? 12 Thou stretchedst out thy right hand, the earth swallowed them. 13 Thou in thy mercy hast led forth the people which thou hast redeemed: thou hast guided them in thy strength unto thy holy habitation."

We are new-creation, *agape*/love warriors, the redeemed from sin and the curse of sin, who are masters of the devil and his works, servant to all men for our Father, who *agape*/loves them, and sons who act just like our Father, as Jesus did.

Luke 17:5 "And the apostles said unto the Lord, Increase our faith. 6 And the Lord said, If ye had faith as a grain of mustard seed, ye might say unto this sycamine tree, Be thou plucked up by the root, and be thou planted in the sea; and it should obey you. 7 But which of you, having a servant plowing or feeding cattle, will say unto him by and by, when he is come from the field, Go and sit down to meat? 8 And will not rather say unto him, Make ready wherewith I may sup, and gird thyself, and serve me, till I have eaten and drunken; and afterward thou shalt eat and drink? 9 Doth he thank that servant because he did the things that were commanded him? I trow not. 10 So likewise ye, when ye shall have done all those things which are commanded you, say, We are unprofitable servants: we have done that which was our duty to do."

When you walk just like Jesus, you, too, will say: "We are unprofitable servants: we have done that which was our duty to do."

There is no problem of faith because this is fact; it is done. Jesus is Lord of Heaven and Earth, and the devil is bruised, abolished, set to nought, as lord of the Earth. We are to enforce that on any work of the devil we see, for and with God.

You don't need faith for facts; you need faith that the spiritual facts will be made real on physical Earth. Eph 1:2 "Grace (*the blessing and ability of God*) be to you, and peace (*victory over the devil and his works in every work of faith*), from God our Father, and from the Lord Jesus Christ. 3 Blessed be the God and Father of our Lord Jesus Christ, who hath blessed us with all spiritual blessings in heavenly places in Christ."

We are His children; therefore all things are ours.

1 Cor 3:21 "… All things are yours."

My granddaughter came to visit one day and wanted to play in her old playhouse, but she saw in it spider webs, spiders and wasp nests. I had forgotten that, the week prior, my son had gone into the playhouse and fumigated it, so all the

DISCOVERING OUR REDEMPTION

wasps and spiders she saw were already dead. But she was terrified of the dead carcasses and thought they were alive. As I listened to her, she described them as alive, and she would not go into the playhouse. I went and spayed again, and then noticed that the insects were already dead, so I stopped spraying. All that really remained was for us to sweep them out. I showed her they were dead, and she happily started to clean her playhouse. In a similar way, the devil has been defeated, and all that remains is for us to sweep him and his works out.

Rev. Bill Johnson told a story on a video I saw in mid-2010. At a large department store, a little child, two years old, said, "Mommy, will Jesus heal that lady in the wheelchair?" Her Mom said, "Yes, He loves her too." So the little girl waddled over to the woman, put her hand on her, and commanded life, in the name of Jesus, just as she had seen her parents do. The woman got up healed. That devil was "swept out" by a two-year-old child. That is a sample of the measure of His victory for us.

In the same manner, a six-year-old prayed, and thirty minutes later a cancer fell off the face of a man (Liardon, p 415). These children saw and delivered the Kingdom of God. They "swept out" devils already defeated by their Lord.

We often make this too hard: Matt 18:2 "And Jesus called a little child unto him, and set him in the midst of them, 3 and said, Verily I say unto you, Except ye be converted, and become as little children, ye shall not enter into the kingdom of heaven. 4 Whosoever therefore shall humble himself as this little child, the same is greatest in the kingdom of heaven. 5 And whoso shall receive one such little child in my name receiveth me."

1 Pet 5:6 "Humble yourselves therefore under the mighty hand of God, that he may exalt you in due time: 7 casting all your care upon him; for he careth for you. 8 Be sober, be vigilant; because your adversary the devil, as a roaring lion, walketh about, seeking whom he may devour: 9 whom resist (*fight, sweep out*) stedfast in the faith, knowing that the same afflictions are accomplished in your brethren that are in the world."

For the one who trusts the Lord: Ps 91:1 "He that dwelleth in the secret place of the most High shall abide under the shadow of the Almighty. 2 I will say of the LORD, He is my refuge and my fortress: my God; in him will I trust."

To that one, the promise is: Ps 91:13 "Thou shalt tread upon the lion and adder: the young lion and the dragon shalt thou trample under feet." Lions, adders and dragons are names for the devil and his works.

Luke 10:18 "And he (*Jesus*) said unto them, I beheld Satan as lightning fall from heaven. 19 Behold, I give unto you power (*authority, commission and the resources of Heaven*) to tread on serpents and scorpions, and over all the power (*ability, works*) of the enemy (*Satan*): and nothing shall by any means hurt you. 20 Notwithstanding in this rejoice not, that the spirits are subject unto you; but rather rejoice, because

Jesus Conquered Satan for Us

your names are written in heaven." Snakes and spiders are also names for and examples of works of the devil.

Tread means to stomp until crushed and no power remains. Whether one step or a thousand, we are made for and equipped to destroy the works of the devil, as Jesus did, as we operate in the Word of God's grace and peace, through Jesus. Acts 10:36 "The word which God sent unto the children of Israel, preaching peace by Jesus Christ: (he is Lord of all:) 37 that word, I say, ye know, which was published throughout all Judaea, and began from Galilee, after the baptism which John preached; 38 how God anointed Jesus of Nazareth with the Holy Ghost and with power: who went about doing good, and healing all that were oppressed (*under the active dominion, reign and lordship*) of the devil; for God was with him." Peace means the devil's works are destroyed, abolished, crushed, gone and healed and God rules instead, i.e., His Kingdom is come.

This is how Father answers the prayer: Luke 11:2 "And he (*Jesus*) said unto them, When ye pray, say, Our Father which art in heaven, Hallowed be thy name. Thy kingdom come. Thy will be done, as in heaven, so in earth ... ." He answers by having us do what Jesus did.

We need not have faith for the things that are ours, and we should not proclaim our ignorance and unbelief by asking for what we already have. We can ask for wisdom to learn, understand and walk in it, but we should not ask for what we already have. For example, we have:

1 Cor 1:30 "But of him are ye in Christ Jesus, who of God is made unto us wisdom, and righteousness, and sanctification, and redemption."

1 Cor 2:16 "For who hath known the mind of the Lord, that he may instruct him? But we have the mind of Christ."

2 Cor 5:17 "Therefore if any man be in Christ, he is a new creature: old things are passed away; behold, all things are become new. 18 And all things are of God, who hath reconciled us to himself by Jesus Christ, and hath given to us the ministry of reconciliation; 19 to wit, that God was in Christ, reconciling the world unto himself, not imputing their trespasses unto them; and hath committed unto us the word of reconciliation. 20 Now then we are ambassadors for Christ, as though God did beseech you by us: we pray you in Christ's stead, be ye reconciled to God. 21 For he hath made him to be sin for us, who knew no sin; that we might be made the righteousness of God in him. 6:1 We then, as workers together with him, beseech you also that ye receive not the grace of God in vain. 2 (For he saith, I have heard thee in a time accepted, and in the day of *soteria*/salvation have I succoured thee: behold, now is the accepted time; behold, now is the day of *soteria*/salvation.)"

Eph 1:2 "Grace be to you, and peace, from God our Father, and from the Lord Jesus Christ. 3 Blessed be the God and Father of our Lord Jesus Christ, who hath blessed us with all spiritual blessings in heavenly places in Christ: 4 according as

DISCOVERING OUR REDEMPTION

he hath chosen us in him before the foundation of the world, that we should be holy and without blame before him in *agape*/love: 5 having predestinated us unto the adoption of children by Jesus Christ to himself, according to the good pleasure of his will, 6 to the praise of the glory of his grace, wherein he hath made us accepted in the *agape*/beloved. 7 In whom we have redemption through his blood, the forgiveness (*remission, obliteration, putting away and purging*) of sins, according to the riches of his grace."

Eph 1:13 "In whom ye also trusted, after that ye heard the word of truth, the gospel of your *soteria*/salvation: in whom also after that ye believed, ye were sealed with that holy Spirit of promise, 14 which is the earnest of our inheritance until the redemption of the purchased possession, unto the praise of his glory."

Eph 2:4 "But God, who is rich in mercy, for his great *agape*/love wherewith he *agape*/loved us, 5 even when we were dead in sins, hath quickened us together with Christ, (by grace ye are *sozo*/saved;) 6 and hath raised us up together, and made us sit together in heavenly places in Christ Jesus: 7 that in the ages to come he might shew the exceeding riches of his grace in his kindness toward us through Christ Jesus. 8 For by grace are ye *sozo*/saved through faith; and that not of yourselves: it is the gift of God: 9 not of works, lest any man should boast. 10 For we are his workmanship, created in Christ Jesus unto good works, which God hath before ordained that we should walk in them."

We are to dwell on these Redemption facts, to make our faith effectual in bringing the Kingdom of God to the Earth. Philem 6 "That the communication of thy faith may become effectual by the acknowledging of every good thing which is in you in Christ Jesus."

The devil is defeated.

Col 2:13 "And you, being dead in your sins and the uncircumcision of your flesh, hath he quickened together with him, having forgiven you all trespasses; 14 blotting out the handwriting of ordinances that was against us, which was contrary to us, and took it out of the way, nailing it to his cross; 15 and having spoiled (*overthrown, made of no effect, made impotent, destroyed, set to nought*) principalities and powers, he made a shew of them openly, triumphing over them in it."

A triumph is the celebration after the enemy is totally defeated. It is not a battle. It is when the battle or war has been won and the enemy is made captive in chains and marched behind the conqueror, as slave of the victor.

We do need faith to access the Word of God, to apply it and sweep out the devil and his works, to the glory of God, by faith in the body and blood of Jesus. We make our testimony those things we have in Jesus; we proclaim, trust in and rely upon "by His stripes (*on His body*) we were healed," and the power of that eternal, redeeming blood of Jesus; and we do not let our souls keep us confused in evil circumstances, but remain focused on what God says we are, who we are, and on Holy Spirit dwelling in us, as described in the Scriptures.

Rev 12:10 "And I heard a loud voice saying in heaven, Now is come *soteria*/salvation, and strength, and the kingdom of our God, and the power of his Christ: for the accuser of our brethren is cast down, which accused them before our God day and night. 11 And they (*the believers*) overcame him (*Satan*) by the blood of the Lamb, and by the word of their testimony; and they *agape*/loved not their *psuche*/lives (*souls*) unto the death."

Just as God gave the Promised Land to the people of Israel under Moses, our battle is against the devil and his lies and works. These are the giants and walled cities we are to fight, not people, and not God. But the devil and his works are not really giants, not when a two-year-old, a five-year-old or a ninety-year-old can pray and the devil's works be destroyed.

We do need an *agape*/love-warrior's attitude to enforce what God had given us in Jesus and Jesus has commanded us to do.

If you do not have that kind of righteous *agape*/love warrior attitude, ask Him for it, because it is what you are made for, and you can be sure you will never know true happiness and peace until you also can experience: Ps 91:13 "Thou shalt tread upon the lion and adder: the young lion and the dragon shalt thou trample under feet."

Let us thank God and then go out and enforce, by faith, working in *agape*/love, the fullness of this marvelous Redemption.

Confidence comes from knowing. Knowing comes from believing. Believing comes from repetition and persuasion from the Word of God. This process of repetition and persuasion is called abiding in the Word and renewing the mind into the Word of Christ.

John 15:5 "I am the vine, ye are the branches: he that abideth in me, and I in him, the same bringeth forth much fruit: for without me ye can do nothing. 6 If a man abide not in me, he is cast forth as a branch, and is withered; and men gather them, and cast them into the fire, and they are burned. 7 If ye abide in me, and my words abide in you, ye shall *aiteo*/ask (*require, demand and expect as due by convent promise*) what ye will, and it shall be done unto you. 8 Herein is my Father glorified, that ye bear much fruit; so shall ye be my disciples. 9 As the Father hath *agape*/loved me, so have I *agape*/loved you: continue ye in my *agape*/love. 10 If ye keep my commandments, ye shall abide in my *agape*/love; even as I have kept my Father's commandments, and abide in his *agape*/love."

1 John 3:23 "And this is his commandment, That we should believe on the name of his Son Jesus Christ, and *agape*/love one another, as he gave us commandment. 24 And he that keepeth his commandments dwelleth in him, and he in him. And hereby we know that he abideth in us, by the Spirit which he hath given us."

DISCOVERING OUR REDEMPTION

Luke 17:10 "So likewise ye, when ye shall have done all those things which are commanded you, say, We are unprofitable servants: we have done that which was our duty to do."

Jesus has defeated Satan; the strongman has been bound, and we are to spoil the devil's "goods." Matt 12:28 "But if I cast out devils by the Spirit of God, then the kingdom of God is come unto you. 29 Or else how can one enter into a strong man's house, and spoil his goods, except he first bind the strong man? and then he will spoil his house."

Jesus has bound the "strong man." Eph 4:7 "But unto every one of us is given grace according to the measure of the gift of Christ. 8 Wherefore he saith, When he ascended up on high, he led captivity *(Satan and sin)* captive *(bound and paraded captive in triumph)*, and gave gifts unto men."

Col 2:15 "And having spoiled principalities and powers, he *(Jesus)* made a shew of them *(Satan and his armies)* openly, triumphing over them in it."

1 Cor 2:6 "Howbeit we speak wisdom among them that are perfect: yet not the wisdom of this world, nor of the princes of this world, that come to nought *(dethroned, bruised, crushed, made ineffective)*."

Jesus now has all authority, and every work of the devil is a lie and a rebellion we are to destroy in the name of the Lord Jesus Christ. We are to set every captive free and destroy every evil work of the devil. Luke 10:19 "Behold, I give unto you power *(authority, commission and the resources of Heaven)* to tread on serpents and scorpions, and over all the *dunamis*/power *(ability and works)* of the enemy: and nothing shall by any means hurt you. 20 Notwithstanding in this rejoice not, that the spirits *[Satan and his abilities]* are subject unto you; but rather rejoice, because your names are written in heaven."

No wonder Jesus said: John 14:12 "Verily, verily, I *(Jesus)* say unto you, He that believeth on me, the works that I do shall he do also; and greater works than these shall he do; because I go unto my Father. 13 And whatsoever ye shall *aiteo*/ask *(require, demand and expect as due by covenant promise)* in my name, that will I do, that the Father may be glorified in the Son. 14 If ye shall *aiteo*/ask *(require, demand and expect as due by covenant promise)* any thing in my name, I will do it."

Rom 16:20 "And the God of peace shall bruise Satan under your feet *as shattered glass*. The grace of our Lord Jesus Christ be with you *(to will, be, think, speak and do this, just like Father God did in Jesus)*. Amen."

CHAPTER 14

JESUS BECAME OUR HIGH PRIEST

In Matthew 28:6, the angel said to the women who had come to finish the embalming of Jesus that Lord's Day morning: "Ye seek Jesus who was crucified; He is not here. He is risen. Come, see the place where the Lord lay."

He died a Lamb; He arose the Lord, High Priest of the New Creation.

When Jesus died as a lamb, that ended the need for any other animals to be sacrificed to shed blood for the sins of man. The Lamb of God had done His job. Through that blood, God could pass over the threshold of our flesh and enter into the spirit of man, by Holy Spirit. Before God could be with a man, but now He could dwell in man. This ended the blood sacrifices of the temple and replaced them with the onetime sacrifice of Jesus. John 1:29 "The next day John seeth Jesus coming unto him, and saith, Behold the Lamb of God, which taketh away the sin of the world."

The function of the Mosaic High Priest was to take the blood of animal sacrifices into the Holy of Holies and sprinkle in on the Mercy Seat to atone for the sins of the people. This was done once a year on the Day of Atonement. That animal blood did not remove sin; it only covered it. But it did remove the curse of sin, so blessing could flow. No one could enter that Most Holy Place and live, so access to God was limited to once a year and to one man at a time (the High Priest).

DISCOVERING OUR REDEMPTION

On the Day of Atonement the High Priest placed his hands on two goats. One was slain, and the blood placed on the High Priest and the Mercy Seat, representing the blood of Jesus to come. The second goat, known as the scapegoat, was led into the wilderness, outside the walls of Jerusalem, there to be killed by wild animals, as Jesus was to be slain by Gentiles, whom the Jews called dogs or animals. Heb 13:11 "For the bodies of those beasts, whose blood is brought into the sanctuary by the high priest for sin, are burned without the camp. 12 Wherefore Jesus also, that he might sanctify the people with his own blood, suffered without the gate."

Thus, Jesus was both the Lamb slain, this time not atoning for, but redeeming and propitiating the sins of mankind, and the Scapegoat, to bear all the punishment for the people, so that not only the Jews, but all men could live in health, prosperity and victory in battle over the devil and his works.

Jesus, as our High Priest, has entered into the Heavenly Holy Place, and His blood never dies, but continually washes mankind of sin. Therefore, as High Priest, Jesus is a constant reminder that by His blood we are redeemed from our sins and the curse of sin paid for 2000 years ago. That blood is still more than sufficient.

Under the Law of Moses, the High Priest was appointed by God to handle the sins of the nation of Israel. Jesus was appointed by God, under the order of Melchisedec, to handle the sins of the world, for all time—past, present and future.

Heb 7:14 "For it is evident that our Lord sprang out of Juda; of which tribe Moses spake nothing concerning priesthood. 15 And it is yet far more evident: for that after the similitude of Melchisedec there ariseth another priest, 16 who is made, not after the law of a carnal commandment, but after the power of an endless *zoe*/life. 17 For he testifieth, Thou art a priest for ever after the order of Melchisedec. 18 For there is verily a disannulling of the commandment going before for the weakness and unprofitableness thereof. 19 For the law made nothing perfect, but the bringing in of a better hope did; by the which we draw nigh unto God. 20 And inasmuch as not without an oath he was made priest: 21 (for those priests were made without an oath; but this with an oath by him that said unto him, The Lord sware and will not repent, Thou art a priest for ever after the order of Melchisedec:) 22 by so much was Jesus made a surety of a better testament. 23 And they truly were many priests, because they were not suffered to continue by reason of death: 24 but this man, because he continueth ever, hath an unchangeable priesthood."

This priesthood of Jesus is forever.

Heb 7:25 "Wherefore he is able also to *sozo*/save them to the uttermost that come unto God by him, seeing he ever *zao*/liveth to make intercession for them. 26 For such an high priest became us, who is holy, harmless, undefiled, separate from sinners, and made higher than the heavens; 27 who needeth not daily, as those high priests, to offer up sacrifice, first for his own sins, and then for the people's: for this he did once, when he offered up himself. 28 For the law maketh men high priests which have infirmity; but the word of the oath, which was since the law, maketh the Son, who is consecrated for evermore."

1 John 2:1 "My little children, these things write I unto you, that ye sin not. And if any man sin, we have an advocate with the Father, Jesus Christ the righteous: 2 and he is the propitiation for our sins: and not for ours only, but also for the sins of the whole world."

You may remember, from John 20, that Mary saw Him after His resurrection. When she discovered who He was, she fell at His feet.

He said to her, John 20:17 "Touch me not; for I am not yet ascended unto the Father: but go unto my brethren, and say to them, I ascend unto my Father and your Father, and my God and your God."

What did Jesus mean by this?

For one thing, He meant that He was not there at that particular time to bring in the Kingdom, the Rule of God, as a physical King, to restore the financial, military and political power of Israel. That would come later, but not right then. There would be no mighty armies or wonders of God to destroy the Roman legions. Jesus said the same thing when the disciples questioned Him just before He ascended into Heaven.

They had left their homes and business and risked all to join the Messiah's program. Their hope of achieving physical, financial, military and political power, in the same way as David and Solomon had, or even wealth and power as Abraham and Job had, or the destruction of armies, as with Hezekiah, was not what Father God intended. Yes, they could have those things, but not in the way they expected. They would not come by sword, but by Holy Spirit operating freely in the hearts of men.

As Jesus was departing, His disciples asked Him once again. Acts 1:6 "When they therefore were come together, they asked of him, saying, Lord, wilt thou at this time restore again the kingdom to Israel? 7 And he said unto them, It is not for you to know the times or the seasons, which the Father hath put in his own power. 8 But ye shall receive *dunamis*/power, after that the Holy Ghost is come upon you: and ye shall be witnesses unto me both in Jerusalem, and in all Judaea, and in Samaria, and unto the uttermost part of the earth." They would conquer the Earth for God and release the vast blessing, not with Jesus at the head of an army, but with Jesus dwelling comfortably in their hearts by Holy Spirit.

The events of the next several days after Jesus said, "Touch me not," to Mary Magdalene, tell us this did not mean that He was going right then to present His blood; it meant that she was not to become attached to His presence. He would not be physically on the Earth for much longer.

Note, the Scriptures do not say directly when Jesus carried His blood to the real Mercy Seat in Heaven.

DISCOVERING OUR REDEMPTION

The obvious choices are:
1. When Jesus took captivity captive and dead people resurrected and walked in Jerusalem after He rose from the dead. Matt 27:52 "And the graves were opened; and many bodies of the saints which slept arose, 53 and came out of the graves after his resurrection, and went into the holy city, and appeared unto many." But in the resurrection from the dead scriptures, it does not say Jesus ascended to Heaven.
2. Or it was when He ascended, to send back Holy Spirit.

When He warned Mary not to touch Him, Jesus specifically said He had not yet ascended to the Father. We assume the ascension was for the purpose of the propitiation and His coronation and glorification on the Throne of God. In Acts 1, it does say He ascended to His Father. From our perspective, we know that propitiating blood was placed on the true Mercy Seat and Jesus could sit down at the right hand of the Father, therefore, that job was done.

For us it is simple: Jesus is now our High Priest: Heb 9:11 "But Christ being come an high priest of good things to come, by a greater and more perfect tabernacle, not made with hands, that is to say, not of this building; 12 neither by the blood of goats and calves, but by his own blood he entered in once into the holy place, having obtained eternal redemption for us."

As the High Priest, Jesus took His own blood and carried it up to the Heavenly Holy of Holies and there presented it to God.

The sacrifice of Jesus is eternal, forever, beyond time.

The daily and annual sacrifices for daily and annual sin are gone. The one-time sacrifice of Jesus covers it all, not just for the Jews, but for all mankind—past, present and future.

Heb 7:26 "For such an high priest became us, who is holy, harmless, undefiled, separate from sinners, and made higher than the heavens; 27 who needeth not daily, as those high priests, to offer up sacrifice, first for his own sins, and then for the people's: for this he did once, when he offered up himself."

Heb 9:26 "For then must he often have suffered since the foundation of the world: but now once in the end of the world hath he appeared to put away sin by the sacrifice of himself. 27 And as it is appointed unto men once to die, but after this the judgment: 28 so Christ was once offered to bear the sins of many; and unto them that look for him shall he appear the second time without sin unto *soteria*/salvation."

That blood was accepted, and that red seal is upon the document of our Redemption. That blood ever lives on the true heavenly altar of God.

The blood of Jesus Christ, God's Son, is the eternal witness of His finished work for us, of our legal right to eternal *zoe* life, and sonship with all its privileges.

On the basis of that blood, we are more than conquerors. That blood is more than sufficient.

Jesus Became Our High Priest

Satan has no legal dominion over us. His dominion is utterly broken. That blood is more than sufficient.

Any dominion the devil exercises now is that of a rebel against God, and the ignorance and apathy of sin-conscious people. We are to enforce the victory of Jesus on the devil and his works and set the captives free. The blood is more than sufficient.

The tokens of that victory in Jesus are continually before the Father. The blood is more than sufficient.

Heb 7:22 "By so much also hath Jesus become the surety of a better covenant."

If you are in grave danger, or Satan is pressing hard upon you, or you see someone in need, you turn to your Father and His unfailing Word in the Scriptures, and you stir yourself in your rights and responsibilities, that are guaranteed on the ground of that blood, and you speak to that mountain and the devil behind it, and command it to go, in the name of Jesus, because the blood is more than sufficient.

Rev 12:11 "And they overcame him (*Satan*) because of the blood of the Lamb, and because of the word of their testimony, and *agape*/loved not their *psuche*/lives (*souls*) unto the death."

You have a legal right to the name of Jesus that casts out demons and breaks Satan's power.

You have a legal right to the name of Jesus that moves mountains and makes the blind to see.

John 16:23 "If ye shall *aiteo*/ask (*require, demand and expect as due by covenant promise*) anything of the Father, he will give it you in my name." RSV

All things are possible to you, because you are fully in the family. You have the perfect protection and the perfect access that the blood guarantees, to be about the Father's business.

That blood is more than sufficient!

You have the right to act just like Jesus and do what Father God would do if He were here.

Ps 103:1 "Bless the LORD, O my soul: and all that is within me, bless his holy name. 2 Bless the LORD, O my soul, and forget not all his benefits: 3 who forgiveth all thine iniquities; who healeth all thy diseases; 4 who redeemeth thy life from destruction; who crowneth thee with *chesed*/lovingkindness and *racham*/tender mercies; 5 who satisfieth thy mouth with good things; so that thy youth is renewed like the eagle's. 6 The LORD executeth righteousness and judgment for all that are oppressed.

"7 He made known his ways unto Moses, his acts unto the children of Israel. 8 The LORD is merciful and gracious, slow to anger, and plenteous in *chesed*/mercy. 9 He will not always chide: neither will he keep his anger for ever. 10 He hath not dealt with us after our sins; nor rewarded us according to our iniquities. 11 For as the heaven is high above the earth, so great is his *chesed*/mercy toward them that fear him. 12 As far as the east is from the west, so far hath he removed our transgressions from us. 13 Like as a father pitieth his children, so the LORD pitieth them that fear him. 14 For he knoweth our frame; he remembereth that we are dust."

Mark 16:15 "And he (*Jesus*) said unto them, Go ye into all the world, and preach the gospel to every creature. 16 He that believeth and is baptized shall be *sozo*/saved; but he that believeth not shall be damned. 17 And these signs shall follow them that believe; In my name shall they cast out devils; they shall speak with new tongues; 18 they shall take up serpents; and if they drink any deadly thing, it shall not hurt them; they shall lay hands on the sick, and they shall recover. 19 So then after the Lord had spoken unto them, he was received up into heaven, and sat on the right hand of God. 20 And they went forth, and preached everywhere, the Lord working with them, and confirming the word with signs following. Amen."

Heb 4:14 "Seeing then that we have a great high priest, that is passed into the heavens, Jesus the Son of God, let us hold fast our profession. 15 For we have not an high priest which cannot be touched with the feeling of our infirmities; but was in all points tempted like as we are, yet without sin. 16 Let us therefore come boldly unto the throne of grace, that we may *lambano*/obtain mercy (*kindness*), and find (*perceive*) grace to help in time of need."

Heb 2:14 "Forasmuch then as the children are partakers of flesh and blood, he also himself likewise took part of the same; that through death he might destroy him that had the power of death, that is, the devil; 15 and deliver them who through fear of death were all their lifetime subject to bondage. 16 For verily he took not on him the nature of angels; but he took on him the seed of Abraham. 17 Wherefore in all things it behoved him to be made like unto his brethren, that he might be a merciful and faithful high priest in things pertaining to God, to make reconciliation for the sins of the people. 18 For in that he himself hath suffered being tempted, he is able to succour them that are tempted."

As High Priest, Jesus is also our Advocate, ever in the face of the Father. 1 John 2:1 "My little children, these things write I unto you, that ye sin not. And if any man sin, we have an advocate with the Father, Jesus Christ the righteous: 2 and he is the propitiation for our sins: and not for ours only, but also for the sins of the whole world." *Advocate* means "one who is in the face of a king or judge for the benefit of another."

Heb 7:25 "Wherefore he (*Jesus*) is able also to *sozo*/save them to the uttermost that come unto God by him, seeing he ever *zao*/liveth to make intercession for them. 26 For such an high priest became us, who is holy, harmless, undefiled, separate from sinners, and made higher than the heavens."

Can God look on sin to know it is there? Yes! Can He be one with it? No! He had Jesus do that for Him. God defines sin as the absence of Himself, darkness, for

Jesus Became Our High Priest

He is light. But as He always has since the foundation of the Earth was laid, He sees all sin through the blood of Jesus. Before it was by faith, but now it is by fact. Jesus has died and is risen!

Thus, because Jesus is High Priest for the human race, every time Father God looks at us, He sees the face of Jesus and our Reconciliation. So Father only sees man through the blood of Jesus, though His own wisdom in Jesus, His righteousness in Jesus, His sanctification in Jesus, His Redemption in Jesus, His grace in Jesus and His peace in Jesus.

As our Advocate, Jesus' presence and His words ever proclaim that we are redeemed. 1 Cor 1:30 "But of him (*Father God*) are ye in Christ Jesus, who of God is made unto us wisdom, and righteousness, and sanctification, and redemption."

Heb 3:1 "Wherefore, holy brethren, partakers of the heavenly calling, consider the Apostle and High Priest of our profession, Christ Jesus." Because He is our High Priest, the Mercy Seat is propitiated, once for all time. As our Apostle, the one who carries our message, Jesus takes what we think, say and do in God's grace and truth, and proclaims them in Heaven, so Father's Kingdom can come to Earth.

No wonder Holy Spirit says: Heb 13:5 "Let your conversation be without covetousness; and be content with such things as ye have: for he hath said, I will never leave thee, nor forsake thee. 6 So that we may boldly say, The Lord is my helper, and I will not fear what man shall do unto me."

Chapter 15

Jesus Worked So the Veil Was Torn

When the veil of the temple was torn from top to bottom, God ended the Mosaic priesthood, the temple and anything that separated God from dwelling in and with men. The action of rending the veil was a God-action, not done by man. Through this act, God declared that the real veil, the body of Jesus, was more than sufficient to make the way for men to come to God, and no priesthood like Aaron's or the accompanying animal sacrifices were needed anymore.

Matt 27:50 "Jesus, when he had cried again with a loud voice, yielded up the ghost. 51 And, behold, the veil of the temple was rent in twain from the top to the bottom; and the earth did quake, and the rocks rent; 52 and the graves were opened; and many bodies of the saints which slept arose, 53 and came out of the graves after his resurrection, and went into the holy city, and appeared unto many."

Mark 15:37 "And Jesus cried with a loud voice, and gave up the ghost. 38 And the veil of the temple was rent in twain from the top to the bottom."

Luke 23:44 "And it was about the sixth hour, and there was a darkness over all the earth until the ninth hour. 45 And the sun was darkened, and the veil of the temple was rent in the midst. 46 And when Jesus had cried with a loud voice, he said, Father, into thy hands I commend my spirit: and having said thus, he gave up the ghost."

Jesus Worked So the Veil Was Torn

John 19:30 "When Jesus therefore had received the vinegar, he said, It is finished: and he bowed his head, and gave up the ghost."

Few understood the depth of what Jesus said about the temple. John 2:17 "And his disciples remembered that it was written, The zeal of thine house hath eaten me up. 18 Then answered the Jews and said unto him, What sign shewest thou unto us, seeing that thou doest these things?"

They were looking for signs, like manna from Heaven, water turning into blood or the land being covered with darkness. They wanted the signs of Moses, thinking they were greater because they could be seen by flesh-ruled men. But they missed the lesson: even these massive signs did not convert the Egyptians or that generation of Israelites that saw them.

Instead, Jesus said the issue is in the spirit of man and the way man accesses God: John 2:19 "Jesus answered and said unto them, Destroy this temple, and in three days I will raise it up. 20 Then said the Jews, Forty and six years was this temple in building, and wilt thou rear it up in three days? 21 But he spake of the temple of his body. 22 When therefore he was risen from the dead, his disciples remembered that he had said this unto them; and they believed the scripture, and the word which Jesus had said."

Jesus said He was going to remove the entire Mosaic system and, along with it, the priesthood, the Levites and anything else of the old system. In modern language, He said He was going to "lay off" thousands of temple related functionaries and suspend their functions and related businesses, such as money-changing and selling animals suitable for sacrifice.

Jesus said concerning the temple: Matt 23:38 "Behold, your house is left unto you desolate. 39 For I say unto you, Ye shall not see me henceforth, till ye shall say, Blessed is he that cometh in the name of the Lord." See also Luke 13:35.

At the death of Jesus, John recorded the words of Jesus as "It is finished." Luke recorded that He said "Father, into thy hands I commend my spirit: and having said thus, he gave up the ghost." Since one of the purposes of John's gospel was to fill in missing gaps, we can use the sequential logic of Jesus proclaiming "It is finished," then commending His spirit to God, and then giving up His ghost/spirit in death, i.e., separation of the spirit and soul from the body.

Even though Jesus was crucified (to kill Him), He left His body before it could no longer sustain Him. Death did not kill Jesus. Instead, Jesus entered into death by His own will. He gave up His life, to take it up again. He left His body, to go into mortal combat with the devil for all mankind, to please His Father.

John 10:17 "Therefore doth my Father *agape*/love me, because I lay down my *psuche*/life (*soul*), that I might take it again. 18 No man taketh it from me, but I lay it down of myself. I have power to lay it down, and I have power to take it again. This commandment have I received of my Father."

DISCOVERING OUR REDEMPTION

While the entire Bible has a chronology, it is not written to provide a chronological record. It is written to tell us what we need to know to know and walk successfully with God in our time. The exact details of the crucifixion vary slightly among the Gospels, as is expected for eye-witness recordings. The exact sequence is not as important as what occurred; otherwise Holy Spirit would have handled that detail more directly.

The synoptic gospels—Matthew, Mark and Luke—record the death of Christ (when He gave up His ghost or His spirit) and the fact that it was accompanied by miraculous signs. These signs were God speaking and confirming Jesus in the language of supernatural wonders. There was the sign of the rending of the veil in the Temple from top to bottom (Mt. 27:51; Mk. 15:38), and right down the middle (Luke 23:45).

Unlike Matthew and Mark, which place this event chronologically in their accounts, Luke places it after the three hours of darkness. Luke 23:44 "And it was about the sixth hour, and there was a darkness over all the earth until the ninth hour. 45 And the sun was darkened, and the veil of the temple was rent in the midst. 46 And when Jesus had cried with a loud voice, he said, Father, into thy hands I commend my spirit: and having said thus, he gave up the ghost."

The earthquake, the rending of the rocky cliffs, the opening of the tombs and the resurrection of many saints are only recorded in Matthew's gospel (27:51-53). Although the events have a certain order in Matthew's narrative (1. Jesus crying with a loud voice, 2. Jesus giving up His spirit from His body or flesh, 3. The rending of the veil, 4. An earthquake, 5. The rending of the rocks, 6. The opening of tombs, and 7. The Raising of dead saints), it is very likely most of these events occurred almost simultaneously, the moment that Jesus died. The last event, the resurrection of the saints to walk through Jerusalem, occurred after Jesus' resurrection.

The rending of the veil is not mentioned directly after the Gospels. The central element that is taught in the Epistles is that the covenant of Moses was superseded and replaced with the covenant of Jesus, and that the temple and all the related activities, sacrifices, jobs and culture were replace by the order of the New Covenant in Jesus. Thus, the rending of the veil is part of the process of removing or replacing the covenant of Moses.

Jesus even said the temple was to be a house of prayer. In the Jewish manner, people met daily for prayer at the temple, in homes or in synagogues. It usually took ten men to make a "prayer quorum," so prayer was by group as well as individual. Most prayer had the focus of the town and nation, not the individual. The temple, as a gathering place for prayer, was not destroyed by Jesus. The early disciples continued to go to the temple and synagogues for prayer, thanksgiving, praise, worship and scripture study until the Jews found ways to expel them.

JESUS WORKED SO THE VEIL WAS TORN

The real veil was not in the temple, but the flesh of Jesus. Heb 10:18 "Now where remission of these is (*sins and iniquities*), there is no more offering for sin (*in the physical temple or altars by a priesthood*). 19 Having therefore, brethren, boldness to enter into the (*true, heavenly or spiritual*) holiest by the blood of Jesus, 20 by a new and *zao*/living way, which he hath consecrated for us, through the veil, that is to say, his flesh ..."

When Jesus gave up His spirit, the temple veil was rent, showing that God had accepted the bodily sufferings of Jesus as the more-than-sufficient price for man to be healed. Isa 53:5 "But he was wounded for our transgressions, he was bruised for our iniquities: the chastisement of our peace was upon him; and with his stripes we are healed."

The first recorded healing in the Bible was when Abraham prayed and healed an entire household. Gen 20:17 "So Abraham prayed unto God: and God healed Abimelech, and his wife, and his maidservants; and they bare children. 18 For the Lord had fast closed up all the wombs of the house of Abimelech, because of Sarah Abraham's wife." This was healing even before the Old Testament, or Law of Moses.

Note, this prayer by Abraham is an example of household salvation. Abimelech got a partial salvation in healing, and we are promised the entire blessing—the Salvation of God for our households: Acts 16:31 "And they said, Believe on the Lord Jesus Christ, and thou shalt be *sozo*/saved, and thy house."

After Jesus struggled in the Garden with the path of God for Him to be made sin, under the dominion of Satan and no longer united in spirit with His Father, Jesus rose as a determined King ready to do battle on the path chosen for Him.

As men came to arrest Him, Jesus performed the last recorded healing under the Old Testament, the Mosaic Law. Luke 22:49 "When they (*the disciples*) which were about him saw what would follow, they said unto him, Lord, shall we smite with the sword? 50 And one of them smote the servant of the high priest, and cut off his right ear. 51 And Jesus answered and said, Suffer ye thus far. And he touched his ear, and healed him."

The first recorded healing in the Blood Covenant of Jesus is actually in the Gospels: Mark 16:15 "And he said unto them, Go ye into all the world, and preach the gospel to every creature. 16 He that believeth and is baptized shall be *sozo*/saved; but he that believeth not shall be damned. 17 And these signs shall follow them that believe; In my name shall they cast out devils; they shall speak with new tongues; 18 they shall take up serpents; and if they drink any deadly thing, it shall not hurt them; they shall lay hands on the sick, and they shall recover. 19 So then after the Lord had spoken unto them, he was received up into heaven, and sat on the right hand of God. 20 And they went forth, and preached everywhere, the Lord working with them, and confirming the word with signs following. Amen."

DISCOVERING OUR REDEMPTION

Father God has always been a healing God, so He did not leave man defenseless when the veil was rent. Instead, He made it a firm command that all believers, like Abraham, could heal the sick and set people free of the oppressions of the devil, just as Jesus had done.

1 Pet 2:24 "Who his own self bare our sins in his own body on the tree, that we, being dead to sins, should *zao*/live unto righteousness: by whose stripes ye were healed. 25 For ye were as sheep going astray; but are now returned unto the Shepherd and Bishop of your *psuche*/souls (*lives*)."

Peace means everything working, nothing missing and nothing broken, to the abundance and glory of God. This includes: Deut 28:6 "Blessed shalt thou be when thou comest in, and blessed shalt thou be when thou goest out. 7 The Lord shall cause thine enemies that rise up against thee to be smitten before thy face: they shall come out against thee one way, and flee before thee seven ways." Peace is not the lack of enemies, but knowing you will have victory in God, when enemies do arise.

This is the kind of warrior or police-officer peace Jesus gave the disciples: John 14:26 "But the Comforter, which is the Holy Ghost, whom the Father will send in my name, he shall teach you all things, and bring all things to your remembrance, whatsoever I have said unto you. 27 Peace I leave with you, my peace I give unto you: not as the world giveth, give I unto you. Let not your heart be troubled, neither let it be afraid."

Yes, with Holy Spirit, the Administrator of the power of God, we can bring peace, just like Jesus did. Acts 10:36 "The word which God sent unto the children of Israel, preaching peace by Jesus Christ: (he is Lord of all:) 37 that word, I say, ye know, which was published throughout all Judaea, and began from Galilee, after the baptism which John preached; 38 how God anointed Jesus of Nazareth with the Holy Ghost and with power: who went about doing good, and healing all that were oppressed (*under the active dominion, rule or lordship*) of the devil; for God was with him."

Here peace specifically means the ability to demonstrate the Kingdom of God by "doing good and healing all that were oppressed of the devil." And this is done by the power of Holy Spirit, released by right-thinking-and-acting men and women.

When Jesus gave up the ghost, His sufferings in the body were over. The physical part of Redemption was done, yet there still remained more in the spirit and soul aspects. Peace means removing every evil and hindrance unto full reconciliation, which includes everything in this life running like God wants, from government to how you feel when you get up in the morning. God's definition of peace is everything running like Heaven on Earth. All aspects, large and small, of this life were totally healed by the chastisement and Jesus' stripes.

Isa 53:5 "But he was wounded for our transgressions, he was bruised for our iniquities: the chastisement of our peace was upon him; and with his stripes we are healed." All of these cruel actions were on Jesus' body. As He received them, He took our entire curse due us, so, in the absence of the curse, we are whole and prosperous. This is God's declaration about healing. As far as God is concerned, the work of the cross declares all men are healed by the stripes of Jesus.

The stripes were given at the whipping post. The wounding, bruising and chastisement (every penalty for anything we do that is not just like God) were done starting with the binding in the Garden until Jesus gave up His spirit. All of this was suffering on and in His body. And it was sufficient. It was due each one of us, and Jesus took it, so men need never bear it, even though we are the ones who think, speak and do the iniquity that caused this suffering.

This is not about our love; it is about the fact that God *agape*/loves us, all mankind and each one individually, as a perfect father would, and all of mankind and each one individually was totally healed in Jesus by His stripes. We incurred the debt of sin, and Jesus paid it, to the pleasure of the Father. We incur the curse of sin, and Jesus suffered the curse fully for man.

Jesus obtained healing, blessing and prosperity greater than that available under the Law of Moses. That is, removal of the curse of sin for blessings in this life, as sin was atoned for by the sacrifice of the blood of animals. The suffering of Jesus' body and His blood was sufficient for all sins. So no longer would there ever need to be another blood sacrifice of any kind. The ordinances specifying the temple and the rituals were done away by God. There was no longer a need for a special priesthood made up of the only ones allowed to access God for blessing.

The atonement of Moses was superseded by the propitiation of Jesus in a better and greater covenant. It is as if with the death of Jesus, when His spirit and soul left His body and was carried to Hades, all that could be given in forgiveness and blessing under the Old, or replaced, Testament, was fully released and, thus, the temple was no longer necessary for that purpose. The physical blessing of Moses, as administered in the temple, were fully realized, and now Jesus was would go and make the new creation, in a renewed (the meaning of the Greek word *kainos is* renewed or restored to newness) and better covenant, possible.

2 Cor 3:5 "Not that we are sufficient of ourselves to think any thing as of ourselves; but our sufficiency is of God; 6 who also hath made us able ministers of the new testament; not of the letter, but of the spirit: for the letter killeth, but the spirit giveth *zoe*/life. 7 But if the ministration of death, written and engraven in stones (*under Moses*), was glorious, so that the children of Israel could not stedfastly behold the face of Moses for the glory of his countenance; which glory was to be done away: 8 how shall not the ministration of the spirit (*in the covenant of Jesus*) be rather glorious? 9 For if the ministration of condemnation be glory (*Holy Spirit empowered blessing and prosperity, rivers made dry to cross over, giants killed, and the legendary wisdom and wealth of Solomon*), much more doth the ministration of righteousness (*in*

DISCOVERING OUR REDEMPTION

Jesus) exceed in glory (*making possible Heaven to come to Earth through new creation people, with indwelling Holy Spirit*). 10 For even that which was made glorious had no glory in this respect (*the glory under Moses is as if it were nothing compared to the glory of Holy Spirit released, under Jesus*), by reason of the glory that excelleth. 11 For if that which is done away (*of the covenant of Moses*) was glorious, much more that which remaineth (*of the covenant in Jesus*) is glorious."

Acts 13:38 "Be it known unto you therefore, men and brethren, that through this man is preached unto you the forgiveness (*remission, removal and putting away*) of sins: 39 and by him all that believe are justified from all things, from which ye could not be justified by the law of Moses."

Heb 8:5 "Who serve unto the example and shadow of heavenly things, as Moses was admonished of God when he was about to make the tabernacle: for, See, saith he, that thou make all things according to the pattern shewed to thee in the mount. 6 But now hath he (*Jesus*) obtained a more excellent ministry, by how much also he is the mediator of a better covenant, which was established upon better promises. 7 For if that first covenant (*of Moses*) had been faultless, then should no place have been sought for the second (*in Jesus*)."

Heb 12:24 "And to Jesus the mediator of the *kainos*/new covenant, and to the blood of sprinkling, that speaketh better things than that of Abel."

The sins of the human race were remitted, purged, obliterated, and put away by the one sacrifice of Jesus. Heb 9:24 "For Christ is not entered into the holy places made with hands, which are the figures of the true; but into heaven itself, now to appear in the presence of God for us: 25 nor yet that he should offer himself often, as the high priest entereth into the holy place every year with blood of others; 26 for then must he often have suffered since the foundation of the world: but now once in the end of the world hath he appeared to put away sin by the sacrifice of himself. 27 And as it is appointed unto men once to die, but after this the judgment: 28 so Christ was once offered to bear the sins of many … ."

Jesus gave His body for healing and, when His spirit was "rent" from His body and He died, the fullness of physical healing was fully paid for. Isa 53:4 "Surely he hath *nasa*/borne our griefs (*infirmities*), and *cabal*/carried our sorrows (*sicknesses*): yet we did esteem him stricken, smitten of God, and afflicted. 5 But he was wounded for our transgressions, he was bruised for our iniquities: the chastisement of our peace was upon him; and with his stripes we are healed."

That healing included Jew and Gentile, as one man before God. Eph 2:13 "But now in Christ Jesus ye who sometimes were far off are made nigh by the blood of Christ. 14 For he is our peace, who hath made both one, and hath broken down the middle wall of partition between us; 15 having abolished in his flesh the enmity, even the law of commandments contained in ordinances; for to make in himself of twain one new man, so making peace; 16 and that he might reconcile both unto

Jesus Worked So the Veil Was Torn

God in one body by the cross, having slain the enmity thereby: 17 and came and preached peace to you which were afar off, and to them that were nigh. 18 For through him we both have access by one Spirit unto the Father."

In Jesus' flesh, He abolished the curse of the law, the law of enmity, the law that says you sin and you die from the curse, and He did it for all men.

In His flesh, Jesus abolished the separation between men who were Jews (near) and Gentiles (far).

Isa 57:18 "I have seen his ways, and will heal him: I will lead him also, and restore comforts unto him and to his mourners. 19 I create the fruit of the lips; Peace, peace to him that is far off, and to him that is near, saith the Lord; and I will heal him."

So, not just Jews, but all men were included in the propitiation of Jesus by the cross. 1 John 2:1 "My little children, these things write I unto you, that ye sin not. And if any man sin, we have an advocate with the Father, Jesus Christ the righteous: 2 and he is the propitiation for our sins: and not for ours only, but also for the sins of the whole world."

When we take the Lord's Supper, we apply this truth to our bodies, and we are healed. 1 Cor 11:23 "For I have received of the Lord that which also I delivered unto you, That the Lord Jesus the same night in which he was betrayed took bread: 24 and when he had given thanks, he brake it, and said, Take, eat: this is my body, which is broken (*lacerated*) for you: this do in remembrance of me."

Do it wrong, and you will stay sick, you will not be healed by the Lord and will stay under the curse of the law: 1 Cor 11:28 "But let a man examine himself, and so let him eat of that bread, and drink of that cup. 29 For he that eateth and drinketh unworthily, eateth and drinketh damnation to himself, not discerning the Lord's body (*that was broken for your healing and physical peace, also releasing the blood of Jesus*). 30 For this cause (*failure to properly apply, in faith, to your present condition, the propitiation of Jesus, as described in Isaiah 53 and the Gospels*) many are weak and sickly among you, and many sleep. 31 For if we would judge ourselves, we should not be judged. 32 But when we are judged, we are chastened of the Lord, that we should not be condemned with the world."

So, instead of going to the temple to get healed, you can take Communion wherever you are and get the same result.

In this way, God removed the need for a physical temple. Every person could get healed, not through the blood of animals in a temple sacrifice, but through the breaking of the bread and judging their physical ailments and limitations, their poverty and lack, and anything else that is not the peace of God, judging any and all evil on Jesus in His sacrifice, and receiving the healing and blessing, as you eat the bread, knowing "by His stripes we are healed." This is believing God for your healing, based on the onetime sacrifice of Jesus, for Father God to heal His family, mankind.

DISCOVERING OUR REDEMPTION

This now could happen anywhere men would remember the Lord's death in the Lord's Supper and judge themselves rightly in Jesus. No temple or building or a special priesthood was required, just faith in the work of God by the cross, by the breaking of bread and drinking of wine.

The Hebrew word translated *worship* has within it the meaning of how you function in this Earth. It means to bow down on the ground in homage and surrender before one who is greater. The same word is also translated as *serve*, meaning how you live your life before and honoring and in agreement with the presence of God. So worship has two aspects: one, in some sort of ceremony or outward actions before God, and, second, in how you live your life before and in God. Men may focus on the temple or church worship, but that is not the full meaning of a meaningful worship to God.

The Greek word *zoe*, translated as life or eternal life, means the life force that you are operating under and in, as shown in what thoughts you allow and ponder on, what imaginations you accept and dwell on, your dreams, hopes and desires, what gives you pleasure, satisfaction and peace, what words you speak and agree with, and what you do and do not do. This is very similar to the meaning of the original language words translated as *worship*, *serve*, and to *fear* God. They are all related.

Jesus spoke to the woman at the well: John 4:19 "The woman saith unto him, Sir, I perceive that thou art a prophet. 20 Our fathers worshipped in this mountain; and ye say, that in Jerusalem is the place where men ought to worship. 21 Jesus saith unto her, Woman, believe me, the hour cometh, when ye shall neither in this mountain, nor yet at Jerusalem, worship the Father. 22 Ye worship ye know not what: we know what we worship: for *soteria*/salvation (*the release of bondages to the devil, danger and lack, so that Heaven comes to dwell on Earth*) is of the Jews. 23 But the hour cometh, and now is, when the true worshippers shall worship the Father in spirit and in truth: for the Father seeketh such to worship him. 24 God is a Spirit: and they that worship him must worship him in spirit and in truth."

Here Jesus indicated that place would no longer define where men would worship God. Worship was now entirely within the spirit of man. The key aspect of the temple was this: it was where the name of God resided. Now, however, that name rests within the Christian. An earthly place of worship is simply a location where multiple people come to express the ceremonial aspects of worship in individual or group thanksgiving, praise, rejoicing, the ministering of alms, the helping of widows and orphans and other physical needs, public Bible reading and proclaiming the Gospel or teaching the Bible, but its effectiveness is dependent upon whether or not you are operating in the Spirit of Christ. It has always been God's desire that men walk before Him in every aspect of life.

Jesus Worked So the Veil Was Torn

When the temple veil was rent, God was making a formal declaration: This place is no longer the access to God for forgiveness and blessing or release of Holy Spirit to do good. This meaning was included in the rending of the true veil, Christ's body, as it was manifested in the rending of the veil of the temple.

God would no longer deal with men through a physical building or animal sacrifices, but He still had a priesthood of the believers. A priest is one who is appointed by God and goes from the physical to the spiritual to get spiritual benefits or effects released back into the physical world. So a priest goes to God to remove sins and the curse of sin and to get blessing for men. When done in faith, this produced the great blessings that Abraham, King David and King Solomon enjoyed.

In the New Testament, believers (individually and corporately) are the temple of God. Inside Christians is where God now dwells, not just His name, but Himself by Holy Spirit. 1 Cor 3:16 "Know ye not that ye are the temple of God, and that the Spirit of God dwelleth in you?"

2 Cor 6:16 "And what agreement hath the temple of God with idols? for ye are the temple of the *zao*/living God; as God hath said, I will dwell in them, and walk in them; and I will be their God, and they shall be my people."

1 Cor 6:19 "What? know ye not that your body is the temple of the Holy Ghost which is in you, which ye have of God, and ye are not your own?"

Eph 2:20 "And are built upon the foundation of the apostles and prophets, Jesus Christ himself being the chief corner stone; 21 in whom all the building fitly framed together groweth unto an holy temple in the Lord: 22 in whom ye also are builded together for an habitation of God through the Spirit."

The believer being a temple and a priest means wherever you go, God goes with you, and God is immediately accessible for you and through you. Do this right, and wherever you go there will be a "move of God," and whatever you do will be a "move of God." This shows our potential, or the hope of glory of Christ, within each Christian. We are to take the needs of ourselves, our families, other Christians and all people and get God's blessings for them, by His Word of reconciliation, in Jesus.

As priests, we are to be organs of thanksgiving, praise, worship, prayer and communication for and about God. 1 Pet 2:5 "Ye also, as *zao*/lively stones, are built up a spiritual house, an holy priesthood, to offer up spiritual sacrifices, acceptable to God by Jesus Christ. ... 9 But ye are a chosen generation, a royal priesthood, an holy nation, a peculiar people; that ye should shew forth the praises of him who hath called you out of darkness into his marvellous light." This means you are to be continually thanking and praising God and showing forth, in signs and wonders, His goodness and His *agape*/love.

As an individual temple of God, we are also houses of prayer. Matt 21:13 "And (*Jesus*) said unto them (*concerning the temple*), It is written, My house shall be called

DISCOVERING OUR REDEMPTION

the house of prayer; but ye have made it a den of thieves. 14 And the blind and the lame came to him in the temple; and he healed them."

In verse 13, Jesus defines the purpose of the temple as a house of prayer; in verse 14, He shows one of the main purposes of that prayer, getting physical healing, which is deliverance from the oppressions of the devil for people in need of it. As the temple of God, we are also to be sources of God-level healing.

Jesus gave the Parable of the Good Samaritan both to show the priests of His day their true mission and also where they were falling short. Another meaning for the word *righteousness*, besides total acceptance, as if you had never sinned or will ever sin again, is "acts of kindness," or "propensity to do only good deeds, as God would." Healing is an act of God's *chesed* kindness.

For us today, we, as kings and priests for and of God, we are not to walk below our calling, but to rise up into that calling. We have more than the saints of the Old Testament did. We have a better and greater covenant, and we have indwelling Holy Spirit, who sees all men as oppressed by the one who only comes to steal, kill and destroy. As we walk in the "hope of our calling," we will not pass by people in need, but do even more for them with our greater resources and abilities.

Luke 10:29 "But he, willing to justify himself, said unto Jesus, And who is my neighbour? 30 And Jesus answering said, A certain man went down from Jerusalem to Jericho, and fell among thieves, which stripped him of his raiment, and wounded him, and departed, leaving him half dead. 31 And by chance there came down a certain priest that way: and when he saw him, he passed by on the other side. 32 And likewise a Levite, when he was at the place, came and looked on him, and passed by on the other side. 33 But a certain Samaritan, as he journeyed, came where he was: and when he saw him, he had compassion on him, 34 and went to him, and bound up his wounds, pouring in oil and wine, and set him on his own beast, and brought him to an inn, and took care of him. 35 And on the morrow when he departed, he took out two pence, and gave them to the host, and said unto him, Take care of him; and whatsoever thou spendest more, when I come again, I will repay thee. 36 Which now of these three, thinkest thou, was neighbour unto him that fell among the thieves? 37 And he said, He that shewed mercy on him. Then said Jesus unto him, Go, and do thou likewise."

We are in a better covenant with better promises and much greater facts of Redemption. We can do the man-level acts of mercy, as did the Good Samaritan, or we can do God-level acts and divinely heal the sick, as Jesus did.

Any believer can proclaim the forgiveness of sin in Jesus over anyone. John 20:23 "Whose soever sins ye remit, they are remitted unto them; and whose soever sins ye retain, they are retained." Not only can you break the power of the devil in sin over anyone, including yourself and your family, but if you do not remit their sins, by your silence of either not directly remitting their sin or not telling them of the remission of sins in Jesus, you leave them in their sin and the effect of the curse of the law, and the kingdom of darkness remains intact, with the devil lording it over God's legally redeemed people. This is the opposite of the *chesed*, grace or lovingkindness of God.

A simple way to handle this is to say, "God Bless you." *Bless* means to release Holy Spirit to do what He wants and is best for them right now, if you do not direct it otherwise. By your intention, this can include breaking the power of the devil over them, getting them healed and remitting any sins they may have committed. You can say all this in a blessing or prayer either out loud, under your breath, or in intentional attitude, as you say "God Bless you." [Note: In my own experience, I have seen God heal people by just shaking their hand and saying "God Bless you," with this kind of intentionality. In these cases, I am actually commanding a blessing and then I let Holy Spirit sort it out. I am a Christian, and this is what I am made to do. 1 Pet 3:9 "Not rendering evil for evil, or railing for railing: but contrariwise blessing; knowing that ye are thereunto called, that ye should inherit a blessing." Rom 12:14 "Bless them which persecute you: bless, and curse not."]

Sin, sickness and forgiveness are so closely related that when a mature one (an elder, or one able to release healing life) ministers healing, any sins not confessed are also forgiven. James 5:14 "Is any sick among you? let him call for the elders (*mature ones, those with enough knowledge and attitude to get the job done right*) of the church; and let them pray over him, anointing him with oil in the name of the Lord: 15 and the prayer of faith shall *sozo*/save the sick, and the Lord shall raise him up; and if he have committed sins, they shall be forgiven him."

Bless means to speak good things that happen. When a king blesses, good things happen. You walk and cooperate in the benefit of the king's blessing, if you believe him, and enforce that blessing on and by the king's government, against all resistors to that decree. To bless in the name of the Lord, or the blessing of God, is Holy Spirit moving upon your thoughts and words to do good for man. This is the job of every priest, which means every Christian.

To bless the name of the Lord means that it is not taken in vain, and those do who use it grow in faith and, thus, release Holy Spirit (the source of the *dunamis* power of God) in that name. So for healing, you could say "I bless you, in the name of Jesus" or "Be healed, in the name of Jesus." The potential for healing is in both expressions. It depends on us, not God.

This blessing the name of the Lord is part of the "Our Father." Matt 6:9 "After this manner therefore pray ye: Our Father which art in heaven, Hallowed be thy name. 10 Thy kingdom come. Thy will be done in earth, as it is in heaven." So the first part of this prayer is blessing the name of the Lord and then, in verse 10, praying that His Kingdom come and reign on Earth, as seen in the ministry of Jesus.

DISCOVERING OUR REDEMPTION

This is the same as God taught through the Psalms. Ps 145:1 "I will extol thee, my God, O king; and I will bless thy name for ever and ever. 2 Every day will I bless thee; and I will praise thy name for ever and ever. 3 Great is the Lord, and greatly to be praised; and his greatness is unsearchable. 4 One generation shall praise thy works to another, and shall declare thy mighty acts."

In verse 1 of Psalm 145, we are encouraged and told that one of our jobs, now and forever, is to bless the name of the Lord and to bless the Lord Himself. The name of the Lord is how we bring Heaven to Earth. To bless the Lord is how we maintain the Kingdom, or presence, of God. Continually blessing is one foundation of our mission, as kings and priests of God, as proclaimed here and as commanded by Jesus in the "Our Father." Ps 145:3 is a praise of God and verse 4 is a proclamation, command and prophecy that every generation should do this. [Note: prayer journals and diaries with answers are great for this.]

This mix of prophecy, praise and command is found throughout this psalm and also throughout the Bible. This is not just the job of mature Christians, those who walk just like Jesus, but any Christian, no matter how imperfect their current walk. Doing this daily, or better yet, hourly is one of the ways to renew our minds, to purge any iniquity from our hearts or minds.

All sins of mankind were remitted in Jesus 2000 years ago, yet we still sin, until we are walking exactly like Jesus walked. 1 John 2:1 "My little children, these things write I unto you, that ye sin not. And if any man sin, we have an advocate with the Father, Jesus Christ the righteous: 2 and he is the propitiation for our sins: and not for ours only, but also for the sins of the whole world. 3 And hereby we do know that we know him, if we keep his commandments. 4 He that saith, I know him, and keepeth not his commandments, is a liar, and the truth is not in him. 5 But whoso keepeth his word, in him verily is the *agape*/love of God perfected: hereby know we that we are in him. 6 He that saith he abideth in him ought himself also so to walk, even as he walked."

1 John 5:2 "By this we know that we *agape*/love the children of God, when we *agape*/love God, and keep his commandments. 3 For this is the *agape*/love of God, that we keep his commandments: and his commandments are not grievous."

The issue is not that we are perfect, but will we agree with God that when we sinned we did something that cost Jesus His life, that God cursed Jesus for, and, through Him, healed us of 2000 years ago. Or will we be like Adam, who blamed God for giving him a wife who led him into sin. If God counted your sins, then you could never have Holy Spirit dwelling in you.

When a person becomes a biblical Christian, a new creation being, his spirit is born again, but his soul (his heart, mind, will and emotions) is not born again. He gets a part of his heart circumcised, and Holy Spirit dwells in his spirit and in that circumcised region of his heart. But all parts of his soul need to be renewed or reprogrammed so the devil's ways are no longer his ways. When we sin, it is a soul (heart, mind, will and emotions) problem, and must be dealt with to clear our soul. So the issue with God, in this life, is the state of your soul and sin.

If we do not agree with God over our sins, then we will reap the curse of what we sow. This reaping is not an active judgment of God, but a simple consequence of unconfessed sin and the law of sowing and reaping. It is a judgment, just as gravity is a judgment. Ignore the law of gravity and jump off a high cliff, and you will have to deal with the consequences. Sin and deal with the consequences, or walk in the fruit of sin, the curse of sin. We can remove the curse (the reaping of the negative consequences of sin, the curse of the law) though confession and right communion in the Lord's Supper.

The issue with God is not that we sin, but will we agree with Him that we sinned and that it was totally healed in Jesus. Failure in either part, agreeing that it was sin or removing the curse unto healing, will cause us to reap the evil that we sow.

This is the message of God: 1 John 1:5 "This then is the message which we have heard of him, and declare unto you, that God is light, and in him is no darkness at all. 6 If we say that we have fellowship with him, and walk in darkness, we lie, and do not the truth: 7 but if we walk in the light, as he is in the light, we have fellowship one with another, and the blood of Jesus Christ his Son cleanseth us from all sin. 8 If we say that we have no sin, we deceive ourselves, and the truth is not in us. 9 If we confess our sins, he is faithful and just to forgive us our sins, and to cleanse us from all unrighteousness. 10 If we say that we have not sinned, we make him a liar, and his word is not in us. 2:1 My little children, these things write I unto you, that ye sin not. And if any man sin, we have an advocate with the Father, Jesus Christ the righteous: 2 and he is the propitiation for our sins: and not for ours only, but also for the sins of the whole world."

Heb 7:25 "Wherefore he is able also to *sozo*/save them to the uttermost that come unto God by him, seeing he ever *zao*/liveth to make intercession for them."

Father God is faithful and just to forgive because He already did that in Jesus 2000 years ago and wants you to know it. He cannot lie, and He cannot and will not repeal the work of Jesus, the Mighty Arm of God. If He did repeal it, then the foundation of the Earth would be destroyed, and He will not do that, as the Earth is the Lord's and is His footstool. So the proper response of the believer is: "Thank You," and not "Please forgive me," as if Jesus had never died and obtained remittance, forgiveness and healing 2000 years ago.

Amazingly, as we minister healing for sickness, unconfessed sins are forgiven, even if the person does not confess them. Faith in the blood of Jesus applied in either forgiveness or healing is more than sufficient to heal the situation. God's attitude seems to be that the gratitude for being healed will allow Holy Spirit to deal

DISCOVERING OUR REDEMPTION

with the corrupt attitudes of heart that led to sin as the person walks in gratitude over the healing and tells others of the goodness of God. Rom 2:4 "Or despisest thou the riches of his goodness and forbearance and longsuffering; not knowing that the goodness of God leadeth thee to repentance?" Prov 16:6 "By *chesed*/mercy (*kindness, grace*) and truth iniquity is purged: and by the fear of the Lord men depart from evil." Certainly being healed is a grace, and the truth that leads to healing often starts with the phrase "Jesus is Lord."

One observation seems to be that part of this is based on our intentions when we minister. Minister healing, and if there is any sin, it is forgiven. Forgive sin without the attitude of healing, and healing may still be needed. This is why taking communion properly is so important, as both healing and forgiveness are covered, when done properly. The evidence of doing it right is in the health and long life of the Christian.

1 Cor 11:29 "For he that eateth and drinketh unworthily, eateth and drinketh damnation to himself, not discerning the Lord's body. 30 For this cause many are weak and sickly among you, and many sleep (*die early or are asleep in sin and need revival*). 31 For if we would judge ourselves, we should not be judged. 32 But when we are judged, we are chastened of the Lord, that we should not be condemned with the world."

This is not an active judgment of God, as many think. The Lord typically holds back judgment, when we sin, to give time for repentance, but sin still is sowing to the flesh, and if left unresolved in Jesus, leads to reaping corruption and death.

Gal 6:7 "Be not deceived; God is not mocked: for whatsoever a man soweth, that shall he also reap. 8 For he that soweth to his flesh shall of the flesh reap corruption; but he that soweth to the Spirit shall of the Spirit reap *zoe*/life everlasting. 9 And let us not be weary in well doing: for in due season we shall reap, if we faint not. 10 As we have therefore opportunity, let us do good unto all men, especially unto them who are of the household of faith."

God sees sin and the consequence of sin as all being one thing and never separates the one from the other. Often, in the Scriptures where God is talking about sin or iniquity, you have to read closely to see if it is referring to the thoughts that lead to sin, the act of the sin, the curse of sin, or the spreading of corruption for failure to properly and fully deal with sin. For teaching purposes, we may separate them, but it is like the human neck or wrist. You can see the head and the body, but where the neck ends and the body starts is hard to determine.

The sins of the human race are remitted, put away, by the blood Jesus, a one-time act completed 2000 years ago, but we still need to apply it, in faith, per our current situation, to remain in agreement with God. We have union eternally, but we must maintain communion/fellowship/relationship now or face our failure on the Day of Judgment.

Jesus Worked So the Veil Was Torn

Notice: The Christians in 1 Cor 11 had their sins remitted, were born again, with Holy Spirit indwelling, but still suffered the effects of the law of sin and death, by not properly applying, in faith, the work of the body and blood of Jesus to their lives. Failure to address our sins when they occur gives place to the devil to put the law of sin and death in motion. God gave the Earth to man, but if we will not maintain it in Jesus; the devil will maintain his world system on us. That is God's judgment. 1 Cor 11:31 "For if we would judge ourselves, we should not be judged. 32 But when we are judged, we are chastened of the Lord, that we should not be condemned with the world."

The law of sin and death is a subset, or a portion, of the law of sowing and reaping. The law of sin and death is composed of the negative aspects. The law of the Spirit of zoe/life in Jesus is the blessing part. Applying our salvation in Jesus, by one of several means, directly attacks the devil and sets the sinner free from the law of sin and death, and into the blessing of God, for healing or recovery from the curse of sin.

The act of sin is sowing to the flesh and releases death into our lives. The act of receiving our Redemption in the blood of Jesus unto healing is an act of the Spirit and produces zoe/life, which includes restoration and more prosperity. Failure to sow to the Spirit leaves us in death, the consequence of sin.

Christians are warned that the law of sowing and reaping also applies to them, and the negative consequence(s) of wrong sowing is just as evil for Christians as it is for non-Christians in this life. The Christian has eternal salvation, but how much of that salvation we walk in now is determined by how much we sow to the Spirit and not the flesh now, in this life. We control the sowing, not God.

Gal 6:7 "Be not deceived; God is not mocked: for whatsoever a man soweth, that shall he also reap. 8 For he that soweth to his flesh shall of the flesh reap corruption; but he that soweth to the Spirit shall of the Spirit reap zoe/life everlasting. 9 And let us not be weary in well doing: for in due season we shall reap, if we faint not. 10 As we have therefore opportunity, let us do good unto all men, especially unto them who are of the household of faith."

God calls this receiving, or breaking, of the negative consequences of the law of sowing and reaping, forgiveness, and it applies to the Christian and non-Christian alike. Forgiveness is the removal of the curse of the sin and the fellowship that was broken. Remittance is a legal fact of the removal of sin from the person obtained by the Redemption of Jesus for all mankind. The new birth is when a non-Christian receives our adoption, the work of Redemption, and enters into the legal status of Salvation with God. The key to the treasure and the treasury of God is faith in the work of Father God in Jesus.

God describes forgiveness as a relationship issue, to allow the sinner to enter into the legal remittance for healing and blessing, unto prosperity and the peace

DISCOVERING OUR REDEMPTION

of God, i.e., to walk in salvation and see it manifested into the Earth. All the sin of mankind is remitted and propitiated in Jesus but, for this life now, the benefits (*sozo*) are released from faith to faith. You enter in by faith, and you release Holy Spirit into the Earth, to activate or deliver His benefits, by faith, continually. We control this by what promise of God we exercise faith for. God does not make the decisions as to who to bless today; we do, by what faith paths we build, so God can build His Kingdom through us. Eph 1:2 "Grace be to you, and peace, from God our Father, and from the Lord Jesus Christ. 3 Blessed be the God and Father of our Lord Jesus Christ, who hath blessed us with all spiritual blessings in heavenly places in Christ."

Remittance is greater than forgiveness, so remittance includes forgiveness. When sins are forgiven, people on Earth receive the breaking of the law of sin and death over them, in a vital and living way. The legal is now applied in spirit and can be manifested into the Earth, by faith in Father God's work in Jesus.

So forgiveness (*aphiemi*) is obtained for immediate healing or other earthly benefits of salvation, currently being held back by the law of sin and death, when:
- A Christian speaks remittance (*aphesis*) in words or prayer
- One ministers healing/deliverance by prayer or the laying on of hands
- We properly judge the body of Jesus in communion
- We properly judge the blood of Jesus in communion
- We confess, agree a sin is real and cost Jesus His life, and was healed by His stripes and resurrection, as prompted by Holy Spirit

The wonder is that any of these can be applied to others or yourself.

In essence, any of these methods is breaking the judgment of the devil in enforcing the law of sin and death, with the judgment of God on Jesus and against the devil, and God's judgment for the oppressed. John 16:8 "And when he (*Holy Spirit*) is come, he will reprove the world of sin, and of righteousness, and of judgment: 9 of sin, because they believe not on me; 10 of righteousness, because I go to my Father, and ye see me no more; 11 of judgment, because the prince of this world is judged (*against*)."

Ps 103:2 "Bless the Lord, O my soul, and forget not all his benefits: 3 who forgiveth all thine iniquities; who healeth all thy diseases; 4 who redeemeth thy life from destruction; who crowneth thee with *chesed*/lovingkindness and *racham*/tender mercies; 5 who satisfieth thy mouth with good things; so that thy youth is renewed like the eagle's. 6 The Lord executeth righteousness and judgment for all that are oppressed." This executing of righteousness is healing, restoration and blessing in direct judgment against, attacks on, or destroying of the works of the devil.

But until someone applies these reconciliation facts to each situation, in faith, the devil is left to work his misery. The more you understand and know these redemption facts, the greater your intensity of purpose and firmness in dealing with the devil. As we become more prompt, faithful and loving when anyone sins, the kingdom of darkness will be destroyed. Here is a command to put priestly *agape/love* in action. Gal 6:1 "Brethren, if a man be overtaken in a fault [*sickness, failure, error or lust*], ye which are spiritual, restore such an one in the spirit of meekness; considering thyself, lest thou also be tempted. 2 Bear ye one another's burdens, and so fulfil the law of Christ."

The newspaper and other media can become a source of information, as people's sins and failures are identified, and we obey Gal 6:1-2 for them and get them healed. Since sin is primarily a soul issue, especially as corruption in the heart, a simple blessing, said with godly intentionality, can be very powerful. Such a simple command can be, "Lord, bless their hearts." Or you can use a much more extensive prayer. Holy Spirit will guide you on this.

On the Mount of Transfiguration, the light of Jesus shown out into the Earth, and Peter, James and John got to see a bit of His fullness. Luke 9:28 "And it came to pass about an eight days after these sayings, he took Peter and John and James, and went up into a mountain to pray. 29 And as he prayed, the fashion of his countenance was altered, and his raiment was white and glistering." This appears to be an event in which the spirit of Jesus, Holy Spirit, shone through Jesus' flesh.

God reconciled man through Jesus' death by the cross. The torn temple veil meant that man was able to come directly into the presence of God, without the intervention of an earthly priest, but with Jesus as his intermediary, seated at the right hand of the Father. Jesus is ever there, as our Advocate. 1 John 2:1 "My little children, these things write I unto you, that ye sin not. And if any man sin, we have an advocate (*one who is in the face of a judge or king for your benefit*) with the Father, Jesus Christ the righteous: 2 and he is the propitiation (*remittance unto aggressive blessing*) for our sins: and not for ours only, but also for the sins of the whole world."

Father God reconciled man unto full, complete and total peace by the blood of Jesus and reconciled us, by Jesus' body of flesh, through death on the cross. Col 1:19 "For it pleased the Father that in him should all fulness dwell; 20 and, having made peace through the blood of his cross, by him to reconcile all things unto himself; by him, I say, whether they be things in earth, or things in heaven. 21 And you, that were sometime alienated and enemies in your mind by wicked works, yet now hath he reconciled 22 in the body of his flesh through death, to present you holy and unblameable and unreproveable in his sight."

Eph 2:15 "Having abolished in his flesh the enmity, even the law of commandments contained in ordinances; for to make in himself of twain one new man, so making peace; 16 and that he might reconcile both unto God in one body by the cross, having slain the enmity thereby."

DISCOVERING OUR REDEMPTION

Jesus abolished the law as the way to God and the way to handle sin. Jesus is now the only way to Father God and the only way to handle sin.

Many have no problem with God as the Just One, far away, stern and aloof. But to know God as Father and meet the heartcry of every human to know God's security, identity and love, we are to know Jesus and what He accomplished for us at the command of our Father God.

John 14:6 "Jesus saith unto him, I am the way, the truth, and the *zoe*/life: no man cometh unto the Father, but by me. 7 If ye had known me, ye should have known my Father also: and from henceforth ye know him, and have seen him."

Heb 10:20 "By a new and *zao*/living way, which he hath consecrated for us, through the veil, that is to say, his flesh."

When the veil of Herod's temple was torn, the priesthood passed from a select group to all mankind and, specifically, to all Christians; and as we mature and walk in this truth of Jesus, we get to deliver the same kind of *agape*/love that Jesus did, wherever we go and with whomever we bless.

As new believers, we can walk in power, and as we mature, we will walk in more *agape*/love. Mark 16:17 "And these signs shall follow them that believe … ."

As priests, we deal with praise, Gospel proclamation, Kingdom demonstration, forgiveness and being peacemakers. Rev 1:5 "And from Jesus Christ, who is the faithful witness, and the first begotten of the dead, and the prince of the kings of the earth. Unto him that *agape*/loved us, and washed us from our sins in his own blood, 6 and hath made us kings and priests unto God and his Father; to him be glory and dominion for ever and ever. Amen."

As kings, we decide, or judge, what needs to change and then go change it, with Holy Spirit power. Our model is as a warrior and a restoring and building king. Our example of a king is Jesus, and, of course, the right actions of King David.

Or, to put it simply, we evaluate any situation and anything that is wrong, and then we, as a priest, go into the spirit realm and get God's blessing; and, as king, implement that blessing into the Earth. What kings say, what they decree, happens. As we speak for Jesus, God's will happens, as we build the faith path God can inhabit to blessing. Thus, we are temples of God, individually and jointly, who operate as Jesus did, for God, as king-priests and priest-kings, to release the *agape*/love of God into the Earth.

We use the right thoughts and intentions in our mind and heart, and then build a faith path by our thoughts, words or actions, that God can inhabit, and Holy Spirit can deliver Father's *chesed* mercy and grace in *dunamis* power. We major on truth and *agape* love and deliver grace. This is what we are made for and find the most joy in. This is the answer to the prayer: "Thy kingdom come, thy will be done on earth as it is in heaven." It is to come through us, the Body of Christ.

Jesus Worked So the Veil Was Torn

Matt 16:18 "… I (*Jesus*) will build my church; and the gates of hell shall not prevail against it. 19 And I will give unto thee the keys of the kingdom of heaven: and whatsoever thou shalt bind on earth shall be bound in heaven: and whatsoever thou shalt loose on earth shall be loosed in heaven."

John 16:23 "And in that day ye shall *aiteo*/ask (*require, demand and expect as due by covenant promise*) me nothing. Verily, verily, I say unto you, Whatsoever ye shall *aiteo*/ask (*require, demand and expect as due by covenant promise*) the Father in my name, he will give it you. 24 Hitherto have ye *aiteo*/asked (*required, demanded and expected as due by covenant promise*) nothing in my name: *aiteo*/ask (*require, demand and expect as due by covenant promise*), and ye shall receive, that your joy may be full."

Now each Christian is qualified, as the temple of God and the agent to release God into the world, to produce Heaven on Earth, for God. This is the liberty we are to walk in. We control the power of God mostly by our words. Prov 18:21 "Death and life are in the power of the tongue: and they that love it shall eat the fruit thereof."

Remember, God is in control, as we reign for Him on the Earth. If we do not reign, He is not in control on the Earth. Rom 5:17 "For if by one man's offence death reigned (*as a cruel and powerful king*) by one; much more they which (*continually*) *lambano*/receive abundance of grace and of the gift of righteousness shall reign (*as powerful and merciful kings*) in *zoe*/life by one, Jesus Christ.) … 20 Moreover the law entered, that the offence might abound. But where sin abounded, grace did much more abound: 21 that as sin hath reigned (*as a cruel and powerful king*) unto death, even so might grace reign (*as powerful and merciful kings*) through righteousness unto eternal *zoe*/life by Jesus Christ our Lord."

We offer thanksgiving, praise and worship to God, and then we deliver God to men, through acts, by Holy Spirit. What a wonder: "Christ in us the hope of glory!" That is, the release of Holy Spirit into the Earth, to manifest the *agape*/love of God in good works of "the God kind."

Titus 2:13 "Looking for that blessed hope, and the glorious appearing of the great God and our Saviour Jesus Christ; 14 who gave himself for us, that he might redeem us from all iniquity, and purify unto himself a peculiar people, zealous of good works. 15 These things speak, and exhort, and rebuke with all authority. Let no man despise thee."

Scripture reading, study, memorization, answering Bible questions, prayer, fasting, giving alms, acts of kindness and generosity, helping widows and orphans, spiritual disciplines, right judging, and affirmations, proclamations, confessions, thanksgiving and praise in thoughts, words, chants, songs and shouts are man-level steps. One key God-level step is private praying in tongues. These are the starting and maintaining actions of faith. The end is not found in these and our education is incomplete until we do good works (God-level results), in faith working by *agape*/love, as Jesus did.

Heb 10:23 "Let us hold fast the profession of our faith without wavering; (for he is faithful that promised;) 24 and let us consider one another to provoke unto *agape*/love and to good works."

The veil of Jesus' body was rent, the temple veil was rent, and God now dwells in men by Holy Spirit, just like Jesus. Our job, as kings and priests, is to do those things that He can inhabit to deliver His goodness, His grace into the Earth.

Chapter 16

Jesus Sat Down

The climax of Redemption was the seating of the Lord Jesus.

After He had been made sin, after He had paid the penalty for our relationship with Satan, after He was made a curse for us, after He had suffered all that Justice demanded of us, then Christ, with us, arose from the dead. Jesus could not be raised from the dead or seated in Heaven until we also were justified with Him. The goal of God was that man could be made the righteousness of God in Christ Jesus.

Rom 4:24 "But for us also, to whom it (*righteousness*) shall be imputed, if we believe on him that raised up Jesus our Lord from the dead; 25 who was delivered for our offences, and was raised again for our justification (*or when we were justified, with the righteousness of Father God, in Christ Jesus*). 5:1 Therefore being justified by faith, we have peace with God through our Lord Jesus Christ: 2 by whom also we have access by faith into this grace wherein we stand, and rejoice in hope of the glory of God."

2 Cor 5:17 "Therefore if any man be in Christ, he is a new creature: old things are passed away; behold, all things are become new. 18 And all things are of God, who hath reconciled us to himself by Jesus Christ, and hath given to us the ministry of reconciliation; 19 to wit, that God was in Christ, reconciling the world unto

DISCOVERING OUR REDEMPTION

himself, not imputing their trespasses unto them; and hath committed unto us the word of reconciliation. 20 Now then we are ambassadors for Christ, as though God did beseech you by us: we pray you in Christ's stead, be ye reconciled to God. 21 For he hath made him to be sin for us, who knew no sin; that we might be made the righteousness of God in him."

What Jesus got, the righteousness of God, in the very pit of Hell, all men got as a gift, by the grace of God. It is there for us, and we enter into it by faith in the resurrection of Jesus by Father God.

To be made righteous means that, independent of our current Earth walk, we are made the righteousness of God in Christ Jesus, because, when Jesus was made righteous from all the sin and curse of sin, mankind was also raised and made righteous with and in Him.

Col 1:19 "For it pleased the Father that in him should all fulness dwell; 20 and, having made peace through the blood of his cross, by him to reconcile all things unto himself; by him, I say, whether they be things in earth, or things in heaven. 21 And you, that were sometime alienated and enemies in your mind by wicked works, yet now hath he reconciled 22 in the body of his flesh through death, to present you holy and unblameable and unreproveable in his sight."

This is the righteousness and reconciliation we are to remind ourselves and others of:

- That we have free and unhindered access to God because of Jesus
- That we are God's agents of right kindness and mercy for Him on the Earth
- That, for the new creation, we have a spirit and the mind of the Spirit of God that only wants to do the will of God

All of this is included in being made the righteousness of God in Christ Jesus.

2 Cor 6:1 "We then, as workers together with him, beseech you also that ye receive not the grace of God in vain. 2 (For he saith, I have heard thee in a time accepted, and in the day of *soteria*/salvation have I succoured thee: behold, now is the accepted time; behold, now is the day of *soteria*/salvation.)"

Because of the work of Redemption by Jesus, every aspect of God's Salvation is now open to mankind. Most would be pleased to know this means earthly health, wealth and prosperity, but there is more.

We were raised with and in Jesus, not just to the level of Earth, but to the highest of all there is, the very throne of God over the entire Universe. This exaltation of man came when Jesus was raised to sit beside the Father.

Eph 2:4 "But God, who is rich in mercy, for his great *agape*/love wherewith he *agape*/loved us, 5 even when we were dead in sins, hath quickened us together with Christ, (by grace ye are *sozo*/saved;) 6 and hath raised us up together, and made us sit together in heavenly places in Christ Jesus: 7 that in the ages to come he might shew the exceeding riches of his grace in his kindness toward us through Christ Jesus."

Jesus Sat Down

Rom 8:10 "And if Christ be in you, the body is dead because of sin; but the Spirit is *zoe*/life because of righteousness. 11 But if the Spirit of him that raised up Jesus from the dead dwell in you, he that raised up Christ from the dead shall also quicken your mortal bodies by his Spirit that dwelleth in you."

Col 2:12 "Buried with him in baptism, wherein also ye are risen with him through the faith of the operation of God, who hath raised him from the dead."

Col 3:1 "If ye then be risen with Christ, seek those things which are above, where Christ sitteth on the right hand of God. 2 Set your affection on things above, not on things on the earth. 3 For ye are dead, and your *zoe*/life is hid with Christ in God."

He declared we were seated together with Christ.

Eph 2:6 "And raised us up with him, and made us to sit with him in the heavenly places, in Christ Jesus." RSV (emphasis added)

This was the highest honor that God had ever conferred upon man.

It is hard to conceive of a higher honor, Jesus, the man, is seated at the right hand of Father God. Where else could be higher? Everything is below this position, and the only one higher is Father God.

Eph 1:19 "And what is the exceeding greatness of his power to us-ward who believe, according to the working of his mighty power, 20 which he wrought in Christ, when he raised him from the dead, and set him at his own right hand in the heavenly places, 21 far above all principality, and power, and might, and dominion, and every name that is named, not only in this world, but also in that which is to come: 22 and hath put all things under his feet, and gave him to be the head over all things to the church, 23 which is his body, the fulness of him that filleth all in all."

The Son became a man, identified Himself with the human race, delivered the human race from the authority of Satan, and carried His blood into the Holy of Holies, to make the Eternal Redemption.

Then He sat down at the right hand of the Majesty on High, in governmental position, as joint King.

We have a man seated at God's right hand, and He is our representative, for He is there to represent us.

1 John 2:1 "My little children, these things write I unto you, that ye sin not. And if any man sin, we have an advocate with the Father, Jesus Christ the righteous: 2 and he is the propitiation for our sins: and not for ours only, but also for the sins of the whole world."

This is the crowning event in Redemption, a man seated at God's right hand, and that man is the head of the new body, the Church.

Is it any wonder he shouts: Eph 1:3 "Blessed be the God and Father of our Lord Jesus Christ, who hath blessed us with all (*every*) spiritual blessings in heavenly places in Christ."

DISCOVERING OUR REDEMPTION

A more literal translation of this passage is: "Blessed be the God and Father of our Lord Jesus Christ, who hath spoken every good thing it is possible to say in the spirit concerning us in heavenly places in Christ [*and ready for delivery to Earth, to bring the Kingdom of God to Earth*]."

Not only are we seated in the highest governmental and love position in the Universe, but we are also blessed with every spiritual blessing that is necessary to maintain our place, as members of His glorious body, and to bring Heaven to Earth.

In the mind of God, every one of us is in Christ now, and He sees us in Him.

When we go to the throne of grace in prayer, it is as though Jesus were going there. When we come in the name of Jesus, we are also acknowledging the greatness of Jesus and His work of Redemption.

Col 3:3 "For ye died, and your *zoe*/life is hid with Christ in God."

We are hidden from the adversary, but we are visible to the Father.

Heb 9:24 "For Christ entered not into a holy place made with hands, like in pattern to the true; but into heaven itself, now to appear before the face of God for us." RSV

Jesus is there, at the right hand of the Father, as our representative, as our Lord, and as our Lover, who gave Himself for us.

We can see that our Redemption is a completed, finished thing.

If Christ sat down at God's right hand, it is because the Father accepted Him and accepted what He did for us as full and complete.

Jesus has been declared Lord of Lords and King of Kings. The coronation is complete. The triumph of the plan of God was not only to re-seat His King over the Earth, but His people as well. Phil 2:5 "Let this mind be in you, which was also in Christ Jesus: 6 who, being in the form of God, thought it not robbery to be equal with God: 7 but made himself of no reputation, and took upon him the form of a servant, and was made in the likeness of men: 8 and being found in fashion as a man, he humbled himself, and became obedient unto death, even the death of the cross. 9 Wherefore God also hath highly exalted him, and given him a name which is above every name: 10 that at the name of Jesus every knee should bow, of things in heaven, and things in earth, and things under the earth; 11 and that every tongue should confess that Jesus Christ is Lord, to the glory of God the Father."

This statement, "Let this mind be in you which was in Christ Jesus," says that our current body, with a born-again spirit, is adequate and capable of thinking like or having a mind like Jesus, at the highest level. How awesome to think of the possibilities, once we decide to serve God, as Jesus did!

The fact that Jesus is seated there at the right hand of Father God is the seal of our acceptance in the Beloved. It is the seal that the work of the great Mighty Arm of God was sufficient. Isa 53:1 "Who hath believed our report? and to whom is the arm of the Lord revealed?"

Jesus Sat Down

This is the work planned before the foundation of the Earth was laid, before man was created on and of the Earth.

Rom 16:25 "Now to him that is of power to stablish you according to my gospel, and the preaching of Jesus Christ, according to the revelation of the mystery, which was kept secret since the world began, 26 but now is made manifest, and by the scriptures of the prophets, according to the commandment of the everlasting God, made known to all nations for the obedience of faith: 27 to God only wise, be glory through Jesus Christ for ever. Amen."

1 Pet 1:18 "Forasmuch as ye know that ye were not redeemed with corruptible things, as silver and gold, from your vain conversation received by tradition from your fathers; 19 but with the precious blood of Christ, as of a lamb without blemish and without spot: 20 who verily was foreordained before the foundation of the world, but was manifest in these last times for you, 21 who by him do believe in God, that raised him up from the dead, and gave him glory; that your faith and hope might be in God."

Change your thinking to that of a priest and king for God. Col 3:1 "If ye then be risen with Christ, seek those things which are above, where Christ sitteth on the right hand of God. 2 Set your affection on things above, not on things on the earth. 3 For ye are dead, and your *zoe*/life is hid with Christ in God. 4 When Christ, who is our *zoe*/life, shall appear, then shall ye also appear with him in glory."

This is the kind of repentance Jesus was talking about and was revealed to Paul. Luke 24:46 "And said unto them, Thus it is written, and thus it behoved Christ to suffer, and to rise from the dead the third day: 47 and that repentance and remission of sins should be preached in his name among all nations, beginning at Jerusalem."

Jesus is seated there until Father God, through the Church, puts all His enemies, Satan and his works, under Jesus' feet, as a footstool.

Heb 10:12 "But this man (*Jesus of Nazareth*), after he had offered one sacrifice for sins for ever, sat down on the right hand of God; 13 from henceforth expecting till his enemies be made his footstool. 14 For by one offering he hath perfected for ever them that are sanctified. 15 Whereof the Holy Ghost also is a witness to us: for after that he had said before, 16 this is the covenant that I will make with them after those days, saith the Lord, I will put my laws into their hearts, and in their minds will I write them; 17 and their sins and iniquities will I remember no more. 18 Now where remission of these (*sins and iniquities*) is, there is no more offering for sin."

Eph 3:8 "Unto me, who am less than the least of all saints, is this grace given, that I should preach among the Gentiles the unsearchable riches of Christ; 9 and to make all men see what is the fellowship of the mystery, which from the beginning of the world hath been hid in God, who created all things by Jesus Christ: 10 to the intent that now unto the principalities and powers in heavenly places might be

DISCOVERING OUR REDEMPTION

known by the church (*of new creation men and women*) the manifold wisdom of God, 11 according to the eternal purpose which he purposed in Christ Jesus our Lord: 12 in whom we have boldness and access with confidence by the faith of him."

Rom 16:20 "And the God of peace shall bruise (*crush totally*) Satan under your feet shortly (*as shattered glass*). The grace of our Lord Jesus Christ be with you [*to think, know, will, be and do this*]. Amen."

The final act of His redemption work was for Jesus to send the promised Holy Spirit. God had given the Law until Jesus, the seed of Abraham, came and delivered the promise God had given Abraham. Gal 3:19 "Wherefore then serveth the law? It was added because of transgressions, till the seed should come to whom the promise was made; and it was ordained by angels in the hand of a mediator. 20 Now a mediator is not a mediator of one, but God is one. 21 Is the law then against the promises of God? God forbid: for if there had been a law given which could have given zoe/life, verily righteousness should have been by the law. 22 But the scripture hath concluded all under sin, that the promise by faith of Jesus Christ might be given to them that believe."

Notice that the covenant of Abraham was really God's covenant with Jesus through Abraham, as the representative of Jesus, as the body of Jesus was in the loins of Abraham. Thus, Abraham was the substitute ... until Jesus could complete the covenant Himself. Jesus is that seed. God, in His mercy, established the Law of Moses as a temporary tool for zoe/life and covering of sin and breaking the curse, until Jesus came. Gal 3:16 "Now to Abraham and his seed were the promises made. He saith not, and to seeds, as of many; but as of one, and to thy seed, which is Christ. 17 And this I say, that the covenant, that was confirmed before of God in Christ, the law, which was four hundred and thirty years after, cannot disannul, that it should make the promise of none effect. 18 For if the inheritance be of the law, it is no more of promise: but God gave it to Abraham by promise."

Here is the promise given Abraham: Gen 12:2 "And I will make of thee a great nation (*kingdom*), and I will bless thee, and make thy name great (*authority*); and thou shalt be a blessing (*source of Holy Spirit abundance in the Earth*): 3 and I will bless them that bless thee, and curse him that curseth thee: and in thee shall all families of the earth be blessed." How few understood that "in thee shall all families of the earth be blessed" means that Holy Spirit would dwell in men to deliver the Kingdom of God to Earth though them.

The great purpose of Jesus coming in the flesh, as a carpenter from Nazareth, was that God could fulfill the promise He had given Abraham. Gal 3:6 "Even as Abraham believed God, and it was accounted to him for righteousness. 7 Know ye therefore that they which are of faith, the same are the children of Abraham. 8 And the scripture, foreseeing that God would justify the heathen through faith, preached before the gospel unto Abraham, saying, In thee shall all nations be blessed. 9 So then they which be of faith are blessed with faithful Abraham. 10 For as many as are of the works of the law are under the curse: for it is written, Cursed is every one that continueth not in all things which are written in the book of the law to do them. 11 But that no man is justified by the law in the sight of God, it is evident: for, The just shall *zao*/live by faith. 12 And the law is not of faith: but, The man that doeth them shall *zao*/live in them. 13 Christ hath redeemed us from the curse of the law (*summarized in Deuteronomy 28*), being made a curse for us: for it is written, Cursed is every one that hangeth on a tree: 14 that the blessing of Abraham might come on the Gentiles through Jesus Christ; that we might receive the promise of the Spirit through faith."

We are justified by grace, through the Redemption in the blood of Jesus. Jesus did not just make Propitiation; He is our Propitiation, through faith in what His blood accomplished for us. Rom 3:24 "Being justified freely by his grace through the redemption that is in Christ Jesus: 25 whom God hath set forth to be a propitiation through faith in his blood, to declare his righteousness for the remission of sins that are past, through the forbearance of God."

One of the great fruits of Redemption is that we can now have Holy Spirit dwelling in us 1 Cor 6:19 "What? know ye not that your body is the temple of the Holy Ghost which is in you, which ye have of God, and ye are not your own? 20 For ye are bought with a price: therefore glorify God in your body, and in your spirit, which are God's."

There is no darkness in Father God, Jesus or Holy Spirit. For Holy Spirit to be joined to us and dwell in us, we are made new creations and justified with the righteousness of Father God in Jesus. 1 Cor 6:17 "But he that is joined unto the Lord is one spirit."

This is not a theological justification or some legal decree, while we remain the same, but a change in the very substance and nature of our spirit.

Holy Spirit comes to dwell in us by our believing the Gospel of our Salvation in Jesus. Eph 1:13 "In whom ye also trusted, after that ye heard the word of truth, the gospel of your *soteria*/salvation: in whom also after that ye believed, ye were sealed with that holy Spirit of promise, 14 which is the earnest of our inheritance until the redemption of the purchased possession, unto the praise of his glory."

Rom 4:5 "But to him that worketh not, but believeth on him that justifieth the ungodly, his faith is counted for righteousness."

Notice how being born again, being made righteous (justified), experiencing Salvation, eternal *zoe*/life, indwelling Holy Spirit, and being sealed by Holy Spirit so God can make sure He gets what He paid for in your redemption are all part of the same process, upon believing in the resurrection of Jesus, as Lord. 1 Pet 1:23 "Being born again, not of corruptible seed, but of incorruptible, by the word of God, which *zao*/liveth and abideth for ever. 24 For all flesh is as grass, and all the

DISCOVERING OUR REDEMPTION

glory of man as the flower of grass. The grass withereth, and the flower thereof falleth away: 25 but the word of the Lord endureth for ever. And this is the word which by the gospel is preached unto you."

Rom 5:18 "Therefore as by the offence of one judgment came upon all men to condemnation; even so by the righteousness of one the free gift came upon all men unto justification of *zoe*/life."

John 20:31 "But these are written, that ye might believe that Jesus is the Christ, the Son of God; and that believing ye might have *zoe*/life through his name."

Rom 10:9 "That if thou shalt confess with thy mouth the Lord Jesus, and shalt believe in thine heart that God hath raised him from the dead, thou shalt be *sozo*/saved. 10 For with the heart man believeth unto righteousness; and with the mouth confession is made unto *soteria*/salvation. 11 For the scripture saith, Whosoever believeth on him shall not be ashamed. 12 For there is no difference between the Jew and the Greek: for the same Lord over all is rich unto all that call upon him. 13 For whosoever shall call upon the name of the Lord shall be *sozo*/saved."

Holy Spirit, as given by Jesus before the Day of Pentecost, was not of the same measure as mankind could receive after the Day of Pentecost, as seen in Acts chapter 2. Men could not be born again of the baptism of Holy Spirit, as given by Jesus, until that Day of Pentecost. Jesus had given Holy Spirit to help the disciples learn of Jesus in the forty days after the resurrection. It is rather obvious that they had not learned what they needed in the time they had spent with Him. Holy Spirit was with them but not in them.

John 20:20 "And when he had so said, he shewed unto them his hands and his side. Then were the disciples glad, when they saw the Lord. 21 Then said Jesus to them again, Peace be unto you: as my Father hath sent me, even so send I you. 22 And when he had said this, he breathed on them, and saith unto them, Receive ye the Holy Ghost: 23 whose soever sins ye remit, they are remitted unto them; and whose soever sins ye retain, they are retained."

Acts 1:2 "Until the day in which he (*Jesus*) was taken up, after that he through the Holy Ghost had given commandments unto the apostles whom he had chosen: 3 to whom also he shewed himself alive after his passion by many infallible proofs, being seen of them forty days, and speaking of the things pertaining to the kingdom of God."

In Luke, Jesus told these followers to go and disciple the nations, but first they should wait until they had received power from Heaven. Then they could go. Acts 1:4 "And, being assembled together with them, commanded them that they should not depart from Jerusalem, but wait for the promise of the Father, which, saith he, ye have heard of me. 5 For John truly baptized with water; but ye shall be baptized with the Holy Ghost not many days hence. 6 When they therefore were come together, they asked of him, saying, Lord, wilt thou at this time restore again the kingdom to Israel? 7 And he said unto them, It is not for you to know the times or the seasons, which the Father hath put in his own power. 8 But ye shall receive power, after that the Holy Ghost is come upon you: and ye shall be witnesses unto me both in Jerusalem, and in all Judaea, and in Samaria, and unto the uttermost part of the earth. 9 And when he had spoken these things, while they beheld, he was taken up; and a cloud received him out of their sight."

Thus, on that Day of Pentecost, which celebrated the giving of the Law after the escape from Egypt, Jesus sent the baptism of Holy Spirit, which John the Baptist had said was why the Messiah had come. Matt 3:9 "And think not to say within yourselves, We have Abraham to our father: for I say unto you, that God is able of these stones to raise up children unto Abraham. 10 And now also the axe is laid unto the root of the trees: therefore every tree which bringeth not forth good fruit is hewn down, and cast into the fire. 11 I indeed baptize you with water unto repentance: but he that cometh after me is mightier than I, whose shoes I am not worthy to bear: he shall baptize you with the Holy Ghost, and with fire: 12 whose fan is in his hand, and he will throughly purge his floor, and gather his wheat into the garner; but he will burn up the chaff with unquenchable fire."

Baptism means to totally immerse so that all interior and exterior is soaked, or filled, with water. If you immersed a bottle that was still sealed, and no water could get into it, it would not be fully baptized. In order to be baptized, the seal or stopper of the bottle must be removed, and the water then fills the interior of the bottle. So the baptism of Jesus fills our deepest interior with Holy Spirit, and we are given Holy Spirit as a seal, when we believe the Gospel of our Salvation in Jesus. This is the receiving of Holy Spirit that occurred on the Day of Pentecost and was then made available to all people. Jesus ascended, and Holy Spirit took His place on the Earth. Jesus is officially, governmentally, seated in Heaven now, and Holy Spirit is officially, or in governmental position, here on Earth now.

We are made kings, for Holy Spirit to reign through and bring Heaven to Earth. Rom 5:17 "For if by one man's offence death reigned (*as king*) by one; much more they which (*continually*) lambano/receive (*hold on to, never let go of the*) abundance of grace and of the gift of righteousness shall reign (*as kings*) in zoe/life by one, Jesus Christ.) 18 Therefore as by the offence of one judgment came upon all men to condemnation; even so by the righteousness of one the free gift came upon all men unto justification of zoe/life. 19 For as by one man's disobedience many were made sinners, so by the obedience of one shall many be made righteous. 20 Moreover the law entered, that the offence might abound. But where sin abounded, grace did much more abound: 21 that as sin hath reigned (*as king*) unto death, even so might grace reign (*as king*) through righteousness unto eternal zoe/life by Jesus Christ our Lord."

Peter explained on that Day: Acts 2:14 "But Peter, standing up with the eleven, lifted up his voice, and said unto them, Ye men of Judaea, and all ye that dwell

DISCOVERING OUR REDEMPTION

at Jerusalem, be this known unto you, and hearken to my words: 15 for these are not drunken, as ye suppose, seeing it is but the third hour of the day. 16 But this is that which was spoken by the prophet Joel; 17 and it shall come to pass in the last days, saith God, I will pour out of my Spirit upon all flesh: and your sons and your daughters shall prophesy, and your young men shall see visions, and your old men shall dream dreams: 18 and on my servants and on my handmaidens I will pour out in those days of my Spirit; and they shall prophesy: 19 and I will shew wonders in heaven above, and signs in the earth beneath; blood, and fire, and vapour of smoke: 20 the sun shall be turned into darkness, and the moon into blood, before that great and notable day of the Lord come: 21 and it shall come to pass, that whosoever shall call on the name of the Lord shall be *sozo*/saved."

Peter declared Salvation is now open to all men, "whosoever," and was no longer just for the Jews.

With the birth of the New Creation Church on the Day of Pentecost, God delivered what He had promise to Abraham so long ago. Gal 3:14 "That the blessing of Abraham might come on the Gentiles through Jesus Christ; that we might receive the promise of the Spirit through faith."

Acts 3:13 "The God of Abraham, and of Isaac, and of Jacob, the God of our fathers, hath glorified his Son Jesus; whom ye delivered up, and denied him in the presence of Pilate, when he was determined to let him go."

John 7:37 "In the last day, that great day of the feast, Jesus stood and cried, saying, If any man thirst, let him come unto me, and drink. 38 He that believeth on me, as the scripture hath said, out of his belly shall flow rivers of *zao*/living water. 39 (But this spake he of the Spirit, which they that believe on him should receive: for the Holy Ghost was not yet given; because that Jesus was not yet glorified.)"

This glorification and coronation was accomplished when Jesus was seated above every name that is named, by the work of mighty Holy Spirit. Eph 1:19 "And what is the exceeding greatness of his power to us-ward who believe, according to the working of his mighty power, 20 which he wrought in Christ, when he raised him from the dead, and set him at his own right hand in the heavenly places, 21 far above all principality, and power, and might, and dominion, and every name that is named, not only in this world, but also in that which is to come: 22 and hath put all things under his feet, and gave him to be the head over all things to the church, 23 which is his body, the fulness of him that filleth all in all."

Rom 1:3 "Concerning his Son Jesus Christ our Lord, which was made of the seed of David according to the flesh; 4 and declared to be the Son of God with power, according to the spirit of holiness, by the resurrection from the dead."

Jesus was offered for our sins, and He was raised, when we were justified. Jesus would still be in Hades, if He had not gotten the job done. Rom 4:24 "But for us also, to whom it (*righteousness*) shall be imputed (*granted and credited*), if we believe on him that raised up Jesus our Lord from the dead; 25 who was delivered for our offences, and was raised again for our justification (*or when we were justified*)."

Peter also explained that this sending forth of the promise of God was because Jesus has been declared both Lord and Christ, and is seated, in governmental position in Heaven, as Lord. Acts 2:29 "Men and brethren, let me freely speak unto you of the patriarch David, that he is both dead and buried, and his sepulchre is with us unto this day. 30 Therefore being a prophet, and knowing that God had sworn with an oath to him, that of the fruit of his loins, according to the flesh, he would raise up Christ to sit on his throne (*as King*); 31 he seeing this before spake of the resurrection of Christ, that his *psuche*/soul (*life*) was not left in hell, neither his flesh did see corruption. 32 This Jesus hath God raised up, whereof we all are witnesses. 33 Therefore being by the right hand of God exalted, and having received of the Father the promise of the Holy Ghost, he hath shed forth this, which ye now see and hear. 34 For David is not ascended into the heavens: but he saith himself, The Lord said unto my Lord, Sit thou on my right hand, 35 until I make thy foes thy footstool. 36 Therefore let all the house of Israel know assuredly, that God hath made that same Jesus, whom ye have crucified, both Lord and Christ."

So Jesus' first recorded governmental action was to send Holy Spirit in a way that He could inhabit men and fill them, so they could operate as Jesus did. Acts 10:36 "The word which God sent unto the children of Israel, preaching peace by Jesus Christ: (he is Lord of all:) 37 that word, I say, ye know, which was published throughout all Judaea, and began from Galilee, after the baptism which John preached; 38 how God anointed Jesus of Nazareth with the Holy Ghost and with power: who went about doing good, and healing all that were oppressed (*under the active dominion, reign and lordship*) of the devil; for God was with him."

Because men can now have Holy Spirit dwelling in them, because of this baptism, men can also have all the promises of God, because, in Holy Spirit, we have all that God is and can do in man, and because of the great work of the Mighty Arm of God, Jesus of Nazareth. 2 Cor 1:19 "For the Son of God, Jesus Christ, who was preached among you by us, even by me and Silvanus and Timotheus, was not yea and nay, but in him was yea. 20 For all the promises of God in him are yea, and in him Amen, unto the glory of God by us. 21 Now he which stablisheth us with you in Christ, and hath anointed us, is God; 22 who hath also sealed us, and given the earnest of the Spirit in our hearts."

This sealing process, we understand, is when the old man of sin is cut away from being part of the believer, by God, and Holy Spirit is sealed to the believer, in the circumcision of Christ. God warns us to never let this completeness and simplicity in Jesus be lost to our minds. Col 2:8 "Beware lest any man spoil you through philosophy and vain deceit, after the tradition of men, after the rudiments of the world, and not after Christ. 9 For in him dwelleth all the fulness of the God-

DISCOVERING OUR REDEMPTION

head bodily. 10 And ye are complete in him, which is the head of all principality and power: 11 in whom also ye are circumcised with the circumcision made without hands, in putting off the body of the sins of the flesh by the circumcision of Christ: 12 buried with him in baptism, wherein also ye are risen with him through the faith of the operation of God, who hath raised him from the dead. 13 And you, being dead in your sins and the uncircumcision of your flesh, hath he quickened together with him, having forgiven you all trespasses; 14 blotting out the handwriting of ordinances that was against us, which was contrary to us, and took it out of the way, nailing it to his cross; 15 and having spoiled principalities and powers, he made a shew of them openly, triumphing over them in it."

Since Jesus destroyed Satan and made an open show of Him, in the process of our Redemption, Salvation, Deliverance, Justification, Peace and Reconciliation, Father God said by men moved by Holy Spirit, who is to teach us all things concerning Jesus: Rom 16:20 "And the God of peace shall bruise (*crush totally*) Satan under your feet shortly (*as shattered glass*). The grace of our Lord Jesus Christ be with you [*to know, will, be and do this*]. Amen."

Jesus is our Peace, Propitiation, Salvation, Redemption, Sanctification, Wisdom, our Head (leader, brains, and mind of Christ) and our Lord, and we are His body and have the same anointing, same Spirit and same call of God. John 20:21 "Then said Jesus to them again, Peace be unto you: as my Father hath sent me, even so send I you."

Gal 4:4 "But when the fulness of the time was come, God sent forth his Son, made of a woman, made under the law, 5 to redeem them that were under the law, that we might receive the adoption of sons. 6 And because ye are sons, God hath sent forth the Spirit of his Son into your hearts, crying, Abba, Father. 7 Wherefore thou art no more a servant, but a son; and if a son, then an heir of God through Christ."

Jesus explained: John 14:16 "And I will pray the Father, and he shall give you another Comforter, that he may abide with you for ever; 17 even the Spirit of truth; whom the world cannot receive, because it seeth him not, neither knoweth him: but ye know him; for he dwelleth with you, and shall be in you. 18 I will not leave you comfortless: I will come to you."

The Holy Spirit indwelling is what makes a human into a Christian, and because He is there and sealed, Jesus says: Matt 28:18 "And Jesus came and spake unto them, saying, All power is given unto me in heaven and in earth. 19 Go ye therefore, and teach all nations, baptizing them in the name of the Father, and of the Son, and of the Holy Ghost: 20 teaching them to observe all things whatsoever I have commanded you: and, lo, I am with you alway, even unto the end of the world. Amen."

Luke 11:20 "But if I with the finger of God (*Holy Spirit*) cast out devils, no doubt the kingdom of God is come upon you."

Jesus Sat Down

Matt 12:28 "But if I cast out devils by the Spirit of God, then the kingdom of God is come unto you. 29 Or else how can one enter into a strong man's house, and spoil his goods, except he first bind the strong man? and then he will spoil his house."

Jesus has defeated the strong man, to spoil his goods, the captives, people in any oppression of the devil through lies and evil works, and we have the same Holy Spirit for the same purpose: Luke 4:18 "The Spirit of the Lord is upon me, because he hath anointed me to preach the gospel to the poor; he hath sent me to heal the brokenhearted, to preach deliverance to the captives, and recovering of sight to the blind, to set at liberty them that are bruised, 19 to preach the acceptable year of the Lord. 20 And he closed the book, and he gave it again to the minister, and sat down. And the eyes of all them that were in the synagogue were fastened on him."

And, if you have ears to hear: Luke 4:21 "And he (*Jesus*) began to say unto them, This day is this scripture fulfilled in your ears." This is now our day!

The axe has been laid at the root of sin, and we have been commanded by the seated, glorified Lord Christ. Even to those of us hardened by unbelief, Jesus commands: Mark 16:14 "Afterward he appeared unto the eleven as they sat at meat, and upbraided them with their unbelief and hardness of heart, because they believed not them which had seen him after he was risen. 15 And he said unto them, Go ye into all the world, and preach the gospel to every creature. 16 He that believeth and is baptized shall be *sozo*/saved; but he that believeth not shall be damned. 17 And these signs shall follow them that believe; In my name shall they cast out devils; they shall speak with new tongues; 18 they shall take up serpents; and if they drink any deadly thing, it shall not hurt them; they shall lay hands on the sick, and they shall recover. 19 So then after the Lord had spoken unto them, he was received up into heaven, and sat on the right hand of God. 20 And they went forth, and preached everywhere, the Lord working with them, and confirming the word with signs following. Amen."

CHAPTER 17

JESUS AND THE 52 DAYS THAT CHANGED THE UNIVERSE

Jesus has been declared Lord of Heaven and Earth. Heaven is where the stars and galaxies of the Universe are, so the coronation of Jesus is Lord of all the work of God's hand. Here are some key changes to the Universe through the work of Jesus in those 52 awesome days 2000 years ago.

Heb 1:10 "And, Thou, Lord, in the beginning hast laid the foundation of the earth; and the heavens are the works of thine hands: 11 they shall perish; but thou remainest; and they all shall wax old as doth a garment; 12 and as a vesture shalt thou fold them up, and they shall be changed: but thou art the same, and thy years shall not fail."

1. Before the foundation of the Earth was laid, Jesus was slain, so He was slain to uphold those foundations. 1 Pet 1:17 "And if ye call on the Father, who without respect of persons judgeth according to every man's work, pass the time of your sojourning here in fear: 18 forasmuch as ye know that ye were not redeemed with corruptible things, as silver and gold, from your vain conversation received by tradition from your fathers; 19 but with the precious blood of Christ, as of a lamb without blemish and without spot: 20 who verily was foreordained before the foundation of the world, but was manifest in these last times for you."

Jesus and the 52 Days that Changed the Universe

2. God has spoken in the past by the prophets, but has now spoken by Jesus. Heb 1:1 "God, who at sundry times and in divers manners spake in time past unto the fathers by the prophets, 2 hath in these last days spoken unto us by his Son, whom he hath appointed heir of all things, by whom also he made the worlds; 3 who being the brightness of his glory, and the express image of his person, and upholding all things by the word of his power, when he had by himself purged our sins, sat down on the right hand of the Majesty on high."
3. The covenant of Jesus included all the work of God's hands, all Creation, and all Creation is now under, or subject to, the cleansing of the blood of Jesus. Col 1:20 "And, having made peace through the blood of his cross, by him to reconcile all things unto himself; by him, I say, whether they be things in earth, or things in heaven."
4. Jesus is lifted above every name in all creation, for this age and the age to come. Phil 2:9 "Wherefore God also hath highly exalted him (*Jesus*), and given him a name which is above every name: 10 that at the name of Jesus every knee should bow, of things in heaven, and things in earth, and things under the earth; 11 and that every tongue should confess that Jesus Christ is Lord, to the glory of God the Father."
5. Jesus has prepared the Church, the Body of Christ, by which He will fill all of creation, the Universe. Eph 1:19 "And what is the exceeding greatness of his power to us-ward who believe, according to the working of his mighty power, 20 which he (*God, by the Spirit of Holiness*) wrought in Christ, when he raised him from the dead, and set him at his own right hand in the heavenly places, 21 far above all principality, and power, and might, and dominion, and every name that is named, not only in this world, but also in that which is to come: 22 and hath put all things under his feet, and gave him to be the head over all things to the church, 23 which is his body, the fulness of him that filleth all in all." Eph 2:5 "Even when we were dead in sins, hath quickened us together with Christ, (by grace ye are *sozo*/saved;) 6 And hath raised us up together, and made us sit together in heavenly places in Christ Jesus: 7 that in the ages to come he might shew the exceeding riches of his grace in his kindness toward us through Christ Jesus."
6. When Jesus was declared both Lord and Christ, He was also declared owner of the Universe. Acts 2:36 "Therefore let all the house of Israel know assuredly, that God hath made that same Jesus, whom ye have crucified, both Lord and Christ."
7. Every knee will bow and every tongue, in all creation, will confess Jesus as Lord. Phil 2:10 "That at the name of Jesus every knee should bow, of

things in heaven, and things in earth, and things under the earth; 11 and that every tongue should confess that Jesus Christ is Lord, to the glory of God the Father."

8. Holy Spirit was released from Heaven in a new way on the Day of Pentecost, as never before seen. Acts 2:32 "This Jesus hath God raised up, whereof we all are witnesses. 33 Therefore being by the right hand of God exalted, and having received of the Father the promise of the Holy Ghost, he hath shed forth this, which ye now see and hear."

9. God now dwells in men and not temples, so where man goes, the God of all Creation goes. 1 Cor 6:19 "What? know ye not that your body is the temple of the Holy Ghost which is in you, which ye have of God, and ye are not your own?"

10. The timetable for the new Heaven and the new Earth was moved forward and can never go backward. Isa 66:22 "For as the new heavens and the new earth, which I will make, shall remain before me, saith the Lord, so shall your seed and your name remain." Isa 51:6 "Lift up your eyes to the heavens, and look upon the earth beneath: for the heavens shall vanish away like smoke, and the earth shall wax old like a garment, and they that dwell therein shall die in like manner: but my salvation shall be for ever, and my righteousness shall not be abolished." Matt 24:35 "Heaven and earth shall pass away, but my (Jesus') words shall not pass away." 1 Cor 15:24 "Then cometh the end, when he (Jesus) shall have delivered up the kingdom to God, even the Father; when he shall have put down all rule and all authority and power. 25 For he must reign, till he hath put all enemies under his feet. 26 The last enemy that shall be destroyed is death. 27 For he hath put all things under his feet. But when he saith, all things are put under him, it is manifest that he is excepted, which did put all things under him. 28 And when all things shall be subdued unto him, then shall the Son also himself be subject unto him that put all things under him, that God may be all in all."

11. The Bosom of Abraham was emptied. Matt 27:51 "And, behold, the veil of the temple was rent in twain from the top to the bottom; and the earth did quake, and the rocks rent; 52 and the graves were opened; and many bodies of the saints which slept arose, 53 and came out of the graves after his resurrection, and went into the holy city, and appeared unto many." 1 Pet 3:18 "For Christ also hath once suffered for sins, the just for the unjust, that he might bring us to God, being put to death in the flesh, but quickened by the Spirit: 19 by which also he went and preached unto the spirits

in prison; 20 which sometime were disobedient, when once the longsuffering of God waited in the days of Noah, while the ark was a preparing, wherein few, that is, eight souls were *sozo*/saved by water." 1 Pet 4:6 "For, for this cause was the gospel preached also to them that are dead, that they might be judged according to men in the flesh, but live according to God in the spirit."

12. Man was restored to his official position of under-ruler for God in Jesus. Heb 2:6 "But one in a certain place testified, saying, What is man, that thou art mindful of him? or the son of man, that thou visitest him? 7 Thou madest him a little lower than the angels (*Elohim, God*); thou crownedst him with glory and honour, and didst set him over the works of thy hands: 8 thou hast put all things in subjection under his feet. For in that he put all in subjection under him, he left nothing that is not put under him. But now we see not yet all things put under him. 9 But we see Jesus, who was made a little lower than the angels for the suffering of death, crowned with glory and honour; that he by the grace of God should taste death for every man. 10 For it became him, for whom are all things, and by whom are all things, in bringing many sons unto glory, to make the captain of their *soteria*/salvation perfect through sufferings."

13. Jesus earned the keys to universal death and Hell/Hades. Rev 1:17 "And when I saw him (*Jesus*), I fell at his feet as dead. And he laid his right hand upon me, saying unto me, Fear not; I am the first and the last: 18 I am he that liveth, and was dead; and, behold, I am *zao*/alive for evermore, Amen; and have the keys of hell and of death."

14. A man is now seated with the God of all Creation. Heb 10:12 "But this man (*Jesus*), after he had offered one sacrifice for sins for ever, sat down on the right hand of God; 13 from henceforth expecting till his enemies be made his footstool."

15. The center stage for all Creation occupies the Throne of the God of the Universe in the return of His Son, Jesus of Nazareth, to Earth, to set the Throne of God on Earth with men. Rev 21:1 "And I saw a new heaven and a new earth: for the first heaven and the first earth were passed away; and there was no more sea. 2 And I John saw the holy city, new Jerusalem, coming down from God out of heaven, prepared as a bride adorned for her husband. 3 And I heard a great voice out of heaven saying, Behold, the tabernacle of God is with men, and he will dwell with them, and they shall be his people, and God himself shall be with them, and be their God. 4 And God shall wipe away all tears from their eyes; and there shall be no

more death, neither sorrow, nor crying, neither shall there be any more pain: for the former things are passed away. 5 And he that sat upon the throne said, Behold, I make all things new. And he said unto me, Write: for these words are true and faithful."

16. God has decreed that He will reign as God of Creation through man. Rom 5:17 "For if by one man's offence (*Adam*) death reigned by one; much more they (*men*) which (*continually*) *lambano*/receive abundance of grace and of the gift of righteousness shall reign in *zoe*/life by one, Jesus Christ.) 18 Therefore as by the offence of one (*Adam*) judgment came upon all men to condemnation; even so by the righteousness of one (*Jesus*) the free gift came upon all men unto justification of *zoe*/life. 19 For as by one man's disobedience (*Adam*) many were made sinners, so by the obedience of one (*Jesus*) shall many be made righteous. 20 Moreover the law entered, that the offence might abound. But where sin abounded, grace did much more abound: 21 that as sin hath reigned (*as a cruel king*) unto death, even so might grace reign (*as a greater king*) through righteousness unto eternal *zoe*/life by Jesus Christ our Lord."

This is not the entire list, but enough to show the Universe was changed forever in those mighty 52 days. It was a work worthy of the Son of God!

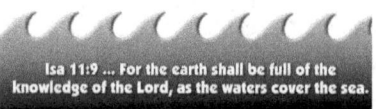

Isa 11:9 ... For the earth shall be full of the knowledge of the Lord, as the waters cover the sea.

Part IV

Understanding Who We Are in Christ

CHAPTER 18

WE WERE CRUCIFIED WITH JESUS

When Paul said, "I have been crucified with Christ," it meant he had been judged, condemned, cast out, stripped naked and nailed to the cross in Jesus, and he had received that identification.

The very thought of crucifixion, to a Jew, and especially to a Pharisee, brought a sense of shame and horror, for to be hung on a cross, tree or stake, made one a curse. Yet, this is exactly what Jesus told us we must do: Matt 16:24 "Then said Jesus unto his disciples, If any man will come after me, let him deny himself, and take up his cross, and follow me."

This is the shame of doing things God's way and not man's way, of wealth, prestige and power, in the world's system. Saul of Tarsus, operating in this world system, persecuted and killed Christians.

When Saul later identified himself with the man Jesus, believed in his heart that God had raise Him from the dead and confessed Him as his Lord, at that moment he became alive to God, sealed with Holy Spirit, a crucified man and a public enemy to those who had crucified Jesus. But this identification process caused Saul, later called Paul, to be born again, to get a renewed, re-born or recreated spirit.

As Paul later wrote: Rom 10:9 "That if thou shalt confess with thy mouth the Lord Jesus, and shalt believe in thine heart that God hath raised him from the dead,

DISCOVERING OUR REDEMPTION

thou shalt be *sozo*/saved. 10 For with the heart man believeth unto righteousness; and with the mouth confession is made unto *soteria*/salvation. 11 For the scripture saith, Whosoever believeth on him shall not be ashamed. 12 For there is no difference between the Jew and the Greek: for the same Lord over all is rich unto all that call upon him. 13 For whosoever shall call upon the name of the Lord shall be *sozo*/saved."

Paul became an outcast to the religious leaders who would not acknowledge Jesus as the Christ.

No wonder he said, in Gal 6:14, that the world had been crucified unto him, and he had been crucified unto the world. Paul had seen the shame of a godless and loveless religion of Law that lived for the power and praise of men, and not the power and praise of God. The world system had been stripped naked before Paul. 1 John 2:15 "*Agape*/love not the world, neither the things that are in the world. If any man *agape*/love the world, the *agape*/love of the Father is not in him. 16 For all that is in the world, the lust of the flesh, and the lust of the eyes, and the pride of *bios*/life, is not of the Father, but is of the world. 17 And the world passeth away, and the lust thereof: but he that doeth the will of God abideth for ever." 1 Tim 6:9 "But they that will be rich fall into temptation and a snare, and into many foolish and hurtful lusts, which drown men in destruction and perdition. 10 For the *agape*/love of money is the root of all evil: which while some coveted after, they have erred from the faith, and pierced themselves through with many sorrows."

As Jesus said: John 5:37 "And the Father himself, which hath sent me, hath borne witness of me. Ye have neither heard his voice at any time, nor seen his shape. 38 And ye have not his word abiding in you: for whom he hath sent, him ye believe not. 39 Search the scriptures; for in them ye think ye have eternal *zoe*/life: and they are they which testify of me. 40 And ye will not come to me, that ye might have *zoe*/life. 41 I receive not honour from men. 42 But I know you, that ye have not the *agape*/love of God in you. 43 I am come in my Father's name, and ye receive me not: if another shall come in his own name, him ye will receive. 44 How can ye believe, which receive honour one of another, and seek not the honour that cometh from God only?"

There was no longer any delusion in regard to the way of men. Prov 14:12 "There is a way which seemeth right unto a man, but the end thereof are the ways of death." And again: Prov 16:25 "There is a way that seemeth right unto a man, but the end thereof are the ways of death."

Because he had lived it, Paul understood: Rom 8:5 "For they that are after the flesh do mind the things of the flesh; but they that are after the Spirit the things of the Spirit. 6 For to be carnally minded is death; but to be spiritually minded is *zoe*/life and peace. 7 Because the carnal mind is enmity against God: for it is not subject to the law of God, neither indeed can be. 8 So then they that are in the flesh cannot please God."

WE WERE CRUCIFIED WITH JESUS

For clarity, see God's definition of peace: Acts 10:36: "The word which God sent unto the children of Israel, preaching peace by Jesus Christ: (he is Lord of all:) 37 that word, I say, ye know, which was published throughout all Judaea, and began from Galilee, after the baptism which John preached; 38 how God anointed Jesus of Nazareth with the Holy Ghost and with power: who went about doing good, and healing all that were oppressed (*under the active dominion, reign, control and lordship*) of the devil; for God was with him." If we are to preach God's Gospel of Peace, our preaching should look much like the way Jesus preached, demonstrated, and proclaimed it. Walking in the Spirit of God will produce the Jesus-kind of peace.

Concerning the ways of the flesh: Phil 3:3 "For we are the circumcision, which worship God in the spirit, and rejoice in Christ Jesus, and have no confidence in the flesh. 4 Though I might also have confidence in the flesh. If any other man thinketh that he hath whereof he might trust in the flesh, I more: 5 circumcised the eighth day, of the stock of Israel, of the tribe of Benjamin, an Hebrew of the Hebrews; as touching the law, a Pharisee; 6 concerning zeal, persecuting the church; touching the righteousness which is in the law, blameless. 7 But what things were gain to me, those I counted loss for Christ. 8 Yea doubtless, and I count all things but loss for the excellency of the *epignosis*/knowledge of Christ Jesus my Lord: for whom I have suffered the loss of all things, and do count them but dung, that I may win Christ, 9 and be found in him, not having mine own righteousness, which is of the law, but that which is through the faith of Christ, the righteousness which is of God by faith."

Paul could no longer be deceived by the world's religions and the power of the flesh. There is no righteousness that a man can do that is adequate before God; God-level righteousness must be from God Himself, not only legally, but in your heart.

Paul knew false religion's cruelty, and he had inflicted much of that cruelty.

In his zeal, he had actually fought God. Acts 9:4 "And he (*Saul*) fell to the earth, and heard a voice saying unto him, Saul, Saul, why persecutest thou me? 5 And he said, Who art thou, Lord? And the Lord said, I am Jesus whom thou persecutest: it is hard for thee to kick against the pricks." Notice that Jesus identified Himself as the same as those Saul had persecuted, thus declaring that all Christians and He were the same. This is Identification.

That little Jew, with his mighty message, and his tremendous power in prayer, had now been crucified to the world. Gal 2:21 "I do not frustrate the grace of God: for if righteousness come by the law, then Christ is dead in vain."

Rom 10:2 "For I bear them record that they (*Jews who deny that Jesus is the Christ*) have a zeal of God, but not according to knowledge. 3 For they being ignorant of God's righteousness, and going about to establish their own righteousness, have not submitted themselves unto the righteousness of God. 4 For Christ is the end of the law for righteousness to every one that believeth."

We understand what crucifixion actually meant in the plan of God. Paul saw his Identification with Christ in Jesus' crucifixion. Paul was united with Jesus' shame and nakedness as a convicted felon of the imperial government of Rome, the rulers of the temple, and of the people of God.

We understand that crucifixion, by itself, did not mean just death.

It was a place of suffering and shame, as a warning to all: Don't fight the world system.

It signifies our union with Christ in His disgrace and suffering.

Rom. 6:6 "Knowing this, that our old man was crucified with him, that the body of sin might be done away, that so we should no longer be in bondage to sin."

Crucifixion points the way to death; it is the cursed place of physical suffering unto death.

In Holy Spirit's great argument of our Identification with Christ, He said, through Paul, that our old man, our spirit, the real man, who was filled with spiritual death in satanic nature, was nailed to the cross in Christ.

Gal 6:14 "But God forbid that I should glory, save in the cross of our Lord Jesus Christ, by whom the world is crucified unto me, and I unto the world. 15 For in Christ Jesus neither circumcision availeth anything, nor uncircumcision, but a new creature (*new creation, born again in Spirit of God*)."

Christ went to the cross, not for Himself, and not as a martyr, but as a Substitute for fallen man.

We were nailed to the cross with Him.

We were crucified with Him.

Gal 2:20 "I am (*have been*) crucified with Christ: nevertheless I zao/live; yet not I, but Christ zao/liveth in me: and the life which I now zao/live in the flesh I zao/live by the faith of the Son of God, who agape/loved me, and gave himself for me. 21 I do not frustrate the grace of God: for if righteousness come by the law, then Christ is dead in vain."

Col 2:11 "In whom (*Jesus Christ*) also ye are circumcised with the circumcision made without hands, in putting off the body of the sins of the flesh by the circumcision of Christ: 12 buried with him in baptism, wherein also ye are risen with him through the faith of the operation of God, who hath raised him from the dead. 13 And you, being dead in your sins and the uncircumcision of your flesh, hath he quickened together with him, having forgiven you all trespasses."

The object of the crucifixion of Jesus, in the mind of the mob, was to get rid of this Man, whom they hated.

In the mind of Justice, it meant Jesus' Identification with humanity in its sin, consequences and suffering, and our Identification with Jesus in His whipping, crucifixion, death, resurrection and glorification. Jesus took the full penalty of sin for all of mankind and paid the full price and consequence of it for us. Justice got all it demanded, for all the sin of mankind. Sin was not just wiped away; it was fully paid in the torment of the damned.

Instead of man actually being crucified, Jesus became all of man, and what Jesus received, man received. What man was due, Jesus took. This is the great covenant Identification of God by Jesus.

Now we can appreciate what God says through Paul better. Rom 8:29 "For whom he did foreknow, he also did predestinate to be conformed to the image of his Son, that he might be the firstborn among many brethren. 30 Moreover whom he did predestinate, them he also called: and whom he called, them he also justified: and whom he justified, them he also glorified *[note this is past tense when He did these in and by Jesus]*."

31 "What shall we then say to these things *[as we finally grasp the immensity of the work of the Mighty Arm of God]*? If God be for us, who can be against us? 32 He that spared not his own Son, but delivered him up for us all *[to crucifixion, suffering death and Hell]*, how shall he *(Father God)* not with him *(Jesus)* also freely give us all things? 33 Who shall lay any thing to the charge of God's elect? It is God that justifieth. 34 Who is he that condemneth? It is Christ that died, yea rather, that is risen again, who is even at the right hand of God, who also maketh intercession for us.

35 "Who shall separate us from the *agape*/love of Christ? shall tribulation, or distress, or persecution, or famine, or nakedness, or peril, or sword? 36 As it is written, For thy sake we are killed all the day long; we are accounted as sheep for the slaughter *[by our enemies]*. 37 Nay, in all these things we are more than conquerors *[over any and all works of the devil]* through him that *agape*/loved us *[by His suffering death, resurrection and glorification]*. 38 For I am persuaded, that neither death, nor life, nor angels, nor principalities, nor powers, nor things present, nor things to come, 39 nor height, nor depth, nor any other creature, shall be able to separate us from the *agape*/love of God, which is in Christ Jesus our Lord."

We constantly renew our minds in these Redemption truths to become and stay fully persuaded also. As you do you will change your identity to the One who was crucified, to the One who was resurrected, and to the One, Jesus our Magnificent Lord, who is now glorified, and Father God made us one with and in Him in Jesus in every step of the way. So each one of us can say: "I was crucified with Him." "I was resurrected with Him." "I was and am now glorified with Him."

This is how we are to start making our crucifixion with Jesus effective in this life. We do not stop at the cross, but keep going to all God has given us in Jesus. We go from "was" to now "is." Otherwise we only get a taste and not the full meal the Lord offers for this life, now.

Chapter 19

We Died with Jesus

Jesus died twice on the cross.
Isaiah 53:9 reveals this to us.
"And they made his grave with the wicked, and with a rich man in his deaths."
The word *death* is plural in the Hebrew.
If you have Bibles with marginal renderings, you will notice this.
That is because Jesus died two deaths on the cross: He died spiritually before He died physically.
In John 10:18, He said that no one could take His life from Him.
John 10:17 "Therefore doth my Father *agape*/love me, because I lay down my *psuche*/life (*soul*), that I might take it again. 18 No man taketh it from me, but I lay it down of myself. I have power to lay it down, and I have power to take it again. This commandment have I received of my Father."
He could not be killed; He could not die. He left His body only when He was ready to do so.
John 19:30 "When Jesus therefore had received the vinegar, he said, It is finished: and he bowed his head, and gave up the ghost. ... 33 But when they came to Jesus, and saw that he was dead already, they brake not his legs: 34 but one of the soldiers with a spear pierced his side, and forthwith came there out blood and water."

We Died with Jesus

Why could Jesus not die? Because His body was not mortal.

He had a body like Adam's before he sinned.

It was a perfect, human body, not mortal, nor immortal.

It was a body that could not die ... until sin had taken possession of Jesus' spirit.

Mortal means to be subject to death and, thus, subject to Satan. *Immortal* is the opposite of mortal and means it can never die and can never be subject to Satan. Only after Adam sinned could he die. Adam died in spirit first, and then his body followed. The angel was posted to keep Adam from eating of the Tree of Life, the Tree of Immortality, so Adam could not be forever dead to God, like Satan is.

Gen 3:22 "And the Lord God said, Behold, the man (*Adam*) is become as one of us, to know good and evil: and now, lest he put forth his hand, and take also of the tree of life, and eat, and live for ever: 23 therefore the Lord God sent him forth from the garden of Eden, to till the ground from whence he was taken. 24 So he drove out the man; and he placed at the east of the garden of Eden Cherubims, and a flaming sword which turned every way, to keep the way of the tree of life."

Prior to that sin, Adam had a body that was not subject to death, but through sin, could die. It was never meant to be immortal ... until Adam ate of the Tree of Life. Jesus had a body, with God as Father, but woman as mother. His flesh was from man; His spirit from God.

One could argue that Jesus, in His incarnation, was like what the Greeks called a demigod, but He chose to be only a man and, thus, not a demigod. Jesus was all of God and all of man. This is the acid test of spiritual truth. 1 John 4:2 "Hereby know ye the Spirit of God: Every spirit that confesseth that Jesus Christ is come in the flesh is of God: 3 and every spirit that confesseth not that Jesus Christ is come in the flesh is not of God: and this is that spirit of antichrist, whereof ye have heard that it should come; and even now already is it in the world."

Jesus is the "last Adam." (1 Cor 15:45-47) As such, the Scriptures indicate that this means His incarnate body was like Adam's. 1 Cor 15:20 "But now is Christ risen from the dead, and become the firstfruits of them that slept. 21 For since by man (*Adam*) came death, by man (*Jesus*) came also the resurrection of the dead. 22 For as in Adam all die, even so in Christ shall all be made *zao*/alive."

Had Jesus sinned, His body also would also have died, just like Adam's did. Thus, Jesus was tempted in all manner of things, like as we are. So Jesus was incarnated in a human body and tempted in every way that a human can be tempted.

Heb 4:14 "Seeing then that we have a great high priest, that is passed into the heavens, Jesus the Son of God, let us hold fast our profession. 15 For we have not an high priest which cannot be touched with the feeling of our infirmities; but was in all points tempted like as we are, yet without sin."

DISCOVERING OUR REDEMPTION

Hallelujah! Jesus, as a man, never sinned. He was the spotless Lamb of God.

Heb 2:16 "For verily he (*Jesus*) took not on him the nature of angels; but he took on him the seed of Abraham. 17 **Wherefore in all things it behoved him to be made like unto his brethren,** that he might be a merciful and faithful high priest in things pertaining to God, to make reconciliation for the sins of the people. 18 For in that he himself hath suffered being tempted, he is able to succour them that are tempted."

Jesus came in a human body, without sin, because His Father was God, and not Adam. He was incarnated in a body from the Earth by a woman. He was the seed of that woman's faith. Matt 1:18 "Now the birth of Jesus Christ was on this wise: When as his mother Mary was espoused to Joseph, before they came together, she was found with child of the Holy Ghost."

Luke 1:37 "For with God nothing shall be impossible. 38 And Mary said, Behold the handmaid of the Lord; be it unto me according to thy word. And the angel departed from her."

Jesus was the One long-promised at the Fall of Adam. Gen 3:15 "And I will put enmity between thee and the woman, and between thy seed **and her seed**; it shall bruise (*crush*) thy head (*governmental authority and ability*), and thou shalt bruise his heel."

Just as with everything else of God, Mary's faith in the Word of God for her situation produced the life and impossible ability of God on the Earth.

Heb 2:14 "Forasmuch then as the children are partakers of flesh and blood, he (*Jesus*) also himself likewise took part of the same; that through death he might destroy him that had the power of death, that is, the devil."

1 John 3:8 "He that committeth sin is of the devil; for the devil sinneth from the beginning. For this purpose the Son of God was manifested, that he might destroy the works of the devil."

When Jesus was raised from the dead, He got an eternal, immortal body. A wonder of the ages is that He, who was made sin in spirit and the curse of sin in body, was raised the righteousness of God. And He could not be raised until each and every human was also made the righteousness of God in Christ Jesus. This is a wondrous fact, prepared for those who enter by faith into the resurrection of Jesus.

Rom 4:24 "But for us also, to whom it shall be imputed, if we believe on him that raised up Jesus our Lord from the dead; 25 who was delivered for our offences, and was raised again for our justification [*and when we were justified unto the righteousness of God in Christ Jesus unto* zoe/life]."

One proof of this is that Jesus was raised in that immortal body, just as we are promised will be true of us.

1 Cor 15:21 "For since by man came death, by man came also the resurrection of the dead. 22 For as in Adam all die, even so in Christ shall all be made *zao*/alive. 23 But every man in his own order: Christ the firstfruits; afterward they that are Christ's at his coming."

WE DIED WITH JESUS

When Jesus became sin, on that awesome and awful crucifixion day, His body then became subject to death and Satan, and He could die under the law of sin and death.

God had spoken the law of sin and death into existence in the beginning. Gen 2:17 "But of the tree of the knowledge of good and evil, thou shalt not eat of it: for in the day that thou eatest thereof thou shalt surely die."

But when Adam sinned, he did not die right away. He was cast out of the Garden, and later he died physically. Death worked in his body over time until it eventually killed him. Gen 5:5 "And all the days that Adam lived were nine hundred and thirty years: and he died."

When Adam sinned, he died in spirit, and his body followed later. [We assume Adam died like other men, in that he aged first and then died with a body no longer able to carry on, and /or he got sick and died.]

In a similar manner, Jesus had to die spiritually before He could die physically.

If Jesus' body had been like yours and mine, then He would not have been Deity, He would not have been a Substitute, and He could not have died for our sins as the spotless Lamb. As an un-born-again man, He merely would have died as a martyr.

But if He had a body like the first man Adam's body prior to the fall, (not mortal or subject to death and, therefore, not subject to Satan, the prince of death, the ability of death), then He was Deity, the Son of God. (Lk 3:23-38)

John 5:18 "Therefore the Jews sought the more to kill him, because he not only had broken the sabbath, but said also that God was his Father, making himself equal with God."

In this, we see the human race died with the Crucified One.

Paul says, 2 Tim 2:11 "It is a faithful saying: For if we be dead with him, we shall also *zao*/live with him."

Rom 6:8 "Now if we be dead with Christ, we believe that we shall also *zao*/live with him."

In these scriptures, we notice we died with Christ, when He died.

This is a reference to the time after Jesus died in spirit, because man was already dead in spirit. When Jesus was made sin, He died in spirit to be just like mankind.

When He died in the flesh, we died with Him.

Rom 6:3 "Know ye not, that so many of us as were baptized (*immersed, saturated, united*) into Jesus Christ were baptized (*immersed, saturation, united*) into his death? 4 Therefore we are buried with him by baptism (*immersion, saturation, unity*) into death: that like as Christ was raised up from the dead by the glory of the Father, even so we also should walk in newness of *zoe*/life. 5 For if we have been planted together in the likeness of his death, we shall be also in the likeness of his

DISCOVERING OUR REDEMPTION

resurrection: 6 knowing this, that our old man is crucified with him, that the body of sin might be destroyed, that henceforth we should not serve sin. 7 For he that is dead is freed from sin. 8 Now if we be dead with Christ, we believe that we shall also *zao*/live with him."

He was our Substitute.

We were one with Him on the cross.

We were one with Him in His physical death.

And we were already dead spiritually.

He joined us in our spiritual death, our unity with Satan.

Our dead old man was nailed with Jesus and killed by the cross.

Eph 4:22 "That ye put off concerning the former conversation the old man, which is corrupt according to the deceitful lusts."

Rom 6:6 "*Ginosko*/knowing this, that our old man is crucified with him, that the body of sin might be destroyed, that henceforth we should not serve sin."

He died under our judgment, in our stead.

He died because He was made sin.

He died because He *agape* loves us, and Father God *agape* loves us.

If we believe Him, there can be no judgment for us.

Isa 53:10 "Yet it pleased the Lord to bruise him; he hath put him to grief: when thou shalt make his soul an offering for sin, he shall see his seed, he shall prolong his days, and the pleasure of the Lord shall prosper in his hand. 11 He shall see of the travail of his soul, and shall be satisfied: by his knowledge shall my righteous servant justify many; for he shall *cabal*/bear their iniquities. 12 Therefore will I divide him a portion with the great, and he shall divide the spoil with the strong; because he hath poured out his soul unto death: and he was numbered with the transgressors; and he *nasa*/bare the sin of many, and made intercession for the transgressors."

That sounds just like Paul's revelation, doesn't it?

The Pauline Revelation is an unveiling of what happened from the time Jesus was made sin, sometime after the Garden of Gethsemane, until He sat down at the right hand of God and sent forth Holy Spirit on the Day of Pentecost, to birth the Church of the new creation people.

Nowhere else can we find this knowledge.

This is Substitution.

This is absolute Identification.

Jesus died for us, and we died with Him.

This is a part of the great Substitutionary truth in prophecy.

He poured out His *psuche*/soul/life unto death.

Isa 53:12 "Therefore will I divide him a portion with the great, and he shall divide the spoil with the strong; because he hath poured out his soul unto death:

and he was numbered with the transgressors; and he *nasa*/bare the sin of many, and made intercession for the transgressors."

Hos 6:1 "Come, and let us return unto the Lord: for he hath torn, and he will heal us; he hath smitten, and he will bind us up. 2 After two days will he revive us: in the third day he will raise us up, and we shall live in his sight."

Through that death, we were made alive.

It was our sin that slew Him.

He became our curse for us, so we do not have to bear the curse.

It is His righteousness that gives us life, the *zoe*/life of God.

He drank the cup of death, that we might drink the cup of life.

In that mighty ministry before He arose from the dead, He destroyed death's lordship.

When death slew Him, it slew itself.

Jesus said what would happen. Read the whole parable in Mark 12 and Luke 20.

Note how God sends His own Son. Mark 12:5 "And again he sent another; and him they killed, and many others; beating some, and killing some. 6 Having yet therefore one son, his wellbeloved, he sent him also last unto them, saying, They will reverence my son. 7 But those husbandmen said among themselves, This is the heir; come, let us kill him, and the inheritance shall be ours. 8 And they took him, and killed him, and cast him out of the vineyard."

Jesus is the great ambush of God against the devil. They had killed the prophets for centuries, and it was no wonder that they killed the greatest prophet among men, John the Baptist, and the greatest prophet of all, Jesus of Nazareth.

1 Cor 2:6 "Howbeit we speak wisdom among them that are perfect: yet not the wisdom of this world, nor of the princes of this world, that come to nought (*dethroned*): 7 but we speak the wisdom of God in a mystery, even the hidden wisdom, which God ordained before the world unto our glory: 8 which none of the princes of this world knew: for had they known it, they would not have crucified the Lord of glory."

Jesus conquered sin when He allowed it to overcome Him.

Isa 53:8 "He was taken from prison and from judgment: and who shall declare his generation? for he was cut off out of the land of the living: for the transgression of my people was he stricken. 9 And he made his grave with the wicked, and with the rich in his death; because he had done no violence, neither was any deceit in his mouth. 10 Yet it pleased the LORD to bruise him; he hath put him to grief: when thou shalt make his soul an offering for sin, he shall see his seed, he shall prolong his days, and the pleasure of the LORD shall prosper in his hand. 11 He shall see of the travail of his soul, and shall be satisfied: by his knowledge shall my righteous servant justify many; for he shall *cabal*/bear their iniquities."

He conquered Satan, when He let Satan gain the mastery over Him.

DISCOVERING OUR REDEMPTION

Dan 9:26 "And after threescore and two weeks shall Messiah be cut off, but not for himself ... ."

Zech 13:7 "Awake, O sword, against my shepherd, and against the man that is my fellow, saith the Lord of hosts: smite the shepherd, and the sheep shall be scattered: and I will turn mine hand upon the little ones." (Mk 14:22)

Eph 5:2 "And walk in *agape*/love, as Christ also hath *agape*/loved us, and hath given himself for us an offering and a sacrifice to God for a sweetsmelling savour."

1 Pet 3:18 "For Christ also hath once suffered for sins, the just for the unjust, that he might bring us to God, being put to death in the flesh, but quickened by the Spirit."

Jesus made the one who enforced the captivity of death captive.

Ps 68:17 "The chariots of God are twenty thousand, even thousands of angels: the Lord is among them, as in Sinai, in the holy place. 18 Thou hast ascended on high, thou hast led captivity captive: thou hast received gifts for men; yea, for the rebellious also, that the Lord God might dwell among them. 19 Blessed be the Lord, who daily loadeth us with benefits, even the God of our salvation. Selah. 20 He that is our God is the God of salvation; and unto God the Lord belong the issues from death. 21 But God shall wound the head of his enemies, and the hairy scalp of such an one as goeth on still in his trespasses."

Jesus led captivity captive when He defeated Satan and made an open display of him.

Col 2:15 "And having spoiled principalities and powers, he made a shew of them openly, triumphing over them in it."

Eph 4:8 "Wherefore he saith, When he ascended up on high, he led captivity captive, and gave gifts unto men."

He conquered disease when He let disease take possession of Him.

Col 2:15 "[God] disarmed the principalities and powers that were ranged against us and made a bold display and public example of them, in triumphing over them in Him and in it [the cross]." AMP

He became one with Satan in spiritual death, to make us one with God in spiritual life.

2 Cor 5:21 "For he hath made him to be sin for us, who knew no sin; that we might be made the righteousness of God in him."

He became one with us in weakness, in sin, in disease, in alienation from God, and in spiritual death, that He might make us one with Himself in righteousness, perfect health and fellowship with the Father.

Jesus became death's prisoner in order to set us free.

In the mind of Justice, we died to sin and its dominion when we died with Christ.

Rom 6:7 "He that hath died is justified from sin." DBY

We Died with Jesus

In that He already died, He is free from the lordship of spiritual death.

There was in God's mind, at the crucifixion, a perfect oneness of Christ with us, and in the resurrection and new birth, a perfect oneness of us in Christ.

Just as Jesus conquered death by submitting to it, we, in the New Creation, conquer Satan by submitting to the Lordship of Jesus.

James 4:6 "But he giveth more grace. Wherefore he saith, God resisteth the proud, but giveth grace unto the humble. 7 Submit yourselves therefore to God. Resist the devil, and he will flee from you."

We and our diseases were laid on Him, and became a part of Him when He was made sin with our sin. Isa 53:3 "He was despised and rejected and forsaken by men, a Man of sorrows and pains, and acquainted (*unified, made one*) with grief and sickness; and like One from Whom men hide their faces He was despised, and we did not appreciate His worth or have any esteem for Him." AMP

We are healed by becoming partakers of Christ's divine nature.

Isa 53:5 "But he was wounded for our transgressions, he was bruised for our iniquities: the chastisement of our peace was upon him; and with his stripes we are healed."

Disease and sickness do not belong to the new creation.

It is an abnormal thing, in the mind of the Father, for a child of God to be sick.

We died with Him.

We died to the dominion of sin.

We died to the dominion of disease.

We died to the dominion of evil circumstances and habits.

We died to the dominion of demons.

We died to the dominion of the curse of sin.

We died to the dominion of the curse of men.

God did not try to improve you; He killed your old man in Jesus.

1 Pet 2:24 becomes a reality. "Who his own self bare our sins in His body upon the tree, that we, having died unto sins, might *zao*/live unto righteousness; by whose stripes ye were healed." RSV

This is Identification, our utter oneness with Him in sin and judgment on the cross.

"That we, having died unto sins." His death and our death are identical.

This is not just His physical death.

This is also spiritual.

He died twice on Calvary, once in the spirit, and once in the physical.

He partook of our spiritual death, and we were utterly one with Him in that judgment.

He partook of our physical death, and we were utterly one with Him in that judgment.

DISCOVERING OUR REDEMPTION

"That we might *zao*/live unto righteousness." Or, that we might partake of His righteousness, as He partook of our sins, that we might be righteous, as He became sin with our sins.

Then the next marvelous statement: "By whose stripes ye were healed."

Jesus not only had our sin nature, but He also had our diseases.

He took over our diseases, and He put them away when He put sin away.

"By His stripes we are healed."

Here the actual Greek word is singular, *stripe*, meaning that His back was one massive stripe of shredded flesh and blood. In the Roman process of scourging, Jesus' back, sides, chest, legs, head and even face would have been cut and shredded by the cruel Roman whip.

These were the stripes of punishment: Deut 25:2 "Then if the guilty man deserves to be beaten, the judge shall cause him to lie down and be beaten in his presence with a certain number of stripes according to his offense. 3 Forty stripes may be given him but not more, lest, if he should be beaten with many stripes, your brother should [be treated like a beast and] seem low and worthless to you."AMP

Jesus was beaten, not within the limits of the Law of Moses, but with the unlimited measure of Imperial Rome. He was beaten as one "low and worthless," less than an animal. To the Romans, He was already a conquered dog, He had no rights, except those granted by Rome. It was as if they said, "Receive pain, bear that pain, and in the scars of it, ever remember, you are worth less than a beast."

Stir yourself to enjoy the wonder of it. As Jesus put our sin and diseases away, by becoming sin and disease for us, so we partake of His righteousness and healing, when we believe in His work for us.

Christ has died once for all as our Sin Substitute.

He, in judgment, met the demands of Justice for us.

He took them with Him when He went to the place of Substitution, the place of Judgment, the place of suffering.

I am convinced that the Father sees us in Christ as perfect, as the finished work of Christ is perfect. Remember, He is a faith God and calls those things that be not as if they are, and they become, when united by faith. Since Jesus was slain before the foundation of the world was laid, God has always dealt with man through the blood of Jesus. It has been man, with a corrupted heart, that resisted God.

Gen 3:8 "And they heard the voice of the LORD God walking in the garden in the cool of the day: and Adam and his wife hid themselves from the presence of the LORD God amongst the trees of the garden. 9 And the LORD God called unto Adam, and said unto him, Where art thou? 10 And he said, I heard thy voice in the garden, and I was afraid, because I was naked; and I hid myself."

How tragic! Even when in trouble and God came to help, as He did so, His love object, His man, ran from Him, rather than to Him.

We Died with Jesus

God loved man before He formed us, and has never had any other intention for us.

Jer 29:11 "For I know the thoughts and plans that I have for you, says the Lord, thoughts and plans for welfare and peace and not for evil, to give you hope in your final outcome." AMP

As you are going through trials, shout these truths to the devil and to stir your heart. YOU ARE LOVED!

God saw that our union with Satan was a perfect union. (Eph 2:1, 5)

We were one with the devil.

He laid our spiritual union with Satan, our death, on Christ.

Eph 2:10 "For we are His workmanship, created in Christ Jesus."

That work was wrought by the great master workman, Christ, before He arose from the dead. God worked and put us on Christ, and when Jesus rose from the dead, He worked in us the same work. By His stripes we were healed and made prosperous for this life. We got this, even before the cross, at the whipping post.

But God did not stop there, although most of us would think that would be enough and the answer to most of our prayers. By the death and resurrection of Jesus, we could become new creations, creatures whose spirits wanted only to please Father God, just like Jesus, and seated in Jesus, to be with Him forever.

Isa 53:11 "He shall see [the fruit] of the travail of His soul and be satisfied; by His knowledge of Himself [which He possesses and imparts to others] shall My [uncompromisingly] righteous One, My Servant, justify many and make many righteous (upright and in right standing with God), for He shall *cabal*/bear (*to strong labor, never to be carried again*) their iniquities and their guilt [with the consequences, says the Lord]. 12 Therefore will I divide Him a portion with the great [kings and rulers], and He shall divide the spoil with the mighty, because He poured out His life unto death, and [He let Himself] be regarded as a criminal and be numbered with the transgressors; yet He *nasa*/bore [and took away] (*carried to completion, never to be carried again*) the sin of many and made intercession for the transgressors (the rebellious). [Luke 22:37.]" AMP

This work was so great that, even in our imperfections in this life, Jesus is not ashamed to call us His brethren. Jesus is looking at something far greater than any present sin we walk in. He knows the work He did in and for us by the cross. He knows the work Father God did, when Father raised Him from the dead.

Heb 2:10 "For it became him, for whom are all things, and by whom are all things, in bringing many sons unto glory, to make the captain (*author*) of their *soteria*/salvation perfect through sufferings. 11 For both he that sanctifieth and they who are sanctified are all of one: for which cause he is not ashamed to call them brethren, 12 saying, I will declare thy name unto my brethren, in the midst of the church will I sing praise unto thee. 13 And again, I will put my trust in him. And again, Behold I and the children which God hath given me. 14 Forasmuch then as

DISCOVERING OUR REDEMPTION

the children are partakers of flesh and blood, he also himself likewise took part of the same; that through death he might destroy him that had the power of death, that is, the devil; 15 and deliver them who through fear of death were all their lifetime subject to bondage."

The Father sees us now in all our beauty and perfection in Christ.

Eph 1:3 "Blessed be the God and Father of our Lord Jesus Christ, who hath blessed us with all spiritual blessings in heavenly places in Christ: 4 according as he hath chosen us in him before the foundation of the world, that we should be holy and without blame before him in *agape*/love: 5 having predestinated us unto the adoption of children by Jesus Christ to himself, according to the good pleasure of his will, 6 to the praise of the glory of his grace, wherein he hath made us accepted in the *agape*/beloved. 7 in whom (*Jesus Christ*) we have redemption through his blood, the forgiveness (*remission, obliteration and putting away*) of sins, according to the riches of his grace."

This beauty is all His own. He made us to please His own heart.

We died to sin once for all in Christ.

We died to Satan's dominion.

We died to the old habits that held us in bondage.

We died to our imperfect childhood that did not raise us in Heaven on Earth.

We died to every event in our lives that tried to offend, cripple or kill us.

We died to every limitation that the world might impose on us.

We died to every limitation that we impose on ourselves.

We died to every false sense of self outside of God.

We died to every false sense of security outside of God.

We died to every false and failed love outside of the love of God.

We died to every aspect of evil fear.

We do not need to die again.

The theory of our dying daily with Christ comes from the KJV, "I am crucified," which is an incorrect translation of Gal 2:20. It should be "I have been crucified ... ."

Another passage for dying daily is 1 Cor 15:31, where it is speaking of Paul's living in the presence of physical death, the expectation of being thrown to the lions in the arena. This is not emotion or attitude, but the reality of people trying to kill him every day of his life.

How we overcome Satan is described this way: Rev 12:11 "And they overcame him (*Satan*) by the blood of the Lamb, and by the word of their testimony; and they *agape*/loved not their *psuche*/lives (*souls*) unto the death." This is not denying the new man self, but resisting the old man of the flesh unto death, as Jesus did, ever looking to His resurrection. It is walking in: Rom 6:11 "Likewise reckon ye also yourselves to be dead indeed unto sin, but *zao*/alive unto God through Jesus Christ our Lord."

WE DIED WITH JESUS

Jesus talked about losing our souls/lives to gain His. Luke 14:25 "And there went great multitudes with him: and he (*Jesus*) turned, and said unto them, 26 if any man come to me, and hate not his father, and mother, and wife, and children, and brethren, and sisters, yea, and his own *psuche*/life (*soul*) also, he cannot be my disciple. 27 And whosoever doth not bear his cross, and come after me, cannot be my disciple." So here the process is based on the kinds of choices we make and the attitudes we maintain.

Matt 16:24 "Then said Jesus unto his disciples, If any man will come after me, let him deny himself, and take up his cross, and follow me. 25 For whosoever will *sozo*/save his *psuche*/life (*soul*) shall lose it: and whosoever will lose his *psuche*/life (*soul*) for my sake shall find it. 26 For what is a man profited, if he shall gain (*win*) the whole world, and lose his own *psuche*/soul (*life*)? or what shall a man give in exchange for his *psuche*/soul (*life*)? 27 For the Son of man shall come in the glory of his Father with his angels; and then he shall reward every man according to his works."

Notice how we manage our souls is related to our outcome on the Day of Judgment, where our works are to be tested. On that day, any work not of God is called wood, hay and stubble and will not survive. That which survives and for which you get a reward is called silver, gold and jewels (see 1 Cor 3:11-15).

Mark 8:36 "For what shall it profit a man, if he shall gain the whole world, and lose his own *psuche*/soul (*life*)? 37 Or what shall a man give in exchange for his *psuche*/soul (*life*)? 38 Whosoever therefore shall be ashamed of me and of my words in this adulterous and sinful generation; of him also shall the Son of man be ashamed, when he cometh in the glory of his Father with the holy angels."

Luke 17:32 "Remember Lot's wife. 33 Whosoever shall seek to save (*purchase*) his *psuche*/life (*soul*) shall lose it; and whosoever shall lose his life shall preserve it."

Luke 21:17 "And ye shall be hated of all men for my name's sake. 18 But there shall not an hair of your head perish. 19 In your patience (*endurance, faithfulness and consistency*) possess (*obtain, purchase and win*) ye your *psuche*/souls (*lives*)."

Acts 20:24 "But none of these things move me (*Paul*), neither count I my *psuche*/life (*soul*) dear unto myself, so that I might finish my course with joy, and the ministry, which I have received of the Lord Jesus, to testify the gospel of the grace of God."

This process is to get control of our souls against the pulls of the world system, run by the devil, to let God's life, His Word and His ways run your souls. We overcome the devil by not holding our souls, our flesh mind, or our carnal nature as stronger than the Word of God. Rom 8:5 "For they that are after the flesh do mind the things of the flesh; but they that are after the Spirit the things of the Spirit. 6 For to be carnally minded is death; but to be spiritually minded is *zoe*/life and peace (*victory over the oppressions of the devil*). 7 Because the carnal mind is enmity against

DISCOVERING OUR REDEMPTION

God: for it is not subject to the law of God, neither indeed can be. 8 So then they that are in the flesh cannot please God."

Gal 5:16 "This I say then, Walk in the Spirit (*the Word of the new creation in Christ*), and ye shall not fulfil the lust of the flesh. 17 For the flesh lusteth against the Spirit, and the Spirit against the flesh: and these are contrary the one to the other: so that ye cannot do the things that ye would."

In every situation, we have the Word of God versus the facts of the situation. Whose report will you believe and cling to? The facts can change to the truth of God's Word, by faith in God. By not letting our soul run away in emotion and offense, we keep our heart pure. The devil's goal is to get us offended in God so that we say faith in God by His Word is not working.

This is described in the Parable of the Sower and the Seed. In this parable, the devil attacks the Word in a variety of ways. If your soul is un-renewed or has gotten corrupted, you will not *lambano*/receive, hold on to, no matter what, the Word of God and produce the results of that Word, as described in verse 23 below. Matt 13:18 "Hear ye therefore the parable of the sower. 19 When any one heareth the word of the kingdom, and understandeth it not, then cometh the wicked one, and catcheth away that which was sown in his heart. This is he which received seed by the way side. 20 But he that received the seed into stony places, the same is he that heareth the word, and anon with joy receiveth it; 21 yet hath he not root in himself, but dureth for a while: for when tribulation or persecution ariseth because of the word, by and by he is offended. 22 He also that *lambano*/received seed among the thorns is he that heareth the word; and the care of this world, and the deceitfulness of riches, choke the word, and he becometh unfruitful. 23 But he that *lambano*/received seed into the good ground is he that heareth the word, and understandeth it; which also beareth fruit, and bringeth forth, some an hundredfold, some sixty, some thirty."

The temptation could be having to miss lunch or people tormenting and trying to kill you for following Jesus. We are warned that we will be persecuted and have many troubles. Ps 34:19 "Many are the afflictions of the righteous: but the Lord delivereth him out of them all."

In all cases, you have to hold on to the promises of God that go past death and not let yourself be terrified in the situation. Yes, some will die as martyrs. Yes, your fleshly standards and idolatries will be tested. If it happens, God will help you, with His Spirit of glory. Your new creation man, your new nature, is just like Jesus and understands the right priorities.

Trust in God to produce God's results. You trust by faith actions. Start confessing everything God did for you in Jesus. Watch your heart and mind like a hawk, and, at the slightest anxiety, launch into obeying: Phil 4:4 "Rejoice in the Lord alway: and again I say, Rejoice. 5 Let your moderation be known unto all men.

We Died with Jesus

The Lord is at hand. 6 Be careful (*anxious, fearful*) for nothing; but in every thing by prayer and supplication with thanksgiving (*in loud shouts, praises and thanks, until you feel thankful and you have written God's inability to lie and His love for you in that situation on your heart*) let your *aiteo*/requests (*requirements, demands and expectations, as due by covenant promise*) be made known unto God. 7 And the peace of God, which passeth all understanding (*because you have done these actions of living trust and faith in God*), shall keep your hearts and minds through Christ Jesus. 8 Finally, brethren, whatsoever things are true, whatsoever things are honest, whatsoever things are just, whatsoever things are pure, whatsoever things are lovely, whatsoever things are of good report; if there be any virtue, and if there be any praise, think on these things."

As you do these trust actions, not just once or twice, but daily for months (90 days minimum) you write God's Word, His faithfulness and His love on your heart. This is how you *lambano* the Word of God to effective results. It is hard work. There is nothing casual about trusting or *lambanoing*. They are both words of intense action. As you do this, then the awesome spiritual truths of God's work in these 52 days by Jesus become as real to you as they are to Him.

Rom 6:10 "For in that he died, he died unto sin once: but in that he *zao*/liveth, he *zao*/liveth unto God. 11 Likewise reckon ye also yourselves to be dead indeed unto sin, but *zao*/alive unto God through Jesus Christ our Lord."

Notice there are two reckonings here. The first is that, like Jesus, you are dead to sin. And the second that, like Jesus, you are now *zao*/alive to God. You only have to reckon if it does not appear that way now. That means something in your life and behavior does not look like Jesus. This could be sickness, lack or sin. So you reckon, based on the facts of Redemption, whenever you discover you are walking in a manner less than Jesus. As you reckon, do it in faith, expecting God to manifest the proper Jesus behavior and character in you.

This is part of the process of abiding in Jesus, your Salvation. Heb 10:38 "Now the just shall *zao*/live by faith: but if any man draw back, my soul shall have no pleasure in him." Faith means you do not see it yet and have to believe God to keep His Word to bring that promise to pass.

Rom 5:1 "Therefore being justified by faith, we have peace with God through our Lord Jesus Christ: 2 by whom also we have access by faith into this grace wherein we stand, and rejoice in hope of the glory of God."

John 15:3 "Now ye are clean through the word which I have spoken unto you. 4 Abide in me, and I in you. As the branch cannot bear fruit of itself, except it abide in the vine; no more can ye, except ye abide in me. 5 I am the vine, ye are the branches: he that abideth in me, and I in him, the same bringeth forth much fruit: for without me ye can do nothing. 6 If a man abide not in me, he is cast forth as a branch, and is withered; and men gather them, and cast them into the fire, and they

DISCOVERING OUR REDEMPTION

are burned. 7 If ye abide in me, and my words abide in you, ye shall *aiteo*/ask what ye will, and it shall be done unto you. 8 Herein is my Father glorified, that ye bear much fruit; so shall ye be my disciples."

Jesus knows very well if we are walking in the fullness of what He paid for. We are the Bride whom He is cleansing. It starts by us agreeing with what He has done for us in His Great Work and reckoning that over the current manifestations of the kingdom of darkness in our lives.

Yes, hate your old-man life and nature, but *agape*/love what God has made you in Jesus. To only die to the old man is incomplete and will not lead to you walking in your Redemption. That Jesus died for our sins is only half the story. The second and greater is that we are made alive in Him. The new birth is far beyond what the old man was. God identified Jesus with man; now man must identify with Jesus, as He is, not as He was.

1 John 4:16 "And we have known and believed the *agape*/love that God hath to us. God is *agape*/love; and he that dwelleth in *agape*/love dwelleth in God, and God in him. 17 Herein is our *agape*/love made perfect, that we may have boldness in the day of judgment: because as he is, so are we in this world."

No longer know yourself, Jesus or any other man after the flesh, but only in the new creation, your born-after-God self.

2 Cor 5:16 "Wherefore henceforth know we no man after the flesh: yea, though we have known Christ after the flesh, yet now henceforth know we him no more."

The wonder of the ages is not that we died in Christ, great as that is, but that when He rose from the dead, we were in Him and got all that He got from the Father.

Rom 8:15 "For ye have not received the spirit of bondage again to fear; but ye have received the Spirit of adoption, whereby we cry, Abba (*Daddy*), Father. 16 The Spirit itself beareth witness with our spirit, that we are the children of God: 17 and if children, then heirs; heirs of God, and joint-heirs with Christ ... ." Joint-heirs means equal to, or the same as, or having the same portion as Jesus!

Rom 4:25 "Who was delivered for our offences, and was raised again for our justification (*or when we were justified*)."

God's answer for how we can grow in Christ is to grow in knowledge of who and what we are in Christ. When we sin, we are not just to die to the old-man-self, but also to acknowledge the mighty work of Jesus on and by the cross in the new creation: Rom 13:10 "*Agape*/love worketh no ill to his neighbour: therefore *agape*/love is the fulfilling of the law. 11 And that, knowing the time, that now it is high time to awake out of sleep: for now is our *soteria*/salvation nearer than when we believed. 12 The night is far spent, the day is at hand: let us therefore cast off the works of darkness, and let us put on the armour of light. 13 Let us walk honestly, as in the day; not in rioting and drunkenness, not in chambering and wantonness, not in strife and envying. 14 But put ye on the Lord Jesus Christ, and make not provision for the flesh, to fulfil the lusts thereof."

How bold is that, when you discover you are in sin? Don't spend much time agonizing over your sinfulness. God already said the only answer for you is death, and Jesus took that death and the torments of Hell for you. Jesus was condemned and damned, so you would not be condemned and damned to Hell. Instead, make your faith work and obey: Rom 13:14 "But put ye on the Lord Jesus Christ, and make not provision for the flesh, to fulfil the lusts thereof."

That includes the lust of feeling sorry for yourself, or denying what God did in Jesus. If you are a Christian, you already have Redemption, the Remission of sins, Adoption, Reconciliation and the New Birth, with indwelling Holy Spirit. Glorify God in His great work and not your sin.

Acknowledge that the old man, who is less than Jesus in any way, died in Jesus, and now you are a new person in Christ Jesus, made in His image and complete in Him. Your old man is dead. He may live in your memories and habits, but he is dead to God, and you believe God's report, not the world's.

Eph 4:20 "But ye have not so learned Christ; 21 if so be that ye have heard him, and have been taught by him, as the truth is in Jesus: 22 that ye put off concerning the former conversation the old man, which is corrupt according to the deceitful lusts; 23 and be renewed in the spirit of your mind; 24 and that ye put on the new man, which after God is created in righteousness and true holiness."

Col 3:9 "Lie not one to another, seeing that ye have put off the old man with his deeds; 10 and have put on the new man, which is renewed in knowledge after the image of him that created him."

Rom 6:9 "Knowing that Christ being raised from the dead dieth no more; death hath no more dominion over him. 10 For in that he died, he died unto sin once: but in that he *zao*/liveth, he *zao*/liveth unto God. 11 Likewise reckon ye also yourselves to be dead indeed unto sin, but *zao*/alive unto God through Jesus Christ our Lord."

We are not to die daily to our new man; we are to daily and hourly, or even second by second, reckon our old man dead and that we are now alive in Christ. Your new self is like Jesus. Technically, you cannot die to that which will live forever, but you can die to a self-identity with what was killed 2000 years ago in Jesus, that part of you, which is, in any way, less than Jesus, the way of the flesh. No longer know yourself by the flesh, but rather by what the Word of God says you are. That is how to walk in the Spirit.

Whose report will you believe?

Rom 6:9 "Knowing that Christ being raised from the dead dieth no more; death hath no more dominion over him. 10 For in that he died, he died unto sin once: but in that he *zao*/liveth, he *zao*/liveth unto God. 11 Likewise reckon ye also

DISCOVERING OUR REDEMPTION

yourselves to be dead indeed unto sin, but *zao*/alive unto God through Jesus Christ our Lord."

The key is in the knowing, not just reading and studying.

Isa 53:1 "Who hath believed our report? and to whom is the arm of the LORD revealed?" (John 12:38; Rom 10:16)

This is not so much sadness that we were sinners, but rejoicing that we are born again, and Jesus is not ashamed to call us His brethren! Or you His brother, or His sister, or His family, in spite of your sin!

That sin and everything with it was healed 2000 years ago, that nature that accepts sin in any form also died 2000 years ago, and when you believed the Gospel of the resurrection of Jesus, you were made righteous with His righteousness. That is the new you, your new-creation man.

Heb 2:10 "For it became him, for whom are all things, and by whom are all things, in bringing many sons unto glory, to make the captain of their *soteria*/salvation perfect through sufferings. 11 For both he that sanctifieth and they who are sanctified are all of one: for which cause he is not ashamed to call them brethren."

These scriptures all tell us to identify ourselves with our new man, created in righteousness and true holiness, and no longer acknowledge our sins as part of us. Yes we did them, and if we do not handle them in Jesus, the law of sowing and reaping will cause misery in our present life.

Instead, break the power of sin; call God true and Satan a liar. Cast off your sins in your heart and confess you are a new man, and your true nature is to be just like Jesus. Make your confession that Jesus is Lord and this flesh thing, this lust thing, this old man thing you walked in is dead, and you are now alive to God by Jesus. Make your confession that as you proclaim this God truth, this spiritual reality, the Lord Jesus will make it physical reality in your life.

This is how you bring salvation to your soul, where the old man lives in your memory, past habits and evil lust attractions.

You do this once, to enter in legally, and then you continue to make it a reality in your life. This is what you are to renew your mind into–the Gospel of Christ in you, the hope of glory.

When you join or enlist in the military, you are fully a soldier of the government you enlist with. Yet you may not yet have the skills or attitudes of a competent soldier. Typically it takes six to twelve months to develop the basic attitudes of a soldier and, depending on what skills you need, anywhere from six months to two years to develop the basic skills for your required tasks as a soldier. Yet the moment you enlist, you fully belong to that government, even though you are not of much use without training and practice in functional skills.

When you are born again, you are born complete; all the parts are there, a new spirit, Holy Spirit indwelling, the mind of Christ, and your heart circumcised.

WE DIED WITH JESUS

God needs to add nothing else to you in basic structure, yet you are not a master craftsman in knowing the Lord, to walk as Jesus walked. That takes development or maturity.

So, like a prince who does not learn the skills of being a prince, the calling is there, but the skills are not yet developed. A strong man and a weak man have all the same muscle structure, yet the strong man has developed his muscles for more strength. The issue is not what you are, when you are born again, but what will you develop and who will you mature into.

A child born a king but raised a pauper will live and think like a pauper, even though he is a king. If, however, he learns who and what he is, and starts to think like a king, eventually he will be the king he is. His mind needs to be renewed from the limited thinking of a pauper to the expansive thinking of a king.

Rom 10:8 "But what saith it? The word is nigh thee, even in thy mouth, and in thy heart: that is, the word of faith, which we preach; 9 that if thou shalt confess with thy mouth the Lord Jesus, and shalt believe in thine heart that God hath raised him from the dead, thou shalt be *sozo*/saved. 10 For with the heart man believeth unto righteousness; and with the mouth confession is made unto *soteria*/salvation."

Remember, salvation has two main components: a God part and a man part. The God part is where God enforces His grace and the price that He paid to redeem and own you through Jesus, His Most Precious Son. He enforces this in your new birth, the indwelling of Holy Spirit, and in your eternal home with Him, because of Jesus. The second, or man, part, is your believing the Gospel that allows God to recreate you in the new birth, and then it requires your enforcement of this reality in your present life to manifest His salvation as a believer on the Earth (here and now) with indwelling Holy Spirit.

Make, reckon, yourself a new man in Christ Jesus and start to glorify His great work in you. This is the exact opposite of dying daily; it is living daily in the confession of what God has done for and in you. This is the testimony that overcomes the devil.

Hold not your old man dear, but hold your new man dear, to the glory of God. His work is good, and if His work is good, and you are His workmanship in Jesus, the real you is God-level good. So die to the old man and put on the new.

Rom 13:14 "But put ye on the Lord Jesus Christ, and make not provision for the flesh, to fulfil the lusts thereof." This is walking in the Spirit. This is walking in the Word of God.

We are told we make our faith effectual by majoring, not in what we were, but what we now are.

Philem 6 "That the communication of thy faith may become effectual by the *epignosis*/acknowledging of every good thing which is in you in Christ Jesus."

DISCOVERING OUR REDEMPTION

You become what you focus on. Focusing on the dead old man is glorifying what Satan has built in you and makes it big in you. Your walk is a reflection of what your soul believes to be truth. God's answer is to focus on what you are now in Christ. You are and become what you see yourself to be.

2 Cor 3:17 "Now the Lord is that Spirit: and where the Spirit of the Lord is, there is liberty (*to be all of what God has made you in Jesus*). 18 But we all, with open face beholding as in a glass (*mirror*) the glory of the Lord, are changed into the same image from glory to glory, even as by the Spirit of the Lord."

We died once with Christ.

Now we live with Him, and we reign with Him, in faith, working by *agape* love.

His perfect Redemption is ours.

His perfect Righteousness is ours.

All He is and had done is ours.

All we are is His. God gets sons whom He can deliver His goodness through to bless His other children.

Because Jesus and the Father are one, the Father made us one with Himself in Christ.

Eph 2:13 "But now in Christ Jesus ye who sometimes were far off are made nigh by the blood of Christ. 14 For he is our peace, who hath made both one, and hath broken down the middle wall of partition between us; 15 having abolished in his flesh the enmity, even the law of commandments contained in ordinances; for to make in himself of twain one new man, so making peace; 16 and that he might reconcile both unto God in one body by the cross, having slain the enmity thereby: 17 and came and preached peace to you which were afar off, and to them that were nigh. 18 For through him we both have access by one Spirit unto the Father. 19 Now therefore ye are no more strangers and foreigners, but fellowcitizens with the saints, and of the household of God."

Eph 4:4 "There is one body, and one Spirit, even as ye are called in one hope of your calling; 5 one Lord, one faith, one baptism, 6 one God and Father of all, who is above all, and through all, and in you all. 7 But unto every one of us is given grace according to the measure of the gift of Christ."

How much grace has God given us? To the measure of Christ!

What is left after that? Nothing! In Christ, you have all there is!

Start rejoicing you have it and start to act like you have it, and you will walk in it.

Dr. John G. Lake said: "It is a law of the human mind that you can act yourself quicker into believing than you can believe yourself into acting." Go and do *agape* love and you will understand *agape* love. [Blake, Curry. *The Voice of Healing* (KWHB Television Broadcast, Episodes 1 and 2, Tulsa, OK, March 2007)

We Died with Jesus

Christ lives in you!

Agape/love lives in you!

Co-labor with God in His Word of our Redemption to let Him manifest through you into the world.

Jesus did this, knowing what He was going to accomplish in the spirit realm. The thief crucified at the same time said: Luke 23:42 "And he (*the repentant thief*) said unto Jesus, Lord, remember me when thou comest into thy kingdom. 43 And Jesus said unto him, Verily I say unto thee, To day shalt thou be with me in paradise."

There is no punctuation in the original texts, so it could read just as well, "I say unto thee today, thou shalt be with me in paradise." Based on the facts of the resurrection, Jesus would be in Hades, not Paradise on that day. We do not have all the spiritual events in clear order, but, without a doubt, Jesus first went to suffer for mankind in Hell/Hades and there pay the full price for our Redemption.

Both Jesus and the thief knew they would die, but the thief did not know the mighty work Jesus had yet to do. However, since all men died in Jesus, the thief also died in Him when Jesus died first in spirit and then in the flesh. According to the events, Jesus died in the flesh first, before either of the thieves died.

Luke 23:44 "And it was about the sixth hour, and there was a darkness over all the earth until the ninth hour. 45 And the sun was darkened, and the veil of the temple was rent in the midst. 46 And when Jesus had cried with a loud voice, he said, Father, into thy hands I commend my spirit: and having said thus, he gave up the ghost."

After Jesus died physically, He went to suffer as the most damned One of all, for He was all the sin of man. We are to use the great facts of Romans 6:3, 6 and 9 to govern our lives by Rom 6:11.

Rom 6:3 "**Know** ye not, that so many of us as were baptized into Jesus Christ were baptized into his death? 4 Therefore we are buried with him by baptism into death: that like as Christ was raised up from the dead by the glory of the Father, even so we also should walk in newness of *zoe*/life. 5 For if we have been planted together in the likeness of his death, we shall be also in the likeness of his resurrection."

Rom 6:6 "**Knowing** this, that our old man is crucified with him, that the body of sin might be destroyed, that henceforth we should not serve sin. 7 For he that is dead is freed from sin. 8 Now if we be dead with Christ, we believe that we shall also *zao*/live with him."

Rom 6:9 "**Knowing** that Christ being raised from the dead dieth no more; death hath no more dominion over him. 10 For in that he died, he died unto sin once: but in that he *zao*/liveth, he *zao*/liveth unto God."

When you know these great "knowings," by constant repetition (for at least 3 months, in diligent, daily effort), you can begin to walk in the proper reckoning of God.

DISCOVERING OUR REDEMPTION

Rom 6:11 "Likewise reckon (*count in spite of the conflicting evidence or symptoms before you or in your feelings*) ye also yourselves to be dead indeed unto sin, but *zao*/alive unto God through Jesus Christ our Lord."

This is a two-step process to walk in our death in Jesus. First, you reckon yourself dead to sin and every failure and evil circumstance. And then you reckon yourself *zao*/alive to God. This first step can be rather short, the second step a lifestyle, but it is now your real life before God.

As you do this, then you can obey with effectiveness: Rom 6:12 "Let not sin therefore reign in your mortal body, that ye should obey it in the lusts thereof."

Sin, in the mind, is composed of the wicked thoughts that lead to wicked words and behaviors. You attack, "let not" with God's Word in your mouth, by controlling the words out of your mouth, to match only what God says. Then you may cast out any demons protecting these wicked lies in your heart or the hearts of others.

Sin, in the body, is composed of addictions, damage, sickness and disease of any kind. You exercise and enforce the benefits of the cruel death of Jesus by using His name to blast the devil out of yourself and others.

This takes these facts of our death with Jesus from theology to life in Jesus.

Rom 6: 4 "Therefore we are buried with him by baptism into death: that like as Christ was raised up from the dead by the glory of the Father, even so we also should walk in newness of *zoe*/life. 5 For if we have been planted together in the likeness of his death, we shall be also in the likeness of his resurrection."

If we are "in the likeness of His resurrection," that means: 1 John 4:17 "Herein is our *agape*/love made perfect, that we may have boldness in the day of judgment: because as he is, so are we in this world."

2 Cor 5:14 "For the *agape*/love of Christ constraineth us; because we thus judge, that if one died for all, then were all dead: 15 and that he died for all, that they which *zao*/live should not henceforth *zao*/live unto themselves, but unto him which died for them, and rose again." As we renew our minds into the Gospel of "Christ in you the hope of glory," by the new creation, we will proclaim "Peace" just like Jesus did (Acts 10:32-38) and thus walk out Rom 16:20. This is how we mortify our flesh mind: proclaim our old man dead in Christ, our new creation by Jesus' resurrection, and go do *agape* love in *dunamis* power and the "mind of Christ."

Rom 8:13 "For if ye *zao*/live after the flesh, ye shall die: but if ye through the Spirit *[the Gospel of Christ in you the hope of glory, the reign of Holy Spirit through and in men]* do mortify *(call dead and useless)* the deeds of the body *[by obeying Rom 6:11]*, ye shall *zao*/live. 14 For as many as are led by the Spirit of God, they are the *(mature)* sons of God. 15 For ye have not received the spirit of bondage again to fear; but ye have received the Spirit of adoption, whereby we cry, Abba, *(Daddy)* Father. 16 The Spirit itself beareth witness with our spirit, that we are the children of God: 17 and if children, then heirs; heirs of God, and joint-heirs with Christ; if so be that we suffer with him, that we may be also glorified together."

CHAPTER 20
WE WERE BURIED WITH JESUS

Jesus had proclaimed that He would be dead 3 days and then rise again. Matt 12:39 "But he answered and said unto them, An evil and adulterous generation seeketh after a sign; and there shall no sign be given to it, but the sign of the prophet Jonas: 40 for as Jonas was three days and three nights in the whale's belly; so shall the Son of man be three days and three nights in the heart of the earth."

John 2:19 "Jesus answered and said unto them, Destroy this temple, and in three days I will raise it up. 20 Then said the Jews, Forty and six years was this temple in building, and wilt thou rear it up in three days? 21 But he spake of the temple of his body."

Matt 27:40 "And saying, Thou that destroyest the temple, and buildest it in three days, *sozo*/save thyself. If thou be the Son of God, come down from the cross."

Matt 27:63 "Saying, Sir, we remember that that deceiver said, while he was yet alive, After three days I will rise again."

Jesus went to do even greater work in the heart of the Earth. He was going to a mighty faith battle in Hades, the place of the damned, and the so-far uncontested kingdom of the devil.

We have seen how Jesus became sin with our sin, how He became our Substitute, bearing our diseases.

DISCOVERING OUR REDEMPTION

We have seen Him under the absolute dominion and power of the adversary on the cross, under the authority and control of evil men, who were glad to see Him die. They knew they were putting to an end this self-proclaimed "Messiah."

They stubbornly refused to acknowledge Him as the true Messiah, as Peter said: Acts 2:22 "Ye men of Israel, hear these words; Jesus of Nazareth, a man approved of God among you by miracles and wonders and signs, which God did by him in the midst of you, as ye yourselves also know."

In Isaiah 53, we saw Jesus leave the cross, in the spirit, bearing our diseases and sins away, as He was conveyed to our place of confinement in Sheol/Hades.

We can imagine Satan's gratification at this point. Ps 2:1 "Why do the heathen rage, and the people imagine a vain thing? 2 The kings of the earth set themselves, and the rulers take counsel together, against the Lord, and against his anointed, saying, 3 Let us break their bands asunder, and cast away their cords from us."

We can see great celebration in Hell, when Satan brought Jesus, as a captive, into the prison house of Hades.

Acts 2:22 "Ye men of Israel, hear these words; Jesus of Nazareth, a man approved of God among you by miracles and wonders and signs, which God did by him in the midst of you, as ye yourselves also know: 23 him, being delivered by the determinate counsel and foreknowledge of God, ye have taken, and by wicked hands have crucified and slain: 24 whom God hath raised up, having loosed the pains of death: because it was not possible that he should be holden of it. 25 For David speaketh concerning him, I foresaw the Lord always before my face, for he is on my right hand, that I should not be moved: 26 therefore did my heart rejoice, and my tongue was glad; moreover also my flesh shall rest in hope: 27 because thou wilt not leave my *psuche*/soul (*life*) in hell (*Hades*), neither wilt thou suffer thine Holy One to see corruption. 28 Thou hast made known to me the ways of *zoe*/life; thou shalt make me full of joy with thy countenance.

"29 Men and brethren, let me freely speak unto you of the patriarch David, that he is both dead and buried, and his sepulchre is with us unto this day. 30 Therefore being a prophet, and knowing that God had sworn with an oath to him, that of the fruit of his loins, according to the flesh, he would raise up Christ to sit on his throne; 31 he seeing this before spake of the resurrection of Christ, that his *psuche*/soul (*life*) was not left in hell (*Hades*), neither his flesh did see corruption. 32 This Jesus hath God raised up, whereof we all are witnesses. 33 Therefore being by the right hand of God exalted, and having received of the Father the promise of the Holy Ghost, he hath shed forth this, which ye now see and hear. 34 For David is not ascended into the heavens: but he saith himself, The Lord said unto my Lord, Sit thou on my right hand, 35 until I make thy foes thy footstool. 36 Therefore let all the house of Israel know assuredly, that God hath made that same Jesus, whom ye have crucified, both Lord and Christ."

We Were Buried with Jesus

You may remember how the Philistines rejoiced over the capture of Samson, and with what joy they put out his eyes and bound him in helplessness.

What a gala day it must have been in Hell when Jesus, who had raised Lazarus from the dead, had destroyed the power of death and disease, had ruled the winds and the waves, had fed the hungry, cast out demons and defeated Satan in open combat, was conquered and made one with the devil.

He had suffered at the whipping post under Roman law for our healing.

They had pierced His hands and feet and nailed Him to a cross.

He was made sick.

Isa 53:3 "He is despised and rejected of men; a man of sorrows, and acquainted (*knew intimately, made one*) with grief (*sickness*): and we hid as it were our faces from him; he was despised, and we esteemed him not."

They could see in Him all the diseases of the ages.

What an hour it must have been!

When the disciples took Jesus' body from the cross, embalmed it, and laid it in the tomb of Joseph of Arimathea, how little they appreciated what He was going through, and what His sufferings were.

They were weeping over their own lost dreams, while Jesus was suffering the damnation of the damned and then defeating the devil in mortal combat with the Word of God in His heart.

How very little the world appreciated where Jesus was and what He was doing!

The disciples of Jesus were looking at the flesh, and the reality of His physical death was assaulting their senses.

They laid His body in the tomb, and the Roman government sealed it and set guards to keep watch, to see that His body was not stolen.

They had heard Him cry, "My God, my God, why hast thou forsaken me?" If Jesus had given up, how could they be expected to stand?

Little did they know that Jesus was fulfilling scripture from the Psalms. Ps 22:1 "My God, my God, why hast thou forsaken me? why art thou so far from helping me, and from the words of my roaring?"

To the disciples and the crowd, it was the cry of the lost. To Jesus, it was the cry of victory, and He quoted the Psalms to go into the greatest faith battle this Universe has ever seen.

They saw His wounds. They saw His blood. They may even have had some of it on their feet.

To the disciples, it appeared that God had forsaken Him whom they loved.

They now lost all hope. They had thought that it was He who would redeem Israel.

They thought only in terms of a physical, financial and political redemption.

DISCOVERING OUR REDEMPTION

For three days and three nights the Lamb of God was our Substitute in Hell.

He was there for us.

He was bearing our pains and our diseases, our sins and our iniquities.

He was there suffering and paying ... until the claims of Justice for man were fully met.

Such an hour had never been and never can be again.

There had to be an adequate meeting of the penalties for the transgressions of the human race, and Jesus met them all.

He became one with Satan, when He became sin, as we now become one with Him, when we are recreated.

Jesus became sin and the consequences of sin, the curse. So we can look to Jesus and see that the thing that is killing us, sin and its consequences, the curse, were killed by Father God when Jesus offered up Himself by the cross.

John 3:14 "And as Moses lifted up the serpent in the wilderness, even so must the Son of man be lifted up: 15 that whosoever believeth in him should not perish, but have eternal *zoe*/life."

John 12:31 "Now is the judgment of this world: now shall the prince of this world be cast out. 32 And I, if I be lifted up from the earth, will draw all men unto me. 33 This he said, signifying what death he should die."

Father put us in Jesus, and when Jesus was buried, we were buried with Him.

Rom 6:3 "Know ye not, that so many of us as were baptized into Jesus Christ were baptized into his death? 4 Therefore we are buried with him by baptism into death: that like as Christ was raised up from the dead by the glory of the Father, even so we also should walk in newness of *zoe*/life. 5 For if we have been planted together in the likeness of his death, we shall be also in the likeness of his resurrection."

Col 2:8 "Beware lest any man spoil you through philosophy and vain deceit, after the tradition of men, after the rudiments of the world, and not after Christ. 9 For in him dwelleth all the fulness of the Godhead bodily. 10 And ye are complete in him, which is the head of all principality and power: 11 in whom also ye are circumcised with the circumcision made without hands, in putting off the body of the sins of the flesh by the circumcision of Christ: 12 buried with him in baptism, wherein also ye are risen with him through the faith of the operation of God, who hath raised him from the dead. 13 And you, being dead in your sins and the uncircumcision of your flesh, hath he quickened together with him, having forgiven you all trespasses."

We were in Jesus when He was buried. You enter into this fact, first, by the immersion of Holy Spirit when you are born again, and then, second, you seal it into your conscious when you submit to water baptism.

1 Pet 3:20 "... when once the longsuffering of God waited in the days of Noah, while the ark was a preparing, wherein few, that is, eight *psuche*/souls (*lives*) were

We Were Buried with Jesus

sozo/saved by water. 21 The like figure whereunto even baptism doth also now *sozo*/save us (not the putting away of the filth of the flesh, but the answer of a good conscience toward God,) by the resurrection of Jesus Christ: 22 who is gone into heaven, and is on the right hand of God; angels and authorities and powers being made subject unto him."

Death is an irrevocable act, as enforced by the devil, who has the power of death. But death is defeated in Jesus.

Rom 8:2 "For the law of the Spirit of *zoe*/life [which is] in Christ Jesus [the law of our new being] has freed me from the law of sin and of death." AMP

1 Cor 15:54 "So when this corruptible shall have put on incorruption, and this mortal shall have put on immortality, then shall be brought to pass the saying that is written, Death is swallowed up in victory. 55 O death, where is thy sting? O grave, where is thy victory? 56 The sting of death is sin; and the strength of sin is the law. 57 But thanks be to God, which giveth us the victory through our Lord Jesus Christ. 58 Therefore, my *agape*/beloved brethren, be ye stedfast, unmoveable, always abounding in the work of the Lord, forasmuch as ye know that your labour is not in vain in the Lord."

When you enter in, by faith in God, and do the action of water baptism, you tell your conscious, that tool of the unconscious mind, that you permanently identify yourself with the death of Jesus, and you permanently identify yourself into the covenant of Jesus, His resurrection and His new birth in you.

This is not just a legal fact; God handles it in the records of Heaven for you. He circumcises a part of your heart and seals it with Holy Spirit. It is how much you *epignosis*/know these Redemption facts, as a master craftsman in the glory of God, that makes your faith effectual in this life.

2 Cor 13:5 "Examine yourselves, whether ye be in the faith; prove your own selves. Know ye not your own selves, how that Jesus Christ is in you, except ye be reprobates (*like garbage, useless in the new creation reality, useless in your faith to produce the power of God*)?"

Instead, know you died in Him, and you were buried in that tomb with Him.

CHAPTER 21

WE HAVE BEEN MADE ALIVE WITH JESUS

When Jesus was made alive in spirit, we were made alive with Him.

Col 2:13 "And you, being dead through your trespasses and the uncircumcision of your flesh, you I say, did he make *zao*/alive together with Him." RSV

Eph 2:5 "Even when we were dead through our trespasses, made us *zao*/alive together with Christ."

This is the heart of Redemption.

Not only were we made alive in spirit, when Jesus was made alive in spirit, but we will also get a new body, just like He got when He arose from the dead.

Rom 6:5 "For if we have become united with him in the likeness of his death, we shall be also in the likeness of his resurrection."

Here we witness the miracle of the eternities. It took place in that subterranean prison house of death. Jesus was made alive from death.

Acts 13:33 "God hath fulfilled the same unto our children, in that he raised up Jesus; as also it is written in the second psalm, Thou art My Son, this day have I begotten thee." RSV

This was the day Jesus was made alive in spirit, right in the center of Hades, to conquer its works.

WE HAVE BEEN MADE ALIVE WITH JESUS

Paul, by the Spirit, gave us Col 1:18: "And he is the head of the body, the church: who is the beginning, THE FIRSTBORN FROM THE DEAD; that in all things he might have the preeminence." RSV (emphasis added)

Jesus was dead with our death. He had died twice: first spiritually and then physically.

1 Pet 3:18 "Because Christ also suffered for sins once, the righteous for the unrighteous, that he might bring us to God; being put to death in the flesh, but made *zao*/alive in the (or His) spirit." RSV

This was not the Holy Spirit; this was Jesus' spirit.

What a transformation must have taken place!

Rom 8:2 "For the law of the Spirit of *zoe*/life in Christ Jesus hath made me free from the law of sin and death."

How it must have shaken the foundation of that awful place, when the demons of Hades saw Jesus made alive, break the bonds of spiritual death, and hurl back the forces of death that had overwhelmed Him on the cross.

Now we can understand Eph 2:10: "We are his workmanship, created in Christ Jesus."

When were we created? In the mind of Justice, it was when Jesus was recreated down there.

This is the legal side of Redemption by the great Judge, Father God.

Rom 3:23 "For all have sinned, and come short of the glory of God; 24 being justified freely by his grace through the redemption that is in Christ Jesus: 25 whom God hath set forth to be a propitiation through faith in his blood, to declare his righteousness for the remission of sins that are past, through the forbearance of God; 26 to declare, I say, at this time his righteousness: that he might be just, and the justifier of him which believeth in Jesus."

God did not just remove our sins and diseases; He had Jesus pay for them fully, so that all the demands of justice were fully met in Jesus. This was full payment, the full ransom, not a simple wiping away of sin. He paid the full bill and removed forever any requirement for it to be paid again. 1 Tim 2:5 "For there is one God, and one mediator between God and men, the man Christ Jesus; 6 who gave himself a ransom for all, to be testified in due time."

That word *propitiation* means not only a removal of all those things that offend, so that the blessing can now flow, but also the aggressive pouring out of blessings, the grace of God. Rom 5:17 "For if by one man's offence death reigned (*as king*) by one; much more they which (*continually*) *lambano*/receive abundance of grace and of the gift of righteousness shall reign (*as a greater, stronger and conquering king*) in *zoe*/life by one, Jesus Christ.)"

That great blessing is Holy Spirit now dwelling in men. God's greatest gift is Himself, in Holy Spirit, in the Christian. He may lie untapped because the just shall

DISCOVERING OUR REDEMPTION

zao/live (release God, in His Word into the Earth) by faith. When we are born again by Holy Spirit, we are made part of the Body of Christ and part of the Church of God. When we operate by faith in God, by His Word, we are being the Church. Then we build that path for Holy Spirit to release the *zoe* life of God to make Heaven on Earth.

That Day of Pentecost was when the Christian Church was really born of God.

Father had faith that, through all the physical, soulish and spiritual suffering He must bear for us, Jesus would not let go of His trust that Father God would vindicate Him and raise Him from death. By His faith, Jesus enabled Father God to raise Him up.

Luke 18:31 "Then he (*Jesus*) took unto him the twelve, and said unto them, Behold, we go up to Jerusalem, and all things that are written by the prophets concerning the Son of man shall be accomplished. 32 For he shall be delivered unto the Gentiles, and shall be mocked, and spitefully entreated, and spitted on: 33 and they shall scourge him, and put him to death: and the third day he shall rise again."

God is a faith God. He counted the things that were not as though they were.

Jesus is a faith man. He counted the things that were not as though they were.

Down there in Hell, when Father God made Jesus alive by the Spirit of Holiness, He counted us righteous, and He counted us alive. Rom 1:4 "And declared to be the Son of God with power, according to the spirit of holiness, by the resurrection from the dead."

This started the fruit of Jesus' suffering in this manner, to fully redeem man.

He counted us new creations, His sons and daughters before the day of Pentecost came, and the first contingent of the Body of Christ came into being.

He counted the things that were not as though they were, and they became.

The moment we believe God raised Jesus from the dead unto righteousness and *zoe*/life, this new birth is made a reality in us. Salvation is brought to Earth by the confession that Jesus is Lord.

Rom 5:18 "Therefore as by the offence of one judgment came upon all men to condemnation; even so by the righteousness of one the free gift came upon all men unto justification of *zoe*/life." Jesus was justified to the level of the *zoe*/life of God. So the very force of His being is the *zoe*/life of God.

Chapter 22
We Were Raised with Jesus

Hear Jesus' statement of faith and affirmation before His crucifixion. Matt 20:17 "And Jesus going up to Jerusalem took the twelve disciples apart in the way, and said unto them, 18 behold, we go up to Jerusalem; and the Son of man shall be betrayed unto the chief priests and unto the scribes, and they shall condemn him to death, 19 and shall deliver him to the Gentiles to mock, and to scourge, and to crucify him: and the third day he shall rise again."

Even in the midst of the crucifixion and in the depths of Hades, Jesus had submitted Himself to the Father's desire to raise Him from the dead. This is what His faith battle looked like.

Ps 42:6 "O my God, my soul is cast down within me: therefore will I remember thee from the land of Jordan, and of the Hermonites, from the hill Mizar. 7 Deep calleth unto deep at the noise of thy waterspouts: all thy waves and thy billows are gone over me. 8 Yet the LORD will command his *chesed*/lovingkindness in the daytime, and in the night his song shall be with me, and my prayer unto the God of my life."

Here this is described, in the complete Psalm 22, written centuries before the actual event.

DISCOVERING OUR REDEMPTION

Psalm 22:1 "My God, my God, why hast thou forsaken me? why art thou so far from helping me, and from the words of my roaring? 2 O my God, I cry in the daytime, but thou hearest not; and in the night season, and am not silent. 3 But thou art holy, O thou that inhabitest the praises of Israel. 4 Our fathers trusted in thee: they trusted, and thou didst deliver them. 5 They cried unto thee, and were delivered: they trusted in thee, and were not confounded. 6 But I am a worm, and no man; a reproach of men, and despised of the people. 7 All they that see me laugh me to scorn: they shoot out the lip, they shake the head saying, 8 He trusted on the Lord that he would deliver him: let him deliver him, seeing he delighted in him. 9 But thou art he that took me out of the womb: thou didst make me hope when I was upon my mother's breasts. 10 I was cast upon thee from the womb: thou art my God from my mother's belly. 11 Be not far from me; for trouble is near; for there is none to help.

"12 Many bulls have compassed me: strong bulls of Bashan have beset me round. 13 They gaped upon me with their mouths, as a ravening and a roaring lion. 14 I am poured out like water, and all my bones are out of joint: my heart is like wax; it is melted in the midst of my bowels. 15 My strength is dried up like a potsherd; and my tongue cleaveth to my jaws; and thou hast brought me into the dust of death. 16 For dogs have compassed me: the assembly of the wicked have inclosed me: they pierced my hands and my feet. 17 I may tell all my bones: they look and stare upon me. 18 They part my garments among them, and cast lots upon my vesture. 19 But be not thou far from me, O Lord: O my strength, haste thee to help me. 20 Deliver my soul from the sword; my darling from the power of the dog. 21 Save me from the lion's mouth: for thou hast heard me from the horns of the unicorns.

"22 I will declare thy name unto my brethren: in the midst of the congregation will I praise thee. 23 Ye that fear the Lord, praise him; all ye the seed of Jacob, glorify him; and fear him, all ye the seed of Israel. 24 For he hath not despised nor abhorred the affliction of the afflicted; neither hath he hid his face from him; but when he cried unto him, he heard. 25 My praise shall be of thee in the great congregation: I will pay my vows before them that fear him. 26 The meek shall eat and be satisfied: they shall praise the Lord that seek him: your heart shall live for ever. 27 All the ends of the world shall remember and turn unto the Lord: and all the kindreds of the nations shall worship before thee. 28 For the kingdom is the Lord's: and he is the governor among the nations. 29 All they that be fat upon earth shall eat and worship: all they that go down to the dust shall bow before him: and none can keep alive his own soul. 30 A seed shall serve him; it shall be accounted to the Lord for a generation. 31 They shall come, and shall declare his righteousness unto a people that shall be born, that he hath done this."

WE WERE RAISED WITH JESUS

The resurrection of the Lord Jesus is the proof of Satan's defeat, of man's Redemption, of God's legal right to make the believer a New Creation, and of His *agape* love toward mankind.

Eph 1:7 stands out with powerful implications and encouragement: "In Him we have redemption (deliverance and salvation) through His blood, the remission (forgiveness, *purging, removal, putting away and washing*) of our offenses (shortcomings, *sins* and trespasses), in accordance with the riches and the generosity of His gracious favor." AMP

God promised we would live with Him on the third day, but few knew this meant the Messiah rising from the dead as our covenant substitute. Hos 6:1 "Come, and let us return unto the LORD: for he hath torn, and he will heal us; he hath smitten, and he will bind us up. 2 After two days will he revive us: in the third day he will raise us up, and we shall live in his sight. 3 Then shall we know, if we follow on to know the Lord: his going forth is prepared as the morning; and he shall come unto us as the rain, as the latter and former rain unto the earth."

Since Jesus rose from the dead, we can live in God, with God, by God and for God. Rom 6:9 "Knowing that Christ being raised from the dead dieth no more; death hath no more dominion over him. 10 For in that he died, he died unto sin once: but in that he *zao*/liveth, he *zao*/liveth unto God. 11 Likewise reckon ye also yourselves to be dead indeed unto sin, but *zao*/alive unto God through Jesus Christ our Lord." This is in spite of your present walk that is not just like Jesus.

Matt 12:39 "But he answered and said unto them, An evil and adulterous generation seeketh after a sign; and there shall no sign be given to it, but the sign of the prophet Jonas: 40 for as Jonas was three days and three nights in the whale's belly; so shall the Son of man be three days and three nights in the heart of the earth."

Mark 8:31 "And he began to teach them, that the Son of man must suffer many things, and be rejected of the elders, and of the chief priests, and scribes, and be killed, and after three days rise again."

John 2:19 "Jesus answered and said unto them, Destroy this temple, and in three days I will raise it up."

We have our Redemption. It is not something we have to pray for or ask for.

When you understand and appreciate the greatness of this Redemption properly, you will be continually thanking Him for your and our Redemption in Him.

Col 1:12 "Giving thanks (*continually*) unto the Father, which hath made us meet to be partakers of the inheritance of the saints in light: 13 who hath delivered us from the power of darkness, and hath translated us into the kingdom of his *agape*/dear Son: 14 in whom we have redemption through his blood, even the forgiveness (*remission, putting away, obliteration, and removal*) of sins."

Your confession will be: Gal 2:20 "I am (*have been*) crucified with Christ: nevertheless I *zao*/live; yet not I, but Christ *zao*/liveth in me: and the life which I now

DISCOVERING OUR REDEMPTION

zao/live in the flesh I *zao*/live by the faith of the Son of God, who *agape*/loved me, and gave himself for me. 21 I do not frustrate the grace of God: for if righteousness come by the law, then Christ is dead in vain."

Col 2:13 "And you, being dead in your sins and the uncircumcision of your flesh, hath he quickened together with him, having forgiven (*pardoned, with the removal of all curses and stopping any curse in action*) you all trespasses."

You don't ask for what you already have. Instead, you thank God for what He has done 2000 years ago in Jesus. Then you enter in by believing and confession, per Romans 10:8-13.

We have the *agape*/love of God poured out on us by the work of Jesus by the cross, we have Redemption, we have Forgiveness, we have Remission, we have Sanctification, we have Reconciliation, we have the wisdom of God, we have all the blessings of God, and we have peace with God.

What is amazing is that no matter what problem we have, the answer from God is to grow in knowledge of God and Jesus. God has set up a system so that as much as you know God you will overcome any lack or evil in this present world system by and through Him. 2 Pet 1:2 "Grace and peace be multiplied unto you through the *epignosis*/knowledge of God, and of Jesus our Lord, 3 according as his divine power hath given unto us all things that pertain unto *zoe*/life and godliness, through the knowledge of him that hath called us to glory and virtue: 4 whereby are given unto us exceeding great and precious promises: that by these ye might be partakers of the divine nature, having escaped the corruption that is in the world through lust."

It is by partaking of the promises, by faith in the work of Jesus, that we share in the divine nature of God.

So if you are poor, know Jesus and what He accomplished more.

If you have trouble at work, know Jesus and what He accomplished more.

If you have enemies out to kill you, know Jesus and what He accomplished more.

If you are depressed, know Jesus and what He accomplished more.

If your marriage is in trouble, know Jesus and what He accomplished more.

If you are sick, know Jesus and what He accomplished more.

God's answer for everything is more knowledge of Him and His ways in Jesus. Hos 4:6 "My people are destroyed for lack of knowledge: because thou hast rejected knowledge, I will also reject thee, that thou shalt be no priest to me: seeing thou hast forgotten the law of thy God, I will also forget thy children."

His answer for effective faith, effective answers to prayer and power with God is the same: Philem 6 "That the communication of thy faith may become effectual by the *epignosis*/acknowledging of every good thing which is in you in Christ Jesus."

WE WERE RAISED WITH JESUS

We are to know that when we get born again we have the mind of Christ, we have a new spirit, we are re-created in the righteousness and true holiness of God, we have Holy Spirit dwelling in us, we can have Holy Spirit sealed in and to us unto the Day of Redemption, and we can have His great Salvation.

The moment we are re-created, born again, at that very moment Redemption is ours. Before, there was a legal condition on how God could treat all mankind. After your new creation, however, it becomes what you are and can be in Christ, not later in Heaven, but now on Earth, in this life—right now.

As we know and enforce this, Satan's dominion over us ends.

As we grow in this, our life of servitude and fear comes to an end.

As we renew our mind into the new-creation realities of our Redemption, we are transformed. Rom 12:2 "And be not conformed to this world: but be ye transformed by the renewing of your mind, that ye may prove what is that good, and acceptable, and perfect, will of God.

Rom 13:14 "But put ye on the Lord Jesus Christ, and make not provision for the flesh, to fulfil the lusts thereof."

We have these things by our Redemption in Jesus. That Redemption is according to the riches of His grace.

Eph 4:7 "But unto every one of us is given grace according to the measure of the gift of Christ."

Satan cannot legally hold any part of creation in his terrible bondage, when we know who we are, our calling in God, the truth of the work of Jesus and the power He has given us to bring the Kingdom of God to Earth.

We are free to fulfill all the purpose God has for man. 2 Cor 3:17 "Now the Lord is that Spirit: and where the Spirit of the Lord is, there is liberty. 18 But we all, with open face beholding as in a glass (*mirror*) the glory of the Lord, are changed into the same image from glory to glory, even as by the Spirit of the Lord."

We are free to continue the work given Adam: to subdue and establish Father's dominion throughout the Earth. We are free to be the answer to His prayer: "Thy Kingdom come, Thy will be done on earth as it is in heaven."

We are born again, we are sealed with Holy Spirit, the legal fact of all men in Jesus is now given to us, and Holy Spirit is sealed into us.

Eph 1:13 "In Him (*Jesus*) you also who have heard the Word of Truth, the glad tidings (Gospel) of your *soteria*/salvation, and have believed in and adhered to and relied on Him, were stamped with the seal (*showing qualification, acceptance, authority and ownership*) of the long-promised Holy Spirit. 14 That [Spirit] is the guarantee of our inheritance [the firstfruits, the pledge and foretaste, the down payment on our heritage], in anticipation of its full redemption and our acquiring [complete] possession of it - to the praise of His glory." AMP

DISCOVERING OUR REDEMPTION

In the preceding chapters, we have had an opportunity to see the wealth and riches of the Father's Grace in His Substitutionary work in Christ.

Eph 2:6 "And He raised us up together with Him (*Jesus*) and made us sit down together [giving us joint seating with Him] in the heavenly sphere [by virtue of our being] in Christ Jesus (the Messiah, the Anointed One)." AMP

We were chosen in Him, crucified with Him, died with Him, were buried with Him, suffered with Him, were justified with Him, were made alive with Him, conquered Satan with Him, and were raised together with Him, and now we are seated beside the Father with Christ, glorified by Holy Spirit with Him and guaranteed eternal *soteria*/salvation with and in Him.

The resurrection of Jesus is proof of our victory over the adversary.

It is a proof that cannot be denied. Every person who believes in his heart that God raised Jesus from the dead, in the mind of God, and in the records of the Supreme Court of Creation, is a victor over the adversary. Then, as we confess Jesus as Lord with our mouths, we exercise our dominion over the devil and bring God's salvation to Earth.

So few of the Father's children have seen this mighty truth, the truth that our victory was in the victory of Christ.

1 Cor 15:57 "But thanks be to God, which giveth us the victory through our Lord Jesus Christ. 58 Therefore, my *agape*/beloved brethren, be ye stedfast, unmoveable [*in spite of the failures, trials and delays of life*], always abounding in the work of the Lord, forasmuch as ye know that your labour is not in vain in the Lord."

When Jesus broke the bars of death, having conquered death, Satan and sin, it was our victory.

Col 3:1 "If then ye were raised together with Christ," and we *were* raised together with Christ.

In the mind of the Father, it was our translation out of the kingdom of darkness and into the Kingdom of the Son of His *agape*/love.

It was our Redemption.

We, in Jesus, had broken Satan's dominion over our body, soul and spirit in Christ.

Perhaps the greatest message of our perfect victory over the adversary is found in Eph 1:19 "And [so that you can know and understand] what is the immeasurable and unlimited and surpassing greatness of His power in and for us who believe, as demonstrated in the working of His mighty strength, 20 which He exerted in Christ when He raised Him from the dead and seated Him at His [own] right hand in the heavenly [places], 21 far above all rule and authority and power and dominion and every name that is named [above every title that can be conferred], not only in this age and in this world, but also in the age and the world which are to come. 22 And He has put all things under His feet and has appointed

We Were Raised with Jesus

Him the universal and supreme Head of the church [a headship exercised throughout the church], [Ps 8:6.]" AMP

Notice the fruit of this victory is that Jesus is given as Head of the Church for the benefit of the Church, He being able to do our calling in Him.

The same ability that worked in the dead spirit and body of Jesus to reanimate it and fill it with immortality is today in the believer.

Rom 8:11 "And if the Spirit of Him Who raised up Jesus from the dead dwells in you, [then] He Who raised up Christ Jesus from the dead will also restore to *zoe*/life your mortal (short-lived, perishable) bodies through His Spirit Who dwells in you." AMP

We are today more than conquerors because of the life of God that was imparted to us in our new creation.

Rom 8:36 "As it is written, For thy sake we are killed all the day long; we are accounted as sheep for the slaughter [*by our enemies*]. 37 Nay, in all these things we are more than conquerors through him that *agape*/loved us."

1 Cor 15:55 "O death, where is thy sting? O grave, where is thy victory? 56 The sting of death is sin; and the strength of sin is the law. 57 But thanks be to God, which giveth us the victory through our Lord Jesus Christ. 58 Therefore, my *agape*/beloved brethren, be ye stedfast, unmoveable, always abounding in the work of the Lord, forasmuch as ye know that your labour is not in vain in the Lord."

It is the ability of God unveiled in that Resurrection that so shook the foundations of Hell, so that today, when the believers know that they were raised together with Christ, they also know they are victors in every field and over every circumstance, and they may go on from victory to victory and triumph to triumph in the confidence of God's Word and His Identification of them with Christ.

That Identification is so great that, in spite of what you see in your life now, you are destined: Eph 4:13 "Till we all come in the unity of the faith, and of the *epignosis*/knowledge of the Son of God, unto a perfect man, unto the measure of the stature of the fulness of Christ: 14 that we henceforth be no more children, tossed to and fro, and carried about with every wind of doctrine, by the sleight of men, and cunning craftiness, whereby they lie in wait to deceive; 15 but speaking the truth in *agape*/love, may grow up into him in all things, which is the head, even Christ."

You are part of this "all" in verse 13, and His is the "all" we are to become. You cannot be more identified than that. God will not be satisfied until you are mature in all things, just as Jesus is now.

God has lifted the believer above all rule and authority and power and dominion, not only in this age, but in that which is to come.

He put all things in subjection under the believer's feet.

He gave Christ, who is the Head of the Body, to be Master over all the forces of the Universe.

DISCOVERING OUR REDEMPTION

Jesus gave to the believer a legal right to the use of His name.

He actually gave him the power of attorney so that, in the name of Jesus, every demon and every power should obey that name, on the lips of the believer.

John 15:7 "If ye abide in me, and my words abide in you, ye shall *aiteo*/ask (*require, demand and expects as due by covenant promise, knowing all the promises are fulfilled in Jesus*) what ye will, and it shall be done unto you. 8 Herein is my Father glorified, that ye bear much fruit; so shall ye be my disciples."

There isn't anything too hard for God.

Jer 32:17 "Ah Lord God! behold, thou hast made the heaven and the earth by thy great power and stretched out arm, and there is nothing too hard for thee."

Luke 1:37 "For with God nothing shall be impossible."

Mark 10:27 "And Jesus looking upon them saith, With men it is impossible, but not with God: for with God all things are possible."

God's ability is the ability that He gives to us, so His resurrection is the proof of our right to reign over Satan and demons.

The proof of the triumph is in the Word of God, it is in Jesus being raised and seated at the right hand of the Father, and it is in the stripes on Jesus' back. When you are assailed with doubts, fears and delays, that is when you need to look for the evidence of your Redemption, and the devil's submission to the name of Jesus. You look to the record of the mighty work of God in Jesus in the Scriptures of you being raised and seated with Christ now. And that is the report you believe.

Make these your testimony, and you will overcome the devil's resistance.

Rev 12:11 "And they overcame him (*Satan, the accuser of the brethren*) by the blood of the Lamb, and by the word of their testimony; and they *agape*/loved not their *psuche*/lives (*souls*) unto the death."

Jesus conquered the devil in Hades, and we were in Jesus when He did it, we were there as one with Him, so we conquered the devil there also with Jesus.

Col 2:13 "And you, being dead in your sins and the uncircumcision of your flesh, hath he quickened together with him, having forgiven (*pardoned, removed and paid in full for*) you all trespasses; 14 blotting out the handwriting of ordinances that was against us, which was contrary to us, and took it out of the way, nailing it to his cross; 15 and having spoiled principalities and powers, he made a shew of them openly, triumphing over them in it."

He was raised because He had conquered and triumphed over Satan in our stead, so that we should no longer live in fear of the unseen forces of darkness.

Heb 2:14 "Forasmuch then as the children are partakers of flesh and blood, he also himself likewise took part of the same; that through death he might destroy (*dethrone, render powerless*) him that had the power of death, that is, the devil; 15 and deliver them who through fear of death were all their lifetime subject to bondage."

WE WERE RAISED WITH JESUS

1 Cor 15:20 "But now is Christ risen from the dead, and become the firstfruits of them that slept. 21 For since by man came death, by man came also the resurrection of the dead. 22 For as in Adam all die, even so in Christ shall all be made alive."

Eph 2:4 "But God, who is rich in mercy, for his great *agape*/love wherewith he *agape*/loved us, 5 even when we were dead in sins, hath quickened us together with Christ, (by grace ye are *sozo*/saved;) 6 and hath raised us up together, and made us sit together in heavenly places in Christ Jesus."

1 Pet 3:18 "For Christ also hath once suffered for sins, the just for the unjust, that he might bring us to God, being put to death in the flesh, but quickened by the Spirit."

Col 2:13 "And you, being dead in your sins and the uncircumcision of your flesh, hath he quickened (*made you alive*) together with him, having forgiven you all trespasses."

If you have believed God raise Jesus from the dead unto righteousness, this is now your reality: Rom 8:10 "And if Christ be in you, the body is dead because of sin; but the Spirit (*your spirit*) is *zoe*/life because of righteousness."

This is included in, but way beyond physical resurrection. That stops at Earth. Instead we were raised with and in Jesus to the highest position possible. Not only in Jesus, beside the Father at the throne of God, but made joint, equal heirs with Jesus. What Jesus got and now gets, you now get. Not the suffering servant of the cross, but the exalted Lord Christ of Revelation.

God's Redemption in Jesus is so "over the top" that it completely satisfies anything that could ever limit the fullness of God and His *agape* love dwelling and operating in you forever. Eph 3:19 "And to know the *agape*/love of Christ, which passeth knowledge, that ye might be filled with all the fulness of God." Whatever your opinion of man, and even the people you know personally, God says our Redemption is so complete and total that we are raised to full sonship and joint rulership with, in and by Jesus.

Not only that, but we Christians are commanded to keep our minds there, no matter what happens here on Earth. Col 3:1 "If ye [*know that you*] then be risen with Christ, seek those things which are above, where Christ sitteth on the right hand of God. 2 Set your affection on things above, not on things on the earth. 3 For ye are dead, and your *zoe*/life is hid with Christ in God." You are to approach every issue of life in the dominion, confidence, trust and love of God in Christ, not in the problem, but from the perspective of God's throne.

And here is a snapshot of what some of that looks like: Col 3:16 "Let the word of Christ dwell in you richly in all wisdom; teaching and admonishing one another in psalms and hymns and spiritual songs, singing with grace in your hearts to the Lord. 17 And whatsoever ye do in word or deed, do all in the name of the Lord Jesus, giving thanks to God and the Father by him."

Chapter 23

We Have Been Given a New Identity in Jesus

We have seen that the New Creation is utterly one with Christ.

Mankind is totally redeemed back into the family of God in the court records of the Supreme Court of Creation.

You are totally redeemed back into the family of God.

Jesus says you are the same as He is: <u>Acts 22:7</u> "And I (*Paul on the road to Damascus*) fell unto the ground, and heard a voice saying unto me, Saul, Saul, why persecutest thou me? 8 And I answered, Who art thou, Lord? And he said unto me, I am Jesus of Nazareth, whom thou persecutest."

Meditate (put those words in your mouth and chew on them) on the fact that Jesus said Saul was persecuting, not His people, but Himself ("Me"). If men touch you, they touch Jesus. This is Jesus identifying with His Body.

Your *agape*/love and confidence in God's power over all the works of the enemy grows, as you know that, legally, God has redeemed all of mankind back into the family.

God has made His statement of His *agape* love for you and His attitude toward any and all works of the devil.

<u>1 John 2:1</u> "My little children, these things write I unto you, that ye sin not. And if any man sin, we have an advocate with the Father, Jesus Christ the righ-

teous: 2 and he is the propitiation for our sins: and not for ours only, but also for the sins of the whole world."

You love others as you are loved, so you major in just how loved you are.

Therefore you also major in how forgiven you are.

You are not afraid to expose, reprove and confess your sins, and *lambano*/receive the forgiveness and healing given 2000 years ago. The blood of Jesus is more than sufficient for them all.

Matt 5:43 "Ye have heard that it hath been said, Thou shalt *agape*/love thy neighbour, and hate thine enemy. 44 But I say unto you, *Agape*/love your enemies, bless them that curse you, do good to them that hate you, and pray for them which despitefully use you, and persecute you; 45 that ye may be the children of your Father which is in heaven: for he maketh his sun to rise on the evil and on the good, and sendeth rain on the just and on the unjust. 46 For if ye *agape*/love them which *agape*/love you, what reward have ye? do not even the publicans the same? 47 And if ye salute your brethren only, what do ye more than others? do not even the publicans so? 48 Be ye therefore perfect, even as your Father which is in heaven is perfect."

How can we love our neighbor, unless we first know we are *agape* loved? We must major in knowing how loved we are. Jude 20 "But ye, *agape*/beloved, building up yourselves on your most holy faith, praying in the Holy Ghost, 21 keep yourselves in the *agape*/love of God, looking for the mercy of our Lord Jesus Christ unto eternal *zoe*/life. 22 And of some have compassion, making a difference: 23 and others *sozo*/save with fear, pulling them out of the fire; hating even the garment spotted by the flesh."

The Father delights in you, for He sees you complete in Jesus, the fullness of what He has made you to be. He does not see what you are in the eyes of fallen man, but, rather, what He has made you in His workmanship. He sees you in your glorious future in Him, and everything standing in the way of that will go, one way or the other. You will do it by faith now, or He will do it after, or as part of, the Day of Judgment.

God declares His love for you every time you remember and stir yourself up in His great work of Redemption and Reconciliation in Jesus.

John 17:25 "O righteous Father, the world hath not known thee: but I have known thee, and these have known that thou hast sent me. 26 And I have declared unto them thy name, and will declare it: that the *agape*/love wherewith thou hast *agape*/loved me may be in them, and I in them."

1 John 4:9 "In this was manifested the *agape*/love of God toward us, because that God sent his only begotten Son into the world, that we might *zao*/live through him."

We have seen that the New Creation is one with Love, one with the God of love, and Love is one with the New Creation.

DISCOVERING OUR REDEMPTION

The New Creation is the Body of Christ.

This living organism, God-dominated, God-filled and love-ruled, is here among men, acting without fear, but rather in boldness, power, *agape*/love and the mind of Christ, by Holy Spirit, in the name of Jesus.

The living organism is acting in His stead, taking over His work, bringing His Kingdom to Earth.

John 20:21 "Then said Jesus to them again, Peace be unto you: as my Father hath sent me, even so send I you."

John 17:18 "As thou hast sent me into the world, even so have I also sent them into the world."

Jesus also said: John 14:27 "Peace I leave with you, my peace I give unto you: not as the world giveth, give I unto you. Let not your heart be troubled, neither let it be afraid."

That word *peace* can be translated as victory over everything so that Heaven comes to Earth, the will of God being done on Earth as it is in Heaven, with nothing missing and nothing broken, and all things working well, including that, when enemies rise up against you, they will flee from you seven ways, so you rest in confidence that all will submit to the Lord Jesus through you. Simply stated, the victory of God, in the name of Jesus, is yours.

What does this Word of peace look like?

Acts 10:36 "The word which God sent unto the children of Israel, preaching peace by Jesus Christ: (he is Lord of all:) 37 that word, I say, ye know, which was published throughout all Judaea, and began from Galilee, after the baptism which John preached; 38 how God anointed Jesus of Nazareth with the Holy Ghost and with power: who went about doing good, and healing all that were oppressed (*under the active dominion, reign or lordship*) of the devil; for God was with him." This is what making peace looks like to God.

In the first chapter of Acts, Luke said, by the Spirit, Acts 1:1 "The things Jesus began to do and teach."

We began where He left off.

We take up the work that He laid down.

He was the Burden-Bearer, the Lover of our souls.

He is acting in us, through us and with us.

God re-created your spirit legally, when Jesus was made alive from the dead. You enter into this vitally when you hear the Gospel and believe God raised Jesus from the dead. You will get a new body at the resurrection. Right now your job is to renew or *sozo*/save your soul into living out God's *zoe* life in every part of daily life now. 1 Pet 2:2 "As newborn babes, desire the sincere milk of the word, that ye may grow thereby."

We Have Been Given a New Identity in Jesus

You renew your mind to this Redemption, this new creation reality, by putting off your old, fallen self-identity and putting on your new identity in Christ. (See *OK, God, Now What?* for how to do this effectively in your heart.)

The same eternal life, or nature of God, that made Jesus righteous has been imparted to us in the new birth.

1 Pet 3:18 "For Christ also hath once suffered for sins, the just for the unjust, that he might bring us to God, being put to death in the flesh, but quickened by the Spirit (*in His spirit*)."

Col 2:13 "And you, being dead in your sins and the uncircumcision of your flesh, hath he quickened together with him, having forgiven you (*pardoned and removed the curse of sin from*) all trespasses."

Rom 1:1 "Paul, a servant of Jesus Christ, called to be an apostle, separated unto the gospel of God, 2 (which he had promised afore by his prophets in the holy scriptures,) 3 concerning his Son Jesus Christ our Lord, which was made of the seed of David according to the flesh; 4 and declared to be the Son of God with power, according to the spirit of holiness, by the resurrection from the dead: 5 by whom we have received grace and apostleship, for obedience to the faith among all nations, for his name: 6 among whom are ye also the called of Jesus Christ."

When we are born again, we are recreated, made alive from death, by the same Spirit that raised Jesus from the dead. We enter into the legal fact of the Redemption of mankind in Jesus, by faith in each believer. It is there for the taking for those who are willing to hear and believe the Gospel.

Rom 8:10 "And if Christ be in you, the body is dead because of sin; but the Spirit (*your spirit*) is *zoe*/life because of righteousness. 11 But if the Spirit of him that raised up Jesus from the dead dwell in you, he that raised up Christ from the dead shall also quicken your mortal bodies by his Spirit that dwelleth in you." Note: the original Greek has no capitalization of the word spirit in verse 10.

We have the same spirit indwelt by Holy Spirit, just like Jesus, for the same calling and job.

Was it any wonder that the Spirit said through John, 1 John 4:17 "As He is, so are we in this world"?

Now we can understand 2 Cor 5:21 "Him who knew no sin he made to be sin on our behalf; that we might become the righteousness of God in him."

Rom 3:26 "That he might himself be righteous, and the righteousness of him that hath faith in Jesus." (Literal translation) [E.W. Kenyon, *Two Kinds of Righteousness*, Pg 25. Kenyon's Gospel Publishing Society, Inc: 2004]

God became the righteousness of Jesus, when He made Him alive from spiritual death in Hades, and the moment we believe that God raised Him from the dead, God becomes our righteousness. We receive, or have executed in us, what Jesus did for us by the cross.

DISCOVERING OUR REDEMPTION

The legal path has been made for each one of us to believe the Gospel, receive and be made that same righteousness.

As God became the righteousness of Jesus, so He becomes the righteousness of the new creation.

As He became the *zoe*/life of Jesus, He becomes the *zoe*/life of the new creation. This truth will revolutionize the Church if men and women can just grasp it.

Eph 2:6 "And raised us up with him, and made us to sit with him in the heavenly places, in Christ Jesus."

This could never have been a part of the revelation, unless you were as righteous as He is.

Can't you see the utter fearlessness this gives you in the presence of all kinds of diseases and of Satan himself? At the gut level, God finds no fault with you, and you enjoy His perfect acceptance, as you go about doing His work for Him, in destroying the works of the devil in any form.

Can't you see what acceptance, joy, boldness and confidence it gives when you enter the Father's presence?

The sense of oneness with Jesus is as real as His sense of oneness was with us, when He was made sin and sickness.

Let us arise and take our place as victors, as conquerors, for we conquered the devil, when Jesus conquered him in Hades, for we were also in Jesus then.

Let us go out and do the work that Jesus began to do when He was here.

We are so identified and made one with Christ that Father God's destiny is for each one of us to mature into Jesus, to be, not just in spirit but also in soul, as Jesus is now.

Eph 4:13 "Till we all come in the unity of the faith, and of the knowledge of the Son of God, unto a perfect man, unto the measure of the stature of the fulness of Christ: ... 15 but speaking the truth in *agape*/love, may grow up into him in all things, which is the head, even Christ."

We are to cooperate in the process now by changing our self-identity into what God has made us now in the new creation: Eph 4:22 "That ye put off concerning the former conversation the old man, which is corrupt according to the deceitful lusts; 23 and be renewed in the spirit of your mind; 24 and that ye put on the new man, which after God is created in righteousness and true holiness."

Rom 13:14 "But put ye on the Lord Jesus Christ, and make not provision for the flesh, to fulfil the lusts thereof." And thus obey Rom 6:11 "Likewise reckon ye also yourselves to be dead indeed unto sin, but *zao*/alive unto God through Jesus Christ our Lord."

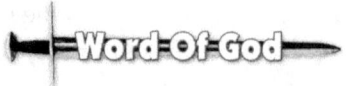

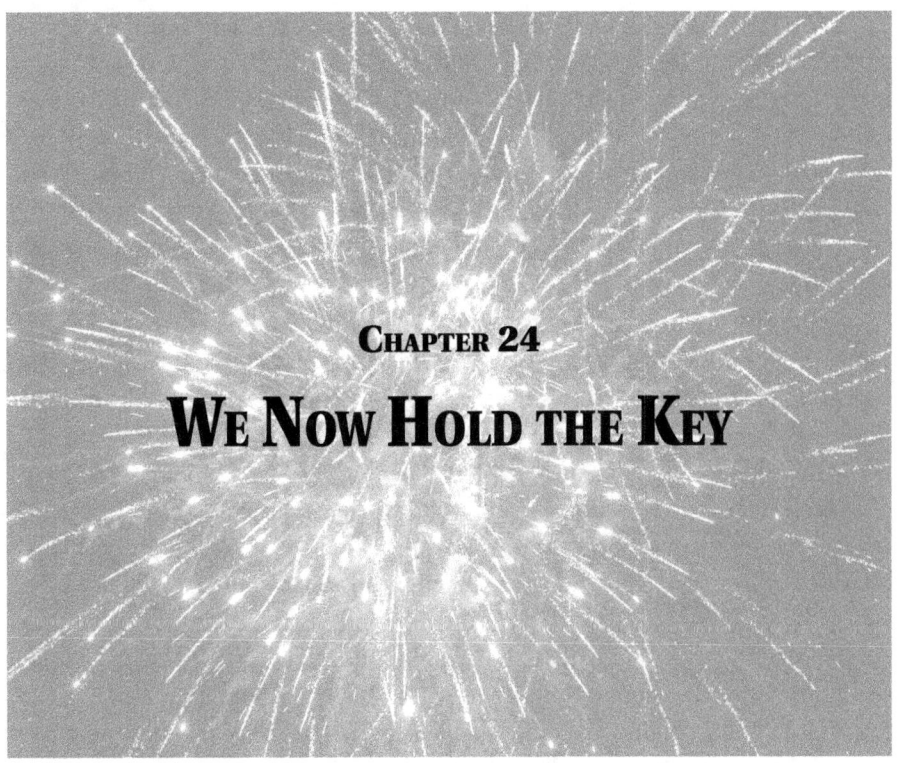

Chapter 24
We Now Hold the Key

God has made His move in Jesus; the next move is always ours.

James 4:8 "Draw nigh to God, and he will draw nigh to you … ."

Shall God be great among men once more?

Shall He heal and save the multitudes?

Shall the vast hordes of men once more hear the message of grace from lips set on fire with love?

Shall Jesus, the Price of *Zoe*/Life, manifest through His Body, the Church?

Shall the Peters once more walk the waves?

Shall we hear them say to the crippled, "Arise; walk!"

Shall we hear them say, as Peter did: Acts 9:33 "And there he found a certain man named Aeneas, which had kept his bed eight years, and was sick of the palsy. 34 And Peter said unto him, Aeneas, Jesus Christ maketh thee whole: arise, and make thy bed. And he arose immediately."

Shall we see men set free from Satan's dominion?

Yes, God has prophesied there will be a generation that will be His gateways.

There will be generations of believers who will believe the Gospel of God, unto doing His will.

DISCOVERING OUR REDEMPTION

Mark 16:15 "And he said unto them, Go ye into all the world, and preach the gospel to every creature. 16 He that believeth and is baptized shall be *sozo*/saved; but he that believeth not shall be damned. 17 And these signs shall follow them that believe; In my name shall they cast out devils; they shall speak with new tongues; 18 they shall take up serpents; and if they drink any deadly thing, it shall not hurt them; they shall lay hands on the sick, and they shall recover."

This is a command and a prophecy. Since this is for our age, you can live it out in your time.

2 Cor 6:1 "We then, as workers together with him, beseech you also that ye receive not the grace of God in vain. 2 (For he saith, I have heard thee in a time accepted, and in the day of *soteria*/salvation have I succoured thee: behold, now is the accepted time; behold, now is the day of *soteria*/salvation.)"

As we do this, God will do as He has always done.

Mark 16:19 "So then after the Lord had spoken unto them, he was received up into heaven, and sat on the right hand of God. 20 And they went forth, and preached everywhere, the Lord working with them, and confirming the word with signs following. Amen."

We are masters for Him, though Him and by Him.

Rom 5:15 "(But not as the offence, so also is the free gift. For if through the offence of one many be dead, much more the grace of God, and the gift by grace, which is by one man, Jesus Christ, hath abounded unto many. 16 And not as it was by one that sinned, so is the gift: for the judgment was by one to condemnation, but the free gift is of many offences unto justification. 17 For if by one man's offence death reigned (*as king, as evidenced by all the evil and sadness in the world, where it is not like Heaven on Earth*) by one; much more they which (*continually*) *lambano*/ receive abundance of grace and of the gift of righteousness shall reign (*as kings for Jesus Christ*) in *zoe*/life by one, Jesus Christ.) 18 Therefore as by the offence of one judgment came upon all men to condemnation; even so by the righteousness of one the free gift came upon all men unto justification of *zoe*/life. 19 For as by one man's disobedience many were made sinners, so by the obedience of one shall many be made righteous. 20 Moreover the law entered, that the offence might abound. But where sin abounded, grace did much more abound: 21 that as sin hath reigned (*as king, through all the forms of death, fast and slow, including sickness and disease*) unto death, even so might grace reign (*as king, to bring Heaven to Earth, by reconciling every evil, including sickness and disease, to make Heaven on Earth*) through righteousness unto eternal *zoe*/life by Jesus Christ our Lord."

The mission given us is certainly of a magnitude to be worthy of the terrible suffering death of His own Beloved Son, Jesus, the Christ of God. He paid the price, and we get the benefits. He did the heavy lifting, the hard work, and we can reap the fruits of abiding in Him.

We are those who continually *lambano* the abundance of grace and the gift of righteousness unto *zoe*/life and unto reigning in grace for Him and crushing death, in every form, for Him. We hold on, by confessing who and what we are in Jesus, in spite of any and all failures and delays, "counting it all joy," until we see the answer. (James 1:2, Rom 5:1-6, 1 Pet 1:3-9)

Heb 3:1 "Wherefore, holy brethren, partakers of the heavenly calling, consider the Apostle and High Priest of our profession (*confession*), Christ Jesus; 2 who was faithful to him that appointed him, as also Moses was faithful in all his house. 3 For this man was counted worthy of more glory than Moses, inasmuch as he who hath builded the house hath more honour than the house. 4 For every house is builded by some man; but he that built all things is God. 5 And Moses verily was faithful in all his house, as a servant, for a testimony of those things which were to be spoken after; 6 but Christ as a son over his own house; whose house are we, if we hold fast the confidence and the rejoicing of the hope firm unto the end."

Father God works with us, as we proclaim His Word of grace, in the name of Jesus.

We have arrived in Jesus.

We know to release God's blessing, someone must have faith, and you have made the decision that the one is you. Just as when Jesus raised the dead boy in Nain (Luke 7:11-17), you see the need and deliver God's goodness, and you have the faith to get the job done. Like Jesus, when others have faith you appreciate it, but each time you pray, you do it as if you were raising a dead boy in an unfriendly city, so it is you, with God, delivering His *agape*/love.

We have the thing the human spirit has craved; we are back home with Father God, who now accepts us based on what He has done in Jesus and for what He will do in us all.

1 John 4:10 "Herein is *agape*/love, not that we *agape*/loved God, but that he *agape*/loved us, and sent his Son to be the propitiation for our sins."

Jesus did not just make Propitiation as an Old Testament priest might try to do; Jesus is the Propitiation!

We are maturing, perfecting ourselves in *agape* love.

1 John 4:17 "Herein is our *agape*/love made perfect, that we may have boldness in the day of judgment: because as he is, so are we in this world. 18 There is no fear in *agape*/love; but perfect *agape*/love casteth out fear: because fear hath torment. He that feareth is not made perfect in *agape*/love. 19 We *agape*/love him, because he first *agape*/loved us."

We are becoming *agape*/love experts, so, when Jesus looks at us, He sees more and more of Himself manifested in us.

DISCOVERING OUR REDEMPTION

We are overcomers over the world system, we have taken those first steps, and now our faith builds the Kingdom of God wherever we aim our faith in God.

1 John 5:5 "Who is he that overcometh the world, but he that believeth that Jesus is the Son of God?"

1 John 5:11 "And this is the record, that God hath given to us eternal *zoe*/life, and this *zoe*/life is in his Son. 12 He that hath the Son hath *zoe*/life; and he that hath not the Son of God hath not *zoe*/life. 13 These things have I written unto you that believe on the name of the Son of God; that ye may know that ye have eternal *zoe*/life, and that ye may believe on the name of the Son of God."

Based on 1 John 4:4, we are whispering now, "Greater is He who is in us, than any opposition or any lack that may confront us."

When you read these scriptures, you hear a voice saying, "This is God speaking."

We remember what manner of men and women He has made us.

We read the Scriptures, the New Testament Redemption revelation, out loud until it captures our hearts, and then continue reading it to keep those hearts pure. We never tire of the knowledge of His Redemption.

1 John 3:2 "*Agape*/beloved, now are we the sons of God, and it doth not yet appear what we shall be: but we know that, when he shall appear, we shall be like him; for we shall see him as he is. 3 And every man that hath this hope in him purifieth himself, even as he is pure."

We fear not.

1 John 4:18 "There is no fear in *agape*/love; but perfect *agape*/love casteth out fear: because fear hath torment. He that feareth is not made perfect in *agape*/love."

We are merciless and relentless, when fears try to take hold of us. We obey: Josh 1:5 "There shall not any man be able to stand before thee all the days of thy life: as I was with Moses, so I will be with thee: I will not fail thee, nor forsake thee. 6 Be strong and of a good courage: for unto this people shalt thou divide for an inheritance the land, which I sware unto their fathers to give them. 7 Only be thou strong and very courageous, that thou mayest observe to do according to all the law, which Moses my servant commanded thee: turn not from it to the right hand or to the left, that thou mayest prosper whithersoever thou goest. 8 This book of the law shall not depart out of thy mouth; but thou shalt meditate therein day and night, that thou mayest observe to do according to all that is written therein: for then thou shalt make thy way prosperous, and then thou shalt have good success. 9 Have not I commanded thee? Be strong and of a good courage; be not afraid, neither be thou dismayed: for the Lord thy God is with thee whithersoever thou goest."

We must constantly mutter, speak, chew and sing the Word of God, especially the Word of Christ and the new creation, to keep our minds renewed so that we can overcome the challenges of every hour and every day.

We Now Hold the Key

We gladly obey: Eph 5:17 "Wherefore be ye not unwise, but understanding what the will of the Lord is. 18 And be not drunk with wine, wherein is excess; but be (*continually being*) filled with the Spirit; 19 [*by*] speaking to yourselves in psalms and hymns and spiritual songs, singing and making melody in your heart to the Lord; 20 giving thanks always for all things unto God and the Father in the name of our Lord Jesus Christ; 21 submitting yourselves one to another in the fear of God."

We obey, knowing that as we give way to small anxieties, nagging fears and cares, and also terrible and massive evil circumstances, we make our minds grow less intelligent and less able to trust God. Or, the more we pray with our minds and our spirits, the more we expand and heal our intellects and ability to hear and work with God.

So, like champions who have not exercised for years, or strong men who discover they are wrapped in ropes, we pull ourselves up and we obey: Phil 4:4 "Rejoice in the Lord alway: and again I say, Rejoice. 5 Let your moderation (*disciplined and diligent manner of loving God in spirit and in truth*) be known unto all men. The Lord is at hand. 6 Be careful (*anxious, fearful, worried or fretful*) for nothing; but in every thing by prayer and supplication with thanksgiving let your *aiteo*/requests (*demands and expectations, per His scripture promises*) be made known unto God. 7 And the peace of God, which passeth all understanding, shall keep your hearts and minds through Christ Jesus. 8 Finally, brethren, whatsoever things are **true**, whatsoever things are **honest**, whatsoever things are **just**, whatsoever things are **pure**, whatsoever things are **lovely**, whatsoever things are of **good report**; if there be any **virtue**, and if there be any **praise**, think on these things. 9 Those things, which ye have both learned, and received, and heard, and seen in me (*Paul*), do: and the God of peace (*who gives victory, as we do the right things*) shall be with you (*and be released in and by those right behaviors, to build the Kingdom of God, per your aiteo/requests*)."

We are relentless. For every evil situation and even mild cares, we search out and confess with our mouths God's overcoming promises. We give thanks that no Word of His is void of power, that all things are possible with God, and that we will see the goodness of the Lord in the land of the living. We speak to believe, and we renew our minds into His truth. We turn those scriptures into songs, confessions and affirmations, and pray, give thanks, praise and rejoice for His glory in each one, according to His Word. Whatever the situation, we join Caleb in making a good report: Num 13:30 "And Caleb stilled the people before Moses, and said, Let us go up at once, and possess it; for we are well able to overcome it [*for the God who melts mountains and humbled mighty Egypt in signs and wonders is with us*]."

Heb 13:5 "Let your conversation be without covetousness; and be content with such things as ye have [*so you are not pulled into making idols of worldly success*]: for he hath said, I will never leave thee, nor forsake thee. 6 So that we may boldly say, The Lord is my helper, and I will not fear what man shall do unto me."

DISCOVERING OUR REDEMPTION

We know world wealth and prosperity is God's desire for us, but not at the expense of loving God. 3 John 2 "*Agape*/beloved, I wish (*pray*) above all things that thou mayest prosper and be in health, even as thy soul prospereth."

It is not money that is the problem; it is the *agape*/love of money that is the problem, because that is operating in the world system, run by the devil. 1 Tim 6:9 "But they that will be rich fall into temptation and a snare, and into many foolish and hurtful lusts, which drown men in destruction and perdition. 10 For the *agape*/love of money is the root of all evil: which while some coveted after, they have erred from the faith, and pierced themselves through with many sorrows. 11 But thou, O man of God, flee these things; and follow after righteousness, godliness, faith, *agape*/love, patience, meekness. 12 Fight the good fight of faith, *lambano*/lay hold on eternal *zoe*/life, whereunto thou art also called, and hast professed a good profession before many witnesses."

1 Tim 6:17 "Charge them that are rich in this world, that they be not highminded, nor trust in uncertain riches, but in the *zao*/living God, who giveth us richly all things to enjoy; 18 that they do good, that they be rich in good works, ready to distribute, willing to communicate; 19 laying up in store for themselves a good foundation against the time to come, that they may *lambano*/lay hold on eternal *zoe*/life."

Knowing Redemption will make you rich beyond measure and fearless in the face of impossible circumstances, you must hold on to, *lambano* it with diligence. 2 Pet 1:8 "For if these things (*of the character, nature and power of God*) be in you, and abound, they make you that ye shall neither be barren nor unfruitful in the *epignosis*/knowledge of our Lord Jesus Christ. 9 But he that lacketh these things (*of the character, nature and power of God*) is blind, and cannot see afar off, and hath forgotten that he was purged from his old sins. 10 Wherefore the rather, brethren, give diligence to make your calling and election sure: for if ye do these things, ye shall never fall: 11 for so an entrance shall be ministered unto you abundantly into the everlasting kingdom of our Lord and Saviour Jesus Christ. 12 Wherefore I will not be negligent to put you always in remembrance of these things, though ye know them, and be established in the present truth [*of our Redemption in Christ*]. 13 Yea, I think it meet, as long as I am in this tabernacle, to stir you up by putting you in remembrance; 14 knowing that shortly I must put off this my tabernacle, even as our Lord Jesus Christ hath shewed me. 15 Moreover I will endeavour that ye may be able after my decease to have these things always in remembrance."

You can know you got and are keeping the message, by measuring your joy and thanksgiving. Col 1:12 "Giving thanks (*continually*) unto the Father, which hath made us meet to be partakers of the inheritance of the saints in light: 13 who hath delivered us from the power of darkness, and hath translated us into the kingdom of his *agape*/dear Son: 14 in whom we have redemption through his blood, even the *aphesis*/forgiveness (*remission, purging, washing, removal, obliteration and putting away*) of sins: 15 who is the image of the invisible God, the firstborn of every creature: 16 for by him were all things created, that are in heaven, and that are in earth, visible and invisible, whether they be thrones, or dominions, or principalities, or powers: all things were created by him, and for him: 17 and he is before all things, and by him all things consist."

1 Pet 1:3 "Blessed be the God and Father of our Lord Jesus Christ, which according to his abundant mercy hath begotten us again unto a *zao*/lively hope by the resurrection of Jesus Christ from the dead, 4 to an inheritance incorruptible, and undefiled, and that fadeth not away, reserved in heaven for you, 5 who are kept by the power of God through faith unto *soteria*/salvation ready to be revealed in the last time. 6 Wherein ye greatly rejoice (*in spite of the evil circumstances and trials you are in and see in the world*), though now for a season, if need be, ye are in heaviness through manifold temptations: 7 that the trial of your faith, being much more precious than of gold that perisheth, though it be tried with fire, might be found unto praise and honour and glory at the appearing of Jesus Christ: 8 whom having not seen, ye *agape*/love; in whom, though now ye see him not, yet believing, ye rejoice with joy unspeakable (*that excites you to shouts without words, incomprehensible for the excitement and the assurance that God cannot lie*) and full of glory: 9 receiving the end of your faith, even the *soteria*/salvation of your *psuche*/souls (*lives*)."

Circumstances may try to pull us into lusts (fear, idolatry, selfishness, self-centeredness, self-preservation and self-righteousness), but we must keep close to God's Word, putting it in our eyes, and our ears and on our lips, proclaiming His love is greater, and we will see the goodness of the Lord in the land of living, in the name of Jesus.

You fight against these lusts by continually stirring up yourself into the truth of your Redemption, the truth of your former purging of sin and the absolute confidence that you are never forsaken, and, instead, you are the gateway of God's power, in the name of Jesus, wherever you are. When you do not feel like it, you exercise great diligence and keep yourself stirred, with acts of thanksgiving, joy, praise, confession of God's truth, affirmations of how they fit in you, speaking and singing in tongues, and you go and do acts of *agape* love, kindness and God's power. You know it is quicker to act your way into believing than to believe your way into right acting.

You fight aggressively any fear that comes at you. In fact, you must not tolerate even a whiff of fear, by obeying: Phil 4:4 "Rejoice in the Lord alway: and again I say, Rejoice. 5 Let your moderation be known unto all men. The Lord is at hand. 6 Be careful (*anxious, fearful, fretful or worried*) for nothing; but in every thing by prayer and supplication with thanksgiving let your *aiteo*/requests (*demand and expectations, per His Bible promises*) be made known unto God. 7 And the peace of God, which passeth all understanding, shall keep your hearts and minds through Christ

DISCOVERING OUR REDEMPTION

Jesus. 8 Finally, brethren, whatsoever things are **true**, whatsoever things are **honest**, whatsoever things are **just**, whatsoever things are **pure**, whatsoever things are **lovely**, whatsoever things are of **good report**; if there be any **virtue,** and if there be any **praise**, think on these things. 9 Those things, which ye have both learned, and received, and heard, and seen in me, do: and the God of peace shall be with you [*to destroy the works of the devil, by healing all who are oppressed by him*]."

Jude 20 "But ye, *agape*/beloved, building up yourselves on your most holy faith, praying in the Holy Ghost, 21 keep yourselves in the *agape*/love of God, looking for the mercy of our Lord Jesus Christ unto eternal *zoe*/life (*in both the answer to every* aiteo/*prayer and in His glorious appearing*). 22 And of some have compassion, making a difference: 23 and others *sozo*/save with fear, pulling them out of the fire; hating even the garment spotted by the flesh. 24 Now unto him that is able to keep you from falling, and to present you faultless before the presence of his glory with exceeding joy, 25 to the only wise God our Saviour, be glory and majesty, dominion and power, both now and ever. Amen."

We are masters at obeying: Philem 6 "That the communication of thy faith may become effectual by the *epignosis*/acknowledging of every good thing which is in you in Christ Jesus." This includes much thanks and long, hard and fast tongues.

At last, we are masters, united with God, the sons He desires to work with and enjoys working with.

1 Cor 3:9 "For we are labourers together with God: ye are God's husbandry, ye are God's building."

We are the God-created, the God-indwelt, the God-empowered and the God-guided.

Prov 3:5 "Trust *(with faith thoughts, words and actions in thanksgiving, praise, rejoicing, confession and affirmations of His Word and love toward you)* in the Lord with all thine heart *(not stopping until your heart is fixed on God by His Word and nothing unsettles you per Phil 4:6-8)*; and lean not unto thine own understanding. 6 In all thy ways acknowledge him *(with faith thoughts, words and actions in thanksgiving, praise, rejoicing, confession and affirmations of His Word and love toward you)*, and he shall direct thy paths."

We are the ones in whom love never fails.

We build for the future, making the unseen of God manifest into the Earth, knowing: Gal 5:6 "For in Jesus Christ neither circumcision availeth anything, nor uncircumcision; but faith which worketh by *agape*/love."

Come, let us go up and take the land! We are well able!

Our battle cry is: Phil 4:13 "I can do all things through Christ which strengtheneth me." Yahoo!

Chapter 25

Because of Jesus, We Have Received a Great Inheritance

Holy Spirit prayed through Paul: Eph 1:15 "Wherefore I also, after I heard of your faith in the Lord Jesus, and *agape*/love unto all the saints, 16 cease not to give thanks for you, making mention of you in my prayers; 17 that the God of our Lord Jesus Christ, the Father of glory, may give unto you the spirit of wisdom and revelation in the knowledge of him: 18 the eyes of your understanding being enlightened; that ye may know what is the hope of his calling, and what the riches of the glory of his inheritance in the saints, 19 and what is the exceeding greatness of his power to us-ward who believe, according to the working of his mighty power, 20 which he wrought in Christ, when he raised him from the dead, and set him at his own right hand in the heavenly places, 21 far above all principality, and power, and might, and dominion, and every name that is named, not only in this world, but also in that which is to come: 22 and hath put all things under his feet, and gave him to be the head over all things to the church, 23 which is his body, the fulness of him that filleth all in all."

This prayer states that, after faith in Christ, comes growing in the knowledge of Him, by His Spirit. Paul started with the overall key, to grow in *epignosis*/knowledge of God. Then he went into specifics. The first two items listed are: Eph 1:18

DISCOVERING OUR REDEMPTION

"... that ye may know what is the hope of his calling, and what the riches of the glory of his inheritance in the saints."

Holy Spirit requires us to pray for God to move in the Earth. Here He requires prayer for us to grow in the Lord, and that growth is to be governed by always keeping our eyes on the target of what we have been called to (the joyful expectation of coming good in His calling for us) and the riches and abundance of resources of God, and for the fullness of Holy Spirit in our souls and body, for what God gets in and out of us in our Redemption in Jesus.

Notice, this is a revelation from God's perspective, not man's. Paul is asking Holy Spirit to grow us into the plans God has for us, rather than our plans for God. He is asking for us to become God-centered and not self-centered.

While we do not have the space to repeat the scriptures, this prayer of Paul is based on Proverbs chapters 1 through 8. God wants us to see with understanding and keep our eyes on the target, so we can have faith for Him to get us there. 2 Cor 3:17 "Now the Lord is that Spirit: and where the Spirit of the Lord is, there is liberty *(for God to do all He wants, in and by you)*. 18 But we all, with open face beholding as in a glass *(mirror)* the glory of the Lord *(in our face, the reflection of Jesus in us, to the fullness of His glory, as He is now)*, are changed into the same image *(of the fullness of Jesus as He is now)* from glory to glory, even as by the Spirit of the Lord."

John G. Lake talked often of seeking the calling of God in our lives, to reflect the fullness of why God has given us the greatest gift in the Universe through Jesus, the indwelling of Holy Spirit. Rev. Lake understood this was the fruit of God in our Redemption. Gal 3:13 "Christ hath redeemed us from the curse of the law, being made a curse for us: for it is written, Cursed is every one that hangeth on a tree: 14 that the blessing of Abraham might come on the Gentiles through Jesus Christ; that we might receive the promise of the Spirit through faith."

The fruit of our working with Holy Spirit will be: 1 John 5:1 "Whosoever believeth that Jesus is the Christ is born of God: and every one that *agape*/loveth him that begat *agape*/loveth him also that is begotten of him. 2 By this we know that we *agape*/love the children of God, when we *agape*/love God, and keep his commandments. 3 For this is the *agape*/love of God, that we keep his commandments: and his commandments are not grievous. 4 For whatsoever is born of God overcometh the world: and this is the victory that overcometh the world, even our faith."

THE ARTICLE

This article by Rev. Lake, from *The Spokane-Review*, Spokane, Washington on October 20, 1918, is amazing in its depth of catching what and why the Father redeemed us in Jesus. (Wyatt, *The Fire of God*, pages 69-78 and is very similar to

"As He Is, So Are We" in Roberts Liardon's book on Lake, pp 926-934). The entire article follows:

"As He is, so are we in the world." 1 John 4:17

The mind of the world is fixed on the Redeemer. The Old Testament Scriptures, looking up to Christ, are particularly prolific in their description of His life, His sorrows, His sufferings, His death, His sacrifice. All these were the qualities of the Redeemer. All these were endured and exercised by the Redeemer in order to obtain something. That something was REDEMPTION.

What Redemption means is best seen by following the chain of Christ's life from the Crucifixion on–not back of the cross, this side of it. If you want to understand the Redeemer, see Him before the cross comes into view. That is, if you want to understand the Redeemer who obtained that Redemption. But if you want to understand the Redemption He obtained, look at this side of Calvary.

The great majority of the Christian world is still weeping at the foot of the cross. The vast majority of Christians are still carrying a little crucifix, representing a dead Christ. The consciousness of man is fixed on the Christ who died, not the Christ who now lives. They are looking back to the Redeemer who was, not the Redeemer who is.

On this side of the cross, we see all the marvel of opposites to what we see in the Christ on the other side of the cross. On the other side of the cross, we see a man of sorrows, and acquainted with sickness, bearing our sicknesses, carrying our sorrows. He had nowhere to lay His head. Poverty was one of His characteristics. Nobody ever stops to think, or rarely so, that He bore His poverty, and what for? Answer: "That through His poverty we might be made rich." He bore our sorrows, what for? That we, through His sorrows, might be made glad. He bore our sufferings, for what? That we, through His stripes, might be healed. He gave His life a sacrifice for sins, for what? That we should know no sin. Then, having completed the Redemption, or purchased the Redemption, that Redemption becomes manifest on this side of Calvary.

I sometimes wish that I could turn the face of the world the other way. You may observe that I rarely turn the face of mankind to the cross. The world looked to the cross until they passed it. But if they had never passed it Redemption would be no more a reality than it was before. Redemption becomes a reality as we obtain the Redemption. To obtain what the Redeemer purchased is the purpose of the Christian life. On this side of the cross, we see the victory, not the suffering, not the humility and dejection and rejection, but the VICTORY.

We see the first glory glimmer of that victory when Jesus, who was crucified as a Redeemer, steps forth as the redeemed. For the Redeemer Himself, the first-fruits of them that slept, BECAME the Redeemer of mankind, or the pattern of Redemption. He was not the pattern of Redemption back there on the other side of the cross. He BECAME the pattern of Redemption. Paul puts it in such terse terms. "He BECAME the author of eternal salvation." Not "was manufactured the author of eternal salvation," not "was born," but BECAME the author of eternal salvation. Why? Because, having, as the Redeemer, entered into the Redemption by Himself, "the first-fruits of them that slept," the first victor, the first example of victory, He became the Manifestor, the Demonstrator, the Revealer, the embodiment of eternal Salvation.

On this side of the cross, there is the victory of His Resurrection, the marvel of all victories, the victory over death, by which He took death captive. A living man Himself, He came forth the Conqueror over death itself, having put all things under His feet. What an ascent into triumph! What a change in His consciousness! What a distinction between the Redeemer and the redeemed! No longer subject to death, but triumphing over it. No longer subject to humiliation, but now, bless God, becoming the exalted One. For in the ascension we see the exaltation of Jesus, instead of the man of sorrows, acquainted with grief, or sickness. We see the living triumphant, exultant Son of God, ascending to the Throne of God, receiving from God, the Father, the superlative gift of gifts, receiving from God, the Father, what Jesus and the Father considered worthy of the suffering and death and sacrifice and Redemption of Jesus Christ, a reward so great that Jesus Himself considered it worth all His sufferings, all His buffetings, His Earth career, His humiliation, His sacrifice and death. It was all given to obtain it, the GIFT OF THE HOLY SPIRIT. (Acts 2:16-18)

On this side of the cross, we see the distributing of His new life. Not the life that was on the other side, but the life that is on this side–the life of triumph, the life of victory, the life of praise, the life of power, the life of glory, exultant, triumphant.

The other night, as I lay in bed, I was thinking and praying over some of the things that were passing through my mind concerning Jesus. The scripture in Rev 1:18 came, with force, to me, where Jesus, not the humiliated Savior, but as a Kingly Conqueror, stands forth with the marvelous declaration: "I am He that liveth, and was dead; and behold, I am alive for evermore, and have the keys of hell and death."

It seems to me that in all the Word of God there is no such shout of triumph as that. Why, it seems to me, as if the very Heaven and the Earth and all that is in them ring with that exultant shout of a real Victor. "I have the keys of hell, and of death." The enemies of man, taken captive by the Son of God, subject to His dictate. That is the Christ that speaks to my soul. That is the Christ on this side of Calvary. That is the Christ my soul worships.

INVOCATION

God, be merciful to us, and bless us, and cause Thy face to shine upon us: that Thy way may be known in the Earth, Thy saving health among all the nation, in the name of Jesus. Amen!

Because of Jesus, We Have Received a Great Inheritance

I am going to tell you a strange thing. I am not much interested in the Christ on the other side of Calvary. Not half so much as I am in the Christ on this side of Calvary. Bless God, I love the Redeemer, but I GLORY in His REDEMPTION.

The marvel of Christianity and the wonder of this scripture that I call your attention to, is that it does not say that "as He WAS" back there, so are we to be in this world. Don't you see, that is where the world fell down, where the Christian life became submerged in a veil of tears and shadows and darkness and poverty and humiliation and suffering. All of which Christian mankind accepted joyfully, because they believed they were exemplifying Jesus Christ, and thinking they were glorifying Him. They still envisioned, not the Christ that IS, but the Christ that WAS [and only on one day of His 33-year life]. The Christ who bore and endured and suffered and died, in order to obtain the privilege of the Christ who is, and to become the Christ who is.

Now, if I could radically turn your minds tonight clear around from that vision of the Christ before the cross, to the vision of the Christ who IS, this fact would mean that your souls must ascend in the consciousness and union with the overcoming Son of God. Not bowed and bound with the humiliated Savior, but joined in holy glory triumph with the Son of God, who obtained the victory and revealed it and distributes its power and glory to the souls of men.

"As He IS," not as He WAS, John said, "so are we in this world." Not in the life to come. The glory is not for the life that is coming, but for the life that is now. The victory is not for the future. It is for the NOW. It is not for the good days bye and bye. It is for the NOW. Not for Heaven to come, but Heaven on Earth NOW.

Sin, sickness and death under His feet. Hell itself taken captive and obedient to His Word. Every enemy of mankind throttled, bound, chained by the Son of God. Mankind joined with Him by the Holy Ghost in living triumph. Why, if I receive of the spirit of Jesus Christ, of the Christ who IS, I receive of the spirit of victory and power and might and dominion of grace, of love, of power, blessed be God, of all the blessed estate of which Jesus Himself is now the conscious Master. All these He gives to the Christian, through imparting to Him the Holy Ghost.

Holy Spirit Message

The Spirit of the Lord says within my soul, that: The universal sound of praise in which angels and men, all creatures in the Earth, the sea and the sky, will eventually join, comes because the consciousness of the overcoming Christ has dawned upon them and possessed their soul.

Some of the final song, the song of the ages, that shout of victory, we find in the 5th chapter of Revelation.

Rev 5:11 "And I beheld, and I heard the voice of many angels round about the throne and the beasts and the elders: and the number of them was ten thousand

DISCOVERING OUR REDEMPTION

times ten thousand, and thousands of thousands; 12 saying with a loud voice, Worthy is the Lamb that was slain to receive power, and riches, and wisdom, and strength, and honour, and glory, and blessing. 13 And every creature which is in heaven, and on the earth, and under the earth, and such as are in the sea, and all that are in them, heard I saying, Blessing, and honour, and glory, and power, be unto him that sitteth upon the throne, and unto the Lamb for ever and ever. 14 And the four beasts said, Amen. And the four and twenty elders fell down and worshipped him that liveth for ever and ever."

Should I carry your soul tonight into the place of victory in God, I must carry it into the consciousness of Christ's overcoming life. All His healing virtue, His saving grace, His transforming spirit, all the angelic communion, the heavenly foretaste, the consciousness of the estate of the redeemed, the glory triumph of Jesus Christ is in the consciousness born from the Resurrection and revealed in the Revelation. "For as He is, so are we in the world."

Jesus, in His Earth life, reached forth in the spirit into that life and kingdom and triumph and exhibited in this world, in a measure, that victory and triumph that His soul knew and envisioned. But when the cross came, He entered, actually and experimentally, into the life that His soul formerly envisioned and knew through the Word of God and the consciousness of God within His heart. And so His ministry in the spirit is a ministry in the ALL POWER, ALL CONSCIOUSNESS, ALL KNOWLEDGE, all grace, all victory, all salvation. Bless God!

I would lift your souls tonight in the spirit of God into that glow and glory of the triumphant life. Do you know that it is only as your mind settles back into the humiliation and suffering and the weakness and the fear and doubting of the dispensation that is past, that you grow weak and sickly and sinful? But as your soul looks forward and possesses, in the present, the glorious victory that Jesus acquired and exhibits and enjoys, does it rise out of its sorrows, out of it sins, into that glorious triumph of the children of God.

PRAYER

God, when earth and sea and sky discover the wonder of the Redemption of Jesus, then, dear God, the heart will turn anew, with a holy love, to the Redeemer, who, by His beauteous grace, dared to endure it all, that we might possess the inheritance.

O God, when we think of the marvel of the souls of the ages breaking into a shout of heavenly glory and praise to Christ, because that on our souls has dawned the wonder of His Redemption, when the world will say again, "Worthy is the Lamb that was slain to receive honor and might and glory and power and blessing." O God, when our hearts comprehend the purpose of Jesus, when our souls possess it, when that Redemption into the likeness and the image and the stature and the fullness of Jesus Christ comes, our souls will worship Thee as they cannot worship Thee this moment.

But, Almighty God, we look forward and throw our hearts open for the almightiness of a Redemption that comprehends the utter transformation of mankind into the image of Jesus Christ. Bless His name forever. Bless His precious name forever! Amen!

It would not be pleasant to always have to live with babies and imbeciles, or with a lot of half-grown-up folks. I want you to sympathize with God. I want you to catch the vision of the ordinary Christian conception. Think of God, having to live forever and ever in association with people who were not half big enough to comprehend His purpose, His desires, or His will. That is not God's purpose. Jesus Christ undertook the biggest contract that Heaven or Earth or Sea or Sky ever knew. He undertook the Redemption of mankind and their transformation, by the Spirit of the living God, into His own likeness and image and stature and understanding, in the grace and power and fullness of His own nature. Jesus Christ is the associate of God, one with Him, and with every son of God. He has purposed that redeemed men, grown up in God, transformed into the very image and likeness and nature and fullness of Jesus Christ, becoming like the Son of God, shall be the associates of God [associate, as in business partners, to further the business of the Kingdom of God together, co-laborers of like mind and purpose].

What did God create mankind for anyway? Answer: "The chief end of man is to [know and] glorify God and enjoy Him forever and a mighty lot more."

God's purpose in the creation of mankind was to develop an association on His own plane. Otherwise God would have been eternally living with babies or imbeciles. He would have been compelled forever to associate with those who were not able to understand or comprehend His nature or character or the marvel of His being or the wonder of His power [and love].

The wonder of the Redemption of Jesus Christ is revealed in the matchlessness of God's purpose to transform man into His very nature and image and likeness and fullness. Thereby men, as sons of God, become, bless God, the associates of Almighty God, on His own plane of life and understanding.

When my soul saw the vision of God Almighty's marvelous purpose, I felt like falling on my face afresh and crying out "Worthy is the Lamb that was slain." For "As He is, so are we in this world." All the glory and power that Jesus knows at the Throne of God, all the wonder of His overcoming grace, all the marvel of the greatness of His power, is yours and mine to receive through faith in the Son of God, yours and mine to expect through the faith of the Son of God, yours and mine to possess and enjoy and reveal to others, to the glory of God.

DISCOVERING OUR REDEMPTION

Prayer

God, one day we must graduate from kindergarten. God, one day our souls must grow up to the stature of men. God, one day our minds must develop to the comprehension and understanding of grown-up souls. God, the world is in kindergarten. The Christian world is drinking milk. God, they have not had the vision; they have not understood the marvel of it all. O God, we bless Thee for the Holy Ghost. We bless Thee for the baptism of the Holy Ghost, which has been the Revealer in our souls of the wonder and magnificence of the eternal exalted Christ.

God, we bless Thee for the grace of God that hath made possible such a union with the Lord Jesus. That being born again of God we have entered into oneness in the Holy Spirit; oneness with Christ that, by His grace, His nature and His power are revealed in us and revealed through us. [Give us a vision of Yourself that causes us to cooperate with You, for us to desire and agree to believe You to release more of You in us, so we go from vision to hope to faith in and by Your Son, Jesus Christ, my Lord.]

And, my God, help us to go one further and say, "Revealed by us to the glory of God, the Father! Amen!"

Let us now give ourselves to God in Holy consecration.

Consecration Prayer

My God and Father,
In Jesus' name, I come to Thee.
Take me as I am. Make me what
I ought to be, in Spirit, in Soul, in Body.
Give me Power to do right. If I have
Wronged any, to repent, to confess, to restore.
No matter what it costs, wash me in the blood
Of Jesus, that I may now become Thy child.
And manifest Thee in a perfect Spirit,
A holy Mind, a Sickless Body ! Amen!

By Rev. John G. Lake, Spokane, Washington

To share with anyone how to receive Holy Spirit and the new birth, we suggest the following:

Here is the basic Gospel: You can only be right with the God of all creation through Jesus Christ: John 14:6 "Jesus saith unto him, I am the way, the truth, and the *zoe*/life: no man cometh unto the Father, but by me. 7 If ye had known me, ye should have known my Father also: and from henceforth ye know him, and have seen him." If you want to know what Father God is really like, just look at Jesus.

Rom 4:24 "But for us also, to whom it (*righteousness*) shall be imputed, if we believe on him that raised up Jesus our Lord from the dead; 25 who was delivered for our offences, and was raised again for our justification (*being made just as if you had never sinned or will sin again, to right standing, as a joint heir with Jesus, as a son of God*)."

1 Cor 15:1 "Moreover, brethren, I declare unto you the gospel which I preached unto you, which also ye have received, and wherein ye stand; 2 by which also ye are (*continuously being*) *sozo*/saved, if ye keep in memory what I preached unto you, unless ye have believed in vain. 3 For I delivered unto you first of all that which I also received, how that Christ died for our sins according to the scriptures; 4 and that he was buried, and that he rose again the third day according to the scriptures." Jesus is now seated at the right hand of the Father. (Act 2:34; Eph 1:20; Heb 1:3)

Rom 10:8 "But what saith it? The word is nigh thee, even in thy mouth, and in thy heart: that is, the word of faith, which we preach; 9 that if thou shalt confess with thy mouth the Lord Jesus, and shalt believe in thine heart that God hath raised him from the dead, thou shalt be *sozo*/saved. 10 For with the heart man believeth unto righteousness; and with the mouth confession is made unto *soteria*/salvation. 11 For the scripture saith, Whosoever believeth on him shall not be ashamed."

A Salvation Prayer:

"Lord Jesus, I believe You died for my sins, were buried and were raised by Father God on the third day for my justification, according to the Scriptures. I make You Lord of my life. Come rule and reign in and through me, my King. Baptize me with Your Holy Spirit and fire. Heal every part of my life. Teach me Your truth, in love, that I may walk to Your glory. Amen! And thank You!"

And a Simpler One:

"Jesus, God raised you from the dead, You are Lord. Fill me with Your Spirit to walk in love. Thank You!"

Now that you are born again by the action of God in your spirit; the next step is for you to get water baptized. Matt 28:19 "Go ye therefore, and teach all nations, baptizing them in the name of the Father, and of the Son, and of the Holy Ghost." You also need fellowship with other believers. We recommend you find a local Christian church to join, and get baptized there.

2 Pet 3:18 "*And* grow in grace, and in the knowledge of our Lord and Saviour Jesus Christ. To him be glory both now and for ever. Amen."

DISCOVERING OUR REDEMPTION

1 Pet 5:10 "*And* the God of all grace, who hath called us unto his eternal glory by Christ Jesus, after that ye have suffered a while, make you perfect, stablish, strengthen, settle you. 11 To him be glory and dominion for ever and ever. Amen."

Isa 11:9 ... For the earth shall be full of the knowledge of the Lord, as the waters cover the sea.

PART V

UNDERSTANDING WHAT IT ALL MEANS TO YOU

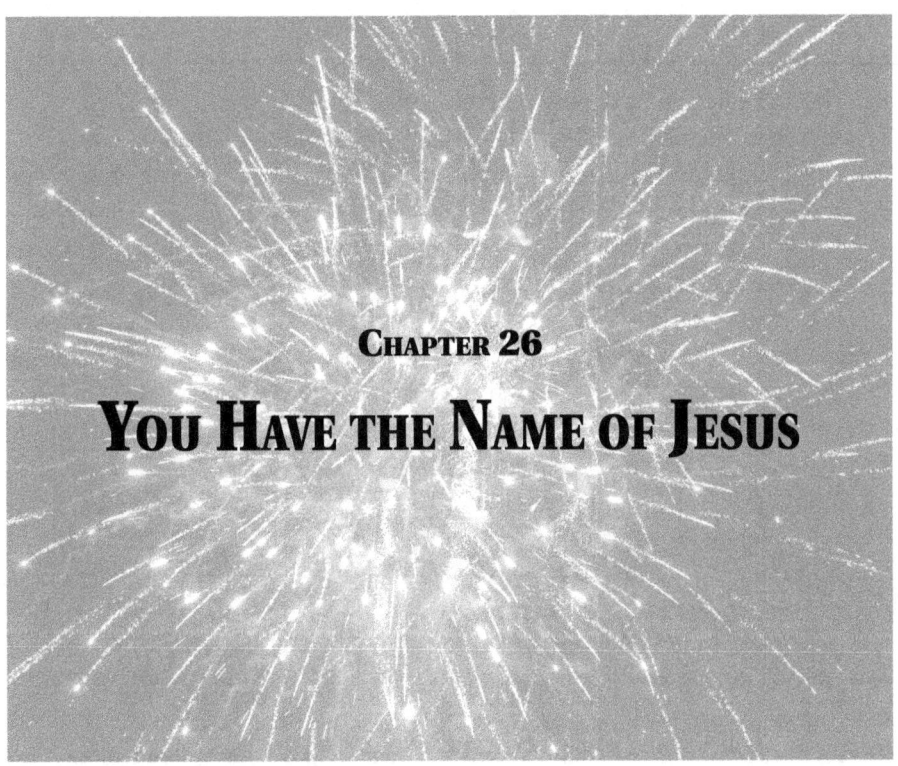

Chapter 26

You Have the Name of Jesus

As you grow in wisdom, you will have committed to memory these scriptures concerning our Redemption in Christ by covenant Identification.

The promises of the Word of God are also prophecies by which we wage effective war. 1 Tim 1:18 "This charge I commit unto thee, son Timothy, according to the prophecies which went before on thee, that thou by them mightest war a good warfare." This is not just personal prophecy, but scripture you have made personal. Eph 6:17 "And take the helmet of *soteria*/salvation, and the sword of the Spirit, which is the word of God."

You know this fighting scripture: John 14:13 "Whatsoever ye shall *aiteo*/ask *(require, demand and expect as due by covenant promise)* in my name, that will I do, that the Father may be glorified in the Son. 14 If ye shall *aiteo*/ask *(require, demand and expect as due by covenant promise)* anything in my name, that will I do."

This is not praying to the Father, nor making a request of Jesus. It is using the name of Jesus, as Peter used it at the beautiful gate, when he set the man free from infantile paralysis. It is demanding the mountains be removed by speaking to them, it is commanding the devil and his works to go and people and situations to be made like Heaven on Earth, and it is commanding the evil forces at work in your neighborhood, town, city, county, state, region, nation, continent, hemisphere,

DISCOVERING OUR REDEMPTION

or the whole Earth to be exposed, broken and destroyed, with both the perpetrators and the victims set free into Jesus.

Here are three levels of *soteria*/salvation:
- Foundational and eternal salvation is your spirit being re-created.
- External or physical salvation is in this life, Heaven on Earth around you and in your body.
- Internal salvation is when your soul has the Word of God fully written on your heart and on your mind, and you walk just as Jesus walked in this life.

Producing *soteria*/salvation is also commanding the forces of darkness to become obedient to the authority of the name of Jesus and seeing God make it so.

That name is yours, even though you may not have taken advantage of it. Father God, through Jesus gave you the power of attorney to use the name of Jesus to do what Jesus did, and even greater things.

John 14:12 "Verily, verily, I say unto you, He that believeth on me, the works that I do shall he do also; and greater works than these shall he do; because I go unto my Father. 13 And whatsoever ye shall *aiteo*/ask (*require, demand and expect as due by covenant promise*) in my name, that will I do, that the Father may be glorified in the Son. 14 If ye shall *aiteo*/ask (*require, demand and expect as due by covenant promise*) any thing in my name, I will do it. 15 If ye *agape*/love me, keep my commandments."

As the Body of Christ, this is not just a power of attorney, for a power of attorney says you are not the person, but can use their name as if they were there, and it is fully legally binding. In the Body of Christ, Jesus is the Head and you are the Body. A body has the same name as the head, so it is your name as well as His. 1 Cor 12:27 "Now ye are the body of Christ, and members in particular."

Here God calls the Christian "Christ": 2 Cor 6:15 "And what concord hath Christ with Belial?" What God calls you, you are!

Jesus and all the power God used to raise Him from the dead, with the sin and consequence of sin of the entire human race, and to seat Him at the head of all is now ours, for Him. Eph 1:19 "And what is the exceeding greatness of his power to us-ward who believe, according to the working of his mighty power, 20 which he wrought in Christ, when he raised him from the dead, and set him at his own right hand in the heavenly places, 21 far above all principality, and power, and might, and dominion, and every name that is named, not only in this world, but also in that which is to come: 22 and hath put all things under his feet, and gave him to be the head over all things to the church, 23 which is his body, the fulness of him that filleth all in all."

We are the means He will use to fill "all in all."

He said, (Matt 28:18-19) "All authority hath been given unto me in heaven and on earth. Go ye therefore, and make disciples of all the nations."

You Have the Name of Jesus

The word *disciple* means student, one who learns to be just like his master. We are to make students of the Word of all nations to be just like Jesus.

We are to teach the world how to operate as Jesus taught His disciples.

You have the ability to go and do it for Him, as His agent and as His Body.

Mark 16:17-18 "In my name they shall cast out demons; ... they shall lay hands on the sick, and they shall recover." RSV

You are a believer now.

That belongs to you now.

Look at how one you are with Christ. This is your identity in Christ!

2 Cor 6:14 "Be ye not unequally yoked together with unbelievers: for what fellowship hath righteousness with unrighteousness? and what communion hath light with darkness? 15 And what concord hath Christ with Belial? or what part hath he that believeth with an infidel? 16 And what agreement hath the temple of God with idols? for ye are the temple of the *zao*/living God; as God hath said, I will dwell in them, and walk in them; and I will be their God, and they shall be my people. 17 Wherefore come out from among them, and be ye separate, saith the Lord, and touch not the unclean thing; and I will receive you, 18 and will be a Father unto you, and ye shall be my sons and daughters, saith the Lord Almighty."

You cannot enter into the fullness until you start with your self-identify in Christ. Look at how God compares you to the un-born again.

In verse 14, He calls you righteousness and them unrighteousness. This is not something you wear; it is what you are.

In verse 14, He calls you light and them darkness. This is what you are.

Eph 5:8 "For ye were sometimes darkness, but now are ye light in the Lord: walk as children of light."

In verse 15, He calls you Christ and them Belial (the god of earthly pleasure and lust). He calls you "Christ," an anointed one, as Jesus is.

In verse 15, He calls you a believer and them an infidel, because you believed one time enough to be born again. This is like pregnancy; you are or you are not. There is no middle zone.

In verse 16, He calls you the temple of God and them the temple of idols.

In verse 16 through 18, He tells you that as you cooperate with Him, starting by changing your self-identity, He will walk in and with you, just as He did with Jesus.

In these verses, He calls you righteousness, light, Christ, believer, the temple of God and sons and daughters.

These are all aspects of having the *zoe*/life of God.

Start to agree with Him in your mind, by the Scriptures, and quit calling Him a liar.

1 John 5:10 "He that believeth on the Son of God hath the witness in himself: **he that believeth not God hath made him a liar;** because he believeth not the

DISCOVERING OUR REDEMPTION

record that God gave of his Son (*specifically the Gospels and Acts*). 11 And this is the record, that God hath given to us eternal *zoe*/life, and this *zoe*/life is in his Son. 12 He that hath the Son hath *zoe*/life; and he that hath not the Son of God hath not *zoe*/life. 13 These things have I written unto you that believe on the name of the Son of God; that ye may know that ye have eternal *zoe*/life, and that ye may believe on the name of the Son of God."

Believing is not mental assent; it is not agreeing it is true without any corresponding thoughts, words and actions. You look at your life, at all of your words and actions, and that is what you believe. *Believe* means that you obey. It is what you really do. What you do is the reflection of what you actually believe. To believe God that you now have Jesus, that you now have eternal *zoe*/life, that you are the righteousness of God in Christ Jesus, and that God, by Holy Spirit, now dwells in you changes your self–identity, and you work to know this in your heart or subconscious mind. (See *OK, God, Now What?* by the author on how to renew your mind effectively for God.)

All of us have a starting place from which we grow into levels of Christian maturity in various aspects of life. You can start in small steps, knowing that the goal is major transformation in God. God is not talking about perfection, but, rather, diligence. Heb 11:6 "But without faith it is impossible to please him: for he that cometh to God must believe that he is, and that he is a rewarder of them that diligently seek him."

How would you act if you knew that you had a trillion dollars in a bank account and that you could draw on it at any time? You have Holy Spirit dwelling in you. You have more resources than a trillion dollars could provide you. You are already rich beyond imagination. All we have to do is to learn how to work with God to release this treasure into the world. A key step is to no longer call God a liar over what you have and who you are, and let the reality of what He has said about you control your self-image. You have the eternal *zoe*/life of God.

The natural version of this kind of life can make a seed grow under a pyramid and spout up through solid concrete. Given half a chance, it will cause barren land to grow with green vegetation. Think what releasing such power in the spirit can do!

Jesus showed us what this *zoe*/life of Father God set free in a human can do.

John 12:50 "And I know that his commandment is *zoe*/life everlasting: whatsoever I speak therefore, even as the Father said unto me, so I speak."

John 1:1 "In the beginning was the Word, and the Word was with God, and the Word was God. 2 The same was in the beginning with God. 3 All things were made by him; and without him was not any thing made that was made. 4 In him was *zoe*/life; and the *zoe*/life was the light of men. 5 And the light shineth in darkness; and the darkness comprehended it not."

You Have the Name of Jesus

Jesus is the light of God. The Gospels portray what Father God looks like and would do in every thought, word and action of Jesus. To know Father God, you have been given the light of Jesus. Just look at Jesus, as He is portrayed in the Scriptures, to know what God is really like.

Heb 1:1 "God, who at sundry times and in divers manners spake in time past unto the fathers by the prophets, 2 hath in these last days spoken unto us by his Son, whom he hath appointed heir of all things, by whom also he made the worlds; 3 who being the brightness of his glory, and the express image of his person, and upholding all things by the word of his power, when he had by himself purged our sins, sat down on the right hand of the Majesty on high."

Jesus is not only the exact representation of Father God, but He is also the Word of God made alive with the *zoe*/life of God. 1 John 1:1 "That which was from the beginning, which we have heard, which we have seen with our eyes, which we have looked upon, and our hands have handled, of the Word of *zoe*/life; 2 (for the *zoe*/life was manifested, and we have seen it, and bear witness, and shew unto you that eternal *zoe*/life, which was with the Father, and was manifested unto us;) 3 that which we have seen and heard (*of Jesus the manifested zoe/life of God*) declare we unto you, that ye also may have fellowship with us: and truly our fellowship is with the Father, and with his Son Jesus Christ. 4 And these things write we unto you, that your joy may be full."

The book of Acts shows what this *zoe*/life can do in believing, born-again men and women.

Acts 5:17 "Then the high priest rose up, and all they that were with him, (which is the sect of the Sadducees,) and were filled with indignation, 18 and laid their hands on the apostles, and put them in the common prison. 19 But the angel of the Lord by night opened the prison doors, and brought them forth, and said, 20 go, stand and speak in the temple to the people all the words of this *zoe*/life."

Your job, as a Christian, is to continually work to be fully convinced, persuaded of the truth of our Redemption in Jesus, and believing will no longer be a problem. That is majoring on the Word of Reconciliation.

Rom 4:20 "He (*Abraham*) staggered not at the promise of God through unbelief; but was strong in faith, giving glory (*loud thanks and praise*) to God; 21 and being fully persuaded that, what he had promised, he was able also to perform."

You start by knowing, thanking and praising God for His great salvation in Jesus. You are on the right track when this leads to rejoicing in God.

You don't have to understand it. If the great and good God gave you a gift, even if you do not understand it, you would say thank you anyway. So give thanks, by what the new covenant says, and you will begin to understand the height, the depth, the strength and the glory of the *agape*/love of God revealed in it.

The age of miracles is your age. It is the present age.

This is the Day of God's Salvation.

DISCOVERING OUR REDEMPTION

2 Cor 6:1 "We then, as workers together with him, beseech you also that ye receive not the grace of God in vain. 2 (For he saith, I have heard thee in a time accepted, and in the day of *soteria*/salvation have I succoured thee: behold, now is the accepted time; behold, now is the day of *soteria*/salvation.)"

You can live and walk in the fullness of God's ability.

You can let that ability loose in you and then out through you, if you will.

This is not about some special anointing; that you already have. 1 John 2:25 "And this is the promise that he hath promised us, even eternal *zoe*/life. 26 These things have I written unto you concerning them that seduce you. 27 But the anointing which ye have received of him abideth in you, and ye need not that any man teach you: but as the same anointing teacheth you of all things, and is truth, and is no lie, and even as it hath taught you, ye shall abide in him."

You do it by laboring with the Word of Christ in you, by the Scriptures, until your heart is transformed.

John 8:31 "Then said Jesus to those Jews which believed on him, If ye continue in my word, then are ye my disciples indeed; 32 and ye shall know the truth, and the truth shall make you free [*to be the full agent of God, as is Jesus*]."

Diligence means hard labor, and it is not fun. But, because of the hope set before us, we are diligent anyway.

2 Pet 1:1 "Simon Peter, a servant and an apostle of Jesus Christ, to them that have obtained like precious faith with us through the righteousness of God and our Saviour Jesus Christ: 2 grace and peace be multiplied unto you through the *epignosis*/knowledge of God, and of Jesus our Lord, 3 according as his divine power hath given unto us all things that pertain unto *zoe*/life and godliness, through the *epignosis*/knowledge of him that hath called us to glory and virtue: 4 whereby are given unto us exceeding great and precious promises: that by these ye might be partakers of the divine nature, having escaped the corruption that is in the world through lust. 5 And beside this, **giving all diligence**, add to your faith virtue; and to virtue knowledge; 6 and to knowledge temperance; and to temperance patience; and to patience godliness; 7 and to godliness brotherly kindness; and to brotherly kindness *agape*/charity. 8 For if these things be in you, and abound, they make you that ye shall neither be barren nor unfruitful in the *epignosis*/knowledge of our Lord Jesus Christ. 9 But he that lacketh these things is blind, and cannot see afar off, and hath forgotten that he was purged from his old sins. 10 Wherefore the rather, brethren, **give diligence** to make your calling and election sure: for if ye do these things, ye shall never fall: 11 for so an entrance shall be ministered unto you abundantly into the everlasting kingdom of our Lord and Saviour Jesus Christ."

You Have the Name of Jesus

This is love's challenge, to let the life of God loose in you, to let the Word of Christ loose in you, to give the name of Jesus its real place in your life, by renewing your mind with all diligence. Philem 6 "That the communication of thy faith may become effectual by the acknowledging of every good thing which is in you in Christ Jesus."

Jesus gave us clear and powerful authority, just as He has, to destroy the work of the devil. Luke 10:19 "Behold (*make this change the way you operate in this world*), I give unto you power (*authority, commission and the resources of Heaven*) to tread on serpents and scorpions, and over all the power (*ability*) of the enemy: and nothing shall by any means hurt you."

And, as Jesus proved, His miracles were exercising the righteous judgment and authority over the devil and thus produced the miracles He did. Acts 10:36 "The word which God sent unto the children of Israel, preaching peace by Jesus Christ: (he is Lord of all:) 37 that word, I say, ye know, which was published throughout all Judaea, and began from Galilee, after the baptism which John preached; 38 how God anointed Jesus of Nazareth with the Holy Ghost and with power: who went about doing good, and healing all that were oppressed of the devil; for God was with him."

Those miracles were the Father showing His *agape*/love through a man who thought like the Father thought. John 14:8 "Philip saith unto him, Lord, shew us the Father, and it sufficeth us. 9 Jesus saith unto him, Have I been so long time with you, and yet hast thou not known me, Philip? he that hath seen me hath seen the Father; and how sayest thou then, Shew us the Father? 10 Believest thou not that I am in the Father, and the Father in me? the words that I speak unto you I speak not of myself: but the Father that dwelleth in me, he doeth the works. 11 Believe me that I am in the Father, and the Father in me: or else believe me for the very works' sake."

Jesus promised that, as we know the Father through Jesus, we will do the same works Jesus did and even greater, as we demand of the Father to do those wondrous things Jesus did. John 14:12 "Verily, verily, I say unto you, He that believeth on me, the works that I do shall he do also; and greater works than these shall he do; because I go unto my Father. 13 And whatsoever ye shall *aiteo*/ask (*require, demand and expect as due by Bible promise*) in my name, that will I do, that the Father may be glorified in the Son. 14 If ye shall *aiteo*/ask (*require, demand and expect as due by Bible promise*) any thing in my name, I will do it."

Jesus even went on to say that if you love Him you will use His name to do the same and even greater God-level works. John 14:15 "If ye *agape*/love me, keep my commandments." His commandment was to use His name to do *aiteo*/asking, requiring, demanding, and expecting God to do miracles (in the name of Jesus) and as we do, Jesus will do those miracles.

DISCOVERING OUR REDEMPTION

Jesus commanded that we are to do what He taught His disciples to do. First He commanded the 12: Matt 10:7 "And as ye go, preach, saying, The kingdom of heaven is at hand. 8 Heal the sick, cleanse the lepers, raise the dead, cast out devils: freely ye have received, freely give."

Luke 9:1 "Then he called his twelve disciples together, and gave them *dunamis*/power and *exousia*/authority over all devils, and to cure diseases. 2 And he sent them to preach the kingdom of God, and to heal the sick."

When the original 12 could not work enough miracles and set the people free, Jesus called and sent 70 (or 72) more to do the same. Luke 10:1 "After these things the Lord appointed other seventy also, and sent them two and two before his face into every city and place, whither he himself would come. 2 Therefore said he unto them, The harvest truly is great, but the labourers are few: pray ye therefore the Lord of the harvest, that he would send forth labourers into his harvest. ... 8 And into whatsoever city ye enter, and they receive you, eat such things as are set before you: 9 And heal the sick that are therein, and say unto them, The kingdom of God is come nigh unto you."

Compassion is a word that requires action. If you are running you are in action and if you are thinking about going on a run, you are thinking about going into action. Compassion is the same kind of word. In compassion, you do, and here Jesus did, by sending others to do what He had been doing, as commanded by the Father. So you will never know Father God fully until you also heal, as Jesus healed. There is an aspect of family you will never know until you use the name of Jesus to set others free.

John 14:8 "Philip saith unto him, Lord, shew us the Father, and it sufficeth us. 9 Jesus saith unto him, Have I been so long time with you, and yet hast thou not known me, Philip? he that hath seen me hath seen the Father; and how sayest thou then, Shew us the Father? 10 Believest thou not that I am in the Father, and the Father in me? the words that I speak unto you I speak not of myself: but the Father that dwelleth in me, he doeth the works. 11 Believe me that I am in the Father, and the Father in me: or else believe me for the very works' sake."

Why did Jesus heal people and why did He send others to heal? Because He saw their pain and suffering, and being the Righteous Shepherd, He must free them or send others to help Him free them of the oppressions, direct rulership, lordship and control of the devil. Matt 9:36 "But when he saw the multitudes, he was moved with compassion on them, because they fainted, and were scattered abroad, as sheep having no shepherd. 37 Then saith he unto his disciples, The harvest truly is plenteous, but the labourers are few; 38 pray ye therefore the Lord of the harvest, that he will send forth labourers into his harvest."

Notice, the harvest of God depends on laborers who do, as Jesus commanded His disciples to do, the works of God. Mark 16:15 "And he (*Jesus*) said unto them,

Go ye into all the world, and preach the gospel to every creature. 16 He that believeth and is baptized shall be *sozo*/saved; but he that believeth not shall be damned. 17 And these signs shall follow them that believe; **In my name** shall they cast out devils; they shall speak with new tongues; 18 they shall take up serpents; and if they drink any deadly thing, it shall not hurt them; they shall lay hands on the sick, and they shall recover. 19 So then after the Lord (*Jesus*) had spoken unto them, he was received up into heaven, and sat on the right hand of God. 20 And they went forth, and preached everywhere, the Lord (*Jesus*) working with them, and confirming the word with signs following. Amen."

Jesus made it clear that getting miracles done is not dependent upon the amount of *agape*/love you walk in. Matt 7:21 "Not every one that saith unto me, Lord, Lord, shall enter into the kingdom of heaven; but he that doeth the will of my Father which is in heaven. 22 Many will say to me in that day, Lord, Lord, have we not prophesied in thy name? and in thy name have cast out devils? and in thy name done many wonderful works? 23 And then will I profess unto them, I never knew you: depart from me, ye that work iniquity."

You can do miracles in the name of Jesus and not walk in the *agape*/love of God. This is stated in Matt 7: 21-23 and, of course, in the loveless mountain-moving faith of 1 Cor 13:1-3. The many who say "Lord, Lord," worked mighty miracles without knowing the God of *agape*/love. They did understand the legal position of Jesus as Lord and the power of His name to release the *zoe*/life of God. And, much like a crooked, or less-than-perfect policeman, even though he may be crooked, that does not change the power of the badge he wears. The name of Jesus as Lord is our badge. Healing, in that sense, is far more mechanical or legal. So using the name of Jesus to work miracles is a starting place, not an ending place.

The problem comes when we believe that healing or miracles are dependent upon our holiness or righteousness. That becomes a limitation that is not from God. If that were true, the only miracles in the Bible would have been those of Jesus, and this is absolutely not the case. Any imperfection of the standard of God Himself is un-holiness.

You are no longer fearful of God but know He is your help. You know that until you are just like Jesus in your entire walk, you have un-holiness in your life. If you insist on focusing on perfection or holiness, then none of the disciples from the Gospels onward would have qualified. The more you walk in *agape*/love the more you can fulfill the purpose for which God saved us, to reflect Himself into the Earth, just as Jesus does, and the less of your life that will burn on the Day of Judgment as wood, hay and stubble (see 1 Cor 3:10-16).

God loves all mankind, and to walk in any offense or unforgiveness means that you have an area in which you and God disagree. As we hold unforgiveness, we are calling ourselves greater than God, and this is a form of idolatry, covetousness

DISCOVERING OUR REDEMPTION

and evil lust. (Col 3:5; Jude 18; 2 Pet 2:10) This is also described in the Scriptures as a lack of fellowship, partnership, agreement, communion or relationship with God, for He sends His rain on the just and the unjust alike. Rom 5:6 "For when we were yet without strength, in due time Christ died for the ungodly."

No one Jesus healed was worthy of healing, and it is no different today. The problem is in us. So, in the same way a police badge gives authority independent of the policeman, it is not our holiness, but the name of Jesus and faith in that name that releases God's love, even though you are not yet perfect in your Christian walk.

As a policeman fires his gun, you keep speaking *aiteo* commands against the devil, and just like the bullets from a gun do their job, when properly aimed, so will your *aiteo* thoughts, words, looks or touch. That is why healing and being healed are of grace and not our holiness. Acts 3:12 "And when Peter saw it, he answered unto the people, Ye men of Israel, why marvel ye at this? or why look ye so earnestly on us, as though by our own power or holiness we had made this man to walk? ... 16 And his name (*Jesus*) through faith in his name hath made this man strong, whom ye see and know: yea, the faith which is by him hath given him this perfect soundness in the presence of you all."

Healing is about Jesus' holiness, not ours. In any healing battle, you can focus only on Jesus as Lord, and for extra punch and personal benefit, God's love for people, and get people healed. Imperfection is not a limitation. This is the miracle of Christ in you, the hope of glory. Keep in the fight, and do not doubt by stopping. Use the Scriptures, the Word of Christ in you, the hope of glory, to stir yourself up into abundant grace and the gift of righteousness, and command life in the name of Jesus.

By the way, since we have been given a job, the Lord will not take our job from us. Rom 11:29 "For the gifts and calling of God are without repentance." He will help you, but we have to do our job or calling. We are to exercise His authority for Him. So commanding healing, like the work of a police officer, is part of our job description. We are to lay hands on the sick; we are to cast out devils, etc.; and everything else can be style. We can ask and require God to strengthen and enforce our words, but we take responsibility and do our work with Holy Spirit.

Jesus said: Luke 10:19 "Behold (*make this change the way you operate in this world*), I give unto you power (*authority, commission and the resources of Heaven*) to tread on serpents and scorpions, and over all the power (*ability*) of the enemy: and nothing shall by any means hurt you." Like a policeman, you do not have to feel the power, but you do have to exercise the authority you have been given. Authority commands and directs.

Jesus did not promise the disciples power first, but authority first; and as they used the authority, the power would be manifest, and the results would follow. ["These signs follow them that believe."]

You Have the Name of Jesus

"Faith steps out to act with the authority of God's Word, seeing yet no sign of the promised power, but believing and acting, as if it were real. As it speaks the word of authority and command [*to creation, the devil and his works*] and puts its foot, without fear, upon the head of its conquered foes, lo, their power is disarmed, and all the forces of the heavenly world are there to make the victory complete." (A. B. Simpson, *The Alliance Weekly*, "The Authority of Faith," p 263)

Jesus gave us *dunamis*/power, ability, on the Day of Pentecost. Acts 1:8 "But ye shall receive *dunamis*/power, after that the Holy Ghost is come upon you: and ye shall be witnesses unto me both in Jerusalem, and in all Judaea, and in Samaria, and unto the uttermost part of the earth."

The ability comes as you exercise the authority as Jesus would, the same way He did, by faith. John 11:41 "Then they took away the stone from the place where the dead was laid. And Jesus lifted up his eyes, and said, Father, I thank thee that thou hast heard me. 42 And I knew that thou hearest me always: but because of the people which stand by I said it, that they may believe that thou hast sent me." Raising the untimely dead is Father's will. There are no limits!

God shows us that His name and Himself are the same: Ps 61:1 "Hear my cry, O God; attend unto my prayer. 2 From the end of the earth will I cry unto thee, when my heart is overwhelmed: lead me to the rock that is higher than I. 3 For thou hast been a shelter for me, and a strong tower from the enemy." Prov 18:10 "The name of the Lord is a strong tower: the righteous runneth into it, and is safe."

God has made His Word greater than His name so we can use His name to bring His Word to manifest in the Earth. Ps 138:1 "I will praise thee with my whole heart: before the gods will I sing praise unto thee. 2 I will worship toward thy holy temple, and praise thy name for thy *chesed*/lovingkindness and for thy truth: for thou hast magnified thy word above all thy name."

It is the name of Jesus that gives us access to God, to both call on and deliver the power of God as needed. Just like Father God needed a man, Jesus, to deliver His healing, Jesus now needs us, His Body on Earth, to do our part.

Acts 3:12 "And when Peter saw it, he answered unto the people, Ye men of Israel, why marvel ye at this? or why look ye so earnestly on us, as though by our own power or holiness we had made this man to walk? 13 The God of Abraham, and of Isaac, and of Jacob, the God of our fathers, hath glorified his Son Jesus; whom ye delivered up, and denied him in the presence of Pilate, when he was determined to let him go. 14 But ye denied the Holy One and the Just, and desired a murderer to be granted unto you; 15 and killed the Prince of *zoe*/life, whom God hath raised from the dead; whereof we are witnesses. 16 And his name through faith in his name hath made this man strong, whom ye see and know: yea, the faith which is by him hath given him this perfect soundness in the presence of you all."

DISCOVERING OUR REDEMPTION

Acts 4:9 "If we this day be examined of the good deed done to the impotent man, by what means he is made whole; 10 Be it known unto you all, and to all the people of Israel, that by the name of Jesus Christ of Nazareth, whom ye crucified, whom God raised from the dead, even by him doth this man stand here before you whole. 11 This is the stone which was set at nought of you builders, which is become the head of the corner. 12 Neither is there *soteria*/salvation in any other: for there is none other name under heaven given among men, whereby we must be *sozo*/saved (*made whole, healed, delivered, rescued, set free and unbound*)."

Using the name of Jesus and knowing Jesus are two different things. But using the name of Jesus as the Lord Almighty and faith in that name, independent of your personal relationship with Him, is the basis of divine healing in our age. Matt 7:22 "Many will say to me in that day, Lord, Lord, have we not prophesied in thy name? and in thy name have cast out devils? and in thy name done many wonderful works? 23 And then will I profess unto them, I never knew you: depart from me, ye that work iniquity." So once again healing and miracles are not part of holiness, per Acts 3:12, or how well you know Jesus.

It is the name of Jesus and faith in His name that release Holy Spirit to heal. Mark 9:38 "And John answered him, saying, Master, we saw one casting out devils in thy name, and he followeth not us: and we forbad him, because he followeth not us. 39 But Jesus said, Forbid him not: for there is no man which shall do a miracle in my name, that can lightly speak evil of me. 40 For he that is not against us is on our part."

Luke 9:49 "And John answered and said, Master, we saw one casting out devils in thy name; and we forbad him, because he followeth not with us. 50 And Jesus said unto him, Forbid him not: for he that is not against us is for us." This one learned how to use the name of Jesus, but was definitely not one of the disciples. One conclusion is that healing, signs and wonders may not be a sign of one's holiness, but the ability of one to believe in the power of the name of Jesus.

1 John 5:12 "He that hath the Son hath *zoe*/life; and he that hath not the Son of God hath not *zoe*/life. 13 These things have I written unto you that believe on the name of the Son of God; that ye may know that ye have eternal *zoe*/life, and that ye may believe on the name of the Son of God."

Here God specifically requests us to use the name of Jesus. 1 John 5:14 "And this is the confidence that we have in him, that, if we *aiteo*/ask (*require, demand and expect as due*) any thing according to his will (*which includes all His covenant promises*), he heareth us: 15 and if we know that he hear us, whatsoever we *aiteo*/ask (*require, demand and expect as due by covenant promise*), we know that we have the petitions that we desired of him."

God gave His name as His presence, awareness and point of power to the people of Israel. They had the name before they built the temple and wanted the name to be in the temple. 1 Kings 8:27 "But will God indeed dwell on the earth? behold, the heaven and heaven of heavens cannot contain thee; how much less this house that I have builded? 28 Yet have thou respect unto the prayer of thy servant (*Solomon*), and to his supplication, O Lord my God, to hearken unto the cry and to the prayer, which thy servant prayeth before thee to day: 29 that thine eyes may be open toward this house night and day, even toward the place of which thou hast said, My name shall be there: that thou mayest hearken unto the prayer which thy servant shall make toward this place. 30 And hearken thou to the supplication of thy servant, and of thy people Israel, when they shall pray toward this place: and hear thou in heaven thy dwelling place: and when thou hearest, forgive."

The temple became the place where a believer could know that God, by His name, dwelt and where He would answer prayer. Ps 118:11 "They compassed me about; yea, they compassed me about: but in the name of the Lord I will destroy them." Ps 124:8 "Our help is in the name of the Lord, who made heaven and earth." Prov 18:10 "The name of the Lord is a strong tower: the righteous runneth into it, and is safe."

Now we, each Christian individually and corporately, are the dwelling place of God. Holy Spirit now dwells in the Christian. 1 Cor 3:16 "Know ye not that ye are the temple of God, and that the Spirit of God dwelleth in you?"

2 Tim 1:14 "That good thing which was committed unto thee keep by the Holy Ghost which dwelleth in us."

Rom 8:11 "But if the Spirit of him that raised up Jesus from the dead dwell in you, he that raised up Christ from the dead shall also quicken your [*current*] mortal bodies by his Spirit that dwelleth in you."

Eph 1:13 "In whom ye also trusted, after that ye heard the word of truth, the gospel of your *soteria*/salvation: in whom also after that ye believed, ye were sealed with that holy Spirit of promise."

Eph 4:30 "And grieve not the holy Spirit of God, whereby ye are sealed unto the day of redemption."

So wherever a Christian is, Holy Spirit is, and we release Him by using the name of the Lord Jesus, who has been declared Lord and Christ by Father God, when He sent His Spirit on the Day of Pentecost. Acts 2:21 "And it shall come to pass, that whosoever shall call on the name of the Lord shall be *sozo*/saved. 22 Ye men of Israel, hear these words; Jesus of Nazareth, a man approved of God among you by miracles and wonders and signs, which God did by him in the midst of you, as ye yourselves also know: 23 him, being delivered by the determinate counsel and foreknowledge of God, ye have taken, and by wicked hands have crucified and slain: 24 whom God hath raised up, having loosed the pains of death: because it was not possible that he should be holden of it. ... 33 Therefore being by the right hand of God exalted, and having received of the Father the promise of the Holy

DISCOVERING OUR REDEMPTION

Ghost, he hath shed forth this, which ye now see and hear. 34 For David is not ascended into the heavens: but he saith himself, The LORD said unto my Lord, Sit thou on my right hand, 35 until I make thy foes thy footstool. 36 Therefore let all the house of Israel know assuredly, that God hath made that same Jesus, whom ye have crucified, both Lord and Christ." So calling on the name of Jesus is the same as calling on the name of the Lord.

John 15:7 "If ye abide in me, and my words abide in you, ye shall *aiteo*/ask (*require, demand and expect as due by covenant promise*) what ye will, and it shall be done unto you. 8 Herein is my Father glorified, that ye bear much fruit; so shall ye be my disciples." So we use the name of Jesus to access God, and it becomes our point of faith as we speak, lay hands, or place anointed cloths, and God does the healing.

It is Jesus now, who, from His exalted position at the right hand of the Father, does the healing though those who use His name. John 14:12 "Verily, verily, I say unto you, He that believeth on me, the works that I do shall he do also; and greater works than these shall he do; because I go unto my Father. 13 And whatsoever ye shall *aiteo*/ask (*require, demand and expect as due by covenant promise*) in my name, that will I do, that the Father may be glorified in the Son. 14 If ye shall *aiteo*/ask (*require, demand and expect as due by covenant promise*) any thing in my name, I will do it."

When we get others healed in the name Jesus, it is Jesus who now does the healing, by Holy Spirit, from the Father. God (Father, Son and Spirit) does the healing through you. Thus we operate as co-laborers with God. Jesus is working through us, as members of His Body, and we cooperate with Him to deliver the healing He already obtained. Acts 4:29 "And now, Lord (*Father God*), behold their threatenings: and grant unto thy servants, that with all boldness they may speak thy word, 30 by stretching forth thine hand to heal; and that signs and wonders may be done by the name of thy holy child Jesus."

Acts 14:3 "Long time therefore abode they speaking boldly in the Lord, which gave testimony unto the word of his grace, and granted signs and wonders to be done by their hands."

James 5:15 "And the prayer of faith shall *sozo*/save the sick, and the Lord shall raise him up; and if he have committed sins, they shall be forgiven him."

Acts 9:34 "And Peter said to him, Aeneas, Jesus Christ (the Messiah) [now] makes you whole. Get up and make your bed! And immediately [Aeneas] stood up." AMP

Mark 16:19 "So then after the Lord had spoken unto them, he was received up into heaven, and sat on the right hand of God. 20 And they went forth, and preached everywhere, the Lord working with them, and confirming the word with signs following. Amen."

We have, posses, have been given, the name of Jesus, to release God into the Earth, to do His will. John 16:23 "And in that day (*when you know who you are in*

You Have the Name of Jesus

Jesus) ye shall *aiteo*/ask (*require, demand, and expect as due by covenant promise*) me nothing. Verily, verily, I say unto you, Whatsoever ye shall *aiteo*/ask (*require, demand, and expect as due by covenant promise*) the Father **in my name**, he will give it you. 24 Hitherto have ye *aiteo*/asked (*required, demanded, and expected as due by covenant promise*) nothing in my name: ask *aiteo*/ask (*require, demand, and expect as due by covenant promise*), and ye shall *lambano*/receive, that your joy may be full."

Heb 13:15 "By him (*Jesus*) therefore let us offer the sacrifice of praise to God continually, that is, the fruit of our lips giving thanks to his name."

Chapter 27

You Have Holy Spirit in You

Jesus promised the disciples that Holy Spirit, who was with them, would be in them.

On the day of Pentecost, after He had recreated them, He entered into their bodies.

What a miracle it is to have God in us!

Holy Spirit is the Administrator of the power of God. He moved to create the Universe as God spoke. Gen 1:1 "In the beginning God created the Heaven and the earth. 2 And the earth was without form, and void; and darkness was upon the face of the deep. And the Spirit of God moved upon the face of the waters. 3 And God said, Let there be light: and there was light."

Holy Spirit is the Mighty Finger of God. His free reign and rule is the Kingdom of God Jesus came to bring. Luke 11:20 "But if I with the finger of God cast out devils, no doubt the kingdom of God is come upon you." Matt 12:28 "But if I cast out devils by the Spirit of God, then the kingdom of God is come unto you." Here Jesus tells us that the Finger of God and Holy Spirit are one and the same.

Notice, in this case, that the rule and reigning of the Kingdom of God is over the devil. Devils and the works of devils are to be commanded and expelled; people are to be helped, loved and enticed into truth with demonstrations of Holy

Spirit power. Luke 10:19 "Behold (*stop, think and let this control you world-view and all your behaviors*), I give unto you *exousia*/power (*commission, authority and the resources of Heaven, including Holy Spirit*) to tread on serpents and scorpions, and over all the *dunamis*/power (*ability and works*) of the enemy: and nothing shall by any means hurt you. 20 Notwithstanding in this rejoice not, that the spirits are subject unto you; but rather rejoice, because your names are written in heaven."

Holy Spirit made it clear that one of Jesus' prime missions was so that men could receive Holy Spirit dwelling in them, in fulfillment of the promise to Abraham. Luke 24:49 "And, behold, I (*Jesus*) send the promise of my Father upon you: but tarry ye in the city of Jerusalem, until ye be endued with power from on high."

Gal 3:13 "Christ hath redeemed us from the curse of the law, being made a curse for us: for it is written, Cursed is every one that hangeth on a tree: 14 that the blessing of Abraham might come on the Gentiles through Jesus Christ; that we might receive the promise of the Spirit through faith."

The active presence of Holy Spirit, where He is operating to produce the goodness of the Lord, is called "blessing." Gal 3:8 "And the scripture, foreseeing that God would justify the heathen through faith, preached before the gospel unto Abraham, saying, In thee shall all nations be blessed. 9 So then they which be of faith are blessed with faithful Abraham."

Per Gal 3:13 above, we see the blessing equals Holy Spirit activity. Thus, when you bless others, you are commanding Holy Spirit to do the will of God, and when you believe God is blessing the work of your hands, you are believing God to empower you and your work by Holy Spirit.

Holy Spirit Baptism: John the Baptist foretold that the Messiah would be the One to send Holy Spirit in a new and different way. Matt 3:11 "I (*John*) indeed baptize you with water unto repentance: but he that cometh after me is mightier than I, whose shoes I am not worthy to bear: he shall baptize you with the Holy Ghost, and with fire: 12 whose fan is in his hand, and he will throughly purge his floor, and gather his wheat into the garner; but he will burn up the chaff with unquenchable fire." (Isa 30:24; Mk 1:7; Lk 3:16; John 1:26; Act 1:5, 2:4, 10:45, 11:15)

Jesus told the disciples to wait, after His ascension, for the long-promised Holy Spirit, who would come in a new and different way. Acts 1:4 "And, being assembled together with them, commanded them that they should not depart from Jerusalem, but wait for the promise of the Father, which, saith he, ye have heard of me. 5 For John truly baptized with water; but ye shall be baptized with the Holy Ghost not many days hence. 6 When they therefore were come together, they asked of him, saying, Lord, wilt thou at this time restore again the kingdom to Israel? 7 And he said unto them, It is not for you to know the times or the seasons, which the Father hath put in his own power. 8 But ye shall receive *dunamis*/power, after that the Holy Ghost is come upon you: and ye shall be witnesses unto me both in

DISCOVERING OUR REDEMPTION

Jerusalem, and in all Judaea, and in Samaria, and unto the uttermost part of the earth. 9 And when he had spoken these things, while they beheld, he was taken up; and a cloud received him out of their sight."

Jesus made it clear that before Holy Spirit had been "with" people, but now, after this event, Holy Spirit would be "in" the believer. John 14:17 "Even the Spirit of truth; whom the world cannot receive, because it seeth him not, neither knoweth him: but ye know him; for he dwelleth with you, and shall be in you."

This is part of the new and different way Holy Spirit would deal with man after that Day of Pentecost 2000 years ago. Since we are talking about the God who is the Creator and Rightful Ruler of the Universe, then the God of the Universe was going to deal with men differently than before.

Peter explained, on that Day of Pentecost, that Jesus had accomplished His Great Mission. Holy Spirit was now coming to Earth in a new and different way. Acts 2:15 "For these are not drunken, as ye suppose, seeing it is but the third hour of the day. 16 But this is that which was spoken by the prophet Joel; 17 and it shall come to pass in the last days, saith God, I will pour out of my Spirit upon all flesh: and your sons and your daughters shall prophesy, and your young men shall see visions, and your old men shall dream dreams."

Jesus got the job done. The intense labor of body, soul and spirit of Jesus was now culminated in being seated at the right hand of God and sending Holy Spirit to Earth in a new and different way. That way was called, by John the Baptist and Jesus, the Baptism of Holy Spirit, as evidenced on that Day of Pentecost 2000 years ago. Acts 2:32 "This Jesus hath God raised up, whereof we all are witnesses. 33 Therefore being by the right hand of God exalted, and having received of the Father the promise of the Holy Ghost, he hath shed forth this, which ye now see and hear."

Throughout this book we talk about Holy Spirit and His involvement with men because He is the One who leads the Body of Christ on Earth with and through men. Acts 15:28 "For it seemed good to the Holy Ghost, and to us... ."

What makes a Christian is Holy Spirit dwelling in a human. Christianity may be the practices, but a Christian is a new kind of creature on the Earth. 2 Cor 5:5 "Now he that hath wrought us for the selfsame thing is God, who also hath given unto us the earnest of the Spirit."

Rom 8:9 "But ye are not in the flesh, but in the Spirit, if so be that the Spirit of God dwell in you. Now if any man have not the Spirit of Christ, he is none of his. 10 And if Christ be in you, the body is dead because of sin; but the Spirit is *zoe*/life because of righteousness. 11 But if the Spirit of him that raised up Jesus from the dead dwell in you, he that raised up Christ from the dead shall also quicken (*in this time on Earth*) your mortal bodies by his Spirit that dwelleth in you."

1 Cor 6:19 "What? know ye not that your body is the temple of the Holy Ghost which is in you, which ye have of God, and ye are not your own? 20 For ye are

bought (*ransomed, redeemed, and delivered*) with a price: therefore glorify God in your body, and in your spirit, which are God's."

All of this is the fruit of the Mighty Arm of God, in His great Redemption of man. 2 Cor 5:17 "Therefore if any man be in Christ, he is a new creature: old things are passed away; behold, all things are become new. 18 And all things are of God, who hath reconciled us to himself by Jesus Christ, and hath given to us the ministry of reconciliation; 19 to wit, that God was in Christ, reconciling the world unto himself, not imputing their trespasses unto them; and hath committed unto us the word of reconciliation. 20 Now then we are ambassadors for Christ, as though God did beseech you by us: we pray you in Christ's stead, be ye reconciled to God. 21 For he hath made him to be sin for us, who knew no sin; that we might be made the righteousness of God in him."

Holy Spirit, the Teacher: Holy Spirit is the One who works in men, and especially the Christian, to will and to do the good pleasure of God. Phil 2:12 "Wherefore, my *agape*/beloved, as ye have always obeyed, not as in my presence only, but now much more in my absence, work out your own *soteria*/salvation with fear and trembling. 13 For it is God which worketh in you both to will and to do of his good pleasure. 14 Do all things without murmurings and disputings: 15 that ye may be blameless and harmless, the sons of God, without rebuke, in the midst of a crooked and perverse nation, among whom ye shine as lights in the world; 16 holding forth the word of *zoe*/life; that I may rejoice in the day of Christ, that I have not run in vain, neither laboured in vain." Notice that the desired outcome is not guaranteed. If you do it wrong, Paul and your other ministers from God will be embarrassed at your performance from their Holy Spirit coaching/ministry/shepherding on the Day of Judgment.

In the same manner, Holy Spirit again speaks in strong words like He uses in Hebrews chapters 3 and 4, if we will hear Him. Rom 2:1 "Therefore thou art inexcusable, O man, whosoever thou art that judgest: for wherein thou judgest another, thou condemnest thyself; for thou that judgest doest the same things. 2 But we are sure that the judgment of God is according to truth against them which commit such things. 3 And thinkest thou this, O man, that judgest them which do such things, and doest the same, that thou shalt escape the judgment of God? 4 Or despisest thou the riches of his goodness and forbearance and longsuffering; not knowing that the goodness of God leadeth thee to repentance? 5 But after thy hardness and impenitent heart treasurest up unto thyself wrath against the day of wrath and revelation of the righteous judgment of God; 6 who will render to every man according to his deeds."

Holy Spirit had already been in the Earth and produced the awesome miracles seen in the Old Testament. Since the New Testament did not start until Jesus either made that Last Supper Passover meal the New Covenant Meal, or until He took

DISCOVERING OUR REDEMPTION

His blood to the true heavenly Mercy Seat, all the miracles Jesus did were as an Old Testament man. So were the miracles that the disciples, the 12 and the 70 performed. So, what was to be new and different? The answer: The power man was to receive was not outside of man, but inside man, with the indwelling of Holy Spirit.

This indwelling Holy Spirit in part is how God is implementing the New Covenant, which includes: Heb 10:15 "Whereof the Holy Ghost also is a witness to us: for after that he had said before, 16 This is the covenant that I will make with them after those days, saith the Lord, I will put my laws into their hearts, and in their minds will I write them; 17 and their sins and iniquities will I remember no more. 18 Now where remission of these is (*sins and iniquities*), there is no more offering for sin." Holy Spirit, by our own personal efforts and the offices of the Body of Christ (apostles, prophets, etc.), is writing His laws into our hearts and minds.

We are commanded to participate in the process. Holy Spirit's primary tool is the Word of God. 1 Pet 2:1 "Wherefore laying aside all malice, and all guile, and hypocrisies, and envies, and all evil speakings, 2 as newborn babes, desire the sincere milk of the word, that ye may grow thereby: 3 if so be ye have tasted that the Lord is gracious." Notice we control our spiritual growth, not God. He commands us to "suck-up" the Word of God like a baby does. If we do not, we are left as carnal-, flesh- and world-circumstances-ruled, and not spirit- or Word-of-God-ruled people.

Thus, even if Jesus Himself is to speak to us, our missing the main messages of the Word of God limits what God can say to us. 1 Cor 3:1 "And I, brethren, could not speak unto you as unto spiritual, but as unto carnal, even as unto babes in Christ. 2 I have fed you with milk, and not with meat: for hitherto ye were not able to bear it, neither yet now are ye able. 3 For ye are yet carnal: for whereas there is among you envying, and strife, and divisions, are ye not carnal, and walk as men?"

Holy Spirit comes to change our world-view, especially our definition of sin, righteousness and judgment: John 16:7 "Nevertheless I tell you the truth; It is expedient for you that I go away: for if I go not away, the Comforter will not come unto you; but if I depart, I will send him unto you. 8 And when he is come, he will reprove the world of sin, and of righteousness, and of judgment: 9 of sin, because they believe not on me; 10 of righteousness, because I go to my Father, and ye see me no more; 11 of judgment, because the prince of this world is judged."

Holy Spirit will instruct us in the knowledge and ways of God, so we can mature into our destiny in Jesus. John 14:26 "But the Comforter (*Encourager, Strengthener, Helper, the One who Stands beside you*), which is the Holy Ghost, whom the Father will send in my name, he shall teach you all things, and bring all things to your remembrance, whatsoever I have said unto you."

John 15:26 "But when the Comforter is come, whom I will send unto you from the Father, even the Spirit of truth, which proceedeth from the Father, he shall testify of me."

You Have Holy Spirit in You

John 16:12 "I (*Jesus*) have yet many things to say unto you, but ye cannot bear them now. 13 Howbeit when he, the Spirit of truth, is come, he will guide you into all truth: for he shall not speak of himself; but whatsoever he shall hear, that shall he speak: and he will shew you things to come. 14 He shall glorify me: for he shall receive of mine, and shall shew it unto you. 15 All things that the Father hath are mine: therefore said I, that he (*Holy Spirit*) shall take of mine, and shall shew it unto you."

Holy Spirit will teach us how to talk like Jesus did, in the language of signs and wonders, driven by *agape*/love. 1 Cor 2:3 "And I was with you in weakness, and in fear, and in much trembling. 4 And my speech and my preaching was not with enticing words of man's wisdom, but in demonstration of the Spirit and of *dunamis*/power: 5 that your faith should not stand in the wisdom of men, but in the *dunamis*/power of God."

We have access to the deep secrets of God by Holy Spirit: 1 Cor 2:9 "But as it is written, Eye hath not seen, nor ear heard, neither have entered into the heart of man, the things which God hath prepared for them that *agape*/love him. 10 But God hath revealed them unto us by his Spirit: for the Spirit searcheth all things, yea, the deep things of God. 11 For what man knoweth the things of a man, save the spirit of man which is in him? even so the things of God knoweth no man, but the Spirit of God. 12 Now we have received, not the spirit of the world, but the spirit which is of God; that we might know the things that are freely given to us of God." Of course this includes the great message of the New Testament, "Christ in you the hope of glory," or the potential of the free reign of Holy Spirit in and by men.

By Holy Spirit, we have the same mind of Christ as Jesus has. 1 Cor 2:16 "For who hath known the mind of the Lord, that he may instruct him? But we have the mind of Christ." Jesus is the living Word of God, so as we reprogram, or renew, our minds into the Word of God, we, too, will become living words of God.

1 John 1:1 "That which was from the beginning, which we have heard, which we have seen with our eyes, which we have looked upon, and our hands have handled, of the Word of *zoe*/life; 2 (for the *zoe*/life was manifested, and we have seen it, and bear witness, and shew unto you that eternal *zoe*/life, which was with the Father, and was manifested unto us;) 3 that which we have seen and heard declare we unto you, that ye also may have fellowship with us: and truly our fellowship is with the Father, and with his Son Jesus Christ. 4 And these things write we unto you, that your joy may be full." (John 1:1-5, 14; Phil 1:4)

We have to work with Holy Spirit to think like Him, so He can move in *dunamis*/power and *agape*/love through us. 2 Tim 1:6 "Wherefore I put thee in remembrance that thou stir up the gift of God, which is in thee by the putting on of my hands. 7 For God hath not given us the spirit of fear; but of *dunamis*/power, and of *agape*/love, and of a sound mind (*like Jesus has*)."

DISCOVERING OUR REDEMPTION

Holy Spirit will always lead us to work with the Word of God because He is the author of it! 2 Pet 1:21 "For the prophecy came not in old time by the will of man: but holy men of God spake as they were moved by the Holy Ghost."

Since Holy Spirit is the one who wrote the Bible, then part of that "mind" includes all scripture. So our first access to that "mind of Christ" is through making the Scriptures primary in our lives. James 1:21 "Wherefore lay apart all filthiness and superfluity of naughtiness, and receive with meekness the engrafted word (*of God, specifically the Word of Christ in you, the hope of glory*), which is able to *sozo*/save your souls. 22 But be ye doers of the word, and not hearers only, deceiving your own selves."

The Word of God is where the power of God is. Isa 55:11 "So shall my word be that goeth forth out of my mouth: it shall not return unto me void, but it shall accomplish that which I please, and it shall prosper in the thing whereto I sent it." The anointing is in you by Holy Spirit and in the Word of God. Put the Word of God in your mouth on Earth, and Holy Spirit can make that Word come to pass.

2 Cor 1:18 "But as God is true, our word toward you was not yea and nay. 19 For the Son of God, Jesus Christ, who was preached among you by us, even by me and Silvanus and Timotheus, was not yea and nay, but in him was yea. 20 For all the promises of God in him (*Jesus*) are yea, and in him Amen, unto the glory of God by us. 21 Now he which stablisheth us with you in Christ, and hath anointed us, is God; 22 who hath also sealed us, and given the earnest of the Spirit in our hearts."

Holy Spirit will lead us to the Scriptures, because this is His primary tool to help us sort between life and death, and soul and spirit. This is part of what He is working on us to "will and to do" of Father God's good pleasure for us. Heb 4:10 "For he that is entered into his rest, he also hath ceased from his own works, as God did from his. 11 Let us labour therefore to enter into that rest, lest any man fall after the same example of unbelief. 12 For the word of God is quick, and powerful, and sharper than any twoedged sword, piercing even to the dividing asunder of soul and spirit, and of the joints and marrow, and is a discerner of the thoughts and intents of the heart. 13 Neither is there any creature that is not manifest in his sight: but all things are naked and opened unto the eyes of him with whom we have to do." Notice this process requires hard and diligent work, or labor on our part, in and with the Word of God.

If you are not doing this "work," then you are not mixing the Word of God as Holy Spirit requires. Heb 3:19 "So we see that they could not enter in because of unbelief. 4 Let us therefore fear, lest, a promise being left us of entering into his rest, any of you should seem to come short of it. 2 For unto us was the gospel preached, as well as unto them: but the word preached did not profit them, not being mixed with faith (*persuadableness, courage, and trust in the God who cannot lie*) in them that heard it."

You Have Holy Spirit in You

Our growth in God and ability to operate in the benefits of His so Great Salvation depend upon our right knowledge of the Scriptures. 2 Tim 3:15 "And that from a child thou hast known the holy scriptures, which are able to make thee wise unto *soteria*/salvation through faith which is in Christ Jesus. 16 All scripture is given by inspiration of God, and is profitable for doctrine, for reproof, for correction, for instruction in righteousness: 17 that the man of God may be perfect, throughly furnished unto all good works."

1 Tim 4:13 "Till I come, give attendance to (*public*) reading (*of the Scriptures*), to exhortation, to doctrine."

Receiving Holy Spirit: Holy Spirit comes when we believe that God raised Jesus from the dead, to make us the righteousness of God. Rom 10:8 "But what saith it? The word is nigh thee, even in thy mouth, and in thy heart: that is, the word of faith, which we preach; 9 that if thou shalt confess with thy mouth the Lord Jesus, and shalt believe in thine heart that God hath raised him from the dead, thou shalt be *sozo*/saved. 10 For with the heart man believeth unto righteousness; and with the mouth confession is made unto *soteria*/salvation. 11 For the scripture saith, Whosoever believeth on him shall not be ashamed. 12 For there is no difference between the Jew and the Greek: for the same Lord over all is rich unto all that call upon him. 13 For whosoever shall call upon the name of the Lord shall be *sozo*/saved."

This righteousness is unto the level of God's *zoe* life. Rom 5:18 "Therefore as by the offence of one judgment came upon all men to condemnation; even so by the righteousness of one the free gift came upon all men unto justification of *zoe*/life."

If you are a Christian, you are in a new class of being, called a son of God. This happens when you are made a new creation in Christ Jesus. And what makes you a son prepares you for the indwelling of Holy Spirit.

Gal 4:5 "... that we might receive the adoption of sons. 6 And because ye are sons [*by the new birth unto being made the righteousness of God in Christ Jesus*], God hath sent forth the Spirit of his Son into your hearts, crying, Abba (*Daddy*), Father. 7 Wherefore thou art no more a servant, but a son; and if a son, then an heir of God through Christ." Notice this position as "son" is both legal (adoption) and paternal (Daddy) and is enabled or empowered (Holy Spirit).

And here is how we are to operate as sons. 1 John 3:23 "And this is his commandment, That we should believe on the name of his Son Jesus Christ, and *agape*/love one another, as he gave us commandment. 24 And he that keepeth his commandments dwelleth in him, and he in him. And hereby we know that he abideth in us, by the Spirit which he hath given us."

1 John 3:1 "Behold (*stop and make this change your world-view so you think desire, speak and act differently*), what manner of *agape*/love the Father hath bestowed upon us, that we should be called the sons of God: therefore the world knoweth us not,

DISCOVERING OUR REDEMPTION

because it knew him not. 2 *Agape*/beloved, now are we the sons of God, and it doth not yet appear what we shall be: but we know that, when he shall appear, we shall be like him; for we shall see him as he is. 3 And every man that hath this hope in him purifieth himself, even as he is pure."

This is how we get the new *zoe* life in Christ Jesus. Rom 8:2 "For the law of the Spirit of *zoe*/life in Christ Jesus hath made me free from the law of sin and death." As we access this *zoe* life in the Word of God, by faith, Holy Spirit can crush any effect of the law of sin and death as we have faith to believe God for it.

1 John 5:9 "If we receive the witness of men, the witness of God is greater: for this is the witness of God which he hath testified of his Son. 10 He that believeth on the Son of God hath the witness in himself: he that believeth not God hath made him a liar; because he believeth not the record that God gave of his Son. 11 And this is the record, that God hath given to us eternal *zoe*/life, and this *zoe*/life is in his Son. 12 He that hath the Son hath *zoe*/life; and he that hath not the Son of God hath not *zoe*/life. 13 These things have I written unto you that believe on the name of the Son of God; that ye may know that ye have eternal *zoe*/life, and that ye may believe on the name of the Son of God."

Another way to describe the mission of Jesus and the purpose of our Redemption is so that men could be made into sons of God by indwelling Holy Spirit. Gal 4:4 "But when the fulness of the time was come, God sent forth his Son, made of a woman, made under the law, 5 to redeem them that were under the law, that we might receive the adoption of sons. 6 And because ye are sons, God hath sent forth the Spirit of his Son into your hearts, crying, Abba (*Daddy*), Father. 7 Wherefore thou art no more a servant, but a son; and if a son, then an heir of God through Christ."

Besides, when we believe that God raised Jesus from the dead, Holy Spirit may also come on and within by the laying on of hands, or when we believe the true Gospel. Eph 1:12 "That we should be to the praise of his glory, who first trusted in Christ. 13 In whom ye also trusted, after that ye heard the word of truth, the gospel of your *soteria*/salvation: in whom also after that ye believed, ye were sealed with that holy Spirit of promise, 14 which is the earnest of our inheritance until the redemption of the purchased possession, unto the praise of his glory."

For those with deep Jewish-type understanding, we get born again through the action of Holy Spirit by believing that Jesus is the Son of God. 1 John 4:13 "Hereby know we that we dwell in him, and he in us, because he hath given us of his Spirit. 14 And we have seen and do testify that the Father sent the Son to be the Saviour of the world. 15 Whosoever shall confess that Jesus is the Son of God, God dwelleth in him, and he in God."

1 John 5:1 "Whosoever believeth that Jesus is the Christ is born of God ... ."

Another way to receive Holy Spirit is to ask Father God for Him in the name of Jesus. Jesus came to baptize men in or with Holy Spirit. Mark 1:7 "And preached, saying, There cometh one mightier than I after me, the latchet of whose shoes I am not worthy to stoop down and unloose. 8 I indeed have baptized you with water: but he shall baptize you with the Holy Ghost."

As Jesus said: Luke 11:13 "If ye then, being evil, know how to give good gifts unto your children: how much more shall your heavenly Father give the Holy Spirit to them that *aiteo*/ask *(require, demand and expect as due by Bible promise)* him?"

So how do you get Holy Spirit, if you do not believe you have Him already? Here is a simple prayer:

"Lord Jesus, I believe You died for my sins, were buried and were raised by Father God on the third day for my justification, according to the Scriptures. I make You, Lord of my life. Come rule and reign in and through me, my King. Baptize me with Your Holy Spirit and fire. Heal every part of my life. Teach me Your truth, in love, that I may walk to Your glory. Amen! And thank You!"

And an even simpler one:

"Jesus, God raised you from the dead; You are Lord. Father, in the name of Jesus, fill me with Your Spirit to walk in love. Thank You!"

Now open your mouth and let a few words or syllables out, to speak in tongues. Go meet with other Christians who speak in tongues. They are known by names such as Pentecostal, Charismatic and Spirit Filled. Ask Father God; He will show you the way.

As Jesus told Nicodemus: John 3:6 "That which is born of the flesh is flesh; and that which is born of the Spirit is spirit. 7 Marvel not that I said unto thee, Ye must be born again. 8 The wind bloweth where it listeth, and thou hearest the sound thereof, but canst not tell whence it cometh, and whither it goeth: so is every one that is born of the Spirit."

The sending of Holy Spirit (so men could be made the righteousness of God in Christ Jesus unto *zoe/life* in the new birth, and then dwell in men) was the goal of the entire 52 days that led to the start or creation of the Church on that Day of Pentecost 2000 years ago. Gal 3:13 "Christ hath redeemed us from the curse of the law, being made a curse for us: for it is written, Cursed is every one that hangeth on a tree: 14 that the blessing of Abraham might come on the Gentiles through Jesus Christ; that we might receive the promise of the Spirit through faith."

Jesus gave the disciples Holy Spirit before He left, but this was not the same as on the Day of Pentecost. John 20:22 "And when he had said this, he breathed on them, and saith unto them, Receive ye the Holy Ghost." Based on the timing of this event, after Jesus' Resurrection and prior to His Ascension, it appears Holy Spirit was given to help the disciples learn and understand the Scriptures concerning the coming Kingdom of God.

Otherwise Jesus would not have said, just before His Ascension: Luke 24:46 "And said unto them, Thus it is written, and thus it behoved Christ to suffer, and

DISCOVERING OUR REDEMPTION

to rise from the dead the third day: 47 and that repentance (*concerning Jesus as Lord*) and *aphesis*/remission (*purging, removal, obliteration and putting away*) of sins should be preached in his name among all nations, beginning at Jerusalem. 48 And ye are witnesses of these things. 49 And, behold, I send the promise of my Father upon you: but tarry ye in the city of Jerusalem, until ye be endued with *dunamis*/power from on high.

"50 And he (*Jesus*) led them out as far as to Bethany, and he lifted up his hands, and blessed them. 51 And it came to pass, while he blessed them, he was parted from them, and carried up into heaven. 52 And they worshipped him, and returned to Jerusalem with great joy: 53 and were continually in the temple, praising and blessing God. Amen."

Since Holy Spirit came to Earth in a new and different way on the Day of Pentecost in Acts 2, He is still here. He is the foretaste of the full presence of God seen in Revelation chapters 21 and 22. None of His gifts have gone, as He is the gift of God. This is part of the definition God gives of His Day of Salvation. 2 Cor 6:1 "We then, as workers together with him, beseech you also that ye receive not the grace of God in vain. 2 (For he saith, I have heard thee in a time accepted, and in the day of *soteria*/salvation have I succoured thee: behold, now is the accepted time; behold, now is the day of *soteria*/salvation.)" Verse 1 tells us that even though we may have Holy Spirit dwelling in us, we may not be working with Him effectively to bring the benefits of the Day of Salvation to Earth. We must participate in the process. Verse 2 makes it plain God is talking about right now, and not some future heavenly state.

Walking with Holy Spirit: God does not want us ignorant of Holy Spirit and His gifts. 1 Corinthians chapters 12-14 detail some of the work and power of Holy Spirit. 1 Cor 12:1 "Now concerning spiritual gifts, brethren, I would not have you ignorant. 2 Ye know that ye were Gentiles, carried away unto these dumb idols, even as ye were led. 3 Wherefore I give you to understand, that no man speaking by the Spirit of God calleth Jesus accursed: and that no man can say that Jesus is the Lord, but by the Holy Ghost. 4 Now there are diversities of gifts, but the same Spirit. 5 And there are differences of administrations, but the same Lord. 6 And there are diversities of operations, but it is the same God which worketh all in all. 7 But the manifestation of the Spirit is given to every man to profit withal. 8 For to one is given by the Spirit the word of wisdom; to another the word of knowledge by the same Spirit; 9 to another faith by the same Spirit; to another the gifts of healing by the same Spirit; 10 to another the working of miracles; to another prophecy; to another discerning of spirits; to another divers kinds of tongues; to another the interpretation of tongues: 11 but all these worketh that one and the selfsame Spirit, dividing to every man severally as he will. 12 For as the body is one, and hath many members, and all the members of that one body, being many, are one body:

so also is Christ. 13 For by one Spirit are we all baptized into one body, whether we be Jews or Gentiles, whether we be bond or free; and have been all made to drink into one Spirit."

In verse 11, He says "to every man," meaning no Christian is exempt. In that same verse, He says "severally as he will." One meaning is that the Holy Spirit is the distributor of the gifts, and this is true. He has the gifts (or is the gift), and He gives them (the manifestation of His power). But that phrase "severally as he will" can also apply to each Christian. We also control what gifts we operate in. Per the instruction in these 3 chapters of 1 Corinthians, we can control when and how they operate. <u>1 Cor 14:32</u> "And the spirits of the prophets are subject to the prophets."

This implies that whatever you focus on of God is what you get "good" at, or your faith grows in. <u>Rom 12:6</u> "Having then gifts differing according to the grace that is given to us, whether prophecy, let us prophesy according to the proportion of faith."

Here we see prophecy is Holy Spirit speaking though a person in their language. Yet what the prophet says is a function of their faith to handle what Holy Spirit is saying. Holy Spirit only speaks pure truth. The prophet is limited by their, at that moment, level, or proportion, of faith. Since faith grows by doing the Word of God, not just hearing it, faith grows the more we learn of God in His Word on a subject and then go and do it.

If you spend your time exercising prophecy and studying the Word of God on it, you will get more confident in prophecy. Your words will be more precise and be spoken with more power. If you spend time with people who operate in healing, or you spend more time in exercising healing and studying the Scriptures on healing, you will see more healing. The promise of God is that He will bless whatever you set your hand to: <u>Deut 28:8</u> "The Lord shall command the blessing upon thee … in all that thou settest thine hand unto … ." You do anything good and godly, and God is with you and for you.

Here, again, is a command to grow in the exercise of walking with Holy Spirit, to release His power into the Earth. <u>1 Pet 4:10</u> "As every man hath *lambano*/received the gift (*Holy Spirit*), even so minister the same one to another, as good stewards of the manifold grace of God. 11 If any man speak, let him speak as the oracles of God; if any man minister, let him do it as of the [*unlimited*] ability which God giveth: that God in all things may be glorified through Jesus Christ, to whom be praise and dominion for ever and ever. Amen."

In verse 10, it is to the level that we hold on to or *lambano* the gift or power of Holy Spirit. Peter was calling the early believers up to operate in the full level, as Jesus did, and not some lower level. Again the emphasis is that, as you operate with Holy Spirit you grow in your ability to release more of Him in what are called "gifts," and they can be developed or made more powerful over time, with study and exercise.

DISCOVERING OUR REDEMPTION

So we see growth in walking with Holy Spirit is not so much God "picking" someone to favor, but those who do the right things allow Holy Spirit to operate. If you want more of God, then the next move is always yours. James 4:6 "But he giveth more grace. Wherefore he saith, God resisteth the proud, but giveth grace unto the humble. 7 Submit yourselves therefore to God. Resist the devil, and he will flee from you. 8 Draw nigh to God, and he will draw nigh to you. Cleanse your hands, ye sinners; and purify your hearts, ye double minded. 9 Be afflicted, and mourn, and weep: let your laughter be turned to mourning, and your joy to heaviness. 10 Humble yourselves in the sight of the Lord, and he shall lift you up."

Operating in or walking in a particular area of Holy Spirit is not a certification of any other part of our life. God called the Corinthian church or gathering of Christians "mere men," or "carnal" and "babes," yet they operated fully and easily in Holy Spirit gifts, to the point that they were overusing them. 1 Cor 3:1 "And I, brethren, could not speak unto you as unto spiritual, but as unto **carnal, even as unto babes** in Christ. 2 I have fed you with milk, and not with meat: for hitherto ye were not able to bear it, neither yet now are ye able. 3 For ye are yet **carnal**: for whereas there is among you envying, and strife, and divisions, are ye not **carnal**, and walk as *(mere unborn-again)* **men**?"

This was a church that allowed sin even worse than that practiced by the heathen Gentiles. 1 Cor 5:1 "It is reported commonly that there is fornication among you, and such fornication as is not so much as named among the Gentiles, that one should have his father's wife. 2 And ye are puffed up, and have not rather mourned, that he that hath done this deed might be taken away from among you." Yet the members of this church operated freely in Holy Spirit gifts. So holiness is not a requirement to operate in the power gifts of Holy Spirit. Since Paul had to correct them on public use, neither is loving or mature good judgment a requirement to operate in the gifts of Holy Spirit.

Still Paul said the Corinthians believers came behind in no gift, meaning that they operated in and with Holy Spirit more than other churches, and had the operation of the full set of gifts, which is even longer than the list of 9 in 1 Cor 12:8-10. 1 Cor 1:5 "That in every thing ye are enriched by him, in all utterance, and in all knowledge; 6 even as the testimony of Christ was confirmed in you: 7 so that ye come behind in no gift; waiting for the coming of our Lord Jesus Christ: 8 who shall also confirm you unto the end, that ye may be blameless in the day of our Lord Jesus Christ. 9 God is faithful, by whom ye were called unto the fellowship of his Son Jesus Christ our Lord." Verse 8 is a profound declaration of the degree of righteousness we are made in Jesus, by the work of Holy Spirit, when He raised Jesus from the dead and recreated us, which we received when we were born again.

Paul never said: "If you do not stop sinning, Holy Spirit will leave." Instead, the message of God is the exact opposite. Hear this declaration to sinning

You Have Holy Spirit in You

Christians, who were obviously grieving Holy Spirit. Eph 4:29 "Let no corrupt communication proceed out of your mouth, but that which is good to the use of edifying, that it may minister grace unto the hearers. 30 And grieve not the holy Spirit of God, whereby ye are sealed unto the day of redemption. 31 Let all bitterness, and wrath, and anger, and clamour, and evil speaking, be put away from you, with all malice: 32 and be ye kind one to another, tenderhearted, forgiving one another, even as God for Christ's sake hath forgiven you." Notice Holy Spirit is sealed in these sinning Christians until the Day of Redemption, which is AFTER the Day of Judgment. Your life may determine the joy of His ride in you, but Holy Spirit is going nowhere.

Thus, this promise still stands: Rom 11:29 "For the gifts and calling of God are without repentance."

Without a doubt, Holy Spirit is the greatest gift of all, for He is God. God has made Himself His gift to us. As described on that wonderful Day of Pentecost 2000 years ago: Acts 2:38 "Then Peter said unto them, Repent (*change your life, knowing that Jesus is Saviour, Lord and Christ*), and be baptized every one of you in the name of Jesus Christ for the *aphesis*/remission (*removal, obliteration, purging, taking away*) of sins, and ye shall receive the gift of the Holy Ghost."

As Peter described to the incredulous disciples, after the wonderful events at the house of Cornelius: Acts 10:45 "And they of the circumcision which believed were astonished, as many as came with Peter, because that on the Gentiles also was poured out the gift of the Holy Ghost. 46 For they heard them speak with tongues, and magnify God. Then answered Peter, 47 Can any man forbid water, that these should not be baptized, which have received the Holy Ghost as well as we?"

Operating by Faith: The operation of Holy Spirit gifts, as are all things of God, is by faith that God will supply the best gift, that which is needed at the time. Notice that even new believers can operate in these gifts, by faith, or believing, or obeying the Word of grace. Mark 16:16 "He that believeth (*the Gospel*) and is baptized shall be *sozo*/saved; but he that believeth not shall be damned. 17 And these signs shall follow them that believe; In my name shall they cast out devils; they shall speak with new tongues; 18 they shall take up serpents; and if they drink any deadly thing, it shall not hurt them; they shall lay hands on the sick, and they shall recover."

Again, this confirms that operation of Holy Spirit gifts is not necessarily a sign of maturity or holiness, but of faith in the Gospel, which means faith in the power of our Redemption in and by Jesus. It is a sign that He loves us so much He will put up with anything we do and is only limited by a lack of faith for Him to operate through. No wonder God said: Rom 1:16 "For I am not ashamed of the gospel of Christ: for it is the *dunamis*/power of God unto *soteria*/salvation (*now or later*) to every one that believeth; to the Jew first, and also to the Greek. 17 For therein is

DISCOVERING OUR REDEMPTION

the righteousness of God revealed from faith to faith: as it is written, The just [*those imputed righteous and/or made the righteousness of God in Christ Jesus*] shall *zao*/live (*release Holy Spirit to bless and do the impossible works of God*) by faith."

Holy Spirit coming on you and controlling you is wonderful, but is a relatively low level of spiritual development. This happened to King Saul, and it did not change him, because he did not successfully graduate from "The School of Holy Spirit" and become wise in the Scriptures in the way of Salvation. 1 Sam 10:6 "And the Spirit of the Lord will come upon thee, and thou shalt prophesy with them, and shalt be turned into another man. 7 And let it be, when these signs are come unto thee, that thou do as occasion serve thee; for God is with thee."

Notice, again, Saul and his men tried to kill David, but Holy Spirit defended him by "overcoming" the attackers, so they could not function. Then, when Holy Spirit had left them, we are told, they still tried to kill David. 1 Sam 19:21 "And when it was told Saul, he sent other messengers, and they prophesied likewise. And Saul sent messengers again the third time, and they prophesied also. 22 Then went he also to Ramah, and came to a great well that is in Sechu: and he asked and said, Where are Samuel and David? And one said, Behold, they be at Naioth in Ramah. 23 And he went thither to Naioth in Ramah: and the Spirit of God was upon him also, and he went on, and prophesied, until he came to Naioth in Ramah. 24 And he stripped off his clothes also, and prophesied before Samuel in like manner, and lay down naked all that day and all that night. Wherefore they say, Is Saul also among the prophets?"

While Holy Spirit gives the gifts, "dividing to every man severally as he will," we are required to seek the gifts. 1 Cor 12:31 "But covet earnestly the best gifts: and yet shew I unto you a more excellent way [*of walking in* agape/*love, so the free operation of Holy Spirit in power and wisdom becomes a natural outflow of walking in* agape/*love*]." 1 Cor 14:1 "Follow after *agape*/charity, and desire spiritual gifts... ." These are clear commands, so no Christian has any excuse for not seeking and operating in Holy Spirit gifts.

Nor does it appear that wisdom or right understanding in God comes without prayer, as Paul prayed. This again shows we have a significant part to play in releasing Holy Spirit as He wills. Eph 1:16 "Cease not to give thanks for you, making mention of you in my prayers; 17 that the God of our Lord Jesus Christ, the Father of glory, may give unto you the spirit of wisdom and revelation in the knowledge of him: 18 the eyes of your understanding being enlightened; that ye may know what is the hope of his calling, and what the riches of the glory of his inheritance in the saints, 19 and what is the exceeding greatness of his power to us-ward who believe, according to the working of his mighty *dunamis*/power, 20 which he wrought in Christ, when he raised him from the dead, and set him at his own right hand in the heavenly places, 21 far above all principality, and power, and might, and dominion, and every name that is named, not only in this world, but also in that which is to come: 22 and hath put all things under his feet, and gave him to be the head over all things to the church, 23 which is his body, the fulness of him that filleth all in all." Again, the answer to this kind of prayer will absolutely change your world-view.

We are to mature to the point we can operate in the Holy Spirit gifts by will and not always being overcome by Holy Spirit. 1 Cor 14:14 "For if I pray in an unknown tongue, my spirit prayeth, but my understanding is unfruitful. 15 What is it then? I will pray with the spirit, and I will pray with the understanding also: I will sing with the spirit, and I will sing with the understanding also." This same principle of exercising Holy Spirit at will applies to any power or wisdom ability of Holy Spirit.

In fact the whole message of the New Testament is to keep your soul in a place where Holy Spirit can operate through you, as you and He will together. Phil 2:12 "Wherefore, my *agape*/beloved, as ye have always obeyed, not as in my presence only, but now much more in my absence, work out your own *soteria*/salvation with fear and trembling. 13 For it is God which worketh in you both to will and to do of his good pleasure. 14 Do all things without murmurings and disputings: 15 that ye may be blameless and harmless, the sons of God, without rebuke, in the midst of a crooked and perverse nation, among whom ye shine as lights in the world; 16 holding forth the word of *zoe*/life; that I may rejoice in the day of Christ, that I have not run in vain, neither laboured in vain."

While Holy Spirit can come, as He did in Acts 2, and apparently force His way upon men, this is not His desired mode for Christian growth. (It may not even be possible, expect as it comes by prayer or prophecy through others.) When you operate by gift it is almost entirely separate from you. When you operate by fruit, you share in the development process and, thus, it is maturity or right *epignosis*/ knowledge of God. Jesus operated by fruit.

Jesus knew He had what He needed from God, when He needed it. So, in this manner, Jesus was the One who, "dividing to every man (*Himself*) severally [*what He needed*] as he (*Jesus*) *willed*." When you have Holy Spirit, you have all of Him, and anything He can do is yours, by faith in God, by His Word. The mature Christian does not operate by gifts, although they may use them. He/she operates by Holy Spirit, knowing whatever is needed is available, by faith in God, by His Word. Thus, you may start with occasional gifts, but the goal is to transition to a lifestyle of fruit. Eph 5:9 "(For the fruit of the Spirit is in all goodness and righteousness and truth.)"

Gal 5:22 "But the fruit of the Spirit (*that brings the Kingdom of God to Earth*) is *agape*/love, joy, peace, longsuffering, gentleness, goodness, faith, 23 meekness, temperance: against such there is no law. 24 And they that are Christ's have cruci-

DISCOVERING OUR REDEMPTION

fied the flesh with the affections and lusts. 25 If we *zao*/live in the Spirit, let us also walk in the Spirit. 26 Let us not be desirous of vain glory, provoking one another, envying one another."

Keeping Filled with Holy Spirit: On that Day in Acts 2, the disciples had been in prayer. Jewish prayer is heavy on the Scriptures and on asking God to do what He has promised. Their prayer would have included the singing of the Psalms. When the Bible talks about being "full of the Spirit," it has two meanings:

1. When you are born again, your spirit is filled and made one with Holy Spirit. 1 Cor 6:17 "But he that is joined unto the Lord is one spirit." This is the meaning of baptize, and, thus, the meaning of being baptized in Holy Spirit. Now your spirit is "full of Holy Spirit."
2. The other is the state of your soul at a point in time. Once you are born again, your spirit is one with Holy Spirit, and He is sealed there unto the Day of Redemption. This means His job is to get the Christian through the Day of Judgment unto the blessed state of the full Redemption of God. Eph 4:30 "And grieve not the holy Spirit of God, whereby ye are sealed unto the day of redemption."

We are told several ways to get "in the Spirit" so our soul (heart, mind, will and emotions) are in full and glad agreement with Holy Spirit. This is a more accurate meaning of being "full of Holy Spirit" as an indication of your walk in the Lord after you are born again.

Acts 6:5 "And the saying pleased the whole multitude: and they chose Stephen, a man full of faith and of the Holy Ghost ... ." Stephen was one of those born again and baptized in Holy Spirit on or after that Day of Pentecost. The statement "full of faith and Holy Spirit" implies a lifestyle and not a single event. Since Stephen is described as different from other new believers, he obviously was doing something different to produce the results he got in working with Holy Spirit. So this is not talking about a onetime event of the baptism of Holy Spirit, but a lifestyle of working with Holy Spirit.

Here is one method of getting "in the Spirit," or "full of faith and of the Holy Ghost," that is very Jewish in nature and probably what the disciples had been doing on that Pentecost morning. Eph 5:14 "Wherefore he saith, Awake thou that sleepest, and arise from the dead, and Christ shall give thee light. 15 See then that ye walk circumspectly, not as fools, but as wise, 16 redeeming the time, because the days are evil. 17 Wherefore be ye not unwise, but understanding what the will of the Lord is. 18 And be not drunk with wine, wherein is excess; but be (*continuously being*) filled with the Spirit; 19 speaking to yourselves in psalms and hymns and spiritual songs, singing and making melody in your heart to the Lord; 20 giving thanks always for all things unto God and the Father in the name of our Lord Jesus Christ; 21 submitting yourselves one to another in the fear of God."

You Have Holy Spirit in You

Again, notice the emphasis on the Word of Christ. Col 3:12 "Put on therefore, as the elect of God, holy and *agape*/beloved, bowels of mercies, kindness, humbleness of mind, meekness, longsuffering; 13 forbearing one another, and forgiving one another, if any man have a quarrel against any: even as Christ forgave you, so also do ye. 14 And above all these things put on *agape*/charity, which is the bond of perfectness. 15 And let the peace of God rule in your hearts, to the which also ye are called in one body; and be ye thankful. 16 Let the word of Christ dwell in you richly in all wisdom; teaching and admonishing one another in psalms and hymns and spiritual songs, singing with grace in your hearts to the Lord. 17 And whatsoever ye do in word or deed, do all in the name of the Lord Jesus, giving thanks to God and the Father by him." [Note: the rest of Ephesians and Colossians, after these verses, continues to describe how to walk "in the Spirit."]

This is much like what God told Joshua it would take to make his way successful in this world. Josh 1:5 "There shall not any man be able to stand before thee all the days of thy life: as I was with Moses, so I will be with thee: I will not fail thee, nor forsake thee. 6 Be strong and of a good courage: for unto this people shalt thou divide for an inheritance the land, which I sware unto their fathers to give them. 7 Only be thou strong and very courageous, that thou mayest observe to do according to all the law, which Moses my servant commanded thee: turn not from it to the right hand or to the left, that thou mayest prosper whithersoever thou goest. 8 This book of the law shall not depart out of thy mouth; but thou shalt meditate therein day and night, that thou mayest observe to do according to all that is written therein: for then thou shalt make thy way prosperous, and then thou shalt have good success. 9 Have not I commanded thee? Be strong and of a good courage; be not afraid, neither be thou dismayed: for the Lord thy God is with thee whithersoever thou goest."

We can be confident that Jesus, a devout Jew, did this also. As He is our example, then we should be doing the same.

Something like Eph 5:14-20, Col 3:12-17 and Josh 1:5-9 is probably what Paul meant when he told Timothy to stir himself up into Holy Spirit. 2 Tim 1:6 "Wherefore I put thee in remembrance that thou stir up the gift of God, which is in thee by the putting on of my hands. 7 For God hath not given us the spirit of fear; but of *dunamis*/power, and of *agape*/love, and of a sound mind (*like Jesus has*)." And this is very much like the commands in Phil 4:4-9.

If you want to know more about how to seek the Lord or stir yourself up into Him, please contact us at www.CovenantPeaceMinistries.com and ask for our article on "How to Seek the Lord the Bible Way." Send your request to: Info@CovenantPeaceMinistries.com.

These other methods were available before the Day of Pentecost, but unique to after that Day of Pentecost is the free use of the gift of tongues. Another way

DISCOVERING OUR REDEMPTION

to increase the Holy Spirit power we operate in is to speak in tongues. 1 Cor 14:4 "He that speaketh in an unknown tongue edifieth himself ... ." Notice this implies either making your spirit stronger and more intense, your soul more accommodating to Holy Spirit in your heart, your soul more able to listen in glad agreement when Holy Spirit speaks, or some combination of all three. For soul work, this means the leverage point, fulcrum or portal, is with the Scriptures already in your heart (subconscious mind) or currently controlling your mind (cognitive mind).

That word *"edifieth,"* and, thus, the benefits of using the gift of tongues includes:
- Strengthening against pressure to break or give up,
- Increase in power, energy and ability,
- Ability to resist and win,
- Ability to exhort and encourage others,
- Ability to understand difficult things,
- Ability to carry others,
- Ability to overcome, remove or destroy,
- Ability to have patience until things do make sense, and
- Ability to endure longer than your enemy to victory.

Since power is about intensity, then the more intense your tongues (loud, hard and fast) the more effective you will be in building power and confidence in God. Many recommend a believer spend at least 2 hours a day in hard, fast and loud tongues, to remain strong in Spirit.

When we are speaking in tongues Holy Spirit is speaking through us in perfect prayer to God for what needs to be done by God's priorities.

As Jesus demonstrated, casting out demons and healing the sick are relatively fast, but changing men's hearts takes longer. 1 Cor 14:2 "For he that speaketh in an unknown tongue speaketh not unto men, but unto God: for no man understandeth him; howbeit in the spirit he speaketh mysteries." Much of the fruit of those who do join Holy Spirit in speaking in tongues seems to be over time in making men's hearts more open to hearing and obeying God.

Please see pages 345-357 in Chapter 32, "Having Faith in God" for more on speaking in tongues.

Feelings versus Faith: To operate in Holy Spirit power is not about in-advance "feelings" or "anointings" of any kind. We see no mention of Jesus operating to perform Holy Spirit-powered miracles where "anointing feelings" came first, nor do we see much of this in Peter or the other apostles. Philip worked many wonders in Samaria, yet there is no mention that he operated by "in-advance feelings," so "special feelings" are obviously not a requirement.

We do see Jesus operating by compassion for healing. Matt 9:35 "And Jesus went about all the cities and villages, teaching in their synagogues, and preaching the gospel of the kingdom, and healing every sickness and every disease among the people. 36 But when he saw the multitudes, he was moved with compassion on them, because they fainted, and were scattered abroad, as sheep having no shepherd." See also Matt 14:14; Mk 1:41; Mk 9:22. Jesus also multiplied bread by compassion (Matt 15:32; Mk 6:42; Lk 9:17; John 6:11). Jesus even calmed the storm in anger or frustration at the disciples' unbelief in Mk 4:37-41 and Lk 9:24-25. And again, with a similar attitude, Jesus cast out a demon when the unbelief in the disciples prevented them. (Matt 17:14-21; Mk 9:15-29 and Lk 9:38-45).

But nowhere is there recorded that Jesus has a special "feeling" that God was going to heal or work miracles at Jesus' judgment against a work of the devil. Instead, Jesus said when He raised Lazarus from the dead: John 11:40 "Jesus saith unto her, Said I not unto thee, that, if thou wouldest believe, thou shouldest see the glory of God? 41 Then they took away the stone from the place where the dead was laid. And Jesus lifted up his eyes, and said, Father, I thank thee that thou hast heard me. 42 And I knew that thou hearest me always: but because of the people which stand by I said it, that they may believe that thou hast sent me. 43 And when he thus had spoken, he cried *(shouted as in battle or passion)* with a loud voice, Lazarus, come forth."

Even the emotion Jesus expressed at the raising of Lazarus seems to be frustration at unbelief and/or Jesus stirring up Himself to command life for His Father. John 11:35 "Jesus wept. 36 Then said the Jews, Behold how he loved him! 37 And some of them said, Could not this man, which opened the eyes of the blind, have caused that even this man should not have died? 38 Jesus therefore again groaning *(stirring or snorting like a war house about to go into battle)* in himself cometh to the grave. It was a cave, and a stone lay upon it." Notice in verse 38 Jesus "again groaned, snorted" implying the "Jesus wept" for verse 35 was a similar stirring up of Himself to war and win.

In one case, we do see Paul exasperated or angered at a woman speaking by a demon. Acts 16:17 "The same followed Paul and us, and cried, saying, These men are the servants of the most high God, which shew unto us the way of *soteria*/salvation. 18 And this did she many days. But Paul, being grieved, turned and said to the spirit, I command thee in the name of Jesus Christ to come out of her. And he came out the same hour." This event does not suggest that Paul was overcome or feeling a special "anointing."

Instead, it appears Paul acted in confidence in what he had, the name of Jesus and faith in that name, to command obedience of a devil, much as Peter explained in one notable miracle (or act of Holy Spirit at the command of a man). Acts 3:12 "And when Peter saw it, he answered unto the people, Ye men of Israel, why marvel ye at this? or why look ye so earnestly on us, as though by our own power or holiness we had made this man to walk? 13 The God of Abraham, and

DISCOVERING OUR REDEMPTION

of Isaac, and of Jacob, the God of our fathers, hath glorified his Son Jesus; whom ye delivered up, and denied him in the presence of Pilate, when he was determined to let him go. 14 But ye denied the Holy One and the Just, and desired a murderer to be granted unto you; 15 and killed the Prince of *zoe*/life, whom God hath raised from the dead; whereof we are witnesses. 16 And his name through faith in his name hath made this man strong, whom ye see and know: yea, the faith which is by him hath given him this perfect soundness in the presence of you all."

Again we see the principle that it is not our holiness that allows Holy Spirit to do what He loves to do, manifest the Kingdom of God on Earth, but faith in the name of Jesus, targeted against a specific work of the devil, much like Jesus did. Acts 10:34 "Then Peter opened his mouth, and said, Of a truth I perceive that God is no respecter of persons: 35 but in every nation he that feareth him, and worketh righteousness, is accepted with him. 36 The word which God sent unto the children of Israel, preaching peace by Jesus Christ: (he is Lord of all:) 37 that word, I say, ye know, which was published throughout all Judaea, and began from Galilee, after the baptism which John preached; 38 how God anointed Jesus of Nazareth with the Holy Ghost and with *dunamis*/power: who went about doing good, and healing all that were oppressed (*under the active lordship, control and rulership*) of the devil; for God was with him."

In all these scriptures, notice we have the same Spirit and the same *dunamis* power for the same job. John 20:21 "Then said Jesus to them again, Peace be unto you: as my Father hath sent me, even so send I you." So if you walk like Jesus in your calling, then your testimony will also be like Acts 10:34-38.

We know Samson operated by faith and not feelings. Heb 11:32 "And what shall I more say? for the time would fail me to tell of Gedeon, and of Barak, and of Samson, and of Jephthae; of David also, and Samuel, and of the prophets: 33 who through faith subdued kingdoms, wrought righteousness, obtained promises, stopped the mouths of lions … ."

Notice Samson was not used to feeling Holy Spirit come on him and could not tell when Holy Spirit was not there. Judg 16:20 "And she said, The Philistines be upon thee, Samson. And he awoke out of his sleep, and said, I will go out as at other times before, and shake myself. And he wist not that the Lord was departed from him." Samson was accustomed to operating in power and yet apparently never "felt" anything when he did.

Feelings are not guaranteed to be part of operating in Holy Spirit power. It is nice when they come, but not the standard. If you have feelings prior to operating in Holy Spirit power, then that is a very low level of faith, if any faith at all. But with faith, you do not have to feel; instead your focus is on the Word of God and His desire and ability to perform it, and not your feelings. 2 Cor 5:7 "For we walk by faith, not by sight [*or any other supporting feelings, except the Word of God*]."

You Have Holy Spirit in You

Releasing Holy Spirit: It is wonderful to have His Word abiding in us, when we realize that the Universe has been created by His Word, and we have that creative ability in us. Jesus, by Holy Spirit, lives in us.

John 15:7 "If ye abide in me, and my words abide in you, ye shall *aiteo*/ask (*require, demand and expect as due by covenant promise, knowing all the requirements have been met in Jesus*) what ye will, and it shall be done unto you. 8 Herein is my Father glorified, that ye bear much fruit; so shall ye be my disciples. 9 As the Father hath *agape*/loved me, so have I *agape*/loved you: continue ye in my *agape*/love."

Now we have God Himself in us, along with His Word.

No wonder He said in 1 John 4:4 "Ye are of God, my little children, and have overcome them: because greater is he that is in you than he that is in the world."

The God in us is the same God who spoke the Universe into being. The same God is in us who walked the sea in Galilee. This same God raised the dead and made Abraham a rich man. This is the very same God and the very same blessing.

The same God is in us who arose from the dead.

Phil 2:13 "For it is God who is at work within you ... ."

We have not taken advantage of the riches of grace that belong to us.

How few of us have let God loose in us and through us.

I can feel Him struggling to have His place and to have His rights, in the individual members of the Body of Christ, and also out into the world.

How He longs to heal the sick, to break the power of Satan over the lives of men through us. He longs to show us the abundance of His riches in the Earth, to bless men in every way.

He is jealous over anything you consider more important than Him, because He knows that limits you and Him in you. James 4:3 "Ye *aiteo*/ask (*require, demand and expect as due by covenant promise*), and receive not, because ye *aiteo*/ask amiss, that ye may consume it upon your lusts. 4 Ye adulterers and adulteresses, know ye not that the friendship of the world is enmity with God? whosoever therefore will be a friend of the world is the enemy of God. 5 Do ye think that the scripture saith in vain, The spirit that dwelleth in us lusteth to envy? 6 But he giveth more grace. Wherefore he saith, God resisteth the proud, but giveth grace unto the humble. 7 Submit yourselves therefore to God. Resist the devil, and he will flee from you. 8 Draw nigh to God, and he will draw nigh to you. Cleanse your hands, ye sinners; and purify your hearts, ye double minded. 9 Be afflicted, and mourn, and weep: let your laughter be turned to mourning, and your joy to heaviness. 10 Humble yourselves in the sight of the Lord, and he shall lift you up."

God longs to solve every problem of mankind ... until Heaven comes to Earth.

Let's let Him loose in us, and through us, to others in *agape*/love.

Fill your mind with the work of Christ by the cross and the dominion of His name, for the Father's glory, and the wonder of "Christ in you the hope of glory."

Chapter 28

You Have Been Made the Righteousness of God

God has said that He will be our righteousness. Isa 54:17 "No weapon that is formed against thee shall prosper; and every tongue that shall rise against thee in judgment thou shalt condemn. This is the heritage of the servants of the Lord, and their righteousness is of me, saith the Lord."

Righteousness is a nature and inner desire demonstrated in thoughts, words and actions. Righteousness is the character of one who is righteous, always doing the right things. Here God promises that He will be your inner desire, on what to do and how to do it. This promise is fulfilled when we operate in the mind of Christ, by Holy Spirit within us.

Isa 45:25 "In the Lord shall all the seed of Israel be justified (*made righteous*), and shall glory."

Righteousness is the legal assessment of an action or of trust in a person. We are justified, made righteous and made the nature, the righteousness of God in Christ Jesus. This makes us, in the new creation, partakers, or sharing in the same thing, His divine nature.

2 Pet 1:2 "Grace and peace be multiplied unto you through the *epignosis/* knowledge of God, and of Jesus our Lord, 3 according as his divine power hath given unto us all things that pertain unto *zoe*/life and godliness, through the *epigno-*

You Have Been Made the Righteousness of God

sis/knowledge of him that hath called us to glory and virtue: 4 whereby are given unto us exceeding great and precious promises: that by these ye might be partakers of the divine nature, having escaped the corruption that is in the world through lust."

This is part of the great work of the Mighty Arm of God, Jesus of Nazareth, the Christ of God. God had already given man imputed or legal righteousness, but without a change in nature. We see this first in Abraham. Gen 15:4 "And, behold, the word of the Lord came unto him, saying, This shall not be thine heir; but he that shall come forth out of thine own bowels shall be thine heir. 5 And he brought him forth abroad, and said, Look now toward heaven, and tell the stars, if thou be able to number them: and he said unto him, So shall thy seed be. 6 And he (*Abraham*) believed in the Lord; and he counted (*imputed*) it to him for righteousness."

While not perfect in his walk, Abraham was still blessed of the Lord. Gen 24:1 "And Abraham was old, and well stricken in age: and the Lord had blessed Abraham in all things."

Gen 25:7 "And these are the days of the years of Abraham's life which he lived, an hundred threescore and fifteen years. 8 Then Abraham gave up the ghost, and died in a good old age, an old man, and full of years; and was gathered to his people." Note Abraham lived 175 years, well past the 120 years of Moses.

The Great Work of God was to give or place in man the righteousness of God in Christ Jesus. Only God could do this. This is the justification of the New Covenant in Jesus. Isa 53:11 "He shall see of the travail of his soul, and shall be satisfied: by his knowledge **shall my righteous servant justify many**; for he shall bear their iniquities. 12 Therefore will I divide him a portion with the great, and he shall divide the spoil with the strong; because he hath poured out his soul unto death: and he was numbered with the transgressors; and he bare the sin of many, and made intercession for the transgressors." Note: this included the new birth/creation.

The Bible talks about three kinds of righteousness:
- Works like God would do. So to obey God's laws means that, as you obey, you do what God wants, and He can inhabit that action, as your right thoughts, words and behaviors make a path for Him into this world, against and over the power of the "god of this world," the devil, to bruise/crush the devil's power and heal the devil's works. This is how God's "blessings" are brought to Earth. Path is one meaning of the word "Torah," and this in the name given to the Pentateuch or the first 5 books of the Bible. The Torah, or Law, had some 613 "paths." The New Testament has some 1,050 commands or "paths," or the single "path" of *agape*/love. Mark 12:29 "And Jesus answered him, The first of all the commandments is, Hear, O Israel; The Lord our God is one Lord: 30 and thou shalt *agape*/love the Lord thy God with all thy heart, and with all thy *psuche*/

soul (*life*), and with all thy mind (*imagination, understanding*), and with all thy *dianoia*/strength (*power, ability and money*): this is the first commandment. 31 And the second is like, namely this, Thou shalt *agape*/love thy neighbour as thyself. There is none other commandment greater than these." Matt 22:40 "On these two commandments hang all the law and the prophets." Gal 5:14 "For all the law is fulfilled in one word, even in this; Thou shalt *agape*/love thy neighbour as thyself." Rom 13:8 "Owe no man any thing, but to *agape*/love one another: for he that *agape*/loveth another hath fulfilled the law. 9 For this, Thou shalt not commit adultery, Thou shalt not kill, Thou shalt not steal, Thou shalt not bear false witness, Thou shalt not covet; and if there be any other commandment, it is briefly comprehended in this saying, namely, Thou shalt *agape*/love thy neighbour as thyself. 10 *Agape*/love worketh no ill to his neighbour: therefore *agape*/love is the fulfilling of the law."

- Imputed or applied righteousness is when God does not count your sins against you. You still have the nature of sin in your spirit, as a result of the sin of Adam, but God does not count your sins against you. This is a legal righteousness and is applied or counted to the person and the curse of sin removed. Isa 61:10 "I will greatly rejoice in the LORD, my soul shall be joyful in my God; for he hath clothed me with the garments of salvation, he hath covered me with the robe of righteousness, as a bridegroom decketh himself with ornaments, and as a bride adorneth herself with her jewels." Rom 4:6 "Even as David also describeth (Ps 32) the blessedness of the man, unto whom God imputeth righteousness without works, 7 saying, Blessed are they whose iniquities are forgiven, and whose sins are covered. 8 Blessed is the man to whom the Lord will not impute sin." Rom 4:22 "And therefore it (*righteousness*) was imputed to him (*Abraham*) for righteousness."

- God imparting His righteous nature and His legal righteousness, so you have imputed righteousness, and your spirit is changed into the righteousness of God unto His *zoe*/life, in your spirit, just like Jesus got, when He was raised from the dead, after being made sin and the curse of sin for mankind. This is the wonder of the new creation and what allows Holy Spirit to enter and dwell in a human, even though we still sin and do not walk just like Jesus all the time. Rom 5:18 "Therefore as by the offence of one (*Adam*) judgment came upon all men to condemnation; even so by the righteousness of one (*Jesus*) the free gift came upon all men unto justification (*being made righteous and the righteousness of God*) of *zoe*/life." Rom 4:24 "But for us also, to whom it (*righteousness*) shall be imputed, if we believe on him that raised up Jesus our Lord from the dead; 25 who

You Have Been Made the Righteousness of God

was delivered for our offences, and was raised again for our justification. 5 Therefore being justified by faith, we have peace with God through our Lord Jesus Christ." 2 Cor 5:17 "Therefore if any man be in Christ, he is a new creature: old things are passed away; behold, all things are become new. 18 And all things are of God, who hath reconciled us to himself by Jesus Christ, and hath given to us the ministry of reconciliation. ... 21 For he hath made him (*Jesus*) to be sin for us, who knew no sin; that we might be made the righteousness of God in him (*Jesus*)." Eph 4:24 "And that ye put on the new man [*in your self-identity and behaviors*], which after God is created in righteousness and true holiness."

Righteous is a legal status or an assessment of the God-like nature of your thoughts, words, actions and results or products. Righteousness is that propensity or nature to do right, or what allows God to move into the Earth through a human. The righteousness of God is the nature to do only what God would do, to the level God would do it. We are made the righteousness of God in Christ by faith.

Justify also has three meanings:
- The process of proving that you did nothing wrong–a legal action
- The process whereby one is declared righteous, a legal state (imputed or reckoned) whether you did wrong or not and depends on your behavior moment by moment
- The process whereby one is made the righteousness of God in Christ Jesus, a change in nature (new creation); it depends on the righteousness of Jesus and not your behavior moment by moment.

2 Cor 5:21 "For he hath made him to be sin for us, who knew no sin; that we might be made the righteousness of God in him."

This is the wonder of the new creation in Christ Jesus. Your spirit is made brand new, after the image of God, in righteousness (nature of God) and true holiness (desiring to only do what God wants and not do any sin or work of the devil, you see yourself as for the exclusive use of God).

Your very new–creation self is the righteousness of God; it is imputed to you and it is now you. This righteousness gives you eternal *zoe* life. Rom 8:10 "And if Christ be in you, the body is dead because of sin; but the Spirit (*your spirit*) is *zoe*/life because of righteousness."

In the new creation, your spirit does not just **have** *zoe* life, it **is** *zoe* life. Abraham had righteousness imputed to him. In the process of your new creation, it is first imputed to you, and then you are made the righteousness of God. This righteousness is an attribute of God in one who is made a new creation, in the image and likeness of God, in "righteousness and true holiness."

Rom 5:18 "Therefore as by the offence of one judgment came upon all men to condemnation; even so by the righteousness of one the free gift came upon all men unto justification of *zoe*/life."

DISCOVERING OUR REDEMPTION

Now God wants us to bear the fruits of righteousness.

2 Cor 9:10 "And increase the fruits of your righteousness."

Isa 32:17 "And the work of righteousness shall be peace; and the effect of righteousness quietness and assurance for ever."

Isa 62:1 "For Zion's sake will I not hold my peace, and for Jerusalem's sake I will not rest, until the righteousness thereof go forth as brightness, and the salvation thereof as a lamp that burneth. 2 And the Gentiles shall see thy righteousness, and all kings thy glory: and thou shalt be called by a new name, which the mouth of the Lord shall name. 3 Thou shalt also be a crown of glory in the hand of the Lord, and a royal diadem in the hand of thy God."

James 3:17 "But the wisdom that is from above is first pure, then peaceable, gentle, and easy to be intreated, full of mercy and good fruits, without partiality, and without hypocrisy. 18 And the fruit of righteousness is sown in peace of them that make peace."

What does this peace look like? God gave us a definition: Acts 10:36 "The word which God sent unto the children of Israel, preaching peace by Jesus Christ: (he is Lord of all:) 37 that word, I say, ye know, which was published throughout all Judaea, and began from Galilee, after the baptism which John preached; 38 how God anointed Jesus of Nazareth with the Holy Ghost and with power: who went about doing good, and healing all that were oppressed of the devil; for God was with him."

Righteousness is a new-spirit nature with the ability to stand in the Father's presence without condemnation, now or ever, as a full joint-heir with Christ, a son of God, whom our elder brother, Jesus, is not ashamed to call the new-creation people, His brethren. (Heb 2:17, 3:1)

Righteousness is that spirit nature that only wants to be God's perfect reflection on this Earth and to run to God with any issue or just to be in His presence.

All the blessings of God belong to the righteous. Righteous acts done in faith of the goodness of the Lord coming to Earth provide the path for God to make Heaven on Earth. The righteous release this into the Earth by faith. Heb 10:38 "Now the just (*righteous*) shall *zao*/live by faith: but if any man draw back, my soul shall have no pleasure in him. 39 But we are not of them who draw back unto perdition (*the law of sin and death ruling over you and yours*); but of them that believe to the *sozo*/ saving of the soul." The righteous one produces the *zoe*/life of God in the Earth, by faith in God, by His Word, i.e., the Bible, which is His covenant promises.

Here is Psalm 112 with a description of a righteous one that does the righteous acts that create the path for God to move on his benefit. Ps 112 "Praise ye the Lord. Blessed is the man that feareth the Lord, that delighteth greatly in his commandments. 2 **His seed shall be mighty upon earth: the generation of the upright shall be blessed. 3 Wealth and riches shall be in his house: and his righteousness** endureth for ever. 4 Unto the upright there ariseth light in the darkness: he is gracious, and full of compassion, and righteous. 5 A good man sheweth favour, and lendeth: he will guide his affairs with discretion. **6 Surely he shall not be moved for ever: the righteous shall be in everlasting remembrance**. 7 He shall not be afraid of evil tidings: his heart is fixed, trusting in the Lord. 8 His heart is established, he shall not be afraid, until he see his desire upon his enemies. 9 He hath dispersed, he hath given to the poor; **his righteousness endureth for ever; his horn shall be exalted with honour**. 10 The wicked shall see it, and be grieved; he shall gnash with his teeth, and melt away: the desire of the wicked shall perish."

You have all the benefits marked in bold above imputed to you by your initial faith in Jesus. You activate your faith, as you do what this righteous one does—the things that are not in bold. The not-bold items can become your confession and affirmations to write these behaviors on your heart so you do more of them. Use the bold items as your confession of what you now have in Jesus. Your confession of these is what activates them in God. Heb 3:1 "Wherefore, holy brethren, partakers of the heavenly calling, consider the Apostle and High Priest of our profession (*confession*), Christ Jesus."

Righteousness, from God's view, means that He can now move in the Earth through you independent of your sin. Your sin will corrupt the way you think, that is your soul, and that will limit your ability to believe God in certain areas. But when your soul lines up with God, by His Word, in any area, then God can move in the Earth, because Jesus is our Sanctification from sin, not our works.

This is how you build a faith path, through which God can operate in power in the Earth.

1 Cor 1:30 "But of him are ye in Christ Jesus, who of God is made unto us wisdom, and righteousness, and sanctification, and redemption: 31 that, according as it is written, He that glorieth, let him glory in the Lord."

This is about Jesus' perfection, not ours. God gives us Jesus' righteousness, so there is no level higher and no greater level of acceptance and *agape*/love. There is no greater channel by which God can operate in the Earth than a new-creation person, the basic Christian.

When God makes you His righteousness in Jesus, in the new birth, He gives all there is for a human to have.

Col 2:10 "And ye are complete in him (*Jesus*), which is the head of all principality and power."

Righteousness gives us the legal right to the use of the name of Jesus, Lord of All.

Righteousness is more than a power of attorney; it is now our name.

We are Christ's body. He is our head. We have the same name. We are one. He, therefore, calls us Christ.

2 Cor 6:15 "And what concord hath Christ with Belial?"

DISCOVERING OUR REDEMPTION

I know this shatters the very roots of the old man in you.

What He calls us is beyond imagination.

Eph 2:10 "For we are his workmanship, created in Christ Jesus unto good works, which God hath before ordained that we should walk in them." RSV

Righteousness gives us the ability to stand in the presence of diseases of all kinds without fear, in the presence of Satan, as an absolute master, to execute the *agape*/love of God, to set people free.

This is Identification; He has given you His nature in Jesus, when He raised Jesus from the dead. When you learn to operate in the mind of Christ, keep yourself stirred up into His Redemption truth, you will operate as Jesus did. This is what it means to have a new spirit, a new nature, a new tendency to do what God would do. 2 Tim 1:6 "Wherefore I put thee in remembrance that thou stir up the gift of God ... . 7 For God hath not given us the spirit of fear; but of *dunamis*/power (*the all things are possible ability of God*), and of *agape*/love, and of a sound mind (*to think, speak and do as Jesus would do*)."

You can stand in front of any evil situation and say, with confidence, "Devil, this victory has already been given me. Your defeat, in this, is a good work already made for me. I will stand, and I will heal any oppression of yours, and the people will go free and prosper in the Lord. Now, in the name of Jesus, Lord of Heaven and Earth, and my Big Brother, GO! And never return! NOW, GO, in the name of Jesus!"

1 John 2:29 "Everyone that doeth righteousness is begotten of God." How few of us have ever done Righteousness. We have thought it meant only conduct, a carefulness in our walk. That is implied, but that is not "doing righteousness."

Doing righteousness is doing the works that Jesus did with the attitude and desires Jesus had, for we are taking Jesus' place. John 6:28 "Then said they unto him, What shall we do, that we might work the works of God? 29 Jesus answered and said unto them, This is the work of God, that ye believe on him whom he hath sent."

John 9:3 "Jesus answered, Neither hath this man sinned, nor his parents: but that the works of God should be made manifest in him. 4 I must work the works of him that sent me, while it is day: the night cometh, when no man can work. 5 As long as I am in the world, I am the light of the world."

Jesus is now in the world by us, you and me, as members of His Body. These are the works of the nature of God, the works of righteousness.

Righteousness gives us the ability to stand in the presence of God anytime, and to stand in the presence of Satan as absolute victors, and the desire to do both. It gives you the right to hold God accountable to perform His Word, as He cannot lie.

You Have Been Made the Righteousness of God

Heb 6:17 "Wherein God, willing more abundantly to shew unto the heirs of promise the immutability of his counsel (*promise*), confirmed it by an oath: 18 that by two immutable things (*promise and an oath*), in which it was impossible for God to lie, we might have a strong consolation, who have fled for refuge to lay hold upon the hope set before us: 19 which hope we have as an anchor of the soul, both sure and stedfast, and which entereth into that within the veil; 20 whither the forerunner is for us entered, even Jesus, made an high priest for ever after the order of Melchisedec."

Notice in this passage God wants you to hold Him accountable to perform His Word!

How little this has been understood. How little we have majored in being made the righteousness of God in Christ Jesus.

Instead of looking at any lack of Heaven on Earth or any lack of Bible promise, we look at what God does say, and, as Paul told Timothy, we learn how to stir ourselves and others to operate by Holy Spirit.

2 Tim 1:6 "Wherefore I put thee in remembrance that thou stir up the gift of God .... 7 For God hath not given us the spirit of fear; but of *dunamis*/power (*the all-things-are-possible ability of God*), and of *agape*/love, and of a sound mind (*to think, speak and do as Jesus would do*)."

Now God is waiting for us to bring this truth to the front. He wants us to begin to know righteousness, live righteousness, practice righteousness, break Satan's dominion, and to speak with authority and confidence, just as Jesus did.

John 11:42 "And I (*Jesus*) knew that thou hearest me always: but because of the people which stand by I said it, that they may believe that thou hast sent me. 43 And when he thus had spoken, he cried with a loud voice, Lazarus, come forth."

Jesus is our righteousness. John 8:28 "Then said Jesus unto them, When ye have lifted up the Son of man, then shall ye know that I am he, and that I do nothing of myself; but as my Father hath taught me, I speak these things. 29 And he that sent me is with me: the Father hath not left me alone; for I do always those things that please him."

Heb 13:5 "... for he (*Father God*) hath said, I will never leave thee, nor forsake thee."

We cannot hear it enough. 2 Cor 5:16 "Wherefore henceforth know we no man after the flesh: yea, though we have known Christ after the flesh, yet now henceforth know we him no more. 17 Therefore if any man be in Christ, he is a new creature: old things are passed away; behold, all things are become new. 18 And all things are of God, who hath reconciled us to himself by Jesus

DISCOVERING OUR REDEMPTION

Christ, and hath given to us the ministry of reconciliation; 19 to wit, that God was in Christ, reconciling the world unto himself, not imputing their trespasses unto them; and hath committed unto us the word of reconciliation. 20 Now then we are ambassadors for Christ, as though God did beseech you by us: we pray you in Christ's stead, be ye reconciled to God. 21 For he hath made him to be sin for us, who knew no sin; that we might be made the righteousness of God in him. 6:1 We then, as workers together with him, beseech you also that ye receive not the grace of God in vain. 2 (For he saith, I have heard thee in a time accepted, and in the day of *soteria*/salvation have I succoured thee: behold, now is the accepted time; behold, now is the day of *soteria*/salvation.)"

Did you know that when God wants to feel good, He looks at you? You are His workmanship in Christ Jesus. You are not only justified, made righteous to the level and satisfaction of God, but you are made the nature of God's righteousness in Jesus.

Here is a brief affirmation: I am born again of God in Jesus. God dwells in me, Jesus dwells in me, Holy Spirit dwells in me, I am His temple. Zeph 3:17 "The LORD *my* God in the midst of *me* is mighty; he *has saved me and He continues to save me*, he rejoices over *me* with joy; he rests in his love *for me*, he joys over *me* with singing." I am God's *agape* beloved. My name is written in Heaven, and I rejoice in it. My true desires are God's desires. I am a new creation, made in true righteousness and holiness, in the image of God, that is the real me in Jesus. I am His workmanship in Christ Jesus. Father God is my righteousness. Jesus is my righteousness. I love to live in *agape* love for God and to others. I love to live in Holy Spirit *dunamis* power, and I love to live in the mind of Christ. I love to live in thanksgiving, praise, joy and *aiteo* in Holy Spirit. I love God in and by the Scriptures. I am valued by God. God paid Jesus to get me, and God loves me. God desires me. I am the apple of His eye. When God wants to feel good, He looks at me. God will never leave me or forsake me because I am in Jesus by God's grace. God has made me the righteousness of God in Jesus. Thank You, Father! In the name of Jesus, thank You!

Chapter 29

You Have God's Wisdom

You might say this is the summation of it all.

If you have God's ability, God's wisdom, God's Spirit, and you let them loose, by renewing your mind, what beyond-imagination abundance and freedom there will be to your ministry of reconciliation?

The fruit is twofold:
- You no longer sin or you sin less, so you do not have to spend time "cleaning up your sins" in restitution, reconciliation and breaking the power of the devil, where your sin has made a path for him.
- You do those actions more often that allow or provide the path for God to move in the Earth.

The way you stop sinning and release the goodness of the Lord in your life and in the lives of others can start by your right "word or mouth work" of scripture and scriptural confessions, proclamations, affirmations, prayers, thanksgiving, praise, rejoicing, spiritual disciplines and *aiteo*/commands. The good news is that your right acts can release God to work, even while you are still not perfect in others parts of your life.

This is how God can say: Rom 2:4 "… the goodness of God leadeth thee to repentance." This happens as you see God move in power, by you and the name of Jesus, in spite of your sins and not because of your holiness.

DISCOVERING OUR REDEMPTION

You do right actions of *agape*/love that make a path for God to bring Heaven to Earth (not sinning is doing right), such as acts of kindness, mercy, alms, generosity, superior workmanship in all things, acts of love to the lovely and unlovely, helping widows and orphans, deliverance, healing, etc.

You are wise enough to be busy doing the "do's" of God and therefore don't have time to do the "do not's." You are wise enough in the ways of God to be doing more of the word or mouth actions above while you work on doing the physical also, knowing that the more of right mouth actions you do, you will also do more of the works of Jesus.

Walking this way is not just a problem of education, but of taking that information and using it to renew your mind, to letting God loose in you, liberating the ability of God that is within you and letting it out into the world to produce the Kingdom of God. It is not a problem of more power; it is a problem of right acknowledging.

Philem 6 "That the communication of thy faith may become effectual (*producing the works of Jesus and even greater works*) by the *epignosis*/acknowledging (*knowing and becoming a master craftsman*) of every good thing which is in you in Christ Jesus."

Your faith becomes effective as you acknowledge everything that is you in the New Creation in Jesus and start to use Him to demonstrate the Kingdom of God in the Earth.

This is the same message as Holy Spirit gives here: 2 Cor 3:17 "Now the Lord is that Spirit: and where the Spirit of the Lord is, there is liberty. 18 But we all, with open face beholding as in a glass (*mirror*) the glory of the Lord, are changed into the same image from glory to glory, even as by the Spirit of the Lord."

We are transformed as we see the glory, the power and the *agape*/love of God in Jesus working in and through our lives. This is the height of creative visualization. This is Identification. This is changing your self-identity.

Look at the Gospels, look at Jesus and see yourself doing what Jesus said and did. As you see a gap, ask Holy Spirit to teach you, and then start doing what Jesus did. God's plan for you excites Him! Don't worry about out-visualizing God. His inheritance in you and for you is greater than you can think or imagine!

2 Cor 4:5 "For we preach not ourselves, but Christ Jesus the Lord; and ourselves your servants for Jesus' sake. 6 For God, who commanded the light to shine out of darkness, hath shined in our hearts, to give the light of the knowledge of the glory of God in the face of Jesus Christ. 7 But we have this treasure in earthen vessels, that the excellency of the power may be of God, and not of us."

Notice that right knowledge of Christ in you means the power of God works through you.

You Have God's Wisdom

While we are to do man-level works, like giving alms, praise, thanksgiving, helping widows and orphans, feeding the hungry and clothing the naked, He is talking about God-level works done in God-level power, like healing the sick, raising the dead, casting out demons, restoring maimed bodies, multiplying food, stopping typhoons, literally moving mountains and stopping the sun in order to battle. He is saying this God-level power can work through us, as we believe Him in His Word.

Your faith in what He has made you in Jesus is how you work with Him to manifest His plan for you in this life. Eph 3:16 "That he would grant you, according to the riches of his glory, to be strengthened with might by his Spirit in the inner man; 17 that Christ may dwell in your hearts by faith; that ye, being rooted and grounded in *agape*/love, 18 may be able to comprehend with all saints what is the breadth, and length, and depth, and height; 19 and to know the *agape*/love of Christ, which passeth knowledge, that ye might be filled with all the fulness of God. 20 Now unto him that is able to do exceeding abundantly above all that we *aiteo*/ask (*require, demand and expect as due by covenant promise*) or think, according to the power that worketh in us, 21 unto him be glory in the church by Christ Jesus throughout all ages, world without end. Amen."

Your growth, or His freedom in you, is limited by what you do, backed by what you study and what you write on your heart. This is a learn-and-then-go-do Gospel. Much of the knowledge will only come as you actually practice, to demonstrate the Kingdom, as Jesus did, and as He instructed His disciples to do.

This is the same message given in: Eph 4:20 "But ye have not so learned Christ; 21 if so be that ye have heard him, and have been taught by him, as the truth is in Jesus: 22 that ye put off concerning the former conversation the old man, which is corrupt according to the deceitful lusts; 23 and be renewed in the spirit of your mind; 24 and that ye put on the new man, which after God is created in righteousness and true holiness."

Put on that new man and start acting like it.

Remember, as Dr. John Lake said, "It is a law of the human mind that I can act myself into believing quicker than I can believe myself into acting." (Blake, *The Voice of Healing*, Episode 2)

Dr. Lake also said something like this, "At some point you have to stop praying and start believing God will do it. So start doing the thing. Use what you have, and God will give you more." (Blake, *Writings from Africa*, p 99.)

One man saw another at a gas station limping. He reached his hand over, as he pumped gas into his own car, grabbed the limping man's hand and commanded life to flow into him. The first time he did this the limping man said he was better. The Christian repeated this about three times. Each time the man got better and more excited. The limping man, who was pumping gas at the same time, got

DISCOVERING OUR REDEMPTION

healed of a back problem and left that day dancing. This does not have to be like a church service. Just minister life wherever you are and you see a need. That is letting Christ's life flow through you. That is letting God loose in you.

Let this challenge you. We claim we have the Gospel story, yet the Scriptures say that if the Gospel is properly preached, the power of God is released, and those who believe that Gospel will go and do or produce the results of God: Mark 16:15 "And he (*Jesus*) said unto them (*the disciples*), Go ye into all the world, and preach the gospel to every creature. 16 He that believeth and is baptized shall be *sozo*/saved; but he that believeth not shall be damned. 17 And these signs shall follow them that believe [*because of what they heard, they will be motivated to go and continually keep doing the following acts, with the following results*]; In my name shall they cast out devils; they shall speak with new tongues; 18 they shall take up serpents; and if they drink any deadly thing, it shall not hurt them; they shall lay hands on the sick, and they shall recover. 19 So then after the Lord had spoken unto them, he was received up into heaven, and sat on the right hand of God. 20 And they went forth, and preached everywhere, the Lord working with them, and confirming the word with signs following. Amen."

Notice that when the proper Gospel is preached, the resulting new believers will go and do, because they believe the Gospel that Jesus commanded to be preached. The measure of your Gospel is whether or not your converts go and do as Jesus said they would. Have we had that Gospel? Do we want that Gospel? Or will we settle for the power of men, and not God? 1 Cor 2:4 "And my speech and my preaching was not with enticing words of man's wisdom, but in demonstration of the Spirit and of power: 5 that your faith should not stand in the wisdom of men, but in the power of God."

Notice something even more amazing. Just before Jesus issued what many consider an impossible command, even to the point of denying it is valid, Jesus chastised the disciples for their unbelief. The cure for obeying Mark 16:15-18 is to heed the admonition of the Lord in verse 14: Mark 16:14 "Afterward he appeared unto the eleven as they sat at meat, and upbraided them with their unbelief and hardness of heart, because they believed not them which had seen him after he was risen. 15 And he said unto them, Go ye into all the world, and preach the gospel to every creature … ."

For more help on how to obey this command, please see our resources at: www.CovenantPeaceMinistries.com.

It is the Word of grace that Jesus confirms and builds us up, to walk as He made us to be: Acts 20:32 "And now, brethren, I commend you to God, and to the word of his grace, which is able to build you up, and to give you an inheritance among all them which are sanctified."

You Have God's Wisdom

Acts 14:3 "Long time therefore abode they (*Paul and Barnabas*) speaking boldly in the Lord, which gave testimony unto the word of his grace, and granted signs and wonders to be done by their hands."

We mature into Christ as we change our self-identity into the New Creation and see ourselves thus in advance of doing it: Eph 4:13 "Till we all come in the unity of the faith, and of the *epignosis*/knowledge of the Son of God, unto a perfect man, unto the measure of the stature of the fulness of Christ: 14 that we henceforth be no more children, tossed to and fro, and carried about with every wind of doctrine, by the sleight of men, and cunning craftiness, whereby they lie in wait to deceive; 15 but speaking the truth in *agape*/love, may grow up into him in all things, which is the head, even Christ."

Locked up in you today, by the New Creation reality, is the ability of God.

As your mind is renewed, you provide the pathway for Him to get out and bless a hurting world with His glory.

Matt 7:14 "Because strait is the gate, and narrow is the way, which leadeth unto *zoe*/life, and few there be that find it."

Jesus has been made wisdom unto us. So we have the wisdom of God to solve every problem there is and bring Heaven to Earth.

1 Cor 1:30 "But of him are ye in Christ Jesus, who of God is made unto us wisdom, and righteousness, and sanctification, and redemption: 31 that, according as it is written, He that glorieth, let him glory in the Lord."

1 Cor 2:12 "Now we have received, not the spirit of the world, but the spirit which is of God; that we might know the things that are freely given to us of God."

John 16:13 "Howbeit when he, the Spirit of truth, is come, he will guide you into all truth: for he shall not speak of himself; but whatsoever he shall hear, that shall he speak: and he will shew you things to come. 14 He shall glorify me: for he shall receive of mine, and shall shew it unto you. 15 All things that the Father hath are mine: therefore said I, that he shall take of mine, and shall shew it unto you."

Jesus made all of creation, so, with access to His mind, we can know all there is to know, to bless mankind. 1 Cor 2:16 "For who hath known the mind of the Lord, that he may instruct him? But we have the mind of Christ."

James told the babes in Christ that if they lacked wisdom they could ask God for it.

James 1:5-8 "And if any one of you is deficient in wisdom, let him *aiteo*/ask (*require, demand and expect as due by covenant promise, knowing all the requirements have been met in Jesus*) God for it, who gives with open hand to all men, and without upbraiding; and it will be given him. But let him *aiteo*/ask in faith and have no doubt; for he who has doubts is like the surge of the sea, driven by the wind and tossed into spray. A person of that sort must not expect to receive anything from the Lord-such a one is a man of two minds, undecided in every step he takes." WYM

DISCOVERING OUR REDEMPTION

The issue is not to be plagued with doubts. Doubts will come, for the devil knows his job, and he is good at it. The issue is entertaining them, tolerating them and fearing them, rather than putting the promises of the Word of God on your lips as a shield of faith and forcing your mind to think on God and His promises instead.

When tempted by the devil, Jesus, our example, responded the way we are to respond: Matt 4:10 "Then saith Jesus unto him, Get thee hence, Satan: for it is written … ."

If you heed the doubts, you will believe a different word. If you diligently fight, by putting the promises of the God who cannot lie on your lips, you will drive them into your heart. Then, when doubts come, you will not tolerate them but respond as Jesus did, "It is written … !"

2 Cor 10:3 "For though we walk in the flesh, we do not war after the flesh: 4 (For the weapons of our warfare are not carnal, but mighty through God to the pulling down of strong holds;) 5 casting down imaginations, and every high thing that exalteth itself against the knowledge of God, and bringing into captivity every thought to the obedience of Christ."

So when you need to know what to do and how to do it, ask God first. He will give you the answer and how to use it. If you think you are in unbelief, ask Him for the wisdom to believe Him in His Word. Go to the Scriptures, and He will be there.

Go to the Scriptures first, then let God lead you to teachers, books, websites, etc.

You are grown up now. You are single minded in God, by His Word. You have passed the period of babyhood, and now you know that Jesus, the living Word, is your wisdom.

You face circumstances, with His Word as the standard, and not what the fleshly parts of your soul, the mind of the flesh, tries to rule you with. You *lambano*, hold on to the Word of righteousness, *zoe*/life and grace to rule by the Word of God, to bring His Kingdom.

Rom 8:4 "That the righteousness of the law might be fulfilled in us, who walk not after the flesh, but after the Spirit (*of the new creation in the Word of God*). 5 For they that are after the flesh do mind the things of the flesh (*no covenant with God, no agape/love of God and no truth that prevails*); but they that are after the Spirit (*new creation scriptures of the God who cannot lie*) the things of the Spirit. 6 For to be carnally minded (*no covenant, no adoption, no truth and no hope in God*) is death; but to be spiritually minded (*in new-creation realities, so that you are adopted as a son of God, like Jesus, having a covenant of hope, in truth that cannot fail*) is *zoe*/life and peace. 7 Because the carnal mind is enmity against God: for it is not subject to the law of God, neither indeed can be. 8 So then they that are in the flesh cannot please God. 9 But ye are not in the flesh, but in the Spirit, if so be that the Spirit of God dwell in you (*and, thus, a new creation*). Now if any man have not the Spirit of Christ, he is none of his."

You Have God's Wisdom

You define your circumstances by His Word and not His Word by any of the circumstances of your failure. You know that the facts of the world must bow to the truth of God's Word, through you, by faith.

You *aiteo* God for wisdom, and you know it is coming. You know you may be challenged, but it is coming, and when it comes, He will have prepared you to handle it to His glory. [Often, He has to prepare you to receive that wisdom, so you can recognize it and understand what to do with it.]

Wisdom is the ability to use knowledge.

You have the knowledge of the life of God that is in you.

You have the knowledge of the power and authority of the Word.

You have the knowledge of your legal right to use the name of Jesus in your combat with spiritual forces and over creation.

You have the knowledge of the fact that God is actually in your body.

Now you are going to use these mighty facts to bless humanity.

The imprisoned God, at last, is set free, with His Bill of Rights in Jesus, to use us as He pleases.

We are no longer hidden.

People know who we are.

There is a path worn to our cottage, no matter where we live, for we have let God loose in us and have given Him His liberty to heal the sick and to bless the world through us, His sons and daughters.

Titus 2:11 "For the grace of God that bringeth *soteria*/salvation hath appeared to all men, 12 teaching us that, denying ungodliness and worldly lusts, we should *zao*/live soberly, righteously, and godly, in this present world; 13 looking for that blessed hope, and the glorious appearing of the great God and our Saviour Jesus Christ; 14 who gave himself for us, that he might redeem us from all iniquity, and purify unto himself a peculiar people, zealous of good (*God-level*) works. 15 These things speak, and exhort, and rebuke with all authority. Let no man despise thee."

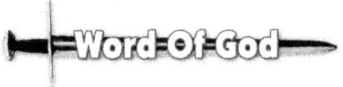

Chapter 30

Why Satan Hates You So Much

Jesus promised or prophesied: <u>Matt 5:10</u> "Blessed and happy and enviably fortunate and spiritually prosperous (in the state in which the born-again child of God enjoys and finds satisfaction in God's favor and salvation, regardless of his outward conditions) are those who are persecuted for righteousness' sake (for being and doing right), for theirs is the kingdom of heaven!" AMP

Then Jesus said: <u>Matt 5:11</u> "Blessed are ye, when men shall revile you, and persecute you, and shall say all manner of evil against you falsely, for my sake. 12 Rejoice, and be exceeding glad: for great is your reward in heaven: for so persecuted they the prophets which were before you."

It may seem that men are persecuting us for righteousness' sake. We heal their sick babies and broken limbs, give their blind sight, raise their dead, cleanse the lepers, cast out devils, give wisdom for great problems and create vibrant economies to feed the people and raise their standard of living, and we receive, in exchange, evil.

But it is really Satan who persecutes us for righteousness' sake.

Satan hates every good and true work of God we do.

Satan fears righteousness more than any other thing.

It is in our continual *lambano*ing for the abundance of grace and the gift of righteousness, through faith in Jesus, that enables us to reign over the devil, for God to bring Heaven to Earth in any situation.

Rom 5:17 "For if by one man's offence death reigned (*as king*) by one; much more they which (*continually*) *lambano*/receive abundance of grace and of the gift of righteousness shall reign (*as a king for Jesus, to bring the Kingdom of God to Earth, as Jesus did*) in *zoe*/life by one, Jesus Christ.)"

On the ground of what God did for us in Christ, when we are born again, we become the righteousness of God, and we have Holy Spirit dwelling in us. That means we have the ability to cast out, to break the power of Satan, to heal the sick, and to raise the dead in the name of Jesus, just as if Jesus were doing it, which He is, through you, right now.

Righteousness by faith in the blood of Jesus gives you confidence to convey deliverance from the fear of Satan and his works, and confidence in God, to fulfill His Word. It is no longer about you; it is about Him and His holiness to bring Heaven to Earth through you.

This brings a new sense of sonship, and this son-consciousness begets a heroic faith. It takes away the sense of spiritual inferiority and utterly destroys the sin-consciousness in us.

We can walk before men just as Jesus did, because we know that we are New Creations. The old life has been utterly destroyed in our spirit, but it does linger in our conscious and unconscious mind. It also lingers in the mind of the devil and the people around you. This is the reason we must renew (and keep renewed) our minds into the mind of Christ.

Every moment of every day you are receiving information that enters your mind and heart, and you must "bring every thought captive to the obedience of Christ," else these thoughts will bring you to the obedience of the devil. You identify and replace all evil thoughts with the Scriptures, that is, with God thoughts. You live out of your heart, your unconscious mind, and that is the reason you must renew your mind. If you do not put in the Spirit-of-God words, the Scriptures, in the Word of grace, you will operate out of the world belief system run by the devil.

Rom 12:2 "Do not be conformed (*continually molded*) to this world (this age), [fashioned after and adapted to its external, superficial customs], but be transformed (changed) by the [entire] renewal of your mind [by its new ideals and its new attitude], so that you may prove [for yourselves] what is the good and acceptable and perfect will of God, even the thing which is good and acceptable and perfect [in His sight for you]." AMP

Here is the self-identity change God commands you to develop in your heart and your mind: Rom 13:10 "*Agape*/love worketh no ill to his neighbour: therefore *agape*/love is the fulfilling of the law. 11 And that, knowing the time, that now it is

DISCOVERING OUR REDEMPTION

high time to awake out of sleep: for now is our *soteria*/salvation nearer than when we believed. 12 The night is far spent, the day is at hand: let us therefore cast off the works of darkness, and let us put on the armour of light. 13 Let us walk honestly, as in the day; not in rioting and drunkenness, not in chambering and wantonness, not in strife and envying. 14 But put ye on the Lord Jesus Christ, and make not provision for the flesh, to fulfil the lusts thereof."

Don't be as a mere man, who looks into the Gospel of the New Creation, the New Testament, and forgets what God has done for him.

James 1:21 "Wherefore lay apart all filthiness and superfluity of naughtiness, and *lambano*/receive with meekness the engrafted word, which is able to *sozo*/save your *psuche*/souls (*lives*). 22 But be ye doers of the word, and not hearers only, deceiving your own selves. 23 For if any be a hearer of the word, and not a doer, he is like unto a man beholding his natural face in a glass (*mirror*): 24 for he beholdeth himself, and goeth his way, and straightway forgetteth what manner of man he was (*your new-creation spirit self*). 25 But whoso looketh into the perfect law of liberty, and continueth therein, he being not a forgetful hearer, but a doer of the work, this man shall be blessed in his deed. 26 If any man among you seem to be religious, and bridleth not his tongue, but deceiveth his own heart, this man's religion (*his walk with God*) is vain (*empty, useless, produces only wood, hay and stubble, which will not survive the Day of Judgment*). 27 Pure religion and undefiled before God and the Father is this, To visit the fatherless and widows in their affliction, and to keep himself unspotted from the world."

You look at yourself, by faith, see Jesus in your face, and then go do what Jesus would do, knowing Holy Spirit is ever there to help you in whatever is needed.

Holy Spirit is there in you, but just like two people speaking languages the other cannot understand, little communication takes place until you can learn a common language. It is up to us to learn the language of Heaven, the language of *agape*/love, the Word of Christ in the Scriptures, to work with and have Holy Spirit effectively help us.

1 Cor 2:16 "For who hath known the mind of the Lord, that he may instruct him? But we have the mind of Christ."

1 Cor 2:12 "Now we have received, not the spirit of the world, but the spirit which is of God; that we might know the things that are freely given to us of God."

We know that every sin we ever committed was remitted 2000 years ago.

Rom 4:25 "Who was betrayed and put to death because of our misdeeds and was raised to secure our justification (our acquittal), [making our account balance and absolving us from all guilt before God *and healing us back to original before-Adam's-sin value and now blessing us in Christ with every spiritual blessing in heavenly places*]." AMP

We know the curse for every sin we commit was healed 2000 years ago. "By His stripes we were healed."

Why Satan Hates You So Much

1 Pet 2:24 "Who his own self bare our sins in his own body on the tree, that we, being dead to sins, should *zao*/live unto righteousness: by whose stripes ye were healed."

Being healed, whole, and strong is righteousness in the body.

Operating in the mind of Christ is righteousness in our soul.

We know that every imperfection we perform or fail to perform was paid for and healed in the body, soul and spirit of Jesus 2000 years ago.

We know that blood was taken to the heavenly Altar for this purpose 2000 years ago and will never die!

This wonderful event occurred 2000 years ago, and yet it is still going strong!

We know that the blood of Jesus never stops healing; that all sufficient blood is more than enough!

Rom 5:8 "But God commendeth his *agape*/love toward us, in that, while we were yet sinners, Christ died for us. 9 Much more then, being now justified by his blood, we shall be *sozo*/saved from wrath through him. 10 For if, when we were enemies, we were reconciled to God by the death of his Son, much more, being reconciled, we shall be *sozo*/saved by his *zoe*/life. 11 And not only so, but we also joy in God through our Lord Jesus Christ, by whom we have now received the atonement (*reconciliation*)."

Heb 12:24 "And to Jesus the mediator of the new covenant, and to the blood of sprinkling, that speaketh better things than that of Abel."

We know that the sins that we committed since we were born again, ignorantly or otherwise, have been forgiven and remitted 2000 years ago, and we stand in the presence of God, just as Jesus did when He walked the Earth, a beloved child in the eyes of a loving Father, who knows all our misdeeds have already been paid for and healed, to the level of Jesus Himself.

Dare we take our stand and make this confession boldly?

Heb 13:15 "Through Him (*Jesus*), therefore, let us constantly and at all times offer up to God a sacrifice of praise, which is the fruit of lips that thankfully acknowledge and confess and glorify His name. [Lev 7:12; Isa 57:19; Hos 14:2.] AMP

Satan seeks to keep us sin conscious and to rob us of our son consciousness.

As long as he can keep us sin conscious, we are whipped; we will have no confidence in God, and it will be all about us and our lack.

As long as the devil can keep us conscious that circumstances are greater than the promises of God, we are whipped. Our emotions are on a roller coaster that only the devil could enjoy.

The devil preaches continually, in evil and unhappy circumstances, thoughts and words, in persecution against us. He knows he cannot get us un-born again, so his best hope is to keep us ignorant to the truth of our Redemption, so we do not act to the level of what God has provided for us.

DISCOVERING OUR REDEMPTION

A great part of the teaching being done in churches today tends to keep the people under condemnation. That creates mental assent, in which they say, "Oh yes, that is a great promise, but I cannot depend on it. Who knows how God might let you down, to teach you a lesson?" Who can stand and fight with such an attitude?

For the most part, the church ministry has never realized that its work is to free men from sin consciousness and make them God conscious, Son conscious, Victory conscious, Faith conscious, Love conscious, Righteousness conscious, Reconciliation conscious, Redemption conscious, Christ's dominion conscious, Christ in you conscious, Adoption, Betrothal, Grace and Christ's power in you conscious.

When we realize that we have been born of love and that we have the love nature of God in us, we will begin to show forth the fragrance of Heaven.

Rom 8:37 "Nay, in all these things we are more than conquerors … ."

To be a conqueror, you have to be in battles and gain victories. You can have your victory or use the power of Jesus' victory. You know you may be knocked down, but you are never out! Phil 4:13 "I can do all things through Christ which strengtheneth me."

When we become Jesus'–victory-in-and-through-us conscious, we will arise as a strong man out of sleep and take our place among the victors.

Rom 13:11 "And that, knowing the time, that now it is high time to awake out of sleep: for now is our *soteria*/salvation nearer than when we believed. 12 The night is far spent, the day is at hand: let us therefore cast off the works of darkness, and let us put on the armour of light. 13 Let us walk honestly, as in the day; not in rioting and drunkenness, not in chambering and wantonness, not in strife and envying. 14 But put ye on the Lord Jesus Christ, and make not provision for the flesh, to fulfil the lusts thereof."

The Son has made us free. Let us stand fast in the liberty wherewith His Redemption has set us free.

Col 3:1 "If ye then be risen with Christ, seek those things which are above, where Christ sitteth on the right hand of God. 2 Set your affection on things above, not on things on the earth. 3 For ye are dead, and your *zoe*/life is hid with Christ in God."

Walk the halls of the Supreme Court of Creation, and see the blood of Jesus that purchased your eternal Redemption and cries better things, from a better covenant than that of Moses.

Acts 13:38 "Be it known unto you therefore, men and brethren, that through this man is preached unto you the *aphesis*/forgiveness (*remission, purging, washing, removal, obliteration and putting away*) of sins: 39 and by him all that believe are justified from all things, from which ye could not be justified by the law of Moses."

Why Satan Hates You So Much

Luke 24:46 "And said unto them, Thus it is written, and thus it behoved Christ to suffer, and to rise from the dead the third day: 47 and that repentance (*that every man will have to acknowledge Jesus as Lord one day, and God, who* agape/*loves you, sent His* agape/*love to Earth through Jesus*) and *aphesis*/remission (*purging, obliteration, removal and putting away*) of sins should be preached in his name among all nations, beginning at Jerusalem."

It is not about your righteousness, but Jesus'. 2 Cor 5:21 "For *Father God* hath made *Jesus* to be sin for us, who knew no sin; that we might be made the righteousness of *Father* God in *Jesus*."

Your sin is not the issue; your receiving and engaging the power of the blood is.

We know Satan attacks the Word, so that we will be offended at God, others or ourselves. Satan does not care who we are offended by or at, just that we are offended, because unforgiveness is his work and produces his fruit. Satan's two primary weapons are idolatry, seeking other sources than God, and offense, or unforgiveness, against God or His people.

Jesus told the Parable of the Sower so we could know the process of how to bring the Word of God to pass in every circumstance, and that our enemy, the devil, will be working to get us offended, if at all possible.

This parable reveals how the devil persecutes us, through ignorance, offense or distraction, to prevent the Word of God from bearing the fruits of righteousness.

Luke 8:10 "And he (*Jesus*) said, Unto you it is given to know the mysteries of the kingdom of God: but to others in parables; that seeing they might not see, and hearing they might not understand. 11 Now the parable is this: The seed is the Word of God."

Matt 13:18 "Hear ye therefore the parable of the sower. 19 When any one heareth the word of the kingdom, and understandeth it not, then cometh the wicked one, and catcheth away that which was sown in his heart. This is he which received seed by the way side. 20 But he that received the seed into stony places, the same is he that heareth the word, and anon with joy *lambano*/receiveth it; 21 yet hath he not root in himself, but dureth for a while: for when tribulation or persecution ariseth because of the word, by and by he is offended. 22 He also that received seed among the thorns is he that heareth the word; and the care of this world, and the deceitfulness of riches, choke the word, and he becometh unfruitful. 23 But he that received seed into the good ground is he that heareth the word, and understandeth it; which also beareth fruit, and bringeth forth, some an hundredfold, some sixty, some thirty."

This is the primary mechanism of bringing the Kingdom of God to Earth and how to defeat the devil in the process. Every act of the Kingdom of God is an act against the kingdom of darkness.

DISCOVERING OUR REDEMPTION

Whenever we hear the Word of God the devil comes and takes away that which we do not understand. Therefore, ignorance and dullness of God in His Word are never bliss!

If we hold on to a promise of God and start to believe it, the devil will attack in ways designed to convince us that it cannot work. If we remain faithful through that, he then attempts to distract us with prosperity and worldly desires. They may not be wrong, but they keep you distracted and your heart divided. The victor counts all this joy and holds on, with a clean heart toward God and man, and, in the end, produces, not normal or man-fruit, but super-normal or God-fruit.

So we are persecuted in the physical world and in our hearts. We are attacked mercilessly, in an attempt to get us to give up and take defeat instead of standing in victory.

2 Cor 10:3 "For though we walk in the flesh, we do not war after the flesh: 4 (for the weapons of our warfare are not carnal, but mighty through God to the pulling down of strong holds;) 5 casting down imaginations, and every high thing that exalteth itself against the knowledge of God, and bringing into captivity every thought to the obedience of Christ; 6 and having in a readiness to revenge all disobedience, when your obedience is fulfilled."

We stand by taking the Word of grace in Jesus and using it to defeat the devil. You *lambano*/hold and proclaim that Word and command the devil and his evil works to go, in the name of Jesus, until you see the victory. You major in the Word of Redemption, Salvation, Peace, Grace, Righteousness, *Zoe* Life, Faith, *Agape* Love, Identification, Adoption, Betrothal, Light, Hope of Glory, Holy Spirit Power, Christ's mind in you, Name of Jesus, Comfort and Reconciliation. This is standing to defeat the devil, as he persecutes righteousness, for this is what you are made for. And the devil has spent 2000 years keeping us ignorant of these facts.

The more we grow in the Gospel, we will: Rom 16:20 "And the God of peace shall bruise Satan under your feet shortly *(as shattered glass)*. The grace of our Lord Jesus Christ be with you *[to know, will, be and do this]*. Amen."

Hos 4:6 "My people are destroyed for lack of knowledge ... ." And the more we *epignosis* know to being master craftsmen in what we have and who we are in Christ the greater our testimony in Christ. Rev 12:11 "And they *(the saints)* overcame him *(Satan)* by the blood of the Lamb, and by the word of their testimony; and they *agape*/loved not their *psuche*/lives *(souls)* unto the death."

Satan cannot get to God, but while we are on this Earth, he can get to us to hurt Father God. The more we grow in the *epignosis* knowledge of God and the work of Jesus in our Redemption, the more we destroy and finally defeat Satan for and through Jesus by Holy Spirit to the glory of Father God.

Isa 11:9 ... For the earth shall be full of the knowledge of the Lord, as the waters cover the sea.

PART VI

UNDERSTANDING WHAT WE NEED TO DO NOW

CHAPTER 31

KNOWING THE WILL OF GOD

This is a problem that bothers most of God's people: How to know the will of the Father.

The will of the Father is wrapped up in His Word. Jesus said, John 6:38 "I came down from heaven not to do mine own will, but the will of Him that sent me." RSV

Jesus knew what the Father's will was. He said, "I always do the things that are pleasing in His sight."

John 8:28 "Then said Jesus unto them, When ye have lifted up the Son of man, then shall ye know that I am he, and that I do nothing of myself; but as my Father hath taught me, I speak these things. 29 And he that sent me is with me: the Father hath not left me alone; for I do always those things that please him."

Paul said, in 2 Cor 5, that he made it his business to be well pleasing to the Father. 2 Cor 5:9 "Wherefore we labour, that, whether present or absent, we may be accepted of him. 10 For we must all appear before the judgment seat of Christ; that every one may receive the things done in his body, according to that he hath done, whether it be good or bad. 11 Knowing therefore the terror of the Lord, we persuade men; but we are made manifest unto God; and I trust also are made manifest in your consciences. 12 For we commend not ourselves again unto you, but give you occasion to glory on our behalf, that ye may have somewhat to answer

DISCOVERING OUR REDEMPTION

them which glory in appearance, and not in heart. 13 For whether we be beside ourselves, it is to God: or whether we be sober, it is for your cause."

If Jesus could please the Father and do His will, and if Paul could please the Father, know His will and do it, then it is possible for us to do it too.

What are the grounds for such an assurance? In the first place, we have God's mind and His will in His Word. It is the surest way for you to deal with God on a personal level.

Heb 4:11 "Let us labour therefore to enter into that rest, lest any man fall after the same example of unbelief. 12 For the word of God is quick, and powerful, and sharper than any twoedged sword, piercing even to the dividing asunder of *psuche/*soul (*life*) and spirit, and of the joints and marrow, and is a discerner of the thoughts and intents of the heart. 13 Neither is there any creature that is not manifest in his sight: but all things are naked and opened unto the eyes of him with whom we have to do. 14 Seeing then that we have a great high priest, that is passed into the heavens, Jesus the Son of God, let us hold fast our profession (*confession of God's* agape/*love toward us in our redemption and new creation benefits in Jesus*). 15 For we have not an high priest which cannot be touched with the feeling of our infirmities; but was in all points tempted like as we are, yet without sin. 16 Let us therefore come boldly unto the throne of grace, that we may *lambano*/obtain mercy, and find (*perceive*) grace to help in time of need."

If we search the Word diligently, allowing Holy Spirit to guide us in it, we will achieve spiritual growth and development through our constant meditations in the Word, so that His will and purpose will become an unconscious consciousness in us. We must be diligent every day, for we know that this means time spent in hours, not minutes, and for at least 90 days, with right emotions, to write particular truths on our hearts so they become life to us. This means many 90-day programs, to write and maintain God's Word in our hearts. We go to the Word as a feast, and if not, we know something is challenging our fellowship with the Father.

He said, "Let the Word of Christ dwell in you richly, admonishing you, building you up."

Col 3:16 "Let the word of Christ dwell in you richly in all wisdom (*building you up to make the right decisions and actions in every way*); teaching and admonishing one another (*to build you up into the* agape/*love of God*) in psalms and hymns and spiritual songs, singing with grace in your hearts to the Lord. 17 And whatsoever ye do in word or deed, do all in the name of the Lord Jesus, giving thanks to God and the Father by him."

When Paul said good-bye to the elders of the Ephesian church, he sent a message through them to their people: "I commend you to the Word of His Grace which is able to build you up and give you the inheritance among them that are sanctified." (Acts 20:32)

Col. 1:9 "For this cause also since the day we heard, do not cease to pray and make request for you, that you may be filled with the *epignosis*/knowledge of His will in all spiritual wisdom and understanding, to walk worthily of the Lord unto all pleasing, bearing fruit in every good work, and increasing in the *epignosis*/knowledge of God."

This word *knowledge* comes from the Greek word *epignosis*, which means correct knowledge, full, complete knowledge where you experience and operate in that knowledge as a master craftsman. It is not just academic or having a low level of skill. It is the knowledge of an expert, a master craftsman, a mature and complete son of God.

We are to be filled with correct knowledge as information, and then the Lord gives us wisdom to use this perfect knowledge by doing the Word. We grow in experiential knowledge, as we do it, to the point we are expert and producing the results associated with that Word.

Someone may say, "It does not seem credible that we could have perfect knowledge." Why shouldn't we? We have a perfect Revelation of God's will. The Bible is a perfect book, Holy Spirit is a perfect teacher, and we are perfect new creations, created in the image of the perfect Christ Jesus. We are made now to God's level of delight and satisfaction. Everything we need is in Jesus: Col 2:9 "For in him (*Jesus*) dwelleth all the fulness of the Godhead bodily. 10 And ye are complete in him, which is the head of all principality and power."

Thus, the promises of God in the Scriptures are not incredible, but highly credible, coming from the God who cannot lie.

Num 23:19 "God is not a man, that he should lie; neither the son of man, that he should repent: hath he said, and shall he not do it? or hath he spoken, and shall he not make it good?"

Jer 1:12 "Then said the LORD unto me, Thou hast well seen: for I will hasten my word to perform it."

God has provided a test for us so that we can know it is He who is speaking to us. Besides having the entire Bible in our hearts, we are told also to deal directly with the spiritual realm, to validate our thoughts, by challenging the source of every thought. 1 John 4:1 "*Agape*/beloved, believe not every spirit, but try the spirits whether they are of God: because many false prophets are gone out into the world. 2 Hereby know ye the Spirit of God: every spirit that confesseth that Jesus Christ is come in the flesh is of God: 3 and every spirit that confesseth not that Jesus Christ is come in the flesh is not of God: and this is that spirit of antichrist, whereof ye have heard that it should come; and even now already is it in the world."

This command is from God and is one of the 1,050 or so New Testament commands for successful Christian life. The *beloved* in verse 1 includes the Christian people John was writing to. A definition for *prophet* is "one who speaks for a

DISCOVERING OUR REDEMPTION

spirit." A false prophet is one who does not speak for God, but, rather, for the devil/spirit of antichrist/error. Any Christian not speaking perfect truth is not speaking perfectly in God and has some degree of error. John was warning the early Christians that error starts with accepting untested apparent truth in our thoughts, leading to more and more vocal/outward deception, so that the evil spirits can then speak freely though Christian people. The same result is even worse among men in general.

A hallmark of our time is deceiving spirits so captivating that they deceive even the elect. Mark 13:22 "For false Christs and false prophets shall rise, and shall shew signs and wonders, to seduce, if it were possible, even the elect." Matt 16:23 "But he (*Jesus*) turned, and said unto Peter, Get thee behind me, Satan: thou art an offence unto me: for thou savourest not the things that be of God, but those that be of men." Luke 9:53 "And they did not receive him, because his face was as though he would go to Jerusalem. 54 And when his disciples James and John saw this, they said, Lord, wilt thou that we command fire to come down from heaven, and consume them, even as Elias did? 55 But he turned, and rebuked them, and said, Ye know not what manner of spirit ye are of." Wow, they were deceived by the devil, even as they talked with Jesus!

There are several specific examples of Christians being deceived in the New Testament. For example, we have the dramatic events related in Galatians, where Peter no longer thought in the mind of Christ (Gal 2:11-16) and was publicly rebuked by Paul. The conclusion of this was the heart of the mighty work of God in Jesus: Gal 2:21 "I do not frustrate the grace of God: for if righteousness come by the law, then Christ is dead in vain."

So Peter was in great deception in this case, not to mention the entire church in Galatia: Gal 3:1 "O foolish Galatians, who hath bewitched you, that ye should not obey the truth, before whose eyes Jesus Christ hath been evidently set forth, crucified among you?"

Concerning other Christians in deception, Paul wrote: 1 Tim 1:19 "Holding faith, and a good conscience; which some having put away concerning faith have made shipwreck: 20 of whom is Hymenaeus and Alexander; whom I have delivered unto Satan, that they may learn not to blaspheme."

Just as Satan deceived Adam and Eve, and the Galatians, with false arguments and doubts that essentially attacked the integrity and honesty of God and the work of Jesus Christ by the cross, the devil is still at it. Here is a source of antichrist and error/deception 1 John 2:15 "*Agape*/love not the world, neither the things that are in the world. If any man *agape*/love the world, the *agape*/love of the Father is not (*operative*) in him. 16 For all that is in the world, the lust of the flesh, and the lust of the eyes, and the pride of *bios*/life, is not of the Father, but is of the world. 17 And the world passeth away, and the lust thereof: but he that doeth the will of God abideth for ever." In this command, Holy Spirit is telling Christians to continually validate who and what we are loving in our thoughts, words and actions.

This passage in 1 John 4:1-3 tells us that many of the thoughts that address or occupy our minds are not just from us, but from other spirits, both God's and the devil's, and we are to directly address the source of our thoughts, to find out their origins. We are to command the source of our thought to confess that "Jesus Christ is come in the flesh"–an exact formula. If the thought is from God, then God will be pleased with your obedience to His Word. After all, this is His command on how to avoid and refute deception and doubts, and Holy Spirit will gladly respond, and devils or lying, antichrist, spirits of error will not.

One way to perform this 1 John 4:1-3 scripture is when you are aware of any important thoughts (especially decisions, scripture interpretations or assessments of people and situations). *Confess* means to agree that it is true by repeating it back. So, in your mind, or out loud, command the source of the thought to confess (i.e., usually confess back to your mind, but if you see angels/spiritual beings that appear in the flesh, follow the same procedure), "Jesus Christ is come in the flesh." This is a command, and you are a child of God, and you should expect to hear the exact wording back. If you do not hear the exact same confession of "Jesus Christ is/has come in the flesh," in reply (and rather quickly), then the source of the thought is not God. Command it to go, in the name of Jesus, and ask the Lord to bring truth into your life in that particular area.

If you hear the exact wording, then the thought is from God, as in verse 4:2. In this case, thank Him for confirming His Word, and respond appropriately to what you have heard. If you want to know the will of God, He has given this method. Like many things of the spirit in God, you will become more proficient the more you do it.

What follows is a simple sequence that can be followed upon becoming aware of a new thought. First ask or think, "Lord, is that You?" Then wait for a yes or no in your mind. Then, whatever you hear (silence is usually the same as a "no"), command that spirit to confess that Jesus Christ is come in the flesh, in the name of Jesus, right now. If you hear, "Jesus Christ is come in the flesh," per verse 1 John 4:2, that is Holy Spirit. If not, command it to go, now, in the name of Jesus, and ignore the thought. Then quote a refuting scripture against the thought, and ask the Lord to teach you His ways in that area.

Jesus said: John 10:27 "My sheep hear my voice, and I know them, and they follow me." First of all, the word for *sheep* in this scripture means a mature ewe/female sheep, not a young lamb. Christian maturity is not measured by how long you have been a Christian, but how much you are like Jesus in your actual walk right now. While healings and miracles are included, even immature Christians can work miracles, per Mark 16 and 1 Cor 12.

DISCOVERING OUR REDEMPTION

If you are mature in Christ, then: 1 John 2:5 "But whoso keepeth his word, in him verily is the *agape*/love of God perfected: hereby know we that we are in him. 6 He that saith he abideth in him ought himself also so to walk, even as he walked." Until we walk in this maturity of perfected *agape*/love, to the measure of the fullness of Christ, and grow into Him in all things, per Eph 4:13-15, we need to obey 1 John 4:1-3.

The person with a Christ-like mind, operating, not in the spirit of fear and unbelief, but in the spirit of power, *agape*/love and a sound mind, wants to know this is God speaking and that they are walking in the light of truth by Holy Spirit and not a deceiving angel of darkness. This is no different than the verification processes used in a bank for cashing a check, or in the military upon receipt of orders of any kind. In both cases, identification and validation are required. This is a war, and you need to know who is talking to you. To a banker or a soldier, verification is a key part of determining correct behavior.

Here is the "doing truth" attitude we should have in this process: John 3:20 "For every one that doeth evil hateth the light, neither cometh to the light, lest his deeds should be reproved. 21 But he that doeth truth cometh to the light, that his deeds may be made manifest, that they are wrought in God."

Eph 5:10 "Proving what is acceptable unto the Lord. 11 And have no fellowship with the unfruitful works of darkness, but rather reprove them. 12 For it is a shame even to speak of those things which are done of them in secret. 13 But all things that are reproved are made manifest by the light: for whatsoever doth make manifest is light. 14 Wherefore he saith, Awake thou that sleepest, and arise from the dead, and Christ shall give thee light. 15 See then that ye walk circumspectly, not as fools, but as wise, 16 redeeming the time, because the days are evil. 17 Wherefore be ye not unwise, but understanding what the will of the Lord is."

1 Thes 5:18 "In every thing give thanks: for this is the will of God in Christ Jesus concerning you. 19 Quench not the Spirit. 20 Despise not prophesyings. 21 Prove all things; hold fast that which is good. 22 Abstain from all appearance of evil. 23 And the very God of peace sanctify you wholly; and I pray God your whole spirit and *psuche*/soul (*life*) and body be preserved blameless unto the coming of our Lord Jesus Christ."

Luke 16:13 "No servant can serve two masters: for either he will hate the one, and *agape*/love the other; or else he will hold to the one, and despise the other. Ye cannot serve God and mammon. ... 15 And he said unto them, Ye are they which justify yourselves before men; but God knoweth your hearts: for that which is highly esteemed among men is abomination in the sight of God."

We have perfect righteousness, the righteousness of God. There is none greater.

We have a perfect relationship, and God says we have become partakers of the very fullness of Christ.

John 1:16 "And of his fulness have all we received, and grace for grace. 17 For the law was given by Moses, but grace and truth came by Jesus Christ."

Our Redemption is perfect, a completed Redemption that meets every need of the human, every desire of God and answers every challenge with divine fullness.

If this is true, I don't know why we cannot have complete knowledge, sufficient to accomplish all God has for us in our generation. I want you to notice, in John 3:3-36, we are born "from above."

The new birth is not a work of psychology or of human philosophy or of human ability.

We are born 1 Pet 1:23 "... not of corruptible things but of incorruptible of the Word of God which *zao*/liveth and abideth for ever."

James tells us that God, of His Own will, begat us. James 1:17 "Every good gift and every perfect gift is from above, and cometh down from the Father of lights, with whom is no variableness, neither shadow of turning. 18 Of his own will begat he us with the word of truth, that we should be a kind of firstfruits of his creatures."

John. 1:13 "We are born not of blood, nor of the will of the flesh nor of the will of man, but of God."

The new creation is God's idea, for His own benefit, and we are the object of His *agape* love.

The new creation is the work of the Holy Spirit through the Word. It is a perfect work.

It makes us complete in Jesus.

Col 2:10 "And ye are complete in him (*Jesus Christ*), which is the head of all principality and power."

Rom 8:1 "There is therefore now no condemnation to them which are in Christ Jesus." If you who read this can accept the Word, you will begin to blossom and bear fruits of righteousness, peace and joy that you have never known before.

We have been preached at for so many years the idea that we are poor, miserable creatures, that we are unworthy and unfit, and this was confirmed through misapplied Scriptures (those that were written to the Jews when they were in apostasy, and not to the church). Also scriptures referring to the unregenerate are often applied to the church until the church has an inferiority complex in regard to sin and the new self-image from the new creation. [Unless a scripture clearly states otherwise, we are to assume every scripture is to and for God's people today. In the New Testament, every scripture is for and directly to Christians. From Romans to Revelation, there are very few, if any, letters written to successful Christians. Instead, like Corinthians, where Paul calls the believers immature and acting like mere normal men, they are written to correct major errors among Christians and have very little to do with non-Christians.]

DISCOVERING OUR REDEMPTION

The church has lived in the realm of sin-consciousness and a sense of unworthiness so long that the Word of God in its totality, and specifically the Word of Christ and of Grace, has little effect upon it.

We want to break these false concepts today. The Word of God is a perfect message, and you may have perfect knowledge of the Father's will through it.

It would be interesting to look up these scriptures in their context.

Eph 1:17 "That the God of our Lord Jesus Christ, the Father of glory, may give unto you the spirit of wisdom and revelation in the *epignosis*/knowledge of him."

It is not the knowledge of the senses, but the knowledge of Him that provides us a path in truth, and Holy Spirit will guide your heart into this.

Eph 4:13 "Till we all come in the unity of the faith and the *epignosis*/knowledge of the Son of God, unto a perfect *full-grown man*, unto the measure of the stature of the fulness of Christ."

There is a complete and full knowledge toward which we are to grow.

This expression occurs 12 or 14 times in the New Testament, especially in the Epistles.

This is a clear indication that the Father expects us to know His will.

Col. 1:12 (Rotherham's translation), "Giving thanks unto the Father who has given us the ability to enjoy our share of the inheritance of the saints in light."

The Greek word *dunamas* or *dunamis* translated "power" means ability.

God has given us His ability to know or share of His will and thus to know what our share is in the inheritance of the saints in light.

For Jesus said: John 14:16 "And I will pray the Father, and he shall give you another Comforter, that he may abide with you for ever; 17 even the Spirit of truth; whom the world cannot receive, because it seeth him not, neither knoweth him: but ye know him; for he dwelleth with you, and shall be in you. 18 I will not leave you comfortless: I will come to you."

John 14:26 "But the Comforter, which is the Holy Ghost, whom the Father will send in my name, he shall teach you all things, and bring all things to your remembrance, whatsoever I have said unto you."

John 16:13 "Howbeit when he, the Spirit of truth, is come, he will guide you into all truth: for he shall not speak of himself; but whatsoever he shall hear, that shall he speak: and he will shew you things to come. 14 He shall glorify me: for he shall receive of mine, and shall shew it unto you. 15 All things that the Father hath are mine: therefore said I, that he shall take of mine, and shall shew it unto you."

1 Cor 2:9 "But as it is written, Eye hath not seen, nor ear heard, neither have entered into the heart of man, the things which God hath prepared for them that *agape*/love him. 10 But God hath revealed them unto us by his Spirit: for the Spirit searcheth all things, yea, the deep things of God. 11 For what man knoweth the things of a man, save the spirit of man which is in him? even so the things of God

knoweth no man, but the Spirit of God. 12 Now we have received, not the spirit of the world, but the spirit which is of God; that we might know the things that are freely given to us of God."

Philem 6 "That the communication of thy faith may become effectual by the acknowledging of every good thing which is in you in Christ Jesus."

We have the ability. It is a God-given ability. It is the ability of God–Holy Spirit. We have Holy Spirit, whom Jesus said would guide us into all truth. He is the same Spirit of Jesus:

Rom 8:11 "But if the Spirit of him that raised up Jesus from the dead dwell in you, he that raised up Christ from the dead shall also quicken your mortal bodies by his Spirit that dwelleth in you."

Gal 4:4 "But when the fulness of the time was come, God sent forth his Son, made of a woman, made under the law, 5 to redeem them that were under the law, that we might receive the adoption of sons. 6 And because ye are sons, God hath sent forth the Spirit of his Son into your hearts, crying, Abba (*Daddy*), Father. 7 Wherefore thou art no more a servant, but a son; and if a son, then an heir of God through Christ."

He is our Teacher, our Guide, our indwelling Instructor.

I cannot see where there is any ground for us to live in weakness and failure and ignorance of the Father's will, of our place and standing in Christ and of our rights and privileges in and for God.

We have no more right to dishonor the Father and dishonor Jesus than Jesus had when He walked here on Earth.

We are the sons and daughters of God. We are heirs of God and joint-heirs with Jesus Christ. Rom 8:16 "The Spirit itself beareth witness with our spirit, that we are the children (*sons*) of God: 17 and if children, then heirs; heirs of God, and joint-heirs with Christ; if so be that we suffer with him, that we may be also glorified together."

We have privileges and rights in the family.

Our first privilege is to make the heart of the Father glad.

We do this by knowing that the Scriptures reveal the Father's will. The Gospels show how to operate in the Father's will. The Epistles teach us to appreciate the Father's will.

The Great Teacher of God is in us, Holy Spirit. As we go to the Word to understand God and how to operate with God, we will learn to know Father's will.

John 7:16 "Jesus answered them, and said, My doctrine is not mine, but his that sent me. 17 If any man will do his will, he shall know of the doctrine, whether it be of God, or whether I speak of myself. 18 He that speaketh of himself seeketh his own glory: but he that seeketh his glory that sent him, the same is true, and no unrighteousness is in him."

DISCOVERING OUR REDEMPTION

We have been commanded to walk in *agape*/love and to believe on the name of Jesus, to use it as a weapon, to bring the *agape*/love of God to Earth. 1 John 3:23 "And this is his commandment, that we should believe on the name of his Son Jesus Christ, and *agape*/love one another, as he gave us commandment."

We can start with these and develop a more perfect understanding of the will of God by renewing our minds with diligent effort. Rom 12:2 "And be not conformed to this world: but be ye transformed by the renewing of your mind, that ye may prove what is that good, and acceptable, and perfect, will of God."

This is His will for the average believer of the Gospel: Mark 16:17 "And these signs shall follow them that believe; In my name shall they cast out devils; they shall speak with new tongues; 18 they shall take up serpents; and if they drink any deadly thing, it shall not hurt them; they shall lay hands on the sick, and they shall recover."

Besides the miracles, exciting tools for the new believer and meat for the mature believer, we are to walk in *agape* love in every aspect of our lives.

On walking in *agape*/love God is talking about walking in all His law, except that which is removed in Jesus (temple, separation, loss of Holy Spirit, etc). If it is not expressly improved in the New Testament, it is still how we are to walk to provide the path that God can inhabit and bring the Kingdom of God to Earth. This has never changed.

Rom 13:7 "Render therefore to all their dues: tribute to whom tribute is due; custom to whom custom; fear to whom fear; honour to whom honour. 8 Owe no man any thing, but to *agape*/love one another: for he that *agape*/loveth another hath fulfilled the law. 9 For this, Thou shalt not commit adultery, Thou shalt not kill, Thou shalt not steal, Thou shalt not bear false witness, Thou shalt not covet; and if there be any other commandment, it is briefly comprehended in this saying, namely, Thou shalt *agape*/love thy neighbour as thyself. 10 *Agape*/love worketh no ill to his neighbour: therefore *agape*/love is the fulfilling of the law."

So it is still the entire will of God now, for all men: Luke 10:25 "And, behold, a certain lawyer stood up, and tempted him, saying, Master, what shall I do to inherit eternal *zoe*/life? 26 He said unto him, What is written in the law? how readest thou? 27 And he (*Jesus*) answering said, Thou shalt *agape*/love the Lord thy God with all thy heart, and with all thy *psuche*/soul (*life*), and with all thy strength (*power, ability, skill, money*), and with all thy mind (*imagination, understanding, hopes and dreams*); and thy neighbour as thyself."

Or the New Testament variation: 1 John 4:18 "There is no fear in *agape*/love; but perfect *agape*/love casteth out fear: because fear hath torment. He that feareth is not made perfect in *agape*/love. 19 We *agape*/love him, because he first *agape*/loved us. 20 If a man say, I *agape*/love God, and hateth his brother, he is a liar: for he that *agape*/loveth not his brother whom he hath seen, how can he *agape*/love God whom he hath not seen? 21 And this commandment have we from him, That he who *agape/loveth* God *agape/love* his brother also."

1 John 5:1 "Whosoever believeth that Jesus is the Christ is born of God: and every one that *agape/loveth* him that begat *agape/loveth* him also that is begotten of him. 2 By this we know that we *agape/love* the children of God, when we *agape/love* God, and keep his commandments. 3 For this is the *agape/love* of God, that we keep his commandments: and his commandments are not grievous."

1 John 3:22 "And whatsoever we *aiteo/ask (require/demand and expect as due by covenant promise)*, we receive of him, because we keep his commandments, and do those things that are pleasing in his sight. 23 And this is his commandment, That we should believe on the name of his Son Jesus Christ, and *agape/love* one another, as he gave us commandment. 24 And he that keepeth his commandments dwelleth in him, and he in him. And hereby we know that he abideth in us, by the Spirit which he hath given us."

So the simple New Testament command of the will of God is to 1 John 3:23 "And this is his commandment, That we should believe on the name of his Son Jesus Christ, and *agape/love* one another, as he gave us commandment."

This is then expanded on in the some 1,050 commands in the New Testament Scriptures. Each one of these commands is the will of God. Each one of these commands is a way to release God into the Earth.

Then what is legalism? By God's definition it is to do acts that create a path for God, but with no faith (absolute assurance of the unseen manifestation of the Word of God unto thanksgiving and joy/hope) that God will inhabit that path to blessing.

Rom 1:16 "For I am not ashamed of the gospel of Christ: for it is the *dunamis/power* of God unto *soteria/salvation* to every one that believeth; to the Jew first, and also to the Greek. 17 For therein is the righteousness of God revealed from faith to faith: as it is written, The just shall *zao/live* by faith (*or the just, those made the righteousness of God in Christ Jesus shall release the* zoe *life of God to bring Heaven to Earth by believing God to perform His Word*)."

Heb 10:38 "Now the just shall *zao/live* by faith: but if any man draw back, my soul shall have no pleasure in him. 39 But we are not of them who draw back unto perdition; but of them that believe to the *sozo/saving* of the soul. 11:1 Now faith is the substance of things hoped for (*unto thanksgiving and rejoicing before you see it*), the evidence of things not seen."

Se when you find yourself in sin, not walking in *agape/love* you are to: Rom 13:10 "*Agape/love* worketh no ill to his neighbour: therefore *agape/love* is the fulfilling of the law. 11 And that, knowing the time, that now it is high time to awake out of sleep: for now is our *soteria/salvation* nearer than when we believed. 12 The night is far spent, the day is at hand: let us therefore cast off the works of darkness,

DISCOVERING OUR REDEMPTION

and let us put on the armour of light. 13 Let us walk honestly, as in the day; not in rioting and drunkenness, not in chambering and wantonness, not in strife and envying. 14 But put ye on the Lord Jesus Christ, and make not provision for the flesh, to fulfil the lusts thereof."

This is a clear command to walk in the New Testament revelation of our total Identification in Christ until our minds are renewed and stay that way. Eph 4:20 "But ye have not so learned Christ; 21 If so be that ye have heard him, and have been taught by him, as the truth is in Jesus: 22 That ye put off concerning the former conversation the old man, which is corrupt according to the deceitful lusts; 23 And be renewed in the spirit of your mind (*in your self identity unto the mind of Christ in your principles, thoughts, words and deeds*); 24 And that ye put on the new man, which after God is created in righteousness and true holiness."

And we do this by obeying what God said earlier in Romans based on the three great knowings of Rom 6:3, 6, and 9: Rom 6:11 "Likewise reckon ye also yourselves to be dead indeed unto sin, but *zao*/alive unto God through Jesus Christ our Lord."

Call your sin what it is, death, and then renew your mind into the New Creation reality of Christ in you the hope of glory. And you produce those desired results, the opposite of the sin and failures you see in your life by obeying: 2 Cor 3:15 "But even unto this day, when Moses is read, the vail is upon their heart. 16 Nevertheless when it shall turn to the Lord, the vail shall be taken away. 17 Now the Lord is that Spirit: and where the Spirit of the Lord is, there is liberty (*to be all what God has made you in Jesus to walk in* agape *love and do the works of the Law*). 18 But we all, with open face beholding as in a glass (*mirror*) the glory of the Lord (*operating in you to make you like Jesus*), are changed into the same image (*that you see of yourself in Jesus with your imagination and words*) from glory to glory, even as by the Spirit of the Lord." Doing this is how you build faith.

So legalism is when you find yourself less than Jesus and do not seek the Lord for what idolatry and hardness of heart you have, for what offense you have toward God or others, and try to do the 1,050 commands of the New Testament without faith.

And you can know you are in faith when you act like Abraham did in his faith work: Rom 4:17 "(As it is written, I have made thee a father of many nations,) before him whom he believed, even God, who quickeneth the dead, and calleth those things which be not as though they were. 18 Who against hope believed in hope, that he might become the father of many nations; according to that which was spoken, So shall thy seed be. 19 And being not weak in faith, he considered not his own body now dead, when he was about an hundred years old, neither yet the deadness of Sara's womb: 20 He staggered not at the promise of God through unbelief; but was strong in faith, giving glory to God (*loud and exuberant thanksgiving, praise and rejoicing*); 21 And being fully persuaded that, what he (*God*) had promised, he was able also to perform. 22 And therefore it was imputed to him for righteousness (*so God could do it*)."

The assumption of many is that they are not in legalism in some way, or in faith in some way. We are creatures of habit and creatures of faith. We drive our cars in faith that we will get where we want and will make it home. This human level faith does not usually need God to be involved. Even though we do not see the items in the store we have faith the store is there and that you will be able to get what you want. If not then you prepare numerous alternative plans to get what you want. Faith it believing in the unseen. Faith in God is believing God will do His currently-unseen promises of the Bible based on your cooperation with Him.

Legalism in Bible meaning is actions without faith in God. They could be faith in the laws of nature or something else. So legalism is when you do not operate in faith in God as exhibited in thanksgiving, praise and rejoicing that God will give it to you per His Bible promises. So two people could be doing the same "Bible thing," with one in faith and the other in legalism. Or one time you could be in faith and the next not. Rom 14:23 " ...for whatsoever is not of faith is sin."

1 Cor 15:56 "The sting of death is sin; and the strength of sin is the law. 57 But thanks be to God, which giveth us the victory through our Lord Jesus Christ. 58 Therefore, my *agape*/beloved brethren, be ye stedfast, unmoveable, always abounding in the work of the Lord, forasmuch as ye know that your labour is not in vain in the Lord."

James 4:17 "Therefore to him that knoweth to do good, and doeth it not, to him it is sin."

1 John 5:17 "All unrighteousness is sin... ."

The opposite of legalism is holiness. Holy means to be set apart for the exclusive use of God, and of course that includes walking just like Jesus. In Jesus we are made in the image of God: Eph 4:24 "And that ye put on the new man, which after God is created in righteousness and true holiness."

Your new man is created in righteousness on God's part, which means perfect and it is totally dedicated and able to serve only God. It is made in holiness which means everything in the new creation is made to operate just like Jesus in every way. So in the new creation you are made the righteousness of God in Christ Jesus to the level and nature of God in Jesus for God.

Walking in holiness is when you know your only purpose it to be used of God to bring Heaven to Earth in partnership with Him, as a co-laborer with Him, and you do those things that God has shown provide the path for Him to bless in the Earth in faith expecting Him to produce that goodness. This means you do those things that God can inhabit. God does not inhabit good works. He inhabits good works done in faith in Him.

DISCOVERING OUR REDEMPTION

Heb 11:6 "But without faith it is impossible to please him: for he that cometh to God must believe that he is, and that he is a rewarder of them that diligently seek him."

You know you will go through times of dryness when there are no accompanying feelings and encouragement, and you must diligently use the mighty tool of God, His Bible, with faith by Holy Spirit help, to hold on to Him in His Word no matter what, i.e., *lambano* God in His Word, per the parable of the sower and the seed (Matt 13, Mark 4, and Luke 8).

And if you are not in glad thanksgiving over what God is going to perform of His Word, you know you are in fear in some form, so you obey as your core set of behaviors: Phil 4:4 "Rejoice in the Lord alway: and again I say, Rejoice. 5 Let your moderation be known unto all men. The Lord is at hand *[in power]*. 6 Be careful (*fretful, worried, fearful, anxious, depressed*) for nothing; but in every thing by prayer and supplication with (*exuberant*) thanksgiving let your *aiteo*/requests (*requirements, demands and expectations per His Bible promises*) be made known unto God. 7 And the peace of God, which passeth all understanding, shall keep your hearts and minds through Christ Jesus. 8 Finally, brethren, whatsoever things are true, whatsoever things are honest, whatsoever things are just, whatsoever things are pure, whatsoever things are lovely, whatsoever things are of good report; if there be any virtue, and if there be any praise, think on these things."

And you do this knowing, maybe starting by confession, but eventually with diligence and much heart writing (in multiple 90 day sessions): Phil 4:13 "I can do all things through Christ which strengtheneth me."

Phil 4:19 "*For* my God shall supply all your need (aiteo *requirements, demands and expectations per His Bible promises*) according to his riches in glory by Christ Jesus. 20 Now unto God and our Father be glory for ever and ever. Amen."

So you know the will of God is for you walk just like Jesus, and anything in you that is not like Jesus you start to exercise faith for Him to change by you renewing your mind in that area and writing that Word on your heart. And you know the will of God is for you to bless others as Jesus did as a way to *agape*/love God. And you walk in the Law of God as a way to walk in *agape*/love of your neighbors.

1 John 5:1 "Whosoever believeth that Jesus is the Christ is born of God: and every one that *agape*/loveth him that begat *agape*/loveth him also that is begotten of him. 2 By this we know that we *agape*/love the children of God, when we *agape*/love God, and keep his commandments. 3 For this is the *agape*/love of God, that we keep his commandments: and his commandments are not grievous."

CHAPTER 32

HAVING FAITH IN GOD

Think of having faith in your own faith in God! Think of the thrill of having your own prayers answered!

I shared these truths with a woman one night and she then went out and laid her hands on a man, and his back was healed, in the middle of a busy room.

A young man heard the nudge of Holy Spirit and went to his little newborn. She was not breathing. He commanded life, in the name of Jesus, and the baby breathed! Over the course of several weeks that baby was delivered four times, once by a saint who was awakened in prayer fifty miles away. Holy Spirit orchestrated the battle, and the baby is now doing fine.

Another woman now goes to the grocery store every week and heals people in the name of Jesus, with no fanfare, in the aisles, as she shops.

Another prayed over some prayer clothes, and, at the last report, had produced ten miracles of demons being cast out and bodies being healed.

None of these were full-time ministers, but they were all believers. "These signs follow those who believe," according to Mark 16:15-20.

This, then, should be the normal experience of every one of us.

God already paid for it in Jesus, so it is waiting in Heaven for any and all of us. Concerning healing, anyone, Christian or not, who calls on God in faith, can

DISCOVERING OUR REDEMPTION

release what is already waiting for them. Rom 10:11 "For the scripture saith, Whosoever believeth on him shall not be ashamed. 12 For there is no difference between the Jew and the Greek: for the same Lord over all is rich unto all that call upon him. 13 For whosoever shall call upon the name of the Lord shall be *sozo*/saved."

Religion has made this way much too hard. We have a doctrine needing a higher life or of being spiritually mature in order to see answered prayer and miracles. Jesus not only said it was the "children's bread," but He said that brand new believers would do these same wondrous things. Mark 16:15 "And he said unto them, Go ye into all the world, and preach the gospel to every creature. 16 He that believeth and is baptized shall be *sozo*/saved; but he that believeth not shall be damned. 17 And these signs shall follow them that believe; In my name shall they cast out devils; they shall speak with new tongues; 18 they shall take up serpents; and if they drink any deadly thing, it shall not hurt them; they shall lay hands on the sick, and they shall recover. 19 So then after the Lord had spoken unto them, he was received up into heaven, and sat on the right hand of God. 20 And they went forth, and preached everywhere, the Lord working with them, and confirming the word with signs following. Amen." This is for new believers, after mature believers have successfully preached to them the Word of grace in Jesus Christ.

When you realize that the great majority of modern Christians never have a prayer answered, you can understand what I mean by having your own faith.

Most Christians are depending upon other people's faith. They can do the praying, but they want someone else to do the believing.

In reality, they are not praying either. They are just repeating words. Prayer, in the New Testament sense, is born of faith, and is always answered.

John Lake said something like this, "You can pray yourself into unbelief. Until you go out and do the thing (lay hands on the sick and command deliverance in the name of Jesus, telling that mountain to go), you will never see more of God. Use what you have, and you will get more. Otherwise, if you just keep praying, all you are doing is keeping yourself in unbelief."

At some point, you must know the scriptures you are basing your prayer on and that God has heard you. If you are not seeing the answer, then get back into the Scriptures and learn God's will on the subject. 1 John 5:13 "These things have I written unto you that believe on the name of the Son of God; that ye may know that ye have eternal *zoe*/life, and that ye may believe on the name of the Son of God. 14 And this is the confidence that we have in him, that, if we *aiteo*/ask (*require, demand and expect as due by covenant promise, based on His holiness*) any thing according to his will, he heareth us: 15 and if we know that he hear us, whatsoever we *aiteo*/ask (*require, demand and expect as due by covenant promise, based on His holiness*), we know that we have the petitions that we *aiteo*/desired (*required, demanded and expected as due by covenant promise, based on His holiness*) of him."

Having Faith in God

The anointing is on the Word of God to perform what God said He wants done. Isa 55:11 "So shall my word be that goeth forth out of my mouth: it shall not return unto me void, but it shall accomplish that which I please, and it shall prosper in the thing whereto I sent it."

Luke 1:37 "For with God nothing is ever impossible and no word from God shall be without power or impossible of fulfillment." AMP

We release that anointing by believing God to perform what we say. John 11:41 "Then they took away the stone from the place where the dead was laid. And Jesus lifted up his eyes, and said, Father, I thank thee that thou hast heard me. 42 And I knew that thou hearest me always: but because of the people which stand by I said it, that they may believe that thou hast sent me. 43 And when he thus had spoken, he cried with a loud voice, Lazarus, come forth."

The Father planned that all should have faith in Him by His Word.

Have you noticed this passage of scriptures in Mark 16:17-18? "These signs shall accompany them that believe: in my name shall they cast out demons; they shall speak with new tongues; they shall take up serpents, and if they drink any deadly thing, it shall in no wise hurt them; they shall lay hands on the sick, and they shall recover." RSV

Of whom is the Lord speaking? He is speaking of the man or the woman who has just believed in their heart that God raised Jesus from the dead and confessed Jesus as Lord.

When the right message is preached, this is what Jesus said the resulting believers will do. There will be no long delay, but it will come right away. Mark 16:15 "These signs shall accompany them that believe ... ." RSV

So a new believer has just received eternal *zoe*/life, and at once, he begins his combat with the unseen forces of darkness. Someone is sick or in bondage, and he exercises his rights. In Jesus' name, he commands the power of Satan to be broken and to leave. The Lord then confirms that Word of reconciliation and the person is healed.

Acts 20:32 shows the place of the Word in the life of the believer: "And now, brethren, I commend you to God, and to the word of his grace, which is able to build you up, and to give you an inheritance among all them which are sanctified." "To build you up" means to build you up in faith, in love, in confidence in God, and in ability to help humanity. It builds you up into God-level things and thinking, desires, speaking and doing.

Your faith may then be developed until it becomes a mighty force. That is the dream of the Father for you. You build yourself up; edify yourself in faith with the Word of God and Holy Spirit. 1 Cor 14:4 "He that speaketh in an unknown tongue edifieth himself ... ."

One way is to pray in tongues as you read the Scriptures. This can accelerate believing: Rom 10:17 "So then faith cometh by hearing, and hearing by the word of

DISCOVERING OUR REDEMPTION

God (*in Christ*)." Read sometimes fast and sometimes slow. Also vary the speed of your tongues as you read.

Another way to build up your faith is to keep praying in tongues. Many recommend that each believer work at 2 hours a day of hard, loud and fast tongues, to build up their faith for whatever comes. You can do this as you drive or do other things. Ask and Holy Spirit will give you wisdom on this. Besides for the needs and opportunities for your own life, do this with an attitude to help others in some way. Show them God's *agape* love. He will do it because He loves them.

Jude 20 "But ye, *agape*/beloved, building up yourselves on your most holy faith, praying in the Holy Ghost, 21 keep yourselves in the *agape*/love of God, looking for the mercy of our Lord Jesus Christ unto eternal *zoe*/life. 22 And of some have compassion, making a difference: 23 and others *sozo*/save with fear, pulling them out of the fire; hating even the garment spotted by the flesh."

Holy Spirit emphasizes that we seek all the gifts, including tongues. 1 Cor 12:30 "Have all the gifts of healing? do all speak with tongues? do all interpret? 31 But covet earnestly the best gifts: and yet shew I unto you a more excellent way."

The more excellent way is to want to use the gifts of the Spirit to demonstrate God's *agape*/love for others. God will heal and deliver because He loves people. As you get in agreement with God in *agape*/love, you and He are thinking more alike, and He can move through you in more and more ways.

1 Cor 14:1 "Follow after *agape*/charity, and desire spiritual gifts, but rather that ye may prophesy. 2 For he that speaketh in an unknown tongue speaketh not unto men, but unto God: for no man understandeth him; howbeit in the spirit he speaketh mysteries. 3 But he that prophesieth speaketh unto men to edification, and exhortation, and comfort. 4 He that speaketh in an unknown tongue edifieth himself; but he that prophesieth edifieth the church."

We need both, self–edification, to be able to believe God in the midst of impossible circumstances, and prophesy, to build up others with words they can understand.

1 Cor 14:14 "For if I pray in an unknown tongue, my spirit prayeth, but my understanding is unfruitful. 15 What is it then? I will pray with the spirit, and I will pray with the understanding also: I will sing with the spirit, and I will sing with the understanding also."

Here we learn that tongues is praying, talking to God to get things done on Earth. You are praying with your spirit, but your mind is not involved and does not know what is being prayed by Holy Spirit through you. So it is praying in, by and with your spirit, as articulated in a language given by Holy Spirit.

So praying in tongues is praying in the Spirit. Jude 20 "But ye, *agape*/beloved, (*constantly*) building up yourselves on your most holy faith, (*constantly*) praying in the Holy Ghost, 21 keep yourselves in the *agape*/love of God, looking for the mercy of our Lord Jesus Christ unto eternal *zoe*/life."

One could argue that praying the Scriptures, especially scripture prayers found in the Bible, is praying "in the Spirit." Since the Word of God is spirit and *zoe*/life, then praying the Scriptures could also be considered as included (to some level) as praying in the Spirit. Yet in praying the Scriptures your mind is praying, which may or may not be fruitful, and there is no guarantee your spirit is involved, and you are using spirit words, the Scriptures.

Jude 20 tells us to continually be building up our most holy faith by means of praying in Holy Spirit. This is a way to:
- Build up yourself properly in the spirit;
- By inference, help your soul get into and accept spiritual truth;
- Help you know how *agape*/loved you are;
- Strengthen you in your ability to see and then deliver, by faith, the unseen things of God, to bring Heaven to Earth, to God's glory; and
- Receive more ability for your spirit to bypass your soul and do the right things anyway.

Certainly the "building up" part is included in praying in tongues.

The apostle Paul tells us that speaking in tongues has its place and is critical to Christian success. 1 Cor 14:18 "I thank my God, I speak with tongues more than ye all: 19 yet in the church I had rather speak five words with my understanding, that by my voice I might teach others also, than ten thousand words in an unknown tongue. 20 Brethren, be not children in understanding: howbeit in malice be ye children, but in understanding (*of the* agape/*love ways of God*) be men."

Paul emphasized praying in tongues for personal development: 1 Cor 14:18 "I thank my God, I speak with tongues more than ye all." So here he was telling us he prayed in tongues (either speaking or singing) more than all the Christians in a city who prayed in tongues too much in public or church gatherings. So, no matter how you count it, Paul spent a lot of time (and assuming a disciplined life) daily in praying and singing in tongues (hours at a time). Remember, a devout Jew spent some 2 to 6 hours a day in praying the Scriptures in a language in which their mind was fruitful, but praying the scripture prayers and the Scriptures is not tongues.

So what do tongues do? They build you up in spirit and humble your soul, so if you are a trumpet, you are not weak and your notes not unclear. It takes humility to spend regular time in which Holy Spirit prays though you, and you do not understand what you are praying, yet God is getting done what He needs by you praying in tongues. If you love God enough to help Him get His priorities done, then spend time praying and singing in tongues.

Paul stated that he prayed in tongues more than the whole Corinthian church. He had a very powerful ministry, with many signs and wonders, and could inspire

DISCOVERING OUR REDEMPTION

and edify even the worst of sinners. He made it clear that he got at least part of his strength from speaking in tongues more than all.

So consider a room full of 100 people, with each one praying 15 minutes in tongues. This would be a combined effect of 25 hours of prayer in tongues. So, for Paul to pray more than the entire church, he would have to pray in the Spirit each week more than 25 hours. In a 7-day week, that would be roughly 4 hours or more a day.

Holy Spirit includes tongues as a gift we are to specifically seek God for. In 1 Cor 12 there is a list of nine gifts, one of which is prophecy. Seek them all, and do not ignore tongues.

Faith is simply to keep commanding and confessing long enough to get the job done. Luke 18:1 "And he (Jesus) spake a parable unto them to this end, that men ought always to pray, and not to faint." Then, being built up in your most holy faith means you will endure through long prayer battles or be more effective and shorten battles as more power is released. The key is focused persistence.

That is the secret of "mustard seed faith." It never gives up until the work is done; it "faints not."

Luke 17:5 "And the apostles said unto the Lord, Increase our faith. 6 And the Lord said, If ye had faith as a grain of mustard seed, ye might say unto this sycamine tree, Be thou plucked up by the root, and be thou planted in the sea; and it should obey you."

So you build your faith, by not looking at small problems, but looking at big events, like moving mountains or making trees walk down the road. Jesus said to work at getting faith for the big things, and then the smaller ones will be easy.

The Word of grace in Christ will build up your sense of Righteousness. I know of nothing that is needed more than this.

Righteousness means that there is no sin so great that Jesus has not already born it and healed it 2000 years ago. The Righteousness of God means that there is nothing you can ever do to deserve it, and once you have it, to lose it. It is the gift of God. Rom 11:29 "For the gifts and calling of God are without repentance."

This righteousness does not depend on you, but on God.

God already set commands that depended on men to perform, and we all failed. Adam failed, and the people of Moses' day failed. Rom 3:10 "As it is written, there is none righteous, no, not one: 11 there is none that understandeth, there is none that seeketh after God. 12 They are all gone out of the way, they are together become unprofitable; there is none that doeth good, no, not one."

Father God set the New Testament based on Jesus' performance, and He did not, nor can He ever fail. Heb 13:8 "Jesus Christ the same yesterday, and to day, and for ever."

Having Faith in God

When we become conscious that we are the righteous of God in Christ Jesus, because of God's love and grace, we will no longer think of our weaknesses and failings.

Isa 32:17 "And the work of righteousness shall be peace; and the effect of righteousness quietness and confidence for ever."

This verse does not belong to just Israel. It is a prophecy for the Church.

The work of righteousness that God wrought in you has brought peace to your heart. *Peace* means tranquility because you know you will win every battle in Jesus. You are no longer under condemnation from God, not ever.

Rom 8:1 "There is therefore now no condemnation to them that are in Christ Jesus."

Any condemnation you experience is your fleshly mind holding you back. Even when you sin, Holy Spirit will direct you how to reconcile or restore what you have done, but never with guilt or condemnation. You now live in perfect quietness and rest.

The effect of righteousness on your heart is a new quietness and a new type of faith.

You know there is nothing to separate you from being loved by Father God.

You understand the depth of the price Father paid in Jesus to get you back to Himself.

You enjoy the effect of your confidence in the finished work of Christ.

You enjoy your confidence in knowing you are totally *agape*/loved by God.

You know He is inside you and can never leave or forsake you.

You fight to keep in the rest of God, against all circumstances where He does the works.

You know, in Jesus, that you are a master of circumstances for God.

You know, in Jesus, that you are a master of demons for God.

You know, in Jesus, that if you lay hands on a sick person, that person will be healed.

The realization of this truth gives you a sense of quietness, a fullness of joy that you have never enjoyed before.

The phrase, "confidence forever," is striking. You have moved out of the restless atmosphere of fear and doubt and into the quiet waters of victory.

You have become a master, where you once served as a slave.

You are more than a conqueror, where once you suffered defeat.

You are bold, where once you shrank back and were ashamed to speak God's Word.

You are now bold, where you once were afraid to tell people God loves them, and then deliver *zoe* life to heal their bodies, ease their minds and give them signs and wonders.

DISCOVERING OUR REDEMPTION

You walk in the light where you once walked in darkness.

You walk in the light of Christ in you the hope of glory where you once walked in sin consciousness, lack, depression and fear.

You enjoy your privileges in Christ as a beloved son, the apple of Father's eye.

You keep in the Scriptures, majoring on the Word of Reconciliation, Redemption, Salvation, Adoption, Betrothal, Righteousness, Victory, Triumph, Truth, Grace and Peace with God through Jesus Christ.

You keep your former purging of sin always in remembrance.

You wrestle your dead old man to silence with your new identity in Christ.

At last, you have your own faith in God by His Word. At last you have arrived.

You know what John 15:5 means: "I am the vine; ye are the branches: he that abideth in me, and I in him, the same beareth much fruit: for apart from me ye can do nothing."

You enjoy the consciousness of the life of the Vine abiding in you and you abiding in the Vine by grace, not by your works. Sin cannot separate you from God, for Jesus has solved the sin problem.

The only thing that can separate you, in your mind and faith, is to forget the depth and the power of His Redemption in the blood of Jesus.

You set the limits or open doors with your faith. Matt 8:13 "And Jesus said unto the centurion, Go thy way; and as thou hast believed, so be it done unto thee. And his servant was healed in the selfsame hour."

You are seizing the promises by *aiteo*/requiring, demanding, and expecting, per covenant promise, for God to perform His words, just like Jesus taught us in the "Our Father," commanding the devil to leave and the body to be healed, all in the name of Jesus.

2 Pet 1:3 "For His divine power has bestowed upon us all things that [are requisite and suited] to *zoe*/life and godliness, through the [full, personal] *epignosis*/knowledge of Him Who called us by and to His own glory and excellence (virtue). 4 By means of these He has bestowed on us His precious and exceedingly great promises, so that through them you may escape [by flight] from the moral decay (rottenness and corruption) that is in the world because of covetousness (lust and greed), and become sharers (partakers) of the divine nature." AMP

You share the divine nature of God, as you seize the promises and obey the commands to do the Word of God.

You are the fruit-bearing part of Christ.

You have been grafted into Him by the new birth.

That graft has given you a new nature.

Abiding in His grace, His *agape*/love and *zoe*/life flow through you to His glory.

Your confession is: "There is nothing in my old man of value, yet Christ now dwells in me. He has made me one with Him."

You bear the Jesus kind of fruit, which is love fruit, faith fruit.

The world is benefited by it. Christians are lifted everywhere you go, into a new consciousness of their rights and privileges in Christ.

You know what John 15:7 means: "If ye abide in me, and my words abide in you, ye shall *aiteo*/ask (*require, demand and expect as due by covenant promise, based on His grace toward you*) whatsoever ye will, and it shall be done unto you."

You know you do abide in Him. You bear the fruitage of His indwelling Word.

You plant the seed of His reconciliation in Jesus in every situation and watch and believe that seed to grow and bear His fruit.

You speak words that give others grace to rise up and walk in their calling.

God's Word on your lips produces real results.

You know it is all by grace, based on His righteousness.

You know, when you *aiteo*, it is by grace that *zoe*/life delivers His salvation.

The Father's Word on Jesus' lips healed the sick, and His Word on your lips does the same.

You know what it means to have legal rights, and whatever you *aiteo*/demand He gives you.

The word *demand* is used in its truest sense.

Jesus said: John 16:23 "And when that time comes, you will ask nothing of Me [you will need to ask Me no questions]. I assure you, most solemnly I tell you, that My Father will grant you whatever you *aiteo*/ask (*require, demand and expect as due by covenant promise*) in My Name [as presenting all that I AM]. 24 Up to this time you have not *aiteo*/asked (*required, demanded and expected as due by covenant promise*) a [single] thing in My Name [as presenting all that I AM]; but now *aiteo*/ask (*require, demand and expect as due by covenant promise*) and keep on *aiteo*/asking and you will *lambano*/receive, so that your joy (gladness, delight) may be full and complete." AMP

The Greek word, *aiteo*, translated as "ask" means "demand as due by promise."

It is not used in the sense that you are commanding God to give something as your inferior, but in the sense that you go into the bank and demand payment on your check. It means that a superior has made a promise based on conditions, and now those conditions have now been met, so the promise is to be delivered. In the same sense, your faith in God takes its rights, its portion and its boldness.

When you use that Word of Reconciliation in Jesus to *aiteo* the devil, his works or any part of creation to manifest God's salvation, it is a demand from a superior to an inferior. Col 3:3 "If ye then be risen with Christ, seek those things which are above, where Christ sitteth on the right hand of God. 2 Set your affection on things

DISCOVERING OUR REDEMPTION

above, not on things on the earth. 3 For ye are dead, and your *zoe*/life is hid with Christ in God."

At last, you know what James 1:22-24 means. "But be ye doers of the word, and not hearers only, deluding your own selves. For if anyone is a hearer of the word and not a doer, he is like unto a man beholding his natural face in a mirror: for he beholdeth himself, and goeth away, and straightway forgetteth what manner of man he was." RSV

You have become a "doer of the Word." You are not just a hearer. You do not delude yourself with false hopes. Instead, you base your hope on God in His Word.

You *lambano* His Word, no matter what. You count it all joy when trials beset you, knowing you will stand and see His glory. You have fits of joy and laughter, while others around you stare in amazement, for you obey: James 1:2 "My brethren, count it all joy when ye fall into divers temptations; 3 knowing this, that the trying of your faith worketh patience. 4 But let patience have her perfect work, that ye may be perfect and entire, wanting nothing."

The worse it gets the louder you shout, in thanksgiving, praise and joy, knowing God cannot lie. Phil 1:28 "And in nothing terrified by your adversaries: which is to them an evident token of perdition, but to you of *soteria*/salvation, and that of God."

Your confidence is in the God who cannot lie. You hold Father God to do it, you hold the devil to get out of it, and you hold creation to obey and get right, per the promises of God.

1 Cor 15:57 "But thanks be to God, which giveth us the victory through our Lord Jesus Christ. 58 Therefore, my *agape*/beloved brethren, be ye stedfast, unmoveable, always abounding in the work of the Lord, forasmuch as ye know that your labour is not in vain in the Lord."

You are in Christ. You are an heir of God and a joint-heir with Jesus Christ.

You know that His Word abides in you and produces results.

You have faith in every Word of Reconciliation you deliver, that it will grow and produce the Reconciliation of God, in healing, blessing, prosperity, wisdom and peace.

Your confession becomes, "I put the Word of God in that situation; now the Word is growing, and it will work. I will see that Word bear fruit. *Agape*/love will triumph." And if needed, with *aiteo* you keep adding *zoe* life until it comes to pass.

You are a producer. You are no longer just marking time.

You know now "what manner of man you are." You know that you are a new creation, empowered by God.

Here is a description of a believer. That man is empowered with God's ability. He laughs at all grades of mountains (trials, tests, temptations and challenges).

He sings his song of triumph, as he goes over in high gear, much like a powerful car goes over a mountain with ease. He is not a subject, a slave. He has passed from that class and into the class of a master.

He remembers in the morning, at noon, at dinner and before sleep what manner of man he is, with thanks, praise, rejoicing, affirmations and good works.

He remembers his former purging of sin in Jesus.

He faces life with a song of victory. The Word of Christ dwells in him richly in all wisdom and prudence (Col 3:16).

The Word has become a part of God to him, a part of the living Christ to him.

Day by day the great, mighty Spirit, who raised Jesus from the dead, builds that Word into his heart consciousness, his conscious and unconscious mind, as he quotes and meditates on the Scriptures all day and night. He has reprogrammed his heart to please his Father, with thanks, praise, rejoicing and affirmations.

He knows faith is a mind and heart matter, a cognitive mind and a subconscious mind matter. If he were to add up the time, each day he spends 2 to 6 hours in some way, working with the Scriptures in thoughts, reading, all manner of words, songs, chants and mutterings, to renew and keep his mind renewed. At first, it was a project, and he took small steps, but now it is a lifestyle. He does it naturally and unconsciously. He knows each step is in at least 90-day sets, before he moves on to more truth.

Christ is being formed in him because he actively works with the Word of God and Holy Spirit.

This developed Christian actively obeys: Phil 2:12 "Wherefore, my *agape*/beloved, as ye have always obeyed, not as in my presence only, but now much more in my absence, work out your own *soteria*/salvation with fear and trembling. 13 For it is God which worketh in you both to will and to do of his good pleasure *(knowing you will have no excuse on the Day of Judgment, because He was faithful to help you but, for anything you would not listen to or obey, will go up in smoke as wood, hay and stubble on that Day)*. 14 Do all things without murmurings and disputing *(as Holy Spirit deals with you to reject the pull and twists of the world)*: 15 that ye may be blameless and harmless, the sons of God, without rebuke, in the midst of a crooked and perverse nation, among whom ye shine as lights in the world; 16 holding forth the word of *zoe*/life; that I may rejoice in the day of Christ, that I have not run in vain, neither laboured in vain."

He labors not for those things he knows will one day be destroyed: John 6:27 "Labour not for the meat which perisheth, but for that meat which endureth unto everlasting *zoe*/life, which the Son of man shall give unto you: for him hath God the Father sealed."

He has set his affections on God, for he does not just believe, but he knows he is risen with Christ. Col 3:1 "If ye then be risen with Christ, seek those things which

DISCOVERING OUR REDEMPTION

are above, where Christ sitteth on the right hand of God. 2 Set your affection on things above, not on things on the earth."

He keeps his ear inclined to Father God and His goodness: Isa 55:1 "Ho, every one that thirsteth, come ye to the waters, and he that hath no money; come ye, buy, and eat; yea, come, buy wine and milk without money and without price. 2 Wherefore do ye spend money for that which is not bread? and your labour for that which satisfieth not? hearken diligently unto me, and eat ye that which is good, and let your soul delight itself in fatness. 3 Incline your ear, and come unto me: hear, and your soul shall live; and I will make an everlasting covenant with you, even the sure mercies of David."

As he goes to the Father, by the Word of Christ, the New Testament Revelation, and is fed by the absolute *agape* love of God, he can then *agape* love others, as he himself (or herself) is *agape* loved. This is the secret to the great commandment of God. You *agape*/love, as you know you are *agape*/loved.

Matt 22:37 "Jesus said unto him, Thou shalt *agape*/love the Lord thy God with all thy heart, and with all thy soul, and with all thy mind. 38 This is the first and great commandment. 39 And the second is like unto it, Thou shalt *agape*/love thy neighbour as thyself. 40 On these two commandments hang all the law and the prophets."

One of these days Christ, in all His fullness, will dominate that man until he will whisper softly: (Gal 2:20) "It is no longer I that *zao*/live, but Christ *zao*/liveth in me ... ."

Col 2:6-7 "As therefore ye received Christ Jesus as Lord, so walk in him, rooted and builded up in him, and established in your faith, even as ye were taught, abounding in thanksgiving." RSV

The Scriptures are real to him. He is governed by Holy Spirit in the Word and not his flesh.

Look at this awesome fact, so often ignored by those who plead for help: Eph 4:7 "But unto each one of us was the grace given, according to the measure of the gift of Christ." RSV

Now we are moving up into the big leagues.

I love what E.W. Kenyon said in his little book, *Identification*: "The guide said, 'In a few minutes we will be in the redwood section, and you will see the giants of the vegetable world.'

"I said softly, as I walked into the prayer meeting, 'We are coming into the spiritual redwoods. We are going to see spiritual giants, supermen. They have God dwelling in them. The Word of Christ is rich upon their lips. The love that relentlessly drove Jesus to the cross has gained possession of them.

"They no longer walk as natural men. They belong to the love class, the miracle class.

Having Faith in God

"They are in the Jesus class.

"They have graduated from the lower class.

"They are the men and women who have 'attained unto the unity of faith and the *epignosis*/knowledge of the Son of God, and have become full-grown men unto the measure of the stature of the fulness of Christ.' (Eph 4:13)

"They have their own faith in God by His Word. They are established in the truth. The Word is real to them.

"They are trusting in the Word of the God who cannot lie.

"They look at the facts of the circumstances; then they look at the eternal truth of God's Word and proclaim and demand that the circumstances bow and conform to that Word in the name of Jesus. They see the facts, they see the Word of God, and they know the Word of God, in faith, will crush and heal the circumstances in the name of Jesus, the Lord of all creation. (Kenyon, *Identification*, page 61.)

"They know they are connected to God. They are God's local representative, to deliver the massive Salvation of our God to the world.

As we see this, we too will cry out: Ps 68:19 'Blessed be the Lord, who daily loadeth us with benefits, even the God of our salvation. Selah. 20 He that is our God is the God of salvation; and unto God the Lord belong the issues from death."

For more on how to build faith, please see our other works, *OK, God, Now What?* and *Battle Prayer for Diving Healing, Field Manual 2*. Go to www.Covenant-PeaceMinistries.com for more details.

CHAPTER 33
DESTROYING SIN-CONSCIOUSNESS

Sin-consciousness is the knowledge or feeling that you are not right with God, there is something missing, and you need to do more for God to bless you. You are not adequate to be in the full presence of God, you have the potential to fail and probably will, and, therefore, God will curse you and punish you.

Sin-consciousness is what Adam walked in after he sinned. God, the only real Friend, came looking for Adam, and Adam and Eve ran from God and not toward Him. Gen 3:7 "And the eyes of them both were opened, and they knew that they were naked; and they sewed fig leaves together, and made themselves aprons. 8 And they heard the voice of the LORD God walking in the garden in the cool of the day: and Adam and his wife hid themselves from the presence of the LORD God amongst the trees of the garden. 9 And the LORD God called unto Adam, and said unto him, Where art thou? 10 And he said, I heard thy voice in the garden, and I was afraid, because I was naked; and I hid myself."

In sin-consciousness you are governed by fear. You are naked before all in shame. Not like a baby, who has no fear, but in shame that you have no real strength, and the world is out to destroy you. Not only that, but you feel that God is too holy and powerful to trust and to be near, and that He is out to hurt you and/or you do not matter to Him.

Destroying Sin-Consciousness

The truth is that we have "eternity hidden in our heart." Eccl 3:11 "He has made everything beautiful in its time. He also has planted eternity in men's hearts and minds [a divinely implanted sense of a purpose working through the ages which nothing under the sun but God alone can satisfy], yet so that men cannot find out what God has done from the beginning to the end." AMP

Rom 1:19 "Because that which may be known of God is manifest in them; for God hath shewed it unto them. 20 For the invisible things of him from the creation of the world are clearly seen, being understood by the things that are made, even his eternal power and Godhead; so that they are without excuse." So, instead we build "fig leaves" of false religion to keep ourselves "safely" separated from God. On the outside, it may look great and attractive, but it is all a false front, a sham.

This inside corruption is sin-consciousness, continual knowledge that you are not right with God, and He is not "safe" to be with or around and that He is very different than you and cannot be trusted.

Sin-consciousness is the opposite or twisting or confusion of the truth of: Col 1:21 "And you, that were sometime alienated and enemies in your mind by wicked works, yet now hath he reconciled 22 in the body of his flesh through death, to present you holy and unblameable and unreproveable in his sight."

Sin-consciousness is the traditions of men that seek to make the Word of God of no effect.

Sin-consciousness is the awareness that you and God are different in substance and nature, and you will never be adequate or accepted enough to please Him. You must pray more, fast more, keep confessing your same sins again and again until you "feel" forgiven, and/or do good more to get right with God, to receive His power.

Sin-consciousness does not look at the work of Jesus in the Scriptures and say, "This is what it says, and it must be truth. My feelings don't matter, only the Word of God does."

Or, instead of religious activity, sin-consciousness lets you know you can never be good enough for God, so why even try? Live your life as you will and just hope God will be merciful to you, a sinner.

All these are the marks of sin-consciousness and denial of the truth of the Gospel of God's goodness released by the suffering, death, resurrection and glorification of Jesus in the Redemption of mankind by His blood, unto the righteousness of God's *zoe*/life, unto the adoption as a child of God and a joint-heir with Jesus.

In sin-consciousness, we reduce our thanksgiving and cannot believe God has qualified us, in Jesus, to be used by Him as was Jesus Himself. Col 1:12 "Giving thanks (*continually*) unto the Father, which hath made us meet to be partakers of the inheritance of the saints in light: 13 who hath delivered us from the power of darkness, and hath translated us into the kingdom of his *agape*/dear Son: 14 in

DISCOVERING OUR REDEMPTION

whom we have redemption through his blood, even the forgiveness (*remission, removal, purging, washing, obliteration and putting away*) of sins: 15 who is the image of the invisible God, the firstborn of every creature."

Peter told us that if we do not know our sins are purged in Jesus 2000 years ago, we cannot grow properly in the knowledge of God and Jesus. 2 Pet 1:8 "For if these things (*of God's nature*) be in you, and abound, they make you that ye shall neither be barren nor unfruitful in the *epignosis*/knowledge of our Lord Jesus Christ. 9 But he that lacketh these things (*of the manifested abundance of the nature and power of God*) is blind, and cannot see afar off, and hath forgotten that he was purged from his old sins."

If you have forgotten your purging in Jesus, if you have not renewed your mind into the truth of our Redemption in and by Jesus, you can rest assured that the devil, the world system, the television, common talk, your family, your friends, your un-renewed conscious and evil circumstances will tell you that you are not perfect, and therefore, in subtle and direct ways, not acceptable to God.

This means you have to keep these truths ever before you. John 8:31 "Then said Jesus to those Jews which believed on him, If ye continue in my word, then are ye my disciples indeed; 32 and ye shall *ginosko*/know the truth, and the truth shall make you free."

Truth has two major aspects. First, that you know it and, second, that it now shapes your life into a new lifestyle. This is what Jesus was talking about, the lifestyle that is no longer darkness, but only light. Eph 5:6 "Let no man deceive you with vain words: for because of these things cometh the wrath of God upon the children of disobedience. 7 Be not ye therefore partakers with them. 8 For ye were sometimes darkness, but now are ye light in the Lord: walk as children of light: 9 (For the fruit of the Spirit is in all goodness and righteousness and truth;) 10 proving (*allow, demonstrate, walking in to show*) what is acceptable (*well pleasing*) unto the Lord [*like Jesus walked*]."

Truth power points:
1. Know the truth, being no longer ignorant
2. Continue in that truth by repetition and study
3. Use the truth to destroy whatever you were believing before
   a. Twists of truth
   b. Replacements/alternates of truth
4. Learn to do the truth
   a. By confession, affirmation and prayer to renew your mind for 3 to 12 months per truth
   b. By actual practice until you become a master craftsman at doing the truth, move from awareness to *ginosko* to *epiginosko*.

As you grow in the truth of what Jesus accomplished in those remarkable 52 days, your confidence in God and His Redemption in Jesus will grow. Done properly, this will make you righteousness-conscious. The free gift of the righteousness of God in Christ Jesus and the abundance of grace to do righteous works righteously. This is where effective Christians walk. Philem 6 "That the communication of thy faith may become effectual by the acknowledging of every good thing which is in you in Christ Jesus."

Sin-consciousness destroys our confidence in God, and confidence in God is the secret of effective faith. The first sign of sin-consciousness is often a lack of thanksgiving toward God for what He has done for you in Jesus. Rom 1:21 "Because that, when they knew God, they glorified him not as God, neither were thankful; but became vain in their imaginations, and their foolish heart was darkened." Darkness now means unable to see the light of Father God in Jesus, to give you hope and confident faith.

There is no evil in God, no iniquity and no condemnation, no darkness, and no sentence of death for you. God is the one who sent Jesus to remove that sentence. 1 Chron 16:31 "Let the heavens be glad, and let the earth rejoice: and let men say among the nations, The Lord reigneth. 32 Let the sea roar, and the fulness thereof: let the fields rejoice, and all that is therein. 33 Then shall the trees of the wood sing out at the presence of the Lord, because he cometh to judge the earth. 34 O give thanks unto the Lord; for he is good; for his *chesed*/mercy endureth for ever. 35 And say ye, Save us, O God of our salvation, and gather us together, and deliver us from the heathen, that we may give thanks to thy holy name, and glory in thy praise."

2 Chron 5:13 "... and praised the Lord, saying, For he is good; for his *chesed*/mercy endureth for ever."

Sin conscious does not walk in thanksgiving or truths like this: 2 Tim 1:8 "... God; 9 who hath *sozo*/saved us, and called us with an holy calling, not according to our works, but according to his own purpose and grace, which was given us in Christ Jesus before the world began, 10 but is now made manifest by the appearing of our Saviour Jesus Christ, who hath abolished death, and hath brought *zoe*/life and immortality to light through the gospel."

When we walk in sin-consciousness, the simple Gospel message does not thrill us, but is only, at best, a historical fact, and of no real benefit to you right now. John 3:16 "For God so *agape*/loved the world, that he gave his only begotten Son, that whosoever believeth in him should not perish, but have everlasting *zoe*/life. 17 For God sent not his Son into the world to condemn the world; but that the world through him might be *sozo*/saved [*made like Heaven on Earth and totally free from any bondage of the law of sin and death or the devil*]."

Luke 24:46 "And (*Jesus*) said unto them, Thus it is written, and thus it behoved Christ to suffer, and to rise from the dead the third day: 47 and that repentance (*from believing that Jesus is not the Christ of God and the judge of all mankind, or to believing that Jesus is the Christ of God and the Judge of all mankind*) and *aphesis*/remis-

DISCOVERING OUR REDEMPTION

sion (*purging, removal, obliteration and putting away*) of sins (*where you are redeemed from sin and the curse of sin into the total* soteria/*salvation of God, with indwelling Holy Spirit*) should be preached in his name among all nations … ,"

It is how effective you are in walking in the spirit of the Word of the Gospel that keeps you in the path of *zoe*/life, peace and victory. Listen to and operate in the mind of the flesh, and you will walk in condemnation and sin-consciousness. That sense of guilt is not from God, but unless you continually dwell on the Word of our Redemption, with the total remission of sin in Jesus, you will walk in condemnation from the devil.

Rom 8:1 "There is therefore now no condemnation to them which are in Christ Jesus, who walk not after the flesh, but after the Spirit. 2 For the law of the Spirit of *zoe*/life in Christ Jesus hath made me free from the law of sin and death. 3 For what the law could not do, in that it was weak through the flesh, God sending his own Son in the likeness of sinful flesh, and for sin, condemned sin in the flesh: 4 that the righteousness of the law might be fulfilled in us, who walk not after the flesh, but after the Spirit. 5 For they that are after the flesh do mind the things of the flesh; but they that are after the Spirit the things of the Spirit. 6 For to be carnally minded is death; but to be spiritually minded is *zoe*/life and peace."

If you want to walk free of condemnation, which is part of sin-consciousness, and in the Spirit of God, work with the Word of Christ in you, the hope, the joyful expectation of coming good, and *lambano*/receive, that is, renew your mind aggressively in the abundance of grace and the gift of the righteousness of God in Christ Jesus. Not by what you do right, your works, but by faith in the effectiveness and sufficiency of the redeeming blood of Jesus. Holy Spirit will tell you that you sinned, and it is paid for, redeemed by the blood of Jesus, and by His stripes it was healed. Now receive that healing, by faith, to the fullness of walking just like Jesus, and walk in the liberty of Holy Spirit, being able to fill every part of your life, as you agree with Him, knowing you are blessed with indwelling Holy Spirit.

Faith, for the Christian, is the substance of things hoped for, or the substance or making real of the joyful expectation of coming good from God, based on His covenant promises, because Jesus has met all the requirements. Dread is based on the assurance of whatever evil you fear. Faith is based on the assurance of love, the goodness of God coming to you. Dread is the fearful expectation of coming evil, because there is no hope or confidence in God to help you. In our day, we call this depression or hopelessness.

The second major sign of sin-consciousness is that your experience and the experience of others is greater than what God says in His Word. These Christians love to hear other people's testimonies, but do not have the Scriptures as their final source, nor do they proclaim the Word of Christ in the new creation as greater than their experiences.

Destroying Sin-Consciousness

1 John 3:21 "*Agape*/beloved, if our heart condemn us not, then have we confidence toward God. 22 And whatsoever we *aiteo*/ask (*require, demand and expect as due by covenant promise*), we receive of him, because we keep his commandments, and do those things that are pleasing in his sight. 23 And this is his commandment, That we should believe on the name of his Son Jesus Christ, and *agape*/love one another, as he gave us commandment. 24 And he that keepeth his commandments dwelleth in him, and he in him. And hereby we know that he abideth in us, by the Spirit which he hath given us."

If you have not been perfect before the Lord, you must know your need of your Redemption in Jesus. 1 John 3:20 "For if our heart condemn us, God is greater than our heart, and knoweth all things." God knows what He paid for in your Redemption.

Confidence comes from knowing or believing facts. You can have confidence in God three ways:

- First, by walking as Jesus walked.
- Second, by knowing you are redeemed, in spite of your current sins.
- And, third, by being an expert in the Word of Righteousness, the Word of Reconciliation, the Word of Redemption and the Word of our *soteria*/Salvation by grace.

God tells us the right process for growing in Him, along with study of the Scriptures, is to continually acknowledge, *epignosis*, what we have in Jesus. The essential element of Christianity is Holy Spirit dwelling in a person in the new creation. So, whether we sin or not, the great knowing is to know that Christ in us, Holy Spirit, is the hope of glory, the One we can count on to receive wonderful joy-filled good.

This is so critical that Holy Spirit warns us that if we do not *epignosis*/know this, our faith is ineffective, like garage, and useless for bringing the Kingdom of God to Earth in right subduing and establishing dominion for and with God. This is the biblical meaning of *reprobate*.

2 Cor 13:4 "For we also are weak in him, but we shall *zao*/live with him by the power of God toward you. 5 Examine yourselves, whether ye be in the faith; prove your own selves. Know ye not your own selves, how that Jesus Christ is in you, except ye be reprobates? (*ineffective, like garage, useless for bringing the Kingdom of God to Earth in right subduing and establishing dominion for and with God*)."

But the simple confession of this without the means to release God's power and glory means your faith is ineffective. God is not about just Holy Spirit in you, but the Lord said: Num 14:21 "But as truly as I live, all the earth shall be filled with the glory of the LORD."

God defines *sin* as anything lacking His glory: Rom 3:23 "For all have sinned, and come short of the glory of God."

DISCOVERING OUR REDEMPTION

The glory of the Lord is Holy Spirit being able to do whatever He wants:

Isa 11:2 "And the spirit of the Lord shall rest upon him, the spirit of wisdom and understanding, the spirit of counsel and might, the spirit of knowledge and of the fear of the Lord; 3 and shall make him of quick understanding in the fear of the Lord: and he shall not judge after the sight of his eyes, neither reprove after the hearing of his ears: 4 but with righteousness shall he judge the poor, and reprove with equity for the meek of the earth: and he shall smite the earth with the rod of his mouth, and with the breath of his lips shall he slay the wicked. 5 And righteousness shall be the girdle of his loins, and faithfulness the girdle of his reins. 6 The wolf also shall dwell with the lamb, and the leopard shall lie down with the kid; and the calf and the young lion and the fatling together; and a little child shall lead them. 7 And the cow and the bear shall feed; their young ones shall lie down together: and the lion shall eat straw like the ox. 8 And the sucking child shall play on the hole of the asp, and the weaned child shall put his hand on the cockatrice' den."

When Jesus worked miracles, that was the glory of the Lord. Not a new way the Earth works, but a blessing, or fixing, of a current condition into the way God wants it, by doing what God has always said or commanded. The Earth was originally made for God to freely dwell in, and it will be again one day. Man was made for God to freely dwell in and with and to operate through. Remember, God does nothing outside His will, and everything Jesus did was perfectly in the will of God.

Eph 1:10 "That in the dispensation of the fulness of times he might gather together in one all things in Christ, both which are in heaven, and which are on earth; even in him: 11 in whom also we have obtained an inheritance, being predestinated according to the purpose of him who worketh all things after the counsel of his own will."

John 8:28 "Then said Jesus unto them, When ye have lifted up the Son of man, then shall ye know that I am he, and that I do nothing of myself; but as my Father hath taught me, I speak these things. 29 And he that sent me is with me: the Father hath not left me alone; for I do always those things that please him."

When Jesus spoke, He had confidence that Father heard Him and would do what Jesus said because Jesus knew He was doing what was commanded Him. Everyone healed was a captive set free. Everyone that heard and understood His teaching was the mentally blind made to see. Every physically blind one healed was the blind also made to see. Jesus was operating under the commandments of God, and so He had confidence that whatever He spoke, consistent with those commandments, His Father would do, because doing the commands of God allows, releases, or pushes or builds, the path for the *zoe*/life of God to move in the Earth to produce the glory of God.

John 14:8 "Philip saith unto him, Lord, shew us the Father, and it sufficeth us. 9 Jesus saith unto him, Have I been so long time with you, and yet hast thou not

Destroying Sin-Consciousness

known me, Philip? he that hath seen me hath seen the Father; and how sayest thou then, Shew us the Father? 10 Believest thou not that I am in the Father, and the Father in me? the words that I speak unto you I speak not of myself: but the Father that dwelleth in me, he doeth the works. 11 Believe me that I am in the Father, and the Father in me: or else believe me for the very works' sake."

John 12:48 "He that rejecteth me, and *lambano*/receiveth not my words, hath one that judgeth him: the word that I have spoken, the same shall judge him in the last day. 49 For I have not spoken of myself; but the Father which sent me, he gave me a commandment, what I should say, and what I should speak. 50 And I know that his commandment is *zoe*/life everlasting: whatsoever I speak therefore, even as the Father said unto me, so I speak."

Jesus was not talking about hearing God all the time, although we believe He was capable of that. Jesus was saying that the written Word of God was also His commandment and that by *lambano*/receiving that commandment, He proceeded to obey it.

The issue is as it always has been, from Adam until now. Will we receive the commandments of God in such a way that they rule us and overrule any other commandments, or will we listen to the voice of another and obey or follow or have confidence in that one instead?

Jesus, in rebuking the religious leaders of His day, said: Matt 15:3 "But he (*Jesus*) answered and said unto them, Why do ye also transgress the commandment of God by your tradition? 4 For God commanded, saying, Honour thy father and mother: and, He that curseth father or mother, let him die the death. 5 But ye say, Whosoever shall say to his father or his mother, It is a gift, by whatsoever thou mightest be profited by me; 6 and honour not his father or his mother, he shall be free. Thus have ye made the commandment of God of none effect by your tradition."

Notice, they made the commandment of God of no effect by giving another commandment that the people obeyed instead. It was not that the commandment of God was bad; it just did not profit the religious leaders in earthly prosperity of the world's system first. 1 Tim 6:9 "But they that will be rich fall into temptation and a snare, and into many foolish and hurtful lusts, which drown men in destruction and perdition. 10 For the *agape*/love of money is the root of all evil: which while some coveted after, they have erred from the faith, and pierced themselves through with many sorrows."

Matt 6:21 "For where your treasure is, there will your heart be also. 22 The light of the body is the eye: if therefore thine eye be single, thy whole body shall be full of light. 23 But if thine eye be evil (*stingy and covetous*), thy whole body shall be full of darkness. If therefore the light that is in thee be darkness, how great is that darkness! 24 No man can serve two masters: for either he will hate the one, and

DISCOVERING OUR REDEMPTION

agape/love the other; or else he will hold to the one, and despise the other. Ye cannot serve God and mammon."

What is "new" is the rule of God in the Gospel of Jesus Christ through men, in spite of their sins, versus the rule of the devil on the Earth. Col 1:27 "To whom God would make known what is the riches of the glory of this mystery among the Gentiles; which is Christ in you, the hope of glory (*the free reign of Holy Spirit in the Earth through men*): 28 whom we preach, warning every man, and teaching every man in all wisdom; that we may present every man perfect in Christ Jesus."

Concerning the miracle of turning water into wine, Holy Spirit tells us: John 2:11 "This beginning of miracles did Jesus in Cana of Galilee, and manifested forth his glory; and his disciples believed on him."

Turning the water into wine is the glory of the Lord.

John 11:39 "Jesus said, Take ye away the stone. Martha, the sister of him that was dead, saith unto him, Lord, by this time he stinketh: for he hath been dead four days. 40 Jesus saith unto her, Said I not unto thee, that, if thou wouldest believe, thou shouldest see the glory of God?"

Raising the dead is the glory of the Lord.

In these cases, the glory of the Lord can be seen in miracles or works of power demonstrating the Kingdom of God in a given situation. God's goal was not just miracles. These were corrective works, where the kingdom of darkness was ruling in some way, and not the Kingdom of God, but the glory fixed a work of the devil.

The Kingdom of God is growing fruits of righteousness, not just correcting the works of the devil. But increasing, or magnifying, the Kingdom of God is the goal until Heaven is established on Earth.

To sin is to fall short of the glory of God: Rom 3:23 "For all have sinned, and come short of the glory of God."

To sin is to be empowered by the devil: 1 John 5:17 "All unrighteousness is sin ... ."

1 John 3:10 "… whosoever doeth not righteousness is not of God … ."

1 John 3:8 "He that committeth sin is of the devil; for the devil sinneth from the beginning. For this purpose the Son of God was manifested, that he might destroy the works of the devil."

Notice, you cannot sin without the devil. You always have a partner when you sin, great or small.

But the next verses after Romans 3:23 tell us the solution to falling short is knowing (active and intense and confident present tense) you have been made out of, or made, the righteousness of God in Christ Jesus.

Rom 3:24 "Being justified freely by his grace through the redemption that is in Christ Jesus: 25 whom God hath set forth to be a propitiation through faith in his blood, to declare his righteousness for the remission of sins that are past, through

Destroying Sin-Consciousness

the forbearance of God; 26 to declare, I say, at this time his righteousness: that he might be just, and the justifier of him which believeth in Jesus. 27 Where is boasting then? It is excluded. By what law? of works? Nay: but by the law of faith. 28 Therefore we conclude that a man is justified by faith without the deeds of the law."

This is the main aspect of the new creation we are to major in, to make our faith effective. Philem 6 "That the communication of thy faith may become effectual by the acknowledging of every good thing which is in you in Christ Jesus."

We may break them apart to study and explain them, but to God they are all united in Jesus.

1 Cor 1:28 "And base (*unlovely*) things of the world, and things which are despised, hath God chosen, yea, and things which are not, to bring to nought (*dethroned*) things that are: 29 that no flesh should glory in his presence. 30 But of him are ye in Christ Jesus, who of God is made unto us wisdom, and righteousness, and sanctification, and redemption: 31 that, according as it is written, He that glorieth, let him glory in the Lord."

So, dethroned, in the work of the Mighty Arm of God by the cross, was the rulership, the reign of sickness, disease, poverty, lack, want, physical power, fear and death. These are the standard power elements of the world system, run and enforced by the devil. We have access to God by the blood of Jesus, and we can release the Kingdom, by faith in the finished work of Christ, so God can and will keep His promises, and our knowing He is able to do what He has promised.

God has done His part; the rest is up to us.

If you are a Christian, you have the same anointing. 2 Cor 1:20 "For all the promises of God in him (*Jesus*) are yea, and in him Amen, unto the glory of God by us. 21 Now he which stablisheth us with you in Christ, and hath anointed us, is God; 22 who hath also sealed us, and given the earnest of the Spirit in our hearts."

That anointing is the seal and the earnest of Holy Spirit. It is not more or less anointing, for the anointing is Holy Spirit. As a person, He cannot be divided. Instead, our actions are in cooperation (more or less) with Holy Spirit. Rather than dwelling on these truths, sin-consciousness looks at the works of the flesh, your everyday failures, not even your major sins, and says they rule and not the Word of God in Jesus. And indwelling Holy Spirit does you no good.

Righteousness in Jesus is total and eternal. Walking in it means first you know the truth that sets you free, that you are righteous, and then you walk in it, to know, be and do the will of God, for that is what you are made to be in Jesus. Walking in the Gospel means you have to steadily work at renewing your mind, continually *lambano*/holding (no matter what) on to the grace of God and gift of righteousness. Rom 5:17 "For if by one man's offence death reigned by one; much more they which (*continually*) *lambano*/receive abundance of grace and of the gift of righteousness shall reign in *zoe*/life by one, Jesus Christ.)"

DISCOVERING OUR REDEMPTION

When you fall short of that, if you do not focus on the finished work of Jesus or indwelling Holy Spirit, then your conscious (the un-renewed part of your soul) condemns you of sin, the devil will persecute you with your sin, other people may remind you, and if you have broken a law of the land, the government will tell you that you have sinned, and, as you focus on the flesh and not the spirit, you will lose your confidence in God.

1 John 3:18 "My little children, let us not *agape*/love in word, neither in tongue; but in deed and in truth. 19 And hereby we know that we are of the truth, and shall assure our hearts before him. 20 For if our heart condemn us, God is greater than our heart, and knoweth all things. 21 *Agape*/beloved, if our heart condemn us not, then have we confidence toward God. 22 And whatsoever we *aiteo*/ask (*require, demand and expect as due by covenant promise*), we receive of him, because we keep his commandments, and do those things that are pleasing in his sight. 23 And this is his commandment, That we should believe on the name of his Son Jesus Christ (*that at the right mention of that name, the glory of the Lord will be manifested in the Earth, to destroy the works of the devil and deliver the salvation of God, in manifesting the Kingdom, the rule, reign and authority of God by grace*), and *agape*/love one another, as he gave us commandment. 24 And he that keepeth his commandments dwelleth in him, and he in him. And hereby we know that he abideth in us, by the Spirit which he hath given us."

Verse 19 tells us that any place in our heart that operates on the righteousness of our works (and we are required to do right works, but any place we trust in our works for righteousness) can quickly throw us into sin-consciousness and condemnation when we have sinned.

Verse 20 says if we have this confidence, then whatever we *aiteo*/demand in the name of Jesus we get. It is our confidence in God that makes the difference. We can have confidence in our right works or our confidence can be in the work of Christ in our Redemption. But when you sin, you have to apply the truth of the Gospel to that sin, or you will lose confidence in God. It is your confidence in God that causes or releases or makes the path for the answer to prayer, not God Himself.

Verse 20 also says your heart is not the ruler, God is and He is greater than your un-renewed, immature Christian heart, if you base your rightness on your works and not Jesus'. So the choice is to either walk like Jesus in right works confidence, or walk in the knowledge of your righteousness in Jesus, independent of the actual holiness (or the lack of holiness) in your present Earth walk.

God wants to answer your right prayer, but what you are placing your confidence in determines your confidence in God and, thus, your answer. Rom 10:4 "For Christ is the end of the law for righteousness to every one that believeth." So the only reason God will answer your prayer is not because of your good works, but because God *agape*/loves you and the people you are praying for.

Then, in verse 23, God tells us what commands we are to obey: love, as seen in proper and good works, and answered prayer and using the name of Jesus to deliver God's acts of miracle power.

In the earlier verse, God tells us Jesus completed the job.

1 John 3:5 "And ye know that he was manifested to take away (*remit, remove, purge and obliterate*) our sins; and in him is no sin." He bore all our sins, and if they are gone from Jesus, then, by covenant Identification, they are gone, remitted, removed and put away from us as well. (Yahoo!)

If you constantly know you are in Him, by grace, this will keep you from sinning. 1 John 3:6 "Whosoever abideth in him sinneth not: whosoever sinneth hath not seen him, neither known him."

But the standard has not changed: do not sin, do not fall short of the glory of God. 1 John 3:7 "Little children, let no man deceive you: he that doeth righteousness is righteous, even as he is righteous. 8 He that committeth sin is of the devil; for the devil sinneth from the beginning. For this purpose the Son of God was manifested, that he might destroy the works of the devil."

So now you have sinned, and your un-renewed heart condemns you. Holy Spirit is not condemning you for your sin; He will convict you of your lack of faith in the work of Jesus, the Mighty Arm of God. God is advertising and emphasizing the greatest work of God in our age, the Redemption of man unto the indwelling Holy Spirit, through Jesus.

John 16:8 "And when he is come, he will reprove the world of sin, and of righteousness, and of judgment: 9 of sin, because they believe not on me; 10 of righteousness, because I go to my Father, and ye see me no more; 11 of judgment, because the prince of this world is judged."

And when we judge the devil, in getting right answers to our *aiteo*/requiring, demanding and expecting as due by covenant promise of God, because all the promises of God in Jesus are Yeah and Amen, we respond properly to the reproving of Holy Spirit.

Our response is not, "Oh, how rotten I am!" but, "Wow! That was/is not like my new man; it is a work of the flesh, and I command it to go in the name of Jesus. I got deceived, and I did it, but that is not me or what I am about. That is not the real me, for I am a new creation in God, in His image. Jesus already paid for this, and I am healed of it; and I now receive that healing in Jesus. Thank You, Father! You are getting me to walk in Jesus more. Thank You!" (For more on this, see Chapter 36, "Dealing with the Burn-It-Now Process.")

This is one way to obey: 2 Cor 3:16 "Nevertheless when it (*any one aware that they are not acting just like the Lord*) shall turn to the Lord, the vail shall be taken

DISCOVERING OUR REDEMPTION

away. 17 Now the Lord is that Spirit: and where the Spirit of the Lord is, there is liberty (*to be all God made you in Jesus*). 18 But we all, with open face beholding as in a glass (*mirror*) the glory of the Lord, are changed into the same image from glory to glory, even as by the Spirit of the Lord."

Sin consciousness says there is no real help in God. So when you finally agree it is sin, you skip the step of faith in God for healing of all that allowed that sin to take place and that all aspects of the situation are already fully healed in Jesus, and you focus on what you need to do to be right. Then when by will power you do avoid sin, you congratulate yourself for doing right, rather than thanking God for answering your prayer. You call them "luck," "good fortune," "right labor" or at best "blessing," but not by faith in God by His Word.

Yes, you need to know the path or steps you need to take to right thoughts and behaviors. The difference is how you handle them. Sin consciousness says, "Here is what I must do," and off you go. Righteousness conscious says, "What I am to do is by God working in me to will and do of His good pleasure to know and understand the Bible paths of God (His laws and Words) and obey them gladly. I am never alone in this. Any resistance is not of God or of my new creation, and thank You, Father, for working in me to walk like Jesus. Any good in me is from You, and I thank You that I will see more of You coming out through me." You are a co-laborer with God to bring Heaven to Earth and never independent of Him. And for each step you give thanks and glory to God in advance, and as they come to pass you continue to give Him thanks, praise and rejoicing per His Word.

In sin consciousness you are independent of God. In God's Righteousness consciousness with indwelling Holy Spirit, it is you and He working together to renew your mind so all His ways are gladness, thanksgiving and praise. You start in faith by renewing your mind into the message of the New Creation in Jesus, giving thanks, praise and rejoicing before your see the answer, while you see the answer and after you see the answer. You major in your Redemption in spite of your sins and failures, and not the false religion of separation by sin or failure.

No one has a problem with sin, guilt and condemnation when they are unaware of sin, and everything is going well. But in the heat of sin and problems, the devil will try to fill you with guilt and condemnation. That sense of shame means you are not walking by the spirit, but by the flesh. And in this state, delivering restitution and reconciliation is very hard.

Rom 8:1 "There is therefore now no condemnation to them which are in Christ Jesus, who walk not after the flesh, but after the Spirit. 2 For the law of the Spirit of *zoe*/life in Christ Jesus hath made me free from the law of sin and death."

If you do not believe the report of the Scriptures, then you stay in the flesh and are ruled by fear. Heb 2:14 "Forasmuch then as the children are partakers of flesh and blood, he also himself likewise took part of the same; that through death he might destroy him that had the power of death, that is, the devil; 15 and deliver them who through fear of death were all their lifetime subject to bondage."

DESTROYING SIN-CONSCIOUSNESS

Faith is the joyful expectation of coming good. Fear is the dread of coming evil. The two do not mix. The amazing thing is that we can have one thought of faith followed by another of fear. 2 Cor 10:3 "For though we walk in the flesh, we do not war after the flesh: 4 (for the weapons of our warfare are not carnal, but mighty through God to the pulling down of strong holds;) 5 casting down imaginations, and every high thing that exalteth itself against the knowledge of God, and bringing into captivity every thought to the obedience of Christ; 6 and having in a readiness to revenge all disobedience, when your obedience is fulfilled."

Holy Spirit will reprove you, make you aware that you have committed a sin and that your answer to that sin is in Jesus, not your flesh. He will reprove you that you are trying to operate in a righteousness of the flesh, not knowing that you are the righteousness of God in Jesus, independent of your works, but by faith in the blood of Jesus, fully healed and made righteous, with *zoe* life and seated with Him at the throne of God.

Holy Spirit will reprove you that the devil has been judged, your sin works destroyed in Jesus, and you are to kick the devil out of the situation and enforce the Kingdom of God, until God's glory is manifested in you and anyone else involved.

Get this right, and you will know your sins are remitted, the entire situation was healed in Jesus. You can then operate in faith to see that healing manifested, and you must work overtime to make sure no one stays offended, and that all the right reconciliations and restitutions are made. Get it wrong, and you will walk in the fear of sin-consciousness and have no faith in God, until you again turn to the Lord in the Word of reconciliation in our Redemption through the more-than-sufficient blood of Jesus, and reprogram your heart.

When you exercise the judgment of God against the devil, in the name of Jesus, you are putting the wrath of God onto the works of the devil, and you are doing works of faith, and it profits you, if you are doing it based on *agape* love. Gal 5:6 "For in Jesus Christ neither circumcision availeth anything, nor uncircumcision; but faith which worketh by *agape*/love."

This is how you can destroy sin-consciousness in your life, by constantly renewing your mind in the Gospel of our *soteria*/salvation in Jesus, and walk in the freedom of Holy Spirit, freely living the *zoe*/life of God in and through you.

As we now know, that mind-renewing process consists of 2 to 6 hours per day with a set of Scriptures daily for at least 90 days (See *OK, God, Now What?* at www.CovenantPeaceMinistries.com for more on this). Since faith is the opposite of fear, as we learn to operate in faith, we will destroy fear and bring God's salvation to Earth. 2 Tim 3:15 "And that from a child thou hast known the holy scriptures, which are able to make thee wise unto *soteria*/salvation through faith which is in Christ Jesus. 16 All scripture is given by inspiration of God, and is profitable for doctrine, for reproof, for correction, for instruction in righteousness: 17 that the man of God may be perfect, throughly furnished unto all good works."

Chapter 34

Working with the Wrath of God

There are two aspects of the so called "wrath of God": One is of God, and the other is of the devil, the dethroned, but obviously still functioning, god of this world.

The great God, Creator of all, is a consuming fire that destroys all not like or of Him. (Heb 12:29, 1 Cor 3:10-14, Matt 3:11-12, Lk 12:49)

The devil, unleashed due to sin in the Earth, in the curse of sin. (Rom 5:12-14)

In general for now, we see very little of the first type; most of the evil seen in the world is the second type.

For the first type, the wrath of God, when you see a prayer answered and some evil had to be removed, that is the wrath of God against that evil. When you see a miracle of healing by God, that is the wrath of God against a work of the devil, in setting that person free. When it is complete, the person has no trace of the disorder, and the person is back to the way God intended. Acts 10:36 "The word which God sent unto the children of Israel, preaching peace by Jesus Christ: (he is Lord of all:) 37 that word, I say, ye know, which was published throughout all Judaea, and began from Galilee, after the baptism which John preached; 38 how God anointed Jesus of Nazareth with the Holy Ghost and with power: who went about doing good, and healing all that were oppressed (*under the active dominion, reign and lordship*) of the devil; for God was with him."

Wrath as a word is an intense application of force to achieve an end result. God's wrath is the force that removes corruption and restores His righteousness on the Earth.

The restoration spoken of in the Book of Revelation, in which all evil is destroyed, Satan bound into the Lake of Fire, and God comes to dwell on the Earth, is a demonstration of His effective wrath. Notice that the intended end result is good; it is "Heaven on Earth."

The devil's wrath destroys all that is like God, in a manner to cause the most fear of the devil among men, the most misery for man, and for men to distrust God and all that is good. (Job 1-3; John 10:10; 1 Pet 5:8; Rev 12-9-12)

There is a third aspect of God's wrath. The negative consequences of violating God's laws are also called His wrath. This is what most people consider His wrath to be. This kind of wrath is the consequences of violation of His laws or of following laws that produce evil consequences. What people tend to forget is that God knows we sin and has solutions for that sin.

The negative consequence is not as sure as the blessed consequences for rightly working with God's laws, as evil is overcome by good, else Jesus never could have healed anyone. James 2:13 "For he shall have judgment without mercy, that hath shewed no mercy; and mercy rejoiceth against judgment (*or mercy triumphs over judgment*)."

If you ignore gravity and jump off a high cliff, the consequences of gravity, the wrath of gravity, will be felt when you hit the ground. God is the one who made gravity and also the parachute, as seen in dandelion seeds and the "wings" of flying squirrels, to show us how to manage the force of gravity and avoid its wrath.

God also showed us the law of flight in birds, that with added energy and right activity, you can fly against the force of gravity. This is the same God and the same law of gravity. It is our choice how we deal with it. Just as with gravity, ignorance of God's law is not bliss. Hos 4:6 "My people are destroyed for lack of knowledge ... ."

The problem is not God, but our not knowing, or ignorance, or misapplication of the facts of Redemption, Reconciliation, Righteousness, Salvation, Sanctification, and Adoption, and then secondarily, not applying them properly, which is Wisdom.

By biblical standards, knowledge that does not cause right behavior as a master craftsman is deception, and not true knowledge. One term for this is mental assent, where you agree it is true, but you do not use it to manifest the Kingdom of God by grace in a situation. You may use law, but you are to reign with grace, not law.

Rom 5:21 "That as sin hath reigned (*as king*) unto death, even so might grace reign (*as a greater king*) through righteousness unto eternal *zoe*/life by Jesus Christ our Lord."

DISCOVERING OUR REDEMPTION

So you are not expert, *epignosis,* knowing the Word of righteousness until you can reign as Jesus would in any situation you are either in or aware of.

In the Garden, when Adam sinned, instead of running to God, because sin had blinded him, he ran *from* God. God went and helped Adam anyway. Gen 3:6 "And when the woman saw that the tree was good for food, and that it was pleasant to the eyes, and a tree to be desired to make one wise, she took of the fruit thereof, and did eat, and gave also unto her husband with her; and he did eat. 7 And the eyes of them both were opened, and they knew that they were naked; and they sewed fig leaves together, and made themselves aprons. 8 And they heard the voice of the Lord God walking in the garden in the cool of the day: and Adam and his wife hid themselves from the presence of the Lord God amongst the trees of the garden. 9 And the Lord God called unto Adam, and said unto him, Where art thou? 10 And he said, I heard thy voice in the garden, and I was afraid, because I was naked; and I hid myself. 11 And he said, who told thee that thou wast naked? Hast thou eaten of the tree, whereof I commanded thee that thou shouldest not eat?"

God knew exactly what happened, but Adam would not speak honestly with God. Adam had released death into the world through his sin. Rom 5:12 "Wherefore, as by one man (*Adam*) sin entered into the world, and death by sin; and so death passed upon all men, for that all have sinned (*having come from the loins of Adam*)."

Now God had to deal with the consequences to save His mankind. So the first thing God did was to limit what Satan could do and to promise that God would one day destroy what Satan had done. Gen 3:12 "And the man said, The woman whom thou gavest to be with me, she gave me of the tree, and I did eat. 13 And the Lord God said unto the woman, What is this that thou hast done? And the woman said, The serpent beguiled me, and I did eat. 14 And the Lord God said unto the serpent, Because thou hast done this, thou art cursed above all cattle, and above every beast of the field; upon thy belly shalt thou go, and dust shalt thou eat all the days of thy life: 15 and I will put enmity between thee and the woman, and between thy seed and her seed; it shall bruise (*crush*) thy head, and thou shalt bruise his heel. 16 Unto the woman he said, I will greatly multiply thy sorrow and thy conception; in sorrow thou shalt bring forth children; and thy desire shall be to thy husband, and he shall rule over thee. 17 And unto Adam he said, Because thou hast hearkened unto the voice of thy wife, and hast eaten of the tree, of which I commanded thee, saying, Thou shalt not eat of it: cursed is the ground for thy sake; in sorrow shalt thou eat of it all the days of thy life; 18 thorns also and thistles shall it bring forth to thee; and thou shalt eat the herb of the field; 19 in the sweat of thy face shalt thou eat bread, till thou return unto the ground; for out of it wast thou taken: for dust thou art, and unto dust shalt thou return."

Working with the Wrath of God

The so called "curses of God" were actually limits on the devil, so the devil could not kill Adam and Eve as he wanted. First, God limited the devil to the Earth. Yes, childbirth would be hard, and yes, man would have to work the land, but, no, the devil could not kill them with starvation, or no children/lack of fertility/infertility, death in child bearing or miscarriage. Because God judged Satan, that means that anytime anyone exercised faith in God, any effect of the law of sin and death could be overcome, because that is what Satan operated on. This was the source of all the goodness and miracles God was able to do before, during and after Jesus was manifested on Earth.

God had promised that from the woman would come a Deliverer who would crush Satan. The devil knew if she lived that One would indeed come. God made sure that, on a cursed Earth, man could still live.

Next, we see the first blood shed in covering sin and establishing covenant relationship. Gen 3:21 "Unto Adam also and to his wife did the LORD God make coats of skins, and clothed them."

But the tragedies managed by the devil had just begun. Eve had two children, Abel and Cain. Abel followed God's laws in covenant sacrifice, and Cain did not. Gen 4:2 "And she again bare his brother Abel. And Abel was a keeper of sheep, but Cain was a tiller of the ground. 3 And in process of time it came to pass, that Cain brought of the fruit of the ground an offering unto the LORD. 4 And Abel, he also brought of the firstlings of his flock and of the fat thereof. And the LORD had respect unto Abel and to his offering: 5 but unto Cain and to his offering he had not respect. And Cain was very wroth, and his countenance fell."

Cain was already into pride, insisting on doing things his own way (a definition of iniquity) and was offended that God did not accept his offering (an attitude of pride and unforgiveness). Yet, instead of rejecting Cain, God tried to help Cain and went to him. Gen 4:6 "And the LORD said unto Cain, Why art thou wroth? and why is thy countenance fallen (*as in a severe depression or temper tantrum*)? 7 If thou doest well, shalt thou not be accepted? and if thou doest not well, sin (*a croucher, demon, monster, hungry beast, guilt or devil*) lieth at the door. And unto thee shall be his desire, and thou shalt rule over him."

God warned Cain that he had sinned and that he could recover by doing right, per God's law. If Cain did not do right, correcting his error and reconciling the sin, then he would be subject to the devil whom his sin had attracted. That devil now desired to control Cain for more evil, and Cain must fight to win freedom from that control. If Cain did not win, the devil would rule or lord over or control Cain, causing him to commit more sin. Rom 6:16 "Know ye not, that to whom ye yield yourselves servants to obey, his servants ye are to whom ye obey; whether of sin unto death, or of obedience unto righteousness?"

Unfortunately Cain did not win the battle. Gen 4:8 "And Cain talked with Abel his brother: and it came to pass, when they were in the field, that Cain rose up

DISCOVERING OUR REDEMPTION

against Abel his brother, and slew him. 9 And the Lord said unto Cain, Where is Abel thy brother? And he said, I know not: Am I my brother's keeper? 10 And he said, What hast thou done? the voice of thy brother's blood crieth unto me from the ground."

Notice that the devil won and tempted Cain to even more anger, resentment and, finally, murder of the one who had done right. Cain killed Abel. The consequence was that Cain received even more of the curse of sin. Gen 4:11 "And now art thou cursed from the earth, which hath opened her mouth to receive thy brother's blood from thy hand; 12 when thou tillest the ground, it shall not henceforth yield unto thee her strength; a fugitive and a vagabond shalt thou be in the earth. 13 And Cain said unto the Lord, My punishment is greater than I can bear. 14 Behold, thou hast driven me out this day from the face of the earth; and from thy face shall I be hid; and I shall be a fugitive and a vagabond in the earth; and it shall come to pass, that every one that findeth me shall slay me."

The first time I understood this I was astounded. Based on the teachings of my past, I thought for sure God would have killed Cain when he killed Abel. Instead, God was merciful to Cain and made it so that Cain would not be killed. Gen 4:15 "And the Lord said unto him, Therefore whosoever slayeth Cain, vengeance shall be taken on him sevenfold. And the Lord set a mark upon Cain, lest any finding him should kill him. 16 And Cain went out from the presence of the Lord, and dwelt in the land of Nod, on the east of Eden."

Look at how God responded to sin in this book of "First Things." First, He went to the aide of Adam and Eve, then He went to correct Cain, to avoid a demonic attack upon him, then He was merciful to Cain and made a way for him to live. So when someone tells you that God hates sin, agree, but respond with something like this: "Yes, God hates everything about sin and He made sure all that hate fell on Jesus, but God loves the sinner." Every miracle Jesus did was an example of God's true attitude toward man. If man could not fix it, God would send someone who could–Jesus, the Messiah, the Mighty Arm of God.

John 3:16 "For God so greatly *agape*/loved and dearly prized the world that He [even] gave up His only begotten (unique) Son, so that whoever believes in (trusts in, clings to, relies on) Him shall not perish (come to destruction, be lost) but have eternal (everlasting) *zoe*/life. 17 For God did not send the Son into the world in order to judge (to reject, to condemn, to pass sentence on) the world, but that the world might find *soteria*/salvation and be made safe and sound through Him. 18 He who believes in Him [who clings to, trusts in, relies on Him] is not judged [he who trusts in Him never comes up for judgment; for him there is no rejection, no condemnation—he incurs no damnation]; but he who does not believe (cleave to, rely on, trust in Him) is judged already [he has already been convicted and has already received his sentence] because he has not believed in and trusted in the name of the only begotten Son of God. [He is condemned for refusing to let his trust rest in Christ's name.]" AMP

Working with the Wrath of God

So God's response is to remove sin, put it away as an issue with Him and, thus, remove the legal grounds for the curse of sin. God hates sin so much that He sent Jesus to suffer and die to resolve it by redemption for the remission, obliteration, purging and putting away of both sin and the curse of sin. Heb 9:26 "For then must he often have suffered since the foundation of the world: but now once in the end of the world hath he appeared to put away sin by the sacrifice of himself."

You cannot sin without the devil, and when you do sin, he is your life source. 1 John 3:8 "He that committeth sin is of the devil; for the devil sinneth from the beginning. For this purpose the Son of God was manifested, that he might destroy the works of the devil."

And just as God warned Cain: Gen 4:7 "If thou doest well, shalt thou not be accepted? and if thou doest not well, sin *(demon, monster, hungering beast, guilt or devil)* lieth at the door. And unto thee shall be his desire, and thou shalt rule over him *(to be free of him)*": that law is still in operation.

Jesus delivered the wrath of God in everyone He healed. Acts 10:36 "The word which God sent unto the children of Israel, preaching peace by Jesus Christ: (he is Lord of all:) 37 that word, I say, ye know, which was published throughout all Judaea, and began from Galilee, after the baptism which John preached; 38 how God anointed Jesus of Nazareth with the Holy Ghost and with power: who went about doing good, and healing all that were oppressed of the devil; for God was with him." This "doing good" included the wrath of God on the rulership/oppression of the devil for everyone that God healed by Jesus.

In our great Redemption, He did the same thing. Acts 10:42 "And he *(Jesus)* commanded us to preach unto the people, and to testify that it is he which was ordained of God to be the Judge of quick and dead. 43 To him give all the prophets witness, that through his name whosoever believeth in him shall receive remission *(purging, removal, obliteration, putting away)* of sins."

When we are born again and our sins are purged in Jesus, that is also the wrath of God, and they are forever destroyed. This is included in what Jesus came to do, that had not been done before. Acts 13:34 "And as concerning that he raised him up from the dead, now no more to return to corruption, he said on this wise, I will give you the sure mercies of David. 35 Wherefore he saith also in another psalm, Thou shalt not suffer thine Holy One to see corruption. 36 For David, after he had served his own generation by the will of God, fell on sleep, and was laid unto his fathers, and saw corruption: 37 but he, whom God raised again, saw no corruption. 38 Be it known unto you therefore, men and brethren, that through this man is preached unto you the *aphesis*/forgiveness *(purging, removal, obliteration, putting away)* of sins: 39 and by him all that believe are justified from all things, from which ye could not be justified by the law of Moses."

In Rev 21 and 22 we see God come to Earth after the wrath destroys all the works of the devil. This Day of Judgment against the devil started with Jesus. This is seen when Jesus cast out a devil who thought it was not yet the time. Matt 8:28 "And when he *(Jesus)* was come to the other side into the country of the Gergesenes, there met him two pos-

DISCOVERING OUR REDEMPTION

sessed with devils, coming out of the tombs, exceeding fierce, so that no man might pass by that way. 29 And, behold, they cried out, saying, What have we to do with thee, Jesus, thou Son of God? art thou come hither to torment us before the time?"

The day of Judgment against the devil with the wrath of God, the finger of God, Holy Spirit, started 2000 years ago and ends in Rev 21 and 22. The wrath of God against the devil is the Kingdom or reign of God removing the reign and effects of the devil. Acts 10:38 "How God anointed Jesus of Nazareth with the Holy Ghost and with power: who went about doing good, and healing all that were oppressed *(under the lordship, rule or reign)* of the devil; for God was with him." Matt 12:28 "But if I cast out devils by the Spirit of God, then the kingdom of God is come unto you." See also Luke 11:20

In this Day of Salvation we are to major on the Grace of Reconciliation in Redemption and do what Jesus commanded. 2 Cor 5:20 "Now then we are ambassadors for Christ, as though God did beseech you by us: we pray you in Christ's stead, be ye reconciled to God. 21 For he *(Father God)* hath made him *(Jesus)* to be sin for us, who knew no sin; that we might be made the righteousness of God in him *(Jesus)*. 6:1 We then, as workers together with him, beseech you also that ye receive not the grace of God in vain. 2 (For he saith, I have heard thee in a time accepted, and in the day of *soteria*/salvation have I succoured thee: behold, now is the accepted time; behold, now is the day of *soteria*/salvation.)"

This is the Day in which we, the Body of Christ, are to exercise the Wrath of God on the works of the devil and set people free into the truth of God. Lk 10:9 "And heal the sick that are therein, and say unto them, The kingdom of God is come nigh unto you." This is part of the "all things" in Matt 28:20 "Teaching them to observe all things whatsoever I have commanded you ... ."

Therefore disciples are to train all others to do the same as Jesus commanded in delivering the wrath of God against the devil and his works. Lk 10:19 "Behold *(perceive and make this change your life)*, I give unto you *exousia*/power *(responsibility, commission and the resources of Heaven)* to tread on *(crush, bruise, destroy, remove, heal)* serpents and scorpions, and over all the *dunamis*/power *(ability, works)* of the enemy: and nothing shall by any means hurt you."

And you can rest assured, that if you are not delivering the Wrath of God against the devil, the devil is putting his wrath on you. 1 Pet 5:8 "Be sober *(no longer drunk and apathetic in the ways of the world)*, be vigilant; because your adversary the devil, as a roaring lion, walketh about, seeking whom he may devour: 9 whom resist *(fight, deliver the wrath of God onto)* stedfast in the faith, knowing that the same afflictions are accomplished in your brethren that are in the world." See also Ephesians 6.

1 Cor 2:4 "And my speech and my preaching was not with enticing words of man's wisdom, but in demonstration of the Spirit and of *dunamis*/power: 5 that your faith should not stand in the wisdom of men, but in the *dunamis*/power of God."

Chapter 35

Facing Off Against the Devil

The pattern seen throughout the Bible is that when men sin, the devil is released to perform great evil and misery on men, by the law of sin and death. This law says: you sin, you die. So we get attacks from the devil when we sin. Rom 5:12 "Wherefore, as by one man sin entered into the world, and death by sin; and so death passed upon all men, for that all have sinned." Rom 5:21 "That as sin hath reigned (*as king*) unto death, even so might grace reign (*to deliver God's salvation to the Earth*) through righteousness unto eternal *zoe*/life by Jesus Christ our Lord." Rom 8:2 "For the law of the Spirit of *zoe*/life in Christ Jesus hath made me free from the law of sin and death." 1 Cor 15:56 "The sting of death is sin; and the strength of sin is the law." James 1:15 "Then when lust hath conceived, it bringeth forth sin: and sin, when it is finished, bringeth forth death." Rom 6:23 "For the wages of sin is death; but the gift of God is eternal *zoe*/life through Jesus Christ our Lord."

So, when we sin, that demon is death coming to work death in our lives. We are sowing to the flesh in evil seeds, and we will reap corruption of the flesh as that evil seed matures.

Since the devil is the enforcer of death, he tempts us to sin so he can enforce the law of sin and death upon us.

DISCOVERING OUR REDEMPTION

Another attack comes when the devil, looking for whomever he can attack, chooses to attack you, whether you have sinned or not. 1 Pet 5:8 "Be sober, be vigilant; because your adversary the devil, as a roaring lion, walketh about, seeking whom he may devour."

So the devil can inflict his wrath, the destruction of anything that looks like God, when we sin and when we do not sin, as long as he is free in this world. So a fuller definition of the law of sin and death is that when you sin death comes in either a fast or slow form, and if you do not sin, because the devil is in the world, he will try to inflict the law of sin and death on you anyway. The less you know about the work of Jesus by the cross, the less you can resist the devil in either kind of attack or oppression.

Most every action we do is designed to bring us good, as we define it at the moment. Even a person committing suicide thinks they are better off dead than alive. Men in combat can be brave and resist the fear, based on a greater good they see at the moment. So almost every action we commit is driven by our perception of what is good right then.

Our minds can be filled with dread, fear of loss or unpleasantness, and what we do now, we think, will make that loss or unpleasantness lessen or go away. If you know the Scriptures, then, at that moment, the Scriptures may seem far away and the pressing need of the moment more important and urgent to act upon.

Remember, when you sin you are either sinning in ignorance or willfully. In either case, you have faith that the sin you commit will get you the good you want in life. So, to sin is to have faith in a lie that activates the law of sin and death, and you must deal with the consequences.

When you do righteous works, per the Word of God, if you have faith in God, you will expect to get:

a) The perceived good and any natural law good (giving alms to the poor helps the poor, and they may thank you = natural good) and

b) Good from God (for you are then operating in faith in God by His Word).

Most actions are:

a) Immediate based on what is already in your heart, so you are almost unaware you did them, or

b) Planned (at least to some level).

In both cases, you are subject to what truth (God's Word) already exists in your heart or what word you are in agreement enough with to do. Ps 119:10 "With my whole heart have I sought thee: O let me not wander from thy commandments. 11 Thy word have I hid in mine heart, that I might not sin against thee. 12 Blessed art thou, O Lord: teach me thy statutes. 13 With my lips have I declared all the judgments of thy mouth."

The point of this is that when you sin you are in faith, but your faith is placed in a lie that will produce death, whether you like it or not. Like Adam and Eve, you are choosing the word of the devil over the Word of God. Or, by your culture and ignorance of the Bible, you are doing what seems right to you, but is, in reality, against the laws of God. Murder is murder, whether you or your culture consider it to be murder or not.

In all cases, the Universe is so designed by God that: Gal 6:7 "Be not deceived; God is not mocked: for whatsoever a man soweth, that shall he also reap. 8 For he that soweth to his flesh shall of the flesh reap corruption; but he that soweth to the Spirit shall of the Spirit reap *zoe*/life everlasting. 9 And let us not be weary in well doing: for in due season we shall reap, if we faint not. 10 As we have therefore opportunity, let us do good unto all men, especially unto them who are of the household of faith."

One possible focus of life is the fact that God is good. He is the source of grace to be and act like Him, so He can bless, and His Word is truth that never changes, in spite of the many conflicting situations and messages of the devil. Ps 100:4 "Enter into his gates with thanksgiving, and into his courts with praise: be thankful unto him, and bless his name. 5 For the Lord is good; his *chesed*/mercy is everlasting; and his truth endureth to all generations."

If you are not in faith in God, by His Word, you are in sin, and that is the devil's territory. Jesus came to destroy the works of the devil. 1 John 3:7 "Little children, let no man deceive you: he that doeth righteousness is righteous, even as he (*Jesus*) is righteous. 8 He that committeth sin is of the devil; for the devil sinneth from the beginning. For this purpose the Son of God was manifested, that he might destroy the works of the devil." This means the wrath of God in raising Jesus from the dead was "destroying" the devil, as was every healing Jesus performed.

In Exodus 4, God gave Moses two signs to convince people he was from God. The first was to put his hand under his robe, and when he removed it, it had become leprous. Then he put it back again, and when he had removed it, it was clean. God does not have leprosy in Heaven, but the devil apparently does have it in Hell. When Moses first put his hand in and removed it, this looked like a work of the devil. When Moses put it in the second time and it came out healed, that was Holy Spirit gladly healing him and destroying that apparent work of the devil.

So we see numerous times in the Bible where a plague came (God sent, or could not stop, it by His laws), and then God was able to heal the people. But God is not confused. Just as with Job, for whatever reason the devil was involved and produced death in some form, and then God was able to heal Job by someone's right action.

Notice, in the case of John 9, the man born blind at birth, that neither the parents nor the man had sinned. This was either an attack of the devil or an accident in this world of sin. What is clear is that God did not make the man blind, else

DISCOVERING OUR REDEMPTION

Jesus would not have healed him. Where would God get blindness in Heaven? In either case, here is what Jesus said: John 9:3 "Jesus answered, Neither hath this man sinned, nor his parents: **but that the works of God should be made manifest in him. 4 I must work the works of him that sent me,** while it is day: the night cometh, when no man can work. 5 As long as I am in the world, I am the light of the world *in showing what God is really like.*"

Like every other healing, this was a judgment of the wrath of God on the devil's work, by a man knowing it was God's will to always heal. Ps 103:3 "Who forgiveth all thine iniquities; who healeth all thy diseases."

Acts 10:36 "The word which God sent unto the children of Israel, preaching peace by Jesus Christ: (he is Lord of all:) 37 that word, I say, ye know, which was published throughout all Judaea, and began from Galilee, after the baptism which John preached; 38 how God anointed Jesus of Nazareth with the Holy Ghost and with power: who went about doing good, and healing all that were oppressed (*under the active lordship and control in some way*) of the devil; for God was with him."

Luke 13:11 "And, behold, there was a woman which had a spirit of infirmity eighteen years, and was bowed together, and could in no wise lift up herself. 12 And when Jesus saw her, he called her to him, and said unto her, Woman, thou art loosed from thine infirmity. 13 And he laid his hands on her: and immediately she was made straight, and glorified God. 14 And the ruler of the synagogue answered with indignation, because that Jesus had healed on the sabbath day, and said unto the people, There are six days in which men ought to work: in them therefore come and be healed, and not on the sabbath day. 15 The Lord then answered him, and said, Thou hypocrite, doth not each one of you on the sabbath loose his ox or his ass from the stall, and lead him away to watering? 16 And ought not this woman, being a daughter of Abraham, whom Satan hath bound, lo, these eighteen years, be loosed from this bond on the sabbath day?"

We understand that the power of God is His *zoe* life. That life is the wrath of God against the devil and his works. We have this *zoe* life because Jesus took all the death due us.

Per Isaiah 53, Jesus took the full wrath of God for us. Heb 10:12 "But this man, after he had offered **one sacrifice for sins for ever**, sat down on the right hand of God; 13 from henceforth expecting till his enemies be made his footstool."

Rom 3:24 "Being justified freely by his grace through the redemption that is in Christ Jesus: 25 whom God hath set forth to be a propitiation through faith in his blood, to declare his righteousness for the remission of sins that are past, through the forbearance of God; 26 to declare, I say, at this time his righteousness: that he might be just, and the justifier of him which believeth in Jesus."

Rom 8:2 "For the law of the Spirit of *zoe*/life in Christ Jesus hath made me free from the law of sin and (*the curse of sin,*) death."

So, before God, there are now no legal attacks from the devil, whether we sin or not. What is missing is our enforcing the law of the spirit of *zoe*/life in Christ Jesus on the works of the devil, as Jesus did.

Luke 10:19 "Behold, I give unto you power (*authority, commission and the resources of Heaven*) to tread on serpents and scorpions, and over all the power (*ability*) of the enemy: and nothing shall by any means hurt you."

Don't blame God for our failure to obey this command and to enforce this responsibility from Jesus. Hear God's answer to Moses, who was "lost in prayer." Moses had prayed the prayer part, so that was done; now God needed faith action, the "go-do part."

Ex 14:13 "And Moses said unto the people, Fear ye not, stand still, and see the salvation of the Lord, which he will shew to you to day: for the Egyptians whom ye have seen to day, ye shall see them again no more for ever. 14 The Lord shall fight for you, and ye shall hold your peace."

This was a great proclamation and prayer and vitally necessary, but God said there was more to do, exercise His Word in command.

Ex 14:15 "And the Lord said unto Moses, Wherefore criest thou unto me? speak unto the children of Israel, that they go forward: 16 but lift thou up thy rod, and stretch out thine hand over the sea, and divide it: and the children of Israel shall go on dry ground through the midst of the sea."

Jesus is the exact way God is, in all a man can be. Heb 1:3 "Who being the brightness of his glory, and the express image of his person, and upholding all things by the word of his power, when he had by himself purged our sins, sat down on the right hand of the Majesty on high."

Col 1:14 "In whom we have redemption through his blood, even the forgiveness of sins: 15 who is the image of the invisible God, the firstborn of every creature." In the Gospels, God, through the life of Jesus, is showing His true nature operating in a man. Every act of healing Jesus did was a judgment of God against the devil for enforcing or implementing the law of sin and death.

Acts 10:34 "Then Peter opened his mouth, and said, Of a truth I perceive that God is no respecter of persons: 35 but in every nation he that feareth him, and worketh righteousness, is accepted with him. 36 The word which God sent unto the children of Israel, preaching peace by Jesus Christ: (he is Lord of all:) 37 that word, I say, ye know, which was published throughout all Judaea, and began from Galilee, after the baptism which John preached; 38 how God anointed Jesus of Nazareth with the Holy Ghost and with power: who went about doing good, and healing all that were oppressed (*under the active dominion, reign or lordship*) of the devil; for God was with him."

Father God used Jesus to destroy the works of the devil. Healing in the name of Jesus is a right act. Destroying sickness, death and disease, in the power and name of Jesus, is the wrath of God against the devil.

DISCOVERING OUR REDEMPTION

When Adam sinned, he released sin and death into the world. Rom 5:14 "Nevertheless death reigned (*as king*) from Adam to Moses, even over them that had not sinned after the similitude of Adam's transgression, who is the figure of him that was to come." Notice, the Law of Moses stopped the free reign of the devil and gave men a way to get *zoe*/life, to counter the law of sin and death until Jesus came.

Acts 13:37 "But he, whom God raised again, saw no corruption. 38 Be it known unto you therefore, men and brethren, that through this man is preached unto you the *aphesis*/forgiveness (*remission, purging, washing, removal, obliteration and putting away*) of sins: 39 and by him all that believe are justified from all things, from which ye could not be justified by the law of Moses."

John 10:10 "The thief cometh not, but for to steal, and to kill, and to destroy: I am come that they might have *zoe*/life, and that they might have it more abundantly."

Rom 5:21 "That as sin hath reigned (*as king, inflicting the curse in fast and slow forms*) unto death, even so might grace reign (*as a conquering king, delivering the salvation of God*) through righteousness unto eternal *zoe*/life by Jesus Christ our Lord."

The devils Jesus cast out thought the Day of God's Judgment against them was far away. Jesus demonstrated that it started with His ministry, as the Day of Salvation, which we are now in.

Matt 8:29 "And, behold, they cried out, saying, What have we to do with thee, Jesus, thou Son of God? art thou come hither to torment (*judge against*) us before the time? 30 And there was a good way off from them an herd of many swine feeding. 31 So the devils besought him, saying, If thou cast us out, suffer us to go away into the herd of swine. 32 And he said unto them, Go. And when they were come out, they went into the herd of swine: and, behold, the whole herd of swine ran violently down a steep place into the sea, and perished in the waters."

By casting out the devils, Jesus judged against them. The judgment was not complete until they were gone and the situation healed, i.e., the judgment was enforced to the final result intended. Ranting at the devil, "You are judged," does no good; deliverance (casting out the devil by *aiteo*/commands to go in the name of Jesus) and healing enforced by faith in the name of Jesus does.

The word *judgment* means a judicial decree for or against someone. The word in Matt 8:29 translated *torment* means misery as a result of a judicial decree against. Jesus issued a judicial decree against the demons and in favor of or for the man controlled by the demons when Jesus said "Go," in verse 32. So, yes, the devils had the timing wrong, and now is the Day of Salvation, which also starts the Day of Judgment against the devil and his works.

2 Cor 6:1 "We then, as workers together with him, beseech you also that ye receive not the grace of God in vain. 2 (For he saith, I have heard thee in a time ac-

cepted, and in the day of *soteria*/salvation have I succoured thee: behold, now is the accepted time; behold, now is the day of *soteria*/salvation.)"

The Day of Salvation means you control whether the heavens are brass or not. God has already spoken; they are open to you in the name of Jesus. That name means "God's Salvation is now and in force." Spoken in faith, He inhabits His name to deliver His salvation.

John 5:27 "And hath given him authority to execute judgment also, because he is the Son of man. 28 Marvel not at this: for the hour is coming, in the which all that are in the graves shall hear his voice, 29 and shall come forth; they that have done good, unto the resurrection of *zoe*/life; and they that have done evil, unto the resurrection of damnation. 30 I can of mine own self do nothing: as I hear, I judge: and my judgment is just; because I seek not mine own will, but the will of the Father which hath sent me."

John 16:8 "And when he is come, he will reprove the world of sin, and of righteousness, and of judgment (*condemnation*): 9 of sin, because they believe not on me; 10 of righteousness, because I go to my Father, and ye see me no more; 11 of judgment, because the prince of this world is judged."

1 John 3:8 "He that committeth sin is of the devil; for the devil sinneth from the beginning. For this purpose the Son of God was manifested, that he might destroy (*execute or deliver or enforce the judgment of God against*) the works of the devil."

The full Day of Judgment will come when God finally cleans the Universe of all of Satan's works. We now, by faith in the power of the blood of Jesus, have salvation from the full wrath of God when He cleans the Universe.

1 Thes 5:8 "But let us, who are of the day, be sober, putting on the breastplate of faith and *agape*/love; and for an helmet, the hope of *soteria*/salvation. 9 For God hath not appointed us to wrath, but to obtain *soteria*/salvation by our Lord Jesus Christ, 10 who died for us, that, whether we wake or sleep, we should *zao*/live together with him."

Rom 5:9 "Much more then, being now justified by his blood, we shall be *sozo*/saved from wrath through him. 10 For if, when we were enemies, we were reconciled to God by the death of his Son, much more, being reconciled, we shall be *sozo*/saved by his *zoe*/life. 11 And not only so, but we also joy in God through our Lord Jesus Christ, by whom we have now received the atonement (*reconciliation*)."

Even though we are "saved," to be in eternity with God, in being born-again, we do not have freedom from our works being judged by the wrath of God on that Day. God has decreed: Num 14:21 "But as truly as I live, all the earth shall be filled with the glory of the LORD." The Day of Judgment is the final cleansing to allow this to happen.

DISCOVERING OUR REDEMPTION

Rom 2:5 "But after thy hardness and impenitent heart treasurest up unto thyself wrath against the day of wrath and revelation of the righteous judgment of God; 6 who will render to every man according to his deeds."

1 Cor 3:12 "Now if any (*Christian*) man build upon this foundation gold, silver, precious stones, wood, hay, stubble; 13 every man's work shall be made manifest: for the day shall declare it, because it shall be revealed by fire; and the fire shall try every man's work of what sort it is. 14 If any man's work abide which he hath built thereupon, he shall receive a reward. 15 If any man's work shall be burned, he shall suffer loss: but he himself shall be *sozo*/saved; yet so as by fire."

Rom 2:16 "In the day when God shall judge the secrets of men by Jesus Christ according to my gospel." In that Day, the Wrath of God will finally destroy all the works of the devil.

In the meantime, Jesus will use us to destroy all the enemies of God. We are to use the name of Jesus to destroy the works of the devil, just as Jesus did! Acts 10:36 "The word which God sent unto the children of Israel, preaching peace by Jesus Christ: (he is Lord of all:) 37 that word, I say, ye know, which was published throughout all Judaea, and began from Galilee, after the baptism which John preached; 38 how God anointed Jesus of Nazareth with the Holy Ghost and with power: who went about doing good, and healing all that were oppressed of the devil; for God was with him."

And, thus, He will fulfill through us, the Body of Christ, Rom 16:20 "And the God of peace shall bruise Satan under your feet *as shattered glass*. The grace of our Lord Jesus Christ be with you *[to know, be and do this]*. Amen."

And this will be our testimony: Rev 12:9 "And the great dragon was cast out, that old serpent, called the Devil, and Satan, which deceiveth the whole world: he was cast out into the earth, and his angels were cast out with him. 10 And I heard a loud voice saying in heaven, Now is come *soteria*/salvation, and strength, and the kingdom of our God, and the *dunamis*/power of his Christ: for the accuser of our brethren is cast down, which accused them before our God day and night. 11 And they (*the saints*) overcame him (*Satan*) by the blood of the Lamb, and by the *logos*/word of their testimony; and they *agape*/loved not their *psuche*/lives (*souls*) unto the death."

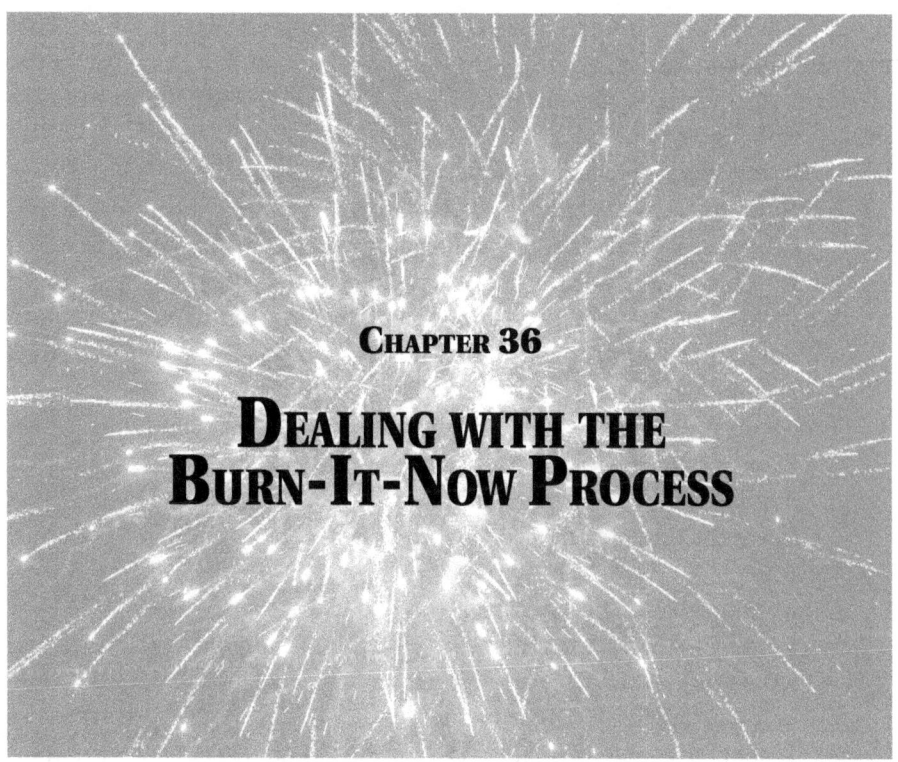

Chapter 36

Dealing with the Burn-It-Now Process

We are commanded to: Rom 8:13 "For if ye *zao*/live after the flesh, ye shall die: but if ye through the Spirit *[the word of the Gospel of Christ]* do mortify *(call or count as dead in Christ by the Word of God)* the deeds of the body, ye shall *zao*/live."

This is similar to these commands: Rom 6:11 "Likewise reckon ye also yourselves to be dead indeed unto sin, but *[reckon yourselves] zao*/alive unto God through Jesus Christ our Lord."

As you become what you look at, do not spend as much time looking at the evil of your sins as the greatness of our salvation in Jesus. 2 Cor 3:17 "Now the Lord is that Spirit: and where the Spirit of the Lord is, there is liberty *[to be all God made you in Jesus]*. 18 But we all, with open face beholding as in a glass *(mirror)* the glory of the Lord *[being manifested in you]*, are changed into the same image from glory to glory, even as by the Spirit of the Lord."

Eph 4:20 "But ye have not so learned Christ; 21 if so be that ye have heard him, and have been taught by him, as the truth is in Jesus: 22 that ye put off *[in your self-image and actions]* concerning the former conversation the old man, which is corrupt according to the deceitful lusts; 23 and be renewed in the spirit of your mind *[in your self-identity, image and actions]*; 24 and that ye put on the new man, which after God is created in righteousness and true holiness *[so you think, desire, speak and do as Jesus would]*."

DISCOVERING OUR REDEMPTION

Notice on the Day of Judgment is the all-consuming fire of God, wrath/judgment, for any work of the devil in anyone's life that is not already destroyed by this 10-step renewing process, based on Isa 53, 1 Pet 2:24, Matt 26:26-28, Rom 6:1-13, Rom 13:11-14, Eph 4:20-32, Eph 6:10-20 and Col 3:5-10:

1. Confessing (agreeing with what Holy Spirit calls sin)
2. Agreeing Jesus died for it and you are forgiven by His blood in the New Covenant 2000 years ago, and, therefore, thanking Him and Father God for sending Jesus
3. Judging that sin and its consequence was put on Jesus' body and remitted, forgiven by His blood, and healed by His stripes and when He was raised from the dead
4. Casting out the devil in the situation or yourself
5. Making any necessary restitution or reconciliation
6. Putting on your mental self, the new man, made after the image of God in true righteousness and true holiness–the real, born-again, new-creation, you
7. Receiving/enforcing any healing needed in Jesus' name
8. Finding specific areas to stop sinning in, confessing that is not your real nature in Jesus and seeing yourself no longer doing that same sin, but, rather, acting like Jesus would
9. Thanking Father God that He is changing you into being more like Jesus every day (obey Phil 4:6-7 when you struggle with this)
10. Going and helping others get free in the same way. You must go and do acts of *agape*/love because that is what Jesus would do and you have "put on Jesus Christ," and should now act like Him.

This is keeping short accounts with God. A contrite heart knows the judgment is there and sure. The only acceptable way to be sorry for your sin is to acknowledge that the Mighty Arm of God, Jesus, bore it for you already, suffered intensely for it, paid for it already and was healed of it already, so that you thank Him for the healing and then expect to receive that healing, to walk more like Him.

Keeping your eye on that Day, while, at the same time, knowing your sins are forgiven is a key to Christian growth: 2 Pet 1:8 "For if these things [*of God's divine nature manifested in abundance in your life*] be in you, and abound, they make you that ye shall neither be barren nor unfruitful in the *epignosis*/knowledge of our Lord Jesus Christ. 9 But he that lacketh these things [*of God's divine nature manifested in abundance in your life*] is blind, and cannot see afar off, and hath forgotten that he was purged from his old sins."

The sins of the human race, the race of Adam, are fully purged in the Record Hall of the Supreme Court of Creation. The blood of Jesus is more than sufficient.

To keep this in continual biblical remembrance is the key.

Dealing with the Burn-It-Now Process

Thus, Paul cried for the mature Christian:

Phil 3:7 "But what things were gain to me, those I counted loss for Christ. 8 Yea doubtless, and I count all things but loss for the excellency of the knowledge of Christ Jesus my Lord: for whom I have suffered the loss of all things, and do count them but dung, that I may win Christ, 9 and be found in him, not having mine own righteousness, which is of the law, but that which is through the faith of Christ, the righteousness which is of God by faith: 10 that I may know him, and the power of his resurrection, and the fellowship of his sufferings, being made conformable unto his death."

God's answer for you committing sin and for you having sin-consciousness is to change your self-identity and to use every opportunity, when you sin or you find sin ruling in others, to proclaim His great Redemption in Jesus. So you can apply the 10-step process to yourself or, in faith, apply and pray for that process in others in the ministry of reconciliation.

Rom 13:10 "*Agape*/love worketh no ill to his neighbour: therefore *agape*/love is the fulfilling of the law. 11 And that, knowing the time, that now it is high time to awake out of sleep: for now is our *soteria*/salvation nearer than when we believed. 12 The night is far spent, the day is at hand: let us therefore cast off the works of darkness, and let us put on the armour of light. 13 Let us walk honestly, as in the day; not in rioting and drunkenness, not in chambering and wantonness, not in strife and envying. 14 But put ye on the Lord Jesus Christ (*as your new-creation self-identity, the new man, made in righteousness and true holiness*), and make not provision for the flesh, to fulfil the lusts thereof."

Phil 2:5 "Let this mind be in you, which was also in Christ Jesus: 6 who, being in the form of God, thought it not robbery to be equal with God: 7 but made himself of no reputation [*against the pull of the world system and the praise of men*], and took upon him the form of a servant, and was made in the likeness of men: 8 and being found in fashion as a man, he humbled himself, and became obedient unto death, even the death of the cross."

Col 3:8 "But now ye also put off all these; anger, wrath, malice, blasphemy, filthy communication out of your mouth. 9 Lie not one to another, seeing that ye have put off the old man with his deeds; 10 and have put on the new man, which is renewed in *epignosis*/knowledge (*learning, doing as a master craftsmen and teaching others to walk as master craftsmen*) after the image of him (*God*) that created him: 11 where there is neither Greek nor Jew, circumcision nor uncircumcision, Barbarian, Scythian, bond nor free: but Christ is all, and in all. 12 Put on therefore, as the elect of God, holy and *agape*/beloved, bowels (*attitudes, self-image, self-identity to doing like Jesus*) of mercies, kindness, humbleness of mind, meekness, longsuffering; 13 forbearing one another, and forgiving one another, if any man have a quarrel against any: even as Christ forgave you, so also do ye. 14 And above all these things put on *agape*/charity, which is the bond of perfectness."

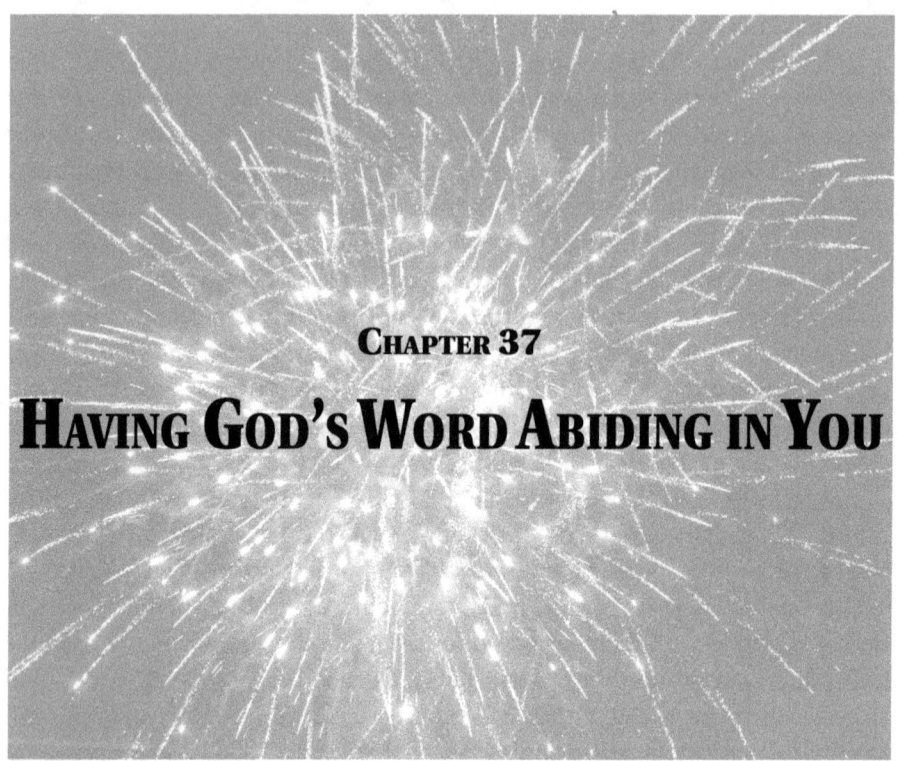

Chapter 37

Having God's Word Abiding in You

Col 3:16 "Let the word of Christ dwell in you richly." RSV

What is it doing there? It is admonishing, it is educating, it is training, it is correcting, and it is building faith and love into your soul in your conscious and unconscious mind.

How? You work with God to do it by your constant attention to that Word of grace in Jesus with timely repetition, study and doing like Jesus would.

Acts 20:32 "Now I commend you to God, and to the word of his grace, which is able to build you up, and to give you the inheritance among all them that are sanctified." RSV

It is not the word of failure, condemnation and sin-consciousness that builds you up into Christ. We are defeated by looking at only our sins, failures and weaknesses, and by constantly being told we are sinners and failures. This is not the message and the work of Jesus. Eph 2:8 "For by grace are ye *sozo*/saved through faith; and that not of yourselves: it is the gift of God: 9 not of works, lest any man should boast. 10 For we are his workmanship, created in Christ Jesus unto good works, which God hath before ordained that we should walk in them."

Rom 11:29 "For the gifts and calling of God are without repentance."

Rom 6:10 "For in that he died, he died unto sin once: but in that he *zao*/liveth, he *zao*/liveth unto God. 11 Likewise reckon ye also yourselves to be dead indeed unto sin, but *zao*/alive unto God through Jesus Christ our Lord."

HAVING GOD'S WORD ABIDING IN YOU

It is that Word of abundant grace and the gift (that cannot be removed) of righteousness in the new creation that tells you Christ is now in you, and He will never give you a writ of divorce, He will never be ashamed to call you His brother/sister, for you have entered in by faith. Father God will never give you a writ to break your adoption; you are sealed to God by Holy Spirit unto the Day of Redemption, which is after and not before the Day of Judgment. Your fate is sealed. God paid for you with the suffering and life of Jesus, and He will get what He paid for. You can come hard or you can come easy, but God is going to posses you one day in fullness. You have a future based on Jesus and not yourself. Father God, Jesus and Holy Spirit say you are worth the price it took to get you to that Day of Redemption.

1 Cor 6:20 "For ye are bought with a price: therefore glorify God in your body, and in your spirit, which are God's." It is in your soul where the issue lies. Either you renew your mind with the *agape*/love of the truth in the word of Christ, or He will do it for you in that Day!

The God who cannot lie has made a promise that must and will happen. Heb 8:7 "For if that first covenant (*under Moses*) had been faultless, then should no place have been sought for the second (*in Jesus*). 8 For finding fault with them, he saith, Behold, the days come, saith the Lord, when I will make a new covenant with the house of Israel and with the house of Judah (*in the Christ or Messiah*): 9 not according to the covenant that I made with their fathers in the day when I took them by the hand to lead them out of the land of Egypt; because they continued not in my covenant, and I regarded them not, saith the Lord. 10 For this is the covenant that I will make with the house of Israel after those days, saith the Lord; I will put my laws into their mind, and write them in their hearts: and I will be to them a God, and they shall be to me a people: 11 and they shall not teach every man his neighbour, and every man his brother, saying, Know the Lord: for all shall know me, from the least to the greatest. 12 For I will be merciful to their unrighteousness, and their sins and their iniquities will I remember no more."

On that day, that which is not like Jesus in our souls will go, and what God is looking for is His *agape*/love working in you. 1 John 4:17 "Herein is our *agape*/love made perfect, that we may have boldness in the day of judgment: because as he is, so are we in this world. 18 There is no fear in *agape*/love; but perfect *agape*/love casteth out fear: because fear hath torment. He that feareth is not made perfect in *agape*/love. 19 We *agape*/love him, because he first *agape*/loved us."

It is a bitter person who will not work to keep themselves knowing how *agape*/loved they are.

Prov 16:6 "By (*chesed*) mercy (*love, kindness and grace*) and truth iniquity is purged: and by the fear of the Lord men depart from evil."

Rom 2:4 "Or despisest thou the riches of his goodness and forbearance and longsuffering; not knowing that the goodness of God leadeth thee to repentance? 5 But after thy hardness and impenitent heart treasurest up unto thyself wrath against the day of

DISCOVERING OUR REDEMPTION

wrath and revelation of the righteous judgment of God; 6 who will render to every man according to his deeds."

Heb 3:12 "Take heed, brethren, lest there be in any of you an evil heart of unbelief (*unpersuadableness, bitterness against God*), in departing from the *zao*/living God. 13 But exhort one another daily, while it is called To day; lest any of you be hardened through the deceitfulness of sin. 14 For we are made partakers of Christ, if we hold the beginning of our confidence stedfast unto the end."

Heb 12:13 "And make straight paths for your feet, lest that which is lame (*lack of thanksgiving, gladness in obedience*) be turned out of the way (*other words or source than God*); but let it rather be healed (*into the mind of Christ*). 14 Follow peace with all men, and holiness, without which no man shall see the Lord: 15 looking diligently lest any man fail of the grace of God; lest any root of bitterness springing up trouble you, and thereby many be defiled."

Just as the people of ancient Israel had to cross the Jordan and kill giants to get their inheritance, so must we take the Word of God and form it or write it into our hearts, so that we, too, can go and slay the giants that hold our land in bondage to the devil and his works.

Jude 20 "But ye, *agape*/beloved, building up yourselves on your most holy faith, praying in the Holy Ghost, 21 keep yourselves in the *agape*/love of God, looking for the mercy of our Lord Jesus Christ unto eternal *zoe*/life. 22 And of some have compassion, making a difference: 23 and others *sozo*/save with fear, pulling them out of the fire; hating even the garment spotted by the flesh. 24 Now unto him that is able to keep you from falling, and to present you faultless before the presence of his glory with exceeding joy, 25 to the only wise God our Saviour, be glory and majesty, dominion and power, both now and ever. Amen."

It is the Word of grace that builds you up.

Acts 20:32 "And now, brethren, I commend you to God, and to the word of his grace, which is able to build you up, and to give you an inheritance among all them which are sanctified."

It is the Word of grace that makes you know of your inheritance.

It is the Word of grace that unveils to you your relationship to the Father, God.

It is the Word of grace that makes you know your rights and privileges in Christ.

It is the Word of grace that tells us what we have in Christ so we can make our faith effectual.

Effectiveness is in answered prayer, signs, wonders and people set free in Jesus and wisdom to remove any problem and to establish prosperity and the abundance of God's goodness.

It is the Word of Christ in you, the hope of glory, that makes our faith effectual.

It is the Word of what and who we are in Christ that Jesus confirms in signs and wonders.

Having God's Word Abiding in You

It is the Word of His grace in His Redemption, Reconciliation, Peace, Salvation, Remission, Justification, Adoption, Betrothal and Glorification that build us up.

He has committed that Word of Reconciliation to us as our ministry, our job, our calling and our joy.

2 Cor 5:18 "And all things are of God, who hath reconciled us to himself by Jesus Christ, and hath given to us the ministry of reconciliation; 19 to wit, that God was in Christ, reconciling the world unto himself, not imputing their trespasses unto them; and hath committed unto us the word of reconciliation. 20 Now then we are ambassadors for Christ, as though God did beseech you by us: we pray you in Christ's stead, be ye reconciled to God. 21 For he hath made him to be sin for us, who knew no sin; that we might be made the righteousness of God in him. 6:1 We then, as workers together with him, beseech you also that ye receive not the grace of God in vain. 2 (For he saith, I have heard thee in a time accepted, and in the day of *soteria*/salvation have I succoured thee: behold, now is the accepted time; behold, now is the day of *soteria*/salvation.)"

You remember it was the words of Christ that healed most of the people who came to Him.

He said they were His Father's words.

The Pauline Revelation is the Father's words about Jesus.

When you say you are a new creation, created in Christ, the Father's words are expressing a fact through your lips.

When you say, "In the name of Jesus, disease, stop being," you are using the Father's words that He spoke through Jesus' lips.

When you step out into your rights of righteousness and begin to bear fruit, it will be the same kind of fruit Jesus bore in His Earth walk.

You are now walking in the calling we have been given.

John 20:21 "Then said Jesus to them again, Peace be unto you: as my Father hath sent me, even so send I you."

You operate as an *agape*/love warrior, fulfilling the command given to Adam: Gen 1:28 "And God blessed them, and God said unto them, Be fruitful, and multiply, and replenish the earth, and subdue it: and have dominion over the fish of the sea, and over the fowl of the air, and over every living thing that moveth upon the earth."

Subdue means to fight as a warrior until you win, and *dominion* means to act as a king and keep it the way God wants. You subdue the devil and his works to establish the dominion, the Kingdom of God. Matt 10:7 "And as ye go, preach, saying, The kingdom of heaven is at hand. 8 Heal the sick, cleanse the lepers, raise the dead, cast out devils: freely ye have received, freely give."

And, thus, delight the Lord Jesus: Luke 10:17 "And the seventy returned again with joy, saying, Lord, even the devils are subject unto us through thy name. 18 And he said unto them, I beheld Satan as lightning fall from heaven. 19 Behold, I give unto you power (*authority, commission and all the resources of Heaven*) to tread on serpents and

DISCOVERING OUR REDEMPTION

scorpions, and over all the power (*ability*) of the enemy: and nothing shall by any means hurt you. 20 Notwithstanding in this rejoice not, that the spirits are subject unto you; but rather rejoice, because your names are written in heaven."

Righteousness means the ability to stand in the Father's presence without a sense of guilt or inferiority, now or ever. It also means you can stand in front of the devil and command him and his works to go without any sense of guilt, inferiority or inadequacy, because of Jesus.

This righteousness becomes yours through believing God raised Jesus from the dead.

Rom 10:9 "That if thou shalt confess with thy mouth the Lord Jesus, and shalt believe in thine heart that God hath raised him from the dead, thou shalt be *sozo*/saved. 10 For with the heart man believeth unto righteousness; and with the mouth confession is made unto *soteria*/salvation."

Rom 4:25 "(*Jesus*) Who was delivered up for our trespasses, and was raised for our justification." RSV A literal translation of this verse reads: "Who was delivered up on account of our trespasses, and was raised when (or because) we were declared righteous."

When the *zoe* life of God is liberated, the ability of God, as described in the Word, is let loose in us, to go out through us. This is how we fulfill our destiny, our calling, as sons of God in Jesus.

The Word of God is called a seed. Trust in that seed. The seed is perfect and incorruptible. Let your confession be that the Word of God is working and growing in you continually. It is the Word of Reconciliation, the Word of Grace, the Word of Christ in you, the hope of glory. That is the word, the seed, growing in you. As you confess and give thanks, it is growing. 1 Pet 1:23 "Being born again, not of corruptible seed, but of incorruptible, by the word of God, which *zao*/liveth and abideth for ever."

The seed is the Word of God. Mark 4:20 "And these are they (*the seeds of the Word of God*) which are sown on good ground; such as hear the word, and *lambano*/receive it, and bring forth fruit, some thirtyfold, some sixty, and some an hundred."

We reign as kings for Jesus where He freely empowers our word of His grace.

Rom 5:16 "And not as it was by one that sinned, so is the gift: for the judgment was by one to condemnation, but the free gift is of many offences unto justification. 17 For if by one man's offence death reigned (*as king*) by one; much more they which (*continually*) *lambano*/receive abundance of grace and of the gift of righteousness shall reign (*as kings for Jesus, doing what Jesus would do in bringing the Kingdom of God to Earth*) in *zoe*/life by one, Jesus Christ.) 18 Therefore as by the offence of one judgment came upon all men to condemnation; even so by the righteousness of one the free gift came upon all men unto justification of *zoe*/life. 19 For as by one man's disobedience many were made sinners, so by the obedience of one shall many be made righteous. 20 Moreover the law entered, that the offence might abound. But where sin abounded, grace did much more abound: 21 that as sin hath reigned (*as king, enforcing the curse of sin*) unto death, even so might grace reign (*as a greater king*) through righteousness unto eternal *zoe*/life by Jesus Christ our Lord."

As He says in Rom 5:17, the key to reigning is how well we *lambano*, hold on to and never let go of, the abundance of grace and the gift of righteousness.

Acts 14:3 "Long time therefore abode they (*Paul and Barnabas*) speaking boldly in the Lord, which gave testimony unto the word of his grace, and granted signs and wonders to be done by their hands."

Acts 2:22 "Ye men of Israel, hear these words; Jesus of Nazareth, a man approved of God among you by miracles and wonders and signs, which God did by him in the midst of you, as ye yourselves also know."

Heb 2:1 "Therefore we ought to give the more earnest heed to the things which we have heard, lest at any time we should let them slip. 2 For if the word spoken by angels was stedfast, and every transgression and disobedience received a just recompence of reward; 3 how shall we escape, if we neglect so great *soteria*/salvation; which at the first began to be spoken by the Lord, and was confirmed unto us by them that heard him. 4 God also bearing them witness, both with signs and wonders, and with divers miracles, and gifts of the Holy Ghost, according to his own will?"

Just as Father did for Jesus, He will confirm the Word of our Redemption, by grace on our lips, for we have been commanded to exercise the ministry of reconciliation.

2 Cor 5:18 "And all things are of God, who hath reconciled us to himself by Jesus Christ, and hath given to us the ministry (*the job, and the work*) of reconciliation; 19 to wit, that God was in Christ, reconciling the world unto himself, not imputing their trespasses unto them; and hath committed unto us the word of reconciliation. 20 Now then we are ambassadors for Christ, as though God did beseech you by us: we pray you in Christ's stead, be ye reconciled to God. 21 For he hath made him to be sin for us, who knew no sin; that we might be made the righteousness of God in him."

John 14:9 "Jesus saith unto him, Have I been so long time with you, and yet hast thou not known me, Philip? He that hath seen me hath seen the Father; and how sayest thou then, Shew us the Father? 10 Believest thou not that I am in the Father, and the Father in me? The words that I speak unto you I speak not of myself: but the Father that dwelleth in me, he doeth the works. 11 Believe me that I am in the Father, and the Father in me: or else believe me for the very works' sake. 12 Verily, verily, I say unto you, He that believeth on me, the works that I do shall he do also; and greater works than these shall he do; because I go unto my Father. 13 And whatsoever ye shall *aiteo*/ask (*require, demand and expect as due by covenant promise*) in my name, that will I do, that the Father may be glorified in the Son. 14 If ye shall *aiteo*/ask (*require, demand and expect as due by covenant promise*) any thing in my name, I will do it. 15 If ye *agape*/love me, keep my commandments."

We have been given the ministry to preach, so God can demonstrate, in signs and wonders, His reconciliation of man by and through the Redemption in the blood of Jesus.

DISCOVERING OUR REDEMPTION

Rom 4:24 "But for us also, to whom it (*righteousness*) shall be imputed, if we believe on him that raised up Jesus our Lord from the dead; 25 who was delivered for our offences, and was raised again for our justification (*or when we were justified*). 5:1 Therefore being justified by faith [*in the propitiation of Jesus by His blood*], we have peace with God through our Lord Jesus Christ: 2 by whom also we have access by faith into this grace wherein we stand, and rejoice in hope of the glory of God."

Col 1:19 "For it pleased the Father that in him (*Jesus*) should all fulness dwell; 20 and, having made peace through the blood of his cross, by him to reconcile all things unto himself; by him, I say, whether they be things in earth, or things in heaven."

What does this Word of Grace, Peace, Reconciliation, Salvation, Adoption, Righteousness, Remission and Redemption look like? Acts 10:36 "The word which God sent unto the children of Israel, preaching peace by Jesus Christ: (he is Lord of all:) 37 that word, I say, ye know, which was published throughout all Judaea, and began from Galilee, after the baptism which John preached; 38 how God anointed Jesus of Nazareth with the Holy Ghost and with power: who went about doing good, and healing all that were oppressed (*under the active rule, reign and lordship*) of the devil; for God was with him. 39 And we are witnesses of all things which he did both in the land of the Jews, and in Jerusalem; whom they slew and hanged on a tree: 40 him God raised up the third day, and shewed him openly; 41 not to all the people, but unto witnesses chosen before of God, even to us, who did eat and drink with him after he rose from the dead. 42 And he commanded us to preach unto the people (*in the ministry of reconciliation*), and to testify that it is he which was ordained of God to be the Judge of quick and dead [*and that right now He is freely judging against the devil through His born-again people*]. 43 To him give all the prophets witness, that through his name whosoever believeth in him shall receive remission of sins [*and, thus, breaking the root of sin that has us bound in lies, lack of knowledge and oppressions of the devil*]."

If you can hear Him, this is Father God speaking to us now. This is our commandment, to *aiteo*, to demonstrate the reconciliation of God where He has made us the righteousness of God in Christ Jesus by grace. You speak His words of grace, you believe you have eternal *zoe*/life, and you believe God to do the same works and even greater works than He did through Jesus through your thoughts, words and actions.

Look at this on the natural level. They tell us there is power enough in an atom to propel a great ship across the ocean. A speck so tiny, one atom, yet it has all this power.

If the power that is invested in releasing the life of God that is in you and the power that is invested in the Word of God (that Word that spoke a whole Universe into being with uncountable numbers of atoms) were let loose in you and through you, things would happen, wouldn't they? What wonders God could do through you!

The object of this message is to let you know that God wants to be set free in you and through you, to be Himself, just as He was in and through Jesus.

John 7:38 "He that believeth on me, as the scripture hath said, out of his belly shall flow rivers of *zao*/living water. 39 (But this spake he of the Spirit, which they that believe on him should receive: for the Holy Ghost was not yet given; because that Jesus was not yet glorified.)".

That river of Holy Spirit *zoe*/life became ours on the Day of Pentecost in Acts 2, and is still flowing now.

Here are two ways to read the Scriptures, to abide in the Jesus who is the living Word of God, which means He is the living Old Testament. Another way to say that is to view the Old Testament in a way that makes the life of Jesus come alive, as to how God always has been. God sent Jesus to clear up His reputation and demonstrate how God really is.

Take Your Time: The first is to take your time and work to let the full meaning of the Word impact your heart. Read it in many different translations, work each phrase and look up each word. Take that scripture (and then entire passages) and sing it, mutter it and chant it. This is you working the Word and inviting Holy Spirit to help you mine the depths of His mercy, truth, grace, understanding and wisdom in each verse and passage. Initially spend most of your time in the New Testament. Typically more revelation of truth comes as you read slower, but test what revelation you get, per 1 John 4:1-3, and even more diligent study.

Take a Word Bath: The second way is called a "Word Bath." This is a simple technique to get your mind back into God's way of thinking. It consists of reading the scriptures rather quickly, not as in studying, but as if the words were a hose, and you are letting a firm stream of words wash over you. Most any good translation will do for this. While many read some of the paraphrased translations here, I find there are too many words in most of them for a good Word bath. The objective is to cover lots of scriptures without too much deep thinking. Go slower than skimming, but faster than studying or contemplating as in step 1 above. It is letting the Word work on you rather than you working the Word.

For a Word Bath keep a note pad handy so you can go back for any special ideas you get. Read until you begin to see that God is indeed in the heavens and, He can run all of history and His Word is true and your problems and dreams are much smaller in size, and you will develop faith that God can do what He said He would do. Also God will get bigger in your eyes and, again, no problem or dream is too big for God to perform, per His Word. In both cases, you will then agree that He indeed will be your helper (see Heb 13:5). Set aside at least an hour for this, or all day.

One of my favorites for a Word Bath is to read in this way the prophets. I start at Isaiah and read until my heart is full of the majesty and purpose of God. Sometimes it may take all the way through Ezekiel. But usually 20 or 30 chapters are sufficient. The goal is to trust the Lord to wash you, as you expose yourself to His Word. Others find the Psalms or the Gospels to be good starting places. Or try Revelation. Just read it over and over until your heart sings, "Even so come Lord Jesus!" Start by asking the Father to wash you with His Word and then begin reading.

DISCOVERING OUR REDEMPTION

You will know that you are "washed" when your heart can freely praise God for His awesome works and His sovereignty. This is more about getting your eyes on what God is doing, rather than what you can get out of God's promises. If you are struggling under heaviness, go to Psalm 19, 23, 91, 103,136, 139 or 145 and repeat them over and over, per Isa 61:3 "To appoint unto them that mourn in Zion, to give unto them beauty for ashes, the oil of joy for mourning, the garment of praise for the spirit of heaviness; that they might be called trees of righteousness, the planting of the Lord, that he might be glorified."

Trust, by confessing out loud, that God is working on you, per Heb 4:12 "For the word of God is quick, and powerful, and sharper than any twoedged sword, piercing even to the dividing asunder of soul and spirit, and of the joints and marrow, and is a discerner of the thoughts and intents of the heart. 13 Neither is there any creature that is not manifest in his sight: but all things are naked and opened unto the eyes of him with whom we have to do."

Here are some of the scriptures this idea of a "word bath" is based on: Eph 5:26 "That he (Jesus) might sanctify and cleanse it with the washing of water by the word, 27 that he might present it to himself a glorious church, not having spot, or wrinkle, or any such thing; but that it should be holy and without blemish."

Ezek 16:9 "Then washed I thee with water; yea, I throughly washed away thy blood from thee, and I anointed thee with oil."

Ezek 36:25 "Then will I sprinkle clean water upon you, and ye shall be clean: from all your filthiness, and from all your idols, will I cleanse you."

Zech 13:1 "In that day there shall be a fountain opened to the house of David and to the inhabitants of Jerusalem for sin and for uncleanness."

Heb 10:22 "Let us draw near with a true heart in full assurance of faith, having our hearts sprinkled from an evil conscience, and our bodies washed with pure water."

John 15:3 "Now ye are clean through the word which I have spoken unto you."

Josh 1:8 "This book of the law shall not depart out of thy mouth; but thou shalt meditate therein day and night, that thou mayest observe to do according to all that is written therein: for then thou shalt make thy way prosperous, and then thou shalt have good success."

Neh 8:1 "And all the people gathered themselves together as one man into the street that was before the water gate; and they spake unto Ezra the scribe to bring the book of the law of Moses, which the Lord had commanded to Israel. 2 And Ezra the priest brought the law before the congregation both of men and women, and all that could hear with understanding, upon the first day of the seventh month. 3 And he read therein before the street that was before the water gate from the morning until midday, before the men and the women, and those that could understand; and the ears of all the people were attentive unto the book of the law."

Neh 9:3 "And they stood up in their place, and read in the book of the law of the Lord their God one fourth part of the day; and another fourth part they confessed, and worshipped the Lord their God."

Having God's Word Abiding in You

One of the challenges of this approach is for those with a strong doctrinal approach to reading the Scriptures. As they read, they apply their pre-defined understanding to each scripture verse or passage. Try to avoid this, when you take a "Word Bath." Read fast enough so that you cannot do it. Instead, have faith and let God's Word, which is "quick, powerful and sharp," work on you. You are looking for both "big picture" and fleeting thoughts as you read, somewhat like looking out the window of a very fast train, bus or car.

It takes a while to reorient your mind to the world of God as revealed in the Scriptures. It may take 5 minutes or several hours. This is the reason you need 20 to 100 chapters to open your heart to the big messages of God.

If you are going to read the Gospels, read all 4 of them along with Acts, not just one. Pick a section of Scripture that is 50 to 150 chapters long and then read it 2 to 6 times over and over. If you feel convicted by Holy Spirit as you read, unless He tells you differently, quickly agree with Him, receive forgiveness, ask for healing or understanding and keep reading. Treat that as a small rest stop, and then get back on the road or in the water.

In the bathing analogy, this is like standing under the shower and enjoying the water running over you. The first method of slow reading is more like scrubbing out a spot with continual rubbing.

A "Word Bath" is usually a trip through the large countryside and not a forest or even "leaf inspection" time. So, if you see something of interest, make a quick note of it and then keep reading. Go back later for deeper meditation and study. As you take the "Word Bath" ask Holy Spirit to show you things, as you exercise faith for Him to "wash you by the water of the Word."

Here is such a prayer for you to pray: Eph 1:17 "That the God of our Lord Jesus Christ, the Father of glory, may give unto *me* the spirit of wisdom and revelation in the knowledge of him: 18 the eyes of *my* understanding being enlightened; that *I* may know what is the hope of his calling *for me*, and what the riches of the glory of his inheritance in the saints, 19 and what is the exceeding greatness of his power to *me* who *believes*, according to the working of his mighty power, 20 which he wrought in Christ, when he raised him from the dead, and set him at his own right hand in the heavenly places, 21 far above all principality, and power, and might, and dominion, and every name that is named, not only in this world, but also in that which is to come: 22 and hath put all things under his feet, and gave him to be the head over all things to the church, 23 which is his body, the fulness of him that filleth all in all." Jude 24 "Now unto *You, Father God*, that is able to keep *me* from falling, and to present *me* faultless before the presence of *Your* glory with exceeding joy, 25 to the only wise God our Saviour, be glory and majesty, dominion and power, both now and ever. Amen."

When should you take a "Word Bath?" It is best before: Mark 4:17 "… when affliction or persecution ariseth for the word's sake, immediately they are offended. 18 And these are they which are sown among thorns; such as hear the word, 19 and the cares of

DISCOVERING OUR REDEMPTION

this world, and the deceitfulness of riches, and the lusts of other things entering in, choke the word, and it becometh unfruitful." If you find yourself wondering where God is, it's definitely time for a "Word Bath."

Alternate approaches to taking a Word Bath include reading along to a scripture recording of the same translation, or praying in tongues while you read. Another powerful way is to do it while fasting. While you may only bathe in this way 5 to 15 minutes at a time, it works best if you can set aside 2- to 4-hour time blocks. The goal is to cover large chunks of scripture and not just take little bites.

A continual washing of the Word keeps the Word abiding in you. It is not just the Word you are feeding yourself, but also it gives you the attitudes of God within that Word. This washes out the buildup of worldly issues, feelings and disappointments and puts your mind back into the Word of Christ.

John 15:3 "Now ye are clean through the word which I have spoken unto you. 4 Abide in me, and I in you. As the branch cannot bear fruit of itself, except it abide in the vine; no more can ye, except ye abide in me. 5 I am the vine, ye are the branches: he that abideth in me, and I in him, the same bringeth forth much fruit: for without me ye can do nothing."

To abide in Jesus, you have to abide in His Word of grace, in our Redemption in Him and our being made the righteousness of God in Christ Jesus unto *zoe* life. Philem 6 "That the communication of thy faith may become effectual by the acknowledging of every good thing which is in you in Christ Jesus."

Notice that we are to do the work of abiding. It is a continual mixing of the Word of Christ into every part of your soul. We do this, first, to establish a foundation, and then continually, to build and maintain. God will help you, but you have to determine to spend the time in the Word daily to make this effective.

God tells us the singular element that confirms His Word is our having *zoe* life. 1 John 5:10 "He that believeth on the Son of God hath the witness in himself: he that believeth not God hath made him a liar; because he believeth not the record that God gave of his Son. 11 And this is the record, that God hath given to us eternal *zoe*/life, and this *zoe*/life is in his Son. 12 He that hath the Son hath *zoe*/life; and he that hath not the Son of God hath not *zoe*/life."

Here is John's summation: 1 John 5:13 "These things have I written unto you that believe on the name of the Son of God; that ye may know (*behold, be aware of continually, consider in a way that changes your world view and behaviors*) that ye have eternal *zoe*/life, and that ye may believe on the name of the Son of God."

Jesus tells us the Word of God, His Word, is *zoe*/life. John 6:63 "It is the spirit that quickeneth; the flesh profiteth nothing: the words that I speak unto you, they are spirit, and they are *zoe*/life."

We are to ever work in getting and keeping this "word-zoe-life" in us. 2 Tim 3:14 "But continue thou in the things which thou hast learned and hast been assured of, knowing of whom thou hast learned them; 15 and that from a child thou hast known the holy scriptures, which are able to make thee wise unto *soteria*/salvation through faith which is in Christ Jesus. 16 All scripture is given by inspiration of God, and is profitable for doctrine, for reproof, for correction, for instruction in righteousness: 17 that the man of God may be perfect, throughly furnished unto all good works."

Then we are to ever be thinking, speaking and doing this Word of *zoe* life. Phil 2:12 "Wherefore, my *agape*/beloved, as ye have always obeyed, not as in my presence only, but now much more in my absence, work out your own *soteria*/salvation with fear and trembling. 13 For it is God which worketh in you both to will and to do of his good pleasure. 14 Do all things without murmurings and disputings: 15 that ye may be blameless and harmless, the sons of God, without rebuke, in the midst of a crooked and perverse nation, among whom ye shine as lights in the world; 16 holding forth the word of *zoe*/life; that I may rejoice in the day of Christ, that I have not run in vain, neither laboured in vain."

The word of the Gospel is where we get the power of God for any part of life. Rom 1:16 "For I am not ashamed of the gospel of Christ: for it is the *dunamis*/power of God unto *soteria*/salvation to every one that believeth; to the Jew first, and also to the Greek. 17 For therein is the righteousness of God revealed from faith to faith: as it is written, The just shall *zao*/live by faith." The wonder-working *zoe* life of God is in His Word. John 6:63 "It is the spirit that quickeneth; the flesh profiteth nothing: the words that I (*Jesus*) speak unto you, they are spirit, and they are *zoe*/life."

2 Tim 3:12 "Yea, and all that will *zao*/live godly in Christ Jesus shall suffer persecution. 13 But evil men and seducers shall wax worse and worse, deceiving, and being deceived. 14 But [*instead*] continue thou in the things which thou hast learned and hast been assured of, knowing of whom thou hast learned them; 15 and that from a child thou hast known the holy scriptures, which are able to make thee wise unto *soteria*/salvation through faith which is in Christ Jesus. 16 All scripture is given by inspiration of God, and is profitable for doctrine, for reproof, for correction, for instruction in righteousness: 17 that the man of God may be perfect, throughly furnished unto all good works."

The power is in the Word: Heb 4:12 "For the word of God is quick, and powerful, and sharper than any twoedged sword … ."

God's Word of grace in Jesus is the secret to unlimited power in prayer and decrees for God. John 15:7 "If ye abide in me (*Jesus*) [*in spite of your sins and failures*], and [*you make*] my words abide in you [*knowing you are made the righteousness of God in Jesus by grace*], ye shall *aiteo*/ask (*demand, require and expect as due by covenant promise knowing Jesus has met all the requirements*) what ye will, and it shall be done unto you. 8 Herein is my Father glorified, that ye bear much fruit; so shall ye be my disciples."

Chapter 38

Working with Propitiation in Communion

The great work of God was Jesus' propitiation through the cross. God did not even start creating the Earth until He had already resolved sin and the curse of sin. His plan was that Jesus was to die and resolve all sin and the effects of sin by redemption through His blood and it was decided before the foundation of the Earth was ever laid. (Rom 6:25; Eph 1:4; Titus 1:2; Rev 3:8)

2 Tim 1:8 "… but be thou partaker of the afflictions of the gospel according to the power of God; 9 who hath *sozo*/saved us, and called us with an holy calling, not according to our works, but according to his own purpose and grace, which was given us in Christ Jesus before the world began, 10 but is now made manifest by the appearing of our Saviour Jesus Christ, who hath abolished death, and hath brought *zoe*/life and immortality to light through the gospel."

1 Pet 1:18 "Forasmuch as ye know that ye were not redeemed with corruptible things, as silver and gold, from your vain conversation received by tradition from your fathers; 19 but with the precious blood of Christ, as of a lamb without blemish and without spot: 20 who verily was foreordained before the foundation of the world, but was manifest in these last times for you."

Col 1:12 "Giving thanks (*continually*) unto the Father, which hath made us meet (*qualified and enabled by grace*) to be partakers of the inheritance of the saints in light:

WORKING WITH PROPITIATION IN COMMUNION

13 who hath delivered us from the power of darkness, and hath translated us into the kingdom of his *agape*/dear Son: 14 in whom we have redemption through his blood, even the forgiveness (*remission, purging, putting away, and obliteration*) of sins: … 20 and, having made peace through the blood of his cross, by him to reconcile all things unto himself; by him, I say, whether they be things in earth, or things in heaven. 21 And you, that were sometime alienated and enemies in your mind by wicked works, yet now hath he reconciled."

We are redeemed by Jesus' blood from the power of the devil and reconciled into His kingdom of *agape*/love. This is the great work of the Mighty Arm of God, Jesus. We are redeemed by His blood from the power of the devil. Redemption from sin and from the curse of sin and healing or salvation are just opposite sides of the same coin.

This is described in Isaiah 53. This chapter is referenced in the New Testament many times as the key act of the Mighty Arm of God for both sin and healing. Here are a few instances: John 12:37 "But though he had done so many miracles before them, yet they believed not on him: 38 that the saying of Esaias the prophet might be fulfilled, which he spake, Lord, who hath believed our report? and to whom hath the arm of the Lord been revealed (*Isa 53:1*)" Acts 8:30 "And Philip ran thither to him (*the Ethiopian eunuch*), and heard him read the prophet Esaias, and said, Understandest thou what thou readest? 31 And he said, How can I, except some man should guide me? And he desired Philip that he would come up and sit with him. 32 The place of the scripture which he read was this, He was led as a sheep to the slaughter; and like a lamb dumb before his shearer, so opened he not his mouth: 33 in his humiliation his judgment was taken away: and who shall declare his generation? for his life is taken from the earth (*Isa 53:7*). 34 And the eunuch answered Philip, and said, I pray thee, of whom speaketh the prophet this? of himself, or of some other man? 35 Then Philip opened his mouth, and began at the same scripture, and preached unto him Jesus." 1 Pet 2:21 "For even hereunto were ye called: because Christ also suffered for us, leaving us an example, that ye should follow his steps: 22 who did no sin, neither was guile found in his mouth: 23 who, when he was reviled, reviled not again; when he suffered, he threatened not; but committed himself to him that judgeth righteously: 24 who his own self bare our sins in his own body on the tree, that we, being dead to sins, should *zao*/live unto righteousness: by whose stripes ye were healed. 25 For ye were as sheep going astray; but are now returned unto the Shepherd and Bishop of your souls (*Isa 53:5-7*)." Matt 8:14 "And when Jesus was come into Peter's house, he saw his wife's mother laid, and sick of a fever. 15 And he touched her hand, and the fever left her: and she arose, and ministered unto them. 16 When the even was come, they brought unto him many that were possessed with devils: and he cast out the spirits with his word, and healed all that were sick: 17 that it might be fulfilled which was spoken by Esaias the prophet, saying, Himself *lambano*/took our infirmities, and bare (*completely*) our sicknesses (*Isa 53:4*)."

In particular, Matt 8:17 shows a more complete translation of Isa 53:4 "Surely he hath *nasa*/borne our griefs (*infirmities*), and *cabal*/carried our sorrows (*sicknesses*): yet we did esteem him stricken, smitten of God, and afflicted." This is concerning infirmities (the inability to operate with power in this physical world) and sicknesses (any and every disease of any kind). Jesus took/bore for us death operating in any form, slow or fast.

While Isaiah 53 uses two different Hebrew words *borne* (*nasa*) and *carried* (*cabal*), both mean to take, carry or bear so that the requirement is now fully carried, contained and removed with nothing left out. It is thus applied in Matt 8:14-17 as specific to physical healing. These same words are used for sin and iniquity in Isa 53:11 "He shall see of the travail of his soul, and shall be satisfied: by his knowledge shall my righteous servant justify many; for he shall **cabal/bear** their iniquities. 12 Therefore will I divide him a portion with the great, and he shall divide the spoil with the strong; because he hath poured out his soul unto death: and he was numbered with the transgressors; and he **nasa/bare** the sin of many, and made intercession for the transgressors."

Thus Jesus bore and carried our infirmities, sicknesses, sin, transgression, iniquities, and curse all in the same mighty work, so there is no requirement from God for any human to ever bear them again. Jesus bore what we deserve, and we receive mercy, not justice. He took our curse upon Himself.

Heb 9:26 "For then must he often have suffered since the foundation of the world: but now once in the end of the world hath he appeared to put away sin by the sacrifice of himself. 27 And as it is appointed unto men once to die, but after this the judgment: 28 so Christ was once offered to bear the sins of many; and unto them that look for him shall he appear the second time without sin unto *soteria*/salvation."

Heb 10:12 "But this man, after he had offered one sacrifice for sins for ever, sat down on the right hand of God; 13 from henceforth expecting till his enemies be made his footstool. 14 For by one offering he hath perfected for ever them that are sanctified. 15 Whereof the Holy Ghost also is a witness to us: for after that he had said before, 16 This is the covenant that I will make with them after those days, saith the Lord, I will put my laws into their hearts, and in their minds will I write them; 17 and their sins and iniquities will I remember no more. 18 Now where remission (*obliteration, removal and putting away*) of these (*sins and iniquities*) is, there is no more offering for sin." (Jer 31:33-34; Isa 54:13; Ezek 36:25-33; Heb 8:10-18)

Matt 26:27 "And he took the cup, and gave thanks, and gave it to them, saying, Drink ye all of it; 28 for this is my blood of the new testament (*covenant*), which is shed for many for the remission (*purging, removal*) of sins."

Acts 13:38 "Be it known unto you therefore, men and brethren, that through this man is preached unto you the forgiveness (*remission, obliteration, removal and putting away*) of sins: 39 and by him all that believe are justified from all things, from which ye could not be justified by the law of Moses."

As far as God is concerned, forgiveness of sin and physical healing were accomplished in the great work of His Mighty Arm, Jesus, the Christ of God, who cut the New Covenant with His own body and blood. Isa 53:1 "Who hath believed our report? and

Working with Propitiation in Communion

to whom is the arm of the LORD revealed? 2 For he shall grow up before him as a tender plant, and as a root out of a dry ground: he hath no form nor comeliness; and when we shall see him, there is no beauty that we should desire him. 3 He is despised and rejected of men; a man of sorrows, and acquainted with grief: and we hid as it were our faces from him; he was despised, and we esteemed him not. 4 Surely he hath *cabal*/borne our griefs (*infirmities*), and *nasa*/carried our sorrows, (*sicknesses*): yet we did esteem him stricken, smitten of God, and afflicted. 5 But he was wounded for our transgressions (*willful sin acts*), he was bruised for our iniquities (*sin thoughts, actions and the curse due*): the chastisement of our peace (*poverty, impotency and misery due for sin*) was upon him; and with his stripes (*tearing, cutting or breaking of His body*) we are *physically* healed. 6 All we like sheep have gone astray; we have turned every one to his own way; and the LORD hath laid on him the iniquity of us all. 7 He was oppressed, and he was afflicted, yet he opened not his mouth: he is brought as a lamb to the slaughter, and as a sheep before her shearers is dumb, so he openeth not his mouth. 8 He was taken from prison and from judgment: and who shall declare his generation? for he was cut off out of the land of the living: for the transgression of my people was he stricken. 9 And he made his grave with the wicked, and with the rich in his death; because he had done no violence, neither was any deceit in his mouth. 10 Yet it pleased the LORD to bruise him; he hath put him to grief (*sickness*): when thou shalt make his soul an offering for sin, he shall see his seed, he shall prolong his days, and the pleasure of the LORD shall prosper in his hand. 11 He shall see of the travail of his soul, and shall be satisfied: by his knowledge shall my righteous servant justify many; for he shall *cabal*/bear their iniquities. 12 Therefore will I divide him a portion with the great, and he shall divide the spoil with the strong; because he hath poured out his soul unto death: and he was numbered with the transgressors; and he *nasa*/bare the sin of many, and made intercession for the transgressors."

This is the propitiation of Jesus, not just the atonement, which is a covering of sin, but remission, a total removal of sin unto blessing in propitiation.

This dual connection of sin and sickness is seen again in: James 5:15 "And the prayer of faith shall *sozo*/save the sick, and the Lord shall raise him up; and if he have committed sins, they shall be forgiven him." Notice the sin forgiveness is the result of praying for healing. So even though there is no confession of sin, the one prayed for is forgiven anyway. See also Matt 9:4-8 in the healing of the man with palsy.

We understand that the bruises and wounds (lacerations or stripes) Jesus received in the crucifixion included the initial binding, followed by the beatings, the lashing at the whipping post, the crown of thorns, the stumbling and falling as He carried the cross, the nails in His hands and feet, the ripping of His back, hands and feet every time He lifted Himself up to breathe when nailed to the cross, and the final spear in His side.

Knowing that sin, sickness and a lack of prosperity (peace) were all healed by Jesus is summarized in Isa 53:5 as part of the New Covenant. Isa 49:8 "Thus saith the LORD, In an acceptable time have I heard thee, and in a

DISCOVERING OUR REDEMPTION

day of salvation have I helped thee: and I will preserve thee, and give thee for a covenant of the people, to establish the earth, to cause to inherit the desolate heritages."

This is also seen in a messianic prophecy: Isa 57:18 "I have seen his ways, and will heal him: I will lead him also, and restore comforts unto him and to his mourners. 19 I create the fruit of the lips; Peace, peace to him that is far off, and to him that is near, saith the LORD; and I will heal him."

While many emphasize eternal rewards, here is what Holy Spirit says this time on Earth is right now: 2 Cor 5:20 "Now then we are ambassadors for Christ, as though God did beseech you by us: we pray you in Christ's stead, be ye reconciled to God. 21 For he hath made him to be sin for us, who knew no sin; that we might be made the righteousness of God in him. 6:1 We then, as workers together with him, beseech you also that ye receive not the grace of God in vain. 2 (For he saith, I have heard thee in a time accepted, and in the day of *soteria*/salvation have I succoured thee: behold, now is the accepted time; behold, now is the day of *soteria*/salvation.)"

Notice the warning of 2 Cor 6:1: it is possible to be born again in this Day of Salvation and yet not walk in the fullness of our salvation. *Vain* means "useless, ineffective, will not survive the Day of Judgment." 2 Cor 6:1 "We then, as workers together with him, beseech you also that ye receive not the grace of God in vain." This means you have to make a choice.

This we are to remember or judge properly when we take communion or the Lord's Supper. 1 Cor 11:24 "And when he had given thanks, he brake it, and said, Take, eat: this is my body, which is broken (*Greek: lacerated*) for you: this do in remembrance of me. 25 After the same manner also he took the cup, when he had supped, saying, This cup is the new testament (*covenant*) in my blood: this do ye, as oft as ye drink it, in remembrance of me. 26 For as often as ye eat this bread, and drink this cup, ye do shew the Lord's death till he come."

Jesus took the stripes and has risen, men can be born again, and now is the Day of the Salvation of God. All of God's benefits are by faith. You believe for them to be manifested based on His Word. You call it done before it is.

The punishment for failure to rightly judge your sins, sicknesses, infirmities, poverty, failures and penalties were all carried and paid for by Jesus in His body and blood 2000 years ago, and that's what it means to take the bread and wine unworthily. We do this in these ways:

- Not remembering the Lord in this meal,
- Not doing it at all; or
- Not doing it properly to acknowledge or show all Jesus accomplished with the terrible price of the cross with His body and blood.

Working with Propitiation in Communion

Heb 10:29 "Of how much sorer punishment, suppose ye, shall he be thought worthy, who hath trodden under foot the Son of God, and hath counted the blood of the covenant, wherewith he was sanctified, an unholy thing, and hath done despite unto the Spirit of grace? 30 For we know him that hath said, Vengeance belongeth unto me, I will recompense, saith the Lord. And again, The Lord shall judge his people."

Heb 2:1 "Therefore we ought to give the more earnest heed to the things which we have heard, lest at any time we should let them slip. 2 For if the word spoken by angels was stedfast, and every transgression and disobedience received a just recompence of reward; 3 how shall we escape, if we neglect so great *soteria*/salvation; which at the first began to be spoken by the Lord, and was confirmed unto us by them that heard him; 4 God also bearing them witness, both with signs and wonders, and with divers miracles, and gifts of the Holy Ghost, according to his own will?"

You may not get the destruction of Jerusalem, but you will get the fruit of any of your wicked ways you do not put under the body and blood of Jesus.

Gal 6:7 "Be not deceived; God is not mocked: for whatsoever a man soweth, that shall he also reap. 8 For he that soweth to his flesh shall of the flesh reap corruption; but he that soweth to the Spirit shall of the Spirit reap *zoe*/life everlasting. 9 And let us not be weary in well doing: for in due season we shall reap, if we faint not. 10 As we have therefore opportunity, let us do good unto all men, especially unto them who are of the household of faith."

If the birth, death, resurrection and glorification of Jesus is the great work of God to man, ignoring it or failing to appreciate and use it is the great insult of man to God. There is no other path to God left for you until you repent and return to Jesus as your total salvation, once for all time. This is what we are to repent of in the Gospel of Jesus Christ

The punishment for failure to apply the methods God has prescribed with the right attitude of heart is that we are judged with the world that has no God, no covenant and no hope, and are, thus, left with the penalties of our sins and failures. Eph 2:12 "That at that time ye were without Christ, being aliens from the commonwealth of Israel, and strangers from the covenants of promise, having no hope, and without God in the world [*or life as a mere man without the God of Israel in power*]."

We do not judge the validity of God's promises by our inability to bring them to Earth, and we do not define the Word of God by our experience. Rather, we define our experience by the Word of God.

Heb 6:18 "That by two immutable things (*the promise Gen 12:1-2, and the oath of the same in Gen 22:15-18*), in which it was **impossible for God to lie**, we might have a strong consolation, who have fled for refuge to lay hold upon the hope set before us: 19 which hope we have as an anchor of the soul, both sure and stedfast, and which entereth into that within the veil; 20 whither the forerunner is for us entered, even Jesus, made an high priest for ever after the order of Melchisedec."

DISCOVERING OUR REDEMPTION

Note: Jesus was able to take His blood to Heaven and to exercise His current High Priest ministry because of the immutable, cannot lie, promise of God to Abraham.

Titus 1:1 "Paul, a servant of God, and an apostle of Jesus Christ, according to the faith of God's elect, and the acknowledging of the truth which is after godliness; 2 in hope of eternal *zoe*/life, which **God, that cannot lie**, promised before the world began."

The path of life in God's great salvation is described in the Scriptures. 2 Tim 3:15 "And that from a child thou hast known the holy scriptures, which are able to make thee wise unto *soteria*/salvation through faith which is in Christ Jesus. 16 All scripture is given by inspiration of God, and is profitable for doctrine, for reproof, for correction, for instruction in righteousness: 17 that the man of God may be perfect, throughly furnished unto all good works."

"Wise unto *soteria*/salvation" means knowing how to apply the facts of salvation to bring the promises from Heaven to Earth.

Eph 1:3 "Blessed be the God and Father of our Lord Jesus Christ, who hath blessed us with all spiritual blessings (*or has spoken every good thing that it is possible to say/promise/proclaim*) in heavenly places in Christ: 4 according as he hath chosen us in him before the foundation of the world, that we should be holy and without blame before him in *agape*/love: 5 having predestinated us unto the adoption of children by Jesus Christ to himself, according to the good pleasure of his will, 6 to the praise of the glory of his grace, wherein he hath made us accepted in the *agape*/beloved. 7 In whom we have redemption through his blood, the forgiveness (*remission, purging, putting away and obliteration*) of sins, according to the riches of his grace; 8 wherein he hath abounded toward us in all wisdom and prudence."

Therefore Jesus said: Matt 6:8 "Be not ye therefore like unto them: for your Father knoweth what things ye have need of, before ye *aiteo*/ask him (*require, demand and expect as due by covenant promise of God*). 9 After this manner therefore pray ye: Our Father which art in heaven, Hallowed be thy name. 10 Thy kingdom come. Thy will be done in earth, as it is in heaven. 11 Give us this day our daily bread. 12 And forgive us our debts, as we forgive our debtors. 13 And lead us not into temptation, but deliver us from evil (*or the evil one*): for thine is the kingdom, and the power, and the glory, for ever. Amen. 14 For if ye forgive men their trespasses, your heavenly Father will also forgive you: 15 but if ye forgive not men their trespasses, neither will your Father forgive your trespasses."

The promise is that Christians should be healthier and live longer than the un-born again. This is the legal side of redemption. The vital side is using the Scriptures to make this a reality in our lives today.

If we are not seeing the blessings, the problem is not God, and it is not the devil. It is us. It is an education and application problem.

2 Cor 4:3 "But if our gospel be hid, it is hid to them that are lost (*have death working in them is some way, fast or slow*): 4 in whom the god of this world hath blinded (*deceived*) the

minds of them which believe not, lest the light of the glorious gospel of Christ, who is the image of God, should shine unto them. 5 For we preach not ourselves, but Christ Jesus the Lord; and ourselves your servants for Jesus' sake."

Many apply this scripture to only those not born again, and it does apply to them, but in the context of verse five, it is also for those born again in the new creation but not fully matured into Christ in His full prosperity.

So the problem is not God, and it is not the devil, for the devil is doing what he does. It is with the Christian, who in either ignorance or deception (remember evil means to twist or corrupt so you cannot tell the difference) is not believing the grace and truth, to walking in God's grace, truth and *agape*/love by His Word.

1 John 1:5 "This then is the message which we have heard of him, and declare unto you, that God is light, and in him is no darkness at all. 6 If we say that we have fellowship with him (*communing, partnering or relating where you are walking, thinking and judging alike*), and walk in darkness, we lie, and do not the truth." 1 Cor 1:10 "Now I beseech you, brethren, by the name of our Lord Jesus Christ, that ye all speak the same thing, and that there be no divisions among you; but that ye be perfectly joined together in the same mind and in the same judgment [*as Holy Spirit*]."

Part of the message of Paul in First and Second Corinthians, and in most of His other letters, indeed in most of the other letters of the New Testament, is that the born again are not fulfilling all God has required of them in the benefits and calling of the new birth.

Eph 5:8 "For ye were sometimes darkness, but now are ye light in the Lord: walk as children of light: 9 (for the fruit of the Spirit is in all goodness and righteousness and truth.)"

Our union with God through the new birth is solid and permanent, but our fellowship, communion, partnership or co-laboring depends on our current thoughts and walk.

Even before Jesus died and rose from the dead, Jesus said healing was part of the bread for the children of God, including deliverance from the effects of evil spirits. How much greater is this for you, if you are a child of God under the New Covenant, and such are you, if you are born again. Whenever Jesus healed anyone, it was God declaring He hates sickness, disease and death in any form, to destroy it.

Mark 7:25 "For a certain woman, whose young daughter had an unclean spirit, heard of him, and came and fell at his feet: 26 the woman was a Greek, a Syrophenician by nation; and she besought him that he would cast forth the devil out of her daughter. 27 But Jesus said unto her, Let the children first be filled: for it is not meet to take the children's bread, and to cast it unto the dogs. 28 And she answered and said unto him, Yes, Lord: yet the dogs under the table eat of the children's crumbs. 29 And he said unto her, For this saying go thy way; the devil is gone out of thy daughter. 30 And when she was come to her house, she found the devil gone out, and her daughter laid upon the bed."

DISCOVERING OUR REDEMPTION

Holy Spirit reaffirmed that every healing and act of God Jesus did was freeing people of oppressions of the devil, i.e., were part of "the children's bread." Acts 10:38 "How God anointed Jesus of Nazareth with the Holy Ghost and with power: who went about doing good, and healing all that were oppressed (*under the active dominion, reign or lordship*) of the devil; for God was with him."

So how do you get this bread? Hear to obedience Jesus' answer: Matt 4:4 "But he answered and said, It is written, Man shall not *zao*/live by bread alone, but by every word (*that you do*) that proceedeth out of the mouth of God."

Failure to operate the instruction manual properly does not mean the instruction manual is wrong. The fault is not with God, but with man. Failure to mix the Word of God with faith such that you obey it has always been the issue for man. The devil will tell you the problem is God, but God says the problem is with man. Heb 4:1 "Let us therefore fear, lest, a promise being left us of entering into his rest, any of you should seem to come short of it. 2 For unto us was the gospel preached, as well as unto them: but the word preached did not profit them, not being mixed with faith in them that heard it."

This is not about your eternal salvation when you get born again. That is settled by grace because of Jesus. Your effectiveness in bringing the Kingdom of God to Earth is based on your effective faith in the more-than-sufficient blood of Jesus.

Judging your circumstances as God's fault or that the Bible is irrelevant or of not enough power will not lead to His blessing. As Jesus said to those who were not effectively believing God: Matt 22:29 "Jesus answered and said unto them, Ye do err, not knowing the scriptures, nor the power of God."

These are all the attitudes of darkness. Eph 5:11 "And have no fellowship with the unfruitful works of darkness, but rather reprove them. 12 For it is a shame even to speak of those things which are done of them in secret. 13 But all things that are reproved are made manifest by the light: for whatsoever doth make manifest is light. 14 Wherefore he saith, Awake thou that sleepest, and arise from the dead, and Christ shall give thee light. 15 See then that ye walk circumspectly, not as fools, but as wise, 16 redeeming the time, because the days are evil."

This has always been God's judgment, as proved by Israel, who for failure to follow the Lord's ways in gladness, was destroyed. Deut 28:47 "Because thou servedst not the LORD thy God with joyfulness, and with gladness of heart, for the abundance of all things; 48 therefore shalt thou serve thine enemies which the LORD shall send against thee, in hunger, and in thirst, and in nakedness, and in want of all things: and he shall put a yoke of iron upon thy neck, until he have destroyed thee."

Verses 1-14 of Deuteronomy 28 describes the blessing for joyful and glad obedience and details some of the terrible penalties for failure, the Law's curse, in verses 15-68 that God could not stop because they would not use God's laws to reconcile them. Here is a New Testament command on how to renew our mind to walk in this gladness to success with God. Eph 5:17 "Wherefore be ye not unwise, but understanding what the will of

WORKING WITH PROPITIATION IN COMMUNION

the Lord is. 18 And be not drunk with wine, wherein is excess; but be (*continuously being*) filled with the Spirit; 19 speaking to yourselves in psalms and hymns and spiritual songs, singing and making melody in your heart to the Lord; 20 (*continually*) giving thanks always for all things unto God and the Father in the name of our Lord Jesus Christ; 21 submitting yourselves one to another in the fear of God."

This same principle or way of God for failure to use what God has given to subdue and establish dominion over the devil is applied to those who do not use or take the Lord's Supper properly. 1 Cor 11:27 "Wherefore whosoever shall eat this bread, and drink this cup of the Lord, unworthily, shall be guilty of the body and blood of the Lord. 28 But let a man examine himself, and so let him eat of that bread, and drink of that cup. 29 For he that eateth and drinketh unworthily, eateth and drinketh damnation to himself, not discerning the Lord's body. 30 For this cause many are weak and sickly among you, and many sleep. 31 For if we would judge ourselves, we should not be judged. 32 But when we are judged, we are chastened of the Lord, that we should not be condemned with the world."

Notice, per verse 30, the effect is that you have the same health and life-span as people in the world who do not know Christ, i.e., you live as a "mere man." Proof you are doing it right includes divine health, prosperity and long life. 3 John 2 "*Agape*/beloved, I wish (*pray*) above all things that thou mayest prosper and be in health, even as thy soul prospereth. 3 For I rejoiced greatly, when the brethren came and testified of the truth that is in thee, even as thou walkest in the truth."

Or because we do not apply the grace of God in faith to our present situation, we live just as the world does: like a people who have not the real God or His covenant promises, driven by dreadful fear and a god who cannot and will not help. Or we live like one who sees no spiritual value in the death and resurrection of Jesus, to the level God has revealed in the Scriptures. Verse 29 does not mean you curse, damn yourself, as if that is something new, it means that you do not push back the death that is all around us with the *zoe*/life of God released in communion. Failure to push back (until you walk just like Jesus walks) means your evil sowing reaps its evil fruit, and the attacks of the devil are not defeated. God does not have to actively judge us by sending the devil, but just like Job, without our properly judging the body and blood of Jesus, He has no way to stop the devil when the devil comes to tempt us. The best He can do is to mitigate what the devil does, as He did with Job. Thus we limit God.

As you eat the bread and drink the wine you can imagine or proclaim that God's *zoe* life is going into your body to heal and make whole against the works of the devil. You can be as general or as specific as you have confidence in God for.

This is one way to obey: 2 Cor 3:18 "But we all, with open face beholding (*in our imagination*) as in a glass (*mirror*) the glory of the Lord (*manifesting what we see in our imagination*), are changed into the same image (*using our imagination as a blueprint*) from glory to glory, even as by the Spirit of the Lord."

DISCOVERING OUR REDEMPTION

You can do this as a process, at the speed of normal digestion, or as the lightning bolts of God in quick deliverance as the elements enter your body. That is up to you and is a matter of what you are believing at the time of release of *zoe* life. The results you get will tell you what you are really believing. Using the Communion Prayer, we have had people report both quick and longer-term divine healings. See *Battle Prayer for Divine Healing – Field Manual 2* for more on this. Ps 18:14 "Yea, he (*God*) sent out his arrows, and scattered them; and he shot out lightnings, and discomfited them." Also see Ps 144:6.

Or, using your imagination, you can visualize eating the bread and drinking the wine for the same effect. Or, as you think of the stripes of Jesus and His blood, visualize the same release of *zoe* life. You can do the same as you minister or pray for yourself or others. So you can imagine God's *zoe* life going in and healing and making whole as needed, as you minster in thoughts, words and/or actions. Since God has provided this method of healing and blessing for Christians for any need, we suggest you start with the actual bread and wine in the Lord's Supper, and plan on growing into the other methods that have less physical elements.

As you release God in *zoe* life in communion, looking to Jesus as our propitiation, go one step further and put on Jesus Christ, and be Jesus to a snake-bitten world, just as Jesus would, as the new-creation person you are.

Rom 13:14 "But put ye on the Lord Jesus Christ (*to think, be and do as He would*), and make not provision for the flesh, to fulfill the lusts thereof."

The issue has never been the will of God for healing. The issue is will we learn of the truth, the right information, and make it part of our lives in true knowledge. Hos 4:6 "My people are destroyed for lack of knowledge: because thou hast rejected knowledge, I will also reject thee, that thou shalt be no priest to me: seeing thou hast forgotten the law of thy God, I will also forget thy children."

Failure to appreciate and apply God's great work in Jesus is included in "lack of knowledge," and it means you live a life as if the work of Jesus had never been done, and you will surely eat the fruit of any wicked seeds you have sown. Gal 6:7 "Be not deceived; God is not mocked: for whatsoever a man soweth, that shall he also reap. 8 For he that soweth to his flesh shall of the flesh reap corruption; but he that soweth to the Spirit shall of the Spirit reap *zoe*/life everlasting. 9 And let us not be weary in well doing: for in due season we shall reap, if we faint not. 10 As we have therefore opportunity, let us do good unto all men, especially unto them who are of the household of faith."

This is all changed by judging your sins, miseries, wicked thoughts, defeats and failures, as being all carried and healed in Jesus, through the actions remembered by the Lord's Supper. Rom 8:2 "For the law of the Spirit of *zoe*/life in Christ Jesus hath made me free from the law of sin and death. 3 For what the law could not do, in that it was weak through the flesh, God sending his own Son in the likeness of sinful flesh, and for sin, condemned sin in the flesh: 4 that the righteousness of the law might be fulfilled in us, who walk not after the flesh, but after the Spirit."

WORKING WITH PROPITIATION IN COMMUNION

Taking communion or the Lord's Supper rightly, per the Word of God, is a right work of the Spirit–the Gospel of Christ in Jesus.

So healing for the Christian is found in the Lord's Supper and in James 5. James 5:13 "Is any among you afflicted? let him pray. Is any merry? let him sing psalms. 14 Is any sick among you? let him call for the elders of the church; and let them pray over him, anointing him with oil in the name of the Lord: 15 and the prayer of faith shall *sozo*/save the sick, and the Lord shall raise him up; and if he have committed sins, they shall be forgiven him. 16 Confess your faults one to another, and pray one for another, that ye may be *iaomai*/healed (*physically*). The effectual fervent prayer of a righteous man availeth much. 17 Elias was a man subject to like passions as we are, and he prayed earnestly that it might not rain: and it rained not on the earth by the space of three years and six months. 18 And he prayed again (*for a total of 8 times*), and the heaven gave rain, and the earth brought forth her fruit. 19 Brethren, if any of you do err from the truth, and one convert him; 20 let him know, that he which converteth the sinner from the error of his way shall *sozo*/save a soul from death, and shall hide a multitude of sins."

The correct response is to show the Lord's death properly in the Lord's Supper and to acknowledge who and what you are now in Christ: Eph 2:13 "But now in Christ Jesus ye who sometimes were far off are made nigh by the blood of Christ. 14 For he is our peace, who hath made both one, and hath broken down the middle wall of partition between us; 15 having abolished in his flesh the enmity, even the law of commandments contained in ordinances; for to make in himself of twain one new man, so making peace (*Isa 53:5*); 16 and that he might reconcile both unto God in one body by the cross, having slain the enmity thereby: 17 and came and preached peace to you which were afar off, and to them that were nigh (*Isa 57:18-19*). 18 For through him we both have access by one Spirit unto the Father. 19 Now therefore ye are no more strangers and foreigners, but fellowcitizens with the saints, and of the household of God; 20 and are built upon the foundation of the apostles and prophets, Jesus Christ himself being the chief corner stone; 21 in whom all the building fitly framed together groweth unto an holy temple in the Lord: 22 in whom ye also are builded together for an habitation of God through the Spirit."

We obtain the benefits by faith in the work of God in Jesus. Here is a prayer to apply these awesome realities during the Lord's Supper or Communion.

A Communion Prayer: Lord Jesus, by Your stripes I was healed 2000 years ago. (*Call to mind any sicknesses, miseries, fears or failures you are aware of and confess them to Him.*) As I eat this bread, I acknowledge all my infirmities and sicknesses were healed by Your stripes 2000 years ago. And, just as sure as this bread is going into my body, Your healing is restoring me right now in every way. Body, be whole, in the name of Jesus, NOW!

DISCOVERING OUR REDEMPTION

Lord Jesus, by Your blood I am redeemed and my sins are remitted 2000 years ago. (*Call to mind any sins you are aware of and confess them to Him.*) As I drink this wine/juice, I acknowledge Your blood redeemed me from all sin and failure, and my sins were purged 2000 years ago in Your death. And just as sure as this drink is going into my body, I receive that forgiveness now. I am redeemed from the curse of the Law, I am made Your righteousness, Holy Spirit dwells in me, and I am in Your Kingdom of *Agape*/love. Lord Jesus, I judge that Your death paid for everything, and Your resurrection healed everything, so I thank You now for forgiveness, health, right thinking and prosperity in You. My life, be whole in the name of Jesus, NOW!

Lord Jesus, by your stripes and Your blood, I proclaim Your life in every part of my life to Your glory, in the name of Jesus, NOW! By You, Lord Jesus, I am now walking in Your Kingdom in righteousness, peace and joy, in Your Holy Spirit of power, *agape*/love and a sound mind. Father, in the name of Jesus, thank You for Your *agape*/love and covenant in Jesus. Thank You!

Our Father, who is in heaven, hallowed, magnified and glorified be Your name, O God, in all the earth and among all peoples. Your Kingdom come. Your will be done on earth as it is in heaven. Give us this day our daily bread. Forgive us our debts as we forgive others, and teach us to forgive. Lead us not into temptation, and deliver us from evil. For Yours, O God, is the Kingdom, the glory and the honor forever. Amen. Thank You. By Your great love I am part of Your Kingdom. By Your great love I am in Jesus, and by Your great love I will be with You forever. Thank You!

Lord Jesus, I know You are coming again, I know the Day of Judgment is coming, and I know I am saved by your grace. Help me live as a member of your Body, representing You and Your awesome *agape* love, mercy, grace, power, and sound mind in every part of my life. You, Lord Jesus, have shown, revealed, and testified of the things of the consummation of this age in Your victory, triumph, and dominion, and You have told us *"Surely I come quickly. Amen."* So my heart cries with You, *"Even so, come, Lord Jesus."* The grace of our Lord Jesus Christ be with me and all I am related to. Amen, and thank You, Father God, in the name of Jesus, thank You!

Please contact us at www.CovenantPeaceMinistries.com for a printable copy of this communion prayer.

For a more expanded discussion on how to make Holy Communion more effective, see our book, *Freedom In A Snake-Bitten World*, also at our website.

Chapter 39

Liberating the Ability of God within You

The most thrilling thing that I have ever learned about Redemption is the marvelous ability of God that is in the believer.

This is released the more we walk in freedom from sin-consciousness, and, instead, in righteousness-consciousness, in dominion and triumph-consciousness in Jesus, as a son of God. The liberty God promised is in Jesus, not our theology.

John 8:31 "Then said Jesus to those Jews which believed on him, If ye continue in my word, then are ye my disciples indeed; 32 and ye shall know the truth, and the truth shall make you free."

That freedom, that liberty, means God can exercise His glory in you anytime you decide to operate on His Word, in faith, and, thus, build a faith path for God to do good on the Earth. You have liberty anytime to release Holy Spirit into anything that brings the Kingdom of God to Earth.

Eph 1:19 "And what is the exceeding greatness of his power to us-ward who believe, according to the working of his mighty power, 20 which he wrought in Christ, when he raised him from the dead, and set him at his own right hand in the heavenly places, 21 far above all principality, and power, and might, and dominion, and every name that is named, not only in this world, but also in that which is to come: 22 and hath put all things under his feet … ."

DISCOVERING OUR REDEMPTION

This is the ultimate power of God for creation, and it is in us and available to us.

We have God's life in us.

2 Cor 5:17 "Wherefore if any man is in Christ, he is a new creation: the old things are passed away; behold, they are become new." RSV

Notice carefully that the believer is a new creation.

He is created in Christ Jesus.

He is the workmanship of God.

Eph 2:10 "For we are his workmanship (*creation*), created in Christ Jesus unto good works, which God hath before ordained that we should walk in them."

This new creation has become a reality to him because he has received the life and nature of God by grace, and then works to renew his mind with the revelation of our Redemption in Christ, that we might be transformed into a functional brother or sister of Jesus.

Rom 12:2 "And be not conformed to this world: but be ye transformed by the renewing of your mind, that ye may prove what is that good, and acceptable, and perfect, will of God."

Eph 4:20 "But ye have not so learned Christ; 21 if so be that ye have heard him, and have been taught by him, as the truth is in Jesus: 22 that ye put off concerning the former conversation the old man, which is corrupt according to the deceitful lusts; 23 and be renewed in the spirit of your mind; 24 and that ye put on the new man, which after God is created in righteousness and true holiness."

With this renewed mind, you know how to effectively walk in this new-creation *zoe*/life of God.

1 John 5:13 "These things I have written unto you, that ye may know that ye have eternal *zoe*/life, even unto you that believe on the name of the Son of God." RSV

You can see now that you have within you, even as you read this (if you are His child), the life and nature of God.

Peter tells us that we have become partakers of the divine nature.

2 Pet 1:4 "Whereby he hath granted unto us his precious and exceeding great promises; that through these ye may become partakers of the divine nature, having escaped from the corruption that is in the world by lust."

As awesome and perhaps incredible as it may sound, God says, if you are a Christian, you have the divine nature of God in you. You partake of it by letting it run or control you in works of *agape*/love.

Jesus emphasizes this by His illustration: John 15:5 "I am the vine, ye are the branches."

When we are born again, we get a brand new spirit. Our bodies are pretty much the same, and our soul (heart, mind, will and emotions) are still mostly the same. We still have the same memories (good and bad, godly and ungodly, along with their interpretations, godly and ungodly), and our desires may be excited to good, but it is our spirit that is reborn. That is where all things are made new.

So we have a process where:

- Jesus redeemed all men back to God legally by the cross of His reconciliation and healed every curse of sin by His stripes. (Isa 53; Rom 4; 2 Cor 5:14-21)
- Each person must believe that God raised Jesus from the dead to receive or have this Redemption "sealed" to them. God calls this the new birth or the new creation. Thus, we are sealed to our eternal salvation in Jesus unto the Day of Redemption. Eph 1:13 "In whom ye also trusted, after that ye heard the word of truth, the gospel of your *soteria*/salvation: in whom also after that ye believed, ye were sealed with that holy Spirit of promise, 14 which is the earnest of our inheritance until the redemption of the purchased possession, unto the praise of his glory."
- Each person is to now work out the saving of their individual souls (heart, mind, will and emotions) in fear and trembling, knowing all works will be judged. (1 Cor 3; 2 Cor 5:1-13; Phil 2:12-18)
- No iniquity or works of iniquity will survive the Day of our God. What will survive are acts of faith in God, working by *agape*/love. In this process, Holy Spirit is your Helper, to write His laws on your heart and your mind, so you only get eternal rewards called gold, silver and jewels on that Day. (Heb 8:7-13; 10:1-39)

The Day of Judgment in which God, through Jesus, by the Word of God, will judge all works by fire. That which is burned will be gone, and that which remains, of silver, gold and jewels, will be of eternal value to God and you. While there is no direct Bible reference, some believe that during the course of the Day of Judgment, God will write any remaining laws on your heart and mind in the judgment and burning process.

On the Day of Redemption, God will take full possession of all He paid for in Jesus, and whatever laws not written on your heart and mind will be written there then, so you are prepared to walk with God in the New Jerusalem and be a blessing.

Heb 4:10 "For he that is entered into his rest, he also hath ceased from his own works, as God did from his. 11 Let us labour therefore to enter into that rest, lest any man fall after the same example of unbelief (*unpersuadableness*)."

Phil 2:12 "Wherefore, my *agape*/beloved, as ye have always obeyed, not as in my presence only, but now much more in my absence, work out your own *soteria*/

DISCOVERING OUR REDEMPTION

salvation with fear and trembling. 13 For it is God which worketh in you both to will and to do of his good pleasure. 14 Do all things without murmurings and disputings: 15 that ye may be blameless and harmless, the sons of God, without rebuke, in the midst of a crooked and perverse nation, among whom ye shine as lights in the world; 16 holding forth the word of *zoe*/life (*in the Gospel of our* soteria/ *salvation*); that I may rejoice in the day of Christ, that I have not run in vain, neither laboured in vain."

1 Cor 3:13 "Every man's work shall be made manifest: for the day shall declare it, because it shall be revealed by fire; and the fire shall try every man's work of what sort it is. 14 If any man's work abide which he hath built thereupon, he shall receive a reward. 15 If any man's work shall be burned, he shall suffer loss: but he himself shall be *sozo*/saved; yet so as by fire."

On that Day, every man's work will be tested by fire. The silver, gold and jewels, those things you have built with God by His Spirit, are eternally yours and of great value. Those works not of God will be burned, as wood, hay and stubble, with not even ashes left to remember what we thought were once so valuable, but on that Day we will be ashamed of. [See our book, *OK God, Now What?*, for more on this.]

The object of Christ's coming was that we might have *zoe*/life, the *zoe* life of God, and have it abundantly.

John 10:10 "I came that they may have *zoe*/life, and may have it abundantly … ." When you were born again by God, you received eternal *zoe*/life. This is past tense, a done deal for you, the new-creation child.

Jesus was the Substitute for all of man, from Adam to the last man; we receive that *zoe*/life by faith, when we become born again in the new creation.

That eternal life is the nature of the Father, as unveiled in Christ.

Heb 1:1 "God, who at sundry times and in divers manners spake in time past unto the fathers by the prophets, 2 hath in these last days spoken unto us by his Son, whom he hath appointed heir of all things, by whom also he made the worlds; 3 who being the brightness of his glory, and the express image of his person, and upholding all things by the word of his power, when he had by himself purged our sins, sat down on the right hand of the Majesty on high."

The words that Jesus spoke were the Father's words.

John 8:28 "Then said Jesus unto them, When ye have lifted up the Son of man, then shall ye know that I am he, and that I do nothing of myself; but as my Father hath taught me, I speak these things. 29 And he that sent me is with me: the Father hath not left me alone; for I do always those things that please him."

Everything Jesus did and said was what pleased the Father: healing the sick, casting out devils, raising the dead, cleansing lepers, doing good works of alms and using forgiveness as a weapon of *agape* love.

LIBERATING THE ABILITY OF GOD WITHIN YOU

John 12:50 "And I know that his commandment is *zoe*/life everlasting: whatsoever I speak therefore, even as the Father said unto me, so I speak."

John 14:10 "Believest thou not that I am in the Father, and the Father in me? the words that I speak unto you I speak not of myself: but the Father that dwelleth in me, he doeth the works. 11 Believe me that I am in the Father, and the Father in me: or else believe me for the very works' sake. 12 Verily, verily, I say unto you, He that believeth on me, the works that I do shall he do also; and greater works than these shall he do; because I go unto my Father. 13 And whatsoever ye shall *aiteo*/ask (*require, demand and expect as due by covenant promise*) in my name, that will I do, that the Father may be glorified in the Son. 14 If ye shall *aiteo*/ask (*require, demand and expect as due by covenant promise*) any thing in my name, I will do it."

As a branch of the Vine, the same life that is manifested in the Vine is flowing out through you and bearing fruit. It is the Vine's life in you that produces the fruitage of love, of faith, and of joy.

This abiding life is released, as we continually acknowledge who and what we are in Christ.

As a branch of the Vine, with the life of Jesus in you, you speak the Father's words, and He does the works, as you speak, just as He did with Jesus.

Philem 6 "That the communication (*Holy Spirit manifestation among people*) of thy faith may become effectual by the acknowledging of every good thing which is in you in Christ Jesus."

At first, you will have to confess it by faith, before you have much of a testimony of your own God-level works. Or, when you sin, you will have to major on this report of God, that your sins do not control your union with God, and you are in Jesus anyway. Keep at it, with the same group of scriptures and scriptural confessions and affirmations for at least 90 days to write His Word on your heart. It will take many 90-day sessions of 2 to 6 hours a day to write the entire Bible on your heart. This is not the same as memorization, although memorization makes this process much easier.

As you mature in Christ, you will look more like Jesus. John 15:7 "If ye abide in me, and my words abide in you, ye shall *aiteo*/ask (*require, demand and expect as due by covenant promise and not your holiness*) what ye will, and it shall be done unto you. 8 Herein is my Father glorified, that ye bear much fruit; so shall ye be my disciples. 9 As the Father hath *agape*/loved me, so have I *agape*/loved you: continue ye in my *agape*/love (*which includes your salvation by grace and not the works of the law*). 10 If ye keep my commandments, ye shall abide in my *agape*/love (*which includes your salvation by grace and not the works of the law*); even as I have kept my Father's commandments, and abide in his *agape*/love (*which includes your salvation by grace and not the works of the law*). 11 These things have I spoken unto you, that my joy might remain in you, and that your joy might be full."

DISCOVERING OUR REDEMPTION

The more you see this, the more Paul's prayer becomes yours, for yourself and those given you.

Eph 1:17 "That the God of our Lord Jesus Christ, the Father of glory, may give unto you the spirit of wisdom and revelation in the *epignosis*/knowledge of him: 18 The eyes of your understanding being enlightened; that ye may know what is the hope of his calling, and what the riches of the glory of his inheritance in the saints, 19 and what is the exceeding greatness of his power to us-ward who believe, according to the working of his mighty power, 20 which he wrought in Christ, when he raised him from the dead, and set him at his own right hand in the heavenly places, 21 far above all principality, and power, and might, and dominion, and every name that is named, not only in this world, but also in that which is to come: 22 and hath put all things under his feet, and gave him to be the head over all things to the church, 23 which is his body, the fulness of him that filleth all in all."

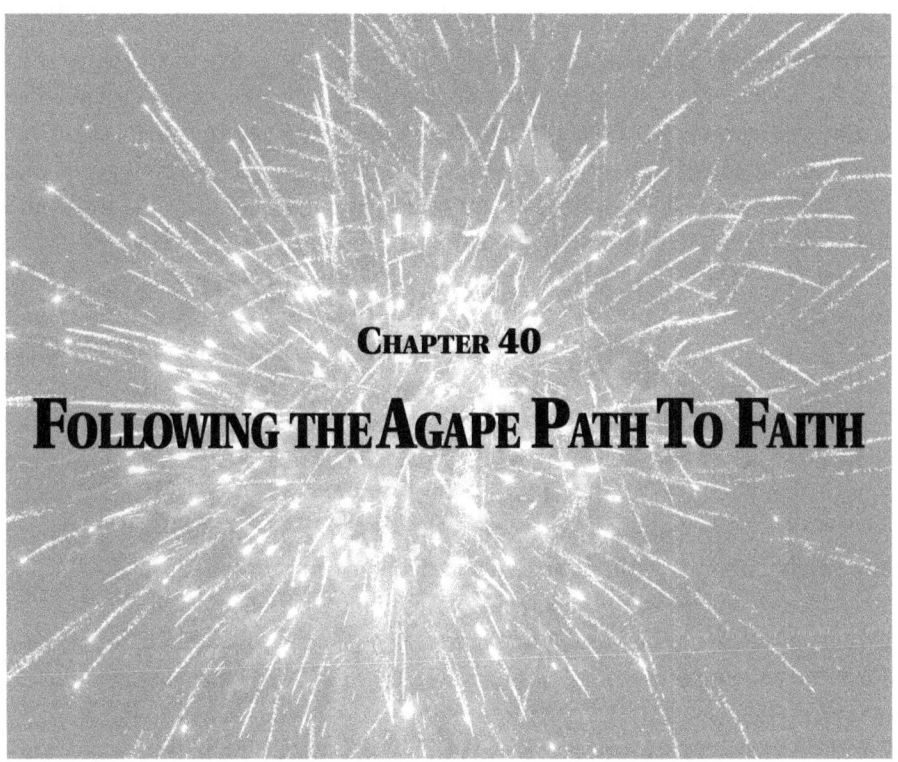

Chapter 40

Following the Agape Path To Faith

God is *agape*/love, and God is a faith God, so the simple answer is to know how *agape*/loved you are by God and let that be the source of your faith in the Word of God. But, for most of us, it takes a bit more than that. So the following is more of a "how to" on the process of knowing God is *agape*/love.

Part of the secret of faith, courage, strength, confidence, trust that does not give up, endurance, persistence and being persuaded of God is to walk in *agape*/love. It is not a requirement for faith, but *agape*/love, which "believes all things," includes faith, confidence, deciding to be fully persuaded, strong and persistent: 1 Cor 13:7 "(Agape/*love*) beareth all things, believeth all things, hopeth all things, endureth all things."

Jesus is the exact representation of how God is, and Jesus is the way back to intimate family life with Father God. This is why God sent Jesus, to redeem us out of the family of Satan and back into the family of God, by adoption. *Adoption* means being known and chosen anyway.

John 14:2 "In my Father's house are many mansions: if it were not so, I would have told you. I go to prepare a place for you. 3 And if I go and prepare a place for you, I will come again, and receive you unto myself; that where I am, there ye may be also. [*Remember, Jesus is seated beside the Father as Ruler, Lord and King of all*

DISCOVERING OUR REDEMPTION

Creation, and Father and Jesus want you there with them, letting Holy Spirit, as the mind and power of God, rule through you also.] 4 And whither I go ye know, and the way [*of walking in the paths of God, so that the Kingdom of God makes Heaven on Earth wherever you are, and whatever you do to fight to establish and enforce the peace of God, as Jesus did*] ye know. 5 Thomas saith unto him, Lord, we know not whither thou goest; and how can we know the way? 6 Jesus saith unto him, I am the way, the truth, and the *zoe*/life: no man cometh unto the Father, but by me. 7 If ye had known me, ye should have known my Father also: and from henceforth ye know him, and have seen him."

Not only are we legally adopted, but we are re-fathered in the new birth by God Himself. By the new birth, God changes our fatherhood from Satan to Himself. John 1:12 "But as many as received him *(Jesus)*, to them gave he power to become the sons of God, even to them that believe on his name: 13 which were born, not of blood, nor of the will of the flesh, nor of the will of man, but of God." So not only is the Christian the legally adopted, known fully before and chosen anyway, but also the desired, wanted and delighted-in love child of God.

This is why we were redeemed by the blood of Jesus, with the awful and loving suffering and death of Jesus. It was all so Father could let His *agape*/love surround and empower every part of your life, as it does in Him. He moves in our acts of righteousness, done by faith in Him, to do His goodness. Eph 5:1 "Be ye therefore followers (*imitators, copycats*) of God, as *agape*/dear children; 2 and walk in *agape*/love, as Christ also hath *agape*/loved us, and hath given himself [*as a ransom*] for us an offering and a sacrifice to God for a sweetsmelling savour."

This is how God has always been, but we could not see it, due to the bitterness of sin. Deut 7:8 "But because the LORD loved you, and because he would keep the oath which he had sworn unto your fathers, hath the LORD brought you out with a mighty hand, and redeemed you out of the house of bondmen, from the hand of Pharaoh king of Egypt."

Isa 63:7 "I will mention the *chesed*/lovingkindnesses (*grace*) of the LORD, and the praises of the LORD, according to all that the LORD hath bestowed on us, and the great goodness toward the house of Israel, which he hath bestowed on them according to his mercies, and according to the multitude of his *chesed*/lovingkindnesses. 8 For he said, Surely they are my people, children that will not lie: so he was their Saviour. 9 In all their affliction he was afflicted, and the angel of his presence saved them: in his love and in his pity he redeemed them; and he bare them, and carried them all the days of old."

But He came and made Himself one with us to *sozo*/save us anyway: Eph 2:1 "And you hath he quickened, who were dead in trespasses and sins; 2 wherein in time past ye walked according to the course of this world, according to the prince of the power of the air, the spirit that now worketh in the children of disobedience:

Following the Agape Path to Faith

3 among whom also we all had our conversation in times past in the lusts of our flesh, fulfilling the desires of the flesh and of the mind; and were by nature the children of wrath, even as others. 4 But God, who is rich in mercy, for his great *agape*/love wherewith he *agape*/loved us, 5 even when we were dead in sins, hath quickened us together with Christ, (by grace ye are *sozo*/saved;) 6 and hath raised us up together, and made us sit together in heavenly places in Christ Jesus: 7 that in the ages to come he might shew the exceeding riches of his grace in his kindness (*chesed*) toward us through Christ Jesus."

This bitterness, this attitude of unforgiveness and offense against God, can color our view of God, so we are blinded to His goodness and truth. These are the attitudes of the devil and, by our joining in these evil thought processes, we become blind to the goodness of the Lord. We are warned not to let this happen to us, as it did the Israelites in the desert with Moses. Heb 12:15 "Looking diligently lest any man fail of the grace of God; lest any root of bitterness springing up trouble you, and thereby many be defiled." Heb 3:10 "Wherefore I was grieved with that generation (*of Israelites in the desert with Moses*), and said, They do alway err in their heart; and they have not known my ways. 11 So I sware in my wrath, They shall not enter into my rest. 12 Take heed, brethren, lest there be in any of you an evil heart of unbelief, in departing from the *zao*/living God. 13 But exhort one another daily, while it is called To day; lest any of you be hardened through the deceitfulness of sin."

Just like them, if we do not mix the Gospel with faith, born-again and dearly loved children of God can live and die as mere men. Heb 4:1 "Let us therefore fear, lest, a promise being left us of entering into his rest, any of you should seem to come short of it. 2 For unto us was the gospel preached, as well as unto them: but the word preached did not profit them, not being mixed with faith (*persuadableness*) in them that heard it."

2 Cor 4:3 "But if our gospel be hid, it is hid to them that are lost (*perishing in the law of sin and death while God is near as did the Israelites in the desert*): 4 in whom the god of this world hath blinded the minds of them which believe not (*remain unpersuadable*), lest the light of the glorious gospel of Christ, who is the image of God, should shine unto them. 5 For we preach not ourselves, but Christ Jesus the Lord; and ourselves your servants for Jesus' sake."

Jesus, as the exact representation of the Father, shows us how the Father really is. He showed us how to really love God and to love our neighbor. All the things that Jesus did were Him loving His Father and, because He loved the Father, He also loved the people God had made. He was also loving His covenant neighbors, the Jewish people.

We can deal with the issues of life, in fear and sympathy, where we agree they are going to have a bad time, or we can agree with God that His *agape*/love is available for them, as a right-thinking human ministers the *zoe*/life of God.

DISCOVERING OUR REDEMPTION

To get rid of fear that God will not hear you, that God does not care, that God maybe will (or maybe not) answer your prayers, search and focus on His Word that God cannot lie and that, most of all, God *agape*/loves people when He can get a right-thinking human to do the "Earth work" of faith in God, by His Word. Such a man is Jesus, and those who walk in Him and like Him. The cure to get rid of all this fear is to know the *agape*/love of God in all its varied and marvelous manifestations.

1 John 4:12 "No man hath seen God at any time. If we *agape*/love one another, God dwelleth in us, and his *agape*/love is perfected (*fulfilled and accomplished continually*) in us. 13 Hereby know we that we dwell in him, and he in us, because he hath given us of his Spirit. 14 And we have seen and do testify that the Father sent the Son to be the Saviour of the world. 15 Whosoever shall confess that Jesus is the Son of God, God dwelleth in him, and he in God. 16 And we have known and believed the *agape*/love that God hath to us. God is *agape*/love; and he that dwelleth in *agape*/love dwelleth in God, and God in him. 17 Herein is our *agape*/love made perfect, that we may have boldness in the day of judgment: because as he is, so are we in this world. 18 There is no fear in *agape*/love; but perfect *agape*/love casteth out fear: because fear hath torment. He that feareth is not made perfect in *agape*/love. 19 We *agape*/love him, because he first *agape*/loved us."

Ps 40:34 "Blessed is that man that maketh the Lord his trust, and respecteth not the proud, nor such as turn aside to lies." *Trust* in this scripture implies courage and strength in the Lord. Today we would call that faith. Trust, in a general sense, is hope; trust for receiving a specific thing, in assurance it is coming, is faith. *Blessed* means empowered to prosper to abundance and to defeat all enemies to the fullness of the goodness of God in the land of the living. A blessed man is walking in the Kingdom of God by the quality of his "trusting." Trust makes blessing work. So we see trust, like faith, operates on quality or endurance, and not on quantity.

Trust or faith is evidenced by what thoughts we allow, what words we speak and what actions we do. Since the mind is not empty, if you are not trusting or having faith in God by His Word, you are trusting or having faith in another word, That "other word" is the lies of the devil, typically by ignorance, deception or offense.

We do the works of trust or faith the way Abraham did. Rom 4:19 "And being not weak in faith, he considered not his own body now dead, when he was about an hundred years old, neither yet the deadness of Sara's womb: 20 he staggered not at the promise of God through unbelief; but was strong in faith, giving glory (*exuberant thanksgiving, praise and rejoicing*) to God; 21 and being fully persuaded (*by continually and repeatedly looking at the promise and character of God over his present circumstances*) that, what he had promised, he was able also to perform."

Trust and faith look the same and are described this way: Phil 4:4 "Rejoice in the Lord alway: and again I say, Rejoice. 5 Let your moderation be known unto all men. The Lord is at hand. 6 Be careful (*anxious, fearful, worried or terrorized*) for nothing; but in every thing by prayer and supplication with (*exuberant and continual*) thanksgiving let your *aiteo*/requests (*requirements, demands and expectations, per Bible promises*) be made known unto God. 7 And the peace of God, which passeth all understanding, shall keep your hearts and minds through Christ Jesus. 8 Finally, brethren, whatsoever things are true, whatsoever things are honest, whatsoever things are just, whatsoever things are pure, whatsoever things are lovely, whatsoever things are of good report; if there be any virtue, and if there be any praise, think on these things."

Doing this continually will make your heart like this: Ps 112:7 "He shall not be afraid of evil tidings: his heart is fixed, trusting in the Lord. 8 His heart is established, he shall not be afraid, until he see his desire upon his enemies."

The Kingdom of God is where things happen as God wants, God's glory is manifested everywhere, and all people are walking in agreement with all of God's authority, ways and laws in *agape*/love all the time. There is no evil fear or fear of lack in God's house, His Kingdom. In His Kingdom, all things operate by faith and continually seeking of God in every part of life. Heb 11:6 "But without faith it is impossible to please him: for he that cometh to God must believe that he is, and that he is a rewarder of them that diligently seek him."

So, in God's Kingdom, not bound by a place, but bound in our hearts, we are continually presenting ourselves and what we do before God. 2 Cor 5:9 "Wherefore we labour, that, whether present or absent, we may be accepted of him."

John 3:19 "And this is the condemnation, that light is come into the world, and men *agape*/loved darkness rather than light, because their deeds were evil. 20 For every one that doeth evil hateth the light, neither cometh to the light, lest his deeds should be reproved. 21 But he that doeth truth cometh to the light, that his deeds may be made manifest, that they are wrought in God."

In Jesus, we have been legally translated out of the kingdom of fear and into the Kingdom of His love. Faith in God, by His Word, lets that *agape*/love of the Father function in this world. If you are united to that *agape*/love, then it benefits you also.

Col 1:12 "Giving thanks (*continually*) unto the Father, which hath made us meet to be partakers of the inheritance of the saints in light: 13 who hath delivered us from the power of darkness, and hath translated us into the kingdom of his *agape*/dear Son: 14 in whom we have redemption through his blood, even the *aphesis*/forgiveness (*purging, removal, washing, obliteration and putting away*) of sins: 15 who is the image of the invisible God, the firstborn of every creature: 16 for by him were all things created, that are in heaven, and that are in earth, visible and invisible, whether they be thrones, or dominions, or principalities, or powers: all things were created by him, and for him: 17 and he is before all things, and by him all things consist."

DISCOVERING OUR REDEMPTION

The fullness of the Kingdom of God includes the total absence of the evil glory, authority, lack, ways and laws of the kingdom of darkness. John 10:10 "The thief cometh not, but for to steal, and to kill, and to destroy [*in the lies and deception he gets us to believe about God*]: I am come that they might have *zoe*/life, and that they might have it more abundantly."

Jesus summarized the Kingdom of God that releases the *zoe*/life of God in Matthew 5 through 8. He said there that we should:
- Keep our attitudes right and avoid self-righteousness;
- Root out unforgiveness and offense in our hearts;
- Give alms and do other man-level good works;
- Maintain a private prayer life with Father God;
- Fast on a regular basis;
- Seek first the Kingdom of God and His righteousness rather than worldly power;
- Develop a heart of *agape*/love for God and our fellowman;
- Know the way we judge God and others is the way we will be judged;
- Do what Jesus says to do, to thrive in the storms of life;
- A*gape*/love, just as Father God *agape*/loves us;
- Judge against the devil and for people;
- Demonstrate what He told the disciples to do: heal the sick, raise the dead, cast out devils, cleanse the lepers and preach the Kingdom is at hand; thus healing the sick, etc., is getting rid of the kingdom of darkness and health is God's desire and Kingdom;
- Participate in public assemblies, just as the Jews went to synagogue regularly.

Jesus promised that if we do these things of the Kingdom: Matt 6:33 "But seek ye first the kingdom of God, and his righteousness; and all these things (*that the Gentiles seek of wealth, power, peace, prosperity and happiness*) shall be added unto you."

The apostle summarizes our efforts in this way: 1 Tim 1:5 "Now the end of the commandment (*teaching, doctrine, instruction*) is *agape*/charity out of a pure heart, and of a good conscience, and of faith unfeigned."

Our goal is to walk in the *agape*/love of God toward God and man.

Here is a summary description of *agape*/love attitudes:

1 Cor 13:4 "*Agape*/love endures long and is patient and

(agape/*love is*) kind (*does good to make better, fill and fix any need, operates in compassion and removes oppression and injustice, feeds the hungry, clothes the naked, heals the sick, redeems the lost and gives Holy Spirit for blessing and gifts of God*);

agape/love never is envious nor boils over with jealousy,

(*agape*/love) is not boastful or vainglorious,

(*agape*/love) does not display itself haughtily.

5 It (*agape*/love) is not conceited (arrogant and inflated with pride);
it (*agape*/love) is not rude (unmannerly) and
(*agape*/love) does not act unbecomingly.
Agape/love (God's love in us) does not insist on its own rights or its own way, for it (*agape*/love) is not self-seeking (*selfish, self-centered, or self-righteous*);
it (*agape*/love) is not touchy or fretful or resentful;
it (*agape*/love) takes no account of the evil done to it
[it (*agape*/love) pays no attention to a suffered wrong].
6 It (*agape*/love) does not rejoice at injustice and unrighteousness, but
(*agape/love*) rejoices when right and truth prevail.
7 *Agape*/love bears up under anything and everything that comes,
(*agape*/love) is ever ready to believe the best of every person,
(*agape*/love) its hopes are fadeless under all circumstances, and
it (*agape*/love) endures everything [without weakening].
8 *Agape*/love never fails [never fades out or becomes obsolete or comes to an end. ...
13 And so faith, hope, *agape*/love abide [faith—conviction and belief respecting man's relation to God and divine things; hope—joyful and confident expectation of *coming good and* eternal *soteria*/salvation; *agape*/love—true affection for God and man, growing out of God's *agape*/love for and in us], these three; but the greatest of these is *agape*/love." AMP

In 1 Cor 13:2, we are told that you can move mountains with faith, but without *agape*/love it profits you nothing. This means that on the Day of Judgment that mountain you moved by faith, but not in *agape*/love, will not be counted as silver, gold or jewels for you on that day. Whoever you moved the mountain for may have gotten blessed, but without *agape*/love, it does not benefit you in the final judgment. For you, on that day, it will be wood, hay or stubble.

1 Cor 3:11 "For no other foundation can anyone lay than that which is [already] laid, which is Jesus Christ (the Messiah, the Anointed One). 12 But if anyone builds upon the Foundation, whether it be with gold, silver, precious stones, wood, hay, straw, 13 the work of each [one] will become [plainly, openly] known (shown for what it is); for the day [of Christ] will disclose and declare it, because it will be revealed with fire, and the fire will test and critically appraise the character and worth of the work each person has done. 14 If the work which any person has built on this Foundation [any product of his efforts whatever] survives [this test], he will get his reward. 15 But if any person's work is burned up [under the test], he will suffer the loss [of it all, losing his reward], though he himself will be *sozo*/saved, but only as [one who has passed] through fire. [Job 23:10.]" AMP

Notice this attribute of *agape*/love: 1 Cor 13:7 "(*Agape/love*) beareth all things, believeth all things, hopeth all things, endureth all things." Based on this, *agape*/

DISCOVERING OUR REDEMPTION

love is the source of God's believing. Even better, the more you walk in the *agape*/love of God, the more you will walk in believing God, which is faith. So *agape*/love is a shortcut to more faith.

When you see someone who is in a sin of any kind, in *agape*/love, you know that that sin is costing them in many ways. They will reap the corruption they are sowing, unless the covenant in Jesus is applied to that situation. The devil, who only comes to rob, kill and destroy, is paying them with malice, fear, loss and torment. The price for unconfessed sin is high and costs the sinner dearly. Thus, one who is in sin is hurting, in confusion and darkness.

The price of any sin is the same—death, and Jesus paid for that sin with His life. So, whether the sin is, in man's eyes, small or large, it cost Jesus His life and unimaginable suffering to pay for that sin. This is Redemption by His blood. So any sin has, as its basis, that God would pay the price, no matter what price man thinks that sin is worth.

The requirement for faith is also total: Rom 14:23 "And he that doubteth is damned (*releasing the law of sin and death*) if he eat, because he eateth not of faith: for whatsoever is not of faith is sin."

When you see the full effect of sin, it is so bad and evil that you would never sin if you knew it in advance. Heb 1:8 "But unto the Son he saith, Thy throne, O God, is for ever and ever: a sceptre of righteousness is the sceptre of thy kingdom. 9 Thou hast *agape*/loved righteousness, and hated iniquity (*evil, sin, and death*); therefore God, even thy God, hath anointed thee with the oil of gladness above thy fellows."

A Christian in sin, whose spirit only acts just like Jesus and is constantly pressuring their soul to stop sinning and to reconcile whatever wrongs are done, is miserable in the process. Isa 48:22 "There is no peace, saith the LORD, unto the wicked."

Thus, a Christian in sin is walking in the carnal mind, the mind of the flesh, and not in the Spirit of God. Rom 8:2 "For the law of the Spirit of *zoe*/life in Christ Jesus hath made me free from the law of sin and death. 3 For what the law could not do, in that it was weak through the flesh, God sending his own Son in the likeness of sinful flesh, and for sin, condemned (*cursed, destroyed*) sin in the flesh: 4 that the righteousness of the law might be fulfilled in us, who walk not after the flesh, but after the Spirit. 5 For they that are after the flesh do mind the things of the flesh; but they that are after the Spirit the things of the Spirit. 6 For to be carnally minded is death; but to be spiritually minded is *zoe*/life and peace. 7 Because the carnal mind is enmity against God: for it is not subject to the law of God, neither indeed can be. 8 So then they that are in the flesh cannot please God. 9 But ye are not in the flesh, but in the Spirit, if so be that the Spirit of God dwell in you. Now if any man have not the Spirit of Christ, he is none of his."

Following the Agape Path to Faith

A Christian does not have two natures. He is born again in spirit, after God, which is his nature now. But his soul (his heart, mind, will and emotions) is not born again. That is to be renewed or rehabilitated or reprogrammed. Rom 12:2 "And be not conformed to this world: but be ye transformed by the renewing of your mind, that ye may prove what is that good, and acceptable, and perfect, will of God."

You are a spirit, you live in a body, and you have a soul. Your spirit works through the soul to get the body to do what the spirit wants. Whatever the soul wants is what the body does. There are a few things the body does without the decisions of the soul, but not many. Breathing and the other autonomic responses of the body are examples. But, without a doubt, a body with two heads will have issues. Jesus is the head of the Body of Christ, but if you do not think like Him, you will rarely cooperate with Him.

When we commit sin, the body is controlled by the soul, actually by evil or ignorant beliefs in the soul. The spirit, due to the fall of Adam, became weaker than the soul. We understand that when Adam died, his spirit died, and his soul became primary. The soul is the connection between the spirit and the body. And, of course, the body is the connection of the soul to the physical world. In general, the human spirit cannot access the physical world except through the soul.

Before he sinned, Adam did not even see that he was naked. Many scholars believe that he was clothed in light, just as when Jesus was transfigured on the mount. But when Adam's spirit died, became one with death, lost its connection to God, his soul and his fleshly senses became stronger, and he saw in a way he could not see before. He became naked and ran from God, his only true Helper. In this way, the spirit became subservient to the soul and body, and the "flesh" or "carnal mind" became stronger. Driven by the senses, the carnal man sees God as a cruel master and enemy, just as Adam did, when he ran from God, who was coming to help him.

Maturity in Christ means that the soul must be renewed in the Word of God to allow the spirit, where Holy Spirit now dwells, to dominate.

Luke 21:19 "By your steadfastness and patient endurance you shall win the true life of your *psuche*/souls (*lives*)." AMP

James 1:2 "Consider it wholly joyful, my brethren, whenever you are enveloped in or encounter trials of any sort or fall into various temptations. 3 Be assured and understand that the trial and proving of your faith bring out endurance and steadfastness and patience. 4 But let endurance and steadfastness and patience have full play and do a thorough work, so that you may be [people] perfectly and fully developed [with no defects], lacking in nothing." AMP

1 Pet 1:22 "Seeing ye have purified your *psuche*/souls (*lives*) in obeying the truth through the Spirit unto unfeigned *phileo*/love of the brethren, see that ye *agape*/love one another with a pure heart fervently."

DISCOVERING OUR REDEMPTION

Thus, for the people under Moses, who were not born again, the soul could be trained to follow God. In the new creation, the spirit is re-created, but still limited by what the soul will accept and agree with. Until the soul is made new in the Word of God, the soul will drive the person and, thus, the body will commit sin, as directed by the soul. The body, by itself, has little to challenge the soul.

Here the psalmist is speaking to his soul, from his spirit or self, for his soul to line up with God: Ps 116:6 "The LORD preserveth the simple: I was brought low, and he helped me. 7 Return unto thy rest, O my soul; for the LORD hath dealt bountifully with thee. 8 For thou hast delivered my soul from death, mine eyes from tears, and my feet from falling."

We live our lives out of our soul (heart), and it is first measured by what you say. Matt 12:34 "O generation of vipers, how can ye, being evil, speak good things? for out of the abundance of the heart the mouth speaketh. 35 A good man out of the good treasure of the heart bringeth forth good things: and an evil man out of the evil treasure bringeth forth evil things. 36 But I say unto you, That every idle word (*that does not produce the Kingdom of God and, therefore, stand on the Day of Judgment*) that men shall speak, they shall give account thereof in the day of judgment. 37 For by thy words thou shalt be justified, and by thy words thou shalt be condemned."

Matt 6:21 "For where your treasure is, there will your heart be also. 22 The light of the body is the eye: if therefore thine eye be single, thy whole body shall be full of light [*whatever light you are constantly looking on or by*]. 23 But if thine eye be evil (*set on fear, stinginess, lack, want, or the world system*), thy whole body shall be full of darkness. If therefore the light that is in thee be darkness, how great is that darkness! 24 No man can serve two masters: for either he will hate the one, and *agape*/love the other; or else he will hold to the one, and despise the other. Ye cannot serve God and mammon."

One answer to releasing our spirit through our soul is to force the soul to operate in spiritual truth with gladness. Remember, if you fake gladness, your unconscious mind cannot tell the difference, even though your cognitive mind can. The heart is the unconscious or subconscious mind. We live out of our subconscious mind, which drives our automatic responses and attitudes. So this is the key: train your heart to do good gladly, by faking it if necessary. Here is how God described one way to do this.

Eph 5:14 "Wherefore he saith, Awake thou that sleepest, and arise from the dead, and Christ shall give thee light. 15 See then that ye walk circumspectly, not as fools, but as wise, 16 redeeming the time, because the days are evil. 17 Wherefore be ye not unwise, but understanding what the will of the Lord is. 18 And be not drunk with wine, wherein is excess; but be (*being*) filled with (*controlled by*) the Spirit; 19 speaking to yourselves in psalms and hymns and spiritual songs, singing and making melody in your heart to the Lord; 20 giving thanks always for all things unto God and the Father in the name of our Lord Jesus Christ; 21 submitting yourselves one to another in the fear of God."

A main Bible message is that a right life is the result of the Word and love of God controlling the heart or soul, by a right programmed mind (conscious and subconscious). Our job in this life is to "save" or reprogram, or re-new our souls with the Word of God, to reach maturity, so we operate wisely in our salvation. The "mind of Christ" within us and a soul in agreement results in us walking by our spirit, which will have free access through a renewed mind, to cause right behavior by the body. This is how we create a path for God to operate in this world.

Therefore we are told one way to *agape*/love God is to *lambano*/receive His Word and keep it in our hearts to do it.

James 1:18 "Of his own will begat he us with the word of truth, that we should be a kind of firstfruits of his creatures. 19 Wherefore, my *agape*/beloved brethren, let every man be swift to hear, slow to speak, slow to wrath: 20 for the wrath of man worketh not the righteousness of God. 21 Wherefore lay apart all filthiness and superfluity of naughtiness, and *lambano*/receive with meekness the engrafted word, which is able to *sozo*/save your *psuche*/souls (*lives*). 22 But be ye doers of the word, and not hearers only, deceiving your own selves."

1 Pet 1:8 "Whom having not seen, ye *agape*/love; in whom, though now ye see him not, yet believing, ye rejoice with joy unspeakable and full of glory: 9 receiving the end of your faith, even the *soteria*/salvation of your *psuche*/souls (*lives*)."

2 Tim 3:15 "And that from a child thou hast known the holy scriptures, which are able to make thee wise unto *soteria*/salvation through faith which is in Christ Jesus."

Failure to accomplish this leaves us as mere men, babes in Christ, who have all they need ("ye are complete in Him"), but have not *lambano*/received the Word of God in a way to mature them into Christ. They are ruled by their souls, filled with and controlled by fleshly, carnal, worldly and demonic values, and not Holy Spirit, in the Word of God.

1 Cor 3:1 "And I, brethren, could not speak unto you as unto spiritual, but as unto carnal, even as unto babes in Christ. 2 I have fed you with milk, and not with meat: for hitherto ye were not able to bear it, neither yet now are ye able. 3 For ye are yet carnal: for whereas there is among you envying, and strife, and divisions, are ye not carnal, and walk as (*mere*) men? 4 For while one saith, I am of Paul; and another, I am of Apollos; are ye not carnal? 5 Who then is Paul, and who is Apollos, but ministers by whom ye believed, even as the Lord gave to every man? 6 I have planted, Apollos watered; but God gave the increase. 7 So then neither is he that planteth any thing, neither he that watereth; but God that giveth the increase."

2 Cor 5:10 "For we must all appear before the judgment seat of Christ; that every one may receive the things done in his body, according to that he hath done,

whether it be good or bad. 11 Knowing therefore the terror of the Lord (*in the absolute assurance that no work of the flesh will survive that Day*), we persuade men; but we are made manifest unto God; and I trust also are made manifest in your consciences. 12 For we commend not ourselves again unto you, but give you occasion to glory on our behalf, that ye may have somewhat to answer them which glory in appearance, and not in heart. 13 For whether we be beside ourselves, it is to God: or whether we be sober, it is for your cause. 14 For the *agape*/love of Christ constraineth us; because we thus judge, that if one died for all, then were all dead: 15 and that he died for all, that they which *zao*/live should not henceforth *zao*/live unto themselves (*in the old man of the flesh*), but unto him which died for them, and rose again. 16 Wherefore henceforth know we no man after the flesh: yea, though we have known Christ after the flesh, yet now henceforth know we him no more."

1 Pet 4:1 "Forasmuch then as Christ hath suffered for us in the flesh, arm yourselves likewise with the same mind: for he that hath suffered in the flesh hath ceased from sin; 2 that he no longer should live (*exist*) the rest of his time in the flesh to the lusts of men, but to the will of God. 3 For the time past of our life may suffice us to have wrought the will of the Gentiles, when we walked in lasciviousness, lusts, excess of wine, revellings, banquetings, and abominable idolatries: 4 wherein they think it strange that ye run not with them to the same excess of riot, speaking evil of you: 5 who shall give account to him that is ready to judge the quick and the dead."

So we can rest assured that even though it may appear that, in this life, we or others do not reap the corruption sown, for sure, on the Day of Judgment, all works will be tested. Col 3:23 "And whatsoever ye do, do it heartily, as to the Lord, and not unto men; 24 knowing that of the Lord ye shall receive the reward of the inheritance: for ye serve the Lord Christ. 25 But he that doeth wrong shall receive for the wrong which he hath done: and there is no respect of persons. 4 Masters, give unto your servants that which is just and equal; knowing that ye also have a Master in heaven."

Eph 6:5 "Servants, be obedient to them that are your masters according to the flesh, with fear and trembling, in singleness of your heart, as unto Christ; 6 not with eyeservice, as menpleasers; but as the servants of Christ, doing the will of God from the heart; 7 with good will doing service, as to the Lord, and not to men: 8 knowing that whatsoever good thing any man doeth, the same shall he receive of the Lord, whether he be bond or free. 9 And, ye masters, do the same things unto them, forbearing threatening: knowing that your Master also is in heaven; neither is there respect of persons with him."

Father God desires that that Day be a Day of Reward of eternal value silver, gold and jewels for all men, and not the destruction by fire of wood, hay and stubble. As a Christian, you are to know this and let *agape*/love drive you to set yourself and others free of the oppressions of the devil, so you and they are free and look forward to that Day in joy.

1 Cor 3:11 "For other foundation can no man lay than that is laid, which is Jesus Christ. 12 Now if any man build upon this foundation gold, silver, precious stones, wood, hay, stubble; 13 every man's work shall be made manifest: for the day shall declare it, because it shall be revealed by fire; and the fire shall try every man's work of what sort it is. 14 If any man's work abide which he hath built thereupon, he shall receive a reward. 15 If any man's work shall be burned, he shall suffer loss: but he himself shall be *sozo*/saved; yet so as by fire. 16 Know ye not that ye are the temple of God, and that the Spirit of God dwelleth in you?"

Whether those sinning are aware of it or not, whether they are so distracted so they cannot feel the pain, they are distressed. Man was created to be a vessel of God and to walk only in *agape*/love; any other condition is an "ill fitting shoe," at best. Men and women who walk in sin don't know the *agape*/love of God in the area where they are not like Jesus. They don't know how loved they are, and only fear and the torments of fear await them. They are lost, in destruction, blinded, miserable, and confused in that part of their life.

They are driven by lusts that can never satisfy. Often they are deceived and cannot even see how and where they are wrong. *Deception* means you are fooled into thinking evil is good, and good is evil. These people are not walking in the righteousness, peace and joy of the Lord. They walk, in that part of their lives (soul or mind), by the spirit of fear and not by Holy Spirit power, *agape*/love and a sound mind, like Jesus would. In that area of their lives, they can perhaps barely see the Kingdom of God, and they definitely cannot produce much of it.

The amazing thing is that the suffering of the sinner, in guilt and condemnation, Jesus bore totally for that sinner, whether they confess their sin or not, so even the sinner's anguish has been healed in Jesus 2000 years ago.

Heb 2:14 "Forasmuch then as the children are partakers of flesh and blood, he (*Jesus*) also himself likewise took part of the same; that through death he might destroy him that had the power of death, that is, the devil; 15 and deliver them who through fear of death were all their lifetime subject to bondage."

Gal 5:19 "Now the works of the (*soul or mind controlled by the*) flesh are manifest, which are these; adultery, fornication, uncleanness, lasciviousness, 20 idolatry, witchcraft, hatred, variance, emulations, wrath, strife, seditions, heresies, 21 envyings, murders, drunkenness, revellings, and such like: of the which I tell you before, as I have also told you in time past, that they which do such things shall not inherit (*walk in and produce or bring to Earth*) the kingdom of God."

When we Christians sin, we are not walking in what we are, or what we are made for. It is always an "ill fitting shoe," and a burden we were not meant to carry. The result is often the development of a touchy, judgmental and self-righteous attitude.

DISCOVERING OUR REDEMPTION

In our culture, we have developed a myriad of ways to hide and pretend these evil shoes are fitting, or we apply a myriad of socially acceptable and unacceptable bandages, crutches, salves and balms, to cover the pain, but in the path of God, we do not go far in that area of our lives, i.e., do not bring the Kingdom of God to make Heaven on Earth.

Prov 4:19 "The way of the wicked is as darkness: they know not at what they stumble."

Prov 13:15 "Good understanding giveth favour: but the way of transgressors is hard."

Remember *inherit* means to move into or to walk in what God has made of us in Jesus. 1 Pet 3:9 "Not rendering evil for evil, or railing for railing: but contrariwise blessing; knowing that ye are thereunto called, that ye should inherit (*bring Heaven to Earth and thus producing*) a blessing."

1 Cor 6:9 "Know ye not that the unrighteous shall not inherit (*bring to Earth*) the kingdom of God? Be not deceived: neither fornicators, nor idolaters, nor adulterers, nor effeminate, nor abusers of themselves with mankind, 10 nor thieves, nor covetous, nor drunkards, nor revilers, nor extortioners, shall inherit (*produce in their evil thoughts, words and actions*) the kingdom of God."

One aspect of God's *agape*/love says, "I care for you and want to be with you, but I cannot inhabit your sin. You are sinning, what you are doing is evil, it is of the devil, and I know you are hurting and confused, all is darkness, and you need help. I will find a way to set you free. You must know My *agape*/love in mercy, grace and truth."

In *agape*/love, we obey: 1 John 5:16 "If any man see his brother sin a sin which is not unto death, he shall *aiteo*/ask, and he shall give him *zoe*/life for them ... ." This is what a heart set on *agape*/love does with the awesome power of answered prayer, as seen in 1 John 5:13-15.

One note: we are not talking about sinners as non-Christians. We are talking about Christians who are sinning, those of the household of faith, as well as non-Christians who are sinning. While a Christian is assured of eternal salvation in the Lord, the penalty in this life, now on earth, is the same for unconfessed sin, whether you are a Christian or not. Rom 1:18 "For the wrath of God is revealed from heaven against all ungodliness and unrighteousness of men, who hold the truth in unrighteousness."

Specifically for Christians: 1 Cor 11:31 "For if we would judge ourselves, we should not be judged. 32 But when we are judged, we are chastened of the Lord, that we should not be condemned with the world."

God is not so unfair as to let the Christian who does not walk in the work of the Mighty Arm of God (judging the body and blood of Jesus as of no benefit for this life, for blessing, reconciliation of sin and removal of the curse of sin) to be free of

Following the Agape Path to Faith

the consequences of sin, when He holds the un-born again to the same standard of holiness. Acts 10:34 "Then Peter opened his mouth, and said, Of a truth I perceive that God is no respecter of persons: 35 but in every nation he that feareth him, and worketh righteousness, is accepted (*approved unto blessing*) with him."

For the Christian and non-Christian: Gal 6:7 "Be not deceived; God is not mocked: for whatsoever a man soweth, that shall he also reap. 8 For he that soweth to his flesh shall of the flesh reap corruption; but he that soweth to the Spirit shall of the Spirit reap *zoe*/life everlasting. 9 And let us not be weary in well doing: for in due season we shall reap, if we faint not. 10 As we have therefore opportunity, let us do good unto all men, especially unto them who are of the household of faith."

Whatever way of sin or error anyone is walking in, they are hurting. If you find fault and pray, because they are sinning, with an attitude of self-righteousness (they are wrong, and you are right), you will sink to religious pride, offense, faultfinding, unforgiveness and bitterness. You will see only evil, and that is what you will become. Heb 12:15 "Looking diligently lest any man fail of the grace of God (*where all sins are remitted in Christ, and no man is better than any other, but all joined for* agape/love); lest any root of bitterness springing up trouble you, and thereby many (*Jews and Christians*) be defiled." Bitterness colors everything you see on a given topic, in offense, faultfinding and contempt, and generally requires more work to resolve to get the bitter one free.

The way of *agape*/love is to get them free because God declares them valuable, in spite of their sin. They are, therefore, worth the price of Jesus, to God, to redeem them from the hand of the enemy, and God is hurting for them in their sin. God knows the price He paid for them, and He wants only His best, in Jesus, for them.

Heb 10:16 "This is the covenant that I will make with them after those days, saith the Lord, I will put my laws into their hearts, and in their minds will I write them; 17 and their sins and iniquities will I remember no more. 18 Now where remission of these is (*sins and iniquities*), there is no more offering for sin."

1 John 3:11 "For this is the message that ye heard from the beginning, that we should *agape*/love one another."

James 5:20 "Let him know, that he which converteth the sinner from the error of his way shall *sozo*/save a soul from death, and shall hide a multitude of sins."

Gal 6:1 "Brethren, if a man be overtaken in a fault (*sin, deception, sickness, disease, lack, poverty, pride, i.e., anything that is not like Heaven on Earth*), ye which are spiritual, restore such an one in the spirit of meekness; considering thyself, lest thou also be tempted. 2 Bear ye one another's burdens, and so fulfil the law of Christ."

You can operate in faith without *agape*/love, but if you operate in *agape*/love, you will operate in faith, so you will believe God by *agape*/love. Now you and God are thinking alike. The answer for faith is to believe God, by His Word, for He is the

DISCOVERING OUR REDEMPTION

God who cannot lie. So the shortcut to faith is to operate in *agape*/love by the Word of God. As you join in with God's *agape*/love for that person or situation and start getting the faith, the answer that needs to be brought to Earth, to bring Heaven to Earth in that situation, you will walk in His Spirit of power, *agape*/love and a sound mind (see 2 Tim 1:7) and be free from fear.

God has paid the full price for the healing of every person from and in any and all sin. God has spoken, whether they are currently a Christian or not, Rom 4:25 "(*Jesus*) Who was delivered for our offences, and was raised again for our justification (*or when we were justified*)."

Rom 4:5 "But to him that worketh not, but believeth on him that justifieth the ungodly, his faith is counted for righteousness."

Rom 5:6 "For when we were yet without strength, in due time Christ died for the ungodly. 7 For scarcely for a righteous man will one die: yet peradventure for a good man some would even dare to die. 8 But God commendeth his *agape*/love toward us, in that, while we were yet sinners, Christ died for us."

This is a clear declaration that sin does not hinder the grace of God.

That *justified* of Rom 4:25 included the healing of everything that is not like Heaven. So God has already healed everyone, Christian or not, 2000 years ago and wants them to walk in that healing now.

Eph 2:4 "But God, who is rich in mercy, for his great *agape*/love wherewith he *agape*/loved us, 5 even when we were dead in sins, hath quickened us together with Christ, (by grace ye are *sozo*/saved;) 6 and hath raised us up together, and made us sit together in heavenly places in Christ Jesus: 7 that in the ages to come he might shew the exceeding riches of his grace in his kindness toward us through Christ Jesus. 8 For by grace are ye *sozo*/saved through faith; and that not of yourselves: it is the gift of God: 9 not of works, lest any man should boast."

Rom 2:4 "Or despisest thou the riches of his goodness and forbearance and longsuffering; not knowing that the goodness of God leadeth thee to repentance?"

Jesus told no one who needed His healing that He could not heal them until they had confessed their sins or stopped sinning, gotten baptized, had enough faith, made restitution, even turned to God, they had not learned their lesson, or it is not the right time. He healed those who came to Him and those He found on the way, as they needed. Luke 9:11 "And the people, when they knew it, followed him: and he received them, and spake unto them of the kingdom of God, and healed them that had need of healing."

If they had need, they qualified for healing by Jesus, which meant that qualified them for Father God.

This is the heart of the Father, and this is *agape*/love. Father believes that if He heals you and gets truth into your heart, you will eventually decide to turn to Him and let Him live His life in and through you. In order to release that *agape*/love, we must apply the Word of Reconciliation to every instance of the devil's oppression with the Word of Peace in Jesus, and set the oppressed free, ourselves included. This process is called "saving our souls," and it is our job in this life.

James 1:21 "Wherefore lay apart all filthiness and superfluity of naughtiness, and receive with meekness the engrafted word, which is able to *sozo*/save your souls. 22 But be ye doers of the word, and not hearers only, deceiving your own selves. 23 For if any be a hearer of the word, and not a doer, he is like unto a man beholding his natural face in a glass (*mirror*): 24 for he beholdeth himself, and goeth his way, and straightway forgetteth what manner of man he was. 25 But whoso looketh into the perfect law of liberty *[from sin to be like Jesus in the new birth]*, and continueth therein, he being not a forgetful hearer, but a doer of the work, this man shall be blessed in his deed. 26 If any man among you seem to be religious, and bridleth not his tongue, but deceiveth his own heart, this man's religion is vain."

So to start walking in *agape*/love, you start doing *agape*/love, for *agape*/love is an action word. You start by doing what good you can do in the natural. Cook a meal, clean a room, give clothes, watch someone's children, help them in writing a report, give money, pray for them to get free of their pain, treat them with respect, etc. Look for both natural and supernatural ways to bless them.

Matt 5:44 "But I say unto you, *agape*/love your enemies, bless them that curse you, do good to them that hate you, and pray for them which despitefully use you, and persecute you; 45 that ye may be the children of your Father which is in heaven: for he maketh his sun to rise on the evil and on the good, and sendeth rain on the just and on the unjust. 46 For if ye *agape*/love them which *agape*/love you, what reward have ye? do not even the publicans the same? 47 And if ye salute your brethren only, what do ye more than others? do not even the publicans so? 48 Be ye therefore perfect, even as your Father which is in heaven is perfect."

Jesus called Himself the Great Shepherd, and everything He said and did was the Father talking. So an under-shepherd is one who ministers the righteousness of the Master Shepherd.

Notice the attitude of the Great Shepherd. He appointed others to go and do what He could not, at that time, for His Father's sheep. Matt 9:36 "But when he saw the multitudes, he was moved with compassion on them, because they fainted, and were scattered abroad, as sheep having no shepherd. 37 Then saith he unto his disciples, The harvest truly is plenteous, but the labourers are few; 38 pray ye therefore the Lord of the harvest, that he will send forth labourers into his harvest. 10 And when he had called unto him his twelve disciples, he gave them power against unclean spirits, to cast them out, and to heal all manner of sickness and all manner of disease."

Notice, Jesus saw the need, asked His disciples to pray to Father God to answer that need, and then appointed them to go supply that need, by healing those

DISCOVERING OUR REDEMPTION

oppressed by the devil, just as Jesus did. By getting the disciples to pray, He expected them to let compassion also work in them, even as they prayed, in becoming one with those in need, and then believing God to heal. So Jesus got them thinking like God thinks, and then sent them out to do like God wants done.

This process qualifies any of us to be the agent that brings Heaven to Earth for Father God. You see people in need, identify with the hurt it is causing them, pray for God to heal them, believe God to heal them through you, and then go heal them with *aiteo*/demands.

For those in sickness, you know sickness is causing them suffering and tempting them to speak words of death in some way. For those in sin, with ungodly words and actions, you know they will pay for them on the Day of Judgment and not receive the silver, gold and jewels God wants for them. Thus, in setting them free to get eternally rich, you get even richer.

James 1:25 "But whoso looketh into the perfect law of liberty, and continueth therein, he being not a forgetful hearer, but a doer of the work, this man shall be blessed in his deed. 26 If any man among you seem to be religious, and bridleth not his tongue, but deceiveth his own heart, this man's religion is vain. 27 Pure religion and undefiled before God and the Father is this, To visit the fatherless and widows in their affliction, and to keep himself unspotted from the world."

In order to not make our religion vain, we must operate in the perfect law of liberty, where we are free to *agape*/love, father and shepherd people who need truth, grace and healing in all forms. In God's principle of enlightened self-interest, you can know you are blessed, made prosperous in all and any ways, for doing the Word of *agape*/love and grace in the ministry of reconciliation.

Matt 7:11 "If ye then, being evil, know how to give good gifts unto your children, how much more shall your Father which is in heaven give good things to them that *aiteo*/ask (*require, demand and expect as due by covenant promise of*) him? 12 Therefore all things whatsoever ye would that men should do to you, do ye even so to them: for this is the law and the prophets."

So you do these acts of *agape*/love to them and for them, as an agent of God, our Father, where He empowers your man-level acts. You live in 1 Cor 13, to meditate there constantly, and you look for ways to bless and make life better for others in small and large ways. You become a master at kindness and goodness. You are taking on the heart of your Father in your soul to see their burdens and bear those burdens for them to deliverance.

You are now becoming united within yourself. You are renewing your soul to match your new creation spirit. You are born from above. Your spirit man is in union with and exactly like your Father. Eph 4:24 "And that ye put on the new man, which after God is created in righteousness and true holiness."

1 Cor 6:17 "But he that is joined unto the Lord is one spirit."

Following the Agape Path to Faith

Your walking in *agape*/love is the good works you are re-created for. Eph 2:10 "For we are his workmanship, created in Christ Jesus unto good works, which God hath before ordained that we should walk in them."

The *agape*/love of God has been and is continually lighting a way for your heart to walk in: Rom 5:5 "And hope maketh not ashamed; because the *agape*/love of God is shed abroad in our hearts by the Holy Ghost which is given unto us."

Your inner eye is becoming single-minded on you *agape*/loving your fellowmen, as the primary way for you to *agape*/love your heavenly Father, His wondrous Son and Holy Spirit. 1 John 3:14 "We know that we have passed from (*operating in*) death unto (*operating in*) zoe/life, because we *agape*/love the brethren. He that *agape*/loveth not his brother abideth in death (*and produces the fruits of death*)."

Matt 6:21 "For where your treasure is, there will your heart be also. 22 The light of the body is the eye: if therefore thine eye be single (*on God as His agent by His Spirit*), thy whole body shall be full of light. 23 But if thine eye be evil (*stingy, fearful, selfish, self-centered and self-justified*), thy whole body shall be full of darkness. If therefore the light that is in thee be darkness, how great is that darkness!"

1 John 4:20 "If a man say, I *agape*/love God, and hateth his brother, he is a liar: for he that *agape*/loveth not his brother whom he hath seen, how can he *agape*/love God whom he hath not seen? 21 And this commandment have we from him, That he who *agape*/loveth God *agape*/love his brother also."

1 John 3:16 "Hereby perceive we the *agape*/love of God, because he laid down his *psuche*/life (*soul*) for us: and we ought to lay down our *psuche*/lives (*souls*) for the brethren. 17 But whoso hath this world's good, and seeth his brother have need, and shutteth up his bowels of compassion from him, how dwelleth the *agape*/love of God in him? 18 My little children, let us not *agape*/love in (*just*) word, neither (*just*) in tongue; but in deed and in truth."

When you are loving, you are doing love things. My wife may love me, but she shows it when she makes me supper or washes my clothes or forgives me if we have a conflict. I may say I love my wife, but I show love by doing acts of love. *Agape*/love is not static, but in action. You can claim you love all you want, but it is measured by what you do, and backed up by what you say. John 3:16 "God so *agape*/loved that He gave His only begotten Son ... ."

You know that sometimes the best way to recover your joy is to go do good deeds for others. Please them and not yourself, and the light of God comes. Isa 58:8 "Then shall thy light break forth as the morning, and thine health shall spring forth speedily: and thy righteousness shall go before thee; the glory of the Lord shall be thy rearward."

Eph 4:29 "Let no corrupt communication proceed out of your mouth, but that which is good to the use of edifying, that it may minister grace unto the hearers.

DISCOVERING OUR REDEMPTION

30 And grieve not the holy Spirit of God, whereby ye are sealed unto the day of redemption. 31 Let all bitterness, and wrath, and anger, and clamour, and evil speaking, be put away from you, with all malice: 32 and be ye kind one to another, tenderhearted, forgiving one another, even as God for Christ's sake hath forgiven you."

So there are two levels of things a Christian can do: the man-level that any human can do and the God-level, which are those things that Holy Spirit can do through us, such as raising the dead, healing the sick, providing words of knowledge, cleansing lepers, etc. 1 John and the rest of the Bible makes it clear we are to do both, not either one or the other.

If we say we love God, that love is not just measured by how much time we spend in church attendance and other church activities. It is not measured only by how well we sing in the choir or teach the Bible class. These are all things that help us and others do the work of the ministry of the Body of Christ, but they are man-level things. We are measured also by the God-level things we do for others, as God's agents, His sons and daughters of *agape*/love.

Jesus defined good this way: Matt 19:16 "And, behold, one came and said unto him, Good Master, what good thing shall I do, that I may have eternal *zoe*/life? 17 And he said unto him, Why callest thou me good? there is none good but one, that is, God: but if thou wilt enter into (*or walk in to produce the*) *zoe*/life (*of God*), keep the commandments." Jesus used the word *good* to mean God-like or *agape*/love acts, for God is *agape*/love.

So, yes, good works are to feed the hungry, but also to multiply the bread, like Jesus did. This is a good work, that is of the Christian, or anointed one, and it is a God-level work. Luke 11:42 "But woe unto you, Pharisees! for ye tithe mint and rue and all manner of herbs, and pass over judgment (*for the oppressed in setting them free from the oppressions of the devil*) and the *agape*/love of God: these ought ye to have done, and not to leave the other undone."

As I do those love things that I can do (man-level), aligned with the Word of God, my heart gets more aligned to believe God for the things I cannot do in my own strength (God-level things), such as heal the sick, raise the dead or cast out devils. That is, when I am doing them for and with God, and not just because I enjoy doing them. John 14:10 "Believest thou not that I am in the Father, and the Father in me? the words that I speak unto you I speak not of myself: but the Father that dwelleth in me, he doeth the works. 11 Believe me that I am in the Father, and the Father in me: or else believe me for the very works' sake."

Even if I like doing such things, I must keep my eye on the fact that this is also what God wants done. That I like it is the gift or grace of God working in me, to will and to do of His good pleasure. The more I make it mine, the more I glory in myself and not God, and that is not *agape*/love for God.

Following the Agape Path to Faith

Philem 6 "That the communication of thy faith may become effectual by the acknowledging of every good thing which is in you in Christ Jesus."

1 Cor 1:29 "That no flesh should glory in his presence. 30 But of him are ye in Christ Jesus, who of God is made unto us wisdom, and righteousness, and sanctification, and redemption: 31 that, according as it is written, He that glorieth, let him glory in the Lord."

As I do the opposite and give God glory, I activate Holy Spirit, who sheds that *agape*/love in my heart. Rom 5:1 "Therefore being justified by faith, we have peace with God through our Lord Jesus Christ: 2 by whom also we have access by faith into this grace wherein we stand, and rejoice in hope of the glory of God. 3 And not only so, but we glory in tribulations also: knowing that tribulation worketh patience; 4 and patience, experience; and experience, hope: 5 and hope maketh not ashamed; because the love of God is shed abroad in our hearts by the Holy Ghost which is given unto us. 6 For when we were yet without strength, in due time Christ died for the ungodly."

Agape love never fails and never gives up. It never gets offended. It is like a mustard seed, that example Jesus gave of faith. It just keeps on day-by-day doing faith things and, as it endures, it grows more and more. As God is *agape*/love, the more you determine to exercise endurance in faith and keep doing those faith actions, you will see the glory of the Lord.

God has declared and established His *agape*/love. Rom 5:8 "But God commendeth his *agape*/love toward us, in that, while we were yet sinners, Christ died for us."

The more you know how forgiven you are (and that does include knowing how evil your sins really are), the more you will grow in that never-failing *agape*/love. Luke 7:47 "Wherefore I (*Jesus*) say unto thee, Her sins, which are many, are forgiven; for she *agape*/loved much: but to whom little is forgiven, the same *agape*/loveth little."

And as you grow in *agape*/love, to operate like God does, by faith, you will move in freedom from fear. 1 John 4:18 "There is no fear in *agape*/love; but perfect *agape*/love casteth out fear: because fear hath torment. He that feareth is not made perfect in *agape*/love. 19 We *agape*/love him, because he first *agape*/loved us."

Thus, as you grow in knowing these Redemption truths, you will grow in *agape*/love, and the character of *agape*/love includes faith. 2 Peter 1:2 "Grace and peace be multiplied unto you through the *epignosis*/knowledge of God, and of Jesus our Lord, 3 according as his divine power hath given unto us all things that pertain unto *zoe*/life and godliness, through the *epignosis*/knowledge of him that hath called us to glory and virtue: 4 whereby are given unto us exceeding great and precious promises: that by these ye might be partakers of the divine nature, having escaped the corruption that is in the world through lust. 5 And beside this,

DISCOVERING OUR REDEMPTION

giving all diligence, add to your faith virtue; and to virtue knowledge; 6 and to knowledge temperance; and to temperance patience; and to patience godliness; 7 and to godliness brotherly kindness; and to brotherly kindness *agape*/charity. 8 For if these things be in you, and abound, they make you that ye shall neither be barren nor unfruitful in the knowledge of our Lord Jesus Christ. 9 But he that lacketh these things is blind, and cannot see afar off, and hath forgotten that he was purged from his old sins."

So to grow in *agape*/love, you major, not on what a great sinner and how inadequate you are, but how forgiven and made new in Jesus you are. Rom 6:10 "For in that he died, he died unto sin once: but in that he *zao*/liveth, he *zao*/liveth unto God. 11 Likewise reckon ye also yourselves to be dead indeed unto sin, but *zao*/alive unto God through Jesus Christ our Lord."

Chapter 41
Growing in Agape Love

There is a big difference between loving your children because they are yours and knowing they are an assignment from God, because they are really His, and your job is to raise them: Eph 4:13 "Till we all come in the unity of the faith, and of the *epignosis*/knowledge of the Son of God, unto a perfect man, unto the measure of the stature of the fulness of Christ: 14 that we henceforth be no more children, tossed to and fro, and carried about with every wind of doctrine, by the sleight of men, and cunning craftiness, whereby they lie in wait to deceive; 15 but speaking the truth in *agape*/love, may grow up into him in all things, which is the head, even Christ."

Thus, my faith and compassion grow as I understand that, whether it is bondage to sickness or evil habits, those I am called to minister to, even though they may be in total agreement with their sin, are deceived and blinded, and they need the freedom God gives. Isa 49:24 "Shall the prey be taken from the mighty, or the lawful captive delivered? 25 But thus saith the Lord, Even the captives of the mighty shall be taken away, and the prey of the terrible shall be delivered: for I will contend with him that contendeth with thee, and I will save thy children."

Isa 43:25 "I, even I, am he that blotteth out thy transgressions for mine own sake, and will not remember thy sins. 26 Put me in remembrance: let us plead together: declare thou, that thou mayest be justified."

DISCOVERING OUR REDEMPTION

As I do these acts of natural, man-level, *agape*/love, it breaks offenses, self-righteousness, bitterness, pride, unbelief and unforgiveness in my own heart. I know I need to do these acts of *agape*/love with a clear and joyful heart. 2 Cor 9:7 "Every man according as he purposeth in his heart, so let him give; not grudgingly, or of necessity: for God *agape*/loveth a cheerful giver."

So, as I do these acts of *agape*/love, I also deal with the ungodly feelings and memories that rise within me. I sacrifice myself for others, expecting no gain or recognition. In this way, I start by doing caring things for others, and, at the same time, I know I am forgiven and loved, so my love grows, as I know how forgiven I am of all the ungodly things that rise, as I do works of *agape*/love. I don't need a special word from God; all I need to do is look and see what I can do for those in need. I also need to do those things that I get by "special word" or wisdom.

When we are born from above, born of God, then we become *agape*/love, as He is. Anything in our heart that resists us walking in *agape*/love is also an "ill fitting shoe." Our new, born-of-God nature is to *agape*/love, just as our Father does. As Jesus is the perfect reflection of the Father, so are we to be. It is the removing of evil in our hearts that allows us to walk in the *agape*/love shed abroad in our hearts by Holy Spirit (see Rom 5:5).

We are not surrendering to God. That implies we are giving up value and potential in surrender. We are not giving up anything, except what evil attributes and penalties from the devil man inherited in the Fall of Adam. We are stripping away that which destroys, to reveal only the light of the *agape*/love of God in the face of Jesus Christ. We are getting rid of that which is not ours. If that hurts, then I am too much in love with the lies of the devil.

The answer is to make that lie submit to God and agree with your new identity in your new creation in Christ. So, as you realize you are thinking wrong thoughts, make them captive, call them what they are, and replace them with right thoughts, especially Scriptures. Speak or sing God's truth instead of the devil's lies. Drive the truth of His *agape*/love into your heart. Wash yourself clean with the Word of God, and, thus, cooperate with Jesus, your Lord. Eph 5:25 "Husbands, *agape*/love your wives, even as Christ also *agape*/loved the church, and gave himself for it; 26 that he might sanctify and cleanse it with the washing of water by the word, 27 that he might present it to himself a glorious church, not having spot wrinkle, or any such thing; but that it should be holy and without blemish."

This process is not a stripping away of you, but the removing of garbage and a building up of who and what you really are in Christ. That is why anything that resists you in walking and loving like Jesus is not born of God and is not of God, and is no longer who or what you are. The problem is a Christian with a corrupt soul (heart, mind, will and emotions) and some area that needs renewing. Renew that part, and in that area you will walk in mercy, grace, truth and *agape*/love.

Growing in Agape Love

1 John 3:9 "No one born (begotten) of God [deliberately, knowingly, and habitually] practices sin, for God's nature abides in him [His principle of *zoe*/life, the divine sperm, remains permanently within him]; and he cannot practice sinning (*comfortably*) because he is born (begotten) of God. 10 By this it is made clear who take their nature from God and are His children (*in how they think, speak and act*) and (*those Christians*) who take their nature from the devil and are his children (*in how they think, speak and act*): no one who does not practice righteousness [who does not conform to God's will in purpose, thought, and action] is of God (*as their source of thoughts, words and actions*); neither is anyone who does not *agape*/love his brother (his fellow believer in Christ). 11 For this is the message (the announcement) which you have heard from the first, that we should *agape*/love one another. … 14 We know (*as our personal litmus test, as to the source of our thoughts, words and acts*) that we have passed over out of death into *zoe*/Life (*in agreeing with God in our thoughts, words and actions, and, thus, have God's zoe/life as our source*) by the fact that we *agape*/love the brethren (our fellow Christians). He who does not *agape*/love abides (remains, *drawing his source of life from,* is held and kept continually) in [spiritual] death (*and, thus, reaping the sad fruit of sowing to the mind of the flesh and not to the Spirit of God*)." AMP

Any resistance in your soul (heart, mind, will or emotions) to walking in *agape*/love is an evil work, a stronghold of the devil's lies, in your soul, and is just as evil as the sin you see in someone else. The penalty for sin, any sin, is death. It is not the size of the sin, but its existence that brings any and all of death. Any sin you see in others that does not cause you to react in *agape*/love and compassion for them, your reaction is not of God. So you react to your evil reaction the same as any sin. This may be harder when your heart is indifferent because, if you are really angry, at least you can be made to see your anger.

The living death of indifference or religious pride sees no need to be involved. That voice says things like, or has the basic attitude of: "I told them where they are wrong; now they can fix it. It's not my job." Or, "I don't like _____, so I just stay away, etc." Rev 3:15 "I (*Jesus*) know thy works, that thou art neither cold nor hot: I would thou wert cold or hot. 16 So then because thou art lukewarm, and neither cold nor hot, I will spue thee out of my mouth."

"Why should I care?" is the voice of indifference and a hardened heart. The proper answer sounds more like: "How can I not care? They are in sin and, therefore, they are in pain. Jesus bore that pain for them so they could be healed. God says they are of extreme value, worth the price of Jesus, and they are living far below what they are created for. Their life is an 'ill-fitting shoe.' They are given to lust that can never satisfy. They have no peace, and they are not walking in the *agape*/love of God in that area. They need help, and the Help of God is in me, to help them, with His power, *agape*/love and a sound mind."

DISCOVERING OUR REDEMPTION

The cure is to spend time learning and knowing how *agape*/loved I am. I seek the Lord for any wicked way in me, so I can focus on Him and His *agape*/love for me. Ps 139:23 "Search me, O God, and know my heart: try me, and know my thoughts: 24 and see if there be any wicked way in me, and lead me in the way everlasting." Ps 86:11 "Teach me thy way, O Lord; I will walk in thy truth: unite my heart to fear thy name. 12 I will praise thee, O Lord my God, with all my heart: and I will glorify thy name for evermore. 13 For great is thy *chesed*/mercy toward me: and thou hast delivered my soul from the lowest hell. 14 O God, the proud are risen against me, and the assemblies of violent men have sought after my soul; and have not set thee before them. 15 But thou, O Lord, art a God full of compassion, and gracious, longsuffering, and plenteous in *chesed*/mercy (*grace*) and truth. 16 O turn unto me, and have mercy upon me; give thy strength unto thy servant, and save the son of thine handmaid. 17 Shew me a token for good; that they which hate me may see it, and be ashamed: because thou, Lord, hast holpen me, and comforted me."

I pray that prayer, and God starts to show me things in the Scriptures and then relates them to my life. His Word is His primary tool. To clean my heart, I must get into His Word and apply it like soap, rubbing again and again until I can see His cleansing action. Eph 5:25 "Husbands, *agape*/love your wives, even as Christ also *agape*/loved the church, and gave himself for it; 26 that he might sanctify and cleanse it with the washing of water by the word, 27 that he might present it to himself a glorious church, not having spot, or wrinkle, or any such thing; but that it should be holy and without blemish. 28 So ought men to *agape*/love their wives as their own bodies. He that *agape*/loveth his wife *agape*/loveth himself."

Notice Jesus gets a Bride who is not clean, the Church, and then cleans that Bride with His Word. 2 Tim 3:15 "And that from a child thou hast known the holy scriptures, which are able to make thee wise unto *soteria*/salvation through faith which is in Christ Jesus. 16 All scripture is given by inspiration of God, and is profitable for doctrine, for reproof, for correction, for instruction in righteousness: 17 that the man of God may be perfect, throughly furnished unto all good works."

Heb 4:12 "For the word of God is quick, and powerful, and sharper than any twoedged sword, piercing even to the dividing asunder of soul and spirit, and of the joints and marrow, and is a discerner of the thoughts and intents of the heart. 13 Neither is there any creature that is not manifest in his sight: but all things are naked and opened unto the eyes of him with whom we have to do."

Thus, I make my heart to be more aligned with Him by His Word, so He and I can work together more effectively and get the sick healed. As I am convicted of sin, I confess I sinned, I acknowledge that that sin cost Jesus His life, and He paid it for me, I thank Him for His great salvation He earned for me, I receive the forgiveness for my sins given 2000 years ago, and receive the healing for those same sins

Growing in Agape Love

given also 2000 years ago, thank and confess I have that healing so I will walk more like Jesus, and, in the process, become as pure as He is pure.

1 John 3:2 "*Agape*/beloved, now are we the sons of God, and it doth not yet appear what we shall be: but we know that, when he shall appear, we shall be like him; for we shall see him as he is. 3 And every man that hath this hope in him purifieth himself, even as he is pure."

Lost in Jesus: Since my goal is to be as pure as Jesus, and the more I learn of Him, the greater He becomes, I do not get lost in self-righteousness over my own purity, but I do get lost in His *agape*/love for me, in spite of my sins. He is even greater than the great price He paid to set me free of those same sins. Jesus is risen; and He is Lord!

Phil 3:8 "Yea doubtless, and I count all things but loss for the excellency of the knowledge of Christ Jesus my Lord: for whom I have suffered the loss of all things, and do count them but dung, that I may win Christ, 9 and be found in him, not having mine own righteousness, which is of the law, but that which is through the faith of Christ, the righteousness which is of God by faith: 10 that I may know him, and the power of his resurrection, and the fellowship of his sufferings, being made conformable unto his death; 11 if by any means I might attain unto the resurrection of the dead. 12 Not as though I had already attained, either were already perfect: but I follow after, if that I may apprehend that for which also I am apprehended of Christ Jesus."

So, whether I put myself in these situations or God does, as I do *agape*/love, I let the situations also lead me to get and keep my heart pure. When I see anyone in sin, I now look for a way to get grace to them, to set them free. Thus, as I bear other's burdens, knowing how sin is eating them up, how they are building sorrow for years to come, I do acts of *agape*/love to help make their lives better and to get them free.

If you find yourself dealing with unforgiveness in yourself, confess it as sin and not from God, put on the new man in Christ and confess your new nature does not sin in unforgiveness, and then pray for those who have offended you. Rom 12:14 "Bless them which persecute you: bless, and curse not. ... 19 Dearly *agape*/beloved, avenge not yourselves, but rather give place unto wrath: for it is written, Vengeance is mine; I will repay, saith the Lord. 20 Therefore if thine enemy hunger, feed him; if he thirst, give him drink: for in so doing thou shalt heap coals of fire on his head. 21 Be not overcome of evil, but overcome evil with good."

Luke 6:27 "But I (*Jesus*) say unto you which hear, *agape*/love your enemies, do good to them which hate you, 28 bless them that curse you, and pray for them which despitefully use you." Notice *agape*/love does good, blesses and prays for those it loves.

With our hearts in unity with *agape*/love, we make the constant affirmation that our purpose is to set others free and to bring about the healing of any bondage

DISCOVERING OUR REDEMPTION

or oppression of the devil, just as Jesus did. 1 John 5:16 "If any man see his brother sin a sin which is not unto death, he shall *aiteo*/ask, and he (*God*) shall give him *zoe*/life for them ... ."

Instead of judging behavior as sin and shunning the person, you will judge it as sin and go into prayer to help them, and not stop until you have gotten them free. If you talk to them, you will heed the warning of: Gal 6:1 "Brethren, if a man be overtaken in a fault, ye which are spiritual, restore such an one in the spirit of meekness; considering thyself, lest thou also be tempted. 2 Bear ye one another's burdens, and so fulfil the law of Christ."

Jesus gave the example of how to deliver hard words: John 5:24 "Verily, verily, I say unto you, He that heareth my word, and believeth on him that sent me, hath everlasting *zoe*/life, and shall not come into condemnation; but is passed from death unto *zoe*/life." If your hard words can deliver the grace and *zoe*/life of God, then speak on. Otherwise, seek the Lord until you can give *zoe*/life and not the dead letter of the law. Eph 4:29 "Let no corrupt communication proceed out of your mouth, but that which is good to the use of edifying, that it may minister grace unto the hearers. 30 And grieve not the holy Spirit of God, whereby ye are sealed unto the day of redemption."

When only law and not *agape*/love becomes dominate, you are ready to point out sins and failures, your "eye becomes evil," and you become an expert fault finder, but you will not do the spiritual labor with God and His Word that purges your old man lusts, and you do not set people free with mercy, *agape*/love, grace and truth.

2 Cor 3:5 "Not that we are sufficient of ourselves to think any thing as of ourselves; but our sufficiency is of God; 6 who also hath made us able ministers of the new testament; not of the letter (*of the law identifying what is wrong and telling them to get right*), but of the spirit (*I see your sin, I will go to God and get* zoe/life *for you and get grace and truth into you*): for the letter killeth, but the spirit giveth *zoe*/life. 7 But if the ministration of death (*you are wrong and will die by the curse of the law*), written and engraven in stones, was glorious, so that the children of Israel could not stedfastly behold the face of Moses for the glory of his countenance; which glory was to be done away: 8 how shall not the ministration of the spirit (*of* agape/love *in Jesus, who healed all, independent of their sins or* agape/love *for God*) be rather glorious?"

This is the selfless love Jesus gave an example of when He washed the disciples' feet. John 13:14 "If I then, your Lord and Master, have washed your feet; ye also ought to wash one another's feet. 15 For I have given you an example, that ye should do as I have done to you. 16 Verily, verily, I say unto you, The servant is not greater than his lord; neither he that is sent greater than he that sent him. 17 If ye know these things, happy are ye if ye do them." Doing just this would radically change the conversations most people engage in and definitely change the flavor of the nightly news.

Growing in Agape Love

I must relate to others with a tenderness, knowing that they are God's children and God's *agape*/love objects, and I do it not just for Him, but with Him, in *agape*/love. Gal 2:20 "I am (*have been*) crucified with Christ: nevertheless I *zao*/live; yet not I, but Christ *zao*/liveth in me: and the life which I now *zao*/live (*of God*) in the flesh I *zao*/live by the faith of the Son of God, who *agape*/loved me, and gave himself for me. 21 I do not frustrate the grace of God: for if righteousness come by the law, then Christ is dead in vain."

The great good news is that every miracle Jesus did was *agape*/love crushing the consequences of the law of sowing and reaping in the law of sin and death. Rom 8:1 "There is therefore now no condemnation to them which are in Christ Jesus, who walk not after the flesh, but after the Spirit. 2 For the law of the Spirit of *zoe*/life in Christ Jesus hath made me free from the law of sin and death."

As my mind is set on the flesh, I am sinning, and while I do this, I am walking in a condemnation from the devil and not the reconciliation of God. But, in evil religious passion, I will assign that condemnation to God. Once I see I am sinning and respond like God wants, then I know I am forgiven, and I know I am *agape*/loved. Rom 13:10 "*Agape*/love worketh no ill to his neighbour: therefore *agape*/love is the fulfilling of the law. 11 And that, knowing the time, that now it is high time to awake out of sleep (*in walking in the mind of the flesh and, thus, also doing acts of sin*): for now is our *soteria*/salvation nearer than when we believed. 12 The night is far spent, the day is at hand: let us therefore cast off the works of darkness (*the fruit of a mind set on the flesh, or a carnal mind, and acting like a "mere" man*), and let us put on the armour of light. 13 Let us walk honestly, as in the day; not in rioting and drunkenness, not in chambering and wantonness, not in strife and envying. 14 But put ye on the Lord Jesus Christ, and make not provision for the flesh, to fulfil the lusts thereof."

When you find yourself in sin, and you moan that it is not you, that you are a new creation, born after the image of God, and your true nature is to be just like Jesus, your faith is being made effective. Philem 6 "That the communication of thy faith may become effectual by the *epignosis*/acknowledging of every good thing which is in you in Christ Jesus."

I can look at the problem and pray from the perspective of a victim in the problem or in sympathy with the people in the problem and the greatness of its evil, or I can pray from the perspective that, by the covenant in the blood of Jesus, it has no right to be there, Jesus destroyed its right and power to be there, that I have the Word of God in the Bible to know God's mind and His will, and, in compassion that delivers, I will use the name of Jesus to declare God's will. Then I cast that devil out and tell that problem to go in the name of Jesus, and God brings His will, Heaven to Earth, as I *aiteo* for Him in that situation. The choice is mine. God has already spoken and made the covenant in the blood of Jesus.

DISCOVERING OUR REDEMPTION

Luke 13:15 "The Lord then answered him, and said, Thou hypocrite, doth not each one of you on the sabbath loose his ox or his ass from the stall, and lead him away to watering? 16 And ought not this woman, being a daughter of Abraham, whom Satan hath bound, lo, these eighteen years, be loosed from this bond on the sabbath day?"

Or I can choose to moan in the sin I see in me and join the devil in agreeing that I am not a new creation and resolve to do better, or I can act as God tells me by the Scriptures. As I see my sin, I return to my new-creation identity in Jesus, call that sin not of God and not of me, cast it and the devils in it out, and put on Jesus in my self-identity and reality with God, receive the remission given 2000 years ago in the covenant blood of Jesus, receive my healing ("by His stripes I am healed") to walk in Jesus where I once sinned, and then I thank Him that He is *agape*/love and He cannot lie and I will see His will in the land of the living. This is how I glorify God in His mighty work in Jesus and get my heart converted at the same time. 1 Cor 1:29 "That no flesh should glory in his presence. 30 But of him are ye in Christ Jesus, who of God is made unto us wisdom, and righteousness, and sanctification, and redemption: 31 that, according as it is written, He that glorieth, let him glory in the Lord."

As I know how *agape*/loved I am, I can then *agape*/love others. Luke 7:47 "… to whom little is forgiven, the same *agape*/loveth little." Mark 12:31 "And the second is like, namely this, Thou shalt *agape*/love thy neighbour as thyself. There is none other commandment greater than these."

When I realize my sin, if I stop at my rottenness and unworthiness, it is still all about me. Sin, by its nature, is selfish, self-centered, self-righteous and self-serving. So, yes, I am worthy of death; yes, I have been empowered by the devil to sin; yes, I have hated God by sinning. But, because of God's *agape*/love and patience, I am not lost. Jesus so *agape*/loved me, Father God so *agape*/loved me, and Holy Spirit so *agape*/loved me that when Jesus died, I died. When Jesus suffered, He suffered for me. When Jesus defeated Satan in Hell, I was there also. When Jesus was raised, so was I. When Jesus was born again from death, so was I. So that, when I believed in the resurrection, when I believed Father God, by Holy Spirit, raised Jesus from the dead, I was made, by grace, His righteousness, and the real me is no longer a sinner. I may still sin, but it is not my nature anymore.

2 Cor 5:16 "Wherefore henceforth know we no man after the flesh: yea, though we have known Christ after the flesh, yet now henceforth know we him no more. 17 Therefore if any man be in Christ, he is a new creature: old things are passed away; behold, all things are become new. 18 And all things are of God, who hath reconciled us to himself by Jesus Christ, and hath given to us the ministry of reconciliation; 19 to wit, that God was in Christ, reconciling the world unto himself, not imputing their trespasses unto them; and hath committed unto us the word of reconciliation."

Growing in Agape Love

I can approach myself as God requires, in the Word of Reconciliation, and not in the word of condemnation. I can see the horror of sin and know that God's *agape*/love looked past my sin. I know that His Word says in the New Covenant He will remember my sins and iniquities no more, and He will walk with me, and He knows my potential, that I am His, and He said I am worth the spirit, soul, body, blood, suffering and death of Jesus, to redeem me. When I receive this, even force it into my soul, I am filled with thanks and praise and return *agape*/love to Him, who first *agape*/loved me. If I am well trained in the Spirit, I will start giving thanks for my Redemption even before I feel anything.

Col 3:17 "And whatsoever ye do in word or deed, do all in the name of the Lord Jesus, giving thanks to God and the Father by him."

Heb 13:15 "By him (*Jesus*) therefore let us offer the sacrifice of praise to God continually, that is, the fruit of our lips giving thanks to his name (*and making confession in His name*)."

1 Thes 5:18 "In every thing give thanks: for this is the will of God in Christ Jesus concerning you."

If I do not feel or have to force myself into thanksgiving, then I can know that I am still offended in my soul somewhere, at God or others, that I am still blinded to His *agape*/love, that I am still blinded by the devil, and I am still not receiving, *lambano*ing the *agape*/love of the grace and truth in Jesus, unto continual thanksgiving. As I see this sin yet remaining in my heart and attitude, Holy Spirit is ever prompting me to know that I can, by faith, receive healing for this offense, unforgiveness, blindness and lack of thanksgiving and trust Father to set me free into more *agape*/love and thanksgiving. By His stripes, we have been healed of EVERYTHING that is not like Jesus!

So, at whatever level of faith I can muster, I can still say, "Thank You, Father. You are still working in me, to will and to do of Your good pleasure, and I will yet walk in thanksgiving!" Thus, I can look at my sins without fear, and, instead, judge rightly the body and blood of Jesus by His great work of the cross and get free.

Phil 2:12 "Wherefore, my *agape*/beloved, as ye have always obeyed, not as in my presence only, but now much more in my absence, work out your own *soteria*/salvation with fear and trembling. 13 For it is God which worketh in you both to will and to do of his good pleasure. 14 Do all things without murmurings and disputings: 15 that ye may be blameless and harmless, the sons of God, without rebuke, in the midst of a crooked and perverse nation, among whom ye shine as lights in the world; 16 holding forth the word of *zoe*/life; that I may rejoice in the day of Christ, that I have not run in vain, neither laboured in vain."

Thus, I know that if I don't care for others, if I don't have compassion, then I am in offense and self-righteousness in some way, and I need help. I may agree that anything in my life that is not just like Jesus is sin, but I do not dwell there. I am

DISCOVERING OUR REDEMPTION

the living dead and away from the *zoe*/life of God in that area of my life. As I see I should be in *agape*/love and am not, He says to me: Eph 5:13 "But all things that are reproved are made manifest by the light: for whatsoever doth make manifest is light. 14 Wherefore he saith, Awake thou that sleepest, and arise from the dead, and Christ shall give thee light. 15 See then that ye walk circumspectly, not as fools, but as wise, 16 redeeming the time, because the days are evil. 17 Wherefore be ye not unwise, but understanding what the will of the Lord is. 18 And be not drunk with wine, wherein is excess; but be *continually being* filled with the Spirit; 19 speaking to yourselves in psalms and hymns and spiritual songs, singing and making melody in your heart to the Lord; 20 giving thanks always for all things unto God and the Father in the name of our Lord Jesus Christ; 21 submitting yourselves one to another in the fear of God."

So I start singing His Word, starting with the Psalms, washing my heart with His Word, until I start to know and even feel His *agape*/love, in spirit and in truth, and respond in thanksgiving. [If you are serious in this, ignore most other music for now, and work with only the Psalms or scripture songs. For this renewing process, you want to stay with the exact Scriptures in song as much as possible. The singing group known as the Sons of Korah have some excellent versions of the Psalms set to modern music. Also you can do an Internet search for scripture in song, or scripture memory songs.]

Part of the secret of knowing how *agape*/loved you are is to know how forgiven you are. Col 3:12 "Put on therefore, as the elect of God, holy and *agape*/beloved, bowels of mercies, kindness, humbleness of mind, meekness, longsuffering; 13 forbearing one another, and forgiving one another, if any man have a quarrel against any: even as Christ forgave you, so also do ye."

You do this by continually: Eph 4:22 "… *putting* off concerning the former conversation the old man, which is corrupt according to the deceitful lusts; 23 and be renewed in the spirit of your mind [*as a new functioning attitude, to walk just like Jesus, as the real you*]; 24 and that ye put on the new man, which after God is created in righteousness and true holiness." Phil 2:5 "Let this mind be in you, which was also in Christ Jesus." Rom 13:14 "But put ye on the Lord Jesus Christ, and make not provision for the flesh, to fulfil the lusts thereof."

You first have to identify some aspect of you that is not just like Jesus. For that, we have the Gospels and the rest of the Bible. But then, instead of wallowing in shame, fear, evil anger, inadequacy, separation and condemnation, wallow in the Word of Grace, Adoption, Betrothal, right mind and A*gape*/Love in Christ Jesus.

So when you sin and become aware that it is sin, you confess your sin, you ask for grace to make any restitution or reconciliation necessary, you acknowledge that your sin cost Jesus His life and suffering, and He paid it for you out of *agape*/love. You acknowledge that His blood is more than sufficient, and you are redeemed out of the hand of the enemy by that awesome and eternal blood, you are redeemed from the curse of that sin by that same wonderful blood of Jesus. You thank Him for His *agape*/love, you receive forgiveness, you receive healing by thanking Father you will now have it, and you receive that you have not a spirit of fear, but of power (the ability to do anything that is impossible), the spirit of *agape*/love (that gives unto death, and holds not the soul unto death), and a sound mind to think and do as Jesus would, including knowing how *agape*/loved you are and that you are made to give that *agape*/love to others. With all this grace, you then go and make those restitutions and reconciliations you may need to do from the sin you discovered in yourself.

As you walk in this *agape*/love, you know it is based on God's Word, and you start to believe God in His Word even more, i.e., you know forgiveness more = your belief grows = your faith grows = your mountain moving grows. Then your goal becomes the good of others at your expense, for God, by His Word. So faith for healing and any other needed help increases.

Now you are loving yourself according to the Scriptures, as Holy Spirit has said, and now you can use this same attitude to *agape*/love others in their sin. Start with those who have offended you, those you find fault with, who irritate you, whom you disagree with, whom you don't like, and those who do not like you or find fault with you. These are all good candidates. In fact, usually they are *agape*/love assignments from God.

The first act is to immediately forgive them, remove any separation in your heart against them and then seek to know how to set them free. Matt 22:37 "Jesus said unto him, Thou shalt *agape*/love the Lord thy God with all thy heart, and with all thy soul, and with all thy mind. 38 This is the first and great commandment. 39 And the second is like unto it, Thou shalt *agape*/love thy neighbour as thyself [*with all thy heart, and with all thy soul, and with all thy mind*]."

Now that you are *agape*/loving yourself, with no condemnation, you can also *agape*/love your neighbor with no condemnation, when you see them in any fault, i.e., any area of their life where the devil is reigning unto death in any form, and *zoe*/life is not. 1 John 5:16 "If any man see his brother sin a sin which is not unto death, he shall *aiteo*/ask (*require, demand and expect as due by covenant promise of God*), and he (*God*) shall give him *zoe*/life for them ... ."

Eph 4:29 "Let no corrupt communication proceed out of your mouth, but that which is good to the use of edifying, that it may minister grace unto the hearers. 30 And grieve not the holy Spirit of God, whereby ye are sealed unto the day of redemption. 31 Let all bitterness, and wrath, and anger, and clamour, and evil speaking, be put away from you, with all malice: 32 and be ye kind one to another, tenderhearted, forgiving one another, even as God for Christ's sake hath forgiven you."

DISCOVERING OUR REDEMPTION

So now, as you know how *agape*/loved you are, by how forgiven you are, your ability to believe God by His Word grows and more of Heaven is brought to Earth. Evil fear is losing its grip on you. He is not the God of evil fear, but the God of *agape*/love, who is *agape*/love. 1 John 4:17 "Herein is our *agape*/love made perfect (*mature, complete*), that we may have boldness in the day of judgment: because as he is, so are we in this world. 18 There is no fear in *agape*/love; but perfect *agape*/love casteth out fear: because fear hath torment. He that feareth is not made perfect in *agape*/love. 19 We *agape*/love him, because he first *agape*/loved us."

You no longer believe the devil's lies: that God lies, that God does not have your best interests at heart, that God has evil in Him, that God is withholding good from you by His ways, that God is not always with you, and that His Word is not true. As that evil stronghold is weakened, thanksgiving starts to rise within you (that God is good, that this will pass, that it could be worse, that God cannot lie, that His Word is truth, that He allows you to plant the seed of His Word into that situation, and you will see the promise of God manifested), and you start to overcome all those things that man received from the fall of Adam, when Adam believed the devil over God and put his faith in the devil and away from God. You do this, as you have that same faith in God by His Word for others and learn to apply it to yourself. So it works both ways. You grow in *agape*/love by loving others, and you grow in *agape*/love by knowing how forgiven you are. The net effect is your faith, your ability to believe God, grows.

James 1:13 "Let no man say when he is tempted, I am tempted of God: for God cannot be tempted with evil, neither tempteth he any man: 14 but every man is tempted, when he is drawn away of his own lust, and enticed. 15 Then when lust hath conceived, it bringeth forth sin: and sin, when it is finished, bringeth forth death. 16 Do not err, my *agape*/beloved brethren. 17 Every good gift and every perfect gift is from above, and cometh down from the Father of lights, with whom is no variableness, neither shadow of turning. 18 Of his own will begat he us with the word of truth, that we should be a kind of firstfruits of his creatures."

So, when you see someone in sin, whether it is a drug gang, a criminal, a gossip, a backbiter, a crooked government leader, a minister you do not agree with, etc, you know that Jesus died for them at total cost, without asking, to set them free of the oppressions of the devil. You turn immediately to the Word of Reconciliation of God in Jesus. You know more completely that sin, or, more particularly, the sins they are in, is the devil lording it over God's creation in the iniquity they are thinking, the sins they commit and the reaping of the law of sin and death, all of which God reconciled in Jesus 2000 years ago.

Rom 5:20 "Moreover the law entered, that the offence might abound. But where sin abounded, grace did much more abound: 21 that as sin hath reigned (*as king*) unto death, even so might grace reign (*to destroy the works of the kingdom of darkness and demonstrate the light of the Gospel of the Kingdom of God in Jesus Christ to Earth, by setting people free from the oppressions of the devil)* through (*the gift of*) righteousness (*by faith in the blood of Jesus*) unto eternal *zoe*/life by Jesus Christ our Lord (*and overcome any death working in any situation in any way and replace it with the* agape/*love,* zoe/*life of God, making Heaven on Earth*)."

Because the devil is lording it over them in their sin, by what they believe, God is not reigning directly in that situation. Notice, sin starts in the way we think and then manifests in our words and actions. Death, through evil ideas, thoughts, attitudes, prejudices, lusts, sickness, disease, lack, poverty, hate and fear is ruling instead. The kingdom of darkness is growing, and the Kingdom of God is limited by the lies and confusion of the devil they are believing, doing and bound by. Thus, they are denying God what He paid for in Jesus, and, if they were free to see, they would reject that evil now.

Your enemy becomes the devil and his lies and his works, and your tool is God's Word and the Lordship of Jesus released in the name of Jesus over that devil. 2 Cor 10:3 "For though we walk in the flesh, we do not war after the flesh: 4 (for the weapons of our warfare are not carnal, but mighty through God to the pulling down of strong holds;) 5 casting down imaginations, and every high thing that exalteth itself against the knowledge of God, and bringing into captivity every thought to the obedience of Christ; 6 and having in a readiness to revenge all disobedience, when your obedience is fulfilled."

Eph 6:10 "Finally, my brethren, be strong in the Lord, and in the power of his might. 11 Put on the whole armour of God, that ye may be able to stand against the wiles of the devil. 12 For we wrestle not against flesh and blood, but against principalities, against powers, against the rulers of the darkness of this world, against spiritual wickedness in high places."

Acts 4:10 "Be it known unto you all, and to all the people of Israel, that by the name of Jesus Christ of Nazareth, whom ye crucified, whom God raised from the dead, even by him doth this man stand here before you whole. 11 This is the stone which was set at nought of you builders, which is become the head of the corner. 12 Neither is there *soteria*/salvation in any other: for there is none other name under heaven given among men, whereby we must be *sozo*/saved."

Sinners are not your enemies. They are lost, hurting, confused and blind to the power of God's *agape*/love. Their prime driver is fear. The devil, his lies and death are your real enemies. You want the grace and truth of Jesus to triumph in the people Satan has afflicted and to set them free. Your enemy is not flesh and blood, people, yourself included, but the devil, with his lies and works.

When you see and pray for a situation and the devil says, "No, I will not move," you respond with getting more into the Word of God, the Spirit of God, and the strength of the Lord, and then you resist the devil by persistent *aiteo* commands

DISCOVERING OUR REDEMPTION

and prayer in the name of Jesus, and more thanksgiving, joy and praise, until the bound are free, because *agape*/love never gives up and believes God in all things.

You set people free and bring Heaven to Earth as an under-ruler, a king for Jesus. Rom 5:17 "For if by one man's offence death reigned (*as king to enforce the curse of sin*) by one; much more they which (*continually*) *lambano*/receive (*hold on to, cling to and not let go of the*) abundance of grace and of the gift of righteousness shall reign (*what they say happens, just as with a king*) in *zoe*/life by one, Jesus Christ.)" See also 1 Cor 2:3.

In the sinner, you see the devil denying God what He declared free in Jesus 2000 years ago. You know it is the devil preaching to you his lordship in the evil circumstances and people you see or are aware of in any sin or curse of sin. Thus, disease of any kind is a declaration that the devil is ruling and not God. Your enemy is the devil, and your weapon is the *agape*/love and power of God, to get the devil off of the afflicted by you operating in the mind of Christ, i.e., the way you think, in accordance with and by the Word of God. This is walking in the Spirit.

You know any resistance to the will of God in you or others is a lie that is being believed and/or a devil in control. You get out lies with truth, grace and power in the Word of God, and you cast out devils and tell the mountains to go, believing God has already answered, and you will see that answer, all in the name of Jesus.

Conversely, sin is a way of thinking that leads to sinful actions. 2 Cor 4:3 "But if our gospel be hid, it is hid to them that are lost (*walking in and reaping death, confusion and darkness*): 4 in whom the god of this world hath blinded the minds of them which believe not, lest the light of the glorious gospel of Christ, who is the image of God, should shine unto them. 5 For we preach not ourselves, but Christ Jesus the Lord; and ourselves your servants for Jesus' sake."

To counter the lordship of the devil is the Gospel of the Lordship of Jesus Christ, and it is to be preached, not just in the wisdom of men, but in the power of God. Rom 15:17 "I have therefore whereof I may glory through Jesus Christ in those things which pertain to God. 18 For I will not dare to speak of any of those things which Christ hath not wrought by me, to make the Gentiles obedient, by word and deed, 19 through mighty signs and wonders, by the power of the Spirit of God; so that from Jerusalem, and round about unto Illyricum, I have fully preached the gospel of Christ."

So one way to look at it is that the sinner (*Christian or non-Christian*) is missing the knowledge of the *agape*/love of God for them by either our failure or some other Christian's failure to properly get to them the Gospel and to persuade them of the *agape*/love of the truth. 2 Thes 2:9 "Even him, whose coming is after the working of Satan with all power and signs and lying wonders, 10 and with all deceivableness of unrighteousness in them that perish (*remain in the law of sin and death, and minds set on the flesh and not the spirit in the Gospel*); because they received not the *agape*/love of the truth, that they might be *sozo*/saved."

Growing in Agape Love

The message is simple: In any area of life you receive not, *lambano* not, hold not on to, no matter what, the *agape*/love of the truth of God's *agape*/love manifested in Jesus, you operate in death and not *zoe*/life.

We are free from the limitations of our lack of holiness in Jesus. In spite of our sins, we use the name of Jesus, in faith, working by *agape*/love, we are preaching, proclaiming, demonstrating and enforcing the Kingdom of God over the kingdom of darkness. Since the devil competes with his lying signs and wonders, we must, in *agape*/love, seek to operate in the way of God's signs and wonders, that those blinded can have the opportunity to see and hold on to the *agape*/love of the truth in Jesus.

Titus 3:3 "For we ourselves also were sometimes foolish, disobedient, deceived, serving divers lusts and pleasures, *zao*/living in malice and envy, hateful, and hating one another. 4 But after that the kindness and *agape*/love of God our Saviour toward man appeared, 5 not by works of righteousness which we have done, but according to his mercy he *sozo*/saved us, by the washing of regeneration, and renewing of the Holy Ghost; 6 which he shed on us abundantly through Jesus Christ our Saviour; 7 that being justified by his grace, we should be made heirs according to the hope of eternal *zoe*/life. 8 This is a faithful saying, and these things I will that thou affirm constantly, that they which have believed in God might be careful to maintain good works. These things are good and profitable unto men."

Jude 20 "But ye, *agape*/beloved, building up yourselves on your most holy faith, praying in the Holy Ghost, 21 keep yourselves in the *agape*/love of God, looking for the mercy of our Lord Jesus Christ unto eternal *zoe*/life. 22 And of some have compassion, making a difference: 23 and others *sozo*/save with fear, pulling them out of the fire; hating even the garment spotted by the flesh. 24 Now unto him that is able to keep you from falling, and to present you faultless before the presence of his glory with exceeding joy, 25 to the only wise God our Saviour, be glory and majesty, dominion and power, both now and ever. Amen."

Part of the attitude of *agape*/love is that those in sin or any bondage of the curse of sin are under the rulership or lordship of Satan, and we are to enforce the victory of Jesus over the devil. The sinner is both hurting and building more hurt, as they remain in bondage to sin. Rom 6:20 "For when ye were the servants of sin, ye were free from righteousness. 21 What fruit had ye then in those things whereof ye are now ashamed? For the end of those things is death. 22 But now being made free from sin, and become servants to God, ye have your fruit unto holiness, and the end everlasting *zoe*/life. 23 For the wages of sin is death; but the gift of God is eternal *zoe*/life through Jesus Christ our Lord."

Holy Spirit has come to keep us in the right perspective. John 16:7 "Nevertheless I tell you the truth; It is expedient for you that I go away: for if I go not away, the Comforter will not come unto you; but if I depart, I will send him unto you. 8 And when he is come, he will reprove the world of sin, and of righteousness, and

DISCOVERING OUR REDEMPTION

of judgment: 9 of sin, because they believe not on me; 10 of righteousness, because I go to my Father, and ye see me no more; 11 of judgment, because the prince of this world is judged."

You can exercise the Lordship of Jesus, with faith in the name of Jesus, against the devil. You do this by faith in the name of Jesus, and operate much as is recorded in the book of Acts. This is portrayed as the power of God crushing the power of the devil. The message is one of war and power in the Word of God and the name of Jesus. The words *love, beloved* or *charity* are not found in the book of Acts except here: Acts 15:25 "It seemed good unto us, being assembled with one accord, to send chosen men unto you with our *agape*/beloved Barnabas and Paul, 26 men that have hazarded their lives for the name of our Lord Jesus Christ." Even here the *agape*/love is directed at men in warrior attitude.

We are told we can operate in total faith without *agape*/love or charity and do mighty things. 1 Cor 13:2 "And though I have the gift of prophecy, and understand **all mysteries**, and **all knowledge**; and though I have **all faith**, so that I could **remove mountains**, and have not *agape*/charity, I am nothing."

If *agape*/love is not also developed, this leads to: Matt 7:22 "Many will say to me (*Jesus*) in that day, Lord, Lord, have we not prophesied in thy name? And in thy name have cast out devils? And in thy name done many *dunamis*/wonderful works (*miracles, mountain moving*)? 23 And then will I profess unto them, I never knew you: depart from me, ye that work iniquity."

Anytime Holy Spirit can set a person free of any oppression of the devil, that is God's reconciliation in action. It is not about our perfection or holiness, but Jesus' perfection. You believe that He is in you and will come out through you to deliver people, because He *agape*/loves people. It is not about you, but Him. Of course the more self-focused you are, you have a hard time believing it is about Him and not about you. So, until then, we can operate with faith in the name of Jesus and mature in *agape*/love.

This is independent of your holiness. You just have to believe in the name of Jesus and be persistence enough to get the job done. If the minister is not in agreement with God and not in *agape*/love, that does not stop the *agape*/love of God from healing the person or situation. God *agape*/loves people so much He gave Jesus and did it all at once, and for all. 1 John 2:1 "My little children, these things write I unto you, that ye sin not. And if any man sin, we have an advocate with the Father, Jesus Christ the righteous: 2 and he is the propitiation (*remittance unto aggressive blessing*) for our sins: and not for ours only, but also for the sins of the whole world."

God wants sinners free, whether the minister is a vessel of honor or a vessel of dishonor. Just being a vessel is sufficient, and if you are a new creation, you are a vessel of God.

GROWING IN AGAPE LOVE

2 Tim 2:19 "Nevertheless the foundation of God standeth sure, having this seal, The Lord knoweth them that are his. And, Let every one that nameth the name of Christ depart from iniquity. 20 But in a great house there are not only vessels of gold and of silver, but also of wood and of earth; and some to honour, and some to dishonour. 21 If a man therefore purge himself from these, he shall be a vessel unto honour, sanctified, and meet for the master's use, and prepared unto every good work."

Knowing you are a vessel is key to working your faith for God: 2 Cor 13:5 "Examine yourselves, whether ye be in the faith; prove your own selves. Know ye not your own selves, how that Jesus Christ is in you, except ye be reprobates (*useless, impotent, ineffective, and worthless as garbage*)?"

If you take your assigned responsibility to become pure like Jesus, you can use the name of Jesus in faith, hope and *agape*/love for and with God, based on God's Word and not your feelings. As with most things in God, you start acting in *agape*/love in obedience, and then you become *agape*/love.

2 Cor 4:5 "For we preach not ourselves, but Christ Jesus the Lord; and ourselves your servants for Jesus' sake. 6 For God, who commanded the light to shine out of darkness, hath shined in our hearts, to give the light of the knowledge of the glory of God in the face of Jesus Christ. 7 But we have this treasure in earthen vessels, that the excellency of the power may be of God, and not of us."

When you see the sinner hurting, you see more the devil resisting God and God hurting for the sinner ... until the devil is out and Holy Spirit, righteousness, peace, joy, boldness, power, *agape*/love, the mind of Christ, mercy, grace and truth reign in and by those people, to the glory of God by Jesus Christ.

So, for yourself, you say: "Father, thank You for healing me in Jesus because You *agape*/love me."

And for others: "Father, thank You for healing them in Jesus because You *agape*/love them."

And your confession becomes: "Father, I thank You that the love I feel, or the obedience I am in, is a gift from You and a portion of Your *agape*/love for them. Thank You for building that in me, and now I set them free in the name of Jesus, because You *agape*/love them, and I am Your agent of *agape*/love for them." This confession is the same for your own child or a stranger on the street. Your focus is on Father's *agape*/love for them and not what you personally want.

By acknowledging any good thing in you, even things that are normal to "good" people, but giving God the credit for it being there, you are obeying: Philem 6 "That the communication of thy faith may become effectual (*in the power of God*) by the *epignosis*/acknowledging of every good thing which is in you in Christ Jesus."

DISCOVERING OUR REDEMPTION

And you are demonstrating that: James 1:17 "Every good gift and every perfect gift is from above, and cometh down from the Father of lights, with whom is no variableness, neither shadow of turning."

These actions make your faith more effective, as you co-mingle and cooperate with the *agape*/love of God, by Holy Spirit within you. Prov 3:5 "Trust in the LORD (*or set your trust in the LORD*) with all thine heart; and lean not unto thine own understanding. 6 In all thy ways acknowledge him, and he shall direct thy paths. 7 Be not wise in thine own eyes: fear the LORD, and depart from evil. 8 It shall be health to thy navel, and marrow to thy bones."

Acknowledging every good and right thing in you as a gift from God, even the desire to build it or the pressure to make you comply, allows God then to direct you and bless you in every way. This makes every "natural inclination" or "stiff upper lip obedience" a gift from God and a pathway for His blessing. He will then lead you to more blessing and more *agape*/love. The key is your confession of truth in God.

Your battle is with the devil, not the people. You start to see that the devil was totally defeated in the work of Reconciliation in Jesus, and the devil must be made to obey Jesus, through you, because you are made the righteousness of God in Jesus by the new birth, Holy Spirit dwells within you, and you are the devil's master in Jesus and man's servant, knowing you are a child and agent of God to use that name of Jesus to deliver the Reconciliation of God in Jesus.

2 Cor 5:19 "To wit, that God was in Christ, reconciling the world unto himself, not imputing their trespasses unto them; and hath committed unto us the word of reconciliation. 20 Now then we are ambassadors for Christ, as though God did beseech you by us: we pray you in Christ's stead, be ye reconciled to God. 21 For he hath made him to be sin for us, who knew no sin; that we might be made the righteousness of God in him. 6:1 We then, as workers together with him, beseech you also that ye receive not the grace of God in vain. 2 (For he saith, I have heard thee in a time accepted, and in the day of *soteria*/salvation have I succoured thee: behold, now is the accepted time; behold, now is the day of *soteria*/salvation.)"

So you operate with a heart of *agape*/love that looks at the pain of the sinner in the consequence of their sin, and the terror for them, of the reaping that what they are sowing will produce, unless you preach so effectively in signs and wonders that they can truly see and receive the *agape*/love of God for them and be delivered. 1 Cor 2:3 "And I was with you in weakness, and in fear, and in much trembling. 4 And my speech and my preaching was not with enticing words of man's wisdom, but in demonstration of the Spirit and of power: 5 that your faith should not stand in the wisdom of men, but in the power of God."

1 Tim 2:3 "For this is good and acceptable in the sight of God our Saviour; 4 who will have all men to be *sozo*/saved, and to come unto the knowledge of the (2

GROWING IN AGAPE LOVE

Thess 2:10 agape *love of the)* truth. 5 For there is one God, and one mediator between God and men, the man Christ Jesus; 6 who gave himself a ransom for all, to be testified in due time. 7 Whereunto I am ordained a preacher, and an apostle, (I speak the truth in Christ, and lie not;) a teacher of the Gentiles in faith and verity (*to deal faithfully or truly with everyone*)."

Jesus went around doing good, and that included alms, but also much preaching of truth, but here is Holy Spirit's summary of a life of *agape*/love: Acts 10:34 "Then Peter opened his mouth, and said, Of a truth I perceive that God is no respecter of persons: 35 but in every nation he that feareth him, and worketh righteousness, is accepted with him. 36 The word which God sent unto the children of Israel, preaching peace by Jesus Christ: (he is Lord of all:) 37 that word, I say, ye know, which was published throughout all Judaea, and began from Galilee, after the baptism which John preached; 38 how God anointed Jesus of Nazareth with the Holy Ghost and with power: who went about doing good, and healing all that were oppressed (*under the active dominion, reign or lordship*) of the devil; for God was with him."

John 20:21 "Then said Jesus to them (*the disciples*) again, Peace be unto you: as my Father hath sent me, even so send I you."

God *agape*/loves people, and, through Jesus, removed sin as an issue, reconciling man to God. 2 Cor 5:19 "To wit, that God was in Christ, reconciling the world unto himself, not imputing their trespasses unto them; and hath committed unto us the word of reconciliation. 20 Now then we are ambassadors for Christ, as though God did beseech you by us: we pray you in Christ's stead, be ye reconciled to God. 21 For he hath made him to be sin for us, who knew no sin; that we might be made the righteousness of God in him."

God heals people because He *agape*/loves people. Until Jesus, He had no pure example to show us of how He wants people helped. Father God considers people without healing and truth as being those without a shepherd. If we are to follow Jesus, we are to *agape*/love people by setting them free for Father God, just as Jesus did. They may be family members or those who have made themselves our enemies, but they are His sheep, and He wants them free.

Question: Who is my neighbor? Answer: Anyone in any oppression of the devil.

John 15:12 "This is my commandment, That ye *agape*/love one another, as I have *agape*/loved you. 13 Greater *agape*/love hath no man than this, that a man lay down his *psuche*/life (*soul*) for his friends."

So, we minister grace and truth in faith, working by *agape*/love, because:
- The sinner is withholding the glory of God in that situation and cooperating with the devil.

DISCOVERING OUR REDEMPTION

- The devil is lording it over God's creation illegally.
- The devil's works are keeping the person or people in bondage against God's will.
- Sin is of the flesh, and a sinner is at war with God when they sin.
- The devil is only paying them with robbery, killing and destruction.
- Because the sinner is in darkness, they continue to make wrong choices and get worse, and the devil reigns more.
- The Kingdom of God, to the glory of God, is not working in that situation.
- In these people, God is not getting what He paid Jesus to get. He knows what it cost Him, and He wants what He paid for.
- The essence of the New Covenant is that God does not hold our sins against us, because the full curse fell on Jesus. We receive that Redemption by faith in His blood.
- God does not ignore our sins; rather He had Jesus bear them fully unto becoming sin and the curse. Justice was pleased to bruise or crush Jesus fully, to justify mankind. God tricked the devil into crucifying Jesus, and then He healed Jesus and, thus, us with Him in the resurrection.
- All men were healed by the stripes of Jesus of every physical effect of sin, so you can set them free now in the name of Jesus. Father God, Jesus and Holy Spirit made sure this happened, so we can deliver salvation now, and that is what you are made for.
- You are God's agent to bring His will to Earth and set the lawful and unlawful prisoner free.
- God wants that person to receive the *agape*/love of the truth so they will get and stay free.
- They are sowing to themselves the law of sin and death, which God has removed in Jesus.
- If they knew the truth, the sinner would turn to Jesus and receive and get His *agape*/love right now.
- All the wrath of God due the sinner fell on and was born fully by Jesus. God now has no wrath toward man, because Jesus *agape*/loved the Father to obey Him and gladly do His will.
- God is not getting glory for His great and mighty work of Reconciliation in Jesus.
- You are not satisfying *agape*/love, that which you are made of, until sinners are set free in the name of Jesus.
- You are God's agent for God to deliver and get what Jesus paid for.
- You have been commanded by Jesus to trample on every ability of the enemy and bring the Kingdom of God to Earth.

GROWING IN AGAPE LOVE

- You are one of God's peacemakers who go about doing good, and healing all that are oppressed (*under the active dominion, reign or lordship*) of the devil, for God is with you.
- Your true, new-creation nature is *agape*/love and has compassion (not sympathy or condemnation) for sinners until they are free.
- As you walk in *agape*/love the only answer is to do what Jesus did in going around and doing good, healing people of the oppressions of the devil.
- As you walk in this attitude of not what you want, but what Father wants, by His Bible, your faith grows, and you deliver more of God's goodness to and for the people Jesus died to save.
- If you find that their sin causes you to sin too, you know there is an area where your soul is not in *agape*/love. You must not allow the devil to trick you into getting offended at them or God.
- You know your ability to set people free is not about your holiness, but Jesus'. Therefore, as for the short term, you will not be perfect like Jesus, and even the Apostle Paul was not, for giving and receiving healing is by grace and not works of righteousness.
- You, like God, are hurting for sinners in compassion that delivers mercy, and you are His hands and His voice to set them free for Him.
- You know you have the ministry of reconciliation, and you will set them free in faith, working by *agape*/love.
- You know, as you speak the words of God's reconciliation in Jesus in *aiteoing* the devil out of that situation, God will confirm that word in signs and wonders, in setting people free from the oppressions of the devil.

Thus, seeking to walk in *agape*/love becomes your shortcut to more effective faith. Gal 5:6 "For in Jesus Christ neither circumcision availeth anything, nor uncircumcision; but faith which worketh by *agape*/love."

Agape/love then becomes, not an event, but a lifestyle. 1 Cor 12:31 "But covet earnestly the best gifts: and yet shew I unto you a more excellent way, [*the lifestyle of* agape/*love*]."

We are vessels of God to release God into the world He *agape*/loves. John 3:16 "For God so *agape*/loved the world, that he gave his only begotten Son, that whosoever believeth in him should not perish, but have everlasting *zoe*/life. 17 For God sent not his Son into the world to condemn the world; but that the world through him might be *sozo*/saved."

Chapter 42

Becoming Burden Bearers

We are now God's burden-bearers.
We carry His load, with His strength.
Gal 6:2 "Bear ye one another's burdens, and so fulfil the law of Christ."
Here is one way we do it, besides physical acts of kindness and generosity.
1 John 5:13 "These things have I written unto you that believe on the name of the Son of God; that ye may know that ye have eternal *zoe*/life, and that ye may believe on the name of the Son of God. 14 And this is the confidence that we have in him, that, if we *aiteo*/ask any thing according to his will, he heareth us: 15 and if we know that he hear us, whatsoever we *aiteo*/ask (*requiring, demanding, expecting as due by covenant promise*), we know that we have the *aiteo*/petitions that we *aiteo*/desired (*requiring, demanding and expecting as due by covenant promise*) of him. 16 If any man see his brother sin a sin which is not unto death, he shall *aiteo*/ask (*requiring, demanding and expecting as due by covenant promise*), and he shall give him *zoe*/life for them ... ."
James 5:19 "Brethren, if any of you do err from the truth, and one convert him; 20 let him know, that he which converteth the sinner from the error of his way shall *sozo*/save a soul from death, and shall hide a multitude of sins."

BECOMING BURDEN BEARERS

Gal 6:1 "Brethren, if a man be overtaken in a fault, ye which are spiritual, restore such an one in the spirit of meekness; considering thyself, lest thou also be tempted."

James 2:12 "So speak ye, and so do, as they that shall be judged by the law of liberty. 13 For he shall have judgment without mercy, that hath shewed no mercy; and mercy rejoiceth against judgment (*or mercy triumphs over negative judgment*)."

We do our Father's will with His ability that dwells within us, Holy Spirit of God.

We do this with His *agape* love that it may profit us. (1 Cor 13)

We do it like George Washington Carver, who saved the Southern United States by using the peanut. He developed the peanut, to provide sustaining food, after the boll weevil destroyed the cotton industry as a cash crop. Then he went to God and got numerous inventions concerning the peanut and created a cash-crop industry. This is what *agape* love does. He was a black man in a period of extreme segregation, yet he saved the black and white southern economy and countless lives because he was driven by *agape* love.

Jesus is living His life in us and out through us, to subdue and establish the dominion of our Father God. What Adam failed to do, God now finishes through us.

We know, though perhaps we do not realize it, that "It is no longer I that *zao*/live, but Christ is *zao*/living in me," as Paul says in Gal 2:20.

We have lost the old landmarks of sense knowledge, since we learned to walk the new Way. We are not governed by what we see, hear, touch, taste or smell; instead, we are now governed by the Word of God. It is the Word that is truth. Rom 3:4 "God forbid: yea, let God be true, but every man a liar; as it is written, That thou mightest be justified in thy sayings, and mightest overcome when thou art judged."

Jesus said, "I am the way." (John 14:6)

It is not a road; it is a person.

It is not a theory; it is a reality.

It is not a doctrine; it is a life.

Dogma and doctrines have finally found their focus in "Christ in you the hope of glory."

Now we are swallowed up in Him.

Rom 15:1-2 "We that are strong ought to bear the infirmities of the weak, and not to please ourselves."

This is the Jesus method.

He was strong. He took our infirmities.

Now His strength has made us strong.

We take over the weaknesses of others.

We are not their critics.

We do not condemn them because they have failed.

DISCOVERING OUR REDEMPTION

We do not get irritated when they will not listen.

We go down and take their burdens and let them walk by our side, free men.

We do not condemn the one who is held in prison by Satan, for we remember that once we were slaves also.

We are the strength-givers, the burden-bearers, the light-leaders in the world of darkness.

We are warriors of *agape*/love.

What a ministry it is to take Jesus' place.

What a life it is to bear the burdens of the weak, carry the loads that others should have had strength to carry, have faith for those who are faithless, courage for those who are whipped, wisdom for those who have long walked in darkness and vanity.

Col 3:14 "And above all these things put on *agape*/charity, which is the bond of perfectness (*maturity*). 15 And let the peace of God rule in your hearts, to the which also ye are called in one body; and be ye thankful. 16 Let the word of Christ dwell in you richly in all wisdom; teaching and admonishing one another in psalms and hymns and spiritual songs, singing with grace in your hearts to the Lord. 17 And whatsoever ye do in word or deed, do all in the name of the Lord Jesus, giving thanks to God and the Father by him."

We are the Jesus men and women of a new age.

Eph 5:1 "Be ye therefore followers (*imitators*) of God, as dear children; 2 and walk in *agape*/love, as Christ also hath *agape*/loved us, and hath given himself for us an offering and a sacrifice to God for a sweetsmelling savour."

He has taken us over so that we might take over His dream for man.

It sounds strange, but it is beautifully true, that we now love as He loved.

We love with His love.

We look upon people through love's eyes. We used to say, "They are reaping what they have sown." We used to see them through sense-knowledge eyes.

Matt 7:1 "Judge (*decide negatively against, take to court quickly or draw an unfair decision*) not, that ye be not judged. 2 For with what judgment ye judge, ye shall be judged: and with what measure ye mete, it shall be measured to you again. 3 And why beholdest thou the mote that is in thy brother's eye, but considerest not the beam that is in thine own eye? 4 Or how wilt thou say to thy brother, Let me pull out the mote out of thine eye; and, behold, a beam is in thine own eye? 5 Thou hypocrite, first cast out the beam out of thine own eye; and then shalt thou see clearly to cast out the mote out of thy brother's eye."

Driven by fear and selfishness, with no Father to protect us, we found fault and accused with the heart of the devil. Now we find ways to get the strength for others to carry their loads and set them patiently on the path to walking in the new-creation truth, until Christ is a reality of love in their lives.

Becoming Burden Bearers

2 Tim 2:14 "Of these things put them in remembrance, charging them before the Lord that they strive not about words to no profit, but to the subverting of the hearers. 15 Study to shew thyself approved unto God, a workman that needeth not to be ashamed, rightly dividing the word of truth. 16 But shun profane and vain babblings: for they will increase unto more ungodliness. 17 And their word will eat as doth a canker: of whom is Hymenaeus and Philetus; 18 who concerning the truth have erred, saying that the resurrection is past already; and overthrow the faith of some. 19 Nevertheless the foundation of God standeth sure, having this seal, The Lord knoweth them that are his. And, Let every one that nameth the name of Christ depart from iniquity. 20 But in a great house there are not only vessels of gold and of silver, but also of wood and of earth; and some to honour, and some to dishonour. 21 If a man therefore purge himself from these, he shall be a vessel unto honour, sanctified, and meet for the master's use, and prepared unto every good work.

22 "Flee also youthful lusts: but follow righteousness, faith, charity, peace, with them that call on the Lord out of a pure heart. 23 But foolish and unlearned questions avoid, knowing that they do gender strifes. 24 And the servant of the Lord must not strive; but be gentle unto all men, apt to teach, patient, 25 in meekness instructing those that oppose themselves; if God peradventure will give them repentance to the acknowledging of the truth; 26 and that they may recover themselves out of the snare of the devil, who are taken captive by him at his will."

Now we judge to see if they need help, and the best way to help them.

Now we say, "Father, help me to help them. I am taking Your wisdom and Your strength to carry the load they have failed to take strength to carry. They have been deceived by sense knowledge. I take their place and carry their burden, as You have taken my place and borne my burden."

Gal 6:2 "Bear ye one another's burdens, and so fulfil the law of Christ."

James 2:8 "If ye fulfil the royal law according to the scripture, Thou shalt *agape*/love thy neighbour as thyself, ye do well."

We now speak of others with love's voice, with love's message, as members of the same family.

Chapter 43

Becoming Gateways for God's Love

Father God's Identification of us with Jesus put us on the throne with Him and in Jesus.

Col 3:1 "If ye then be risen with Christ, seek those things which are above, where Christ sitteth on the right hand of God. 2 Set your affection on things above, not on things on the earth. 3 For ye are dead, and your *zoe*/life is hid with Christ in God."

That *zoe*/life is released as you think, talk and walk like Jesus walked–*agape*/love in action.

Just like Jesus was, we are now the Gateway of God's *agape*/love to man.

His Identification with us puts us in the place of leaders, teachers, comforters, helpers, and burden-bearers.

We bring God to man, just as He came to us.

We are the portals of God for the Earth in Jesus.

We boldly say, "Look on us." (Acts 3:4)

We are Love, as He is Love. We are *Agape* Love's lips, *Agape* Love's hands and feet.

Without wires and gateways to move the power, the mighty generator of a nuclear power plant would be useless.

Becoming Gateways for God's Love

Without transmission lines and gateways, God in all His ability, is helpless, useless to men.

John 15:9-10 "Even as the Father hath *agape*/loved me, I also have *agape*/loved you: abide ye in my *agape*/love. If ye keep my commandments, ye shall abide in my *agape*/love; even as I have kept my Father's commandments, and abide in his *agape*/love."

We are to *agape*/love as He *agape*/loved, pour out our lives as He poured out His, for and with Father God.

Paul saw the real issue and gave it to us in: 2 Cor. 5:13 "For if we have been beside ourselves, it has been for God's glory; or if we are now in our right senses, it is in order to be of service to you. For the *agape*/love of Christ overmasters us, the conclusion at which we have arrived being this that One having died for all, His death was their death, and that He died for all in order that the *zao*/living may no longer *zao*/live to themselves, but to Him who died for them and rose again." WYM

Paul believed in the *agape*/love of God, to the extent that he was believed to be beside himself. His answer was: "The *agape*/love of Christ has taken hold of my heart. I realize that Christ's death was every man's death. I can no longer look at any man except as in relation to the death of Christ." There is no one for whom Jesus did not die, who did not die when Jesus died and who was not raised when Jesus was raised.

We preach the Gospel because we want men to get what God paid so dearly for us to have.

The same love that caused Christ to die for man had constrained Paul's heart and was causing him to live for them.

The attitude of love is this: "I love them as though I had died for them."

Paul is even stronger in his description of Love's Identification, in Rom 9:3 "I suffer endless anguish of heart. I could have wished myself accursed and banished from Christ for the sake of my brothers." MOF

In reading this, we feel we can hardly measure up to it.

But this is not hard, because He has made us Love. He has made us like Himself. Rising in love requires getting rid of un-love, which is not of us. It may be part of the old man that we got from Adam after he sinned, but it is not part of the new-creation man.

Col 3:10 "And have put on the new man, which is renewed in *epignosis*/knowledge (*to operate in God as a master craftsman, as Jesus does*) after the image of him (*Father God*) that created him: 11 where there is neither Greek nor Jew, circumcision nor uncircumcision, Barbarian, Scythian, bond nor free: but Christ is all, and in all. 12 Put on therefore, as the elect of God, holy and *agape*/beloved, bowels of mercies, kindness, humbleness of mind, meekness, longsuffering; 13 forbearing one another, and forgiving one another, if any man have a quarrel against any: even as

DISCOVERING OUR REDEMPTION

Christ forgave you, so also do ye. 14 And above all these things put on *agape*/charity, which is the bond of perfectness *(maturity)*. 15 And let the peace of God rule in your hearts, to the which also ye are called in one body; and be ye thankful."

What Jesus was in His Earth walk, we are now in our Earth walk.

1 John 4:17 "Herein is our *agape*/love made perfect, that we may have boldness in the day of judgment: because as he is *(Father God, Jesus,* agape/*love)*, so are we in this world. 18 There is no fear in *agape*/love; but perfect *agape*/love casteth out fear: because fear hath torment. He that feareth is not made perfect in *agape*/love. 19 We *agape*/love him, because he first *agape*/loved us."

Father's love can find no expression except through the new creation.

1 John 4:20 "If a man say, I *agape*/love God, and hateth his brother, he is a liar: for he that *agape*/loveth not his brother whom he hath seen, how can he *agape*/love God whom he hath not seen? 21 And this commandment have we from him, That he who *agape*/loveth God *agape*/love his brother also."

Those great generators are dependent upon the wires to transmit the power, to do something good.

They and they alone can bear the current that can stir motors and light homes anywhere in the world.

We are simply the wires, delivering God's *agape* love and *zoe* life power.

We are majoring in the Word of Reconciliation, Redemption, Righteousness, Peace, *Agape*/love, Adoption, Mercy, Truth, Grace, Power and Salvation in Jesus.

Can't you see, if you fail Him, He is helpless?

We limit Him, or we allow Him to be limitless. We are the key, the gateway, the portal for God to bring His Kingdom to Earth.

Ps 78:40 "How oft did they provoke him in the wilderness, and grieve him in the desert! 41 Yea, they turned back and tempted God, and limited the Holy One of Israel. 42 They remembered not his hand, nor the day when he delivered them from the enemy." God was near and yet so far, due to the hardness, the offence, the unpersuadableness, the bitterness, based on lies and a twisted view of God and themselves, in their hearts. (Heb 3 and 4; 1 Cor 10:1-15)

This was waiting for them, and the next generation did it. Dan 11:32 "… but the people that do know their God shall be strong, and do exploits."

Prov 28:1 "The wicked flee when no man pursueth: but the righteous are bold as a lion."

God has provided us with the ultimate in righteousness but begs us to be persuaded of His truth: 2 Cor 5:17 "So if any one [be] in Christ, [there is] a new creation; the old things have passed away; behold all things have become new: 18 and all things [are] of the God who has reconciled us to himself by [Jesus] Christ, and given to us the ministry of that reconciliation: 19 how that God was in Christ, reconciling the world to himself, not reckoning to them their offences; and putting in us the word of that reconciliation. 20 We are ambassadors therefore for Christ, God as [it were] beseeching by us, we entreat for Christ, Be reconciled to God. 21 Him who knew not sin he has made sin for us, that we might become God's righteousness in him." DBY

What will it take to work with the Word of Grace until we walk in this? We are in the day we have been waiting for. The time is now; the issue is to renew our minds in this awesome truth.

2 Cor 6:1 "But [as] fellow-workmen, we also beseech that ye receive not the grace of God in vain: 2 (for he says, I have listened to thee in an accepted time, and I have helped thee in a day of *soteria*/salvation: behold, now [is the] well-accepted time; behold, now [the] day of *soteria*/salvation:)" DBY

We have heard God begging us; we are the ones who keep our minds renewed constantly in the grace and *agape*/love of God.

Jude 20 "But ye, *agape*/beloved, building up yourselves on your most holy faith, praying in the Holy Ghost, 21 keep yourselves in the *agape*/love of God, looking for the mercy of our Lord Jesus Christ unto eternal *zoe*/life. 22 And of some have compassion, making a difference: 23 and others save with fear, pulling them out of the fire; hating even the garment spotted by the flesh. 24 Now unto him that is able to keep you from falling, and to present you faultless before the presence of his glory with exceeding joy, 25 to the only wise God our Saviour, be glory and majesty, dominion and power, both now and ever. Amen."

So we constantly recall His acts of love in the Scriptures and *aiteo* command, as He commanded, until we have our own testimonies of His power, in the name of Jesus, setting men free in signs and wonders.

We have been redeemed from the curse of the law. Gal 3:13 "Christ hath redeemed us from the curse of the law, being made a curse for us: for it is written, Cursed is every one that hangeth on a tree."

So let's look at the curse, as described in the Old Testament. Deut 28:58 "If thou wilt not observe to do all the words of this law that are written in this book, that thou mayest fear this glorious and fearful name, THE LORD THY GOD; 59 then the LORD will make thy plagues wonderful, and the plagues of thy seed, even great plagues, and of long continuance, and sore sicknesses, and of long continuance. 60 Moreover he will bring upon thee all the diseases of Egypt, which thou wast afraid of; and they shall cleave unto thee. 61 Also every sickness, and every plague, which is not written in the book of this law, them will the LORD bring upon thee, until thou be destroyed."

Notice these are the results of breaking God's law. The curse in the law of sin and death is the result of the sin we or others commit. This passage is just part of the curses described for sinning, but this is not God's will. He wants us to not sin and not incur these consequences.

DISCOVERING OUR REDEMPTION

Recent Hebrew study has discovered that the verb in verse 59 is a permissive and not a directive verb. So a more accurate translation is "The **Lord cannot stop thy** plagues being so awesome …" as seen in *Young's Analytical Concordance.* If we will not call our sins and hardness of heart what they are and take them to God (as in the past covenant of Moses, to the temple, or now to the communion table in the renewed covenant of Jesus), or, as always, directly to God, in faith of His goodness and receive that forgiveness and healing by faith, we will reap what we have sown, and God cannot stop it. He may be able to mitigate it, as He did for Adam and Eve, or Job, and even Israel's remnant, but He cannot stop it. But it is never His desire for us to live under or in any death of any kind.

Mal 3:6 "For I am the Lord, I change not; therefore ye sons of Jacob are not consumed."

Ezek 33:11 "Say unto them, As I live, saith the Lord GOD, I have no pleasure in the death of the wicked; but that the wicked turn from his way and live: turn ye, turn ye from your evil ways; for why will ye die, O house of Israel?" See also Ezek 18:32.

With all of this evil reaping we are redeemed from by the blood of Jesus, none of it is legal on any human or creature in God's creation. "By His stripes we are healed" means Jesus took what we deserve for us, so we do not have to ever bear it.

Even if we miss the power of His stripes, by His resurrection, when Jesus was made alive from the dead and His body totally filled with Holy Spirit and healed in fullness, so were we. Rom 4:25 "Who was delivered for our offences, and was raised again for our justification (*or when we were justified, made perfect in every way*)."

Rom 6:23 "For the wages of sin is death; but the gift of God is eternal *zoe*/life through Jesus Christ our Lord."

Rom 8:2 "For the law of the Spirit of *zoe*/life in Christ Jesus hath made me free from the law of sin and death."

Rom 8:10 "And if Christ be in you, the body is dead because of sin; but the Spirit is *zoe*/life because of righteousness. 11 But if the Spirit of him that raised up Jesus from the dead dwell in you, he that raised up Christ from the dead shall also *zao*/quicken your mortal bodies (*the current one we have now, for our resurrection bodies will be immortal*) by his Spirit that dwelleth in you [*now*]."

We are redeemed from sin and the curse of sin, and none of this evil is from God. Our ministry of reconciliation is to blast the devil and his works off of people, others and ourselves, in the name of Jesus.

2 Cor 5:17 "Therefore if any man be in Christ, he is a new creature: old things are passed away; behold, all things are become new. 18 And all things are of God, who hath reconciled us to himself by Jesus Christ, and hath given to us the ministry of reconciliation (*making things right, to just like they are in Heaven, to bring Heaven to Earth*); 19 to wit, that God was in Christ, reconciling the world unto himself, not

imputing their trespasses unto them; and hath committed unto us the word of reconciliation (*that because of Jesus we are to make things right, to just like they are in Heaven, to bring Heaven to Earth*). 20 Now then we are ambassadors for Christ, as though God did beseech you by us: we pray you in Christ's stead, be ye reconciled to God (*knowing that God has removed all war from you in Jesus*). 21 For he hath made him to be sin for us, who knew no sin; that we might be made the righteousness of God in him. 6:1 We then, as workers together with him, beseech you also that ye receive not the grace of God in vain. 2 (For he saith, I have heard thee in a time accepted, and in the day of *soteria*/salvation have I succoured thee: behold, now is the accepted time; behold, now is the day of *soteria*/salvation.)"

We know we and all mankind are redeemed from sin and the curse of sin.

Gal 3:13 "Christ hath redeemed us from the curse of the law, being made a curse for us: for it is written, Cursed is every one that hangeth on a tree."

Eph 1:6 "To the praise of the glory of his grace, wherein he hath made us accepted in the *agape*/beloved. 7 In whom we have redemption through his blood, the *aphesis*/forgiveness (*remission, removal, purging, obliteration, and putting away*) of sins, according to the riches of his grace; 8 wherein he hath abounded toward us in all wisdom and prudence; 9 having made known unto us the mystery of his will, according to his good pleasure which he hath purposed in himself."

Eph 1:12 "That we should be to the praise of his glory, who first trusted in Christ. 13 In whom ye also trusted, after that ye heard the word of truth, the gospel of your *soteria*/salvation: in whom also after that ye believed, ye were sealed with that holy Spirit of promise, 14 which is the earnest of our inheritance until the redemption of the purchased possession, unto the praise of his glory."

Col 1:19 "For it pleased the Father that in him (*Jesus*) should all fulness dwell; 20 and, having made peace through the blood of his cross, by him to reconcile all things unto himself; by him, I say, whether they be things in earth, or things in heaven. 21 And you, that were sometime alienated and enemies in your mind by wicked works, yet now hath he reconciled (*in spite of your wicked works and corrupt minds*) 22 in the body of his flesh through death, to present you holy and unblameable and unreproveable in his sight (*in spite of your wicked works and corrupt minds*)."

As agents of the peace He has already made, we are to enforce that peace to remove all enemies of God, just as Jesus did.

Acts 10:34 "Then Peter opened his mouth, and said, Of a truth I perceive that God is no respecter of persons: 35 but in every nation he that feareth him, and worketh righteousness, is accepted with him. 36 The word which God sent unto the children of Israel, preaching peace by Jesus Christ: (he is Lord of all:) 37 that word, I say, ye know, which was published throughout all Judaea, and began from Galilee, after the baptism which John preached; 38 how God anointed Jesus of Nazareth with the Holy Ghost and with power: who went about doing good, and healing

DISCOVERING OUR REDEMPTION

all that were oppressed (*under the active dominion, reign or lordship*) of the devil; for God was with him. 39 And we are witnesses of all things which he did both in the land of the Jews, and in Jerusalem; whom they slew and hanged on a tree: 40 him God raised up the third day, and shewed him openly; 41 not to all the people, but unto witnesses chosen before of God, even to us, who did eat and drink with him after he rose from the dead. 42 And he commanded us to preach unto the people, and to testify that it is he which was ordained of God to be the Judge of quick and dead. 43 To him give all the prophets witness, that through his name whosoever believeth in him shall receive remission (*purging, removal, washing, obliteration and putting away*) of sins. 44 While Peter yet spake these words, the Holy Ghost fell on all them which heard the word."

This is the kind of peace Jesus delivered in word and demonstration: Ps 103:2 "Bless the Lord, O my soul, and forget not all his benefits: 3 who forgiveth all thine iniquities; who healeth all thy diseases; 4 who redeemeth thy life from destruction; who crowneth thee with *chesed*/lovingkindness and *racham*/tender mercies; 5 who satisfieth thy mouth with good things; so that thy youth is renewed like the eagle's. 6 The Lord executeth righteousness and judgment for all that are oppressed."

Jesus has the same Spirit He has given us. That is how identified we are with Jesus and Father God.

Gal 4:4 "But when the fulness of the time was come, God sent forth his Son, made of a woman, made under the law, 5 to redeem them that were under the law, that we might receive the adoption of sons. 6 And because ye are sons, God hath sent forth the Spirit of his Son into your hearts, crying, Abba (*Daddy*), Father."

Therefore you have the same Spirit as Jesus has and for the same purpose.

Luke 4:18 "The Spirit of the Lord is upon me, because he hath anointed me to preach the gospel to the poor; he hath sent me to heal the brokenhearted, to preach deliverance to the captives, and recovering of sight to the blind, to set at liberty them that are bruised, 19 to preach the acceptable year of the Lord."

Because we have the same Spirit with the same job, we continually know: 2 Tim 1:6 "Wherefore I put thee in remembrance that thou stir up the gift of God … . 7 For God hath not given us the spirit of fear; but of *dunamis*/power (*the impossible ability of God*), and of *agape*/love, and of a sound mind (*just like Jesus has, the mind of Christ*)."

So we stir ourselves up into this Redemption truth and go out and make some peace wherever the enemy of God is reigning, death by the devil, and deliver the Salvation of God, knowing we have remission, purging, removal, washing, obliteration and putting away of sins.

As Peter said in his most important message: 2 Pet 1:13 "Yea, I think it meet, as long as I am in this tabernacle, to stir you up by putting you in remembrance; 14 knowing that shortly I must put off this my tabernacle, even as our Lord Jesus

Christ hath shewed me. 15 Moreover I will endeavour that ye may be able after my decease to have these things always in remembrance."

What is so critical to keep in remembrance? Part of it is this: 2 Pet 1:8 "For if these things (*of the nature of God*) be in you, and abound, they make you that ye shall neither be barren nor unfruitful in the *epignosis*/knowledge of our Lord Jesus Christ. 9 But he that lacketh these things [*the abundance of the nature and characteristics of God, like Jesus*] is blind, and cannot see afar off, and hath forgotten that he was purged from his old sins (*redemption unto remission, washing, obliteration, and putting away of sin*). 10 Wherefore the rather, brethren, give diligence to make your calling and election sure: for if ye do these things, ye shall never fall."

We know that we can act our way quicker into believing than we can believe our way into acting.

For many ages, the power and ability of the mighty atom was never utilized.

In the same way, for nearly 2000 years, the limitless ability of God by Jesus has been unused.

After the first 300 years or so of its history, the church has been largely weak and powerless.

Christians can see miracles and focus on what failed and never recall what God was able to do.

We have majored on the wisdom of men and not the *dunamis* power of God: 1 Cor 2:1 "And I, brethren, when I came to you, came not with excellency of speech or of wisdom, declaring unto you the testimony of God. 2 For I determined not to know any thing among you, save Jesus Christ, and him crucified. 3 And I was with you in weakness, and in fear, and in much trembling. 4 And my speech and my preaching was not with enticing words of man's wisdom, but in demonstration of the Spirit and of power: 5 that your faith should not stand in the wisdom of men, but in the power of God."

Since the first years of the church, we have not seen the Gospel preached fully, as God intended. Rom 15:19 "Through mighty signs and wonders, by the power of the Spirit of God; so that from Jerusalem, and round about unto Illyricum, I have fully preached the gospel of Christ."

The anointing is in the Word and in you. Put that Word in you and on your lips, and God can set the oppressed free though you. This is not about your holiness. Trust the Word of God to do what only the Word of God can do—reveal, in grace, truth and mercy, Jesus and the awesome facts of Redemption unto Salvation.

It is the Word of grace that produces this revelation and God confirms: Acts 14:3 "Long time therefore abode they speaking boldly in the Lord, which gave testimony unto the word of his grace, and granted signs and wonders to be done by their hands."

DISCOVERING OUR REDEMPTION

Instead, sin has reigned as master, and the church has served as slave.

We have preached guilt, condemnation, sin and ignorance of God's ways.

Still, this weakened church represents the new creation, which is a Satan-conqueror.

Rev 12:11 "And they overcame him *(Satan)* by the blood of the Lamb, and by the word of their testimony; and they *agape*/loved not their *psuche*/lives *(souls)* unto the death."

Shall we allow our current situation to continue?

It is time to major on the majors of God, the great work of the Mighty Arm of God, and magnify that work to all men, starting with yourself, daily.

Heb 3:12 "Take heed, brethren *(fellow Christians)*, lest there be in any of you an evil heart of unbelief, in departing from the *zao*/living God. 13 But exhort one another daily, while it is called To day; lest any of you be hardened *[in soul-heart, mind, will and emotions]* through the deceitfulness of sin. 14 For we are made partakers of Christ, if we hold the beginning of our confidence stedfast unto the end; 15 while it is said, To day if ye will hear his voice, harden not your hearts, as in the provocation *(rebellion in the desert, where they refused to give up their offense in God and be persuaded of His goodness, of Redemption truths, so they could cross the river and conquer a land of giants)*."

You have seen the truth in this mighty message of Identification, the loving embrace, the marriage offer of Redemption.

Now what are you going to do with it?

By Christ's great Redemption we are made priests and kings, to do God's will His way.

Rev 1:5 "And from Jesus Christ, who is the faithful witness, and the first begotten of the dead, and the prince of the kings of the earth. Unto him that *agape*/loved us, and washed us from our sins in his own blood, 6 and hath made us kings and priests unto God and his Father; to him be glory and dominion for ever and ever. Amen."

Our strength is His strength, and we are to be strong in it.

Eph 6:10 "Finally, my brethren, be strong in the Lord, and in the power of his might. 11 Put on the whole armour of God, that ye may be able to stand against the wiles of the devil. 12 For we wrestle not against flesh and blood, but against principalities, against powers, against the rulers of the darkness of this world, against spiritual wickedness in high places."

Ps 99:4 "The king's strength also loveth judgment; thou dost establish equity, thou executest judgment and righteousness in Jacob. 5 Exalt ye the Lord our God, and worship at his footstool; for he is holy."

Ps 103:2 "Bless the Lord, O my soul, and forget not all his benefits: 3 who forgiveth all thine iniquities; who healeth all thy diseases; 4 who redeemeth thy life from destruction; who crowneth thee with *chesed*/lovingkindness and *racham*/tender mercies."

BECOMING GATEWAYS FOR GOD'S LOVE

We have been redeemed from the curse of the law, so no affliction of the devil is now legal.

Christ's Redemption is now, and it delivers the captives.

Ps 111:7 "The works of his hands are verity and judgment; all his commandments are sure. 8 They stand fast for ever and ever, and are done in truth and uprightness. 9 He sent redemption unto his people: he hath commanded his covenant for ever: holy and reverend is his name. 10 The fear of the Lord is the beginning of wisdom: a good understanding have all they that do his commandments: his praise endureth for ever."

Ps 103:6 "The Lord executeth righteousness and judgment for all that are oppressed."

Ps 89:13 "Thou hast a mighty arm: strong is thy hand, and high is thy right hand. 14 Justice and judgment are the habitation of thy throne: *chesed*/mercy (*grace*) and truth shall go before thy face. 15 Blessed is the people that know the joyful sound: they shall walk, O Lord, in the light of thy countenance. 16 In thy name shall they rejoice all the day: and in thy righteousness shall they be exalted. 17 For thou art the glory of their strength: and in thy favour our horn shall be exalted. 18 For the Lord is our defence; and the Holy One of Israel is our king."

Ps 146:5 "Happy is he that hath the God of Jacob for his help, whose hope is in the Lord his God: 6 which made heaven, and earth, the sea, and all that therein is: which keepeth truth for ever: 7 which executeth judgment for the oppressed: which giveth food to the hungry. The Lord looseth the prisoners: 8 the Lord openeth the eyes of the blind: the Lord raiseth them that are bowed down: the Lord loveth the righteous: 9 the Lord preserveth the strangers; he relieveth the fatherless and widow: but the way of the wicked he turneth upside down. 10 The Lord shall reign for ever, even thy God, O Zion, unto all generations. Praise ye the Lord."

Isa 49:24 "Shall the prey be taken from the mighty, or the lawful captive delivered? 25 But thus saith the Lord, Even the captives of the mighty shall be taken away, and the prey of the terrible shall be delivered: for I will contend with him that contendeth with thee, and I will save thy children."

Ps 107:1 "O give thanks unto the Lord, for he is good: for his *chesed*/mercy (*grace*) endureth for ever. 2 Let the redeemed of the Lord say so, whom he hath redeemed from the hand of the enemy."

Will we fight the fight of faith and defeat the devil?

1 Tim 6:11 "But thou, O man (*or woman*) of God, flee these things (*of the carnal mind and the mind of the flesh*); and follow after righteousness, godliness, faith, *agape*/love, patience, meekness. 12 Fight the good fight of faith, *lambano*/lay hold on eternal *zoe*/life, whereunto thou art also called, and hast professed a good profession before many witnesses."

DISCOVERING OUR REDEMPTION

We have the same Spirit as did Jesus for the same job; it is in our new-creation nature, the basis of our born-of-God spirit. Gal 4:4 "But when the fulness of the time was come, God sent forth his Son, made of a woman, made under the law, 5 to redeem them that were under the law, that we might receive the adoption of sons. 6 And because ye are sons, God hath sent forth the Spirit of his Son into your hearts, crying, Abba (*Daddy*), Father. 7 Wherefore thou art no more a servant, but a son; and if a son, then an heir of God through Christ."

John 1:12 "But as many as received him, to them gave he power to become the sons of God, even to them that believe on his name: 13 which were born, not of blood, nor of the will of the flesh, nor of the will of man, but of God. 14 And the Word was made flesh, and dwelt among us, (and we beheld his glory, the glory as of the only begotten of the Father,) full of grace and truth. 15 John bare witness of him, and cried, saying, This was he of whom I spake, He that cometh after me is preferred before me: for he was before me. 16 And of his fulness have all we received, and grace for grace. 17 For the law was given by Moses, but grace and truth came by Jesus Christ. 18 No man hath seen God at any time; the only begotten Son, which is in the bosom of the Father, he hath declared him [*as to the Father's true nature and fidelity*]."

2 Cor 1:21 "Now he which stablisheth us with you in Christ, and hath anointed us, is God; 22 who hath also sealed us, and given the earnest of the Spirit in our hearts."

There is only one Holy Spirit, and He is sealed within you, the Christian. So, your confession is now: Luke 4:18 "The Spirit of the Lord is upon me, because he hath anointed me to preach the gospel to the poor; he hath sent me to heal the brokenhearted, to preach deliverance to the captives, and recovering of sight to the blind, to set at liberty them that are bruised, 19 to preach the acceptable year of the Lord."

It is the same anointing, same calling, and same Spirit for the same job: Acts 10:38 "how God anointed [*you in*] Jesus of Nazareth with the Holy Ghost and with power: [*for you to act as a king for Jesus, in going*] about doing good, and healing all that [*are*] oppressed (*under the active dominion, reign or lordship*) of the devil; for God is with [*you in*] him."

We are the gateway, the portal of God, to Earth. As Smith Wigglesworth said: "If the spirit is not moving, I move the spirit." And John Lake said: "It is a law of the human mind that I can act myself into believing quicker than I can believe myself into acting." (Blake, *The Voice of Healing*, Episodes 1 and 2)

2 Tim 1:6 "Wherefore I put thee in remembrance that thou stir up the gift of God ... . 7 For God hath not given us the spirit of fear; but of *dunamis*/power (*of His unlimited ability, where all things are possible*), and of *agape*/love, and of a sound mind (*to think, know, be and do like Jesus would*). 8 Be not thou therefore ashamed of the

testimony of our Lord, nor of me his prisoner: but be thou partaker of the afflictions of the gospel according to the power of God."

The problem is not that God is not speaking; it is that we are not aware or listening in a way that produces glad obedience, to go do acts of faith. We are lost in the now and not what could be because of Jesus. What Wigglesworth was really saying is that if your soul is so distracted and lost in large and small offenses, so you cannot hear Holy Spirit to glad obedience, then grab hold of the Word of God and stir yourself up, much like a coach in a half-time locker room, to a team that is losing, and get excited in God, who dwells within you, to think and act like He would.

Here is a simple prayer from our book, *Battle Prayer for Divine Healing, Field Manual 2*. For more information please go to www.CovenantPeaceMinistries.com. The words are not as important as the intent, and who is speaking–you speak for God, and many have used this as a way to get started.

Use this prayer to become that Gateway of *agape*/love that God paid such a high price for in our Redemption through the blood of Jesus, because He *agape*/loves us all.

Father, in the name of Jesus, I/we thank You this is already done. And, Father, in the name of Jesus, right now, (*Person's name*), I speak to the devil and take authority over you and bind you to obey me, in the name of Jesus. I speak to this (*Problem area*), and I speak to your body, (*Person's name*), and I say, in the name of Jesus Christ of Nazareth, the Lord of Heaven and Earth, that RIGHT NOW all works of (*Problem*) will GO, (*infection and disease will die*), and none of this will ever return. Any pain, I break you, command you to go and never return. In the name of Jesus, fear of this (*disease, problem and/or pain*) will leave and never return, RIGHT NOW, in the name of JESUS. (*Person*), you will be absolutely healed and normal, you and your body will operate normally, you will do all things well and normally, and you will be a testimony to God. In the name of Jesus, so be it! RECEIVE, NOW, in the name of Jesus of Nazareth, by His blood and His stripes. Amen! So be it!

Or simply: "Freedom, in the name of JESUS! Amen!"

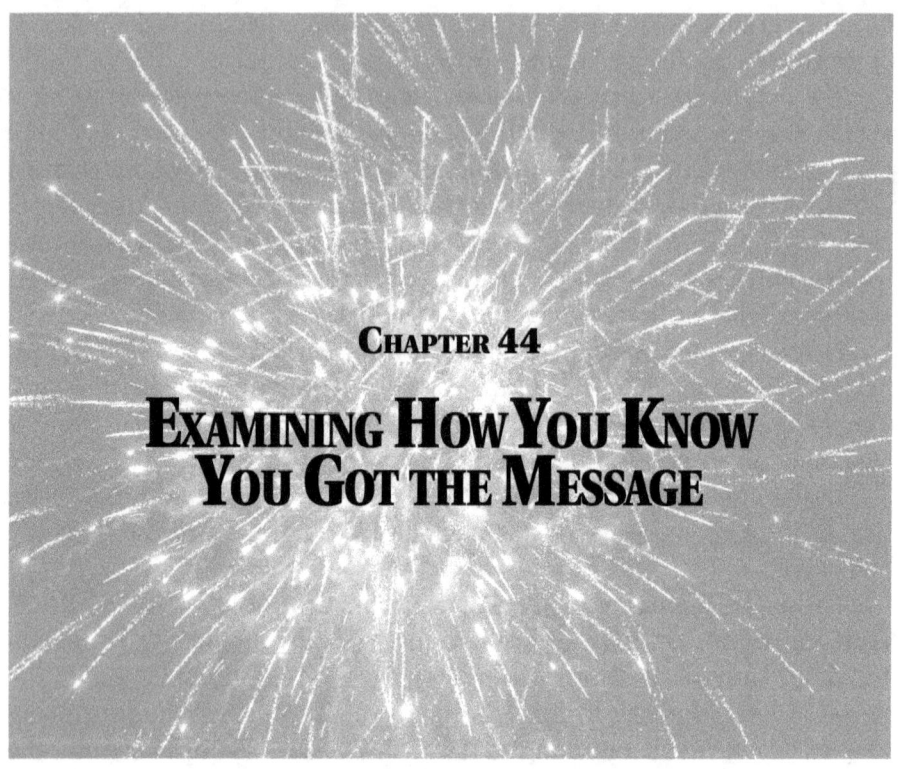

Chapter 44

Examining How You Know You Got the Message

This revelation, in detail, is part of the unique contribution of Paul to the understanding of the things of God. It is no wonder Paul gave this great praise: Eph 3:20 "Now unto him that is able to do exceeding abundantly above all that we *aiteo*/ask (*require, demand and expect as due by covenant promise*) or think (*imagine, visualize*), according to the power that worketh in us, 21 unto him be glory in the church by Christ Jesus throughout all ages, world without end. Amen."

[*Aiteo* is a Greek word often translated in the KJV as "ask" and "desire." It means to ask or require of a superior who made a promise based on requirements, and the requirements have now been met, so the superior is to deliver that which was promised. Thus, alternate meanings include "require," "demand," and "expect." God has stated: Isa 45:11 "Thus saith the Lord, the Holy One of Israel, and his Maker, Ask (*require and demand*) me of things to come concerning my sons, and concerning the work of my hands command ye me." Here the Old Testament word translated as *ask* also includes "require" and "demand: in its meaning.]

As we understand this great work, the effect should be: Ps 107:1 "O give thanks unto the Lord, for he is good: for his *chesed*/mercy endureth for ever. 2 Let the redeemed of the Lord say so, whom he hath redeemed from the hand of the enemy."

EXAMINING HOW YOU KNOW YOU GOT THE MESSAGE

God says the response of your understanding is proper if you are: Col 1:12 "Giving thanks (*continually*) unto the Father, which hath made us meet (*fully qualified and empowered by grace*) to be partakers of the inheritance of the saints in light: 13 who hath delivered us from the power of darkness, and hath translated us into the kingdom of his *agape*/dear Son: 14 in whom we have redemption through his blood, even the forgiveness (*remission, obliteration and putting off*) of sins: 15 who is the image of the invisible God, the firstborn of every creature: 16 for by him were all things created, that are in heaven, and that are in earth, visible and invisible, whether they be thrones, or dominions, or principalities, or powers: all things were created by him, and for him: 17 and he is before all things, and by him all things consist. 18 and he is the head of the body, the church: who is the beginning, the firstborn from the dead; that in all things he might have the preeminence. 19 For it pleased the Father that in him should all fulness dwell; 20 and, having made peace through the blood of his cross, by him to reconcile all things unto himself; by him, I say, whether they be things in earth, or things in heaven."

If you are not continually thankful, these verses state that you have yet to understand what Jesus accomplished in His great work by the cross. That work, as revealed in the Scriptures, is so great it boggles or numbs the mind. As Kenneth Wuest states in his translation, because of the limitations of our language: 2 Cor 4:7 "But we have this treasure [the reflection of the light of the knowledge of the glory of God in the face of Christ] in earthenware containers, in order that the **super-excellence** of the *dunamis*/power might be from God as a source and not from us." KSW

Again, the KJV states it this way: Eph 1:5 "Having predestinated us unto the adoption of children by Jesus Christ to himself, according to the good pleasure of his will, 6 to the praise of the glory of his grace, wherein he hath made us accepted in the *agape*/beloved. 7 In whom we have redemption through his blood, the forgiveness (*remission*) of sins, according to the riches of his grace; 8 wherein he hath **abounded** (*AMP: super-abounded*) toward us in all wisdom and prudence."

God also calls it the "Reconciliation," and the news of it is so great that men have a hard time receiving it, and must be continually challenged to keep it in mind, not because it is so hard, but because it is so wonderful. This is the challenge of God's spiritual knowledge and economy to flesh or natural man's knowledge and economy. Who can handle the immensity of the power of the work of the Mighty Arm of God in His great work by the cross of Jesus Christ?

Isa 53:1 "Who hath believed our report? and to whom is the arm of the Lord revealed?"

2 Cor 5:14 "For the *agape*/love of Christ constraineth us; because we thus judge, that if one died for all, then were all dead: 15 and that he died for all, that they which *zao*/live should not henceforth *zao*/live unto themselves, but unto him

DISCOVERING OUR REDEMPTION

which died for them, and rose again. 16 Wherefore henceforth know we no man after the flesh: yea, though we have known Christ after the flesh, yet now henceforth know we him no more. 17 Therefore if any man be in Christ, he is a new creature: old things are passed away; behold, all things are become new. 18 And all things are of God, who hath reconciled us to himself by Jesus Christ, and hath given to us the ministry of reconciliation; 19 to wit, that God was in Christ, reconciling the world unto himself, not imputing their trespasses unto them; and hath committed unto us the word of reconciliation.

"20 Now then we are ambassadors for Christ, as though God did beseech you by us: we pray you in Christ's stead, be ye reconciled to God. 21 For he hath made him to be sin for us, who knew no sin; that we might be made the righteousness of God in him. 6:1 We then, as workers together with him, beseech you also that ye receive not the grace of God in vain. 2 (For he saith, I have heard thee in a time accepted, and in the day of *soteria*/salvation have I succoured thee: behold, now is the accepted time; behold, now is the day of *soteria*/salvation.)"

This is the time and day we are in now, the time and day of the Salvation of God.

From Peter, we have another command to keep this in remembrance and a warning that without labor, we will lose it. 2 Pet 1:12 "Wherefore I will not be negligent to put you always in remembrance of these things, though ye know them, and be established in the present truth *[of our Redemption in the blood of Jesus]*. 13 Yea, I think it meet, as long as I am in this tabernacle, to stir you up by putting you in remembrance; 14 knowing that shortly I must put off this my tabernacle, even as our Lord Jesus Christ hath shewed me. 15 Moreover I will endeavour that ye may be able after my decease to have these things always in remembrance. 16 For we have not followed cunningly devised fables, when we made known unto you the power and coming of our Lord Jesus Christ, but were eyewitnesses of his majesty. 17 For he received from God the Father honour and glory, when there came such a voice to him from the excellent glory, This is my *agape*/beloved Son, in whom I am well pleased."

So the four signs that you got the message are:
- Continual thanksgiving
- Continual stirring of yourself into remembrance, so you also walk in continual thanksgiving and manifestation of "good works"
- Stirring up other Christians to walk in continual thanksgiving and manifestation of "good works"
- Continually renewing your mind in the Word of Christ in the New Testament, to not let these truths drift away from their power

This is what the Scriptures define as the way to know you got the message of our Redemption.

EXAMINING HOW YOU KNOW YOU GOT THE MESSAGE

As you look at this list, take a look at your life. Which actions are you continually doing now, and which action do you need to increase? What things are you doing now that need to decrease, so you can prepare yourself to be doing these things that reflect a proper understanding of what God did in Jesus by the cross? What are you now planning to do?

> Isa 11:9 ... For the earth shall be full of the knowledge of the Lord, as the waters cover the sea.

Part VII

The Conclusion

CHAPTER 45

SOME CONCLUDING THOUGHTS

God long ago promised: Isa 44:22 "I have blotted out, as a thick cloud, thy transgressions, and, as a cloud, thy sins: return unto me; for I have redeemed thee." Yet, notice, in the midst of this glorious declaration, God cries, "return unto me."

This sounds much like: 2 Cor 5:18 "And all things are of God, who hath reconciled us to himself by Jesus Christ, and hath given to us the ministry of reconciliation; 19 to wit, that God was in Christ, reconciling the world unto himself, not imputing their trespasses unto them; and hath committed unto us the word of reconciliation. 20 Now then we are ambassadors for Christ, as though God did beseech you by us: we pray you in Christ's stead, be ye reconciled to God. 21 For he hath made him to be sin for us, who knew no sin; that we might be made the righteousness of God in him. 6:1 We then, as workers together with him, beseech you also that ye receive not the grace of God in vain. 2 (For he saith, I have heard thee in a time accepted, and in the day of *soteria*/salvation have I succoured thee: behold, now is the accepted time; behold, now is the day of *soteria*/salvation.)"

Even though He had done a mighty work of Redemption, who will heed it and take it to heart? Sin had never been the real issue; what has been the issue is who will come to the Lord? God has made the way. He has removed sin and the curse of sin for all mankind, through the body, soul, spirit and blood of Jesus, His

DISCOVERING OUR REDEMPTION

beloved Son. As we come to Him through Jesus, He will give us His Salvation, to be manifested in the Earth.

Isa 53:1 "Who hath believed our report? and to whom is the arm of the Lord revealed?" Who will come to God's great work of Redemption and hear what He says? If you have read this far, He is calling you, He is speaking to you, and He wants you to know the love He has for you and placed within you in your new birth, unto the righteousness of God in Christ Jesus, the moment you believed that God raised Jesus from the dead.

It is not enough to know it merely as academic fact. For that, there are many great books and study programs. No, it is not just the facts that release you into that which you truly are, an *agape*/love warrior of God's peace, who preaches and demonstrates the Word of God's peace, just like Jesus did. Only the reality of the facts in your soul can accomplish that: Acts 10:36 "The word which God sent unto the children of Israel, preaching peace by Jesus Christ: (he is Lord of all:) 37 that word, I say, ye know, which was published throughout all Judaea, and began from Galilee, after the baptism which John preached; 38 how God anointed Jesus of Nazareth with the Holy Ghost and with power: who went about doing good, and healing all that were oppressed (*under the active dominion, reign or lordship*) of the devil; for God was with him."

The challenge of the Bible is that it is God speaking to us. Put it in your mouth, and it becomes God speaking through you. We have an expression, "What God is trying to say … ." This is very dangerous. It is fine to say of humans that we are tying to say something, but God speaks in the manner He has chosen, and we have to ask Him for help to understand it. Every verse in the Scriptures is a request from God to come to Him and learn from Him.

Right knowledge of God's work in Redemption is to cause you to be: Col 1:12 "giving thanks (*continually*) unto the Father, which hath made us meet (*qualified, empowered and enabled*) to be partakers of the inheritance of the saints in light [*by operating in faith in God, by His Word*]: 13 who hath delivered us from the power of darkness, and hath translated us into the kingdom of his *agape*/dear Son: 14 in whom we have redemption through his blood, even the forgiveness (*remission, removal, purging, obliteration and putting away*) of sins: 15 who is the image of the invisible God, the firstborn of every creature: 16 for by him were all things created, that are in heaven, and that are in earth, visible and invisible, whether they be thrones, or dominions, or principalities, or powers: all things were created by him, and for him: 17 and he is before all things, and by him all things consist."

If this does not cause you thanksgiving, praise and joy, to jumping up and dancing, then you have missed the message, and it does not change God's laws, but there is something in your heart that either was never built or has gotten corrupted.

Some Concluding Thoughts

God's lament is that: "My people are destroyed for lack of knowledge." We are destroyed, operating in less than Heaven on Earth in any part of life, but, instead, experiencing the devil's cruel rule. This evil subjugation is not because of a lack of anointing, impartation or anything else. It is a lack of the Word of God mixed into our hearts, unto glad obedience. Hos 4:6 "My people are destroyed for lack of knowledge: because thou hast rejected knowledge, I will also reject thee, that thou shalt be no priest to me: seeing thou hast forgotten the law of thy God, I will also forget thy children."

These are strong words, but the reality is that Redemption is God's Great Work, planned from before the foundation of the Earth was laid, and made at the price of unimaginable suffering and battle by Jesus for you. God places tremendous value on each one of us, but you must make the sacrifice of Christ yours by renewing your mind.

Jesus came in the flesh, and yet He was not received. His response was not, "Well, I guess I need a different message," or "I need to say it a different way." Instead, He said: Matt 13:15 "For this people's heart is waxed gross, and their ears are dull of hearing, and their eyes they have closed; lest at any time they should see with their eyes, and hear with their ears, and should understand with their heart, and should be converted, and I should heal them."

Jesus came to heal, but the people of His day would not or could not hear Him, because their hearts were not prepared to hear unto glad obedience. This is still the message for today: Heb 1:1 "In many separate revelations [each of which set forth a portion of the Truth] and in different ways God spoke of old to [our] forefathers in and by the prophets, 2 [But] in the last of these days He has spoken to us in [the person of a] Son, Whom He appointed Heir and lawful Owner of all things, also by and through Whom He created the worlds (*Universe*) and the reaches of space and the ages of time [He made, produced, built, operated, and arranged them in order]. 3 He is the sole expression of the glory of God [the Light-being, the out-raying or radiance of the divine], and He is the perfect imprint and very image of [God's] nature, upholding and maintaining and guiding and propelling the universe by His mighty word of power. When He had by offering Himself accomplished our cleansing of sins and riddance of guilt, He sat down at the right hand of the divine Majesty on high, 4 [Taking a place and rank by which] He Himself became as much superior to angels as the glorious Name (title) which He has inherited is different from and more excellent than theirs. 5 For to which of the angels did [God] ever say, You are My Son, today I have begotten You [established You in an official Sonship relation, with kingly dignity (*when God raised Jesus from the dead*)]? And again, I will be to Him a Father, and He will be to Me a Son? [2 Sam 7:14; Ps 2:7.]" AMP

Their healing was there, but they missed hearing Jesus speak. Instead, they listened to the devil, like Adam and Eve did, the devil who continually says it is

DISCOVERING OUR REDEMPTION

God's fault. God gave the message, in the life of Jesus, before, during and after the cross, and by Holy Spirit, who today is still giving the message He has chosen to give, because any other message is not how you are built. It is humbling to think that God holds us accountable for what He has said, regardless of:
- Whether we ever heard it or not
- Whether we did or did not understand it
- Whether we lost what we had or not

If this book has not done its job, then you read this as simple information, to be put on a shelf, have a theological debate or get a seminary degree. If you read this in awe and trembling, then we did a better job in getting the message of the Scriptures across.

If, when you have read this, you walk in signs and wonders, because you now have the message of grace in our Redemption that God can confirm, and you are walking in *agape*/love because you got the revelation of how *agape*/loved you are, then we did the job of the Gospel.

We do not claim any special expertise, which is why this book has so much scripture in it. The issue is: "What is God saying?" This is a fear-and-trembling word to Christians: Heb 4:6 "Seeing therefore it remaineth that some must enter therein, and they to whom it was first preached entered not in because of unbelief (*unpersuadableness, believing a different word, lack of confidence and offense toward God, so you make Him a liar*): 7 again, he limiteth a certain day, saying in David, To day, after so long a time; as it is said, To day if ye will hear his voice, harden not your hearts. 8 For if Jesus (*Joshua of the Old Testament*) had given them rest, then would he not afterward have spoken of another day. 9 There remaineth therefore a rest to the people of God. 10 For he that is entered into his rest, he also hath ceased from his own works, as God did from his. 11 Let us labour therefore to enter into that rest, lest any man fall after the same example of unbelief (*unpersuadableness, believing a different word, lack of confidence and offense toward God, so you make Him a liar*). 12 For the word of God is quick, and powerful, and sharper than any twoedged sword, piercing even to the dividing asunder of (*psuche*) soul and spirit, and of the joints and marrow, and is a discerner of the thoughts and intents of the heart. 13 Neither is there any creature that is not manifest in his sight: but all things are naked and opened unto the eyes of him with whom we have to do."

Here is the message we have been given: 2 Cor 5:19 "To wit, that God was in Christ, reconciling the world unto himself, not imputing their trespasses unto them; and hath committed unto us the word of reconciliation. 20 Now then we are ambassadors for Christ, as though God did beseech you by us: we pray (*beg*) you in Christ's stead, be ye reconciled to God. 21 For he hath made him to be sin for us, who knew no sin; that we might be made the righteousness of God in him. 6:1 We then, as workers together with him, beseech you also that ye receive not the grace

Some Concluding Thoughts

of God in vain. 2 (For he saith, I have heard thee in a time accepted, and in the day of *soteria*/salvation have I succoured thee: behold, now is the accepted time; behold, now is the day of *soteria*/salvation.)"

As verses 6:1-2 clearly state, it is so different, so wonderful that we can miss it or not hold on to it effectively, to bring the Kingdom of God to Earth, as did Jesus. John 20:21 "Then said Jesus to them again, Peace be unto you: as my Father hath sent me, even so send I you."

We are not to do less than Jesus, but MORE! John 14:10 "Believest thou not that I (*Jesus*) am in the Father, and the Father in me? the words that I speak unto you I speak not of myself: but the Father that dwelleth in me, he doeth the works. 11 Believe me that I am in the Father, and the Father in me: or else believe me for the very works' sake. 12 Verily, verily, I say unto you, He that believeth on me, the works that I do shall he do also; and greater works than these shall he do; because I go unto my Father. 13 And whatsoever ye shall *aiteo*/ask (*require, demand and expect as due by covenant promise*) in my name, that will I do, that the Father may be glorified in the Son. 14 If ye shall *aiteo*/ask (*require, demand and expect as due by covenant promise*) any thing in my name, I will do it. 15 If ye *agape*/love me, keep my commandments."

If you can receive it, John 14:10-14 is His commandment and is included in: 1 John 3:23 "And this is his commandment, That we should believe on the name of his Son Jesus Christ, and *agape*/love one another, as he gave us commandment."

The Bible is your "special word." Many look for special verbal words, yet we have the written and unchanging covenant contract of God with man in the Bible. In a court of law, the written agreement codifies the intent of the relationship, and so does the Bible. At the end of the day, it is the Word of God that will give you the faith to walk in this so Great Salvation. Rom 10:2 "For I (*Paul*) bear them (*the Jews*) record that they have a zeal of God, but not according to knowledge. 3 For they being ignorant of God's righteousness, and going about to establish their own righteousness, have not submitted themselves unto the righteousness of God. 4 For Christ is the end of the law for righteousness to every one that believeth. 5 For Moses describeth the righteousness which is of the law, That the man which doeth those things shall *zao*/live by them. 6 But the righteousness which is of faith speaketh on this wise, Say not in thine heart, Who shall ascend into heaven? (that is, to bring Christ down from above:) 7 Or, Who shall descend into the deep? (that is, to bring up Christ again from the dead.) 8 But what saith it? The word is nigh thee, even in thy mouth, and in thy heart: that is, the word of faith, which we preach; 9 that if thou shalt confess (*agree that it is truth*) with thy mouth the Lord Jesus, and shalt believe in thine heart that God hath raised him from the dead, thou shalt be *sozo*/saved. 10 For with the heart man believeth unto righteousness; and with the mouth confession is made unto *soteria*/salvation. 11 For the scripture saith, Whoso-

DISCOVERING OUR REDEMPTION

ever believeth on him shall not be ashamed. 12 For there is no difference between the Jew and the Greek: for the same Lord over all is rich unto all that call upon him. 13 For whosoever shall call upon the name of the Lord shall be *sozo*/saved. 14 How then shall they call on him in whom they have not believed? and how shall they believe in him of whom they have not heard? and how shall they hear without a preacher? 15 And how shall they preach, except they be sent? as it is written, How beautiful are the feet of them that preach the gospel of peace, and bring glad tidings of good things! 16 But they have not all obeyed the gospel. For Esaias saith, Lord, who hath believed our report? 17 So then faith cometh by hearing, and hearing by the word of God (*in Christ*)."

What is this Word we are to hear unto obedience? Gal 2:21 "I do not frustrate the grace of God: for if righteousness come by the law, then Christ is dead in vain." 2 Cor 5:18 "And all things are of God, who hath reconciled us to himself by Jesus Christ, and hath given to us the ministry of reconciliation; 19 to wit, that God was in Christ, reconciling the world unto himself, not imputing their trespasses unto them; and hath committed unto us the word of reconciliation. 20 Now then we are ambassadors for Christ, as though God did beseech you by us: we pray you in Christ's stead, be ye reconciled to God. 21 For he hath made him to be sin for us, who knew no sin; that we might be made the righteousness of God in him. 6:1 We then, as workers together with him, beseech you also that ye receive not the grace of God in vain. 2 (For he saith, I have heard thee in a time accepted, and in the day of *soteria*/salvation have I succoured thee: behold, now is the accepted time; behold, now is the day of *soteria*/salvation.)"

The good news of God is that the reign of God, the Kingdom of God, is now in the Day of His Salvation and, thus, judgment against the devil. Rom 5:14 "Nevertheless death reigned (*as king*) from Adam to Moses, even over them that had not sinned after the similitude of Adam's transgression, who is the figure of him that was to come. 15 But not as the offence, so also is the free gift. For if through the offence of one (*Adam*) many be dead, much more the grace of God, and the gift by grace, which is by one man, Jesus Christ, hath abounded unto many. 16 And not as it was by one that sinned, so is the gift: for the judgment was by one to condemnation, but the free gift is of many offences unto justification. 17 For if by one man's offence death reigned (*as king*) by one; much more they which (*continually*) *lambano*/receive abundance of grace and of the *permanent* gift of righteousness shall reign (*as kings*) in *zoe*/life by one, Jesus Christ.) 18 Therefore as by the offence of one judgment came upon all men to condemnation; even so by the righteousness of one the free *and permanent* gift came upon all men unto justification of *zoe*/life [Rom 11:29 "*For the gifts and calling of God are without repentance.*"]. 19 For as by one man's disobedience many were made sinners, so by the obedience of one shall many be made righteous. 20 Moreover the law entered, that the offence might abound. But

Some Concluding Thoughts

where sin abounded, grace did much more abound: 21 that as sin hath reigned (*as king*) unto death, even so might grace reign (*as king*) through righteousness unto eternal *zoe*/life by Jesus Christ our Lord."

What will these kings of grace and righteousness do for Jesus? Rom 16:20 "And the God of peace shall bruise (*crush*) Satan under your feet shortly (*as shattered glass*). The grace of our Lord Jesus Christ be with you [*to think, believe, know, be and do this*]. Amen."

To those who wanted a dead man to come back and tell the living of the truth of God, Jesus said, Luke 16:31 "And he (*Jesus*) said unto him, If they hear not Moses and the prophets, neither will they be persuaded, though one rose from the dead." Jesus' answer is that if you will not search to know God in the Scriptures, to believe Him, in the Bible, even if a man came back from the dead, you would not believe what that man said.

To those who knew Jesus as a boy from Nazareth and struggled to believe that this one, whom they had known all His life, was the Messiah, the one who would redeem Israel, Jesus declared Himself: John 6:43 "Jesus therefore answered and said unto them, Murmur not among yourselves. 44 No man can come to me, except the Father which hath sent me draw him: and I will raise him up at the last day. 45 It is written in the prophets, And they shall be all taught of God. Every man therefore that hath heard, and hath learned of the Father, cometh unto me. 46 Not that any man hath seen the Father, save he which is of God, he hath seen the Father. 47 Verily, verily, I say unto you, He that believeth on me hath everlasting *zoe*/life. 48 I am that bread of *zoe*/life. 49 Your fathers did eat manna in the wilderness, and are dead. 50 This is the bread which cometh down from heaven, that a man may eat thereof, and not die. 51 I am the *zao*/living bread which came down from heaven: if any man eat of this bread, he shall *zao*/live for ever: and the bread that I will give is my flesh, which I will give for the *zoe*/life of the world."

It is the same today. We may have been around the Scriptures all our lives, yet we do not know our Redemption in such a way that releases the Salvation of God into the Earth, including our hearts. The way to know it is when a hospital is a rare thing in our land, because we, His disciples, have taught the world how to live and establish the divine health of God in His Kingdom. Matt 10:7 "And as ye go, preach, saying, The kingdom of heaven is at hand. 8 Heal the sick, cleanse the lepers, raise the dead, cast out devils: freely ye have received, freely give."

God declares His Word is alive and powerful, yet we have plenty of evidence that you can memorize the Scriptures and die a mere man. What is the difference? Jesus' answer is for us to come to the Word of God and ask God to make it alive to us and to let us walk in the *zoe* life that is in Jesus, and *aiteo* demand, as due by covenant promise, that He will teach us of Himself, what He has done in the great work of His Mighty Arm.

DISCOVERING OUR REDEMPTION

Isa 45:11 "Thus saith the Lord, the Holy One of Israel, and his Maker, Ask (*require and demand*) me of things to come concerning my sons, and concerning the work of my hands command ye me." It is up to us to demand of God that He teach us of Himself. John 6:45 "It is written in the prophets, And they shall be all taught of God. Every man therefore that hath heard, and hath learned of the Father, cometh unto me (*Jesus*)."

Like the Jews of Jesus' day, you may have been around the Scriptures all your life, yet the secret belongs to those who take those Scriptures and let themselves be taught of God. This is not just the all-powerful and distant God, but the God who is their loving Father. It is you who must stay in the Word of God. Prov 4:20 "My son (*or daughter*), attend to my words; incline thine ear unto my sayings. 21 Let them not depart from thine eyes; keep them in the midst of thine heart. 22 For they are life unto those that find them, and health to all their flesh. 23 Keep thy heart with all diligence; for out of it are the issues of life. 24 Put away from thee a froward mouth, and perverse lips put far from thee. 25 Let thine eyes look right on, and let thine eyelids look straight before thee. 26 Ponder the path of thy feet, and let all thy ways be established. 27 Turn not to the right hand nor to the left: remove thy foot from evil. 5:1 My son (*or daughter*), attend unto my wisdom, and bow thine ear to my understanding."

Mark 12:24 "And Jesus answering said unto them, Do ye not therefore err, because ye know not the scriptures, neither the power of God?"

Or, as God said to the people in the desert (and to us again) in the book of Hebrews: Heb 4:7 "… To day if ye will hear his voice, harden not your hearts."

Here is such an ancient prayer: Ps 119:4 "Thou hast commanded us to keep thy precepts diligently. 5 O that my ways were directed to keep thy statutes! 6 Then shall I not be ashamed, when I have respect unto all thy commandments. 7 I will praise thee with uprightness of heart, when I shall have learned thy righteous judgments. … 17 Deal bountifully with thy servant, that I may live, and keep thy word. 18 Open thou mine eyes, that I may behold wondrous things out of thy law. … 33 Teach me, O Lord, the way of thy statutes; and I shall keep it unto the end. 34 Give me understanding, and I shall keep thy law; yea, I shall observe it with my whole heart. 35 Make me to go in the path of thy commandments; for therein do I delight. 36 Incline my heart unto thy testimonies, and not to covetousness. 37 Turn away mine eyes from beholding vanity; and quicken thou me in thy way. 38 Stablish thy word unto thy servant, who is devoted to thy fear."

It sounds harsh to many modern ears, yet the ancient path is still the right path. Change the evil culture of the lack of the true knowledge of God in your own home, your city, your state and even your nation by praying out loud at least half the psalms every day and spending at least an hour a day in the New Testament. Make sure you include at least 30 minutes reading out loud the Gospels, looking at

Some Concluding Thoughts

Jesus, as the exact revelation of the nature and character of God, and your example on how you will imitate God, per Eph 5:1 "Be ye therefore followers (*imitators, copycats*) of God as *agape*/dear children (*sons*)."

It takes about 4 hours to pray out loud all the psalms (1 through 150), and about 2 hours to pray out loud half of them (1 through 75 or 76 through 150). As you do this, trust God to teach you. This becomes a lifestyle. It may start as a project, but as the Word works into you, it will become your very life. Heb 4:11 **"Let us labour therefore to enter into that rest**, lest any man fall after the same example of unbelief (*unpersuadableness, who did not work to make the Word of God persuade them, to glad obedience*)." It is very simple: no right labor equals no right results.

There is not more anointing to seek, nor more impartation. The anointing is in the Word of God, and the impartation is when the Word of God becomes your rule for thought, motive, words and action. Acts 10:34 "Then Peter opened his mouth, and said, Of a truth I perceive that God is no respecter of persons: 35 But in every nation he that feareth him, and worketh righteousness, is accepted with him."

If you are waiting for a flash of lightening to open your eyes, look no further. While that is possible, it is not the typical way a tender heart responds to God. Go to the Word of God in the New Testament revelation of God's Redemption and there learn of your Redemption. Make it go from academic facts to life transformation. The secret of Christianity is in being what God has made you. Heb 3:16 "For some, when they had heard, did provoke: howbeit not all that came out of Egypt by Moses (*in that great Redemption*). 17 But with whom was he grieved forty years [*after that great Redemption*]? was it not with them that had sinned, whose carcases fell in the wilderness? 18 And to whom sware he that they should not enter into his rest, but to them that believed not (*who did not work to make the Word of God persuade them, to glad obedience*)? 19 So we see that they could not enter in because of unbelief (*in failure to work to make the Word of God persuade them, to glad obedience*). 4:1 Let us therefore fear, lest, a promise being left us of entering into his rest, any of you should seem to come short of it. 2 For unto us was the gospel preached, as well as unto them: but the word preached did not profit them, not being mixed with faith in them that heard it (*in failure to work to make the Word of God persuade them, to glad obedience and fearless confidence in God by His Word*)."

You will get flashes of revelation and great insights. Try the spirit behind them, per 1 John 4:1-3 (see pages 313-316), and enjoy them when they are from God. But remember, we have been commanded to make renewing and keeping renewed our mind into the Word of Christ as our life effort: Rom 12:2 "And be not conformed (*molded, shaped and fitted under constant pressure*) to this world: but be ye transformed (*shaped and kept shaped into the reflection of your new-creation self*) by the (*continual*) renewing of your mind, that ye may prove what is that good, and acceptable, and perfect, will of God."

DISCOVERING OUR REDEMPTION

Eph 4:20 "But ye have not so learned Christ; 21 If so be that ye have heard him, and have been taught by him, as the truth is in Jesus: 22 that ye put off concerning the former conversation the old man, which is corrupt according to the deceitful lusts; 23 and be renewed in the spirit of your mind (*in your self-identity and lifestyle*); 24 and that ye put on the new man (*just like Jesus has*), which after God is created in righteousness and true holiness."

Col 3:8 "But now ye also put off all these; anger, wrath, malice, blasphemy, filthy communication out of your mouth. 9 Lie not one to another, seeing that ye have put off the old man with his deeds (*in the new creation*); 10 And have put on the new man, which is renewed in *epignosis*/knowledge (*unto doing as a master craftsman*) after the image of him that created him (*in the new birth/creation*): 11 where there is neither Greek nor Jew, circumcision nor uncircumcision, Barbarian, Scythian, bond nor free: but Christ is all, and in all. 12 Put on therefore, as the elect of God, holy and *agape*/beloved, bowels of mercies, kindness, humbleness of mind, meekness, longsuffering; 13 forbearing one another, and forgiving one another, if any man have a quarrel against any: even as Christ forgave you, so also do ye. 14 And above all these things put on *agape*/charity, which is the bond of perfectness. 15 And let the peace of God rule in your hearts, to the which also ye are called in one body; and be ye thankful. 16 Let the word of Christ dwell in you richly in all wisdom; teaching and admonishing one another in psalms and hymns and spiritual songs, singing with grace in your hearts to the Lord. 17 And whatsoever ye do in word or deed, do all in the name of the Lord Jesus, giving thanks to God and the Father by him."

Rom 13:10 "*Agape*/love worketh no ill to his neighbour: therefore *agape*/love is the fulfilling of the law. 11 And that, knowing the time, that now is high time to awake out of sleep: for now is our *soteria*/salvation nearer than when we believed. 12 The night is far spent, the day is at hand: let us therefore cast off the works of darkness, and let us put on the armour of light. 13 Let us walk honestly, as in the day; not in rioting and drunkenness, not in chambering and wantonness, not in strife and envying. 14 But put ye on the Lord Jesus Christ (*as your new self identity and life-style*), and make not provision for the flesh, to fulfil the lusts thereof."

Wash yourself with His Word of His great Redemption in Jesus until your heart rejoices in His so Great Salvation. To those who do this, then: Heb 4:9 "There remaineth therefore a rest to the people of God. 10 For he that is entered into his rest, he also hath ceased from his own works, as God did from his. 11 **Let us labour** (*in mixing the Word of God into our hearts, to persuade ourselves that God can do it in and through us, because of the great work of Jesus*) **therefore to enter into that rest**, lest any man fall after the same example of unbelief (*unpersuadableness, who did not work to make the Word of God persuade them, to glad obedience*). 12 For (*to those who do work to make the Word of God persuade them, to glad obedience*) the word of

Some Concluding Thoughts

God is quick, and powerful, and sharper than any twoedged sword, piercing even to the dividing asunder of soul and spirit, and of the joints and marrow, and is a discerner of the thoughts and intents of the heart. 13 Neither is there any creature that is not manifest in his sight: but all things are naked and opened unto the eyes of him with whom we have to do. 14 Seeing then that we have a great high priest, that is passed into the heavens, Jesus the Son of God, let us hold fast our profession. 15 For we have not an high priest which cannot be touched with the feeling of our infirmities; but was in all points tempted like as we are, yet without sin. 16 Let us therefore come boldly unto the throne of grace, that we may *lambano*/obtain (*hold on to it, knowing we already have*) mercy, and find (*perceive, so it changes our lives*) grace to help in time of need."

We are redeemed! The more we understand this, the more we will be: Col 1:12 "giving thanks (*continually*) unto the Father, which hath made us meet to be partakers of the inheritance of the saints in light: 13 who hath delivered us from the power of darkness, and hath translated us into the kingdom of his *agape*/dear Son: 14 in whom we have redemption through his blood, even the *aphesis*/forgiveness (*remission, purging, obliteration, washing, removal and putting away*) of sins."

As this truth takes hold of you, you will find the Word of God a source of life. You will watch yourself looking eagerly to get into the Scriptures and receive life. Your mouth will change, and you will include thanksgivings, affirmations and confessions of God's truth for yourself, as did Paul: Gal 2:20 "I am (*have been*) crucified with Christ: nevertheless I *zao*/live; yet not I, but Christ *zao*/liveth in me: and the life which I now *zao*/live in the flesh I *zao*/live by the faith of the Son of God, who *agape*/loved me, and gave himself for me. 21 I do not frustrate the grace of God: for if righteousness come by the law, then Christ is dead in vain."

Or, as did David: Ps 23:1 "The LORD is my shepherd, I shall not want ... ."

If you are diligent in daily labor with the Word of God, by tithing at least 10 percent of your 24-hour day (or 2.4 hours per day), you will begin to see this start to rise in you within the first 60 to 120 days or so. Your attitude will become: 1 Cor 15:55 "O death, where is thy sting? O grave, where is thy victory? 56 The sting of death is sin; and the strength of sin is the law. 57 But thanks be to God, which giveth us the victory through our Lord Jesus Christ. 58 Therefore, my *agape*/beloved brethren, be ye stedfast, unmoveable, always abounding in the work of the Lord, forasmuch as ye know that your labour is not in vain in the Lord."

Sadly, the reverse is also true. We are living creatures, which means we are always growing in one direction or another. Men and women who are weak in faith or had it once and lost it:

- Have stopped feeding on the Word of God and stopped enjoying intimate time with God over the Scriptures
- Have reduced or stopped their thanksgiving, praise, joy and prayer

DISCOVERING OUR REDEMPTION

- Have stopped making affirmations and confessions of themselves in God's Salvation in Jesus.

And, if they are not doing these things of God, they are doing other things, and that only leaves the things of the devil's world system to fill their thoughts, words and actions. Prov 18:20 "A man's belly shall be satisfied with the fruit of his mouth; and with the increase of his lips shall he be filled. 21 Death and life are in the power of the tongue: and they that love it shall eat the fruit thereof." It's your tongue, and you choose whose words you fill it with.

We are commanded: Col 3:14 "And above all these things put on *agape*/charity, which is the bond of perfectness. 15 And let the peace of God rule in your hearts, to the which also ye are called in one body; and be ye thankful. 16 Let the word of Christ dwell in you richly in all wisdom; teaching and admonishing one another in psalms and hymns and spiritual songs, singing with grace in your hearts to the Lord. 17 And whatsoever ye do in word or deed, do all in the name of the Lord Jesus, giving thanks to God and the Father by him."

Every moment of every day we are ingesting into our hearts facts and attitudes of one kind or another. If you are not taking in God's eternal truth in Jesus, you are taking in the devil's temporary vanity of momentary facts or conditions that will be destroyed on the Day of Judgment. If you are not actively mixing in the Word of Christ, you are mixing in the devil's lies that you do not have the mighty Redemption of God in Jesus for you to use to bring His Salvation to Earth at every point of need.

Words are also eating and drinking, so whose words are you living on? John 10:10 "The thief cometh not, but for to steal, and to kill, and to destroy: I am come that they might have *zoe*/life, and that they might have it more abundantly."

Matt 4:4 "But he (*Jesus*) answered and said, It is written, Man shall not *zao*/live by bread alone, but by every *rhema*/word (*that you do*) that proceedeth out of the mouth of God."

John 8:31 "Then said Jesus to those Jews which believed on him, If ye continue in my word, then are ye my disciples indeed; 32 and ye shall know the truth, and the truth shall make you free (*to think, know, be and do all God has created you for*)."

John 15:7 "If ye abide in me, and my words abide in you, ye shall *aiteo*/ask (*require, demand and expect as due by covenant promise, knowing all the requirements have been met in Jesus*) what ye will, and it shall be done unto you. 8 Herein is my Father glorified, that ye bear much fruit; so shall ye be my disciples."

Just as sure as God redeemed Israel from Egypt under Moses for a physical redemption, we have both a spiritual and a physical Redemption by the blood of Jesus. Deut 7:8 "But because the LORD loved you, and because he would keep the oath which he had sworn unto your fathers, hath the Lord brought you out with a mighty hand, and redeemed you out of the house of bondmen, from the hand of Pharaoh king of Egypt."

Some Concluding Thoughts

Every time we see Pharaoh's army swallowed up in the Red See, we see Jesus: Col 2:15 "And having spoiled principalities and powers, he made a shew of them openly, triumphing over them in it."

Jesus got the job done. We have the full spiritual Redemption now, and when Jesus returns and God sets up His footstool on Earth, per Revelation chapters 21 and 22, we will have the consummation of our wedding day. In the meantime, we, the Bride, now deliver His Salvation by our acts of faith working by *agape*/love, as we prepare ourselves for that great wedding day, the consummation of our Redemption. Rev 19:6 "And I heard as it were the voice of a great multitude, and as the voice of many waters, and as the voice of mighty thunderings, saying, Alleluia: for the Lord God omnipotent reigneth. 7 Let us be glad and rejoice, and give honour to him: for the marriage of the Lamb is come, and his wife hath made herself ready. 8 And to her was granted that she should be arrayed in fine linen, clean and white: for the fine linen is the righteousness of saints."

We have a commission from Jesus to bring Heaven to Earth now, by faith, working by *agape*/love: Matt 28:18 "And Jesus came and spake unto them, saying, All power is given unto me in heaven and in earth. 19 Go ye therefore, and teach all nations, baptizing them in the name of the Father, and of the Son, and of the Holy Ghost: 20 teaching them to observe all things whatsoever I have commanded you: and, lo, I am with you alway, even unto the end of the world. Amen."

The legal basis for our Redemption unto Salvation was laid from that Passover of crucifixion to the 50^h day of Pentecost, when Jesus sent Holy Spirit and sat down 2000 years ago. Heb 10:12 "But this man (*Jesus*), after he had offered one sacrifice for sins for ever, sat down on the right hand of God; 13 from henceforth expecting till his enemies be made his footstool."

Jesus started His great work at that Passover meal where He instituted the Lord's Supper, as a covenant remembrance meal for us, a betrothal with His Bride, in the bread and the wine, to commemorate His great work, to identify Himself with mankind, and to receive healing and blessing for His great propitiation for our sins and healing from the curse of sin. On the same day (as the Jews count days starting at one sunset and going to the following sunset) He suffered, shed His redeeming blood, died for all men and went to Hell as the damned of the damned, to win our freedom.

1 Cor 15:3 "For I (*Paul*) delivered unto you first of all that which I also received, how that Christ died for our sins according to the scriptures; 4 and that he was buried, and that he rose again the third day according to the scriptures: 5 and that he was seen of Cephas, then of the twelve: 6 after that, he was seen of above five hundred brethren at once; of whom the greater part remain unto this present, but some are fallen asleep. 7 After that, he was seen of James; then of all the apostles. 8 And last of all he was seen of me (*Paul*) also, as of one born out of due time."

DISCOVERING OUR REDEMPTION

Jesus remained from the 3rd day until the 43rd day, teaching the disciples. Then at the end of 40 days of teaching He ascended to His Father and our God. Then 7 days later, on the 50th day, He sent the promised Holy Spirit to birth the new Church with new-born, new-creation men and women. Acts 1:1 "The former treatise have I made, O Theophilus, of all that Jesus began both to do and teach, 2 Until the day in which he was taken up, after that he through the Holy Ghost had given commandments unto the apostles whom he had chosen: 3 to whom also he shewed himself alive after his passion by many infallible proofs, being seen of them forty days, and speaking of the things pertaining to the kingdom of God: 4 and, being assembled together with them, commanded them that they should not depart from Jerusalem, but wait for the promise of the Father, which, saith he, ye have heard of me. 5 For John truly baptized with water; but ye shall be baptized with the Holy Ghost not many days hence. 6 When they therefore were come together, they asked of him, saying, Lord, wilt thou at this time restore again the kingdom to Israel? 7 And he said unto them, It is not for you to know the times or the seasons, which the Father hath put in his own power. 8 But ye shall receive *dunamis*/power (*ability*), after that the Holy Ghost is come upon you: and ye shall be witnesses unto me both in Jerusalem, and in all Judaea, and in Samaria, and unto the uttermost part of the earth. 9 And when he had spoken these things, while they beheld, he was taken up; and a cloud received him out of their sight. 10 And while they looked stedfastly toward heaven as he went up, behold, two men stood by them in white apparel; 11 which also said, Ye men of Galilee, why stand ye gazing up into heaven? This same Jesus, which is taken up from you into heaven, shall so come in like manner as ye have seen him go into heaven."

No man could become the righteousness of God, to be born again, until Jesus rose from the dead. Gal 2:21 "I do not frustrate the grace of God: for if righteousness come by the law, then Christ is dead in vain."

Rom 4:24 "But for us also, to whom it (*the righteousness of God in Christ Jesus*) shall be imputed, if we believe on him that raised up Jesus our Lord from the dead; 25 who was delivered for our offences, and was raised again for our justification (*or when we were justified*)."

Father God is making His enemies His footstool through and by the Church now: Eph 3:9 "And to make all men see what is the fellowship of the mystery, which from the beginning of the world hath been hid in God, who created all things by Jesus Christ: 10 to the intent that now unto the principalities and powers in heavenly places might be known by the church the manifold wisdom of God,"

Rom 16:20 "And the God of peace shall bruise (*crush*) Satan under your feet shortly (*as shattered glass*). The grace of our Lord Jesus Christ be with you (*to think, know, be and do this*). Amen."

Some Concluding Thoughts

God has given the Christian His Holy Spirit to enable us to accomplish our job of manifesting His great Salvation in bringing Heaven to Earth: 2 Tim 1:7 "For God hath not given us the spirit of fear; but of *dunamis*/power (*God's wonder working ability*), and of *agape*/love, and of a sound mind (*to operate just like Jesus in the mind of Christ*)."

Jesus made the renewed covenant by and in His blood. Heb 10:14 "For by one offering he (*Jesus*) hath perfected for ever them that are sanctified. 15 Whereof the Holy Ghost also is a witness to us: for after that he had said before, 16 this is the covenant that I will make with them after those days, saith the Lord, I will put my laws into their hearts, and in their minds will I write them; 17 and their sins and iniquities will I remember no more. 18 Now where remission of these is, there is no more offering for sin. 19 Having therefore, brethren, boldness to enter into the holiest by the blood of Jesus, 20 by a new and *zao*/living way, which he hath consecrated for us, through the veil, that is to say, his flesh; 21 and having an high priest over the house of God; 22 let us draw near with a true heart in full assurance of faith, having our hearts sprinkled from an evil conscience, and our bodies washed with pure water."

Jesus bore our sins, sicknesses, and pains and took the chastisement for our peace, so that man never has to bear them ever again. Isa 53:4 "Surely he hath *nasa*/borne our griefs (*and infirmities*), and *cabal*/carried our sorrows (*pains and sicknesses*): yet we did esteem him stricken, smitten of God, and afflicted. 5 But he was wounded for our transgressions, he was bruised for our iniquities: the chastisement of our peace was upon him; and with his stripes we are healed. 6 All we like sheep have gone astray; we have turned every one to his own way; and the Lord hath laid on him the iniquity of us all."

We are redeemed from sin and the curse of sin. Gal 3:13 "Christ hath redeemed us from the curse of the law, being made a curse for us: for it is written, Cursed is every one that hangeth on a tree: 14 that the blessing of Abraham might come on the Gentiles through Jesus Christ; that we might receive the promise of the Spirit through faith."

When these Redemption truths really gain the ascendancy in us, they will make us spiritual supermen, masters of evil circumstances, demons and diseases, warriors of the *agape*/love of God.

By His blood we have remission of sins, freedom from the curse of the law, open access to God anytime in His throne room, peace with God, overcoming ability over the devil, and Jesus as our High Priest and King. This is our Redemption by His blood, and that blood is more than sufficient.

This is an unveiling of what we are in Christ, how the Father sees us in the Son.

It will be the end of weakness and failure. There will be no more struggles for faith, for all things are ours, and we have written this Redemption into our hearts with diligence.

DISCOVERING OUR REDEMPTION

There will be no more praying for power; we will finally believe unto being zealous for good works, in faith, working by *agape*/love, that He is in us and wants out through us, for this is why we were created. 2 Cor 4:5 "For we preach not ourselves, but Christ Jesus the Lord; and ourselves your servants for Jesus' sake. 6 For God, who commanded the light to shine out of darkness, hath shined in our hearts, to give the light of the knowledge of the glory of God in the face of Jesus Christ. 7 But we have this treasure in earthen vessels, that the excellency of the *dunamis*/power may be of God, and not of us."

We already have all the power there is, Holy Spirit dwelling in us.

We know that no matter what, God in us makes us greater than any situation we find ourselves in.

Gal 4:4 "But when the fulness of the time was come, God sent forth his Son, made of a woman, made under the law, 5 to redeem them that were under the law, that we might receive the adoption of sons. 6 And because ye are sons, God hath sent forth the Spirit of his Son into your hearts, crying, Abba, (*Daddy*) Father."

There will no longer be the awful bondage of sin-consciousness, for we are the Righteousness of God in Christ.

There is no more crying for forgiveness for we know it was given 2000 years ago.

Eph 1:7 "(*Jesus*) in whom we have redemption through his blood, the *aphesis*/forgiveness (*remission, obliteration and putting off*) of sins, according to the riches of his grace."

We no longer cry for what we already have in Christ.

We may cry out for how to use it better and *agape*/love God and people better, but we give thanks for what we already have, to make our faith effectual, to drive that knowledge deep into our hearts. Philem 6 "That the communication of thy faith may become effectual by the *epignosis*/acknowledging of every good thing which is in you in Christ Jesus."

We are learning to see ourselves though God's eyes and not the eyes of fallen man. Col 3:1 "If ye then be risen with Christ, seek those things which are above, where Christ sitteth on the right hand of God. 2 Set your affection on things above, not on things on the earth. 3 For ye are dead, and your *zoe*/life is hid with Christ in God."

We are learning to see our value and potential to God, by the price He paid for us in Jesus. Rom 5:8 "But God commendeth his *agape*/love toward us, in that, while we were yet sinners, Christ died for us. 9 Much more then, being now justified by his blood, we shall be *sozo*/saved from wrath through him. 10 For if, when we were enemies, we were reconciled to God by the death of his Son, much more, being reconciled, we shall be saved by his *zoe*/life. 11 And not only so, but we also joy in God through our Lord Jesus Christ, by whom we have now received the atonement (*reconciliation*)."

Some Concluding Thoughts

Notice, in verse 11, that when we *lambano*/receive our Reconciliation in Christ, we will walk in joy and not the so-called "silent" joy. This is not what this word means. Rather, it means a contained explosion. Dancing, shouting, yelling, arm waving, screaming and running are the signs of this kind of joy. You have two choices:
- You can read this book until you experience it
- You can do the action of joy, while proclaiming these truths until you do feel it.

We have gotten wise now; we major on knowing these new-creation truths.

Rom 13:14 "But put ye on the Lord Jesus Christ, and make not provision for the flesh, to fulfil the lusts thereof."

The first lust is to say it cannot be true, and that is the first lust you make no provision for.

We know what we are in Christ.

We know Christ is in us.

We rightly judge the body and blood of Jesus.

We do not let offense of any kind rule in us. Unforgiveness is our hated enemy.

Any attitude of resentment, fault-finding, irritation, strife, etc. we root out of ourselves, and when we see them in others, we show them mercy and set them free from the oppressions of the devil.

Gal 6:4 "But let every man prove (*examine and judge*) his own work, and then shall he have rejoicing in himself alone, and not in another."

John 3:19 "And this is the condemnation, that light is come into the world, and men *agape*/loved darkness rather than light, because their deeds were evil. 20 For every one that doeth evil hateth the light, neither cometh to the light, lest his deeds should be reproved. 21 But he that doeth truth cometh to the light, that his deeds may be made manifest, that they are wrought in God."

We judge ourselves freely in communion at the Lord's Table, so we are not judged by the devil, that we do not know of our Redemption in Jesus' blood, and healing in Jesus' body. 1 Cor 11:27 "Wherefore whosoever shall eat this bread, and drink this cup of the Lord, unworthily, shall be guilty of the body and blood of the Lord. 28 But let a man examine himself, and so let him eat of that bread, and drink of that cup. 29 For he that eateth and drinketh unworthily, eateth and drinketh damnation to himself, not discerning the Lord's body. 30 For this cause many are weak and sickly among you, and many sleep. 31 For if we would judge ourselves, we should not be judged. 32 But when we are judged, we are chastened of the Lord, that we should not be condemned with the world."

We are not afraid of our sins; instead, we eagerly seek them out and root them out and get healing for them, knowing that: Isa 53:4 "Surely he (*Jesus*) hath *cabal*/borne our griefs, and *nasa*/carried our sorrows: yet we did esteem him stricken, smitten of God, and afflicted. 5 But he was wounded for our transgressions, he was

DISCOVERING OUR REDEMPTION

bruised for our iniquities: the chastisement of our peace was upon him; and with his stripes we are healed."

We know God's goal for us is that we prosper and be in health in our souls, to be just like Jesus.

This knowledge fills us with the joyful expectation of coming good, now, in this life, and eternally with Him.

Eph 4:22 "That ye put off concerning the former conversation the old man, which is corrupt according to the deceitful lusts; 23 and be renewed in the spirit of your mind; 24 and that ye put on the new man, which after God is created in righteousness and true holiness."

We make our identity in Christ our only identity. We no longer identify with sin or failure.

We are transformed by hope and deliver it, by faith in Him, who is *agape*/love.

We are the beloved, for whom God gladly paid such a price.

John 3:16 "For God so *agape*/loved the world, that he gave his only begotten Son, that whosoever believeth in him should not perish, but have everlasting *zoe*/life. 17 For God sent not his Son into the world to condemn the world; but that the world through him might be *sozo*/saved."

We know that He dwells in us.

We are in the family, no longer orphans, lonely and selfish, fearful and depraved.

We cry with Jesus: "Our Father!"and "Daddy!"

Matt 7:11 "If ye then, being evil, know how to give good gifts unto your children, how much more shall your Father which is in heaven give good things to them that *aiteo*/ask (*require, demand and expect as due by covenant promise of*) him?"

We cry with Holy Spirit, "Abba, Daddy! Father!"

We know the authority of His name.

We know His name releases the power in the Word of God, and the devil and his works must bow at that wonderful name of Jesus Christ of Nazareth, once a carpenter but now, Lord of Lords and King of Kings.

We know that when Jesus defeated the devil and made an open show of him, the devil was commanded to obey, in the name of Jesus.

Col 2:13 "And you, being dead in your sins and the uncircumcision of your flesh, hath he quickened together with him, having forgiven you all trespasses; 14 blotting out the handwriting of ordinances that was against us, which was contrary to us, and took it out of the way, nailing it to his cross; 15 and having spoiled principalities and powers, he made a shew of them openly, triumphing over them in it."

The prince of this world has been judged against and defeated by the Prince of *Zoe*/Life.

Some Concluding Thoughts

Matt 28:18 "And Jesus came and spake unto them, saying, All power is given unto me in heaven and in earth."

Rom 14:11 "For it is written, As I *zao*/live, saith the Lord, every knee shall bow to me, and every tongue shall confess to God."

Phil 2:9 "Wherefore God also hath highly exalted him, and given him a name which is above every name: 10 that at the name of Jesus every knee should bow, of things in heaven, and things in earth, and things under the earth; 11 and that every tongue should confess that Jesus Christ is Lord, to the glory of God the Father."

We are now experts at using that name of Jesus to bring salvation to Earth for any need.

Acts 4:12 "Neither is there *soteria*/salvation in any other: for there is none other name under heaven given among men, whereby we must be *sozo*/saved."

We don't debate; we simply lay hands on the sick, so Jesus heals them, and let that be our response to debate.

And we see this prayer answered every day: Acts 4:29 "And now, Lord, behold their threatenings: and grant unto thy servants, that with all boldness they may speak thy word, 30 by stretching forth thine hand to heal; and that signs and wonders may be done by the name of thy holy child Jesus."

Your confidence grows as you put your trust in Him: 2 Cor 5:18 "And all things are of God, who hath reconciled us to himself by Jesus Christ, and hath given to us the ministry of reconciliation; 19 to wit, that God was in Christ, reconciling the world unto himself, not imputing their trespasses unto them; and hath committed unto us the word of reconciliation. 20 Now then we are ambassadors for Christ, as though God did beseech you by us: we pray you in Christ's stead, be ye reconciled to God. 21 For he hath made him to be sin for us, who knew no sin; that we might be made the righteousness of God in him. 6:1 We then, as workers together with him, beseech you also that ye receive not the grace of God in vain. 2 (For he saith, I have heard thee in a time accepted, and in the day of *soteria*/salvation have I succoured thee: behold, now is the accepted time; behold, now is the day of *soteria*/salvation.)"

We keep ourselves stirred up and encouraged in our confidence in Him by His Word and long, hard, loud and fast speaking and singing in tongues.

We don't seek just exuberant emotion, no matter how much fun, but have also learned how to rise in the spirit with the Word of God, with Holy Spirit, to keep ourselves stirred up into His power, *agape*/love and the mind of Christ. We cooperate with Holy Spirit, to walk in Righteousness, Peace, Joy, Mercy, Grace, Truth, New Birth, Identification, Adoption, Betrothal, Reconciliation and Redemption. We no longer settle for mere human emotion, but have learned how to live in and by His Spirit.

John 4:23 "But the hour cometh, and now is, when the true worshippers shall worship the Father in spirit and in truth: for the Father seeketh such to worship

DISCOVERING OUR REDEMPTION

him. 24 God is a Spirit: and they that worship him must worship him in spirit and in truth."

As Jesus said: John 17:17 "*(Father,)* sanctify them through thy truth: thy word is truth."

James 1:17 "Every good gift and every perfect gift is from above, and cometh down from the Father of lights, with whom is no variableness, neither shadow of turning. 18 Of his own will begat he us with the word of truth, that we should be a kind of firstfruits of his creatures."

John 6:63 "It is the spirit that quickeneth; the flesh profiteth nothing: the words that I speak unto you, they are spirit, and they are *zoe*/life."

We are God-inside minded. We are walking- and living-scripture minded. We are the-God-of-the-Scriptures minded.

We are no longer orphans; we have arrived in a family that can never leave us. We have an adoption that can never be revoked.

Gal 4:4 "But when the fulness of the time was come, God sent forth his Son, made of a woman, made under the law, 5 to redeem them that were under the law, that we might receive the adoption of sons. 6 And because ye are sons, God hath sent forth the Spirit of his Son into your hearts, crying, Abba *(Daddy),* Father."

1 Cor 2:16 "For who hath known the mind of the Lord, that he may instruct him? But we have the mind of Christ."

Rom 5:5 "And hope maketh not ashamed; because the *agape*/love of God is shed abroad in our hearts by the Holy Ghost which is given unto us. 6 For when we were yet without strength, in due time Christ died for the ungodly."

We have His ability.
We have His wisdom.
We have His love.
We know we are loved.
We are made of His love.
We are made to love, and the more we know of this love the more we become like Him.

Eph 3:16 "That he would grant you, according to the riches of his glory, to be strengthened with might by his Spirit in the inner man; 17 that Christ may dwell in your hearts by faith; that ye, being rooted and grounded in *agape*/love, 18 may be able to comprehend with all saints what is the breadth, and length, and depth, and height; 19 and to know the *agape*/love of Christ, which passeth knowledge, that ye might be filled with all the fulness of God."

We know the story of Redemption is the story of God's so great love to us.

1 John 3:16 "Hereby perceive we the *agape*/love of God, because he laid down his *psuche*/life *(soul)* for us: and we ought to lay down our *psuche*/lives *(souls)* for the brethren."

Some Concluding Thoughts

Rom 5:7 "For scarcely for a righteous man will one die: yet peradventure for a good man some would even dare to die. 8 But God commendeth his *agape*/love toward us, in that, while we were yet sinners, Christ died for us. 9 Much more then, being now justified by his blood, we shall be *sozo*/saved from wrath through him. 10 For if, when we were enemies, we were reconciled to God by the death of his Son, much more, being reconciled, we shall be *sozo*/saved by his *zoe*/life. 11 And not only so, but we also joy in God through our Lord Jesus Christ, by whom we have now received the atonement (*reconciliation*).

Rev 5:9 "And they sung a new song, saying, Thou art worthy to take the book, and to open the seals thereof: for thou wast slain, and hast redeemed us to God by thy blood out of every kindred, and tongue, and people, and nation; 10 and hast made us unto our God kings and priests: and we shall reign on the earth (*to establish and maintain the Kingdom of God for Jesus*)."

We are His Righteousness.

He lives in us.

He planned it so we will be with Him forever.

We are seated with Him on His throne.

Eph 2:4 "But God, who is rich in mercy, for his great *agape*/love wherewith he *agape*/loved us, 5 even when we were dead in sins, hath quickened us together with Christ, (by grace ye are *sozo*/saved;) 6 and hath raised us up together, and made us sit together in heavenly places in Christ Jesus."

His lordship is a reality. Jesus is Lord.

His Word is present tense to our hearts.

The darker it gets, the more we focus on His Word, His promises, His *agape*/love and His joy.

We have learned how to tell others of our troubles. 2 Cor 1:8 "For we would not, brethren, have you ignorant of our trouble which came to us in Asia, that we were pressed out of measure, above strength, insomuch that we despaired even of life: 9 but we had the sentence of death in ourselves, that we should not trust in ourselves, but in God which raiseth the dead: 10 who delivered us from so great a death, and doth deliver: in whom we trust (*by doing those faith actions of thanksgiving, praise, joy, affirmations and confession*) that he will yet deliver us."

We call those things of His Word that are not yet, to be, until they are.

2 Cor 4:17 "For our light affliction, which is but for a moment, worketh for us a far more exceeding and eternal weight of glory; 18 while we look not at the things which are seen, but at the things which are not seen: for the things which are seen are temporal; but the things which are not seen are eternal."

We have a standing invitation to His throne room.

We are invited to come boldly into His presence.

DISCOVERING OUR REDEMPTION

Eph 2:13 "But now in Christ Jesus ye who sometimes were far off are made nigh by the blood of Christ."

Eph 3:12 "In whom we have boldness and access with confidence by the faith of him."

Heb 10:19 "Having therefore, brethren, boldness to enter into the holiest by the blood of Jesus, 20 by a new and *zao*/living way, which he hath consecrated for us, through the veil, that is to say, his flesh; 21 and having an high priest over the house of God; 22 let us draw near with a true heart in full assurance of faith, having our hearts sprinkled from an evil conscience, and our bodies washed with pure water. 23 Let us hold fast the profession of our faith without wavering; (for he is faithful that promised;) 24 and let us consider one another to provoke unto *agape*/love and to good works: 25 not forsaking the assembling of ourselves together, as the manner of some is; but exhorting one another: and so much the more, as ye see the day approaching."

We spend time with Him, discovering His plans for the future and enjoying His love today for us and through us.

We are seated with Him in Heaven.

He is with us on Earth. Heb 13:5 "... for he hath said, I will never leave thee, nor forsake thee."

In the presence of these tremendous realities, we arise and take our place. We go out and live as supermen, indwelt by God.

Rom 8:37 "Nay, in all these things we are more than conquerors through him that *agape*/loved us."

Ps 107:1 "O give thanks unto the Lord, for he is good: for his *chesed*/mercy endureth for ever. 2 Let the redeemed of the Lord say so, whom he hath redeemed from the hand of the enemy."

Col 1:12 "Giving thanks (*continually*) unto the Father, which hath made us meet to be partakers of the inheritance of the saints in light: 13 who hath delivered us (*Jew and Gentile*) from the power of darkness, and hath translated us into the kingdom of his *agape*/dear Son: 14 in whom we have redemption through his blood, even the forgiveness (*remission, obliteration, removal and putting away*) of sins."

Isa 51:11 "Therefore the redeemed of the Lord shall return, and come with singing unto Zion; and everlasting joy shall be upon their head: they shall obtain gladness and joy; and sorrow and mourning shall flee away."

Jer 31:11 "For the Lord hath redeemed Jacob, and ransomed him from the hand of him that was stronger than he. 12 Therefore they shall come and sing in the height of Zion, and shall flow together to the goodness of the Lord, for wheat, and for wine, and for oil, and for the young of the flock and of the herd: and their soul shall be as a watered garden; and they shall not sorrow any more at all."

Some Concluding Thoughts

Rev 5:9 "And they sung a new song, saying, Thou (*Jesus, the Lamb of God*) art worthy to take the book, and to open the seals thereof: for thou wast slain, and hast redeemed us to God by thy blood out of every kindred, and tongue, and people, and nation; 10 and hast made us unto our God kings and priests: and we shall reign on the earth (*to establish and maintain the Kingdom of God on Earth for Jesus*)."

Here is how we are to do it:

Rom 5:16 "And not as it was by one that sinned, so is the gift: for the judgment was by one to condemnation, but the free gift is of many offences unto justification. 17 For if by one man's offence death reigned (*as king, to enforce the law of sin and death, to corruption of the entire world*) by one; much more they which (*continually*) *lambano*/receive abundance of grace and of the *permanent* gift of righteousness shall reign (*as kings with Jesus Christ, to bring the Kingdom of God to Earth in their lifetimes, by crushing the works of darkness and death*) in zoe/life by one, Jesus Christ.) [Rom 11:29 "For the gifts and calling of God are without repentance."]18 Therefore as by the offence of one judgment came upon all men to condemnation; even so by the righteousness of one the (*permanent*) free gift came upon all men unto justification of zoe/life. 19 For as by one man's disobedience many were made sinners, so by the obedience of one shall many be made (*permanently*) righteous. 20 Moreover the law entered, that the offence might abound. But where sin abounded, grace did much more abound: 21 that as sin hath reigned (*as a cruel and merciless king*) unto death, even so might grace reign (*in faith, working by* agape *love, mercy, grace and truth, bring the Kingdom of God to Earth, by crushing the oppressions of the devil everywhere and anywhere they are*) through righteousness unto eternal zoe/life by Jesus Christ our Lord."

We are experts at keeping ourselves stirred up in the Spirit of God's wonderful Salvation truth in our Redemption unto Reconciliation by the remission of sins and the curse of sin by the blood of Jesus along with long, loud, hard and fast tongues.

We know we are God's sons by permanent adoption, sealed by Holy Spirit unto the Day of Redemption, and the apple of His eye.

We know Jesus is in us and wants to deliver the Kingdom of God through us.

We know we have an eternal Salvation reserved for us in Heaven for that last Day.

We can bring portions of that Salvation to Earth, in our lives and in the lives of others, now.

We know we have a destiny that is the dream of the ages.

We know we are loved, and faith in God, by His Word, will overcome anything.

We are the devil's master, to his fear, whenever we move in God's faith, hope and *agape*/love.

We know, unto bold and righteous confidence, that greater is He that is in us than he that is in the world.

DISCOVERING OUR REDEMPTION

We are men's servants, setting them free and encouraging them in the Lord.

God's power by us is released, knowing we are, by grace, the righteousness of God in Christ Jesus, and not by how well we do right.

We know that giving salvation to others, by Holy Spirit power, is grace, and receiving the manifested Holy Spirit salvation is also by grace.

Eph 2:4 "But God, who is rich in mercy, for his great *agape*/love wherewith he *agape*/loved us, 5 even when we were dead in sins, hath quickened us together with Christ, (by grace ye are *sozo*/saved (*made whole, delivered, bondages broken, unto the free reign of the* agape/love *of God in His Kingdom*);) 6 and hath raised us up together, and made us sit together in heavenly places in Christ Jesus: 7 that in the ages to come he might shew the exceeding riches of his grace in his kindness toward us through Christ Jesus. 8 For by grace are ye *sozo*/saved (*made whole, delivered, bondages broken, unto the free reign of the* agape/love *of God in His Kingdom*) through faith; and that not of yourselves: it is the gift of God: 9 not of works, lest any man should boast. 10 For we are his workmanship, created in Christ Jesus unto good works, which God hath before ordained that we should walk in them."

Yes, we have salvation in the sweet bye and bye, but we can also have as much of that salvation, being made whole, healing, prosperity, blessing, abundance and victory, as we will believe God for now.

We are so busy doing the "do's" that we don't have time to do the "do nots."

We reign for Jesus, by holding on to that grace, in spite of our failures, sins or present conditions.

We know that, because of the Redemption in the blood of Jesus, there is no sin so great as to stop it, and it is from God, so there is nothing we can do to deserve it.

We are experts at knowing we are redeemed by the blood of Jesus.

We are experts at knowing that the blood of Jesus, the Son of God, is more than sufficient.

We are experts at giving and receiving by grace.

We are experts at knowing we are the righteousness of God in Christ Jesus by grace.

We are experts rooting out evil fear by obeying: Phil 4:4 "Rejoice in the Lord alway: and again I say, Rejoice. 5 Let your moderation be known unto all men. The Lord is at hand. 6 Be careful (*anxious, fearful, fretful, irritable or terrorized*) for nothing; but in every thing by prayer and supplication with (*loud, boisterous, and continual*) thanksgiving let your *aiteo*/requests (*requirements, demands and expectations per His covenant promises*) be made known unto God. 7 And the peace of God, which passeth all understanding, shall keep your hearts and minds through Christ Jesus. 8 Finally, brethren, whatsoever things are **true**, whatsoever things are **honest**, whatsoever things are **just**, whatsoever things are **pure**, whatsoever things are **lovely**, whatsoever things are of **good report**; if there be any **virtue**, and if there be

Some Concluding Thoughts

any **praise**, think on these things. 9 Those things, which ye have both learned, and received, and heard, and seen in me *(Paul)*, do: and the God of peace *(who brings His overcoming and Heaven-creating power as we believe Him)* shall be with you."

As we grow in the Lord and actually walk in righteousness more and more, we join with Paul in continually crying: Phil 3:8 "Yea doubtless, and I count all things but loss for the excellency of the *ginosko*/knowledge of Christ Jesus my Lord: for whom I have suffered the loss of all things, and do count them but dung, that I may win Christ, 9 and be found in him, not having mine own righteousness, which is of the law, but that which is through the faith of Christ, the righteousness which is of God by faith."

We are experts in the *agape*/love of God.

We are experts at showing others how *agape*/loved they are.

We are experts at keeping ourselves in the *agape*/love of God.

We are experts in delivering Holy Spirit salvation, by grace, in the name of Jesus, through faith that works by *agape*/love in *dunamis*/power.

We know we were chosen for this time. We are not accidents; we were chosen by God for this time. And you, too, have things in you that you were created to deliver in your time. God has a plan for you that can only be fulfilled with you in Jesus and Jesus in you, with you working together with Him for your time. By His grace, you also are expert at working with Him, by His Word, to think, know, be and do what you are made for in Jesus.

This wonder of the ages is only fully released when you are made a new creation. Eph 2:8 "For by grace are ye *sozo*/saved *(from any and all limitations, for you not to be just like Jesus in position and action)* through faith; and that not of yourselves: it is the gift of God: 9 not of works, lest any man should boast. 10 For we are his workmanship, created in Christ Jesus unto good works, which God hath before ordained that we should walk in them."

You walk in confidence, knowing: 1 John 4:4 "Ye are of God, *(one of His)* little children, and have overcome them: because greater is he that is in you, than he that is in the world."

The works you are created for are bigger than your natural man, or any natural man. Phil 4:13 "I can do all things through Christ *who* strengtheneth me."

The devil is committed to keeping you in the flesh mind, like a "mere" man, to stop you.

You are an expert in bringing the Word to abundant fruit, per the parable of the sower and the seed of Matt 13, Mark 4 and Luke 8, and ever *lambanoing* the Word of the abundance of grace and the gift of righteousness, to reign as a king in *zoe*/life for, by, with, through and in Jesus.

God (who cannot lie, and it is impossible for Him to lie) is willing and able to do anything it takes, by His covenant promises in the Bible, to set you and anyone

DISCOVERING OUR REDEMPTION

you associate yourself with free of every oppression, rule, lordship and control of the devil into the Kingdom of God on Earth.

God has available everything for you, by Him, in His Word, to produce every work you are made for. God, by His Word alone, is sufficient. You only need add faith in Jesus and His work to produce the works of God.

John 6:28 "Then said they unto him, What shall we do, that we might work the works of God? 29 Jesus answered and said unto them, This is the work of God, that ye believe on him whom he hath sent."

Your potential is only limited by the imagination of God in His Word! John 15:7 "If ye abide in me *(Jesus)*, and my words abide in you, ye shall *aiteo*/ask *(require, demand and expect as due by Bible promise)* what ye will, and it shall be done unto you. 8 Herein is my Father glorified, that ye bear much fruit; so shall ye be my disciples."

Therefore, you are expert at keeping your soul renewed into the new creation, spirit man, made after the image of God, in true righteousness and holiness, just like Jesus, for the Bible tells you so.

You are expert in knowing that everything in God is produced by faith in Him, by His Word, the Bible. Heb 10:38 "Now the just *(the new-creation people)* shall *zao*/live [*bring Heaven to Earth, just like and even greater than Jesus did*] by faith: but if any man draw back, my *psuche*/soul *(life)* shall have no pleasure in him. 39 But we are not of them who draw back unto perdition; but of them that believe to the *sozo*/saving of the *psuche*/soul *(life)*."

You are an expert at renewing your mind, so that what God says in His Word is more than sufficient, no matter what comes, no matter how small or great the issues in life that find you or you are given.

You do not let the world, your 5 sense or your circumstances determine reality and what will be. For you, the Word of God is more real than the flesh and bone you live in, and you will only call things what God says they are. If it is not, you will proclaim the Word of God over the current facts with *aiteo*, thanksgiving, praise and rejoicing, in God's power, faithfulness, *agape*/love and reliability, until God changes those facts to the truth of His Word, His Holy Scriptures.

Everything or anything that can stop you from fulfilling your destiny in God, for success on the Day of Judgment, was solved by Jesus in His great work of Redemption, Atonement, Propitiation and Reconciliation. Isa 53:4 "Surely he hath *cabal*/borne our griefs, and *nasa*/carried our sorrows: yet we did esteem him stricken, smitten of God, and afflicted. 5 But he was wounded for our transgressions, he was bruised for our iniquities: the chastisement of our peace *(for anything that could stop our total success in God)* was upon him; and with his stripes we are healed *(of anything that could stop or limit our total success in God, to bring Heaven to Earth in this life)*. 6 All we like sheep have gone astray; we have turned every one to

Some Concluding Thoughts

his own way; and the Lord hath laid on him the iniquity (*anything in our life that is not just like Jesus*) of us all."

We have chosen whose report we will believe, no voice is louder than God's, and if we need to, we will shout His words until we can no longer hear any other voice! Rom 10:9 "That if thou shalt confess with thy mouth the Lord Jesus, and shalt believe in thine heart that God hath raised him from the dead, thou shalt be *sozo*/saved. 10 For with the heart man believeth unto righteousness; and with the mouth confession is made unto *soteria*/salvation. 11 For the scripture saith, Whosoever believeth on him shall not be ashamed. 12 For there is no difference between the Jew and the Greek: for the same Lord over all is rich unto all that call upon him. 13 For whosoever shall call upon the name of the Lord shall be *sozo*/saved. 14 How then shall they call on him in whom they have not believed? and how shall they believe in him of whom they have not heard? and how shall they hear without a preacher? 15 And how shall they preach, except they be sent? as it is written, How beautiful are the feet of them that preach the gospel of peace, and bring glad tidings of good things (*that God reigns is us by faith because of Jesus*)! 16 But they have not all obeyed (*believed, been persuaded by and had confidence in God in*) the gospel. For Esaias saith, Lord, who hath believed our report? 17 So then faith cometh by hearing, and hearing (*unto believing and releasing the power of God*) by the word of God (*in Christ*)."

The first and last thing (and as many times as needed in between) you will say over any situation, "Father, thank You this is already done. This is a good work You have made for me to exercise the dominion of Jesus in for You. Jesus is Lord! Jesus has suffered, died and been raised from the dead to become Lord of Heaven and Earth. Situation, get right, like Jesus wants it, and like He died and paid for. Devil, go and never return, now in the name of Jesus. *Zoe*/life of God, come and make Heaven on Earth, now, in the name of Jesus! Thank You, Father, in the name of Jesus, thank You!"

Going Forward: Settle it in your heart; Jesus has done His great work by the cross. There is more to come, but for all mankind, we now have Adoption and Redemption by the Remission of sins and the curse of sin, unto Reconciliation, unto Peace, unto Salvation, by the Propitiation of Jesus, unto the Righteousness of God in Christ Jesus, unto the *zoe*/life of God with indwelling Holy Spirit.

We enter into our Adoption, Reconciliation, Peace and Redemption by faith in the work of that holy blood of God in Jesus. Acts 20:28 "Take heed therefore unto yourselves, and to all the flock, over the which the Holy Ghost hath made you overseers, to feed the church of God, which he hath purchased with his own blood."

The greatness of this so-great Salvation boggles the mind.

James 4:6 "But he (*Father God*) giveth more grace. Wherefore he saith, God resisteth the proud, but giveth grace unto the humble. 7 Submit yourselves therefore

DISCOVERING OUR REDEMPTION

to God. Resist the devil, and he will flee from you. 8 Draw nigh to God, and he will draw nigh to you. Cleanse your hands, ye sinners; and purify your hearts, ye double minded."

2 Cor 5:20 "Now then we are ambassadors for Christ, as though God did beseech you by us: we pray you in Christ's stead, be ye reconciled to God. 21 For he hath made him to be sin for us, who knew no sin; that we might be made the righteousness of God in him. 6:1 We then, as workers together with him, beseech you also that ye receive not the grace of God in vain. 2 (For he saith, I have heard thee in a time accepted, and in the day of *soteria*/salvation have I succoured thee: behold, now is the accepted time; behold, now is the day of *soteria*/salvation.)"

Isa 52:7 "How beautiful upon the mountains are the feet of him that bringeth good tidings, that publisheth peace; that bringeth good tidings of good, that publisheth salvation; that saith unto Zion, Thy God reigneth!"

What does this Salvation, this good news, this reign of God look like?

Acts 5:16 "There came also a multitude out of the cities round about unto Jerusalem, bringing sick folks (*to the disciples*), and them which were vexed with unclean spirits: and they were healed every one."

Luke 1:37 "For with God nothing is ever impossible and no word from God shall be without power or impossible of fulfillment." AMP

Gen 18:14 "Is anything too hard for the Lord?"

Isa 52:1 "Awake, awake; put on thy strength, O Zion; put on thy beautiful garments, O Jerusalem, the holy city: for henceforth there shall no more come into thee the uncircumcised and the unclean. 2 Shake thyself from the dust; arise, and sit down, O Jerusalem: loose thyself from the bands of thy neck, O captive daughter of Zion. 3 For thus saith the Lord, Ye have sold yourselves for nought; and ye shall be redeemed without money. 4 For thus saith the Lord God, My people went down aforetime into Egypt to sojourn there; and the Assyrian oppressed them without cause. 5 Now therefore, what have I here, saith the Lord, that my people is taken away for nought? they that rule over them make them to howl, saith the Lord; and my name continually every day is blasphemed. 6 Therefore my people shall know my name: therefore they shall know in that day that I am he that doth speak: behold, it is I. 7 How beautiful upon the mountains are the feet of him that bringeth good tidings, that publisheth peace; that bringeth good tidings of good, that publisheth salvation; that saith unto Zion, Thy God reigneth!"

Rom 10:8 "But what saith it? The word is nigh thee, even in thy mouth, and in thy heart: that is, the word of faith, which we preach; 9 that if thou shalt confess with thy mouth the Lord Jesus, and shalt believe in thine heart that God hath raised him from the dead, thou shalt be *sozo*/saved (*made whole, delivered, healed and God's reign manifested*). 10 For with the heart man believeth unto righteousness; and with the mouth confession is made unto *soteria*/salvation (*made whole, delivered, healed and*

Some Concluding Thoughts

God's reign manifested). 11 For the scripture saith, Whosoever believeth on him shall not be ashamed. 12 For there is no difference between the Jew and the Greek: for the same Lord over all is rich unto all that call upon him. 13 For whosoever shall call upon the name of the Lord shall be *sozo*/saved (*made whole, delivered, healed and God's reign manifested*). 14 How then shall they call on him in whom they have not believed? and how shall they believe in him of whom they have not heard? and how shall they hear without a preacher? 15 And how shall they preach, except they be sent? as it is written, How beautiful are the feet of them that preach the gospel of peace, and bring glad tidings of good things! 16 But they have not all obeyed the gospel. For Esaias saith, Lord, who hath believed our report? 17 So then faith cometh by hearing, and hearing by the word of God (*in Christ*). 18 But I say, Have they not heard? Yes verily, their sound went into all the earth, and their words unto the ends of the world."

What does this Peace, this good news, look like?

Acts 10:34 "Then Peter opened his mouth, and said, Of a truth I perceive that God is no respecter of persons: 35 but in every nation he that feareth him, and worketh righteousness, is accepted with him. 36 The word which God sent unto the children of Israel, preaching peace by Jesus Christ: (he is Lord of all:) 37 that word, I say, ye know, which was published throughout all Judaea, and began from Galilee, after the baptism which John preached; 38 how God anointed Jesus of Nazareth with the Holy Ghost and with power: who went about doing good, and healing all that were oppressed of the devil; for God was with him. 39 And we are witnesses of all things which he did both in the land of the Jews, and in Jerusalem; whom they slew and hanged on a tree: 40 him God raised up the third day, and shewed him openly."

Rom 3:21 "But now the righteousness of God without the law is manifested, being witnessed by the law and the prophets; 22 even the righteousness of God which is by faith of Jesus Christ unto all and upon all them that believe: for there is no difference: 23 for all have sinned, and come short of the glory of God; 24 being justified freely by his grace through the redemption that is in Christ Jesus: 25 whom God hath set forth to be a propitiation through faith in his blood, to declare his righteousness for the remission of sins that are past, through the forbearance of God; 26 to declare, I say, at this time his righteousness: that he might be just, and the justifier (*and healer*) of him which believeth in Jesus."

Rom 5:8 "*For* God commendeth his *agape*/love toward us, in that, while we were yet sinners, Christ died for us. 9 Much more then, being now justified by his blood, we shall be *sozo*/saved (*made whole, delivered, healed and God's reign manifested*) from wrath through him (*on the last day, as well as from every oppression of the devil now*). 10 For if, when we were enemies, we were reconciled to God by the death of his Son, much more, being reconciled, we shall be *sozo*/saved (*made whole, delivered,*

DISCOVERING OUR REDEMPTION

limitations removed, healed and God's reign manifested) by his *zoe*/life. 11 And not only so, but we also joy in God through our Lord Jesus Christ, by whom we have now received the atonement (*and not just atonement, but propitiation unto the reconciliation of God, unto the level of God, by God*)."

Matt 25:23 "His lord said unto him, Well done, good and faithful servant; thou hast been faithful over a few things, I will make thee ruler over many things: enter thou into the joy of thy lord."

Hallelujah! Jesus got the job done! We are redeemed by His blood!

Rev 5:9 "And they sung a new song, saying, (*Jesus, the Lamb of God*) Thou art worthy to take the book, and to open the seals thereof: for thou wast slain, and hast redeemed us to God by thy blood out of every kindred, and tongue, and people, and nation; 10 and hast made us unto our God kings and priests: and we shall reign on the earth (*to establish and maintain the Kingdom of God on Earth for, through, by and with Jesus*)."

Acts 10:42 "And he (*Jesus*) commanded us to preach unto the people, and to testify that it is he which was ordained of God to be the Judge of quick and dead. 43 To him give all the prophets witness, that through his name whosoever believeth in him shall receive remission (*removal, purging, obliteration and putting away*) of sins." Ps 107:1 "O give thanks unto the Lord, for he is good: for his *chesed*/mercy (*grace*) endureth for ever. 2 Let the redeemed of the Lord say so, whom he hath redeemed from the hand of the enemy."

Shout with me: "I am redeemed from the hand of the enemy, by the blood of Jesus!" Hallelujah!

Rev 12:11 "And they overcame him (*Satan*) by the blood of the Lamb, and by the word of their testimony; and they *agape*/loved not their *psuche*/lives unto the death."

Our testimony is that we have been redeemed by the propitiation of Jesus, by faith in His blood, unto righteousness of God in Christ Jesus, into *zoe*/life, with indwelling Holy Spirit, and to the full adoption back into the family of God.

Jesus got the job done. We are reconciled back to God!

I have believed God raised Jesus from the dead; I have confessed with my mouth Jesus is Lord!

Shout with me: I am home! I have a Father who loves me beyond measure. I am *agape*/loved by God! Hallelujah!

Isa 11:9 ... For the earth shall be full of the knowledge of the Lord, as the waters cover the sea.

APPENDICES

BIBLIOGRAPHY AND RECOMMENDED READING

1. Blake, Curry, comp., *John G. Lake"s Writings from Africa* (Longwood, FL, Xulon Press: 2005)
   "Pray and pray and pray yourself into unbelief," p 99
2. Blake, Curry, *The Official Teaching of the John G. Lake Healing Rooms* (Edgewater, CO, JGLM Publishing: 2006)
   "The only hindrance to healing is that if the Christian thinks there is a hindrance to healing." p10
   "Anything between the promise of God and its fulfillment is an enemy for you to grasp, to beat and to defeat." p204
3. Blake, Curry, The Voice of Healing (KWHB Television Broadcast, Episode 2, in first 10 minutes, Tulsa OK, March 2007)
   Lake: "It is a law of the human mind that one can act themselves into believing quicker than they can believe themselves into acting."
   Wigglesworth: "If the spirit is not moving, I move the spirit."
4. Kenyon, E.W., *Identification* (Lynwood, Washington, Kenyon Gospel Publishing Society: 2004)
5. Kenyon, E.W., *Two Kinds of Righteousness* (Lynnwood, WA, Kenyon Gospel Publishing Society: 2004)
6. Liardon, Roberts, compiler and editor, *John G. Lake: The Complete Collection of His Life Teachings* (New Kensington, PA, Whitaker House: 1999)
7. Mann, Donald C. http://blog.covenantpeace.com/2013/03/30/how-many-days-from-passover-to-pentecost-when-jesus-was-crucified/
8. Robertson, A.T., *A Harmony of the Gospels for Students of the Life of Christ*, Harper, San Francisco, 1922, pp 279-291.
9. Simpson, A.B., "The Authority of Faith" (The Christian and Missionary Alliance, The Alliance Weekly, New York, New York, April 23, 1938)
10. Thomas, Robert L., and Gundry, Stanley N., *A Harmony of the Gospels*, Harper, San Francisco, 1978, reprinted in 1991, pp 320-323.
11. Wuest, Kenneth, *The New Testament, An Expanded Translation* (Grand Rapids, MI, Wm. B. Eerdmans Publishing Company: 1961)

APPENDICES

12. Wyatt, Brett, compiler and editor, *The Fire of God: Pillars of Faith, Book 1, John G. Lake in Spokane* (Spokane, WA, Riley Christian Media: 2002)

Of great help have been several other books by E.W. Kenyon:

- *The Bible in the Light of Our Redemption*, Kenyon's Gospel Publishing Society npp; 16 edition (March 1, 1989) and
- *What Happened from the Cross to the Throne*, Kenyon's Gospel Publishing Society npp (March 1, 1989)
  * Kenyon's Gospel Publishing Society, PO Box 973, Lynnwood, WA 98046-0973 1-866-743-4243, www.Kenyons.org.

Note: Much of Dr. Kenyon's writing is of the highest caliber and demonstrates much time spent with the Lord. While we all need improvement in our theology, Dr. Kenyon's books espouse that the Mosaic covenant, removed in Jesus, was also the Abrahamic covenant. This was popular Christian thinking until Israel was restored in 1948 (the same year Dr. Kenyon died), proving that the Abrahamic covenant still applies to Israel, Jews and Christians. Galatians chapter 3 makes it clear that the Abrahamic covenant was made with Christ and, thus, is still very much in force. See Galatians 3:16-17 and 29. For more on this see www.JaySnell.org for detailed explanations. For most of Dr. Kenyon's work, if you replace his wording of Abrahamic covenant with Mosaic covenant, you will improve your understanding. I believe that is one of the reasons Dr. Kenyon is not as referenced as he should be, for many modern men and women of God started or were significantly helped with his materials, as I have been. I have taught from Dr. Kenyon's materials for so many years I feel he is a good friend, and hopefully some of his unique writing style has improved mine.

Other resource also used:

Bodily Healing and the Atonement, Dr. T. J. McCrossan, re-edited by R. Hicks and K. Hagin (Tulsa, OK, Kenneth Hagin Ministries: 1982) pp 1-49)
The Blood Covenant, H. Clay Trumbull (Kirkwood, MO, Impact Books: 1975)
The Threshold Covenant, H. Clay Trumbull (Kirkwood, MO, Impact Books: 2000)

GLOSSARY CONTENTS

Agape	521
Aiteo	521
Aphesis	522
Bios	522
Cabal	522
Chesed	522
Dianoia	523
Diasozo	523
Dunamis	523
Epignosis	523
Exousia	525
Fear of God, the	525
Glory	533
Grace	535
Ginosko	536
Hugies	536
Iaomai	536
Iniquity	536
Ischus	538
Justified/Justification	538
Kainos	539
Kardia	539
Lambano	540
Leb/Lebab	540
Logos	540
Meod	541
Mercy	541
Nasa	541
Neos	541
Nephesh	541
Peace	541
Phileo	544
Phobos	544
Pneuma	544
Psuche	545
Propitiation	545
Racham	546
Redeem/Ransom	546
Rhema	547
Righteousness	549
Sin/Transgressions	555
Sozo/Soteria	556
Spirit/Soul/Body	557
Zao/Zoe	563

A GLOSSARY OF OFT-MISUNDERSTOOD BIBLICAL WORDS

These are definitions for everyday use in effective ministry. For more academic definitions, I suggest you start with *Strong's Exhaustive Concordance*. Also our books, *The Prayer Cards* and *OK, God, Now What,* have extensive discussions and Scripture references.

AGAPE

Agape (*Strong's* NT 25, pronounced: ag-ah'pay) is a Greek word (*agape*, the noun form, *agapao*, the verb form, *Strong's* NT 24) which, in the KJV, is translated as love and charity, i.e. caring in action, and has within its meaning an aggressive working for another's benefit, total good at your own expense, with no expectation of recognition, appreciation, reciprocation or honor and a desire to always be with the one loved. The definition of *charity,* love (*agape*) in 1 Corinthians 13 describes the basic nature of God and the true nature of Christians, as born-again ones, what Holy Spirit fills our hearts with, and what we are to walk in. *Agape* always is ever-ready and seeking a way to help or do the one loved good. Because *agape* has an emotional content, it is much like the best of a perfect father's and/or a perfect mother's love. John 3:16 "For God so *agape*/loved the world, that he gave his only begotten Son, that whosoever believeth in him should not perish, but have everlasting *zoe*/life. 17 For God sent not his Son into the world to condemn the world; but that the world through him might be *sozo*/saved." *Agape* means not without trouble, but one with you in all trouble. *Agape* is related to the Hebrew word *racham*. In this book, *agape* is used when other forms are the actual word to show the root.

AITEO

Aiteo (*Strong's* NT 154, pronounced: ahee-teh'-o) is the Greek word translated ask or desire in many New Testament scriptures related to prayer. It means to ask or demand of one in authority because that one made a promise based on requirements, and now the requirements have been met, so the one who promised is now to give what has been promised and desired by the one asking. It also includes the sense that you have intensity or focus in your desire to see the request fulfilled. For example: you are working on a task, and you promised your little daughter that you would take her for an ice cream cone or some other treat when you were done. You are now done and your daughter *aiteo*/demands, by saying, "You are finished. You said you would take me when you were done. You are done; please take me now." Or, in a legal sense, such as in a situation where you fell behind in your property taxes and, as authorities come to kick you out, you get the money and pay the taxes. Then you wave your paid-up receipt and *aiteo*/say, "I paid my taxes; now take your people and go!" Or you pawned an item, and now you have the money to redeem it. You *aiteo*/say, as you wave the pawn ticket, "Here is the money; give it back, now!" Even if the pawnshop owner had a better offer for that item, he must give it back to you. *Aiteo* is not a quiet or polite word in this sense. There is another sense in which you follow all the procedures, and the appropriate results will come. If you go to a bank and have the proper verification, checks, signatures and sufficient balance, you can cash a check. This is also included in the meaning of *aiteo*.

APHESIS

Aphesis (*Strong's* NT, 859, pronounced: af'-es-is) means remitted and paid for is such a way that there is no evidence of the debt ever existing, which is stronger and more complete than forgiveness.

BIOS

Bios (*Strong's* NT, 979, pronounced: bee'-os) means period of life, natural life and not just human life.

CABAL

Cabal (*Strong's* OT, 5445, pronounced: saw-bal') means to totally carry a burden that is heavy or massive so nothing is left out, strong labor, complete removal and delivery.

CHESED

Chesed (*Strong's* OT 2617, pronounced: keh'-sed) is an Old Testament word often translated in the KJV as mercy, kindness, lovingkindness, goodness or favor. It is only defined by covenant, which is stronger than a contract or modern marriage agreement, and can never be broken. It is the absolute commitment to fulfill the legal covenant conditions, even at the expense of your life, as demonstrated by what you actually do or cause to happen. It is to do good as promised, no matter what. It is only defined by action, not thoughts. The modern world has lost much of this concept, so it is hard to understand in today's Western world-view. 1 Samuel 18 shows David and Jonathan cutting a covenant, 2 Samuel 9 shows how *chesed* is implemented. In vs. 3, it is called the "*chesed*/kindness of God." It is similar to New Testament grace in concept, as grace has a legal and royal meaning.

APPENDICES

DIANOIA

Dianoia (*Strong's* NT 1271, pronounced: dee-an'-oy-ah) means deep thought, mind, understanding, visualization, imagination or the faculty of using the mind.

DIASOZO

Diasozo (*Strong's* NT, 1295, pronounced: dee-as-odze'-o) means saved, rescued, made whole, or healed totally or throughout, to cure, preserve or rescue; limitations removed totally.

DUNAMIS

Dunamis (*Strong's* NT, 1411, pronounced: doo'-nam-is) means strong capacity, continuous power, ability, miracles or acts of great power and effectiveness.

EPIGNOSIS

Epignosis (*Strong's* NT, 1922, pronounced: ep-ig'-no-sis) means full knowing and discernment so you are an expert at doing it, more than just book learning or awareness, but deep experience and superior performance, knowing completely with nothing else to learn about it or to do it in a superior manner with ease and confidence. This would be a master chef whereas *ginosko* means a chef or even one who knows about cooking, but may not cook.

The New Testament Greek root word is *ginosko* (*Strong's* NT 1097), meaning knowledge by experience and observation, experiential knowledge or full and complete knowledge or understanding. *Epignosis* (*Strong's* NT 1922) is even a deeper knowing, a knowledge that perfectly unites the person with the subject at all levels. This is the knowledge from expert, reliable and repeatable doing, not just study or a few practice efforts.

Many swim, but few are Olympic swimmers, and even fewer have gold medals. Many can read the instructions on how to make a cake. Make a few acceptable cakes, and you begin to *ginosko* cake making. It takes a master bakery chef with years of experience to make a repeatable and proper cake. This is *epignosis* (or *epiginosko*). In modern times, with our classroom and few laboratory sessions, head or basic familiarization is talked about as knowing, even to an "A" or 100% grade on a test, but it does not meet the meaning of the word *ginosko*, much less *epignosis*.

In the Bible sense, it is a knowing that unites with the *zoe*/life of God and produces "God-results" in the Earth. So whether it is a godly businessman, Samson ripping off gates to a city, or raising the dead, the knowing is only effective if God's life mixes with man's life and produces results on a repeatable or "at will" basis. So this is not the typical education process, where students can remember a few facts or get all the questions right in Sunday School, or pass a driver's classroom test.

DISCOVERING OUR REDEMPTION

Even to get a vehicle driver's license, a practical demonstration of basic skills and judgment is required. Just reading the Bible may give you familiarization, but not a personal knowledge of God.

In our modern world, where many have seen or heard about a subject and, thus, become an expert, to the Hebrew or Greek mind, mere mental recognition was of little performance value. Seeing a master musician or ballerina does not make one an expert in either. You may be an expert watcher or listener, but you are not an expert performer. So, in Christianity, until you can do at will a command or demonstrate reliably a desirable characteristic, you are not yet in the realm of *gnosis*, much less *epignosis*. For example, praying for the sick is much different than getting the sick healed by prayer.

The concept is seen in this scripture: Gen 4:1 "And Adam knew Eve his wife; and she conceived, and bare Cain, and said, I have gotten a man from the LORD." Adam and Eve probably had sex many times, but when their union produced a child it was also called "knowing." One level of knowing comes with sex, *ginosko*, but there is a deeper level of knowing when a man and woman create a child together. The first is experiential; the second produces life in union with God.

The Greek word *epignosis* is such a deep knowing, a full knowing. Eph 4:13 "Till we all come in the unity of the faith, and of the *epignosis*/knowledge of the Son of God, unto a perfect man, unto the measure of the stature of the fulness of Christ." Here this knowledge is not talking about what it takes to be born again. That is a relatively low level of agreement with God. As miraculous as it is, it is but a basic beginning. What this scripture is referring to is a "knowledge" that, when complete, you cannot tell the person as different from Jesus in their behavior or their operation in the full power of God. This is Bible "*epignosis*/knowing" and God's goal for each of us.

Here are these two concepts in the same scripture: 1 Cor 13:12 "For now we see through a glass, darkly; but then face to face: now I *gnosis*/know in part; but then shall I *epignosis*/know even as also I am *epignosis*/known." We may start at some level of *ginosko*, but the goal is to *epignosis* God. Eph 4:15 "But speaking the truth in *agape*/ love, may grow up into him in all things, which is the head, even Christ." 2 Pet 1:2 "Grace and peace be multiplied unto you through the *epignosis*/knowledge of God, and of Jesus our Lord, 3 according as his divine power hath given unto us all things that pertain unto life and godliness, through the *epignosis*/knowledge of him that hath called us to glory and virtue."

If this seems like splitting hairs, which would you rather have do a critical brain surgery on you—a medical school student, who read about it in a book, a resident brain surgeon, who has just learned the process, or a fine practicing doctor, who has done the procedure hundreds or thousands of times without failure?

The medical student has familiarization, the resident perhaps *ginosko*; and the fine practitioner has *epignosis* of the procedure and is a master craftsman.

EXOUSIA

Exousia (*Strong's* NT 1849, pronounced: ex-oo-see'-ah) means authority, right or freedom to act, commission, force, and capacity; competency to act, jurisdiction, power and strength to operate.

FEAR OF GOD, THE

The fear of God is designed to keep us from sinning (in which case the devil can try and enforce the law of sin and death, the curses, the wrath of the Law) and for men to want to do righteousness so that God's *agape*/love can fill the Earth. Job 28:28 "And unto man he said, Behold, the fear of the LORD, that is wisdom; and to depart from evil is understanding." Ps 111:7 "The works of his (*the LORD's*) hands are verity and judgment; all his commandments are sure. 8 They stand fast for ever and ever, and are done in truth and uprightness. 9 He sent redemption unto his people: he hath commanded his covenant for ever: holy and reverend is his name. 10 The fear of the LORD is the beginning of wisdom: a good understanding have all they that do his commandments: his praise endureth for ever." Prov 9:9 "Give instruction to a wise man, and he will be yet wiser: teach a just man, and he will increase in learning. 10 The fear of the LORD is the beginning of wisdom: and the knowledge of the holy is understanding. 11 For by me thy days shall be multiplied, and the years of thy life shall be increased."

Thus, the fear of God is to not sin but do the ways of God, so the healing and prospering life of God can fill the Earth. The first level attitude is to fear and avoid violating God's ways, knowing the consequences are death and destruction, but the real secret of fearing God is to do what He wants so His *zoe*/life can fill and prosper all you think, say and do, and, thus, bring Heaven to Earth. Operate in this kind of fear, and you will walk in joy and gladness because of the goodness of the Lord.

For those who think the fear of the Lord is not to be without intensity and control your every thought, word and action: Phil 2:10 "That at the name of Jesus every knee should bow, of things in heaven, and things in earth, and things under the earth; 11 and that every tongue should confess that Jesus Christ is Lord, to the glory of God the Father. 12 Wherefore, my *agape*/beloved, as ye have always obeyed, not as in my presence only, but now much more in my absence, work out your own *soteria*/salvation with fear and trembling. 13 For it is God which worketh in you both to will and to do of his good pleasure. 14 Do all things without murmurings and disputings: 15 that ye may be blameless and harmless, the sons of God, without rebuke, in the midst of a crooked and perverse nation, among whom

DISCOVERING OUR REDEMPTION

ye shine as lights in the world; 16 holding forth the word of *zoe*/life; that I may rejoice in the day of Christ, that I have not run in vain, neither laboured in vain."

Thus every sin committed in either commission or omission is a failure to fear the Lord effectively, like Jesus did, and every sin has consequences. To know the consequences is one of the ways to keep from sinning.

The fear of the Lord is that which causes you to seek and hear God and to obey His Word in gladness. This is described on four levels. All are the territory of a humble (*I repent that I exalted myself against God and did it my way*) and contrite (*I know what I deserve, and I know I will reap evil if I do not fix it with God*) heart.

1) The absolute assurance that all sin, every evil work, will be destroyed and that we will reap whatever evil we sow that we do not confess, agree Jesus died for, make whatever restitution on Earth is required, receive total healing, and put on Jesus Christ over it. This is "knee-knocking" self-preservation, avoid-all-loss fear, and the one most mentioned in the Bible. (Deut 28 has an impressive list of blessing and what to fear for disobedience, 2 Cor 5:10 and Phil 2:12 show the "knee-knocking attitude a Christian is to have.)
2) Awesome reverence that God is great and to be obeyed, for it is to our benefit. This fear is still a form of self-protection. (2 Cor 7:1, Deut 10:20)
3) God is a loving Father, and our sins hurt Him, by cutting off His love in that area. This is a loving fear, where we are more concerned that God does not get all He wants, and we are the reason. This is a loving fear that does not want to offend Him. (Rev 14:7, Heb 12:28)
4) This is walking in *agape*/love, where you are an active agent of God, delivering His *agape*/love in every part of life and, therefore, do not sin and only do righteousness. This is where Jesus and mature Christians walk, as *agape*/love slaves to God, delighting to only please Him in holding on to His Word in trouble and setting others free. (1 John 4:16-19)

Whatever level of fear keeps you from sin and keeps you doing righteousness is the place to start. There are many scriptures showing each aspect; here are a few describing these different aspects of the fear of God. 2 Cor 5:10 "For we must all appear before the judgment seat of Christ; that every one may receive the things done in his body, according to that he hath done, whether it be good or bad. 11 Knowing therefore the terror of the Lord, we persuade men; but we are made manifest unto God; and I trust also are made manifest in your consciences." Phil 2:12 "Wherefore, my beloved, as ye have always obeyed, not as in my presence only, but now much more in my absence, work out your own *soteria*/salvation with fear and trembling." 2 Cor 7:1 "Having therefore these promises, dearly *agape*/beloved, let us cleanse ourselves from all filthiness of the flesh and spirit, perfecting holiness in the fear of God." Deut 10:20 "Thou shalt fear the Lord thy God; him shalt thou serve, and to him shalt thou cleave, and swear by his name. 21 He is thy praise, and he is thy

God, that hath done for thee these great and terrible things, which thine eyes have seen. 22 Thy fathers went down into Egypt with threescore and ten persons; and now the LORD thy God hath made thee as the stars of heaven for multitude." Rev 14:7 "Saying with a loud voice, Fear God, and give glory to him; for the hour of his judgment is come: and worship him that made heaven, and earth, and the sea, and the fountains of waters." Heb 12:28 "Wherefore we receiving a kingdom which cannot be moved, let us have grace, whereby we may serve God acceptably with reverence and godly fear: 29 for our God is a consuming fire." 1 John 4:16 "And we have known and believed the *agape*/love that God hath to us. God is *agape*/love; and he that dwelleth in *agape*/love dwelleth in God, and God in him. 17 Herein is our *agape*/love made perfect, that we may have boldness in the day of judgment: because as he is, so are we in this world. 18 There is no fear in *agape*/love; but perfect *agape*/love casteth out fear: because fear hath torment. He that feareth is not made perfect in *agape*/love. 19 We *agape*/love him, because he first *agape*/loved us."

God does not have to actively judge wrath on us in this life. The laws that He made when He created the Earth and pronounced good do that. Rom 2:11 "For there is no respect of persons with God." Gal 6:7 "Be not deceived; God is not mocked: for whatsoever a man soweth, that shall he also reap. 8 For he that soweth to his flesh shall of the flesh reap corruption; but he that soweth to the Spirit shall of the Spirit reap *zoe*/life everlasting."

These two scriptures tell us a fundamental truth. It does not matter who you are; if you plant and nurture good seed, you will reap good fruit; if you plant and nurture bad seed, you will reap bad fruit. This applies to anyone on the Earth, everyone, and everywhere. This is a basic law of the universe that God has put in place. Like gravity, God does not have to do anything to enforce the law of sowing and reaping. So reaping what we sow, good or bad, is not a direct judgment from God, just the normal process of His existing laws in operation.

In contrast, every healing of Jesus was an example of God actively judging the works of the devil and the application of His wrath against the devil to set people free from either devil attacks, accidents or evil reaping. He gave us that job to continue. Luke 10:19 "Behold, I give unto you power (*authority, commission and the resources of Heaven*) to tread on serpents and scorpions, and over all *dunamis*/power (*ability*) of the enemy: and nothing shall by any means hurt you." As Jesus is the exact representation of God, we can know He delights in judging the devil to freedom for the oppressed through men–you and me.

Many people think that the God of the Old Testament is a God of wrath and the God of the New Testament one of *agape*/love. Well, He is the same God in both and has always been and always will be the same. He is also a God of forgiveness. Hear the cry of God to the people of the Old Testament, who had sown and nurtured bad seed: Hos 10:12 "Sow to yourselves in righteousness, reap in *chesed*/

DISCOVERING OUR REDEMPTION

mercy; break up your fallow ground: for it is time to seek the LORD, till he come and rain righteousness upon you. 13 Ye have plowed wickedness, ye have reaped iniquity; ye have eaten the fruit of lies: because thou didst trust in thy way, in the multitude of thy mighty men [*rather than in God*]."

Look at the example of Job. In Job 1 and 2, we see a throne- or courtroom scene where Satan, the god of this world, accuses God and Job. God does not stop the devil, because the devil is working within God's laws; but God does limit what Satan can do. First, He limits him to not touching Job's life; and then, second, God limits him to not killing Job.

Then we see God go to work. First, in Job 32 He sends Elihu to adjust Job's thinking and help him to quit finding fault with God. Job did well in holding on to God for goodness, no matter what, but he still sinned in accusing God of evil or making a mistake. After Elihu had worked a little humility into Job, God appeared and Job repented.

Here is what God did. First, He got Job to pray as an intercessor for his friends who did not repent. Now Job was thinking like God. Then God blessed. Job got twice as much wealth and a new set of children, and he lived 140 years longer. This was God at work!

In God's history with Israel, they continually would not cooperate with Him, to allow Him to bless them, and, thus, their actions produced the curse and not the blessing. He continually sent prophets, just as He did to Job, to turn men from their sins and get life from Him; but they did not. In spite of this, He mitigated the situation, reducing as much as He could, to save them. Mal 3:6 "For I am the LORD, I change not; therefore ye sons of Jacob are not consumed." It is as if our unresolved sin builds up, and even though God's hand is around us as a wall, the sin overflows the wall, and we reap the judgment of Satan due. God's ultimate triumph is that He can bless the "saved" in Heaven, in spite of our Earth life, because of the right actions of Jesus.

We see this in the numerous times Israel sinned and yet God showed them a way to stop the curse or judgment. In Numbers 12, Miriam contracted leprosy for sinning, but then Moses prayed, and she was healed. In the process, Moses had to forgive Miriam for speaking against his wife. This same series of events happened repeatedly in the Bible. God has always looked for one who will deal with Him so He can heal. Ps 103:3 "Who forgiveth all thine iniquities; who healeth all thy diseases;" When He could find no man, He sent Jesus: Isa 59:16 "And he saw that there was no man, and wondered that there was no intercessor: therefore his arm brought salvation unto him; and his righteousness, it sustained him. 17 For he put on righteousness as a breastplate, and an helmet of salvation upon his head; and he put on the garments of vengeance for clothing, and was clad with zeal as a cloak."

APPENDICES

Here is God's attitude toward death in any form–from a small headache or scrape, to loss of all limbs, to untimely death, to famine and war: Hos 13:14 "I will ransom them from the power of the grave; I will redeem them from death: O death, I will be thy plagues; O grave, I will be thy destruction: repentance shall be hid from mine eyes." 1 Cor 15:26 "The last enemy that shall be destroyed is death." Rev 1:17 "And when I saw him (*Jesus*), I fell at his feet as dead. And he laid his right hand upon me, saying unto me, Fear not; I am the first and the last: 18 I am he that *zao*/liveth, and was dead; and, behold, I am *zao*/alive for evermore, Amen; and have the keys of hell and of death."

Bottom line: Anything anyone needs healed from is an enemy to God. Jesus cast out devils and healed people to show what God delights to do. Jesus made it clear sickness is God's enemy and is to be destroyed by any Christian at any time.

God has no desire for us to suffer any of His wraths. Jesus took all the wrath of God due us on Himself, per Isaiah 53.

Father God sent Jesus to demonstrate His true nature and to "destroy the works of the devil" (1 John 3:8). The word *destroy* could also mean "to exercise wrath." So this could be stated as "God sent Jesus to exercise His wrath and, thus, destroy what the devil has built on the Earth, so men could be saved and Heaven come to Earth."

Zoe/life is the opposite of the effects of sin and death. John 3:16 "For God so *agape*/loved the world, that he gave his only begotten Son, that whosoever believeth in him should not perish, but have everlasting *zoe*/life. 17 For God sent not his Son into the world to condemn the (*people of the*) world; but that the world through him might be *sozo*/saved." In these scriptures, we see God's attitude toward us and the devil; life for us, wrath for the devil and all his works. The problem is, if our hearts and minds are in love with the works of the devil, we will suffer the consequences of evil fruit and loss, along with the devil on that Day, per 1 Cor 3.

Consider: how did Adam and Eve turn this world over to the curse? By disobeying God's word, they gave this Earth to the consequences of sin and the rule of Satan. One of the meanings of the word *god* is source. When they believed Satan rather than God, they made the devil their source of life, releasing sin, Satan's anti-life force, death, into the world or their domain. Rom 5:14 "Nevertheless death reigned from Adam to Moses, even over them that had not sinned after the similitude of Adam's transgression, who is the figure of him that was to come." With Moses, God started to deal with death by giving a more direct and open source of life, until Jesus came.

Consider: 2 Cor 4:4 "In whom the god of this world hath blinded the minds of them which believe not, lest the light of the glorious gospel of Christ, who is the image of God, should shine unto them." Just as he did with Adam and Eve, Satan, the god of this world, is still blinding people's minds to the *agape*/love of God in

DISCOVERING OUR REDEMPTION

Jesus Christ. The Bible tells us that in the end, Jesus will be established as the rightful ruler of this world, and Satan put fully in the Lake of Fire.

The wrath of God is that impartial force of *agape*/love that must clean up sin, all evil that would hurt or hinder His children. God is light, sin is darkness, and light must dispel darkness till darkness is no more. The darkness then feels the "wrath" of the light. The opposite is also true: if light is extinguished, it has felt the wrath of darkness. John 8:12 "Then spake Jesus again unto them, saying, I am the light of the world: he that followeth me (*as I followed and imitated Father God*) shall not walk in darkness, but shall have the light of *zoe*/life (*as seen in Me in your own life*)." Jesus, as seen in the gospels, is the true light of what God is and delights to do good when He finds one who will work with Him to do what He wants. True light is to see Jesus as how Father God really is.

Here is the true nature of the God of the Old Testament. Even when Adam and Eve sinned and, thus, unleashed the entire misery of all history upon the human race, God sought them out, gave them garments and even gave them the promise that one of the woman's seed would "crush Satan's head" (see Genesis 3). Father God could have destroyed Adam and Eve in a heartbeat, but He did not. Instead, He showed them how to live in the mess they had made with the promise of ultimate victory and restored fellowship with Him. In Genesis 3 Adam released the curse into the Earth. God mitigated it so that man could live, but by the sweat of his brow. Otherwise the devil would have killed Eve in childbirth and men in famine. So, even if God must exercise His wrath, His justice, His consequences for sin, He always made a way to bless in the end. He promised One who would "bruise" the devil's head. Because we all sin and fall short of the glory of God, He sent His Son John 3:17 "For God sent not his Son into the world to condemn the world; but that the world through him might be *sozo*/saved," thus "bruising" the devil's head.

Most of what men call judgments of God are simply this:
- Evil sowing and reaping: getting back what we have done to others, or reaping the evil bounty of our own sins
- Attacks of the devil
- Accidents in a world with sin
- Failure to walk effectively in Psalms 23 and 91.

In these cases, it is not God at work, but, rather, the devil.

Ps 34:21 "Evil shall slay the wicked ... ." Ps 18:26 "With the pure thou wilt shew thyself pure; and with the froward thou wilt shew thyself froward." Ps 141:10 "Let the wicked fall into their own nets ... ." Luke 6:37 "Judge not (*against*), and ye shall not be judged (*against*): condemn not, and ye shall not be condemned: forgive, and ye shall be forgiven: 38 give, and it shall be given unto you; good measure, pressed down, and shaken together, and running over, shall men give into your bosom. For with the same measure that ye mete withal it shall be measured to you again." Ezek 18:30 "Therefore I will judge you, O house of Israel, every one according to his ways, saith the Lord GOD. Repent, and turn yourselves from all your transgressions; so iniquity shall not be your ruin. 31 Cast away from you all your transgressions, whereby ye have transgressed; and make you a new heart and a new spirit: for why will ye die, O house of Israel? 32 For I have no pleasure in the death of him that dieth, saith the Lord GOD: wherefore turn yourselves, and live ye." (Notice that, per Heb 8:10 and Ezek 26:36, in the New Covenant of Jesus, God gives us this new heart and this new spirit. And again: Rom 8:15 "For ye have not received the spirit of bondage again to fear; but ye have received the Spirit of adoption, whereby we cry, Abba (*Daddy*), Father.")

God holds back His wrath to give us time to repent and to provide a way of escape, for, through it all, God is calling, "Turn to my Son and live!" It is amazing that people can have faith in God's wrath, but not His blessing. If we confess our sins to God, receive His forgiveness and remission, apply that forgiveness to the consequences of sin and the curse sin brings, and put on the new man in Jesus, with all our defects totally healed, we can destroy the consequences and the curse sin brings, just like Jesus did.

Every healing Jesus performed was an example of God's attitudes to evil that hurts men, when He has someone with His view on His goodness (see Ps 103). King David knew the truth: Ps 86:5 "For thou, Lord, art good, and ready to forgive; and plenteous in *chesed*/mercy unto all them that call upon thee. 6 Give ear, O LORD, unto my prayer; and attend to the voice of my supplications. 7 In the day of my trouble I will call upon thee: for thou wilt answer me."

As we agree with God, we will enforce the benefits of all the wrath due us falling on Jesus, and resist the devil in any of his works, until he flees. Acts 10:34 "Then Peter opened his mouth, and said, Of a truth I perceive that God is no respecter of persons: 35 but in every nation he that feareth him, and worketh righteousness, is accepted with him. 36 The word which God sent unto the children of Israel, preaching peace by Jesus Christ: (he is Lord of all:) 37 that word, I say, ye know, which was published throughout all Judaea, and began from Galilee, after the baptism which John preached; 38 how God anointed Jesus of Nazareth with the Holy Ghost and with power: who went about doing good, and healing (*in judgment against the devil*) all that were oppressed (*under the active dominion, reign or lordship*) of the devil; for God was with him." Notice, in verse 35, using the name of Jesus to get people healed is a work of righteousness. No matter how good or bad at it you are, this makes you acceptable to God. The more you reprogram your heart, the better you will be at using the name of Jesus to put the wrath of God on the devil and his works. God will deal with man and our works on the Day of Judgment, and God is dealing with Satan through the Church in this, the Day of Salvation.

DISCOVERING OUR REDEMPTION

We see, many times, in the Old Testament where men built an altar to make a sacrifice, and God sent fire and consumed it: Gideon (Judg 6:21), David (1 Chron 21:26) and Elijah (1 Kings 18:38). The sacrifice stood for the sin, and God destroyed it by fire. Then God started, through a man, to set things right. When God destroys something, it is all gone. The great flood destroyed all, as did the judgment on Sodom and Gomorrah. Rev 21 and 22 show the Earth fully cleaned and prepared for God to bring Heaven to Earth. Jesus destroyed, purged, and dissolved our sins once for all men 2000 years ago. The job was fully and completely done. God does not live in time, and this work of Jesus was timeless, eternal, once, for all time. This is what He means when Holy Spirit says: Heb 10:10 "By the which will we are sanctified through the offering of **the body of Jesus Christ once for all**. 11 And every priest standeth daily ministering and offering oftentimes the same sacrifices, which can never take away sins: 12 but this man, after he had offered **one sacrifice for sins for ever**, sat down on the right hand of God; 13 from henceforth expecting till his enemies be made his footstool [*by us, the Church*]. 14 For **by one offering he hath perfected for ever** them that are sanctified. 15 Whereof the Holy Ghost also is a witness to us: for after that he had said before, 16 This is the covenant that I will make with them after those days, saith the Lord, I will put my laws into their hearts, and in their minds will I write them; 17 and their **sins and iniquities will I remember no more**. 18 Now where remission of these is, **there is no more offering for sin.**" The wrath due us fell on Jesus. It is done! Our job is to praise God for His work in Jesus, and now deliver the wrath of God on the devil and get people set free. Doing this is how we walk in the fear of God like Jesus did.

Jesus came to baptize with Holy Spirit and fire. That fire burns up all the chaff, the useless parts of the Earth, and chaff is a symbol of any work of the devil. Luke 3:16 "John answered, saying unto them all, I indeed baptize you with water; but one mightier than I cometh, the latchet of whose shoes I am not worthy to unloose: he shall baptize you with the Holy Ghost and with fire: 17 whose fan is in his hand, and he will throughly purge his floor, and will gather the wheat into his garner; but the chaff he will burn with fire unquenchable." The final day is the Day of Judgment. Until then we are to judge the devil by fire, in setting people free of any oppression of the devil, in Jesus' name, in this, the Day of God's Salvation, in judgment against the devil and his works by the Church.

Jesus, by Holy Spirit, burns with fire the works of the devil in men and makes them whole; thus delivering the wrath of God to the devil and not to men. Acts 14:3 "Long time therefore abode they speaking boldly in the Lord, which gave testimony unto the word of his grace, and granted signs and wonders to be done by their hands." Mark 16:19 "So then after the Lord had spoken unto them, he was received up into heaven, and sat on the right hand of God. 20 And they went forth,

APPENDICES

and preached everywhere, the Lord working with them, and confirming the word with signs following. Amen."

And we are to continue that same word, in the same way, against the wrath of the devil by using the wrath of God to create peace like Jesus did. Acts 10:36 "The word which God sent unto the children of Israel, preaching peace by Jesus Christ: (he is Lord of all:) 37 that word, I say, ye know, which was published throughout all Judaea, and began from Galilee, after the baptism which John preached; 38 how God anointed Jesus of Nazareth with the Holy Ghost and with power: who went about doing good, and healing all that were oppressed (*under the active dominion, reign or lordship*) of the devil; for God was with him."

Let us go and do likewise, making peace in the name of Jesus, knowing: Isa 55:11 "So shall my word be that goeth forth out of my mouth (*through you*): it shall not return unto me void, but it shall accomplish that which I please, and it shall prosper in the thing whereto I sent it." Isa 49:24 "Shall the prey be taken from the mighty, or the lawful captive delivered? 25 But thus saith the Lord, Even the captives of the mighty shall be taken away, and the prey of the terrible shall be delivered: for I will contend with him that contendeth with thee, and I will save thy children. 26 And I will feed them that oppress thee with their own flesh; and they shall be drunken with their own blood, as with sweet wine: and all flesh shall know that I the Lord am thy Saviour and thy Redeemer, the mighty One of Jacob." Heb 13:8 "Jesus Christ the same yesterday, and to day, and for ever." He is ever the Healer.

So we see that the fear of the Lord is really two parts. First things not to do because that will be destroyed on the Last Day and as you do them you are sowing to the flesh and will reap corruption in this life. The second is that the fear of the Lord will cause you to go and do those things God requires so you can sow to the Spirit and reap *zoe*/life on the Day of Judgment as rewards of silver, gold and jewels, and the benefits of *zoe*/life in this life now.

GLORY

Means: honor, splendor, shiny, beauty, wealth, the best of, the strength of, or power of, radiance and light. An overall definition is that God's glory is released or dwells when Holy Spirit can freely do all God wants to on the Earth, of His goodness, through His people, i.e., in you. This includes the Shekinah glory filling a place of worship (Ex 40:34-35, 1 Kings 8:11), clouds/mist, or a light or glow on people, such as on Moses and Jesus: Luke 9:29 "And as he (*Jesus*) prayed, the fashion of his countenance was altered, and his raiment was white and glistering. 30 And, behold, there talked with him two men, which were Moses and Elias: 31 who appeared in glory, and spake of his decease which he should accomplish at Jerusalem." The glory of God also includes raising the dead: Rom 6:4 "... as Christ

DISCOVERING OUR REDEMPTION

was raised up from the dead by the glory of the Father ..." Holy Spirit and God's manifested glory are tightly linked.

God defines His glory as (or it is released by) His goodness and His name: Ex 33:18 "And he (*Moses*) said, I beseech thee, shew me thy glory. 19 And he said, I will make all my goodness pass before thee, and I will proclaim the name of the LORD before thee; and will be gracious to whom I will be gracious, and will shew *racham*/mercy on whom I will shew *racham*/mercy. 20 And he said, Thou canst not see my face: for there shall no man see me, and live. 21 And the LORD said, Behold, there is a place by me, and thou shalt stand upon a rock: 22 and it shall come to pass, while my glory passeth by, that I will put thee in a clift of the rock, and will cover thee with my hand while I pass by: 23 and I will take away mine hand, and thou shalt see my back parts: but my face shall not be seen." Ex 34:5 "And the LORD descended in the cloud, and stood with him there, and proclaimed the name of the LORD. 6 And the LORD passed by before him, and proclaimed, The LORD, The LORD God, merciful and gracious, longsuffering, and abundant in *chesed*/goodness and truth, 7 keeping *chesed*/mercy for thousands, forgiving iniquity and transgression and sin, and that will by no means clear the guilty (*those who will not confess their sin to God for forgiveness*); visiting the iniquity of the fathers upon the children, and upon the children's children, unto the third and to the fourth generation (*this visiting iniquity to the 3rd and 4th generation was clarified as non-generational in Ezek 18*). 8 And Moses made haste, and bowed his head toward the earth, and worshipped." This is God's definition of the glory that will fill the Earth.

There are two main aspects of glory revealed in the Scriptures: glory that comes from God in manifestations of Heaven on Earth, and glory that comes from man to God. The word *glory* has the root of heaviness or weighty, implying the true substance, that which lasts when other things pass away. Thus, all righteous works that survive the Day of Judgment, as silver, gold and jewels, are the result of the glory of the Lord (Holy Spirit) and you working together to produce those works. 1 Cor 3:9 "For we are **labourers together with God**: ye are God's husbandry, ye are God's building. 10 According to the grace of God which is given unto me, as a wise masterbuilder, I have laid the foundation, and another buildeth thereon. But let every man take heed how he buildeth thereupon. 11 For other foundation can no man lay than that is laid, which is Jesus Christ. 12 Now if any man build upon this foundation gold, silver, precious stones, wood, hay, stubble; 13 every man's work shall be made manifest: for the day shall declare it, because it shall be revealed by fire; and the fire shall try every man's work of what sort it is. 14 If any man's work abide which he hath built thereupon, he shall receive a reward. 15 If any man's work shall be burned, he shall suffer loss: but he himself shall be *sozo*/saved; yet so as by fire." Wood, hay and stubble are those things not of His glory.

Appendices

The amazing thing is that this same word for glory applies to what man praises and exalts, i.e., gives glory to, be it God, nature or man. The combined effect of the glory of the Lord and the glory of man is found in our thanksgiving, praise, worship and obedience. Ps 149:4 "For the LORD taketh pleasure in his people: he will beautify the meek with salvation. 5 Let the saints be joyful in glory: let them sing aloud upon their beds" Even our mouths are described as our glory or the place where our glory is shown or released: Ps 30:12 "To the end that my glory may sing praise to thee, and not be silent. O LORD my God, I will give thanks unto thee for ever."

No wonder that, when we exalt God, Holy Spirit then inhabits our praise, as He (Holy Spirit) is the administrator of glory/manifestations of God's goodness in the Earth: Ps 22:3 "But thou art holy, O thou that inhabitest the praises of Israel." 1 Pet 2:9 "But ye are a chosen generation, a royal priesthood, an holy nation, a peculiar people; that ye should shew forth the praises of him who hath called you out of darkness into his marvellous light: 10 which in time past were not a people, but are now the people of God: which had not obtained mercy, but now have obtained mercy." Rom 6:4 "Therefore we are buried with him by baptism into death: that like as Christ was raised up from the dead by the glory of the Father, even so we also should walk in newness of *zoe*/life." Rom 8:11 "But if the Spirit of him that raised up Jesus from the dead dwell in you, he that raised up Christ from the dead shall also quicken your mortal bodies by his Spirit that dwelleth in you." 2 Cor 3:18 "But we all, with open face beholding as in a glass (*mirror*) the glory of the Lord, are changed into the same image from glory to glory, even as by the Spirit of the Lord." Related opposites of God's glory include darkness, sin, iniquity and death, none of which will survive the Day of Judgment.

GRACE

Grace is granted by one who has power/authority to one who does not, and is very similar to being blessed or given kindness/*chesed*, in that it is free, unmerited favor that is aggressively applied to you and does good for you. Grace is the free gift of God to be, think, act like and produce the results of Jesus in any situation, i.e., the will of Father God on Earth as it is in Heaven. Grace is always given, not earned, and is greater than ever could be earned. You don't have to seek it, although you are required to; it seeks you, to give you total goodness for any need. Grace is how you get the blessing benefit. It is God's free gift and attitude of favor to give you what you do not deserve, to walk into the blessings of God, to the fullness of Christ in you. As we are "*sozo*/saved by grace," grace is God's goodness empowered to produce blessing after the nature of God, and the result is more than you could ever come close to doing for yourself, but brings Heaven on Earth, both now and in the future. Eph 4:7 "But unto every one of us is given grace according to the measure of the gift of Christ." All of God's grace is available to us in gift, prayer and faith, per Heb 4:16. Grace has aspects of the Hebrew word *chesed*.

GINOSKO

Ginosko (*Strong's* NT, 1097, pronounced: ghin oce'-ko) means knowledge of, awareness, learned or book learned.

HUGIES

Hugies (*Strong's* NT, 5199, pronounced: hooge-ee-ace') means whole, sound, healed, or complete.

IAOMAI

Iaomai (*Strong's* NT, 2390, pronounced: ee-ah'-om-ahee) means physical healing or wholeness.

INIQUITY

Iniquity means every aspect of wrong thoughts and words that lead to sin, the sins themselves, their consequences and the punishment due for sin. It also can mean misfortunes that attack you. Iniquity specifically is those thoughts that are not of God and, therefore, lead you to sin in any act of commission, doing, or omission, not doing. This is called a propensity to sin or a wicked, adulterous heart, when you keep them in your mind. Keeping wicked thoughts in your mind is the start of doing evil, i.e., wickedness, evil, against God and His ways, violation of the covenant with God. Isa 59:7 "Their feet run to evil, and they make haste to shed innocent blood: their thoughts are thoughts of iniquity; wasting and destruction are in their paths. 8 The way of peace they know not; and there is no judgment in their goings: they have made them crooked paths: whosoever goeth therein shall not know peace." Ps 36:3 "The words of his mouth are iniquity and deceit: he hath left off to be wise, and to do good."

The Bible standard is to always control or rein in your thoughts and do not allow them to stray to wickedness or iniquity. 2 Cor 10:5 "Casting down imaginations, and every high thing that exalteth itself against the knowledge of God, and bringing into captivity every thought to the obedience of Christ." Ps 10:4 "The wicked, through the pride of his countenance, will not seek after God: God is not in all his thoughts." Prov 30:32 "If thou hast done foolishly in lifting up thyself, or if thou hast thought evil, lay thine hand upon thy mouth." James 1:14 "But every man is tempted, when he is drawn away of his own lust, and enticed. 15 Then when lust hath conceived, it bringeth forth sin: and sin, when it is finished, bringeth forth death." Another translation for iniquity is lawlessness: the refusal to obey God's known will in His Word and ways, i.e., disobedience, stubbornness, rebellion and accepting no one's rule but one' own, lawless.

God's remission, in the propitiation of Christ, completely forgives and removes the iniquities and sin and heals the punishment or curse due for them. Isa 53:5 "But he was wounded for our transgressions, he was bruised for our iniquities: the chastisement of our peace was upon him; and with his stripes we are healed. 6 All we like sheep have gone astray; we have turned every one to his own way; and the LORD hath laid on him the iniquity of us all. ... 11 He shall see of the travail of his soul, and shall be satisfied: by his knowledge shall my righteous servant justify many; for he shall bear their iniquities."

The propensity to sin is related to what is in our hearts and what we keep thinking on as acceptable. Matt 15:17 "Do not ye yet understand, that whatsoever entereth in at the mouth goeth into the belly, and is cast out into the draught? 18 But those things which proceed out of the mouth come forth from the heart; and they defile the man. 19 For out of the heart proceed evil thoughts, murders, adulteries, fornications, thefts, false witness, blasphemies: 20 these are the things which defile a man: but to eat with unwashen hands defileth not a man." A stingy man will not give even a penny and praises those who act likewise. This is how men reinforce iniquity among themselves. Prov 23:7 "For as he thinketh in his heart, so is he ... ." The opposite is true: think truth and you will do truth; think *agape*/love and you will do *agape*/love.

Iniquity is purged by knowing the *chesed*/grace of God that your sins were purged in Jesus, by the truth, His Word (pray Psalm 119 often), and an absolute assurance that every iniquity will be judged and destroyed on the Day of Judgment, and that while you sin on the Earth you are sowing to yourselves unrighteousness, with its sad and wicked fruit now and on that Day. Prov 16:6 "By *chesed*/mercy and truth iniquity is purged: and by the fear of the LORD men depart from evil." 2 Pet 1:9 "But he that lacketh these things (*of the fruits of abiding in Christ*) is blind, and cannot see afar off, and hath forgotten that he was purged from his old sins (*in the chesed, grace of the New Covenant in the blood of Jesus*)."

The cure to allowing iniquity to dwell in your heart is the ultimate positive attitude: Phil 4:4 "Rejoice in the Lord alway: and again I say, Rejoice. 5 Let your moderation be known unto all men. The Lord is at hand. 6 Be careful for nothing; but in every thing by prayer and supplication with thanksgiving let your *aiteo*/ requests be made known unto God. 7 And the peace of God, which passeth all understanding, shall keep your hearts and minds through Christ Jesus. 8 Finally, brethren, whatsoever things are true (*the Bible*), whatsoever things are honest, whatsoever things are just, whatsoever things are pure, whatsoever things are lovely, whatsoever things are of good report; if there be any virtue, and if there be any praise, think on these things. 9 Those things, which ye have both learned, and received, and heard, and seen in me, do: and the God of peace shall be with you."

Or, as God told Joshua: Josh 1:6 "Be strong and of a good courage: for unto this people shalt thou divide for an inheritance the land, which I sware unto their fathers to give them. 7 Only be thou strong and very courageous, that thou mayest observe to do according to all the law, which Moses my servant commanded thee: turn not from it to the right hand or to the left, that thou mayest prosper whithersoever thou goest. 8 This book of the law shall not depart out of thy mouth; but thou shalt meditate therein day and night, that thou mayest observe to do according to all that is written therein: for then thou shalt make thy way prosperous, and then thou shalt have good success. 9 Have not I commanded thee? Be strong and of a good courage; be not afraid, neither be thou dismayed: for the LORD thy God is with thee whithersoever thou goest."

A hard heart, steeped in iniquity, cannot see the goodness of the Lord. Rom 2:4 "Or despisest thou the riches of his goodness and forbearance and longsuffering; not knowing that the goodness of God leadeth thee to repentance? 5 But after thy hardness and impenitent heart treasurest up unto thyself wrath against the day of wrath and revelation of the righteous judgment of God." A Christian is to know, without doubt, that all iniquity and its fruits/works will be destroyed on the Day of Judgment.

ISCHUS

Ischus (*Strong's* NT, 2479, pronounced: is-khoos') means force, power, might, ability strength, money, armies, or intellect.

JUSTIFIED/JUSTIFICATION

This is the legal/governmental process of removing all elements of sin, enmity, loss, wrath and/or alienation, and making totally blessed, so good from God is forced upon one, i.e., the process by which one is made righteous. For a Christian, we are justified to be made the righteousness of God in Jesus in our spirit, by faith that God raised Him from the dead. Justification/justified has a very similar meaning to reconciliation, but is more legal in nature.

Justification with God through Jesus does not resolve any reconciliation or restitution you have to make with other humans on Earth. God will give you grace to resolve these earthly issues. Rom 5:15 "But not as the offence, so also is the free gift. For if through the offence of one (*Adam*) many be dead, much more the grace of God, and the gift by grace, which is by one man, Jesus Christ, hath abounded unto many. 16 And not as it was by one that sinned, so is the gift: for the judgment was by one to condemnation, but the free gift is of many offences unto justification. 17 For if by one man's offence death reigned by one; much more they which (*continually*) *lambano*/receive abundance of grace and of the gift of righteousness shall reign (*as kings for Jesus*) in *zoe*/life by one, Jesus Christ.) 18 Therefore as by the offence (*sin*) of one judgment came upon all men to condemnation; even so by the righteousness of one the free gift came upon all men unto justification of *zoe*/life."

KAINOS

Kainos (Strong's NT 2537, pronounced: kahee-nos') is a Greek word that means new as in freshness or renovated, but not new in time. New as in renewed or renovated as compared to *neos* – new as never before. *Kainos* is used in New Testament references reference to the New Covenant/Testament or new creation (except once in Hebrews). It describes how the covenant of Jesus is really the renewed covenant of Abraham which is consummated in Jesus. Paul describes how in the covenant of Abraham the covenant was really with Christ by and through Abraham. Gal 3:13 "Christ hath redeemed us from the curse of the law, being made a curse for us: for it is written, Cursed is every one that hangeth on a tree: 14 that the blessing of Abraham might come on the Gentiles through Jesus Christ; that we might receive the promise of the Spirit through faith. 15 Brethren, I speak after the manner of men; though it be but a man's covenant, yet if it be confirmed, no man disannulleth, or addeth thereto. 16 Now to Abraham and his seed were the promises made. He saith not, And to seeds, as of many; but as of one, And to thy seed, which is Christ. 17 And this I say, that the covenant, that was confirmed before of God in Christ, the law, which was four hundred and thirty years after, cannot disannul, that it should make the promise of none effect." So the covenant of Moses could not remove the promise of the covenant of Christ in Abraham and thus the *kainos*/New Testament is the re-activated covenant of Abraham. Also in the *kainos*/new creation the person is not obliterated, cease to exist and then brought back, but renovated in spirit back to the plan God had for Adam, 2 Cor 5:17 "Therefore if any man be in Christ, he is a *kainos*/new creature: old things are passed away; behold, all things are become *kainos*/new." For more detail please see www.JaySnell.org and *The Unbroken Force of Abraham's Blessings*.

KARDIA

Kardia (*Strong's* NT 2588, pronounced: kar-dee'-ah) means both the physical heart and the center of being, the inner man, the center of feelings and mind. It is similar to the Hebrew *leb* in concept.

DISCOVERING OUR REDEMPTION

LAMBANO

Lambano (*Strong's* NT 2983, pronounced: lam-ban'-o) is a Greek word that means to hold on to like a man would hold on to a life preserver when overboard in a raging sea. It is often translated "receive" in the KJV. Here it means to "receive" as if you were a football player trying to catch a ball in the middle of a group of strong defenders. You catch it, and the defenders now try to knock and grab the ball from your hand, so you must defend and keep the ball in your hands, even as you run toward the goal. Another meaning is to carry a very heavy item, like a very heavy bucket and carry it no matter how far or difficult the ground, and deliver it full and on time.

LEB/LEBAB

Leb/Lebab (*Strong's* OT 3820/3823, pronounced: labe/law-babe') means heart, feelings or physical heart. Is a synonym with *lebab*.

LOGOS

Logos (*Strong's* NT 3056, pronounced: lo-gos') means all that something is, message, expression of the full thought, the message of God as God is one with His Word. We are commanded to do *logos* to produce the *zoe*/life of God. James 1:23 "For if any be a hearer of the *logos*/word, and not a doer, he is like unto a man beholding his natural face in a glass."

Matt 7:24 "Therefore whosoever heareth these *logos*/sayings of mine, and doeth them, I will liken him unto a wise man, which built his house upon a rock: 25 and the rain descended, and the floods came, and the winds blew, and beat upon that house; and it fell not: for it was founded upon a rock. 26 And every one that heareth these *logos*/sayings of mine, and doeth them not, shall be likened unto a foolish man, which built his house upon the sand: 27 and the rain descended, and the floods came, and the winds blew, and beat upon that house; and it fell: and great was the fall of it. 28 And it came to pass, when Jesus had ended these *logos*/sayings, the people were astonished at his doctrine."

When you hear a word to obey it, then that *logos*/word becomes *rhema*. In the military, this is very real. Failure to obey a *logos* and make it *rhema* puts you in danger of death because of dereliction of duty or mutiny. Obedience keeps you in the life of the organization. Greek and Roman slaves understood this very well, as has every soldier in all of history. The only thing that matters is what *logos* you do, not what you just study, memorize or quote.

MEOD

Meod (Strong's OT 3966, pronounced: meh-ode') means vehemence, strength, diligence, quick commitment, excited, positive, right attitude and enthusiasm, or eagerly with force and loudness.

MERCY

Mercy is ignoring/forgiving/exonerating all wrongs, so you do not get the full penalty, wrath or evil you deserve; and/or being given a great good you did not earn and are not worthy of. Lam 3:22 "It is of the LORD's *chesed*/mercies that we are not consumed, because his compassions fail not." 1 Pet 1:3 "Blessed be the God and Father of our Lord Jesus Christ, which according to his abundant mercy hath begotten us again unto a *zao*/lively hope by the resurrection of Jesus Christ from the dead, 4 to an inheritance incorruptible, and undefiled, and that fadeth not away, reserved in heaven for you, 5 who are kept by the power of God through faith unto *soteria*/salvation ready to be revealed in the last time."

NASA

Nasa (Strong's OT 5375, pronounced: naw-saw') means to lift, contain or carry so no more can be included and nothing is left out.

NEOS

Neos (Strong's NT 3501, pronounced: neh'-os) is a Greek word that means new in time such as a new born baby or a new-built car. A used car that is new to a buyer is *neos* to that buyer, while the car itself is a *kainos* or refreshed car so it looks like new. Thus to an individual the new birth is *neos*/new to them, but is the activation of the *kainos*/New Covenant in Jesus accomplished 2000 years ago. Please see *kainos* for more details.

NEPHESH

Nephesh (Strong's OT 5315, pronounced: neh'-fesh) means soul, inner man, as exhibited by outward appearance, words and actions, feelings, appetite, greed, desire and behavior.

PEACE

The Bible word translated *peace* is based on the Hebrew word *shalom*, which means calm assurance and confidence in God because all things are working well and in order, with nothing missing, nothing broken and everything producing to the abundance of Heaven on Earth. This is not a passive state, similar to being drugged, but a calm assurance, no matter how bad it is, that God is making it right,

DISCOVERING OUR REDEMPTION

because you have put in process and are continuing to do the things to allow/cause this to happen, i.e., thanksgiving, all kinds of prayer and supplication, praise, alms, legal justice, etc. Phil 4:4 "Rejoice in the Lord alway: and again I say, Rejoice. 5 Let your moderation be known unto all men. The Lord is at hand *(in power)*. 6 Be careful for nothing *(no anxiety)*; but in every thing by prayer and supplication with thanksgiving let your *aiteo*/requests be made known unto God. 7 And the peace of God, which passeth all understanding *(because you have activated godly faith and will see the supernatural power of God, in answer to your aiteo prayers)*, shall keep *(guard, be a fortress around)* your hearts and minds through Christ Jesus. 8 Finally, brethren, whatsoever things are true, whatsoever things are honest, whatsoever things are just, whatsoever things are pure, whatsoever things are lovely, whatsoever things are of good report; if there be any virtue, and if there be any praise, think on these things. 9 Those things, which ye have both learned, and received, and heard, and seen in me, do: and the God of peace shall be with you." Notice, this is actively managing your thoughts and behaviors. The best way to control thoughts is to go and do acts of *agape*/love. Controlling your thoughts is a learned skill.

The meaning of peace also includes the process by which this state is achieved, so it is very closely related to *soteria*/salvation, as a state or condition of being, and to *sozo*/saved, peacemaking on how it is achieved. Rom 16:20 "And the God of peace shall bruise Satan under your feet *as shattered glass*. The grace of our Lord Jesus Christ be with you [*to think, know, be and do this*]. Amen." So to give peace and grace means: all things working well to produce the blessing of Heaven on Earth, and you will destroy and shatter seven ways all your enemies, as you fight as Jesus would. Also, you will have in abundance all things you need to do this work well, in you and yours.

A more complete definition is that peace is: the blessing of God to make and enjoy the Kingdom of God, Heaven on Earth, in every aspect of life and to be doing all the right things to produce Heaven on Earth, now, including destroying all your enemies God's way. This process or warrior definition agrees with: John 14:26 "But the Comforter, which is the Holy Ghost, whom the Father will send in my name, he shall teach you all things, and bring all things to your remembrance, whatsoever I have said unto you *(so you can act as Jesus would)*. 27 Peace *(the ability to fight and bring Heaven on Earth as I did)* I leave with you, my peace *(calm assurance and trust in God that you are doing all things, as Holy Spirit is helping you, to the glory of Father God, to bring the blessing of Heaven to Earth)* I give unto you: not as the world giveth, give I unto you. Let not your heart be troubled, neither let it be afraid." John 16:33 "These things I have spoken unto you, that in me ye might have peace *(calmness, knowing that Jesus has defeated all your enemies, for you to put them under your feet and bring Heaven on Earth, warring, fighting as Jesus taught us)*. In the world ye shall have tribulation: but be of good cheer; I have overcome the world." 1 Cor 15:57 "But thanks be to God, which giveth us the victory through our Lord Jesus Christ. 58 Therefore, my *agape*/beloved brethren, be ye stedfast, unmoveable, always abounding in the work of the Lord, forasmuch as ye know that your labour is not in vain in the Lord." 2 Cor 2:14 "Now thanks be unto God, which always causeth us to triumph in Christ, and maketh manifest the savour of his knowledge by us in every place." And this knowledge includes everything from normal life (clean sheets and efficient garbage collection) to the Lord confirming His Word of grace in power (healing the sick, raising the dead, the blind seeing, the lame walking, etc.). So if you think peace is all about your comfort, so you can only enjoy the pleasures of this world, you have missed the Gospel of God in Jesus Christ.

Notice how this fits with the "peace," or "peacemaker" mission of Jesus: Acts 10:36 "The word which God sent unto the children of Israel, preaching peace by Jesus Christ: (he is Lord of all:) 37 that word, I say, ye know, which was published throughout all Judaea, and began from Galilee, after the baptism which John preached; 38 how God anointed Jesus of Nazareth with the Holy Ghost and with power: who went about doing good, and healing all that were oppressed (*under the active dominion, reign or lordship*) of the devil; for God was with him (*to make peace in this way*)." Luke 4:17 "And there was delivered unto him the book of the prophet Esaias. And when he (*Jesus*) had opened the book, he found the place where it was written, 18 The Spirit of the Lord is upon me, because he hath anointed me to preach the gospel to the poor; he hath sent me to heal the brokenhearted, to preach deliverance to the captives, and recovering of sight to the blind, to set at liberty them that are bruised, 19 to preach (*command, declare, proclaim and demonstrate*) the acceptable year of the Lord."

We have been given that same Spirit of power, *agape*/love and sound mind attitude of an *agape*/love warrior in Jesus: Gal 4:4 "But when the fulness of the time was come, God sent forth his Son, made of a woman, made under the law, 5 to redeem them that were under the law, that we might receive the adoption of sons. 6 And because ye are sons, God hath sent forth the Spirit of his Son into your hearts, crying, Abba (*Daddy*), Father."

Peace is knowing you have done and will continue doing those things that produce Heaven on Earth, to make nothing missing, nothing broken or twisted out of God's purpose, and all things, including your shattering the devil under your feet, are working well to abundance. This gives you a peace, an assurance that the world cannot give.

This also fits right in with the traditional definition of a policeman as a "peace officer," and therefore explains why we are to pray for the government, per 1 Tim 2 and Rom 13:1 "Let every soul be subject unto the higher powers (*government in all forms as they support the righteous work of God*). For there is no power but of God: the powers that be are ordained of God. 2 Who-

DISCOVERING OUR REDEMPTION

soever therefore resisteth the power, resisteth the ordinance of God: and they that resist shall receive to themselves damnation. 3 For rulers are not a terror to good works, but to the evil. Wilt thou then not be afraid of the power? do that which is good, and thou shalt have praise of the same: 4 for he is the minister of God to thee for good. But if thou do that which is evil, be afraid; for he beareth not the sword in vain: for he is the minister of God, a revenger to execute wrath upon him that doeth evil. 5 Wherefore ye must needs be subject, not only for wrath, but also for conscience sake. 6 For this cause pay ye tribute also: for they are God's ministers, attending continually upon this very thing. 7 Render therefore to all their dues: tribute to whom tribute is due; custom to whom custom; fear to whom fear; honour to whom honour. 8 Owe no man any thing, but to *agape*/love one another: for he that *agape*/loveth another hath fulfilled the law."

PHILEO

Phileo (Strong's NT, 5368, pronounced: fil-eh'-o) means brotherly love, friend, affection, love, kiss or feeling.

PHOBOS

Phobos (Strong's NT, 5401, pronounced: fob-os') means that which causes flight in dread or terror of an unpleasant thing, in intense attitude and quick action; exceedingly afraid. It is used in the New Testament to describe the fear of the Lord. This includes that absolute assurance that on the Day of Judgment every man's works will be tested by fire and that which does not survive will be a loss to that person. So we are continually admonished throughout the New Testament to live our lives, knowing they will be tested. If you are a Christian, you are *sozo*/saved (1 Cor 3:7-10), but your works, the fruit of your life, will be tested and that found wanting will be destroyed.

PNEUMA

Pneuma (Strong's NT, 4151, pronounced: pnyoo'mah) means air, breath, current and also spirit. Pneuma is used to describe the spirit of man and the Spirit of God. The spirit is that part of man that comes directly from God in Adam, and because the sin of Adam made the spirit dead and united with and under the authority of the devil by the law of sin and death, man must be recreated with God's *zoe*/life to be reunited with God, as was Jesus by the work of the cross and when Jesus was raised from the dead. When a person is born again, their spirit is recreated and justified unto *zoe*/life, the same as is in Jesus. This is a work God does in the new creation. (See Spirit/Soul/Body for more detail.)

APPENDICES

PSUCHE

Psuche (*Strong's* NT, 5590, pronounced: psoo-khay') means soul or life; that part of a person manifested through their body; a reflection of the inner man of the thoughts, intention, will and emotions exhibited or seen in how a person speaks and acts, not just animal or that the person is alive. The spirit and soul have similar characteristics and, thus, are hard to tell which is in operation, except by the Word of God (Heb 4:12), and, thus, easily confused. The soul is produced by the spirit of man inhabiting a body. The soul, which consists of the heart, mind, will and emotions, must be renewed by the believer with the Word of God, to mature the believer into the fullness of Christ, per Eph 4, Rom 12, Rom 13, Col 3 and many other scriptures. *Psuche* is also translated as life because what you actually say and do is a reflection of what is in your soul. In general, the spirit of man is limited to and must relate to the outside world through or with the soul.

PROPITIATION

When sin is propitiated all wrath is removed, and aggressive blessing is bestowed on the former sinner. If there were no sin, then aggressive blessing is now bestowed from a previous, less-blessed, passive or indifferent position. The Greek word is *hilasterion* (*Strong's* NT 2435), and means to conciliate or make propitious or to cause good things to come. *Random House Dictionary* defines propitiation as: that which propitiates or makes favorably inclined; appease; conciliate. And conciliate means: 1) To overcome the distrust or hostility of; placate; win over: to conciliate an angry competitor. 2) To win or gain (goodwill, regard, or favor). 3) To make compatible; reconcile.

The propitiation process removes all issues for disfavor, if any, and institutes or restores one to a favorable position of aggressive good and identification. This could be either to resolve a difficulty, to "bribe," or to give a token of love for favor. *Favorable* means now disposed to do well toward and wanting to do well toward. So the new position is not neutral or indifferent, but now is a position in which the one favorably inclined or conciliated is openly seeking to do well toward the one reconciled, as if to themselves. In the case of a king, the king does not now simply forgive any wrong or ignore you. Instead, he looks continually for ways to bless or prosper you in any way he can and takes great delight in the bestowment of these benefits. Of course, with this attitude in the king, when the person does come to him for help or a favor of any kind, the king will, gladly and with great cheer and joy, do whatever can be done. Rom 3:23 "For all have sinned, and come short of the glory of God; 24 being justified freely by his grace through the redemption that is in Christ Jesus: 25 whom God hath set forth to be a propitiation through faith in his blood, to declare his righteousness for the remission of sins that are past,

DISCOVERING OUR REDEMPTION

through the forbearance of God; 26 to declare, I say, at this time his righteousness: that he might be just, and the justifier of him which believeth in Jesus." 1 John 2:1 "My little children, these things write I unto you, that ye sin not. And if any man sin, we have an advocate with the Father, Jesus Christ the righteous: 2 and he is the propitiation for our sins: and not for ours only, but also for the sins of the whole world." Eph 1:3 "Blessed be the God and Father of our Lord Jesus Christ, who hath blessed us with all spiritual blessings in heavenly places in Christ." Rom 5:1 "Therefore being justified by faith, we have peace with God through our Lord Jesus Christ." Our propitiation is complete in Christ. Thus, all enmity is reconciled and abundant blessing aggressively directed to man, general good and Holy Spirit in the Christian.

RACHAM

Racham (*Strong's* OT 7533, pronounced: raw-kham') is an Old Testament word often translated as mercy, tender mercies or compassion in the KJV. *Racham* is a deeper word than mercy, which in modern usage is more of a legal term. *Racham* means tender loving care, as a mother for a child, who can see no wrong in the child, no matter what it does; love that sees past our sins for our good. *Racham* has all the best of motherhood and fatherhood in its meaning, where love never stops, no matter what children do, and is similar to the New Testament *agape*/love/charity in concept.

REDEEM/RANSOM

Redeem or ransom is to pay the purchase price to take ownership and set under the control of the one who paid the price. Gal 3:13 "Christ **hath redeemed** us from the curse of the law, being made a curse for us: for it is written, Cursed is every one that hangeth on a tree: 14 that the blessing of Abraham might come on the Gentiles through Jesus Christ; that we might receive the promise of the Spirit through faith." 1 Pet 1:18 "Forasmuch as ye know that ye **were not redeemed** with corruptible things, as silver and gold, from your vain conversation received by tradition from your fathers; 19 but with the precious blood of Christ, as of a lamb without blemish and without spot." Rom 3:23 "For all have sinned, and come short of the glory of God; 24 being justified freely by his grace through the **redemption** that is in Christ Jesus: 25 whom God hath set forth to be a propitiation through faith in his blood, to declare his righteousness for the *aphesis*/remission (*payment in full unto removal, obliteration, cancellation and putting away*) of sins that are past, through the forbearance of God; 26 to declare, I say, at this time his righteousness: that he might be just, and the justifier of him which believeth in Jesus." Eph 1:7 "In whom **we have redemption** through his blood, the *aphesis*/forgiveness (*remission, obliteration, and putting away*) of sins, according to the riches of his grace." 1 Tim 2:5 "For there is one God, and one mediator between God and men, the man Christ Jesus; 6 who **gave himself a ransom** for all, to be testified in due time." Matt 20:28

"Even as the Son of man came not to be ministered unto, but to minister, and to give his *psuche*/life (*soul*) **a ransom** for many." (See Isa 53:11.)

To think your purpose in life is your own is an ultimate level of deception: 1 Cor 6:19 "What? know ye not that your body is the temple of the Holy Ghost which is in you, which ye have of God, and ye are not your own? 20 For ye are bought with a price (*the life, body and blood of Jesus*): therefore glorify God in your body, and in your spirit, which are God's." 1 Cor 7:23 "Ye are bought with a price; be not ye the servants of men." Eph 1:13 "In whom ye also trusted, after that ye heard the word of truth, the gospel of your *soteria*/salvation: in whom also after that ye believed, ye were sealed with that holy Spirit of promise, 14 which is the earnest of our inheritance until the redemption of the purchased possession, unto the praise of his glory." Peace is in those things that fulfill God's goals to produce Heaven on Earth in you and in the Earth through you.

As the redeemed, we are now called by God to fulfill His purpose of making Heaven on Earth through Jesus. We will face troubles, as the devil exalts himself against the knowledge of God, and as God sends us to set others free. Knowing you are bought, and not your own, but God's, is freedom.

RHEMA

Rhema (Strong's NT, 4487, pronounced: hray'mah) means the message that leads to action or obedience; the word of God you do or obey. *Logos* becomes *rhema* as you do it. Hearing the *logos*/Word of God and not doing it is self-deception and produces no *zoe* life. Hearing the *logos*/Word of God and doing it produces *zoe* life. Matt 4:4 "But he (*Jesus*) answered and said, It is written, Man shall not *zao*/live by bread alone, but by every *rhema*/word that proceedeth out of the mouth of God (*that you do*)."

Jesus gave this parable to show it is about what you do, not what you have heard. Matt 21:28 "But what think ye? A certain man had two sons; and he came to the first, and said, Son, go work to day in my vineyard. 29 He answered and said, I will not: but afterward he repented, and went. 30 And he came to the second, and said likewise. And he answered and said, I go, sir: and went not. 31 Whether of them twain did the will of his father? They say unto him, The first. Jesus saith unto them, Verily I say unto you, That the publicans and the harlots go into the kingdom of God before you."

From *Vine's Expository Dictionary of Biblical Words*, copyright © 1985, Thomas Nelson Publishers: "The significance of *rhema* (as distinct from *logos*) is exemplified in the injunction to take 'the sword of the Spirit, which is the word of God,' Eph 6:17; here the reference is not to the whole Bible as such, but to the individual scripture which the Spirit brings to our remembrance for use in time of need, a prerequisite being the regular storing of the mind with scripture."

DISCOVERING OUR REDEMPTION

But this does not in any way imply that *rhema* is not just limited to Holy Spirit giving a special word, but rhema applies to any scripture that you use by repeating and commanding against the devil in any faith battle, for all the promises of God in Jesus are "yea and amen." The emphasis of Eph 6 is what you are to do independent of any special leading or word from Holy Spirit. The *logos* of the word of God becomes *rhema* as you do the *logos*. So even if you do get a special word from Holy Spirit, it is not *rhema* until you obey it to doing it to completion.

Rom 10:17 "So then faith cometh by hearing, and hearing by the *rhema*/word of God (*that you do*)." Hearing the message of salvation and not believing God raised Jesus from the dead will not make you righteous, and not confessing that Jesus is Lord with your mouth will not result in your salvation, per Rom 10:7-13. Conversely hearing that word of your salvation, that God raised Jesus from the dead, will get you made the righteousness of God in Christ Jesus, and confessing Jesus is Lord with your mouth will bring you salvation, according to God's riches.

In the military, *logos*/words of command that are obeyed become *rhema*/words that further the life of the military organization. If those words are not obeyed and remain simply *logos*, the military organization will not be furthered. Failure to know and obey the standing orders of the law, as in traffic signs, will put you on the wrong side of the law and under its wrath, if an accident occurs or if a police officer sees you disobeying the law. Ignorance of the *logos* law does not excuse you, if you disobey that *logos* law.

The message of the Scriptures is that if you do not do the *logos* that proceeds out of the mouth of God in the Scriptures and make it *rhema*, then the devil will enforce the law of sin and death, as the consequences for not doing it God's way. You can consider all of Scripture as a standing, written order to be fully obeyed. Disobedience to the written or spoken word of God is called rebellion or iniquity, and is "as the sin of witchcraft." 1 Sam 15:23 "For rebellion is as the sin of witchcraft, and stubbornness is as iniquity and idolatry. Because thou hast rejected the word (*logos*) of the Lord, he hath also rejected thee from being king."

Conversely, in the covenant in the blood of Jesus, your ability to operate as a king for Jesus and have your words produce the results of Jesus depends on how well you hold on to the redemption truths of being made the righteousness of God in Christ Jesus in the new birth and the abundance of God's grace in and through Jesus. Rom 5:17 "For if by one man's offence death reigned (*as king in enforcing the law of sin and death*) by one (*Adam in his sin in the garden*); much more they which (*continually*) lambano/receive abundance of grace and of the gift of righteousness shall reign (*as a king for Jesus, in enforcing the law of* agape/love) in zoe/life by one, Jesus Christ.)"

In the military, or in any home, there are standing orders, often written, such as: make your beds, take out the trash, do your homework or job on time and do it right, help your fellow soldier, stay on post or in the house until given permission to leave, etc. The New Testament has some 1,050 commands, and many are clearly standing orders, but they are of no effect until you do them. Here are just a few. 1 Thes 5:16 "Rejoice evermore. 17 Pray without ceasing. 18 In every thing give thanks: for this is the will of God in Christ Jesus concerning you. 19 Quench not the Spirit. 20 Despise not prophesyings. 21 Prove all things; hold fast that which is good. 22 Abstain from all appearance of evil." Phil 4:4 "Rejoice in the Lord alway: and again I say, Rejoice. 5 Let your moderation be known unto all men. The Lord is at hand. 6 Be careful for nothing; but in every thing by prayer and supplication with thanksgiving let your *aiteo*/requests *(per His Bible promises)* be made known unto God. 7 And the peace of God, which passeth all understanding, shall keep your hearts and minds through Christ Jesus. 8 Finally, brethren, whatsoever things are true, whatsoever things are honest, whatsoever things are just, whatsoever things are pure, whatsoever things are lovely, whatsoever things are of good report; if there be any virtue, and if there be any praise, think on these things. 9 Those things, which ye have both learned, and received, and heard, and seen in me, do: and the God of peace shall be with you."

Phil 4:7 and 9 make it clear you only get the desired results if you have obeyed, done, what is in the previous verses. These commands are all *logos* and only produce the *zoe*/life of God when you do them and, thus, make them *rhema* and receive the promise. (See also the definition of *logos*.)

RIGHTEOUSNESS

Biblical righteousness has three principle meanings:

1) Righteous acts or works are acts/results that God does through a person so they are perfectly right with God in every way and survive as gold, silver or jewels on the Day of Judgment. This is to obey and do all of God's commandments completely and gladly.
2) A legal state where the one is made as if they had never sinned or will never sin again. This is like being exonerated in a court of law, until you sin or break the law again. This righteousness is conditional, as it is lost when you sin or violate the law again, and you once again become a criminal or a "sinner," with a penalty due, as described in the Law of Moses. Then righteousness must be restored in some way by an action that exonerates, removes or hides the sin from further legal action or curse, and pays or forgives the penalties/curse due for the sin. This is to be legally forgiven of the sin, but your nature remains the same. If you sin again, it is as if you were never righteous, and the full penalty (death) again applies.
3) To be imputed/given the gift of righteousness, which means it is independent of your behavior. The one who is made righteous to this level can produce no

DISCOVERING OUR REDEMPTION

alienation or offence to the court or to the one granting righteousness, no matter what they do, and the one in authority aggressively pours all of the blessing and abundance on them (think spoiled, rich kid with a patient and just father). This righteousness of God does not depend upon your goodness, but Jesus', and is a permanent righteousness. Now your nature is new, and your sins obliterated once, forever, and you are reconciled to God forever, even if you sin again. You are now separated from your sins or evil works, but, until you apply the benefits of the work of Jesus to your current sins and problems, the devil will still try to apply the law of sin and death to you. This level of righteousness allows you to go to God at any time; you are never unclean before Him. God is in Heaven, you are on Earth. If you as a Christian sin, you are righteous with God before and after you sin, but you have to deal with the consequences of sin committed on Earth.

Under the Law of Moses, sins were covered by the annual atonement, but they were never removed or fully paid for, pending the propitiation of Christ. The sins were forgiven, i.e. the penalty of the law of sin and death removed, but the effect was the people were made the second type of righteousness, blessed, but conditional on right behavior. If you sinned again, you released death as the penalty for sin again. Jesus brought forgiveness and remission, the obliteration of sin, to make men the righteousness of God in Jesus and is made effective by faith in the work of Jesus by the cross.

In Christ we are made the third kind of righteousness before God. We died with Him, as our sins are paid in full by His suffering and death for us. Col 3:3 "For ye are dead, and your *zao*/life is hid with Christ in God." Rom 6:2 "God forbid. How shall we, that are dead to sin, *zao*/live any longer therein? 3 Know ye not, that so many of us as were baptized into Jesus Christ were baptized into his death?" Gal 2:19 "For I through the law am dead to the law, that I might *zao*/live unto God. 20 I am crucified with Christ: nevertheless I *zao*/live; yet not I, but Christ *zao*/liveth in me: and the life which I now *zao*/live in the flesh I *zao*/live by the faith of the Son of God, who *agape*/loved me, and gave himself for me. 21 I do not frustrate the grace of God: for if righteousness come by the law, then Christ is dead in vain." Rom 5:9 "Much more then, being now justified by his blood, we shall be *sozo*/saved from wrath through him. 10 For if, when we were enemies, we were reconciled to God by the death of his Son, much more, being reconciled, we shall be *sozo*/saved by his *zoe*/life." Luke 24:47 "And that repentance (*Jesus is Lord and Judge, and everyone will have to deal with Him now and later, and He is your Redeemer, Healer and Judge against the devil and every curse of sin*) and *aphesis*/remission (*payment in full unto removal, purging, washing and putting away*) of sins should be preached in his name among all nations, beginning at Jerusalem."

By this one act of Jesus, sin was remitted once, forever, and we enter into this remission and being made the righteousness of God in Jesus by faith. 2 Cor 5:20

APPENDICES

"Now then we are ambassadors for Christ, as though God did beseech you by us: we pray you in Christ's stead, be ye reconciled to God. 21 For he hath made him to be sin for us, who knew no sin; that we might be made the righteousness of God in him." Rom 3:28 "Therefore we conclude that a man is justified by faith without the deeds of the law. 29 Is he the God of the Jews only? is he not also of the Gentiles? Yes, of the Gentiles also: 30 seeing it is one God, which shall justify the circumcision by faith, and uncircumcision through faith." Rom 4:5 "But to him that worketh not, but believeth on him that justifieth the ungodly, his faith is counted for righteousness." Rom 5:1 "Therefore being justified by faith, we have peace with God through our Lord Jesus Christ."

In 1 Cor 6 Paul upbraids the Corinthians for their sin, yet he still proclaims: 1 Cor 6:11 "And such [*functional sinners*] were some of you: but ye are washed, but ye are sanctified, but ye are justified in the name of the Lord Jesus, and by the Spirit of our God." In spite of their current sin, they still possessed the Type 3 righteousness obtained by the name of Jesus and the power of Holy Spirit.

Under the Law of Moses sin was covered in the annual atonement until Jesus came. This forgiveness by atonement (NT Greek – *aphiemi*) brought the peace and prosperity of Israel. *Remission* (NT Greek – *aphesis, the verb, and aphiemi, the noun*) is the removal, purging, washing, obliteration, destruction and putting away of sin, with no evidence that it was ever there or will be again making us righteous, not just forgiven. Rom 3:25 "Whom God hath set forth to be a propitiation through faith in his blood, to declare his righteousness for the *aphesis*/remission (*full payment unto removal, purging, washing, obliteration and putting away*) of sins that are past, through the forbearance of God; 26 to declare, I say, at this time his righteousness: that he might be just, and the justifier (*the one making righteous*) of him which believeth in Jesus." Heb 9:22 "And almost all things are by the law purged with blood; and without shedding of blood is no *aphesis*/remission." Acts 13:38 "Be it known unto you therefore, men and brethren, that through this man is preached unto you the *aphesis*/forgiveness (*full payment unto remission, obliteration and putting away*) of sins: 39 and by him all that believe are justified from all things, from which ye could not be justified by the law of Moses." Type 3 includes Type 2 with God, but sin and the curse of sin must still be reconciled on Earth.

In Jesus we see the fulfillment of God as our righteousness: Isa 45:24 "Surely, shall one say, in the LORD have I righteousness and strength: even to him shall men come; and all that are incensed against him shall be ashamed. 25 In the LORD shall all the seed of Israel be justified, and shall glory." Jer 23:6 "In his days Judah shall be saved, and Israel shall dwell safely: and this is his name whereby he shall be called, THE LORD OUR RIGHTEOUSNESS." Isa 53:11 "He shall see of the travail of his soul, and shall be satisfied: by his knowledge shall my righteous servant justify (*cleanse and make righteous unto holiness unto the new creation*) many; for he shall

DISCOVERING OUR REDEMPTION

cabal/bear their iniquities."

This is found in the New Covenant through the blood of Jesus. Heb 8:10 "For this is the covenant that I will make with the house of Israel after those days, saith the Lord; I will put my laws into their mind, and write them in their hearts: and I will be to them a God, and they shall be to me a people: 11 and they shall not teach every man his neighbour, and every man his brother, saying, Know the Lord: for all shall know me, from the least to the greatest. 12 For I will be merciful to their unrighteousness, and their sins and their iniquities will I remember no more." Heb 10:4 "For it is not possible that the blood of bulls and of goats should take away sins. ... 16 This is the covenant that I will make with them after those days, saith the Lord, I will put my laws into their hearts, and in their minds will I write them; 17 and their sins and iniquities will I remember no more. 18 Now where *aphesis*/remission (*removal, purging, washing away, obliteration and putting away*) of these (*unrighteousness, sins and iniquities*) is, there is no more offering for sin. 19 Having therefore, brethren, boldness to enter into the holiest by the blood of Jesus..." To have your unrighteousness removed by faith means you are now righteous in spirit. As you confess your current sins, you give thanks for the forgiveness and remission already given 2000 years ago by faith in the work of Jesus by the cross.

And we get it the way it has always been given, by faith: Gen 15:6 "And he (*Abraham*) believed in the LORD; and he counted it to him for righteousness." To be righteous means there is now no wrath, only blessing. Rom 5:10 "For if, when we were enemies, we were reconciled to God by the death of his Son, much more, being reconciled, we shall be *sozo*/saved by his *zoe*/life. 11 And not only so, but we also joy in God through our Lord Jesus Christ, by whom we have now received the atonement (*reconciliation, propitiation*)." Eph 2:13 "But now in Christ Jesus ye who sometimes were far off are made nigh by the blood of Christ. 14 For he is our peace ... ." Col 1:20 "And, having made peace through the blood of his cross, by him to reconcile all things unto himself; by him, I say, whether they be things in earth, or things in heaven. 21 And you, that were sometime alienated and enemies in your mind by wicked works, yet now hath he reconciled 22 in the body of his flesh through death, to present you holy and unblameable and unreproveable in his sight."

A key element is to understand that we, as Christians, are different than our works. We ourselves, our spirits, are *sozo*/saved, already judged dead, made righteous unto new *zoe*/life in Jesus by Holy Spirit. A Christian is one who has received that by faith. We are now dead to the Law, so the Law has no force over us, and we were made legally righteous, to the level of Jesus, before God, to walk in the experiential outworking of right acts (Type 1), even though our current walk is not perfect (until we walk just like Jesus). 2 Cor 5:21 "For he (*God*) hath made him (*Jesus*) to be sin for us, who knew no sin; that we might be made the righteousness

Appendices

of God in him (*Jesus*)." Justified unto the same right nature of God in Jesus.

Christian life works and behaviors will be judged for the Type 1 righteousness, per 1 Cor 3:15, by fire on the Day of Judgment. Yet the born-again, new man spirit is *sozo*/saved and survives that fire because of the third type of righteousness, which is by the faith of/in Christ and not our works (Rom 5:10, Rom 10:6-13). What survives that day you get to keep. 1 Cor 3:12 "Now if any man build upon this foundation gold, silver, precious stones, wood, hay, stubble; 13 every man's work shall be made manifest: for the day shall declare it, because it shall be revealed by fire; and the fire shall try every man's work of what sort it is. 14 If any man;s work abide which he hath built thereupon, he shall receive a reward. 15 If any man's work shall be burned, he shall suffer loss: but he himself shall be *sozo*/saved; yet so as by fire." If you are a Christian, your works may burn, but not you.

God's solution for us was to include us in the death and resurrection of Jesus. This saves our spirit. Yet we will still have our works or "soul fruit" judged: Matt 16:27 "For the Son of man shall come in the glory of his Father with his angels; and then he shall reward every man according to his works." Rom 2:5 "But after thy hardness and impenitent heart treasurest up unto thyself wrath against the day of wrath and revelation of the righteous judgment of God; 6 who will render to every man according to his deeds." 2 Cor 5:10 "For we must all appear before the judgment seat of Christ; that every one may receive the things done in his body, according to that he hath done, whether it be good or bad."

All the blessings of God go to the righteous: those who commit no sin in their Earth walk or who are now clean because they have had their sins forgiven (both the sin action and the curse consequence of sin). Type 2, conditional righteousness, depends on you, i.e., your holiness. Type 3 righteousness depends on Jesus' holiness and not yours. If you are a Christian, Type 2 righteousness no longer applies before God, as Type 3 has superseded it. Rom 5:1 "Therefore being justified by faith, we have peace with God through our Lord Jesus Christ." In peace, God only has favor toward us to produce Heaven on Earth. Eph 1:3 "Blessed be the God and Father of our Lord Jesus Christ, who hath blessed us with all spiritual blessings in heavenly places in Christ." 2 Pet 1:2 "Grace and peace be multiplied unto you through the knowledge of God, and of Jesus our Lord, 3 according as his divine power hath given unto us all things that pertain unto *zoe*/life and godliness, through the knowledge of him that hath called us to glory and virtue: 4 whereby are given unto us exceeding great and precious promises: that by these ye might be partakers of the divine nature, having escaped the corruption that is in the world through lust." We escaped that corruption when we were made the righteousness of God in Christ Jesus by faith. This righteousness depends on the holiness of Jesus and not our own.

If we sin, we have a choice. We can agree with what God says in His written

DISCOVERING OUR REDEMPTION

Word, the Scriptures, or what Holy Spirit convicts us of. As we see that we sinned and call it sin, we are walking in the light. We are seeing clearly. If we do not call our sin as it is, we are walking in darkness and are still deceived in that sin. If we argue with God over what He calls sin, we put ourselves out of fellowship with Him. When we confess that it indeed was sin, that Jesus died for that sin, and that we already have remission for that sin, then this scripture applies. (Notice the first sign that you are out of fellowship, joyful agreement with God, is when your joy is lessened or gone.) 1 John 1:4 "And these things write we unto you, that your joy may be full. 5 This then is the message which we have heard of him, and declare unto you, that God is light, and in him is no darkness at all. 6 If we say that we have fellowship with him, and walk in darkness, we lie, and do not the truth: 7 but if we walk in the light, as he is in the light, we have fellowship one with another, and the blood of Jesus Christ his Son cleanseth us from all sin. 8 If we say that we have no sin, we deceive ourselves, and the truth is not in us. 9 If we confess our sins, he is faithful and just to *aphiemi*/forgive us our sins, and to cleanse us from all unrighteousness. 10 If we say that we have not sinned, we make him a liar, and his word is not in us. 2:1 My little children, these things write I unto you, that ye sin not. And if any man sin, we have an advocate with the Father, Jesus Christ the righteous: 2 and he is the propitiation for our sins: and not for ours only, but also for the sins of the whole world."

Removal of this lack of fellowship issue is called forgiveness, *aphiemi*, in the KJV, but *remission* is more accurate. In the English language, *forgiveness* means "a decision to ignore and wipe away an offense or debt with no payment or restitution required." In remission, the offense or debt is fully paid, and not just removed. God made the decision to forgive man our sin by the process of redemption, through the payment of the blood of Jesus, to give us remission of sins. So, in Jesus, we have the payment fully made, and, as when Jesus was made righteous, fully healed, and justified, so were we, 2000 years ago. Rom 4:24 "But for us also, to whom it (*righteousness*) shall be imputed, if we believe on him that raised up Jesus our Lord from the dead; 25 who was delivered for our offences, and was raised again for our justification (*or when mankind was justified*)." So we now have remission, payment in full, because of the work of Jesus, a past tense, fully completed action that stands forever. Eph 1:7 "In whom (*Jesus*) we have redemption through his blood, the *aphesis*/forgiveness (*payment in full unto remission, removal, purging, obliteration and putting away*) of sins, according to the riches of his grace." And this is the basis for our righteousness in Jesus by grace and not by works.

The thing that dumbfounds the fleshly mind, that makes actions more important than the Word of God, is that even though you sin, you do not lose the righteousness of God in Christ that you are made in the new birth. The new birth is in your spirit, and perhaps in part of your heart, but not in the rest of your soul.

APPENDICES

Soul purity is your goal in the Christian life. For the Christian, or one in permanent covenant with God, *aphiemi* relates to your fellowship or agreement with God as you work out your own salvation in this life. When you receive that forgiveness given 2000 years ago for your present sin, you are then back in fellowship with God, and this is the *aphiemi* forgiveness/remission. Thus, you control whether you walk in *aphiemi* forgiveness/remission and blessing or not.

This is the realm of sowing and reaping. Gal 6:7 "Be not deceived; God is not mocked: for whatsoever a man soweth, that shall he also reap. 8 For he that soweth to his flesh shall of the flesh reap corruption; but he that soweth to the Spirit shall of the Spirit reap *zoe*/life everlasting." This is a clear warning to the sinning Christian. There are no free sins. All words and actions of the Christian constitute our works. The Christian has been separated from their sin works, but all works will be tried on the last Day.

You do not lose righteousness in your spirit for your present sin, but when you sin, you must deal with the devil and his application of the law of sin and death on the Earth. Likewise, you must also deal with God's law of sowing and reaping. Because of lack of confession and lack of application of communion in the bread and wine in truth and faith, you will reap evil or corruption in your physical body and life, in spite of your spirit righteousness. Holy Spirit is sealed in the Christian unto the Day of Redemption, when God will reap in fullness what He has already paid for. Eph 1:13 "In whom ye also trusted, after that ye heard the word of truth, the gospel of your *soteria*/salvation: in whom also after that ye believed, ye were sealed with that holy Spirit of promise, 14 which is the earnest of our inheritance until the redemption of the purchased possession, unto the praise of his glory." So in spite of the Christian who is not just like Jesus in their walk (anything less is sin), Holy Spirit is not going anywhere. God will get what He paid for.

It is not until you apply the truth of the Gospel of Jesus Christ to your sins and/ or the curses operating in your life that you will walk in soul-righteousness and blessing in this life. So this is a case of burn it by the fire of the Gospel now, or it will try to kill you in this life. The spirit-righteousness of God in Christ Jesus in your spirit ensures your final salvation after the Day of Judgment. The reality of your soul-righteousness will determine the quality of your testing on the Day of Judgment.

This explains how the Christian can be the righteousness of God and yet sin, or have sin works. The Christian is separated, sanctified from their sin works and unto God. The source of our sanctification is God, by Jesus, not our works. 1 Cor 1:30 "But of him (*God*) are ye in Christ Jesus, who of God is made unto us wisdom, and righteousness, and sanctification, and redemption." This is part of the Gospel, and is really good news! Rom 6:10 "For in that he (*Jesus*) died, he died unto sin once: but in that he *zao*/liveth, he *zao*/liveth unto God. 11 Likewise reckon ye also yourselves to be dead indeed unto sin, but *zao*/alive unto God through Jesus Christ our Lord."

DISCOVERING OUR REDEMPTION

Those works in your life that are not just like Jesus would do them will not survive the Day of Judgment, yet God, who cannot lie, says the Christian will. 1 Cor 3:12 "Now if any man build upon this foundation gold, silver, precious stones, wood, hay, stubble; 13 every man's work shall be made manifest: for the day shall declare it, because it shall be revealed by fire; and the fire shall try every man's work of what sort it is. 14 If any man's work abide which he hath built thereupon, he shall receive a reward. 15 If any man's work shall be burned, he shall suffer loss: but he himself shall be *sozo*/saved; yet so as by fire. 16 Know ye not that ye are the temple of God, and that the Spirit of God dwelleth in you?" This is a key benefit of being made the Type 3 righteousness of God in Christ Jesus.

SIN/TRANSGRESSIONS

Sin is actually missing any mark or path God has set, whether by commission, by what we do, or by omission, by what we do not do. Transgressions or willful sins are those violations of God's law that are knowingly done, or you may have discovered after the fact that you sinned. Sin includes transgressions and those violations you did not know you committed. Ignorance of the law does not forgive violations of the law, thus sin is sin, whether you know you committed it or not, and, thus, requires levels of restitution or payment on Earth and in Heaven. Per Genesis 2:17, the law of sin and death is to do right and be blessed, or to sin and die. Rom 6:23 "For the wages of sin is death; but the gift of God is eternal *zoe*/life through Jesus Christ our Lord." Ezek 18:4 "Behold, all souls are mine; as the soul of the father, so also the soul of the son is mine: the soul that sinneth, it shall die." Rom 1:18 "For the wrath of God is revealed from heaven against all ungodliness and unrighteousness of men, who hold the truth in unrighteousness." Rom 2:9 "Tribulation and anguish, upon every soul of man that doeth evil, of the Jew first, and also of the Gentile..."

The penalty for sin is death through the curse, which is death in a fast or a slow, or prolonged, form. Deut 28:14 "And thou shalt not go aside from any of the words which I command thee this day, to the right hand, or to the left, to go after other gods to serve them. 15 But it shall come to pass, if thou wilt not hearken unto the voice of the LORD thy God, to observe to do all his commandments and his statutes which I command thee this day; that all these curses shall come upon thee, and overtake thee. ... 61 Also every sickness, and every plague, which is not written in the book of this law, them will the LORD bring upon thee, until thou be destroyed." Gal 3:10 "For as many as are of the works of the law are under the curse: for it is written, Cursed is every one that continueth not in all things which are written in the book of the law to do them."

Christ removed the curse from us to give us the ultimate blessing, God Himself, dwelling in us by His Spirit: Gal 3:13 "Christ hath redeemed us from the curse of the law, being made a curse for us: for it is written, Cursed is every one that hangeth on a tree: 14 that the blessing of Abraham might come on the Gentiles through Jesus Christ; that we might receive the promise of the Spirit through faith." There is now no legal curse upon the Earth for anyone.

Sozo/Soteria

For these Greek words, *sozo* (*Strong's'* NT 4892/4491, pronounced: sode'-zo) is the verb, save, the process through which you become whole and blessed; *soteria* (*Strong's'* NT 4991, pronounced: so-tay-ree'-ah) is the noun, salvation, the state of being whole and blessed, like Heaven on Earth. *Sozo* is the process by which all of Earth and human life is made like Heaven on Earth in the fullness of the glory of God, i.e., that which produces the peace of God or the Kingdom of God, from now to eternity. Physical healing is just a small portion of the meaning. Salvation has an eternal aspect, eternal life with God. The present life aspect is producing Heaven on Earth in your life and in those you are responsible for. *Salvation* means to be made prosperous and successful to the level of God Himself in every way possible, with no limits. So nothing related to the full potential of human life in Christ is left out. The root word from which salvation is derived means open, freedom from restraint. Sickness, poverty, danger, lameness, infirmity, weakness, etc., are all restraints, limits and pressure points. Salvation or wholeness has no restraints, limits or pressure points, and has the full freedom of God's blessings in action to fill the Earth with His glory.

Spirit/Soul/Body

Man is a three-part being, made up of spirit (the real you), soul (heart, mind, will and emotions and how you interface or function with this world through your body), and body (what operates in this earth). From Genesis we see that the addition of the spirit to the body created a living soul. Gen 2:7 "And the LORD God formed man of the dust of the ground, and breathed into his nostrils the breath/*spirit* of life; and man became a living soul."

Your heart is not your spirit, but the heart seems to be that combination of inner life that includes your mind and touches your spirit. 1 Thes 5:23 "And the very God of peace sanctify you wholly; and I pray God your whole **spirit and soul and body** be preserved blameless unto the coming of our Lord Jesus Christ." Heb 4:12 "For the word of God is quick, and powerful, and sharper than any twoedged sword, piercing even to the dividing asunder **of soul and spirit**, and of the joints and marrow, and is a discerner of the **thoughts and intents of the heart**." When you die, your spirit and soul leave your mortal body. James 2:26 "For as the body without the spirit is dead ..." Your heart is to be purified in this life, especially hardness of heart, to God and His Word, by doing the Word and expecting God to do His part (Rom 2:4-5, 1 Tim 1:5, Heb 3:10-12, Eph 4:16-18, James 1:6, 2 Pet 2:14).

DISCOVERING OUR REDEMPTION

We are made righteous by faith in Jesus in our spirits. This is how we are born again, made a new creature in Christ Jesus. We will get a new, immortal body at the resurrection. Our soul is unchanged. Notice all your memories remain the same, before and after being born again. We are made the righteousness of God in Jesus and given zoe/life in our spirits, as Holy Spirit comes to dwell in our spirit.

Our goal in life is to renew our mind, heart or soul to think without iniquity, i.e., just like Jesus. 2 Cor 10:5 "Casting down imaginations, and every high thing that exalteth itself against the knowledge of God, and bringing into captivity every thought to the obedience of Christ." This process is called "saving our souls," or "outworked sanctification," and is demonstrated by how much our walk is like Jesus. This renewing process of the soul comes as we grow in the true knowledge of Jesus, not mere mental facts, but actually working with God, so that the fruits of God are produced in the Earth through you.

2 Pet 1:2 "Grace and peace be multiplied unto you through the *experiential* knowledge of God, and of Jesus our Lord, 3 according as his divine power hath given unto us all things that pertain unto zoe/life and godliness, through the *experiential* knowledge of him that hath called us to glory and virtue: 4 whereby are given unto us exceeding great and precious promises: that by these ye might be partakers of the divine nature, having escaped the corruption that is in the world through lust." Our mental learning is solidified as we go and do agape/love. As we believe, to releasing zoe/life, we do this.

The old man is the un-recreated spirit and way of thinking that produces sin, also called the carnal mind, or the mind of the flesh and lust. An immature Christian thinks like a "mere man" (1 Cor 3:1-3). The old man, the body of sin, is killed in Jesus and recreated into the new man. John 1:12 "But as many as received him, to them gave he power to become the sons of God, even to them that believe on his name: 13 which were born, not of blood, nor of the will of the flesh, nor of the will of man, but of God." Col 3:9 "... seeing that ye have put off the old man with his deeds; 10 and have put on the new man, which is renewed (*made effective*) in knowledge after the image of him that created him." The new birth removes the spirit of the old man, but does not necessarily totally change the old-man-trained soul.

While we are made new creations in the new birth, we have to retrain our minds and hearts so we can walk like Jesus in this earth. Eph 4:22 "That ye put off concerning the former conversation the old man, which is corrupt according to the deceitful lusts; 23 and be renewed in the spirit of your mind; 24 and that ye put on the new man, which after God is created in righteousness and true holiness."

And this new man delights to walk in all the ways of God in *agape*/love. 1 John 5:2 "By this we know that we *agape*/love the children of God, when we *agape*/love God, and keep his commandments. 3 For this is the *agape*/love of God, that we keep his commandments: and his commandments are not grievous." The new man does

APPENDICES

not have any resistance to God, and none of God's commands are grievous to him.

Psuche and bios: The other Greek words translated in the KJV as "life" include *psuche* and *bios*. *Psuche* is also translated as "soul," which has a different connotation than "life." As translated in the Scriptures, there is much confusion between these words. *Zoe* is used in reference to general life and the *life* of God, implying it is what God gives. *Bios* is a general form of life that all living creatures have. *Zoe* is in reference to that which God alone gives. So He gives life to all things, and then Jesus said He came to give *zoe*/life as opposed to all other kinds of life or life force. This is in opposition to whatever form of life force people were operating in at the time. So He either meant that He came to give a different life force or a great increase of the good life force people already operated in.

The meaning for *soul* is even more difficult, in that many do not recognize what is clearly revealed in the Scriptures as a difference between *soul* and *spirit*. The Greek word *psuche* (Strong's NT 5590) is translated "soul" fifty-eight times, "life" forty times, "mind" three times and "heart" once. This shows a lack of understanding on the part of the translators, not on Holy Spirit's part.

From *Vine's* explanation of *psuche* we have the following:

"The language of Heb 4:12 suggests the extreme difficulty of distinguishing between the soul and the spirit, alike in their nature and in their activities. Generally speaking the spirit is the higher, the soul the lower element. The spirit may be recognized as the life principle bestowed on man by God, the soul as the resulting life constituted in the individual, the body being the material organism animated by soul and spirit ... .

"Body and soul are the constituents of the man according to Matt 6:25; 10:28; Luke 12:20; Acts 20:10; body and spirit according to Luke 8:55; 1 Cor 5:3; 7:34; James 2:26. In Matt 26:38 the emotions are associated with the soul, in John 13:21 with the spirit; cf. also Ps 42:11 with 1 Kings 21:5. In Ps 35:9 the soul rejoices in God, in Luke 1:47 the spirit. *(This confusion between Ps 35 and Luke 1 is a good example in which the modern thinkers translating the KJV did not understand that the soul and spirit are different, yet have, what can be described as, similar features.)*

"Apparently, then, the relationships may be thus summed up 'Soma, body, and pneuma, spirit, may be separated, pneuma and psuche, soul, can only be distinguished' (Cremer)." (NT:5590 Soul from *Vine's Expository Dictionary of Biblical Words*: Nashville, Tn., Thomas Nelson Publishers, 1985).

One way to distinguish the soul is that it is the mind, the heart, the will and the emotions of all men, and constitutes that which receives information directly from the senses of the body and also from the spirit. So, concerning our acceptable thoughts, intentions, motives, attitudes of the heart, the soul is the joining and deciding ground between the body and the spirit. Thus, Heb 4:12 takes the Word of God to determine where either the soul or the spirit ends and the other begins. The spirit of the born-again man will always be in harmony with the Word of God. The soul of the born-again or the natural man may or may not be in harmony, agreement and commitment with the Word of God. This latter is more a function of an individual's experiences, culture and training. What one actually does and says is the result of the status of truth in their soul and, thus, the word *psuche* is often translated as "life." What is in your soul or heart is displayed in the life you live.

So when a person is in the spirit, their soul is mostly controlled or in cooperation with the thoughts and attitudes of a spirit being. This is seen when a demon speaks through a person, or Holy Spirit, as in biblical prophecy (also see the meaning of *zoe*). The life force exhibited is a function of whatever unity the soul has with that particular spirit being (life or *zoe*). For example, when one uses the name of Jesus to raise the dead, this is an action in unity with Holy Spirit. When one accepts the death of a person, especially a young one, they are in unity with their body senses, and the person is buried and not raised. In both cases, the soul is the deciding ground of "whose report will you believe?" The resulting behavior is then called the "life " of that person, as seen in the action of either raising the dead or burying them.

This understanding of the difference is seen in both the Hebrew and Greek texts, but not in the KJV and most other modern translations. For example, look at the Hebrew and the Greek and then the English translations relating to these important scriptures. Isa 53:11 "He shall see of the travail of his **soul**, and shall be satisfied: by his knowledge shall my righteous servant justify many; for he shall bear their iniquities." Matt 20:28 "Even as the Son of man came not to be ministered unto, but to minister, and to give his ***psuche/life*** (*soul*) a ransom for many." John 10:15 "As the Father knoweth me, even so know I the Father: and I lay down my ***psuche/life*** (*soul*) for the sheep." According to the original Hebrew and Greek, the meaning is clear and consistent, but not in the English translation.

Also here are both Greek words in the same verse translated as life: John 12:25 "He that loveth his ***psuche/life*** shall lose it; and he that hateth his ***psuche/life*** in this world shall keep it unto ***zoe/life*** eternal." Since we know God does not want us to kill ourselves, the meaning is that if your soul is not just like Father God's, work until it is, and when you do, your soul will release the *zoe*/life of God from your born-again spirit. You work on it according to 2 Cor 3:17 "Now the Lord is that Spirit: and where the Spirit of the Lord is, there is liberty *to be all Father God made you to be in Jesus.* 18 But we all, with open face beholding as in a glass (*mirror, seeing Jesus manifest Himself in and through me*) the glory of the Lord, are changed into the same image from glory to glory, even as by the Spirit of the Lord." Eph 4:22 "That ye put off concerning the former conversation the old man, which is corrupt according to the deceitful lusts; 23 and be renewed in the spirit of your mind; 24 and that ye put on the new man, which after God is created in righteousness and true holiness." The transformation occurs as you continually see aspects of Jesus that you desire and, in faith, see yourself walking in, first unto thanksgiving and joy, and then Holy Spirit will transform your inner man according to your faith, and it will be seen in your outer man or walk. Rom 1:17 "For therein is the righteousness of God revealed from faith to faith: as it is written, The just shall *zao*/live by faith."

As the New Testament describes the heart of the Christian as possibly dead or resistant to God, we do not consider the heart the dwelling place of Holy Spirit. Rom 2:5 "But after thy hardness and impenitent heart treasurest up unto thyself wrath against the day of wrath and revelation of the righteous judgment of God." The heart seems to be better described as that place or part of your soul or subconscious mind that connects to your spirit, and near that place is also the conscience part of your soul (that internal governor that is always judging your actions based on your beliefs and the soul part of your heart). Rom 2:29 "But he is a Jew, which is one inwardly; and circumcision is that of the *kardia*/heart, in *or by* the *pneuma*/spirit, and not in the letter; whose praise is not of men, but of God." The heart and the spirit are different, but closely tied together. A heart fully indwelt by a right spirit is a right heart. Eph 3:17 "That Christ/*Holy Spirit* may dwell (*happily or fully*) in your hearts by faith; that ye, being rooted and grounded in *agape*/love ..."

According to modern science, the cognitive mind is the cerebral cortex, and the unconscious mind is a combination of the rest of the brain and the neural material throughout the body. The term *heart*, as a portion of the soul, implies the part of the soul different than the cognitive mind. The spirit is considered to reside near the physical heart and the solar plexus (behind the stomach).

For the born-again one, the heart can be corrupted, but the spirit cannot. We understand Holy Spirit to be in our spirits, so our spirit can now always be pure, but our heart is included in the process of renewing the mind and must continually be kept clean. The goal of the Christian life is for the spirit to once again rule your soul and body, though a right heart, and not the pre-born-again condition, in which the body and/or soul rule instead.

Notice the warning not to let your heart be corrupted by sin: Heb 3:12 "Take heed, brethren, lest there be in any of you an evil heart of unbelief, in departing from the *zao*/living God. 13 But exhort one another daily, while it is called To day; lest any of you be hardened through the deceitfulness of sin." James 3:14 "But if ye have bitter envying and strife in your hearts, glory not, and lie not against the truth." James 4:8 "Draw nigh to God, and he will draw nigh to you. Cleanse your hands, ye sinners; and purify your hearts, ye double minded." 1 John 3:20 "For if our heart condemn us, God is greater than our heart, and knoweth all things." Thus the heart is in need of constant maintenance to stay in cooperation with Holy Spirit.

Your conscious mind seems to be that active part of the way you think and accesses your memory and the events in the physical world by your senses. Below is a model that shows the distinction between the spirit, soul and body for the new-creation, born-again person:

THE BORN-AGAIN CHRISTIAN

THE SPIRIT WORLD	THE MENTAL WORLD	THE PHYSICAL WORLD
Your Spirit-The Real You	Your Soul	Your Body
	Habits, Attitudes, Desires	Flesh
Hunger for God	Conscience, Memory, Intentions	Senses
Born Again: Bible, Word	Heart, Emotions, Will, Mind	Bible: Word of God
Righteousness-Life-Zoe	Imagination, Cognitive Mind	
Holy Spirit>Jesus>Father	Subconscious Mind	

What this table conveys is that the physical world has a boundary, the world of the spirit, and good portions of the soul do not, or are not of the same kind of "stuff" as the physical universe our bodies inhabit. Note also that automatic responses, such as attitudes, habits, emotions and memory, are highly linked to the physical body in structure and effect. Damage to the physical brain, for example, can have major impacts on these elements of the soul. To be amused means to be without thinking, so the mind is a deeper part of the person. This also indicates the reason the devil has such a strong focus in our modern world on keeping people amused, mindless and entertained. To open your mind in such amusement means that you are programming your subconscious without knowledge. As you are responsible for the shape or godliness of your soul, you are still accountable for the effects, whether you are aware of it or not.

Jesus is the living Word made flesh. In the diagram, the Word of God is seen under the spirit and the body, as this is the only physical link God has given man to the spiritual world, and all godly definitions of the spirit must be consistent with the Bible. Ps 138:2 "I will worship toward thy holy temple, and praise thy name for thy *chesed*/lovingkindness and for thy truth: for thou hast magnified thy word above all thy name." Ps 119:88 "Quicken me after thy *chesed*/lovingkindness; so shall I keep the testimony of thy mouth. 89 For ever, O LORD, thy word is settled in heaven. 90 Thy faithfulness is unto all generations: thou hast established the earth, and it abideth. 91 They continue this day according to thine ordinances: for all are thy servants." 1 Pet 1:23 "Being born again, not of corruptible seed, but of incorruptible, by the word of God, which *zao*/liveth and abideth for ever. 24 For all flesh is as grass, and all the glory of man as the flower of grass. The grass withereth, and the flower thereof falleth away: 25 but the word of the Lord endureth for ever. And this is the word which by the gospel is preached unto you."

In reality, the spirit world is actually more solid or real than the physical world, as is all that physically exists is made from spirit. As with everything God makes, the soul and probably the spirit, is, in structure and operation, far more detailed and complex than described here. But remember, that thing which we call the soul was made to house God and, with you, to operate the universe for and with Him, so it is really quite capable and marvelous. The more you operate in this "completeness" of the new birth, the more you and He actively cooperate to do His will in this universe. The new creation is an instantaneous event of God, by decree; the renewed mind takes time and human effort, in cooperation and effort with Holy Spirit in the Word of God. The Word of God is so important, as it is the only physical link (in its printed form) that we are given to the spirit world and God. To hear the voice of God all you have to do is speak the Scriptures. If it does not sound like God, the problem is you, not it.

So to be "filled" with the Spirit means to have your soul in agreement with Holy Spirit and your behavior or "life" reflecting that agreement. One way to describe this is that God fully possess your soul, or you are "full of" or "filled with" His Spirit. Here is both a command and a description of what that looks like. Eph 5:18 "And be not drunk with wine, wherein is excess; but be filled with the Spirit; 19 speaking to yourselves in psalms and hymns and spiritual songs, singing and making melody in your heart to the Lord; 20 giving thanks always for all things unto God and the Father in the name of our Lord Jesus Christ; 21 submitting yourselves one to another in the fear of God." See *zoe* for more detail on this.

Zao/Zoe

Zao (Strong's NT 2198, pronounced: dzah'-o) is the verb form, *live*; *zoe* (Strong's NT 2222, pronounced: dzo-ah') is the noun, *life*. In the Bible this word generally means the life, power, enthusiasm, and attitude that only comes from the true *zao*/living God. Bringing *zoe* to men was the primary propose of Jesus and the proof that Jesus is from God. All of His actions in demonstrating the *zoe*/life of God in a man in miracles, dying on the cross, resurrecting from the dead and sending Holy Spirit were so that we could be justified unto *zoe*/life, to provide a dwelling place for Holy Spirit within our spirits. This is so that we can do our part in finishing the job of destroying the works of the devil. John 10:10 "The thief cometh not, but for to steal, and to kill, and to destroy: I am come that they might have *zoe*/life, and that they might have it more abundantly." 1 John 5:9 "If we receive the witness of men, the witness of God is greater: for this is the witness of God which he hath testified of his Son. 10 He that believeth on the Son of God hath the witness in himself: he that believeth not God hath made him a liar; because he believeth not the record that God gave of his Son. 11 **And this is the record, that God hath given to us eternal *zoe*/life, and this *zoe*/life is in his Son**. 12 He that hath the Son hath *zoe*/life; and he

DISCOVERING OUR REDEMPTION

that hath not the Son of God hath not *zoe*/life." This *zoe*/life in our spirit, with Holy Spirit indwelling, is a main mark of what a Bible Christian should be.

God's answer for every work of the devil and the path into God's prosperity is the *zoe*/life of God. According to John 10:10, we see that the opposite of anything that steals, kills or destroys is the *zoe* of God. Jesus bears the title of the Prince of *Zoe*/Life. Acts 3:15 "And killed the Prince of *zoe*/life, whom God hath raised from the dead; whereof we are witnesses." Rom 8:2 "For the law of the Spirit of *zoe*/life in Christ Jesus hath made me free from the law of sin and death." Thus, we see that every work of the devil, in death in any form, is overcome and destroyed by the *zoe*/life of God.

In the Greek understanding, a human operated in the *zoe* of a god or spirit when they thought and acted like that god or spirit. A Greek warrior wanted to operate in the full *zoe* of Ares, the god of war, to prosper in battle and vanquish enemies. To do this, a warrior would fill his mind with thoughts and attitudes of war and train with weapons and physical exercise to make himself excel in war. Thus, with enthusiasm and joy, he would train and fight, breathing, or *zao*ing that spirit of war. While not addressing a specific "god," we see similar actions and effects in a team locker room, where the coach inspires his men to get in agreement so that the "in-spirit-dwells," to "inspire" or "pump up" the team or players before the game or at half time, or in a motivational speaker to any group. They are now filled with that spirit-thinking alike, inspired and excited. In fact, the word *enthusiasm* means "one with god," or to be in *zoe*.

This is the same concept for operating in the *zoe* of God. Holy Spirit is within us. According to Eph 4:17-18, it is how we think and then act that releases Him/*zoe* from our spirit into the world to do good. To sin is to operate in the devil's death or darkness (i.e., the devil's anti-*zoe*). 1 John 3:8 "He that committeth sin is of the devil; for the devil sinneth from the beginning. For this purpose the Son of God was manifested, that he might destroy the works of the devil. ... 10 In this the children of God are manifest, and the children of the devil: whosoever doeth not righteousness is not of God *in his actions*, neither he that *agape*/loveth not his brother." Rom 6:21 "What fruit had ye then in those things whereof ye are now ashamed? for the end of those things is death. 22 But now being made free from sin, and become servants to God, ye have your fruit unto holiness, and the end everlasting *zoe*/life. 23 For the wages of sin is death; but the gift of God is eternal *zoe*/life through Jesus Christ our Lord."

For our own motivation into the *zoe*/life of God, Eph 5:18 "And be not drunk with wine, wherein is excess; but be *continually being* filled with the Spirit; 19 speaking to yourselves in psalms and hymns and spiritual songs, singing and making melody in your heart to the Lord; 20 giving thanks always for all things unto God and the Father in the name of our Lord Jesus Christ; 21 submitting yourselves one to another in the fear of God." Col 3:14 "And above all these things put on *agape*/charity, which is the bond of perfectness. 15 And let the peace of God rule in your hearts, to the which also ye are called in one body; and be ye thankful. 16 Let the word of Christ dwell in you richly in all wisdom; teaching and admonishing one another in psalms and hymns and spiritual songs, singing with grace in your hearts to the Lord. 17 And whatsoever ye do in word or deed, do all in the name of the Lord Jesus, giving thanks to God and the Father by him." Notice that right speaking and singing keeps us in God's *zoe*. Obeying these continually, therefore, will cause you to continually operate in the *zoe* of God. This is also a description of what it looks like to operate in the *zoe* of God.

A similar Old Testament word (*sharat* OT 8334), translated as both "worship" and "serve," carries the concept that in all of God-life we breathe and move in Him, thus, echoing the Greek word *zoe*. So when we sin, we are actually serving or worshiping or breathing sin. 1 John 3:8 "He that committeth sin is of the devil; for the devil sinneth from the beginning. For this purpose the Son of God was manifested, that he might destroy the works of the devil." So when we sin, we are *zao*ing the devil. Jesus destroyed the devil and his works in the spirit realm, and we have the job of doing our part now. This job of destroying all the devil's works is complete on the Day of Judgment. Thus, when we operate in Jesus, to set people free, we are delivering judgment to the devil. We do it as we *zao* God on the subject of healing, or for any other answered *aiteo*, for any other part of His salvation.

So, in essence, as part of the Universe and in the Universe, your every thought, word and action is in tune with some level of that Universe. At the top is God; everywhere else is rebellion and the devil. Thus, you cannot think a thought, speak, or do an action of rebellion and be in unity with God, and when you do, you are in unity with the devil, and not God. 1 John 3:8 "He that committeth sin is of the devil; for the devil sinneth from the beginning." You cannot sin in unity with Father God, so, by default, you are in unity with the devil or the god of this world. 2 Cor 4:4 "In whom the god of this world hath blinded the minds of them which believe not, lest the light of the glorious gospel of Christ, who is the image of God, should shine unto them." John 12:31 "Now is the judgment of this world: now shall the prince of this world be cast out." This unity is on a thought-by-thought basis, so each thought must be judged.

Another biblical term for this unity with the god of this world is *iniquity*: Acts 8:23 "For I perceive that thou art in the gall of bitterness, and in the bond of iniquity." Titus 2:14 "Who gave himself for us, that he might redeem us from all iniquity, and purify unto himself a peculiar people, zealous of good works." Heb 1:9 "Thou hast *agape*/loved righteousness, and hated iniquity; therefore God, even thy God, hath anointed thee with the oil of gladness above thy fellows." 2 Pet 2:16 "But was rebuked for his iniquity: the dumb ass speaking with man's voice forbad the madness of the prophet."

DISCOVERING OUR REDEMPTION

The concept described by *zoe* is that you are always in a unity with a spirit of some kind or another. This is very different from most modern Western thinking, where the concept is that you can have a "middle" position, deciding free from either God or the devil. While convenient in this culture, this does not fit the concept of *zoe*, nor does it fit the Scriptures and will lead to great terror on the Day of Judgment. 1 John 5:17 "All unrighteousness is sin … ."

To allow or follow a spirit is a function of where you are or what you choose. For example, you may choose certain clothes to remind you of what spirit you have decided to let operate through you. This is the meaning and purpose of a talisman and carrying about statues of various gods, or, in a milder sense, team colors.

Whereas, as a Christian, you may have Holy Spirit as one with your spirit, but your thoughts, words and actions need to be consistent with Holy Spirit for you to operate "in the spirit of God." Conversely, if you are not operating in the Spirit of God, you are operating in another spirit. As you operate within the Scriptures, your thoughts, words and actions allow God to operate through you, to His glory. If you are not operating out of the Jesus-like parts of scripture, you are *zao*ing out of God and in the spirit of the devil.

So one way to describe the Gospel is that God invites you to operate by His *zoe* in Jesus, knowing that all your failures to operate perfectly in His *zoe* have been paid for by Jesus through the cross, and you can come to God freely at any time to operate in His *zoe*. The more you know this the more your conscience is cleansed of thinking that anything was lacking in the work of Jesus through the cross and resurrection. Col 2:10 "And ye are complete in him, which is the head of all principality and power."

God defines this *zoe* as a distinguishing mark of what He accomplished in Jesus. 1 John 5:10 "He that believeth on the Son of God hath the witness in himself: he that believeth not God hath made him a liar; because he believeth not the record that God gave of his Son. 11 **And this is the record, that God hath given to us eternal *zoe*/life, and this *zoe*/life is in his Son.** 12 He that hath the Son hath *zoe*/life; and he that hath not the Son of God hath not *zoe*/life." Gal 2:20 "I am *(have been)* crucified with Christ: nevertheless I *zao*/live; yet not I, but Christ *zao*/liveth in me: and the life which I now *zao*/live in the flesh I *zao*/live by the faith of the Son of God, who *agape*/loved me, and gave himself for me."

Because God made Jesus sin for us, He can now dwell in us because of Jesus. As we access His *zoe*/life, in spite of our failures, we proclaim the power of the blood of Jesus. Heb 9:14 "How much more shall the blood of Christ, who through the eternal Spirit offered himself without spot to God, purge your conscience from dead works to serve *(operate by the* zoe *of)* the *zao*/living God?"

Here again is a plea to stop operating or serving in the *zoe* of other gods and only operate in the eternal *zoe* of God. 1 Thes 1:9 "For they themselves shew of us what manner of entering in we had unto you, and how ye turned to God from idols to serve the *zao*/living and true God; 10 and to wait for his Son from heaven, whom he raised from the dead, even Jesus, which delivered us from the wrath to come."

Appendices

All of this comes under the area of renewing the mind, so, when Holy Spirit prompts with thoughts and words, we respond quickly in agreement and continue to operate in the *zoe*/life of God. God makes it clear that operating any other way does not bring the Kingdom of God. Gal 5:19 "Now the works of the flesh (*anti*-zoe) are manifest, which are these; Adultery, fornication, uncleanness, lasciviousness, 20 idolatry, witchcraft, hatred, variance, emulations, wrath, strife, seditions, heresies, 21 envyings, murders, drunkenness, revellings, and such like: of the which I tell you before, as I have also told you in time past, that they which do such things shall not inherit *(produce)* the kingdom of God. 22 But the fruit of the Spirit (zoe *of God*) is *agape*/love, joy, peace, longsuffering, gentleness, goodness, faith, 23 meekness, temperance: against such there is no law. 24 And they that are Christ's have crucified the flesh with the affections and lusts. 25 If we *zao*/live in the Spirit, let us also walk in the Spirit. 26 Let us not be desirous of vain glory, provoking one another, envying one another." Verse 25 is a clear command to walk in the *zoe* we now have.

For the Christian, the plea is to no longer do those things that are not God's *zoe*, and, instead, *zao* for and through God. 2 Cor 5:15 "And that he died for all, that they which *zao*/live should not henceforth *zao*/live unto themselves, but unto him which died for them, and rose again."

The concept of *zoe* and Hebrew worship or service is that there are no actions independent of the spirit world and a spirit. We are constantly operating in God or the devil, with no neutral ground. This is a major challenge to modern Western thought, where there are typically three possible choices: a) with God or good; b) with the devil or evil; or c) a neutral ground aligned with neither. The Bible calls this third position deception. James 1:22 "But be ye doers of the word, and not hearers only, deceiving your own selves." 1 Cor 6:9 "Know ye not that the unrighteous shall not inherit *(produce)* the kingdom of God? Be not deceived: neither fornicators, nor idolaters, nor adulterers, nor effeminate, nor abusers of themselves with mankind, 10 nor thieves, nor covetous, nor drunkards, nor revilers, nor extortioners, shall inherit *(produce)* the kingdom of God. 11 And such were some of you: but ye are washed, but ye are sanctified, but ye are justified in the name of the Lord Jesus, and by the Spirit of our God." 1 Cor 15:33 "Be not deceived: evil communications corrupt good manners. 34 Awake to righteousness, and sin not; for some have not the knowledge of God: I speak this to your shame." 1 John 1:8 "If we say that we have no sin, we deceive ourselves, and the truth is not in us." Ps 10:4 "The wicked, through the pride of his countenance, will not seek after God: God is not in all his thoughts."

In summary, 1 Pet 1:18 "Forasmuch as ye know that ye were not redeemed with corruptible things, as silver and gold, from your vain conversation received by tradition from your fathers; 19 but with the precious blood of Christ, as of a lamb without blemish and without spot: 20 who verily was foreordained before the foundation of the world, but was manifest in these last times for you, 21 who by him do believe in God, that raised

DISCOVERING OUR REDEMPTION

him up from the dead, and gave him glory; that your faith and hope might be in God. 22 **Seeing ye have purified your souls in obeying the truth** through the Spirit unto unfeigned love of the brethren, **see that ye *agape*/love one another with a pure heart fervently**: 23 being born again, not of corruptible seed, but of incorruptible, by the word of God, which *zao*/liveth and abideth for ever. 24 For all flesh is as grass, and all the glory of man as the flower of grass. The grass withereth, and the flower thereof falleth away: 25 but the word of the Lord endureth for ever. And this is the word which by the gospel is preached unto you."

To have the *zoe* of God is mind-boggling potential. To operate in *zoe* is to activate the *zoe*/life of God into the people, situations and activities of Earth, to change from the current state to the will of God. As with most things of God, the static and academic status does not produce godly results, until we activate *zoe* by faith and deliver it where needed. This active and deep knowing is how we grow in God. 2 Pet 1:3 "According as his divine power hath given unto us all things that pertain unto *zoe*/life and godliness, through the *deep and experiential epignosos*/knowledge of him that hath called us to glory and virtue." We start with recognition, and then move into being and doing, according to our born-again nature. Eph 4:21 "If so be that ye have heard him, and have been taught by him, as the truth is in Jesus: 22 that ye put off concerning the former conversation the old man, which is corrupt according to the deceitful lusts; 23 and be renewed in the spirit of your mind; 24 and that ye put on the new man, which after God is created in righteousness and true holiness."

Any resistance to this means you have an area or areas where you need to renew (*purify*) your mind to the Christ-mind way of thinking, speaking and doing. 2 Cor 10:3 "For though we walk in the flesh, we do not war after the flesh: 4 (for the weapons of our warfare are not carnal, but mighty through God to the pulling down of strong holds;) 5 casting down imaginations, and every high thing that exalteth itself against the knowledge of God, and bringing into captivity every thought to the obedience of Christ." Notice that this is "our war" or our job in this life now.

As you purify your soul, by *phileo*/brotherly love, you move into *zao*ing God in *agape*/love from a purified heart. It is the way you think that controls your actions and determines whether you walk in the *zoe* of God or not. Eph 4:17 "This I say therefore, and testify in the Lord, that ye henceforth walk not as other Gentiles walk, in the vanity of their mind, 18 having the understanding darkened, **being alienated from the *zoe*/life of God** through the ignorance that is in them, because of the blindness of their heart: 19 who being past feeling have given themselves over unto lasciviousness, to work all uncleanness with greediness."

For a description of how to walk in the *zoe* of God, from one of many in the Bible: Eph 4:20 "But ye have not so learned Christ; 21 if so be that ye have heard him, and have been taught by him, as the truth is in Jesus: 22 that ye put off concerning the former conversation the old man, which is corrupt according to the deceitful lusts; 23 and be

APPENDICES

renewed in the spirit of your mind; 24 and that ye put on the new man, which after God is created in righteousness and true holiness. 25 Wherefore putting away lying, speak every man truth with his neighbour: for we are members one of another. 26 Be ye angry, and sin not: let not the sun go down upon your wrath: 27 Neither give place to the devil. 28 Let him that stole steal no more: but rather let him labour, working with his hands the thing which is good, that he may have to give to him that needeth. 29 Let no corrupt communication proceed out of your mouth, but that which is good to the use of edifying, that it may minister grace unto the hearers. 30 And grieve not the Holy Spirit of God, whereby ye are sealed unto the day of redemption. 31 Let all bitterness, and wrath, and anger, and clamour, and evil speaking, be put away from you, with all malice: 32 and be ye kind one to another, tenderhearted, forgiving one another, even as God for Christ's sake hath forgiven you. 5:1 Be ye therefore followers *(imitators, copy cats)* of God, as dear children; 2 and walk in *agape*/love, as Christ also hath *agape*/loved us, and hath given himself for us an offering and a sacrifice to God for a sweetsmelling savour." This *zoe*/walk description really goes to the root of Eph 6.

To minister healing, or any work of salvation, in the *zoe* of God includes "breathing in" the attitude of God's promises against the devil and his works and, for those who need the blessing, by applying His *zoe* as needed, knowing John 16:11 "… the ruler (evil genius, prince) of this world [Satan] is judged and condemned and sentence already is passed upon him." AMP Luke 10:19 "Behold, I give unto you power *(authority, commission and the resources of Heaven)* to tread on serpents and scorpions, and over all the power *(ability)* of the enemy: and nothing shall by any means hurt you. 20 Notwithstanding in this rejoice not, that the spirits are subject unto you; but rather rejoice, because your names are written in heaven." So we are to be continually Col 1:12 "giving thanks *continually* unto the Father, which hath made us meet to be partakers of the inheritance of the saints in light: 13 who hath delivered us from the power of darkness, and hath translated us into the kingdom of his *agape*/dear Son: 14 in whom we have redemption through his blood, even the forgiveness of sins." Rev 1:5 "… Jesus Christ, who is the faithful witness, and the first begotten of the dead, and the prince of the kings of the earth. Unto him that *agape*/loved us, and washed us from our sins in his own blood, 6 and hath made us kings and priests unto God and his Father; to him be glory and dominion for ever and ever. Amen …. 17 … And he *(Jesus)* … *says to us*, Fear not; I am the first and the last: 18 I am he that *zao*/liveth, and was dead; and, behold, I am *zao*/alive for evermore, Amen; and have the keys of hell and of death." Rom 16:20 "And the God of peace shall bruise Satan under your feet shortly *as shattered glass*. The grace of our Lord Jesus Christ be with you *(to know, be and do this)*. Amen." Ps 103:6 "The LORD executeth righteousness and judgment for all that are oppressed *through us."* For He says, Hos 13:14 "I will ransom them from the power of the grave; I will redeem them from death: O death, I will be thy plagues; O grave, I will be thy destruction: repentance shall be hid from mine eyes." 2 Tim 1:7 "For God hath not given *you* the spirit of fear; but of *dunamis*/power, and of *agape*/love, and of

DISCOVERING OUR REDEMPTION

a sound mind." 1 Tim 6:12 "*So* fight the good fight of faith, lay hold on eternal *zoe*/life, whereunto thou art also called … ." Eph 6:10 "… be strong in the Lord, and in the power of his might," *preaching His word of grace,* Acts 14:3 "… speaking boldly in the Lord, which *gives* testimony unto the word of his grace, and *grants* signs and wonders to be done by *your* hands, *words and actions.*" Acts 19:12 "So that from *your* body *are* brought unto the sick handkerchiefs or aprons, and the diseases *depart* from them, and the evil spirits *go* out of them. *For* Mark 16:20 "… the Lord *is* working with *you*, and confirming the word with signs following. Amen."

Living this way is to walk in the Spirit of God, the *zoe* of God, which is what we are made for. Adam lost it, so man could operate only externally in the *zoe* of God. Jesus is the Prince, the Price and the Gift of *zoe* life for mankind so that the *zoe* of righteousness, the same desires and power to do right as God is in Jesus, can now be in man. Rom 8:2 "For the law of the Spirit of *zoe*/life in Christ Jesus hath made me free from the law of sin and death."

2 Cor 5:16 "16 Wherefore henceforth know we no man after the flesh: yea, though we have known Christ after the flesh, yet now henceforth know we him no more. 17 Therefore if any man be in Christ, he is a new creature: old things are passed away; behold, all things are become new. 18 And all things are of God, who hath reconciled us to himself by Jesus Christ, and hath given to us the ministry of reconciliation; 19 to wit, that God was in Christ, reconciling the world unto himself, not imputing their trespasses unto them; and hath committed unto us the word of reconciliation. 20 Now then we are ambassadors for Christ, as though God did beseech you by us: we pray you in Christ's stead, be ye reconciled to God. 21 For he *(Father God)* hath made him *(Jesus)* to be sin for us, who knew no sin; that we might be made the righteousness *(nature, holiness, desire, power)* of God in him *(Jesus).* 6:1 We then, as workers together with him, beseech you also that ye receive not the grace of God in vain. 2 (for he saith, I have heard thee in a time accepted, and in the day of *soteria*/salvation have I succoured thee: behold, now is the accepted time; behold, now is the day of *soteria*/salvation.)"

Rom 5:18 "Therefore as by the offence of one *(Adam)* judgment came upon all men to condemnation *(death)*; even so by the righteousness *(purity and right desires)* of one *(Jesus)* the free gift came upon all men unto justification of *zoe*/life *[to allow the new creation or new birth with indwelling Holy Spirit]*. 19 For as by one man's disobedience many were made sinners, so by the obedience of one shall many be made righteous *(unblameable, unreproveable, holy and new nature like the resurrected Jesus)*. 20 Moreover the law entered, that the offence might abound. But where sin abounded, grace did much more abound: 21 that as sin hath reigned *(as a cruel king enforcing the law of sin and death)* unto death, even so might grace reign *(as a greater and more powerful king)* through righteousness *[in men by the new creation]* unto eternal *zoe*/life by Jesus Christ our Lord *[to produce Heaven on Earth for Father God]*."

IDENTIFIED
(A Redemption Song)

1. In crucifixion on the cross,
With Jesus Christ identified;
In death for man's eternal loss,
With Jesus Christ identified.

Chorus:
Identified, identified,
With Jesus Christ identified;
In all He was, or is, or shall be.
Eternally identified.

2. In burial 'neath the cursed ground,
With Jesus Christ identified;
In Hell's deep dungeons where He's found,
With Jesus Christ identified.

3. In vict'ry over hell's dark host,
With Jesus Christ identified;
Yes, while He paid sin's awful cost,
With Jesus Christ identified.

4. In resurrection might and pow'r,
With Jesus Christ identified;
At God's right hand this very hour,
With Jesus Christ identified.

5. In coronation's glorious day,
With Jesus Christ identified;
When He by right shall kingdoms sway,
With Jesus Christ identified.

-E.W. Kenyon
from Identification, page 69

Ministry Page

You may contact Don Mann in any of the following ways:

Don Mann
3 Crossan Court
Landenberg, PA 19350

www.CovenantPeaceMinistries.com
eMail: Info@CovenantPeaceMinistries.com

Please share your testimonies with us.

FREE GIFT WITH YOUR PURCHASE:
Visit our Book Store at www.CovenantPeaceMinistries.com to redeem your gift

FREE NEWSLETTER:
Sign up for our free eNewsletter for tools to help you grow in Christ

Did You Borrow This Book? Want a Copy of Your Own?
Need a Great Gift for a Friend or Loved One?
ORDER LIST

☐ Yes I want to invest $29.99 in my future and have a personal copy of this book (in paperback). For simplicity, go to Amazon.com and find *Discovering Our Redemption* by Donald C. Mann, or go to the book store at our website, www.CovenantPeaceMinistries.com and use the Amazon.com link there. Hardback, and eBook versions are also available: Adobe Reader, iBook, Nook, and Kindle.

For the following items, please go to our book store at www.CovenantPeaceMinistries.com to complete your order.

☐ Yes, I want the audio books for *Discovering Our Redemption* as read by the author. Unabridged.*
- Vol 1, Understanding Redemption and What Jesus Accomplished
    - _____ 8 CD Set $39.95
    - _____ 1-2 MP3 $39.95
- Vol 2, Understanding Who We Are in Christ and How to Walk in It
    - _____ 10 CD Set $49.95
    - _____ 1-2 MP3 $39.95

☐ Yes, for my regular ministry use, I want a special durable edition of *Discovering Our Redemption* for $75.00.*

* Prices subject to change without notice, please see our website for current pricing.

QUANTITY ORDERS INVITED
For bulk discount prices for all items, please email us at:
Info@CovenantPeaceMinistries.com

To request Don to Speak to Your Group, or for more Valuable and Powerful Ministry Tools, please go to
www.CovenantPeaceMinistries.com.

Many have been helped by our free materials and videos!

For encouragement and understanding, see: Blog.CovenantPeace.com

Get the Entire POWER TRILOGY
www.CovenantPeaceMinistries.com

OK, God, Now What?
Activating His Ancient Secrets for Success

How to renew your mind for more power with God

This book shows the Bible principles that are changing top sports, sales, business and Christian leaders, and ordinary people to godly success in every part of life.

Gain peace of mind, clarity, purpose, health, wealth and a better life. In just 21, 40 or 90 days you will see dramatic results.

For the new Christian, get started right; for the mature Christian, get revelation, a new fire and peace like you've only dreamed of.

Discovering Our Redemption
How to Be Transformed By the 52 Days that Changed the Universe

Experience the confidence as you know what Jesus did in each step of the critical last 52 days of His ministry 2000 years ago.

Feel your faith rise as you take these historical facts and use them for the foundation for your faith, just like the apostles did.

This book shows what Jesus did from the Last Supper to the Day of Pentecost and how to apply these historical facts to greater growth in God.

Battle Prayer for Healing, Field Manual 2
Releasing God's Healing Power When You Need It

This book is a step-by-step scriptural guide on how to pray so God can heal through you.

Use this book as a spiritual first-aid kit in times of trouble, as a tool for a more effective ministry, and as a study guide so you can grow in Christ and the power of Holy Spirit. For Christians at every level, *Battle Prayer for Divine Healing, Field Manual 2* is for you!

Where are the answers I need?
They are in the *Power Trilogy*.
Get the complete set today and experience the transformation of your life!

- **Faith-building facts** of our Redemption → *Discovering Our Redemption*
- **How to renew your mind** for miracles and blessing in God → *OK, GOD, Now What?*
- **How to release** your faith for healing miracles → *Battle Prayer for Divine Healing-Field Manual 2*

Go to www.CovenantPeaceMinistries.com to get yours today.

IN THE RIGHT HANDS, THIS BOOK WILL CHANGE LIVES!

Most of the people who need this message will not be looking for this book. To change their lives, you need to put a copy of this book in their hands.

Still other seeds fell on fertile soil, and they produced a crop that was thirty, sixty, and even a hundred times as much as had been planted!

Matthew 13:8, NLV

Our ministry is constantly seeking methods to find good ground, the people who need this anointed message to change their lives. Will you help us reach them?

Remember this—a farmer who plants only a few seeds will get a small crop. But the one who plants generously will get a generous crop.

2 Corinthians 9:6, NLV

EXTEND THIS MINISTRY
BY SOWING
3 BOOKS, 5 BOOKS, 10 BOOKS,
OR MORE TODAY
AND BECOME A LIFE CHANGER!

Thanking you in advance,

Harold McDougal, Founder
The Published Word
Since 2004

McDougal & Associates
www.ThePublishedWord.com

Servants of Christ and Stewards of the Mysteries of God
(Your On-Demand Book Publisher and Bookseller)

Visit our newly designed site
www.ThePublishedWord.com

Free Subscription to **M&A Newsletter**
Receive free articles by ThePublishedWord authors, exclusive discounts, and free downloads from our best and newest books

Visit www.ThePublishedWord.com to subscribe

Write to: McDougal & Associates
             18896 Greenwell Springs Road
             Greenwell Springs, LA 70739

Email: orders@thepublishedword.com

For a complete list of our titles or to place an order online,
visit www.ThePublishedWord.com

www.ingramcontent.com/pod-product-compliance
Lightning Source LLC
Chambersburg PA
CBHW060507230426
43665CB00013B/1429